JOHN, PAUL, GEORGE & RINGO

The Definitive Illustrated Chronicle of the Beatles, 1960-1970

TIM HILL

Photographs by Daily Mail

FALL RIVER PRESS

Originally published in Great Britain in 2007 as
The Beatles: Then There Was Music

This 2008 edition published by Fall River Press,
by arrangement with Atlantic Publishing.

Cover and interior design by Smay Design

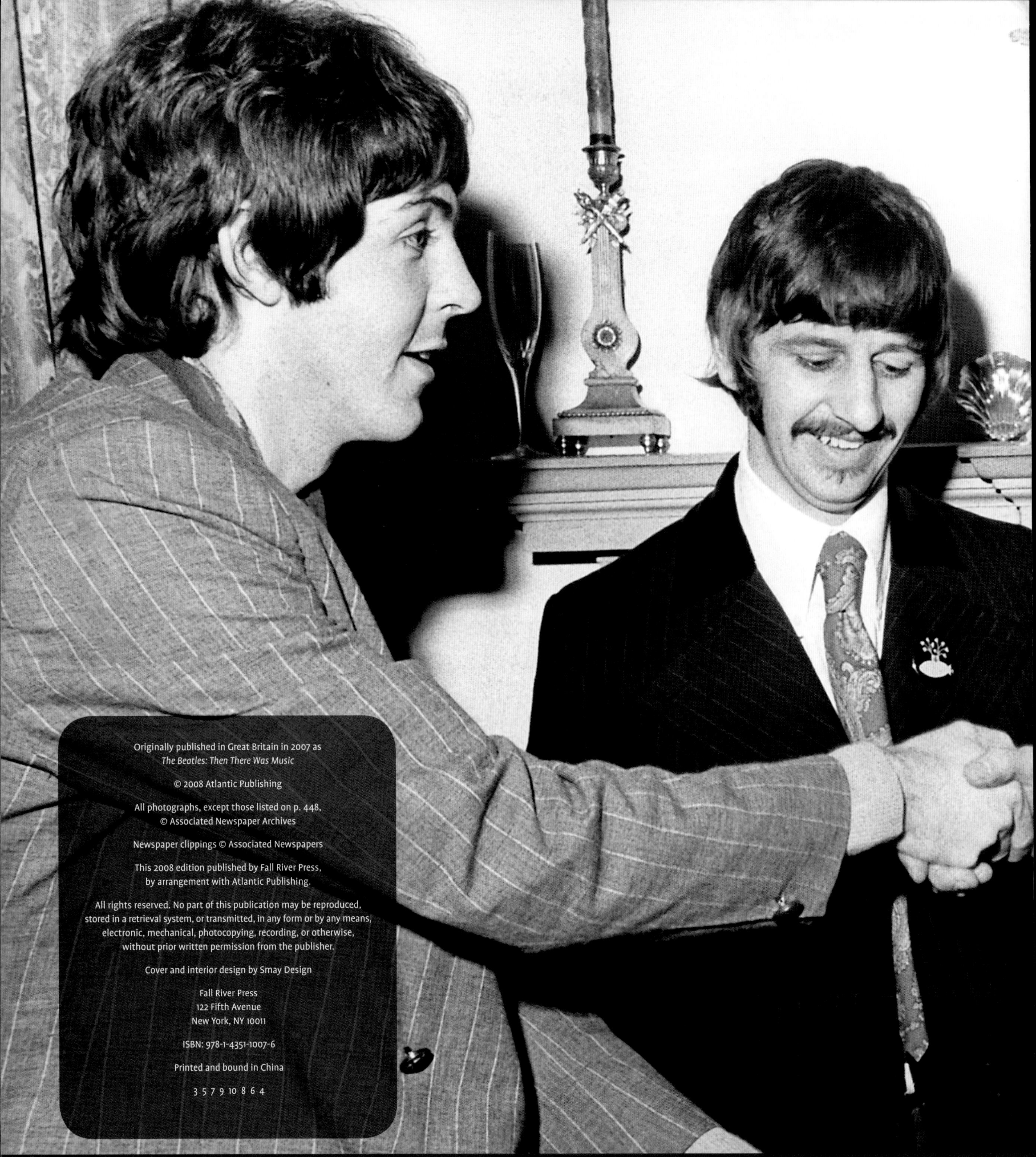

Fall River Press
122 Fifth Avenue
New York, NY 10011

ISBN: 978-1-4351-1007-6

Printed and bound in China

3 5 7 9 10 8 6 4

CONTENTS

Foreword

My first encounter with the Beatles was in 1964. I was in Melbourne Australia, where I had my own photographic studio. I was almost twenty-five years old, enjoying city life with friends that included a number of leading lights in the Australian arts scene. I was asked to photograph Brian Epstein for a newspaper interview. Thousands of people crowded round the Beatles' hotel but we managed to fight our way in. At the end of the interview Brian, curious about the results, asked me if he could see the photographs I had taken. Then he introduced me to the Beatles who were just down the corridor in their own lounge. They were looking at presents given by their fans and every so often they would go to the window and wave to the crowds.

Next day I went back with two large prints of Brian. In the dark room I had introduced a decorative wreath in the background around his head. He was knocked out by what he saw and asked to view more of my work. The same afternoon, Brian called me with an invitation to accompany him to the Beatles' concert at the Festival Hall and photograph them on stage. Finally, he asked me if I would be interested in him managing me as a photographer back in the UK. Later that year I accepted his offer.

Over the next few years I photographed the Beatles all over the world. I watched and captured them on film as they performed countless times to millions of screaming fans who were crazy about them and their music, their energy and enthusiasm for life.

I think the years of learning the entertainment business the hard way with five- or six-hour back-to-back sessions onstage in Hamburg made the Beatles consummate performers in a traditional sense, which is maybe why their variety shows and movies seemed to come so naturally to them. I watched them give their polished stage shows all over the world and their act rarely changed. It bored me eventually and it obviously bored them—especially when their performance couldn't be heard over the screams of the audience.

My pictures often have a theme that can be unlocked with a visual key that's visible in the photograph. On one hand, not taking conventional photos may have narrowed the market for my pictures, on the other hand the unusual staging I created was not only what the Beatles enjoyed and wanted, it also fed the mood of the picture editors and their readers at the time. And those photographs are still very much in demand.

The pictures I took of John and Cynthia at Kenwood were picked up by newspapers all over the world: there had never been coverage like it. I got the inspiration from a book my grandmother gave me in 1955 called *The History of the Camera in Australia*. It included many photographs of early Australian life and that's exactly how I saw John—as a pioneer. If you look closely at the picture you'll see Julian is holding a golden spoon!

All the photo sessions were creative in their own way and I enjoyed each of them. I remember my first shoot in studios in Farringdon Road—I travelled there, down the Strand, with the Beatles in their Rolls-Royce with everyone looking.

For the second studio session I did with them, at Sherriff Road in Hampstead, I had some help from friends at the Royal Academy and we set up this sort of Pop Art stage with strips of different colours and shiny foil. The idea was to create a levitation effect with the boys but we didn't have enough time to achieve that and the session ended with the guys wrapping themselves in polythene, then breaking up big pieces of polystyrene in what Professor David Mellor of Sussex University called the Auto-destruct Session.

The most creative experience I had with the Beatles was in the Tokyo Hilton: we couldn't get out because of the fans. The local promoter asked them to do something for charity; he gave them paper and paints to create a poster. They put a lamp with a circular base in the middle of the paper and each of them took a corner and created their piece of art, each in his own style. When they finished, they took the lamp away and signed their autographs in the central space. It really was a spontaneous work of art.

I felt closest to John: we both had philosophical and artistic ideas about things other than music. Was he a genius, were the others? Lennon and McCartney together achieved outstanding creative success, but when you end a creative partnership it's hard to get the same quality and I think that shows, not just in the individual work of Paul and John after the split but in all of the individual solo careers. In my opinion the greatest genius of the Beatles was in what they did together.

I see the Beatles as a product of their time but it's obvious that they brought with them a new age with completely changed music and values. The young generation, sick of the gloomy postwar society, were ready for the colour and energy of rock 'n' roll. The Beatles had that a-plenty; at first that energy was raw and unsophisticated but as the tedium of live performance hit, they turned their talent to composition and innovation in the recording studio. I'm not alone in thinking they changed the world; they certainly changed mine. I look back with great pride and pleasure to the work I did with them in the photographic studio and, very often, on location. While no one can take away from the Beatles their great talent, they were able to connect with some of the most creative people of their age and gain impetus

OPPOSITE: **John, Cynthia, and Julian photographed at their home, Kenwood.**

ABOVE: **The Beatles at Cliveden in 1965 during the filming of the movie *Help!*.**

RIGHT: **The Beatles dismantle the set after the session at Sherrif Road.**

for their ideas. This added greatness to natural talent: think of the list—George Martin, Klaus Voorman, Peter Blake, Brian Epstein himself, and many more.

My last trip with the Beatles was on the fated Far East tour in 1966: the photos I took on the plane after the chaotic departure from Manila are deceptive in every sense with the Beatles playing cards during the flight after the frightening parting display put on by the Filipino crowds —the only time I heard them being booed. I had been driven to the airport with a pistol pointed

at me. You got used to the drama. The Beatles got off the flight at Delhi and I flew on to Athens. I never saw them together again in person or photographed them as a group after that.

In this book are hundreds of photographs: quite a few are taken by me and I still feel incredibly lucky to have been there. The collection of words and images compressed into these few hundred pages reflects the overwhelming decade of the Beatles' career as a band. In that brief time they exceeded the output and success of most artists' entire careers, yet

they continued solo careers while their classic albums and compilations kept them at the top of the charts. While little can compare with the sheer exhilaration of the 1960s, I hope you get a feel of those adrenalin-rich days as you read the pages that follow.

—Robert Whitaker
London, 2008

Introduction:
Four Lads Who Shook the World

John Lennon said, "Nothing affected me until Elvis." Had he lived, John might have been pleased to hear eminent musicians saying similar things about the Beatles: "No contest. Nothing else comes close." Such was Queen's Brian May's verdict on the "technicolor explosion" that was "I Want To Hold Your Hand", which he unhesitatingly selected as his all-time number one single. In the same poll Phil Collins picked out "She Loves You", which "turned my life around". Brian Wilson virtually gave up the creative ghost after hearing *Sgt. Pepper*, while Eric Clapton felt he was intruding on hallowed ground when invited to Abbey Road to play on "While My Guitar Gently Weeps". Those are just some of the legends lining up with the rest of us to pay homage to the greatest band that ever plugged in a guitar or hit a rim shot. The Beatles reinvented the pop idiom, and in the process inspired not just adoration and respect but awe and reverence.

Despite their domination of the music scene of the '60s and '70s and a vast worldwide following, fans have to accept that recent generations don't know the Beatles as well as before. Moreover, children of our time can't possibly picture the society from which the Beatles emerged to rock the world into modernity. In that world, food was rationed, TV was black and white, and National Service would sort you out. Labouring classes trudged to work (if they were lucky enough to get it) while the upper classes carried out their divinely appointed task—to rule the country.

The Beatles entered the scene in a world that in a way had more resemblance to Dickensian society than any bright new future for heroes, but they fixed that bleak world for a whole generation practically overnight, putting a spring in the step, a sense of optimism and identity, and a new tune in the heads of that generation. But the Beatles couldn't do it by staying in their home city of Liverpool: they had to do their National Service in Hamburg's Reeperbahn—in dingy bars and clubs of the red light district. There they learned to rock and played alongside cult musicians like Little Richard who helped them learn the catalogue of rock 'n' roll that they recreated in the Cavern Club, and that Paul still knows how to belt out.

The Beatles knew they were special: Liverpool and Hamburg figured it out, followed by Brian Epstein and George Martin; then the entire country and, finally, the world. Their tunes were catchy, the rhythms were upbeat, the guitar sound had a new energy, and the lyrics made simple connections with a gritty reality that offered a refreshing change from the sugary stuff mimicking American romantic ballads currently being served up.

The Beatles weren't rock stars to start with, they were four guys with truly remarkable talents, some of which were self-destructive and would ensure the band couldn't survive. Being art students, Paul and John wrapped up their music and their talent in a total package, which was so much more than a few good tunes. Allthough those early tunes carried them to fame, it was their unstinting efforts in the studio that ensured their enduring success.

The Beatles became synonymous with the Swinging Sixties but their iconic reach extended much further in time and far beyond the realms of music and fashion. They didn't just span the decade of the '60s; they defined it. A pop sensation became a cultural phenomenon that endured and whose effects continue to be felt today.

"When you get to the top," wrote poet Philip Larkin, "there is nowhere to go but down." The Beatles, he went on, were an exception to that rule. "There they remain, unreachable, frozen, fabulous." Distance has served only to enhance their reputation, to confirm that genius has no expiration date. Forty years on, Beatles music remains as fresh, vibrant, and innovative as the day it was pressed, a peerless legacy for existing fans to revisit and new ones to discover.

This book tells the story of John, Paul, George, and Ringo: it's illustrated with almost a thousand fabulous classic and rare photographs from the archives of the *Daily Mail* and other picture collections. Facsimile news cuttings and extracts from the newspaper editions of the time chart the key events and big stories as they were experienced. A day-by-day chronicle runs through the book logging the most important events in the life of the Beatles whilst together, and in their careers after the split. Photographs of memorabilia from Beatles concerts and merchandise show how the world celebrated the Beatles in the heady days when they were Fab. Key characters are introduced with bios, stories of how great songs such as "Michelle" and "A Day in the Life" came about are recounted. Every major album is featured with background not just on how it was made but also on the photography and design of the cover.

Read in big chunks, dip in and out, just look at the pictures, or trace the chronicle: this book will dazzle you with its contents and take you on amazing journey with the world's most famous foursome.

The Early Years

It Won't Be Long

The Beatles were confident that they were sprinkled with stardust, but it took five years to form the lineup, hone their act, and decide on the name of the group that would change the face of popular music.

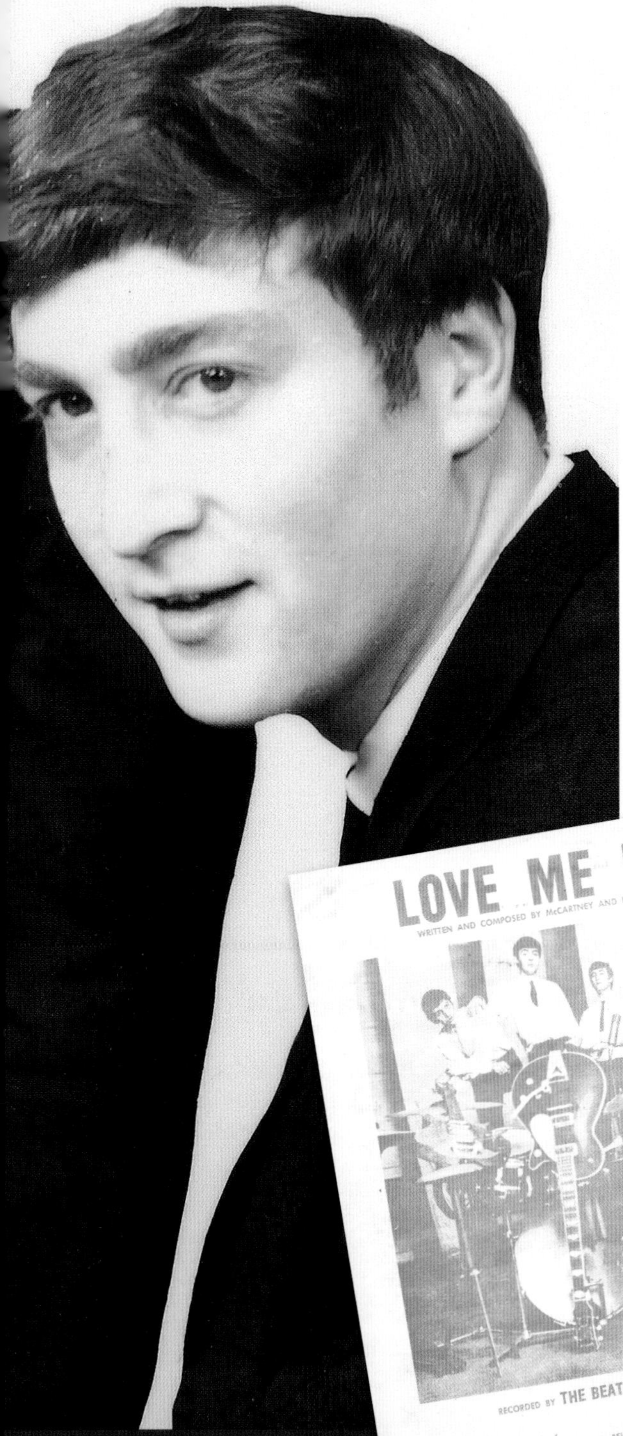

The historic first meeting between John Lennon and Paul McCartney took place on 6 July 1957 at a garden fete in Woolton, where sixteen-year-old John's skiffle band was providing the entertainment. Paul posed a potential threat to John's leadership of the group, but his musicianship earned him an invitation to join the Quarry Men. Fretboard dexterity also gained Paul's young friend, George Harrison, an entrée into the inner circle. There followed many months of unrewarding slog, lineup changes, and rebranding exercises. Stuart Sutcliffe looked the part but was no bass player and happily shuffled off the stage. Drummer Pete Best rode the wave that swept the Beatles to the top of Liverpool's beat group pile and won them a loyal Hamburg following. But his days were numbered when record retailer Brian Epstein decided to diversify into artist management after seeing one of the Beatles' electrifying Cavern performances. Epstein sharpened up their image, instilled professionalism, and secured a recording deal with Parlophone. Best failed the test when the red light went on in the studio, and Ringo Starr was promptly head-hunted from a rival band. The Fab Four lineup was complete in August 1962, and before the end of the year "Love Me Do" had given them their first Top 20 hit. At long last, the Beatles were on their way to the top.

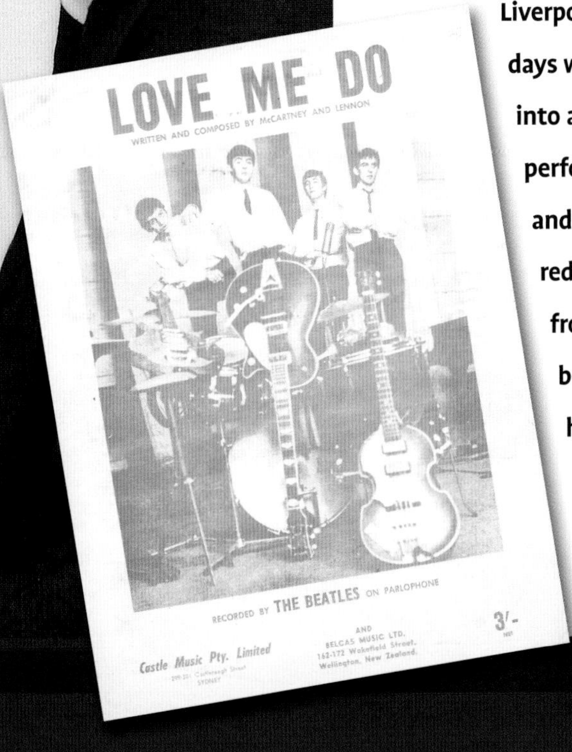

OPPOSITE: **Paul, Pete Best, George, and John.**

LEFT: **Sheet music for "Love Me Do", the Beatles' first single that was released on the Parlophone label on 5 October 1962.**

LEFT: **A postwar picture of Beatle-to-be Paul McCartney (right) at the age of six with his eight-year-old brother Mike, later to become Mike McGear of the Scaffold.**

BELOW: **Paul had been playing with the band for two years but it was his talent as an artist that was picked up by his teachers when he was awarded the Liverpool Institute's art prize.**

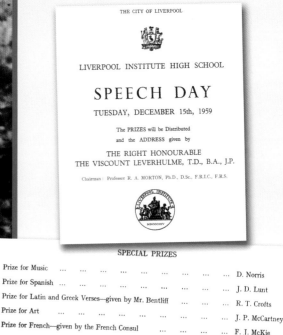

THE CITY OF LIVERPOOL

LIVERPOOL INSTITUTE HIGH SCHOOL

SPEECH DAY

TUESDAY, DECEMBER 15th, 1959

The PRIZES will be Distributed
and the ADDRESS given by

THE RIGHT HONOURABLE
THE VISCOUNT LEVERHULME, T.D., B.A., J.P.

Chairman : Professor R. A. MORTON, Ph.D., D.Sc., F.R.I.C., F.R.S.

SPECIAL PRIZES

Prize for Music ...	... D. Norris
Prize for Spanish ...	... J. D. Lunt
Prize for Latin and Greek Verses—given by Mr. Bentliff	... R. T. Crofts
Prize for Art ...	... J. P. McCartney
Prize for French—given by the French Consul	... F. J. McKie

Meet the Quarry Men

A legend at the site of the Cavern Club bears the inscription: FOUR LADS WHO SHOOK THE WORLD. It wasn't until 1964 that John, Paul, George, and Ringo rocked the planet to its core and changed the course of popular music. The path to global preeminence began almost a decade earlier, a long and circuitous ride in which the group underwent a dizzying number of metamorphoses before the all-conquering four-piece lineup was formed.

From an early age John Lennon thought he was marked out for greatness—either that or an asylum. He was bright but not studious, pugnacious with punier specimens, using his quick-wittedness to outsmart those bigger than he. He had a fertile imagination, a rebellious streak, and a keen sense of the absurd. All were on show in the *Daily Howl*, a paper the young Lennon circulated among his Quarry Bank schoolmates. It was full of cartoons, caricatures, and Edward Lear-style nonsense verse of the kind that would appear in his later published works.

He would remain an inveterate scribbler, but in 1956 he was bitten by a different bug. "Nothing affected me till Elvis," John would say, though when he formed his first band it was a skiffle combo, not least because washboards and tea-chest basses were a cheap and cheerful route to performing on stage. With an inexpensive acoustic guitar and a few banjo chords under his belt, the latter courtesy of his mother, Julia, John was up and running with the Quarry Men.

Paul McCartney had been keener on the big-band sound and show tunes, the influence of

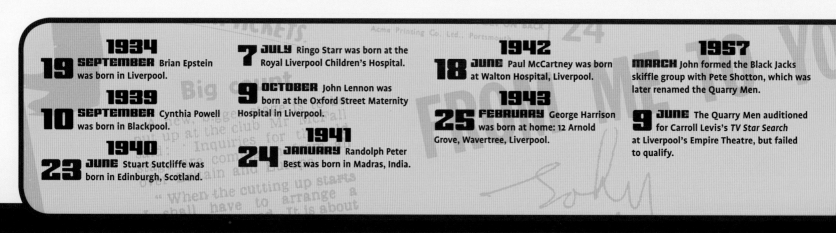

1934
19 SEPTEMBER Brian Epstein was born in Liverpool.

1939
10 SEPTEMBER Cynthia Powell was born in Blackpool.

1940
23 JUNE Stuart Sutcliffe was born in Edinburgh, Scotland.

7 JULY Ringo Starr was born at the Royal Liverpool Children's Hospital.

9 OCTOBER John Lennon was born at the Oxford Street Maternity Hospital in Liverpool.

1941
24 JANUARY Randolph Peter Best was born in Madras, India.

1942
18 JUNE Paul McCartney was born at Walton Hospital, Liverpool.

1943
25 FEBRUARY George Harrison was born at home: 12 Arnold Grove, Wavertree, Liverpool.

1957
MARCH John formed the Black Jacks skiffle group with Pete Shotton, which was later renamed the Quarry Men.

9 JUNE The Quarry Men auditioned for Carroll Levis's *TV Star Search* at Liverpool's Empire Theatre, but failed to qualify.

his trumpet-playing father, Jim. But he too was carried away by the twin seductions of guitar and skiffle. On 6 July 1957 Paul went along to a Woolton Village Church garden fete at the suggestion of his Liverpool Institute pal Ivan Vaughan, who had been at elementary school with the sixteen-year-old fronting the band providing the entertainment that day. Paul was more interested in the chance of picking up girls than listening to the Quarry Men, but the two youngsters did meet. Paul impressed John with his ability to tune a guitar and knowledge of song lyrics, as well as his playing. John was

torn between wanting to improve the band and inviting a possible rival leader to join. He opted for improvement; Paul was in.

Getting George Harrison on board was harder. Paul sang the praises of a guitar-playing friend with whom he shared a bus journey to school. John regarded George, three years his junior, as a young whippersnapper, but once again talent won the day. George's ability to play the rock number "Raunchy" right through unerringly caused John to relent. By February 1958 three quarters of the Beatles' lineup was in place.

ABOVE: **At the Arnhem War Memorial on the way to their all-important first tour of Hamburg. Paul, George, and Pete Best are seated to the right. With them from left of the photo are the promoter, Allan Williams, his wife Beryl, and his business partner, the calypso singer Lord Woodbine. Stuart Sutcliffe stands to the right wearing sunglasses. John is notably absent from the photograph—in the days before the all-invasive interest of the press someone had to take the picture.**

ABOVE INSET : **Fifteen-year-old Paul McCartney was first introduced to John Lennon at St. Peter's Church fete in Woolton on 6 July 1957. Paul's ability impressed John and he was invited to join John's group, the Quarry Men.**

6 JULY Paul met John for the first time when he saw the Quarry Men play at St. Peter's Church garden fete in Liverpool.

20 JULY Paul was invited to join the Quarry Men.

7 AUGUST The Quarry Men performed at the Cavern Club in Liverpool for the first time.

18 OCTOBER Paul's debut performance with the Quarry Men, at the New Clubmore Hall, Liverpool. He played lead guitar, but made a mess of his solo and was demoted to rhythm guitar.

1958
6 FEBRUARY George met the Quarry Men and was later invited to join them because of his growing skill as a guitarist, although he was younger than the others.

15 JULY John's mother, Julia, was killed by a speeding car when crossing the road after leaving his Aunt Mimi's house.

1959
25 MARCH Ringo joined Rory Storm & the Hurricanes, at that time Merseyside's top band.

29 AUGUST The Quarry Men played at the opening night of the

Casbah Club, owned by Pete Best's mother. The group consisted of John, Paul, George, and Ken Brown. They still had no drummer.

10 OCTOBER Ken Brown left the Quarry Men.

15 NOVEMBER As Johnny and the Moondogs, John, Paul, and George made the final audition for Carroll Levis's *TV Star Search* at Liverpool's Empire Theatre.

Rock the Casbah

Over the next eighteen months the group found it tough going. The competition was stiff and plentiful, gigs hard to come by. The Quarry Men did cut their first record in this period, however, paying 17s 6d for the privilege of committing "That'll Be the Day" to acetate. The flipside was a McCartney–Harrison composition titled "In Spite of All the Danger", an early indication of the group's keenness to write their own material. John and Paul were collaborators-in-chief, the two teenagers finding a special bond in the loss of their mothers as well as showing a flair for composition.

By the spring of 1959, the Quarry Men were stumbling along and could easily have folded. George had become a sometime member of another band, the Les Stewart Quartet, and it was this connection that gave John's group a welcome boost. The Les Stewart Quartet was booked to open a new coffee bar, a converted basement in a large Victorian property in West Derby. Mona Best opened the Casbah not simply for commercial gain or to provide kids with a place to hang out. She was ambitious for her unassuming seventeen-year-old son Pete, and

1960

5 MAY The Quarry Men changed their name to the Silver Beetles.

10 MAY The band auditioned for Larry Parnes at the Wyvern Social Club in Liverpool to support Billy Fury's next tour. Although unsuccessful, Parnes offered them the chance to support Johnny Gentle's tour of Scotland.

14 MAY The group played at the Lathom Hall in Liverpool.

20 MAY Johnny Gentle's tour began at the Town Hall in Alloa in Scotland. A friend of John's named Stuart Sutcliffe played bass while Tommy Moore was on drums. For the purpose of the tour Paul called himself Paul Ramon, Stuart was known as Stuart da Stal, and George called himself Carl Harrison.

21 MAY The tour moved to the Northern Meeting Ballroom in Inverness.

23 MAY The next date was the Dalrymple Hall in Fraserburgh, Aberdeen.

25 MAY A tour date at St. Thomas' Hall, Banffshire.

26 MAY A performance at the Town Hall, Forres, Morayshire.

27 MAY A show at the Regal Ballroom, Nairn, Nairnshire.

28 MAY The final tour date at the Rescue Hall in Aberdeen.

30 MAY Back home in Liverpool, they played at the Jacaranda Coffee Bar.

2 JUNE A date at the Institute, Neston, Wirral.

6 JUNE Along with Gerry and the Pacemakers, the Silver Beetles played at the Grosvenor Ballroom in Liskeard, Cornwall. They then continued to perform each Saturday until 30 July, when complaints of noise and rowdiness forced the venue to cancel the shows.

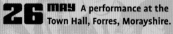
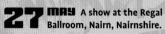
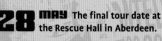

saw the new venture as a way of promoting his career. John, Paul, and George helped decorate the place before its grand opening on 29 August, though only George should have been onstage on the big day. An internal bust-up left the Les Stewart Quartet depleted, and at George's suggestion John and Paul rode to the rescue.

The Quarry Men, plus Les Stewart bass player Ken Brown, became the Casbah's resident band, though Brown was soon shown the door after he received his gig fee despite being too unwell to perform, a clear breach of equity to the other three. It was also the parting of the ways for the Quarry Men and the Casbah, but regular work had buoyed their spirits and persuaded them to keep going. The worst was behind them: 1960 was to be a turning point in their burgeoning careers.

In January of the new year the group became a four-piece again as John's art-college friend Stuart Sutcliffe was recruited to play bass. Sutcliffe was an outstanding artist but could barely play a note. His place in the band rested on John's endorsement and the fact that an art prize funded the purchase of a Hofner President bass guitar. Sutcliffe improved over time, and it is a fallacy that he always played side-on to the audience to mask his lack of ability, but his guitar work remained at a rudimentary level. Not that John seemed to care. Sutcliffe looked the part of a rock 'n' roller, which was more than enough.

Sutcliffe may not have contributed much musically, but he is credited with suggesting that the group change its name along insect lines, a nod toward the much-revered Crickets. Several permutations were tried before they

settled upon the Beatles that summer. Sutcliffe was also the conduit to Allan Williams, the next important figure in the Beatles' story. Williams owned the Jacaranda Coffee Bar and was also a small-time promoter. Sutcliffe, who patronized the Jacaranda, went to Williams scouting for business, an approach that led to the band's first pro tour—crisscrossing Scotland backing Johnny Gentle—and the first of five trips to Hamburg.

Days before the newly constituted Beatles set off for Germany on 16 August 1960, they solved their long-term rhythm-section problem after paying an impromptu return visit to the Casbah. There they found Pete Best on drums in the resident band, which was on the verge of splitting. There was a hasty audition, but with Hamburg looming there was hardly a decision to be made. The helter-skelter trip round Scotland, and arduous sets up to eight hours long in seedy Hamburg clubs, disabused the Beatles of any notion that being a working band was a glamorous pursuit. But hour after hour of beer and Preludin-fuelled stage work honed their live act and made them into a tight professional unit. "Mach schau!" the punters would yell, and make a show they did. One Ringo Starr was also in Hamburg in the autumn of 1960.

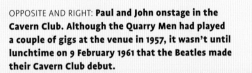
OPPOSITE AND RIGHT: **Paul and John onstage in the Cavern Club. Although the Quarry Men had played a couple of gigs at the venue in 1957, it wasn't until lunchtime on 9 February 1961 that the Beatles made their Cavern Club debut.**

13 JUNE Tommy Moore's last appearance with the band; the venue was the Jacaranda Coffee Bar.

18 JUNE It was Paul's 18th birthday.

13 SEPTEMBER Pete Best passed an audition to join the band as drummer.

17 SEPTEMBER For the first time they played as the Beatles; the venue was the Indra Club in Hamburg, Germany. They were there for 48 days and

played four and a half hours a night with six hours at the weekend. The group now comprised Paul, John, George, Pete, and Stuart.

13 SEPTEMBER The Beatles were moved to the Kaiserkeller after complaints about the noise at the Indra Club. They played here for another 58 nights along with Rory Storm & the Hurricanes.

15 SEPTEMBER Ringo Starr, drummer with Rory Storm & the Hurricanes, filled in for Pete Best although

Best was to continue to play with the Beatles for another two years.

21 NOVEMBER George was deported back to England because he was under 18 and therefore not allowed to be in a nightclub after midnight.

1 DECEMBER Paul and Pete Best were deported—this time after a fire occurred in their hotel room and they were suspected of arson.

10 DECEMBER John returned to England.

27 DECEMBER During a break from the Hamburg dates the Beatles played at Litherland Town Hall in Liverpool.

31 DECEMBER A New Year's Eve performance at the Casbah Coffee Club in West Derby, Liverpool. The club was in the basement of Pete Best's home and was managed by his mother, Mona.

Goodbye Stuart

Liverpool's premier drummer—Ringo Starr—was plying his trade with Rory Storm & the Hurricanes—at the time a bigger name than the Beatles on Merseyside. There was both fraternization and rivalry between the groups, who shared the onerous workload at the Kaiserkeller. The residency ended on a sour note when the Kaiserkeller owner cut up rough after he found the Beatles jamming at a rival club, the Top Ten. After a run-in with the police, all made it back to England except Stuart Sutcliffe, who chose to remain with girlfriend Astrid Kirchherr. She and Klaus Voormann were part of an intellectual set who had befriended the group. Kirchherr didn't suggest that they brush their Teddy boy quiffs forward—but she was responsible for the collarless jackets and a number of stunning monochrome photographs of the Beatles.

Sutcliffe was briefly reunited with the band when they returned to Hamburg in March 1961, but by then Paul was angling to take over on bass. Sutcliffe was sanguine about leaving the Beatles. Never a committed musician, he decided to focus on his art studies and marry Astrid but died from a brain haemorrhage on 10 April 1962, two months before the planned nuptials.

The Beatles, meanwhile, were going from strength to strength. The Hamburg apprenticeship had turned them into electrifying, time-served performers, and they soon became Liverpool's top band. They did the rounds of the plethora of "jive hives" that Liverpool boasted, and on 9 February 1961 took their bow at the venue with which they would become most associated.

1961

5 JANUARY A performance at the Town Hall in Litherland, Liverpool. For the next three months they played at various local venues in their hometown.

9 FEBRUARY The band took to the stage for their first lunchtime show at the Cavern Club in Liverpool.

25 FEBRUARY It was George's 18th birthday.

11 MARCH The boys' Beatles Farewell Show took place at the Aintree Institute in Aintree, Liverpool. The show went on throughout the night, finishing at 8:00 a.m. and included performances from Gerry and the Pacemakers and Rory Storm & the Hurricanes.

15 MARCH Stuart Sutcliffe left the group, remaining in Germany.

1 APRIL A second series of shows in Hamburg, this time at the Top Ten club. They ultimately played every single night until 1 July—a total of 92 appearances.

22 JUNE The band provided the backing track for Tony Sheridan on some tracks produced by Bert Kaempfert.

1 JULY The Beatles signed a one-year contract with Bert Kaempfert.

3 JULY The boys returned to Liverpool.

6 JULY The first edition of *Mersey Beat* was published in Britain and included an essay by John about the band.

7 JULY It was Ringo's 21st birthday.

13 JULY Their first performance back in Liverpool at St. John's Hall in Tuebrook.

14 JULY Then back to the Cavern Club when they played both the lunchtime and evening slot. The Beatles then continued to play regular local gigs, predominantly at the Cavern Club.

20 JULY A report on the boys' contract with Kaempfert was on the front page of *Mersey Beat*.

27 JULY At the Cavern Club they supported Cilla White—later to become Cilla Black.

The Cavern: Home to the Beatles

The Cavern had been a jazz club when it opened its doors in 1957, the management tolerating skiffle but frowning on beat music. Indeed, the Quarry Men had played there in 1957, receiving a dressing-down for slipping some Elvis numbers into their set. Things changed when Ray McFall took over the Mathew Street establishment. Rock 'n' roll was now on the menu, in tandem with jazz initially, though the latter sessions were soon phased out,

ABOVE: **The Beatles onstage in Liverpool in 1962. Pete Best (right) had very little time left playing drums with the band. Just as the Beatles were about to make it to the big leagues, he was sacked.**

ABOVE INSET: **A flyer for an early Beatles performance at Hambleton Hall in January 1961.**

LEFT: **Rory Storm & the Hurricanes, with Ringo standing on the far right.**

OPPOSITE: **George, John, and Paul, the three permanent members of the Quarry Men, outside Paul's house in early 1960.**

31 AUGUST Bob Wooler wrote an article about the Beatles in *Mersey Beat*.

9 OCTOBER It was John's 21st birthday so he and Paul bought bowler hats and hitched to Paris.

17 OCTOBER The band's first fan-club performance took place at the David Lewis Club in Liverpool.

28 OCTOBER At Brian Epstein's NEMS record store, Raymond Jones enquired about the band's record "My Bonnie", which had been released only in Germany. Brian promised to find it.

30 OCTOBER Two more girls asked about "My Bonnie" at Brian's store.

8 NOVEMBER Brian phoned and booked a ticket at the Cavern Club, citing an "important visit".

9 NOVEMBER Brian and Alistair Taylor watched the boys during a lunchtime show at the Cavern Club.

1 DECEMBER The band travelled to London with Brian to meet Colin Borland and Beecher Stevens from Decca to hopefully negotiate a recording contract.

3 DECEMBER The band and Bob Wooler visited Brian at his NEMS store.

4 DECEMBER Deutsche Grammophon representatives met Brian in Liverpool after he had asked if "My Bonnie" could be released as a single in the UK.

6 DECEMBER The boys met Brian again at his shop.

8 DECEMBER Brian contacted Ron White from EMI to try to get a contract with them.

10 DECEMBER Another meeting between Brian and the boys—this time at the Casbah Coffee Club.

13 DECEMBER Dick Rowe, head of Decca's A&R, sent Mike Smith

to watch the band at the Cavern Club. Afterwards Smith recommended that Decca set up a recording audition.

18 DECEMBER Ron White wrote to Brian saying that EMI had rejected the band.

26 DECEMBER The Beatles played at the Big Beat Ball at the Tower Ballroom in New Brighton. They were billed as the "Beetles".

31 DECEMBER The band travelled down to London for an audition at Decca the next day.

THE

BEATLES

Sole Direction :
BRIAN EPSTEIN,
Nems Enterprises Ltd.
12/14 Whitechapel,
Liverpool 1.
ROYal 7895

1962

1 JANUARY The band's audition for Decca took place at the label's studio in West Hampstead. After 15 tracks were recorded Brain Poole and the Tremoloes took their turn. The Tremoloes were subsequently signed up but not the Beatles.

4 JANUARY The Beatles were placed top of the list in *Mersey Beat*'s first poll for the most popular group; this edition of the paper was mainly focused on the band.

5 JANUARY "My Bonnie" was released in the UK.

1 FEBRUARY Brian Epstein made his first booking for the band at the Thistle Café in West Kirby, Cheshire. They continued to play regularly at the Cavern Club and other local venues. The group's management contract signed on 24 January officially began.

5 FEBRUARY Pete Best was ill; Ringo Starr appeared with the group for the first time in England.

6 FEBRUARY Brian Epstein met Dick Rowe and Beecher Stevens from Decca, who informed him that the Beatles had been rejected by the record company.

20 FEBRUARY Brian Epstein wrote to Bert Kaempfert asking him to release the band from their contract.

7 MARCH The Beatles went to the Playhouse Theatre in Manchester to record their performance for the BBC's Light programme *Teenager's Turn (Here We Go)* in front of a live audience.

8 MARCH The band made their radio debut when *Teenager's Turn (Here We Go)* was broadcast.

10 APRIL Stuart Sutcliffe died suddenly from a brain haemorrhage at the age of 21.

unable to survive the shockwaves of the Mersey Beat explosion.

The dank, fetid atmosphere of the underground vault was hardly salubrious, yet with the Beatles as the resident band no one was too bothered about the inadequate ventilation, walls running with condensation, or the stench of disinfectant. They made almost 300 Cavern appearances over the next two and a half years, the last of them when "She Loves You" was about to hit the airwaves. Their fee increased from £5 to £300, though even a sixtyfold increase couldn't contain the Beatles by August 1963.

At the Cavern the group experienced Beatlemania in microcosm. There was fierce rivalry among the girls, who would queue from early morning to secure a good vantage point. Mad scrimmages ensued when the doors opened. The toilets were packed just before the Beatles arrived onstage as the girls dolled themselves up in the hope of being singled out for special attention.

In late June, during their second Hamburg stint, the Beatles attended their first proper recording session. They signed with bandleader Bert Kaempfert after impressing onstage at the Top Ten. It was primarily as a backing group—singer Tony Sheridan was the main attraction—but a milestone nonetheless. They even got to record two songs alone, "Ain't She Sweet" and a Harrison–Lennon instrumental titled "Cry for a Shadow". Polydor released a single comprising two of the Sheridan numbers, "My Bonnie" and "The Saints", with the "Beat Brothers" credited as

The Beatles

the backing group. It made Germany's Top 40 but didn't get a UK release. The Beatles weren't even able to bask in the limelight of their minor Continental success, for by then they were back on the Liverpool circuit, still seeking a breakthrough. It came at the end of the year, and from an unlikely source: a frustrated thespian turned record shop manager.

Enter Brian Epstein

It was furniture, not the entertainment business, that ran in the Epstein family blood. Brian was expected to follow in the family footsteps, but from a young age he had other ideas. After briefly attending RADA, he reluctantly agreed to knuckle down, taking charge of a new division of the family concern, North End Music Stores. Epstein prided himself on the level of customer service NEMS offered. If a particular record wasn't in stock, he guaranteed that a copy would be sourced from somewhere. It was one such request that brought the Beatles to his attention in late October 1961.

The Beatles had brought a few copies of "My Bonnie" home with them, and, not wanting to miss a self-promotional trick, pressed one into the hands of Bob Wooler, the Cavern's resident DJ. Wooler enthusiastically plugged the record, so regular Cavernites would have been very familiar with it. One such fan, Raymond Jones, requested a copy of "My Bonnie" at NEMS, thereby taking his place in the history books as the first person to bring the Beatles to Brian

OPPOSITE: **George at the Cavern Club. After performing at several afternoon sessions, the Beatles were finally promoted to a nighttime slot at the club on 21 March 1961.**

OPPOSITE INSET LEFT: **Cavern Club season ticket holders got to see the Beatles on countless occasions in 1962.**

OPPOSITE INSET RIGHT: **Brian Epstein's business card dating from 1962.**

TOP LEFT: **A publicity picture, featuring Pete Best, shows the boys in the suits that Brian Epstein favoured rather than the leather jackets they had previously worn.**

ABOVE: **The official Beatles fan club was established in 1962, although an unofficial one had been started as early as September 1961.**

BELOW: **Allan Williams is sometimes credited as being the band's first manager, but he is more commonly viewed as the promoter who was responsible for many of the band's bookings during their formative years.**

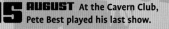

The Beatles

SOLE DIRECTION: A. WILLIAMS TEL. ROYAL 7943

BOOKINGS: TEL. STANLEY 1556

13 APRIL The band returned to Germany to play 48 dates at the Star-Club in Hamburg.

23 APRIL "My Bonnie" was released in the US.

8 MAY During a visit to the HMV store in Oxford Street, London, Brian Epstein met engineer Ted Huntly, who sent Brian to talk to Ardmore & Beechwood, where he met Sidney Colman. Colman arranged a meeting with EMI producer George Martin.

9 MAY Brian Epstein met George Martin at Abbey Road and immediately sent a telegram to the boys, who were in Hamburg.

2 JUNE With the Hamburg contract finished, the boys returned to England.

4 JUNE The band signed a recording contract with EMI.

6 JUNE The Beatles' first trip to the Abbey Road studios to make a recording test for Parlophone records.

9 JUNE They were back at the Cavern Club—their first show after coming back from Germany.

26 JUNE NEMS Enterprises Ltd. was officially formed.

26 JULY The Beatles supported Joe Brown and the Bruvvers at Cambridge Hall, Southport, in a concert promoted by Brian Epstein.

14 AUGUST Brian Epstein asked Ringo Starr to join the band.

15 AUGUST At the Cavern Club, Pete Best played his last show.

16 AUGUST Brian Epstein decided to sack Best a few hours before the evening's show at the Riverpark Ballroom in Chester. Johnny Hutchinson of the Big Three filled in that evening and was offered the chance to replace him but he turned the proposal down.

18 AUGUST Ringo Starr officially joined the band for a gig at the Port Sunlight Horticultural Society's annual show that took place in Birkenhead.

Epstein's attention. Others soon followed, and Epstein made it his business to find out about the group that had prompted the enquiries. He discovered that not only were the Beatles a local band, but they were playing almost on a daily basis at a club a stone's throw away from his store.

On 9 November a besuited Epstein and his assistant Alistair Taylor descended into the Cavern to find out what all the fuss was about. Even had he swapped his pinstripes for more casual attire, the Beatles and regulars would have recognized the twenty-seven-year-old Epstein because they all patronized his store. His presence certainly raised eyebrows and sparked comment. Epstein could have conducted the business at hand quickly by noting down the details of the record Raymond Jones and others had asked for. But he lingered, not just that day but on a number of occasions over the next three weeks. In that time, the idea formed that he might diversify into an altogether different branch of the music business.

Why did Epstein decide to take a leap into the unknown, from record retailing into managing a band? He certainly recognized the stardust, and maybe saw theatrical management as a proxy for his own failed stage ambitions. It also seems clear that the sexual energy exuded by the four leather-clad musicians was a further source of attraction.

The Beatles were impressed with Epstein's pitch. He guaranteed to get them more gigs at better venues with increased fees. He also dangled the carrot of a recording contract, which sealed the deal. A management fee of 25 percent off the top line was something that would grate further down the line, but in December 1961 it was waved away in the rosy afterglow of having acquired as their manager the head of a large record-distribution outlet.

Epstein was an experienced retailer but green when it came to show business management. He had to pick things up as he went along, which would lead to some woeful deals being done on the Beatles' behalf. But he believed in them, as they believed in themselves, and set about

the task of gaining the Beatles an entrée into the big time. It looked as though he had struck gold immediately when he got an A&R man from Decca to pay a visit to the Cavern. In truth, Decca was paying lip service to an important client, NEMS's buying power giving Epstein considerable clout with the record labels. But Mike Smith, the executive dispatched to the far-flung northwestern outpost, actually liked what he saw. The Beatles' performance earned them an audition on New Year's Day 1962.

Unfortunately, they chose the wrong time to have an off day. The group had had a fraught journey in icy conditions, arriving tired and hungry; they were forced to use unfamiliar studio equipment; and the occasion seemed to get to them. Though they failed to re-create the dynamism of their stage show, Smith was still prepared to take a chance. There was a contract opening with Decca, but the Beatles weren't the only band up for consideration. Smith had also auditioned Brian Poole and the Tremeloes, and would happily have signed both groups to the label. A&R boss Dick Rowe, who had seen neither group perform, told Smith he could add only one act to Decca's roster. Smith decided to go with the Tremeloes, the deciding factor being that the Beatles sounded "too much like the Shadows".

The record deal

By the spring of 1962, Epstein had already made good on most of his promises. The Beatles' lot was immeasurably better in terms of the work they were getting, and they were now the undisputed top of the Liverpool pile. If Hamburg had tightened the band, it was Epstein who smartened them up and turned them into a slick, professional outfit. However, the jewel in the crown was a recording contract, and on that issue he was struggling to deliver. He was certain

the Beatles were going to be huge; all he had to do now was convince the industry's movers and shakers ensconced in the capital two hundred miles away.

Epstein did the rounds of all the majors, including Pye, Philips, and EMI, only to be given short shrift by them all. Then, during yet another door-knocking exercise, he passed an HMV shop in Oxford Street that offered the very service he had been looking for. Epstein had been advised that he might have more luck if he left a demo disk rather than an unwieldy tape, and here was just such an outlet.

The engineer who made the copies liked what he heard, and was even more impressed to discover that some of the material was self-penned. This group was clearly a cut above the amateurish dross he often had to deal with. He put Epstein in touch with music publishers Ardmore & Beechwood, an EMI subsidiary located in the very same building. Sid Colman, who ran the operation, offered to put in a word with the Artists & Repertoire department of his parent

OPPOSITE: **The Cavern Club was a dark, poorly ventilated vault in the heart of the city, but many Mersey Beat acts played there, including Cilla Black (left), who was a cloakroom girl at the club when she met the Beatles in 1961.**

OPPOSITE INSETS AND RIGHT: **By 1962, with lots of bands competing for slots on the local scene, the Beatles were able to trade on their new recording contract to their advantage.**

BELOW: **The final lineup. On 18 August 1962, two days after Pete was sacked, Ringo Starr joined the band.**

BELOW INSET: **On 6 June 1962 EMI offered the Beatles a recording contract with their Parlophone label.**

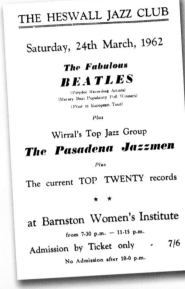

THE HESWALL JAZZ CLUB

Saturday, 24th March, 1962

The Fabulous
BEATLES
(Polydor Recording Artists)
(Mersey Beat Popularity Poll Winners)
(Prior to European Tour)

Plus

Wirral's Top Jazz Group
The Pasadena Jazzmen

Plus

The current TOP TWENTY records

★ ★

at Barnston Women's Institute

from 7-30 p.m. — 11-15 p.m.

Admission by Ticket only   -   7/6

No Admission after 10-0 p.m.

THE BEATLES

PARLOPHONE RECORDS

company. Most of EMI's A&R men were tied up with top-line artists, but there was one who might give the Beatles a hearing.

George Martin headed up Parlophone, a minor EMI label best known for putting out quirky comedy records. It took some time to break down Martin's resistance, an exasperated Epstein once again using the buying power of NEMS as a bargaining chip. Martin relented but was hardly knocked out by what he heard

when the Beatles auditioned on 6 June 1962. The Beatles, fresh from their third Hamburg stint, recorded four songs that day: "Love Me Do", "P.S. I Love You", "Ask Me Why", and a cover that regularly featured in their set, "Besame Mucho." It was adequate, though Martin felt the material wasn't strong enough. But he did think they had something, enough for him to rubber-stamp the precontract agreement already in place.

LA SCALA BALLROOM 166
HIGH STREET · RUNCORN
NEMS ENTERPRISES LTD. Present -
(THE NORTH'S No. 1 ROCK COMBO)
★ THE BEATLES ★
AND OTHER TOP LINE ATTRACTIONS
Tuesday, 11th December 1962
FIRST PERFORMANCE
Commencing 7 p.m.
Ticket 3/-

TOP: **The Beatles posing with their instruments in a small backyard in London in 1963.**

ABOVE: **A ticket from a December 1962 show at La Scala Ballroom.**

OPPOSITE LEFT: **The Beatles are billed to appear with fellow Liverpudlians Gerry and the Pacemakers, who had a hit with "How Do You Do It?", a song the Beatles refused to record.**

continued from page 19

1962

22 AUGUST John married Cynthia Powell at Mt. Pleasant Register Office in Liverpool.

23 AUGUST Granada Television filmed the band during a performance at the Cavern Club.

4 SEPTEMBER The band's first recording session at Abbey Road when "How Do You Do It?" and "Love Me Do" were taped.

11 SEPTEMBER "P.S. I Love You", "Please Please Me", and "Love Me Do" were recorded at Abbey Road. Session drummer Andy White helped on drums while Ringo played percussion.

1 OCTOBER A new contract between Brian Epstein and the band was signed.

5 OCTOBER "Love Me Do"/"P.S. I Love You" was released in the UK. The record was played on Radio Luxembourg.

6 OCTOBER The boys appeared at Dawson's Music Shop in Widnes to sign copies of "Love Me Do", their first single; it was the first of many similar appearances.

8 OCTOBER At EMI House the band made a recording for Radio Luxembourg's *The Friday Spectacular*.

9 OCTOBER The Beatles visited the offices of *Record Mirror* in Shaftesbury Avenue, London.

11 OCTOBER "Love Me Do" was in the listings of favourite songs in *Record Retailer*.

12 OCTOBER The band was one of the support acts for Little Richard at the Tower Ballroom in New Brighton.

17 OCTOBER The Beatles appeared on Granada TV's *People and Places*, their television debut.

25 OCTOBER They recorded an appearance for the BBC's *Here We Go* at the Playhouse Theatre

The first single

When they reconvened at Abbey Road on 4 September, the question of what to put out as a debut single was pressing. Martin strongly urged them to record a catchy Mitch Murray number that had just come his way. Under sufferance the Beatles ran through a lacklustre version of "How Do You Do It?" but were adamant that they wanted to record one of their own songs. "When you can write material as good as this, I'll record it," came the sharp rejoinder. Still the group dug their heels in. From a position of relative weakness, it was remarkable that they overrode Martin's judgment.

So "Love Me Do" it was to be, which at least had a distinctive harmonica riff that Martin liked. But the producer had another concern, and this time he wouldn't give way. Martin had been dissatisfied with Pete Best's drumming on the 6 June recording, and must have been pleased that in the interim the Beatles had replaced him with Liverpool's finest, Ringo Starr. Martin's reservations were undoubtedly a contributory factor in Best's sacking in mid-August, though John, Paul, and George had been pondering the issue for some time. Best may have been hugely popular with the fans—his dismissal provoked a severe backlash—but he was at best

a limited drummer, somewhat taciturn, and had clung to his rock 'n' roller's quiff long after the others had adopted the moptop look. In short, he didn't fit in. Ringo had actually deputized for Best on a couple of occasions in Hamburg; now the Beatles wanted him as a permanent fixture on the drummer's stool. It was perfect timing for Ringo, who thought his career might have stalled as he faced yet another summer season on the holiday-camp circuit.

Unfortunately, at the 4 Sepember session George Martin was also dissatisfied with Ringo's efforts, and "Love Me Do" Take Three was arranged for the following week, this time with top session man Andy White on drums. Ringo was mortified, feeling that his time as a Beatle was over almost before it had started. He was reduced to rattling maracas and shaking a tambourine at that session, in which the Beatles also recorded "P.S. I Love You" and a nascent version of "Please Please Me".

Things weren't as bad as they appeared, however. It wasn't unusual to replace a capable stage drummer with a session musician for the different demands of the recording studio. And in any event, it was the 4 September recording, featuring Ringo, that was chosen for the single release. Strangely, when the group's debut album was put together early the following year, it was the Andy White version that was included in the set, and

subsequent pressings of the single also featured White on drums.

The Beatles were understandably elated when "Love Me Do" started to get airplay and appeared on various charts. Perhaps they wouldn't have been so surprised had they been aware that Epstein had ordered 10,000 copies to fill the NEMS stock cupboards. Even so, "Love Me Do" hovered in the lower reaches of most listings, apart from *Mersey Beat*, where, predictably, it shot to No. 1. It was a steady if unspectacular debut to their recording career. A strong follow-up was needed. Once again, George Martin proposed "How Do You Do It?" And once again, the Beatles had other ideas.

ABOVE: **A ticket and flyer for a Little Richard gig at the Empire Theatre in Liverpool on 28 October 1962. The Beatles were fortunate enough to back the American singer for the second time that month. Both events were arranged by Brian Epstein and were the most ambitious events promoted by NEMS to date.**

---

in Manchester. On the same day they were interviewed for the Cleaver and Clatterbridge Hospital radio station.

26 OCTOBER Here We Go was broadcast at 5 p.m. "Love Me Do" officially entered the chart listings.

28 OCTOBER Their first performance at the Liverpool Empire Theatre, again supporting Little Richard.

1 NOVEMBER The Beatles began a two-week booking at the Star-Club in Hamburg.

7 NOVEMBER They appeared on Granada TV's *People and Places*.

15 NOVEMBER The band returned from Germany.

16 NOVEMBER The Beatles recorded another item for Radio Luxembourg's *The Friday Spectacular*. On the same day they visited the offices of the music paper *Disc*.

17 NOVEMBER Another recording for *People and Places* was made.

26 NOVEMBER Back at Abbey Road to record "Please Please Me" and "Ask Me Why", which were to make up their second single.

30 NOVEMBER Another recording session for "Please Please Me".

2 DECEMBER At the BBC Paris Studio they recorded an appearance for *The Talent Spot*.

4 DECEMBER *The Talent Spot* was broadcast at 5 p.m. They travelled to the Wembley television studios for a live

appearance on Associated-Rediffusion's *Tuesday Rendezvous*.

13 DECEMBER Their appearance on *People and Places* was broadcast.

17 DECEMBER Brian took George Martin to watch the band perform live at the Cavern Club.

18 DECEMBER Still under an existing contract, the Beatles played 12 last dates at the Star-Club.

1963

Then There Was Music

"Beatlemania" entered the English language in 1963 as the Fabs conquered Britain with four infectious singles and back-to-back albums that would top the charts for a year.

At the beginning of the year the Beatles reigned supreme at the Cavern but beyond Merseyside they remained a little-known support band. Hordes of Liverpudlian fans wanted to keep it that way, but the tide was unstoppable. By the time "From Me to You" hit the airwaves in April, the Beatles were top of the bill no matter what the concert flyers said. By the time "She Loves You" was released in August, promoters up and down the land wanted a piece of the most extraordinary pop phenomenon to hit the country since Elvis. There was mass hysteria when the Beatles appeared on *Sunday Night at the London Palladium* in October, and the following month they played the Royal Command Performance, the most prestigious event on the entertainment calendar. The Beatles had made it "to the toppermost of the poppermost" in their home country. Next stop, the world.

OPPOSITE: **The Beatles celebrate winning** *Melody Maker*'s **Top Vocal Group Award on 11 September 1963. Sandwiched in between them is Susan Maughan, who won the award for Top Female Singer.**

THIS PAGE: **Success may have seemed to have come suddenly, but the Beatles worked hard in 1963, playing 219 concerts that year, 75 of them by the end of March, before the release of "From Me to You".**

JANUARY 1963

1 After playing 13 nights at the Star-Club in Hamburg, the group flew back to London.

2 The boys set off to Scotland for their first concert tour but the plane was diverted from Edinburgh to Aberdeen and the initial date was cancelled due to bad weather.

3 The first gig of the tour was played at the Two Red Shoes Ballroom in Elgin.

5 Saturday night's venue was the Museum Hall in Bridge of Allan.

6 The Beach Ballroom in Aberdeen was the final booking of the tour.

8 An appearance was made on the Scottish children's programme *Roundup* when the group mimed to "Please Please Me". The show was filmed at the Scottish Television studios in Glasgow.

10 The Beatles returned to Liverpool to lead a five-act bill including Gerry and the Pacemakers at the Grafton Rooms.

11 The second single, "Please Please Me"/"Ask Me Why" was released in the UK on Parlophone R 4983. A lunchtime performance at the Cavern Club before travelling to the Plaza Ballroom, Old Hill near Dudley, for an evening gig.

12 An evening show was performed at the Invicta Ballroom in Chatham.

13 An appearance on *Thank Your Lucky Stars* was recorded at the Alpha Television Studios in Birmingham.

14 Seven hundred people packed into the Civic Hall in Ellesmore Port when the band played for the Wolverham Welfare Association Dance.

16 A live performance on *People and Places* was given at Granada Studios before moving on to the Playhouse Theatre to record for the *Here We Go* programme.

Finding a follow-up to "Love Me Do"

George Martin's new year's resolutions for 1963 probably included making a wiser choice for the Beatles' next single. He had never been particularly enamoured with the debut single, and must have had a wry smile when it peaked at No. 17 on the UK charts despite Brian Epstein's best efforts to ramp up sales through his NEMS stores. But the boys remained determined to live or die by their own material, so Martin had no choice but to find someone else to record the sure-fire hit "How Do You Do It?". Gerry and the Pacemakers, another recruit to the burgeoning Epstein stable, were the lucky recipients, and the producer's ear for a chart-topper proved to be unerring. Thus, while the Beatles were the first group from the Mersey Sound conveyor belt to chart, it was the Pacemakers who gave Liverpool its first No. 1.

All of which left George Martin with a quandary: what should the Beatles release to build on the moderate success of "Love Me Do"? The options were somewhat thin. The recording sessions of 4 and 11 September 1962 had produced only one other candidate, "Please Please Me", John's self-conscious attempt at writing a "Roy Orbison song". John had recalled a snatch of an old Bing Crosby number "Please", which included the line, "Please lend a little ear to my pleas", and liked the wordplay so much that he gave it the Lennon treatment in his ballad. Out went saccharine sentimentalism, in came provocative lyrics with a sexual undertone, taking the boy-girl pop song a step further into the new permissive era.

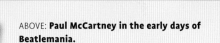

RIGHT: **The boys were beginning to make their mark, and the shows given in early 1963 revealed a band caught between the smalltime and national stardom. Just three days after the Beatles performed on the BBC they were back to playing in minor venues such as the Baptist Youth Club in Darwen, Lancashire (far right). During the spring they toured supporting other acts—first with Helen Shapiro and then Tommy Roe and Chris Montez (right). It wouldn't be long until they would top the bill themselves.**

ABOVE: **Paul McCartney in the early days of Beatlemania.**

OPPOSITE: **The Beatles performing in Birkenhead in April 1963.**

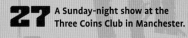

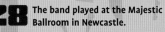

17 A lunchtime show at the Cavern Club was followed by a performance at the Majestic Ballroom, Birkenhead.

19 The band made their national TV debut on *Thank Your Lucky Stars* performing "Please Please Me". "Please Please Me"/"Ask Me Why" entered the UK charts, remaining there for 18 weeks and eventually reaching No. 2.

20 An evening concert was played at the Cavern Club.

21 The Beatles attended a photographic session at Abbey Road with Angus McBean to produce promotional material. A third appearance on Radio Luxembourg's *The Friday Spectacular*.

22 A live appearance on the lunchtime show *Pop Inn* and recording for the television show *The Talent Spot* were made.

23 After a long drive home from London, the Beatles played at the Cavern Club that evening.

24 After appearing at the NEMS Liverpool store, the boys travelled to North Wales for an appearance at the Assembly Hall in Mold.

25 Brian Epstein signed a contract with Vee-Jay Records allowing them to release Beatles discs in the States. The local Baptist Youth Club hosted a dance at the Co-operative Hall in Darwen, with the Beatles topping the bill.

26 The boys played at the El Rio Club in Macclesfield, where they were supported by Wayne Fontana and the Jets. This was followed by a show at the King's

Hall in Stoke-on-Trent. The recording for *Saturday Club* was broadcast.

27 A Sunday-night show at the Three Coins Club in Manchester.

28 The band played at the Majestic Ballroom in Newcastle.

29 *The Talent Spot* was broadcast on BBC Television.

30 The Beatles were on home ground playing at the Cavern Club at lunchtime.

FEBRUARY 1963

1 Two concerts were played in Midlands venues: the Assembly Rooms in Tamworth and Maney Hall in Sutton Coldfield.

2 The band's first full tour of Britain began at the Gaumont Cinema in Bradford with the band at the bottom of a list of five acts supporting Helen Shapiro. The *Evening Standard* was the first London newspaper to write a feature about the Beatles in an article by Maureen Cleave.

3 A rhythm and blues session at the Cavern Club, with the Beatles topping an eight-band bill.

4 The Beatles' last lunchtime session at the Cavern Club.

5 The Shapiro tour continues—this time at the Gaumont Cinema in Doncaster.

7 A drive north to perform at the Regal Cinema in Wakefield.

8 The boys were ejected from a golf-club dance after entering the ballroom in leather jackets after a performance at Carlisle ABC.

9 The first part of the Shapiro tour finished at the Empire Theatre in Sunderland.

10 A photographic session at the Royal Court Hotel with Cyrus Andrews. The band missed the Shapiro

tour that night in order to prepare for a recording session the following day.

11 Ten new tracks were recorded at Abbey Road for their first album *Please Please Me*. It took just under 11 hours with the session finally ending at 10:30 p.m.; the band lasted the day on throat lozenges called "Zubes" assisted by tea, milk, and cigarettes.

12 Two performances in the north; the Arena Ballroom in Sheffield followed by the Astoria Ballroom in Oldham.

13 One show at the Majestic Ballroom in Hull.

"Please Please Me": something raw and vibrant

The wording of "Please Please Me" wasn't a problem for Martin, who knew that a strong melody was far more important than the lyrics, whether or not the latter were suffused with innuendo. But he did think the arrangement was "dreary" and suggested upping the tempo. A decade later, John would claim that "Please Please Me" was recorded exactly as he wrote it, though Paul's memory of events accords with that of the producer. In any case, the Beatles repaired to the studio in late November and belted out the pepped-up number—seventeen times, to be exact. John added a harmonica overdub, reprising the opening strains of "Love Me Do", albeit in up-tempo rather than bluesy form. The Beatles couldn't afford to pass up the opportunity of adding a "signature" instrumental opening, a trick employed widely in the music business to get a band established. It was the final piece of the jigsaw, and Martin had no hesitation in congratulating the boys at having just recorded their first number one.

And he was right—well, almost. "Please Please Me" was released on 11 January 1963 and did indeed shoot to the top of all the main listings, including the prestigious *Melody Maker* and *New Musical Express* publications. But it was denied top spot in *Record Retailer*, the music industry's trade publication, which laid claim to being the "official" UK chart, and was certainly the one the Guinness record compilers used. Frank Ifield's "Wayward Wind" provided the stumbling block; there would be no other in the UK for the next eleven single releases, until Engelbert Humperdinck's "Release Me" denied "Penny Lane"/"Strawberry Fields Forever" top spot in 1967.

"Love Me Do" had received precious little promotion from either EMI or publisher Ardmore & Beechwood, leaving a disgruntled Epstein the unenviable task of trying to drive sales and get airplay for what George Martin regarded as essentially B-side material. "Please Please Me" was a different matter altogether. The country now saw what had held the Cavern-goers spellbound. This was something different, raw, and vibrant, a pulsating two-minute adrenalin-rush of cascading harmonica riffs, ascending guitar chords, and fabulous harmonies.

THE SHAPIRO TOUR

The Beatles were booked for their first national tour supporting sixteen-year-old Helen Shapiro who had been voted Britain's best female singer for two years running. The tour lasted on and off for a month, during which time the Beatles gave fourteen performances and steadily worked their way up the bill, finally being elevated to the privileged position of closing the first half. The boys were able to forgo the van and travel to each tour date on a coach with the other artists. It was on the coach journey from York to Shrewsbury on 28 February that Paul and John wrote their next single, "From Me to You".

GAUMONT :: BRADFORD
THE HELEN SHAPIRO SHOW
2nd Performance 8-30 p.m.
SATURDAY
FEBRUARY 2
CENTRE STALLS 5/6
BLOCK 7 A 8
No ticket exchanged nor money refunded
THIS PORTION TO BE RETAINED

TOP: **John and Paul sharing the vocals.**

ABOVE: **A ticket from the first night of the Beatles' first nationwide tour, supporting Helen Shapiro at the Gaumont Cinema in Bradford.**

OPPOSITE: **The Beatles and George Martin proudly display their silver disc for "Please Please Me" in April 1963. By way of a thank you, the boys performed a private concert for EMI executives.**

14 A performance at the Locarno Ballroom in Liverpool.

15 The concert originally scheduled for 11 January took place at the Ritz Ballroom in King's Heath—although in only five weeks the band had shot from relative anonymity to chart success, making it quite a lucrative booking for the promoters, as the cost stayed the same.

16 The band appeared on the cover of *Record Mirror*, a national music paper. Booked by John Smith, the well-known London promoter, they played at the Carfax Assembly Rooms, Oxford.

17 A second recording for *Thank Your Lucky Stars* was held at Teddington Studio—they were now third in a seven-act lineup with Billy Fury at the top.

18 Two performances at the Queens Hall in Widnes—both sold out.

19 An evening gig at the Cavern Club. Fans stood in line for two days to buy tickets. It was the last time the Beatles saw Pete Best.

20 The Beatles appeared on *Parade of the Pops*, a live lunchtime BBC radio programme transmitted from the Playhouse Theatre.

21 Two houses were played at the Majestic Ballroom, Birkenhead.

22 The Northern Songs Ltd. publishing company was set up by Dick James and John and Paul for the Lennon–McCartney songs, with Brian Epstein as director. The band performed at the Oasis Club in Manchester.

23 The second leg of the Shapiro tour kicked off at the Granada Cinema in Mansfield. Their second appearance on *Thank Your Lucky Stars* was broadcast on television that night.

24 A show at the Coventry Theatre in Coventry.

25 George's 20th birthday. Vee-Jay released the band's first single in the US, containing "Please Please Me" and "Ask Me Why", but it didn't enter the *Billboard* charts. The band's name was misspelled "The Beattles" on the initial pressing.

28 On the journey to the show at the Granada Cinema in Shrewsbury, John and Paul wrote "From Me to You", which was to be their next single. They based the lyrics on the letters page of *New Musical Express*.

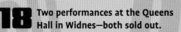

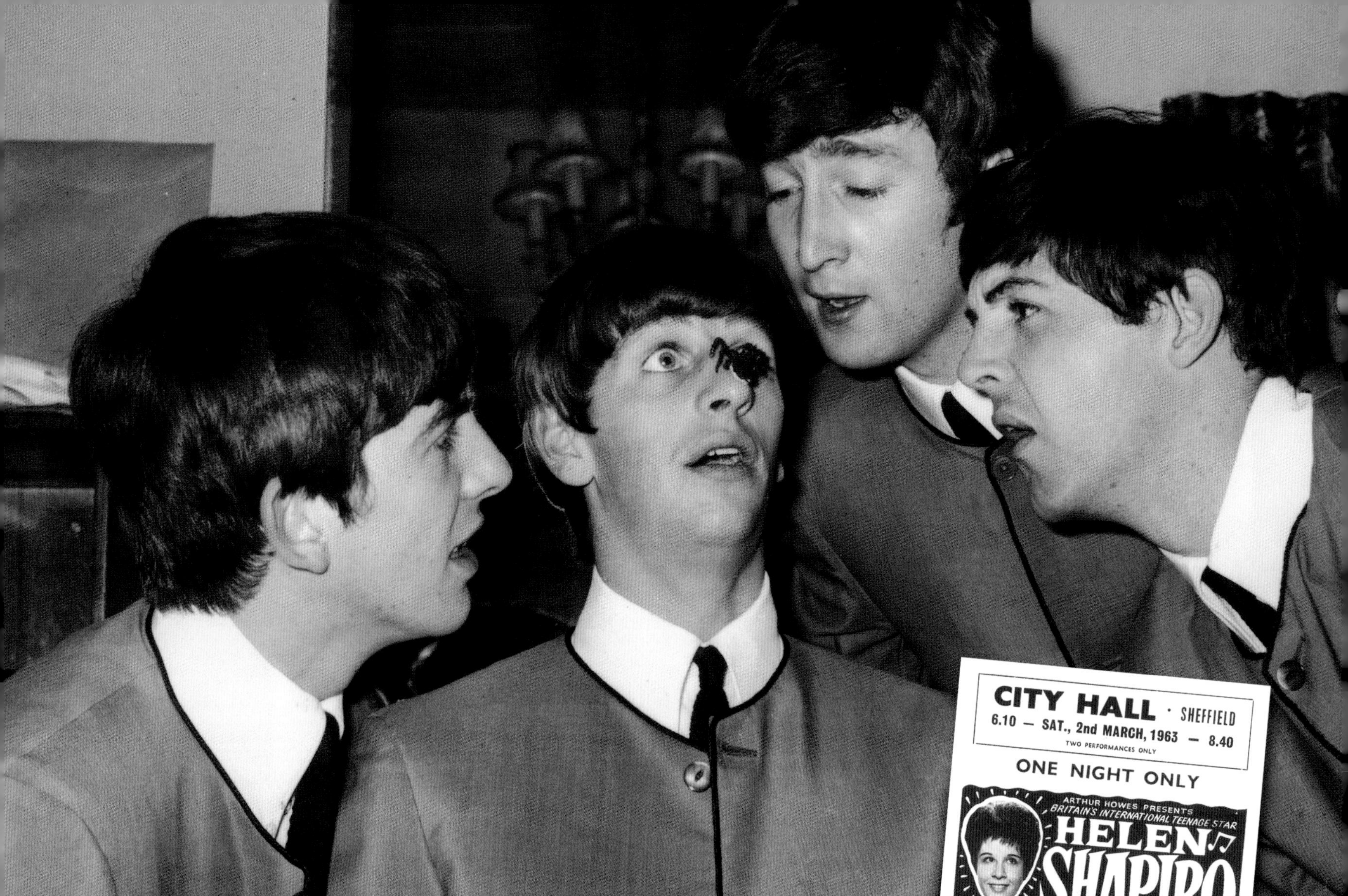

FIRST COVER OF A BEATLES SONG

"Misery" didn't follow the "I-Me-You" pattern, but it was nonetheless a calculated composition. John and Paul wrote it specifically for Helen Shapiro, knowing that to have a major artist record one of their numbers would be a feather in their cap. In fact, Columbia turned the song down before Helen Shapiro got to hear it, and "Misery" wound up as a filler on the *Please Please Me* album. It did become the first Lennon–McCartney song to be recorded by another artist, though. Kenny Lynch, who was also on the bill of the Shapiro tour, jumped at the chance to record it during a break in the tour. The Beatles were less than impressed with Lynch's rendition, but this minor hit marked the inauspicious beginning of a global trend; before long artists the world over, from every musical genre, would be falling over themselves to record the music of Lennon–McCartney.

TOP: **The boys clown for the camera after a show at the London Palladium.**

ABOVE: **The Shapiro tour ended on 3 March: this handbill promotes the penultimate performance in Sheffield.**

CITY HALL · SHEFFIELD
6.10 — SAT., 2nd MARCH, 1963 — 8.40
TWO PERFORMANCES ONLY

ONE NIGHT ONLY

ARTHUR HOWES PRESENTS
BRITAIN'S INTERNATIONAL TEENAGE STAR

HELEN SHAPIRO

THE DYNAMIC "LOVE ME DO" BEATLES

BRITAIN'S TOP VOCAL GROUP
THE KESTRELS

SPECIAL GUEST STAR
DANNY WILLIAMS
"MOON RIVER" "JEANNIE"

THE RED PRICE BAND

THE HONEYS

YOUR COMPÈRE
DAVE ALLEN

"UP ON THE ROOF"
KENNY LYNCH

PRICES 8/6 7/- 6/6 5/6 5/- 4/- 3/6
Booking Agents : Wilson Peck Ltd., 78–84 Fargate, Sheffield

Booking Agents :
Wilson, Peck Ltd.
Fargate, Sheffield 1. Tel. 27074

POSTAL BOOKING FORM
Saturday, 2nd March, 1963
Helen Shapiro Show

Please forward .... Date ....

for the EVENING 6.10 / 8.40 performance on .... SEATS 8/6 7/- 6/6 5/6 5/- 4/- 3/6

I enclose stamped addressed envelope and P.O. / Cheque value £ .... s. d.
(Please delete words not applicable)

NAME ....

ADDRESS .... (Block letters)

Use this form if inconvenient to call at the Theatre The best available seats will be allotted to you

Printed in Empire (Modern) Printing Co. Ltd — Manchester 4

Marathon recording session produces debut album

Martin knew it was vital to catch the wave. Touring commitments left precious few windows of opportunity, but Monday, 11 February was pencilled in for a marathon recording session that would yield material for the first Beatles album. It was back on the road with two gigs in the north of England the following day, so there were no second chances. Martin wasn't fazed, for he wanted to try to capture the raw quality that made the Beatles such a mesmerizing live band. Indeed, he flirted briefly with the idea of making a live album before deciding it was totally impractical.

The gruelling thirteen-hour session did mean there was some fraying at the edges, not least in John's rasping vocals on "Twist and Shout", the last of the eleven songs recorded that remarkable day. John was suffering from a cold, but straining for the notes with a voice that was all but shot gave his performance a maniacal edge that ultimately made this track a tour de force. It wasn't that the verve compensated for any lack of polish. On this barnstorming rocker, and the album as a whole, any rough edges merely added to its visceral appeal.

"Twist and Shout" was one of six covers recorded that day, songs that regularly formed part of the Beatles' set. There were four of their own numbers, though with the A- and B-sides of the two singles fleshing out the fourteen-track album, it meant that Lennon–McCartney held creative sway in the finished piece. The eleventh song they tried during the session was Paul's "Hold Me Tight", which failed to make the cut this time but which would be resurrected on the next album later that year.

MARCH 1963

1 The band played a concert at the Odeon Cinema in Southport.

2 After two performances at the City Hall in Sheffield, the boys travelled to Manchester for a live performance at the Didsbury Studio Centre for the news programme *ABC at Large*. David Hamilton interviewed them with Brian Epstein.

3 The final show of the Shapiro tour was held at the Gaumont Cinema in Hanley.

4 The Beatles were paid £100 for a booking for the first time at the Plaza Ballroom in St. Helens.

5 "From Me to You" was recorded at Abbey Road with "Thank You Girl" as the B-side.

6 The Beatles' fifth and last appearance on the radio show *Here We Go*.

7 The band appeared at the Elizabethan Ballroom, Nottingham, with Gerry and the Pacemakers, the Big Three, and Billy J. Kramer with the Dakotas. The evening, known as the Mersey Beat Showcase, was the first of several organized by NEMS Enterprises with all the acts and fans travelling down to the venue together. It was an original idea from Brian Epstein; the cost to fans was 25 shillings.

8 The boys played the Royal Hall in Harrogate.

9 The band began its second British tour supporting Tommy Roe and Chris Montez at the Granada Cinema in East Ham, London.

10 Disguised as policemen to avoid the fans, the four played the second date of the tour at the Hippodrome Theatre in Birmingham.

11 The Beatles' last appearance for *The Friday Spectacular*, recorded at Abbey Road.

PLEASE PLEASE ME

Released
🇬🇧 22 March 1963 (Parlophone)

Side One:
I Saw Her Standing There
Misery
Anna (Go to Him) (Alexander)
Chains (Goffin–King)
Boys (Dixon–Farrell)
Ask Me Why
Please Please Me

Side Two:
Love Me Do
P.S. I Love You
Baby It's You (David–Williams–Bacharach)
Do You Want to Know a Secret
A Taste of Honey (Scott–Marlow)
There's a Place
Twist and Shout (Medley–Russell)

Cover story

Please Please Me, the Beatles' debut album, was a triumph despite being hastily compiled to cash in on the band's rising popularity. Just two weeks after its release, the boys received their first silver disc, having sold 250,000 copies of the album.

The cover photo was taken in EMI's headquarters at 20 Manchester Sq. by Angus McBean and the sleeve notes are by Tony Barrow. The photographer recalled later: "As I went into the door I was in the staircase well. Someone looked over the banister—I asked if the boys were in the building, and the answer was yes. 'Well', I said, 'get them to look over, and I will take them from here.' I only had my ordinary portrait lens, so to get the picture, I had to lie flat on my back in the entrance. I took some shots and I said, 'That'll do'."

The iconic cover made the staircase so famous that when EMI moved during the '90s, the staircase was dismantled and rebuilt in their new offices. The old building was knocked down and no longer exists.

ABOVE: **As the Beatles' popularity rose, media interest inevitably followed, and the band found itself increasingly asked to pose for official pictures and sign autographs.**

OPPOSITE: **Not only did the boys have to alternate between major gigs and small club venues, they increasingly had to squeeze recordings for TV and radio in between as well.**

continued from previous page

MARCH 1963

12 The third date of the tour was the Granada Cinema in Bedford. The date was missed by John who was ill.

13 John missed the show at the Rialto Theatre in York. The harmonica overdub for "Thank You Girl" was recorded.

14 John missed a third night at the Gaumont Cinema in Wolverhampton. George Martin was involved with another editing and mixing session to work on "From Me to You" in the boys' absence.

15 John was able to rejoin the band for two houses at the Colston Hall in Bristol.

16 The group performed live on *Saturday Club*. The original recording session had been cancelled due to John's illness. This was followed by a performance at Sheffield City Hall.

17 A performance at the Embassy Cinema in Peterborough.

18 A concert at the Regal Cinema in Gloucester.

ON LIFE

"Let's get our kicks today for tomorrow we die, man, that's rot. Some people are like that, thick people blowing up the world. I am interested in what will happen."

—George

ON HIS CAREER

"I don't fancy being a bus conductor. I'd like to be sort of comfortable, with a nice house and a few hairdressing businesses."

—Ringo

19 The Regal Cinema was again the venue for the show, this time in Cambridge.

20 The tour moved on to Romford in Essex, where the boys appeared at the ABC Cinema.

21 The band recorded a segment for *On the Scene*, a BBC radio show, at the BBC Piccadilly Studios.

22 The LP *Please Please Me* was released in the UK on Parlophone PMC 1202 (mono) and PCS 3042 (stereo). Evening performance at the Gaumont, Doncaster.

23 A concert in Newcastle-Upon-Tyne at the City Hall.

24 The boys returned home to play at the Empire Theatre in Liverpool.

25 The band spent the day on location with photographer Dezo Hoffman.

26 The schedule resumed at the Granada Cinema in Mansfield.

27 Next, to the ABC Cinema in Northampton.

28 Moving to the West Country, they played at the ABC Cinema in Exeter.

29 A long drive to London to play the Odeon Cinema in Lewisham.

30 Back west to the Guildhall in Portsmouth.

31 The last night of the Roe–Montez tour at the De Montfort Hall in Leicester.

Publishing deal costs Beatles millions

28 February 1963 witnessed the signing of a deal that would have huge ramifications for the Beatles' business empire. John and Paul had no shortage of confidence in their ability as songwriters—the way they dug their heels in over their debut single bore testament to that—but they were extremely naïve regarding the commercial side of music publishing. They could see the logic of being paid to perform and sell records—and were keen to maximize that potential—but intellectual property rights and royalty deals slipped beneath their radar.

Brian Epstein had handed the rights to "Love Me Do"/"PS I Love You" to Ardmore & Beechwood, the music publisher that had provided the conduit to EMI and George Martin. But Epstein was unimpressed by that firm's efforts to market the debut single, and for "Please Please Me" he wanted someone who would promote as well as publish. Enter Dick James, a 1950s crooner who knew his time in front of the microphone had passed and who had set up his own publishing company in 1961.

James and George Martin were longtime acquaintances. It was James who had sent "How Do You Do It?" to Parlophone, hoping for his first big hit as a publisher. The disappointment at having the song turned down by the Beatles was about to be tempered as Martin recommended his services to Epstein. At the meeting, James was bowled over by an acetate of "Please Please Me" and knew immediately that he was on to a winner. But could he deliver the exposure Epstein wanted? James may not as yet have had much success in his new venture, but he had been in the business a long time and knew a lot of influential people. He immediately opened a very impressive door, getting the Beatles a spot on the prestigious network TV show *Thank Your Lucky Stars* (which aired 19 January 1963).

Any qualms Epstein had immediately melted away. But James had even more to offer. Instead of the usual 50–50 arrangement between publisher and composer, delivered on a song-by-song basis, he suggested forming a company that would publish all Lennon–McCartney music. The Beatles would own half of Northern Songs, James the other half, with the latter also taking a 10 percent handling fee. Epstein sold the deal enthusiastically to John and Paul, who didn't trouble themselves with the small print. Only much later did they realize that they owned a share of a company within a company, and how badly they had been advised. The terms of the deal that established Northern Songs cost the Beatles millions, and at the end of the decade the wrangling over the ownership of the company would prove to be the final nail in the coffin of John and Paul's fractured relationship.

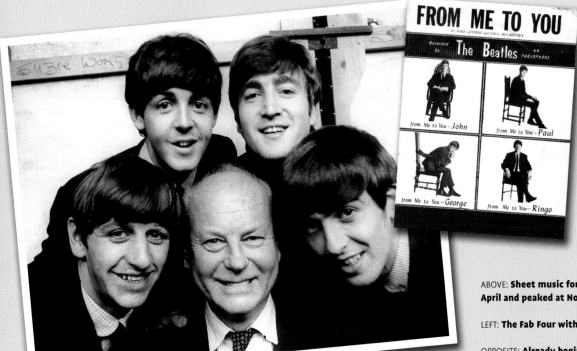

ABOVE: **Sheet music for "From Me to You", the Beatles' third single, released on 11 April and peaked at No. 1.**

LEFT: **The Fab Four with journalist Godfrey Wynn.**

OPPOSITE: **Already beginning to feel the strain of a busy schedule and crazy fans, the boys find time to relax with a new racing track range from Scalextric.**

APRIL 1963

1 Two programmes for the radio series *Side by Side* were recorded in the BBC Piccadilly Studios.

3 The band played three songs for the radio show *Easy Beat*. Paul and John joined the panel that reviewed new singles.

4 At the BBC Paris Studio, London, the Beatles made a third recording for *Side by Side*. Later that afternoon they played to a restrained audience in the Roxburgh Hall at Stowe School, Buckinghamshire, following a request from schoolboy Dave Moores.

5 The boys received their first silver disc after selling 250,000 copies of *Please Please Me*.

6 A day spent travelling north to play at the Pavilion Gardens Ballroom, Buxton.

7 Back to the south to perform at the Savoy Ballroom in Portsmouth.

8 John and Cynthia's son, John Charles Julian, was born.

9 A live radio interview for *Pop Inn* was given at the BBC Paris Studio, London, followed by a live television performance for the children's programme *Tuesday Rendezvous* at Wembley Studios. That night, the band played a concert in the ballroom at the Gaumont State Cinema in Kilburn, London.

10 The Beatles appeared for the last time at the Majestic Ballroom, Birkenhead.

11 The boys' third single, "From Me to You"/"Thank You Girl" was released in the UK on Parlophone R5015.

ON POLITICS

"Politics? I'm not apathetic but I didn't like history at school and it's the same with politics."
—Paul

ON AGING

"The only thing I'm afraid of is growing old. I hate that."
—John

12 Back to the Cavern Club for a rhythm and blues session.

13 The Beatles finally appeared on national BBC television when they record *The 625 Show* at Shepherd's Bush.

14 A third appearance on *Thank Your Lucky Stars* was filmed. Afterwards, the band watched the Rolling Stones at the Crawdaddy Club in Richmond.

15 John visited his wife and first son and named Brian Epstein as the godfather.

16 The Beatles appeared live on Granada Television on *Scene at 6.30*. It clashed with the broadcast of the previously recorded *The 625 Show* that went out at 6:25.

18 The band made their first appearance at the Royal Albert Hall. Later that evening Paul was to meet Jane Asher, who was writing a piece on the band for *Radio Times*.

21 An afternoon performance at the Empire Pool in Wembley. A 14-act bill was headed by Cliff Richard and the Shadows and played to an audience of 10,000.

22 The first *Side by Side* programme was broadcast and included performances of "I Saw Her Standing There" and "From Me to You".

24 Mersey Beat Showcase at the Majestic Ballroom in Finsbury Park.

26 A performance at the Music Hall, Shrewsbury, booked by promoter Lewis Buckley.

27 Saturday night's show at the (Victory) Memorial Hall in Northwich.

28 Finally a break for everyone. John and Brian Epstein opted to fly out to Spain.

29 Paul, George, and Ringo had a holiday in Santa Cruz, Tenerife.

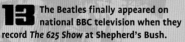

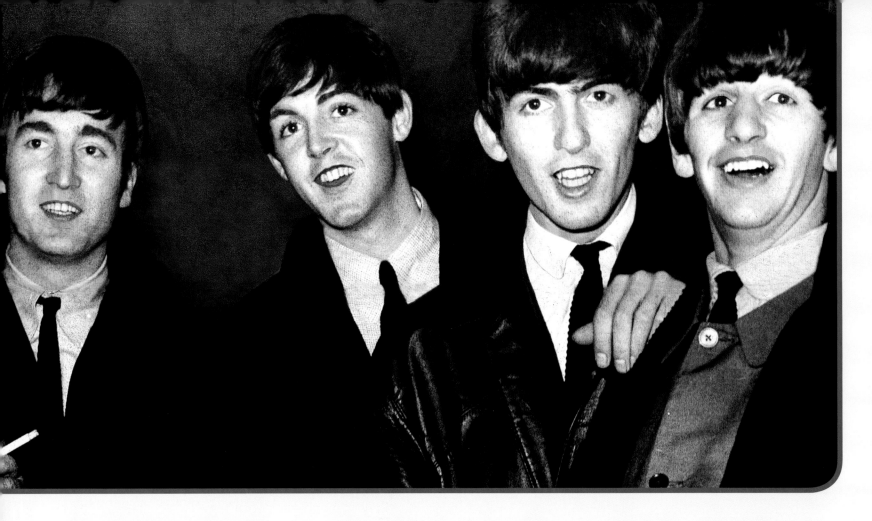

Six months at No.1 for debut album

Please Please Me was a phenomenal success, providing EMI with a very healthy return on the £400 it had cost to produce. It hit the top of the UK album chart on 11 May 1963 and remained anchored there for thirty weeks. The Beatles would have ten more number one albums, but none would match that feat. To this day it remains a record for a pop group. Only the soundtrack albums to *South Pacific*, *The Sound of Music*, and *The King and I* have stayed at the top of the UK chart longer. Simon and Garfunkel's *Bridge Over Troubled Water* did eventually eclipse *Please Please Me*'s total, though that was the aggregate of several stints at number one.

The debut album provided another watershed moment in the group's development. The eight self-penned songs were credited to McCartney–Lennon, the duo having agreed that all their output, whether written individually or collaboratively, should carry a joint credit. How that should be expressed provoked much discussion, with Epstein and newly-appointed publisher Dick James throwing their views into the mix. Various ideas were floated, including alternating between Lennon–McCartney and McCartney–Lennon, and putting the name of the chief contributor first. In the end, alphabetical order—which everyone save McCartney felt sounded better anyway—prevailed, and from that point on the familiar form was adopted.

ABOVE: **The Beatles around the time of the Orbison tour, when their popularity was suddenly and spectacularly burgeoning.**

MAY 1963

1 Tony Barrow became the Beatles' press agent.

2 A photograph of Jane Asher screaming in excitement at the band is published in *Radio Times*.

4 "From Me to You"/"Thank You Girl" reached the top of the UK charts, remaining there for seven weeks.

6 "From Me to You"/"Thank You Girl" was released by Vee-Jay on VJ 522 in the US. It reached only No. 116 in the *Billboard* charts.

11 Back from their respective holidays, the boys played at the Imperial Ballroom in Nelson with 2,000 eager fans packed into the venue. The album *Please Please Me* topped the British charts and remained there for 30 weeks.

12 At the Aston Studios in Birmingham the band finally topped the bill in a recording for *Thank Your Lucky Stars*. They mimed to "From Me to You" and "I Saw Her Standing There".

13 The second *Side by Side* programme was broadcast and included performances of "From Me to You" and "Thank You Girl".

14 A show at the Rank Ballroom, Sunderland.

15 The Royalty Theatre, Chester, was the venue for the evening's performance.

16 Second national live televised performance for the BBC on the children's programme *Pops and Lenny*.

SONG STORY: "I SAW HER STANDING THERE"

Paul recalled writing "I Saw Her Standing There"—whose bass riff he acknowledged was a steal from Chuck Berry's "Talkin' About You"—during one of the many occasions when he and John played hookey from school. John had little recollection of the event, other than the fact that he contributed a few lines. One of those contributions was an amendment to Paul's opening, which rhymed "seventeen" (the song's working title) with "beauty queen". John went for archness over predictability: "She was just seventeen/You know what I mean," a change Paul warmly endorsed. This driving rocker was a feature of the Beatles' set with multiple guitar solos that sometimes ran on for ten minutes. Restraint was needed for the studio version that ended up as the opening track on *Please Please Me* so it was reined in to meet the usual three-minute deadline. The famous "One, two, three, FOUR!" count-in survived the editing process as it enhanced the raw energy of the piece, with a nod towards the pulsating opening of Elvis's "Blue Suede Shoes".

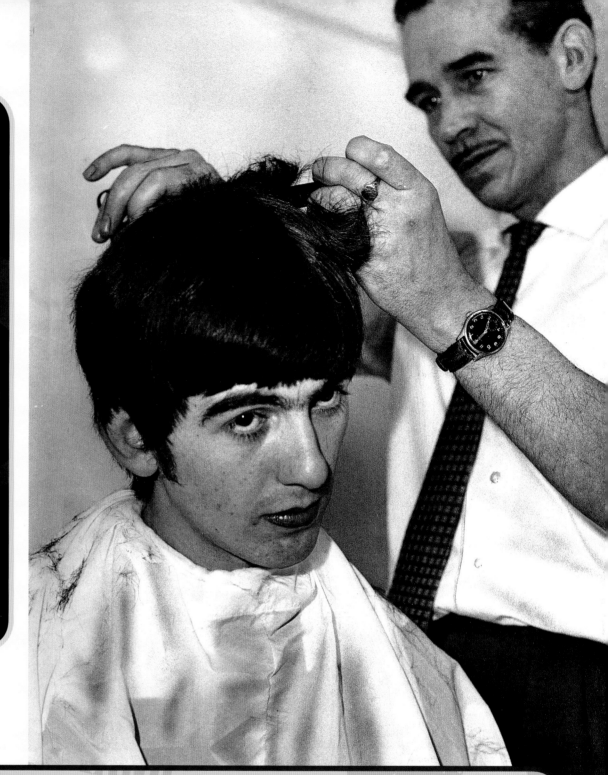

RIGHT: **George's Beatle moptop is kept in trim.**

17 The boys took part in a photo session with Dezo Hoffman. The recording of *Thank Your Lucky Stars* was broadcast. Promoter Carry Clayman booked the band for an appearance at the Grosvenor Rooms in Norwich that evening.

18 The third British tour began, with the first show held at the Adelphi Cinema in Slough. Roy Orbison had initially topped the bill but his top slot was rapidly taken over by the Beatles.

19 The second tour date at the Gaumont Cinema in Henley.

20 Then on to the Gaumont Cinema in Southampton.

21 The band recorded *Saturday Club*, for which they topped the bill. In the evening they returned and recorded a new programme called *Steppin' Out*.

22 The tour continued at the Gaumont Cinema, Ipswich.

23 The band played at the Odeon Cinema in Nottingham.

24 The Beatles recorded the first programme for their own radio series *Pop Go the Beatles* at the Aeolian Studios in New Bond Street. This very successful series was the brainchild of Vernon Lawrence, a studio manager at the BBC. With an initial run of four programmes planned, it took only four weeks to put together.

25 The previously recorded *Saturday Club* was broadcast.

26 The band was back at the Empire Theatre in Liverpool.

27 Moving briefly into Wales, the tour continued at the Capitol Cinema in Cardiff.

28 Another tour date at the Gaumont Cinema in Worcester.

29 On to the Rialto Theatre in York.

30 A date at the Odeon Cinema in Manchester.

31 The Friday night venue was the Odeon Cinema, Southend-on-Sea.

Beatles eclipse established stars

"Beatlemania" may not have officially entered the English language until the autumn of 1963, but the three UK tours in the first half of that year provided ample indication that the Fab Four were about to explode onto the pop scene. Like the crescendo in the middle of "Twist and Shout", the reception the Beatles were given in towns and cities around the country grew from cool restraint to wild abandon. At the start of the first tour they were greeted as a decent support act; by the end of the third there was no doubt who was top of the bill, whatever the flyers said.

The first of those tours had the Beatles at the bottom of a six-act bill whose star turn was teenage sensation Helen Shapiro. Unlike many music business insiders, Shapiro thought "Love Me Do" was terrific and had badgered promoter Arthur Howes to recruit the Beatles for her forthcoming tour. Howes had tried them out on the undercard to yodel king Frank Ifield in December 1962, but they were something of a damp squib. They may have built up a loyal following in Liverpool and Hamburg, where the fans rocked to their sound, but they found Peterborough stoically indifferent to their efforts.

Howes signed them regardless. It proved to be a shrewd move, for although the early dates confirmed that the Peterborough experience was by no means unique, the ripple effect of the recently released "Please Please Me" single soon swelled to tidal wave proportions, engulfing the teenage fans—and leaving the other acts to flounder in the Fab Four's wake. The Beatles were promoted up the bill, but that made little difference. The performers who came on before them had to contend with a palpable air of anticipation; those who appeared afterward were left to struggle with an audience sated by the aural feast they had greedily devoured.

ABOVE: **The Beatles pose with fans at the Gaumont Theatre in Doncaster.**

ABOVE INSET: **The three main acts at the Romford Odeon, the Beatles, Billy J. Kramer and the Dakotas, and Gerry and the Pacemakers, held the top three spots in the British charts when they went onstage at this Mersey Beat Showcase event on 16 June.**

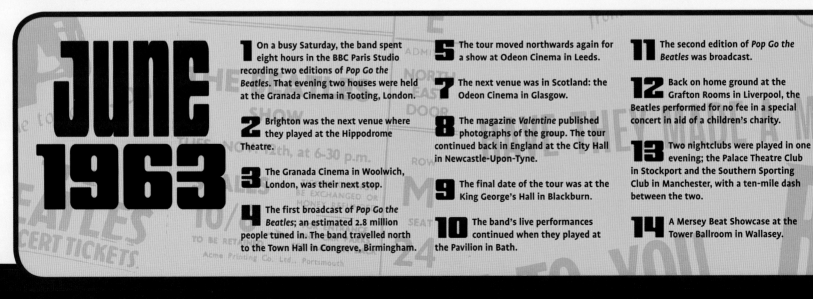

JUNE 1963

1 On a busy Saturday, the band spent eight hours in the BBC Paris Studio recording two editions of *Pop Go the Beatles*. That evening two houses were held at the Granada Cinema in Tooting, London.

2 Brighton was the next venue where they played at the Hippodrome Theatre.

3 The Granada Cinema in Woolwich, London, was their next stop.

4 The first broadcast of *Pop Go the Beatles*; an estimated 2.8 million people tuned in. The band travelled north to the Town Hall in Congreve, Birmingham.

5 The tour moved northwards again for a show at Odeon Cinema in Leeds.

7 The next venue was in Scotland: the Odeon Cinema in Glasgow.

8 The magazine *Valentine* published photographs of the group. The tour continued back in England at the City Hall in Newcastle-Upon-Tyne.

9 The final date of the tour was at the King George's Hall in Blackburn.

10 The band's live performances continued when they played at the Pavilion in Bath.

11 The second edition of *Pop Go the Beatles* was broadcast.

12 Back on home ground at the Grafton Rooms in Liverpool, the Beatles performed for no fee in a special concert in aid of a children's charity.

13 Two nightclubs were played in one evening; the Palace Theatre Club in Stockport and the Southern Sporting Club in Manchester, with a ten-mile dash between the two.

14 A Mersey Beat Showcase at the Tower Ballroom in Wallasey.

"Toppermost of the poppermost"

The schedule was punishing. Howes wasted little time sending them out on a follow-up tour, this time as third on a bill in which Chris Montez and Tommy Roe were the headliners. The pattern was much the same, the fans making it clear who was the real star turn. The Beatles did make their feelings known about the relentless crisscrossing of the country, but lassitude never impinged on their single-minded determination to make it to what John termed "the toppermost of the poppermost".

The number of engagements they fulfilled, the way they were herded around the country, and the accommodations they were given would leave even a C-list act of the modern era at his manager's throat. Add to that the fact that in snatched moments on coach journeys or in hotel rooms, John and Paul were also dashing off more hits. "From Me to You" and "Thank You Girl", the A- and B-sides of their third single, were written during the Shapiro tour. These songs kept up the early—and quite deliberate—trick of including personal pronouns in the title to give them a direct, intimate appeal. "Thank You Girl" was written first and was pencilled in as the new single. But when "From Me to You" came pouring out during the coach journey from York to Shrewsbury, they instantly revised their plan. The inspiration for the song was the From You to Us column in *New Musical Express*. It wouldn't be the last time that a line from a newspaper or magazine would be the springboard for a Lennon–McCartney classic.

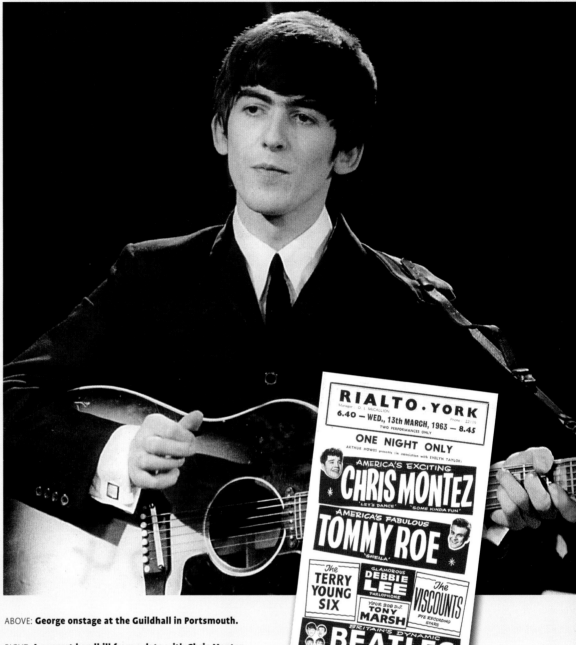

ABOVE: **George onstage at the Guildhall in Portsmouth.**

RIGHT: **A concert handbill from a date with Chris Montez and Tommy Roe.**

15 Fifteen hundred people watched the Beatles perform at the City Hall in Salisbury.

16 The last Mersey Beat Showcase at the Odeon Cinema, Romford, Essex. Brian Epstein had cancelled the future dates planned. Amazingly, the three bands performing held the top three positions in the singles charts that week.

17 The last recording for *Pop Go the Beatles* was made at the Maida Vale Studios near Abbey Road.

18 The third edition of *Pop Go the Beatles* was broadcast. It was Paul's 21st birthday. After a party at Abbey Road, another celebration was held in a marquee in his aunt's garden in Huyton.

19 An edition of *Easy Beat* was recorded at the Playhouse Theatre. Ringo used his Ludwig drum kit live for the first time.

20 The band formed their own company, The Beatles Ltd, to handle their income. Brian Epstein was appointed director.

21 A report in the *Daily Mirror* appeared with the headline BEATLES IN BRAWL. It reported that John, after getting drunk, beat up Cavern DJ Bob Wooler at Paul's 21st birthday party on 18 June. Wooler reportedly accused John of being gay. Epstein paid £200 to stop him suing John. A Friday night show at the Odeon Cinema in Guildford, Surrey.

22 In London, John recorded his appearance on *Juke Box Jury* where he was derogatory about all the singles, including Elvis Presley's "Devil in Disguise". He then flew by helicopter to join the others for a performance at the Ballroom Town Hall in Abergavenny, Wales.

23 Del Shannon's version of "From Me to You" entered the US charts; the first Lennon–McCartney song to achieve this. *Easy Beat* was broadcast. At the Alpha Studios in Birmingham the success of Mersey Beat was celebrated when an edition of *Lucky Stars (Summer Spin)* contained only Liverpool acts. The Beatles topped the bill in this ABC television programme hosted by Pete Murray.

24 Another appearance on *Side by Side* went out on the BBC.

25 The fourth edition of *Pop Go the Beatles* was broadcast.

continued from previous page

JUNE 1963

26 John and Paul wrote "She Loves You" after playing to the Majestic Ballroom in Newcastle-Upon-Tyne, London; their last performance at a Top Rank Ballroom.

27 Paul flew down to London to watch Billy J. Kramer recording at Abbey Road.

28 The band shared the bill with Acker Bilk when they played to an audience of 3,200 at the Queen's Hall in Leeds.

29 An edition of *Saturday Club* was recorded at the Playhouse Theatre and included "Roll Over Beethoven" and "Memphis Tennessee". That evening *Juke Box Jury* was broadcast on BBC Television while *Lucky Stars (Summer Spin)*

went out on ABC, attracting an audience of more than 6 million. The two programmes overlapped by ten minutes.

30 Ted Rogers MCed the first of ten weeks of concerts held in seaside towns at the ABC Cinema in Yarmouth.

ABOVE: **Brian Epstein poses with some of the acts from his stable, including (l–r in the front row) Tommy Quickly, Cilla Black, and Billy J. Kramer.**

ABOVE RIGHT: **Epstein's operation started out as a small family-run business, NEMS Enterprises, but as his stable was ever more successful, his company expanded. By 1966 there would be more than 80 members of staff across five offices.**

OPPOSITE: **Brian's styling of the Beatles and the carefully posed publicity shots helped to counter their reputation for being long-haired and rebellious. You wouldn't mind if these guys moved in next door!**

BIO: BRIAN EPSTEIN

Materially, the first 26 years of Brian Epstein's life were extremely comfortable; emotionally and spiritually it was a very different matter. A homosexual at a time when same-sex relationships were illegal and a businessman when he would have preferred to tread the boards, Epstein led a troubled life before the Beatles gave it meaning and direction.

Epstein's grandfather had started the family furniture business at the turn of the twentieth century. It prospered under his stewardship, and under that of his son Harry, but the retail business didn't light any fires in Harry's firstborn. Nevertheless, Brian dutifully set about learning the ropes on leaving school, before being called up for National Service. The highly strung aesthete found life in the army even less palatable than the furniture trade and suffered badly at the hands of fellow conscripts and officers alike. His early discharge was ostensibly on the grounds that he was "emotionally and mentally unfit to serve", though the authorities clearly recognized that his orientation was key to the depression and anxiety he exhibited.

After a brief, unrewarding spell at RADA, Epstein threw himself into running NEMS, the music arm of the family concern. His personal taste was for Elgar rather than Elvis, but he built up an impressive knowledge of the music scene and established a meticulous stock-control system. If a record was available, NEMS would get a copy. That corporate boast was tested in October 1961, when fans began enquiring about "My Bonnie" by a group called the Beatles. Epstein discovered that they were a local band performing almost daily at a club on his doorstep. On 9 November he went along to the Cavern to see what all the fuss was about. Epstein managed the band until his death on 27 August 1967.

On tour with the "Big O"

With "From Me to You" on its way to becoming the first of eleven straight UK number ones, the Beatles hit the road again in May. Arthur Howes had nothing planned for this period, but Epstein was keen to keep the juggernaut rolling—and this time his boys were promoted to second on the bill, supporting top American star Roy Orbison, who had enjoyed huge success with songs such as "Only the Lonely" and "Crying". The Beatles were fans of the "Big O", and the tour bus provided ample opportunity for "competitive" songwriting. At the concert halls that friendly rivalry took on a slightly different hue. Onstage Orbison was somewhat statuesque and impassive, his lips barely appearing to move. By contrast, the raw energy of the moptops' performances charged the atmosphere in a way not seen since Elvis's lip-curling, gyratory antics of the previous decade. For the teenage girls there were clearly sexual forces at work. For the guys it was all about aspiration: they could dress like a Beatle, adopt the same mannerisms and "in" words. And far from antagonizing the older age group and the establishment—as Elvis had done with his pelvic thrusting—the Beatles had the mums and dads cheerfully tapping their feet too. Their carefully crafted, clean-cut image, cheeky but not rude or subversive, offended no one. What better seal of approval than to have whistled Beatles tunes floating down the corridors of Buckingham Palace? It was all hogwash, of course; the group indulged in all the typical excesses of pop stardom. But perception is reality, and the combination of memorable music and universal appeal was a marketing man's dream.

By May 1963 it was clear that here was a bubble that was growing exponentially. The boys pleaded with Orbison to allow them to close the show, though in truth that decision was virtually inevitable, such was the hysteria being generated.

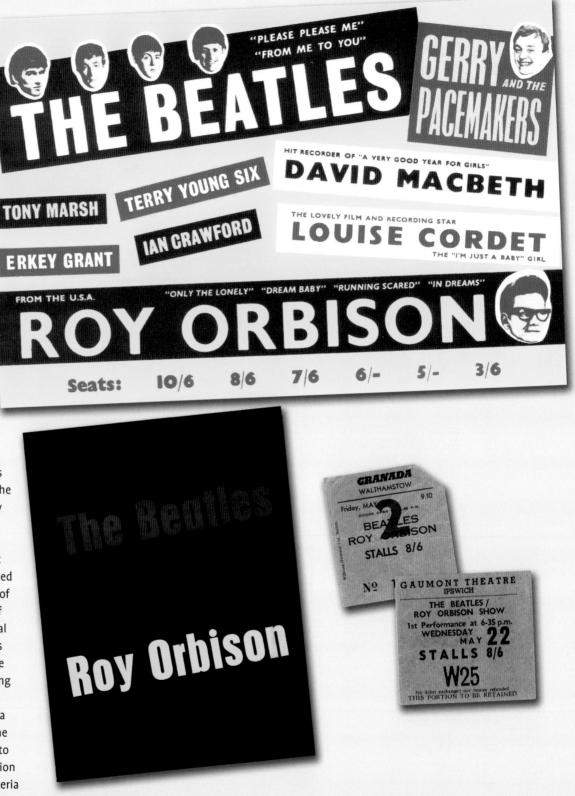

ABC THEATRE
BLACKPOOL   PHONE 24233

BIG
6.0

SUNDAY NIGHT
STAGE SHOW
SUNDAY, SEPT. 8TH   8.15

ONE NIGHT ONLY

THE
BEATLES

CHAS.   SHIRLEY
McDEVITT & DOUGLAS
THE COUNTRYMEN

JACK DOUGLAS | LEE LESLIE

TERRY YOUNG | SONS OF THE PILTDOWN MEN

LEFT: **After missing some tour dates earlier in the year, the Beatles gave a brief tour at the start of September, including dates at Luton, Preston, and Blackpool.**

ABOVE: **The boys relax in the empty stalls of a London theatre ahead of a performance. Brian Epstein was soon to insist that the band no longer play in ballrooms, preferring venues with fixed seating.**

JULY 1963

1 "She Loves You" and the B-side "Get You in the End" (later known as "I'll Get You") were recorded at Abbey Road. The songs reportedly took 345 minutes to record and made up the Beatles' first million-selling single. Unusually, the single was to be No. 1 in the singles charts in two completely separate runs.

2 After the runaway success of *Pop Go the Beatles*, the boys were booked for another 11 programmes. The first of these was recorded at the Maida Vale Studios and included "That's All Right Mama". The host was Rodney Burke.

3 The *Beat Show* was recorded for BBC radio at the Playhouse Theatre.

4 The *Beat Show* was broadcast from 1-1:30 p.m. Meanwhile, at Abbey Road George Martin embarked on the mono mixing of "I'll Get You" and "She Loves You". The band was spotted at the Scene Club that evening watching the Rolling Stones for the second time.

5 Epstein verbally agreed to a tour of Australia for the following year. At a second appearance at the Plaza Ballroom, Old Hill, the band performed with Denny

and the Diplomats (featuring Denny Laine, who eventually joined Paul's group, Wings).

6 Paul crowned the Northwich carnival queen before playing at the (Victory) Memorial Hall that evening.

7 A Sunday night house at the ABC Theatre, Blackpool. It was Ringo's 23rd birthday.

8 The first of a run of six nights, all with two houses, at the Winter Gardens in Margate, Kent.

BIO: NEIL ASPINALL

As driver, aide, roadie, Apple executive, and friend, Neil Aspinall is just about the only cast member of the Beatles' saga to have spanned the entire drama. He was a classmate of Paul's at Liverpool Institute, and during recess George would join both of them in a regular smokers' huddle. But while the Quarry Men were scratching around for gigs, Aspinall collected a sheaf of examination certificates and took the non-rock 'n' roll career path of accountancy.

It was his friendship with Pete Best rather than the school connection that brought Aspinall into the Beatles' orbit. He was lodging at the Bests' Haymans Green home when the basement was converted into a club by the ambitious matriarch, Mona. Aspinall helped prepare some flyers to promote the Beatles' appearance at the Casbah, and at Pete's request took on the job of getting the group and their equipment round the jive hives, for which task he invested £80 in a battered old van. He quickly found that being the Beatles' roadie was not only more glamorous than double-entry bookkeeping but considerably more lucrative, and in the summer of 1962 he made it his full-time occupation. The following year, telecoms worker and Cavern doorman Mal Evans made the same decision, which freed Aspinall to assume a wider PA role.

In August '63 Aspinall's loyalties were tested over the sacking of Pete Best. The sanitized version of events holds that Aspinall offered to quit in sympathy, only to be dissuaded by the charitable Best, who knew the Beatles were going places and didn't see why both men should miss out. A less savoury scenario depicts the embittered drummer giving the lodger an ultimatum: quit the Beatles or start looking for new digs. The picture was further complicated by the fact that Aspinall had fathered a child with Mona; carrying on as a member of the Beatles' inner circle thus meant more than just having to find alternative accommodation.

Aspinall was one of the few to survive the cull when Allen Klein was brought in to put Apple on a sound financial footing. After the Beatles split, he continued to oversee the group's catalogue, merchandising, and legal affairs, stepping down as Apple's CEO in April 2007. Aspinall passed away on 24 March 2008 from lung cancer.

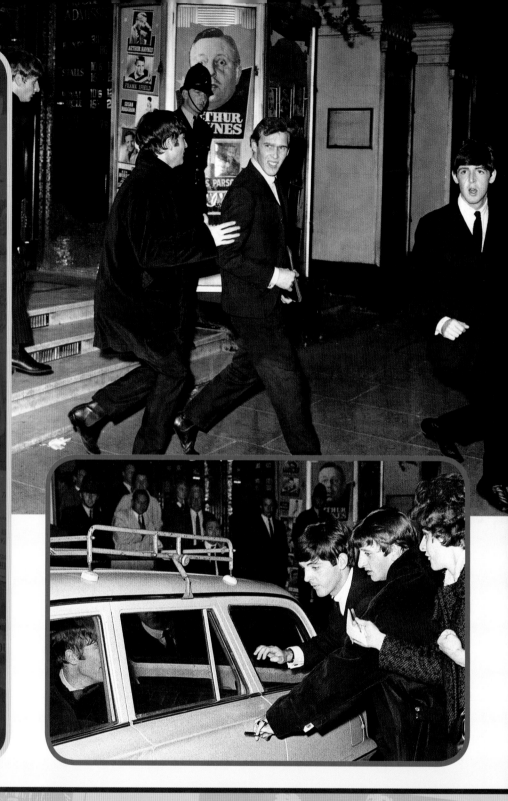

continued from previous page

JULY 1963

9 The second night at the Winter Gardens. Billy J. Kramer and the Dakotas were also on the bill.

10 A brief trip back to London to record two more shows for *Pop Go the Beatles* and then back to Margate for the evening shows.

12 The EP *Twist and Shout* was released on Parlophone GEP 8882 (mono only) in the UK. The A-side featured "Twist and Shout" and "A Taste of Honey", with "Do You Want to Know a Secret" and "There's a Place" on the B-side. NEMS Presentations Ltd, a concert promotions company, was founded with Brian Epstein as one of the directors.

14 A long journey from Kent to Lancashire to play at the ABC Theatre, Blackpool.

15 At Birkenhead Magistrates Court Paul was fined £17 for a speeding offence.

16 An incredible 18 songs were recorded for three episodes of *Pop Go the Beatles*. Guests included the Hollies and the Swinging Blue Jeans. The fifth edition of *Pop Go the Beatles* was broadcast.

17 The contract to play in Paris in January was signed. Another recording for *Easy Beat* at the Playhouse Theatre was made. It included "I Saw Her Standing There" and "Twist and Shout".

OPPOSITE TOP: **After their triumph on *Sunday Night at the London Palladium*, the boys and their road manager Neil Aspinall try to elude the press and fans by leaving through the front entrance rather than the stage door.**

OPPOSITE BOTTOM: **The Beatles make for the getaway car on Argyll Street following the sensational performance at the London Palladium. George Cooper, the theatre's stage doorman, said he hadn't seen scenes like this since Johnnie Ray appeared in 1955.**

ABOVE: **1963 was a particularly demanding time for the Beatles. This was especially so in the autumn when they gave almost daily concerts, crisscrossing the country.**

RIGHT: **Vee-Jay Records had planned to issue the Beatles' first US album, *Introducing the Beatles*, on 22 July 1963. Financial problems prevented the launch going ahead as announced, although some copies of the record were in circulation. It was not until February 1964 that the album was properly released.**

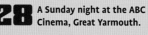
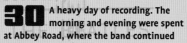

18 Recording continued at the Abbey Road Studios as they started to tape tracks for their second album, *With the Beatles*.

19 The band travelled back to Wales to perform for two nights at the Ritz Ballroom, Rhyl.

21 Sunday night's house was at the Queen's Theatre in Blackpool.

22 The planned release date of the LP *Introducing the Beatles* by Vee-Jay on VJLP 1062 (mono) and SR 1062 (stereo) in the US. The album was only properly issued by Vee-Jay in February 1964. At home there was another six-night concert run—this time at the Odeon Cinema in Weston-Super-Mare. It was here that Dezo Hoffmann spent a day on the beach taking photographs of the boys in Victorian bathing costumes.

23 The sixth edition of *Pop Go the Beatles* was broadcast.

28 A Sunday night at the ABC Cinema, Great Yarmouth.

29 Photo sessions were held at the Washington Hotel with Don Smith and Marc Sharratt.

30 A heavy day of recording. The morning and evening were spent at Abbey Road, where the band continued to tape tracks for their second LP. During the afternoon an interview for *Non Stop Pop* and another session for *Saturday Club* were recorded at the Playhouse Theatre, London. The seventh edition of *Pop Go the Beatles* was broadcast.

31 A frenzied audience watched the band at the Imperial Ballroom in Nelson, Lancashire.

By Daily Mail Reporter

A POLICE chief yesterday attacked the Beatle-mania which caused him to seal off a city's centre and forced policemen to go without rest or food.

It happened in Liverpool, home town of the Beatles. About 12,000 fans turned up to buy tickets for a performance at the Empire Theatre.

Queueing started at 8 a.m. on Saturday. Police told the fans to move on, but they returned at nightfall.

Queueing continued yesterday morning. At one time the queue was a mile long.

More than 100 policemen on foot and a contingent of mounted police were called out to control the crowd.

The Chief Constable of Liverpool, Mr. J. W. T. Smith, who was directing operations, said later: "I am not happy about things today.

Stampede

"I know it is our duty to protect children, but I have had to bring men off the beats in the divisions to control the queues for this commercial venture. Some have been on duty for long stretches today and have had to go without meals.

"I'm going to make recommendations and a report about it all to my watch committee. One thing I would like is for tickets for these sort of shows to be issued through the post."

Hour by hour ambulance officers were called to the queue to deal with casualties from exhaustion, crushing, hysteria and hunger.

At 5 a.m. in a darkened, narrow street, there was a stampede which ended in one gigantic scrum.

SOS note: An Automobile Association patrolman who was called out to repair the Beatles' van at Rushyford, Co. Durham, radioed his H.Q. that he was trapped in a theatre car park by "hundreds of screaming teenagers." Later he escaped.

Beatlemania!

On 14 October the *Daily Mirror* led with a one-word headline: BEATLEMANIA! Like every other national newspaper, the biggest-selling daily gave a detailed account of the frenzied scenes that had attended the Beatles' appearance on *Sunday Night at the London Palladium* the previous day. No other variety show carried more prestige, the very name of the venue being synonymous with the pinnacle of the UK entertainment business. The shenanigans behind the invitation were in themselves revealing. The Palladium show was part of a huge show-business empire run by Lew Grade and his brother Bernard Delfont. They had approached Epstein with a view to buying into NEMS and had been given a peremptory rebuff. It was hardly politic to make enemies of the most powerful impresarios in the land, but the latter were hard-nosed businessmen; they weren't about to let a petty squabble prevent them from booking the top draw in the country.

On the show the group belted out a four-number set: "From Me to You", "I'll Get You", "She Loves You", and "Twist and Shout". But for once the performance was incidental; it was the pandemonium outside the Argyll Street theatre that was the real story. Hordes of fans laid siege to the Palladium, and the group's ploy to wrong-foot them by escaping via the front entrance unravelled as they emerged to find the getaway car had been parked fifty yards up the road.

The police were unprepared for the mass outpouring of emotion they witnessed. In hindsight, it was a release waiting to happen. This was a new, unbuttoned England, immortalized in the famous Philip Larkin lines: "Sexual intercourse began/In nineteen sixty-three/(Which was rather late for me)/Between the end of the *Chatterley* ban/And the Beatles' first LP." The country had recently feasted on the Profumo-Keeler scandal, and Beatlemania was the latest manifestation of the new mood of liberation sweeping the land.

OPPOSITE AND BOTTOM RIGHT: **Beatlemania broke out all over Britain. In South London, policemen were required to control the queue for tickets, which had grown overnight despite the rain; in Portsmouth mothers with prams waited for the box office to open.**

OPPOSITE AND RIGHT INSETS: **Different cities, same story—the *Daily Mail* reports stampedes and riots around the UK and Ireland.**

TOP: **The Beatles try to escape fans on the night of their appearance at the Palladium.**

RIGHT: **The Beatles did not only appeal to a female audience, but it was the swooning and screaming of the girls that made the headlines.**

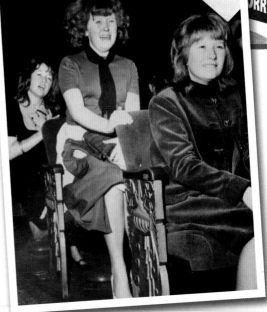

THE IRISH RIOT OVER THE BEATLES

By Daily Mail Reporter

THE Beatles' first visit to Dublin caused a riot last night.

Fans and passers-by were seriously injured. Cases taken to hospital included two fractured ankles and a broken leg.

Several policemen received minor injuries and 50 people fainted. Shop windows and street signs were smashed and three cars were wrecked.

The riot started when a crowd of about 3,000 waited to see the Beatles leave the Adelphi Cinema. A policeman said: "It is ridiculous how this mania turned to barbarism."

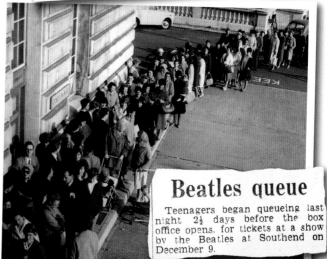

Beatles queue

Teenagers began queueing last night 2½ days before the box office opens, for tickets at a show by the Beatles at Southend on December 9.

LEFT: **In an image typical of the band's playfulness, Paul offers his bandmates cheese on cocktail sticks, but George would rather play with his food at a reception celebrating their forthcoming tour of the UK.**

BELOW: **In Lewisham, South London, fans jubilantly wave the tickets they have just bought for the Beatles concert in November 1963. Meanwhile police hem in the desperate fans still waiting in line.**

OPPOSITE: **In the autumn of 1963, touring meant performing six nights a week with usually a Monday off, but these rest days were often filled with other commitments such as the Royal Command Performance or the *Ken Dodd Show*.**

McCartney Sr. would have preferred "Yes, yes, yes"

As Beatlemania took hold in the UK, John and Paul dashed off the group's fourth single in a provincial hotel room in late June. "She Loves You" was another catchy winner, though with advance sales of almost a quarter of a million the fans were by now taking that for granted. Introducing a third person into the story line hardly represented a huge leap forward in the lyric-writing skills of Lennon–McCartney. And to open a song with a thrice-repeated "She loves you, yeah, yeah, yeah" seemed to be stretching a point too far—certainly EMI sound engineer Norman Smith thought so when he glanced at the lyric sheet prior to the recording session. George Martin was more concerned about the jazzy sixth chord for the final split harmony, thinking it was a corny throwback to the big band era. Paul's dad felt that modern youth was taking too many liberties with the English language and would have preferred "yes, yes, yes" for the refrain. But it is hard to overestimate the extent to which that opening drum roll and driving melody captured the imagination of a nation. The Fab Four performing falsetto "oooos"—accompanied by the neatly choreographed shaking of their moptop hair—and "yeah, yeah, yeah" would become an icon, not only of summer 1963 but the entire decade. "She Loves You" would become the Beatles' best-selling single and set a UK record that would not be broken for fourteen years.

OPPOSITE INSETS: **The Beatles six-night stint in Southport, not far from hometown Liverpoool, gave a real Mersey Sound lineup with Gerry and the Pacemakers sharing the bill, and, (right) sheet music for "She Loves You".**

AUGUST 1963

1 For the first time *The Beatles Book*, a monthly fan-club magazine, was published by Sean O'Mahoney. The 11th and 12th editions of *Pop Go the Beatles* were recorded at the Playhouse Theatre, Manchester.

2 The band's last appearance at the Grafton Rooms in Liverpool.

3 Another last, when they played their final show at the Cavern Club after nearly 300 performances that had shaped their future success. They had been paid £5 for their first show and received £300 for the last.

4 Fans blocked the Queen's Theatre entrance in Blackpool, so the boys had no choice but to clamber onto the roof using some scaffolding and descend through a trap door.

5 David Hamilton hosted an event in a marquee at the Urmston Show in Lancashire. The band appeared with three other acts.

6 It was the turn of the Channel Islands and the Beatles played two nights at the Springfield Ballroom on Jersey. The eighth edition of *Pop Go the Beatles* was broadcast.

8 Travelling by light aircraft, the band played the Auditorium on Guernsey.

11 A Sunday night at the ABC Theatre, Blackpool.

12 The start of a run of performances at the Odeon Cinema, Llandudno, Wales. Two houses were played each night.

13 A second night at the Odeon. The ninth edition of *Pop Go the Beatles* was broadcast.

14 A break from the Wales dates as they came back to Manchester

to record two songs for *Scene at 6.30* at the Granada TV Centre.

17 The last night in Llandudno.

18 En route to Devon, the boys stopped in Birmingham to record a session for *Lucky Stars (Summer Spin)* with host Pete Murray. In Torquay they played two houses at the Princess Theatre.

19 Staying south to perform at the Gaumont Cinema in Bournemouth, they began the six-night stint booked here.

20 The tenth edition of *Pop Go the Beatles* was broadcast.

21 A recording session at Abbey Road. Further editing and mono mixing for the next LP was carried out.

22 Robert Freeman photographed the band at the Palace Court Hotel—the shot used for the cover of the second album. An appearance on *Day by Day*, a Southern television show, was recorded at the television centre in Southampton.

23 "She Loves You"/"I'll Get You" was released on Parlophone R 5055 in the UK.

24 A silver disc was awarded for the EP *Twist and Shout*. The last performance in Bournemouth.

25 Back to Blackpool to play at the ABC Theatre.

26 A six-night, two-house run at the Odeon Cinema, Southport.

27 The start of four days when the band recorded various aspects of a documentary that examined the success of Mersey Beat. On the first day they were recorded playing at the Little Theatre without an audience. The 11th edition of *Pop Go the Beatles* was broadcast.

28 Wednesday's filming concentrated on the boys discussing their future aspirations.

30 Shots were taken of Ringo coming out of his house, getting into George's sports car, then being filmed in a ladies' hairdresser's. The programme that eventually went out in October was called *The Mersey Sound*.

31 The final Saturday night show was at Southport.

Rocking the royals

If there was any lingering doubt that the Beatles cut a swath through the age and class divide, it disappeared when, just three weeks after their barnstorming appearance on *Sunday Night at the London Palladium,* they received the royal seal of approval. There was no greater show-business honour than an invitation to appear on the bill of the *Royal Variety Performance,* and, predictably, it was John who flirted with the idea of subverting the august proceedings at the Prince of Wales Theatre on 4 November. He rehearsed his famous "ad lib" about asking those in the expensive seats to "rattle your jewellery" in accompaniment to "Twist and Shout", omitting the planned expletive at the last moment—much to Brian Epstein's relief.

A total of 40 million people tuned in when these two prestigious London theatre appearances were aired on prime-time television. It was the kind of exposure Epstein could have only dreamt about twelve months earlier, when success had been measured in hearing "Love Me Do" on Radio Luxembourg and seeing it nudge into the Top 20.

Life would never again be the same for the group, though it was actually an incident between those two key London dates that caused them

to realize it. After the Palladium appearance the Beatles had embarked on their first overseas tour proper, to Sweden. That they went down as a storm in Scandinavia was no surprise; they were used to lifting the roof off concert halls. But the boys were taken aback by the chaotic scenes that greeted their arrival back at London Airport on 31 October. Delirious fans swamped the terminal, not in the hope of hearing a note but simply to lay out the welcome mat.

Prime Minister Sir Alec Douglas-Home witnessed the bedlam firsthand. So did Ed Sullivan, presenter of one of the US's top-rated TV shows, who made it his business to discover what all the fuss was about. He was on the lookout for the next big thing, a fresh act that might have the same impact Elvis had had in 1956. Sullivan had a hunch that the Beatles might succeed where the likes of Cliff Richard had failed, and immediately entered into negotiations with Epstein to book the group. If their appeal crossed the Atlantic, he would know he had a scored a major coup; if they bombed, he could put it down as a novelty item from the old mother country.

ABOVE: **Royal Variety Performance souvenir programme. Those not lucky enough to attend could buy the special magazine published by the *Daily Mirror* and read the Beatles' personal account.**

LEFT: **The boys look exhausted as they sign a series of autograph books during the autumn tour.**

LEFT INSET: **Marlene Dietrich takes the stage with the Beatles at the Royal Variety Performance.**

OPPOSITE: **A rehearsal for the Royal Variety Performance on 4 November at the Prince of Wales Theatre. The Beatles were the seventh act of 19, including Marlene Dietrich, Harry Secombe, Tommy Steele, and Pinky and Perky.**

AT THE ROYAL VARIETY PERFORMANCE

"For our last number I'd like to ask your help. Would the people in the cheaper seats, clap your hands? And the rest of you, if you'll just rattle your jewellery."

—John

ABOVE: **John is the centre of attention in the bar after a performance during the autumn tour.**

LEFT: **Anne Escreet enjoys the photo opportunity of a lifetime when she has the attention of all four Beatles in Hull.**

SEPTEMBER 1963

1 A Sunday evening was spent recording for *Big Night Out* at the Didsbury Studio Centre in Manchester. Hosted by Mike and Bernie Winters, this was a variety show for ABC Television.

2 "She Loves You" had sold more than half a million copies in the UK.

3 The last three editions of *Pop Go the Beatles* were taped at the Aeolian Hall in London. The 12th edition of *Pop Go the Beatles* was broadcast.

4 John Smith booked the band for four nights starting with a date at the Gaumont Cinema in Worcester. This booking was possible only because Epstein

had cancelled the rest of the Mersey Beat Showcase dates.

5 The second date at the Gaumont Cinema in Taunton.

6 The EP *Beatles Hits* was released in the UK on Parlophone GEP 8880 (mono only). "From Me to You" and "Thank You Girl" were on the A-side with "Please Please Me" and "Love Me Do" on the B-side. The third date was at the Odeon Cinema in Dunstable.

7 *Big Night Out* was broadcast. The final Smith date was at the Fairfield Hall in Croydon. During the day another session for *Saturday Club* was recorded at

the Playhouse Theatre in London. It was the show's fifth birthday and by now had achieved audience figures of 9 million. The song list included "Happy Birthday Saturday Club"—a short arrangement by John of the traditional song. Following the recording, Paul was interviewed by Rosemary Hart for *A World of Sound*, a radio series for the Home Service.

8 Sunday night's venue was the ABC Theatre in Blackpool.

10 The band received the award for Top Vocal Group of the Year at the Variety Club Awards lunch at the Savoy Hotel, London. Later that afternoon John and Paul watched the

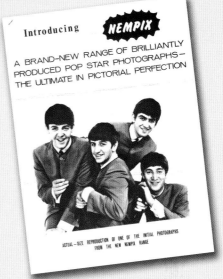

Introducing NEMPIX

A BRAND-NEW RANGE OF BRILLIANTLY PRODUCED POP STAR PHOTOGRAPHS— THE ULTIMATE IN PICTORIAL PERFECTION

ACTUAL-SIZE REPRODUCTION OF ONE OF THE INITIAL PHOTOGRAPHS FROM THE NEW NEMPIX RANGE

London and America resist the tide

The Beatles had proved themselves in both the singles and album charts, and had shown that they could steal any show, no matter what slot they were given on the bill. There were two missing pieces of the jigsaw. One was the print media. The Beatles were getting plenty of coverage in provincial newspapers and music publications, but they weren't national news. Tony Barrow, who wrote a music column in the *Liverpool Echo* under the "Disker" byline, was appointed full-time press secretary to NEMS in May 1963. At first Barrow's efforts to get his press releases into print were met with stony resistance in the capital. The time would come soon enough when London's Fleet Street newspapers would be vying for any snippets Barrow could toss them, pieces that could be worked up into a front-page splash.

The second issue was the lack of impact their records were having on the American charts. The Beatles might have been the biggest fish on the UK pop scene, but across the pond they remained minnows. The group's first two releases, "Please Me" and "From Me to You", sank without trace, largely through the woeful promotional efforts by the distributor. Vee-Jay had picked up the distribution deal after Capitol, which was owned by EMI and had first refusal, had shown itself unwilling to release any Beatles records—or those of any other British artist, for that matter. The timing was unfortunate, for Vee-Jay's president blew a sizeable chunk of the company's operating capital in a gambling spree, which left a gaping hole in any plans to promote a record by an unknown British band. In short, cracking America would take a little while longer.

Rolling Stones rehearsing. The *Daily Mirror* published a long interview with the Beatles describing them as "Four frenzied Little Lord Fauntleroys who are making £50,000 every week". The 13th edition of *Pop Go the Beatles* was broadcast.

11 Another recording session at Abbey Road when they continued to work on material for the second album, *With the Beatles*. Three new songs by Paul and John were taped: "Little Child", "All I've Got to Do", and "I Wanna Be Your Man". In the evening, George's first song, "Don't Bother Me", was recorded.

12 The Beatles' fame was spreading to Australia so at Abbey Road the boys recorded four separate messages that could be broadcast down under featuring their usual witty repartee.

13 After the Friday night show at the Public Hall in Preston, Paul drove to Nelson to judge the Imperial Miss 1963 contest at the Imperial Ballroom.

14 Another date at the (Victory) Memorial Hall in Northwich. Brian Epstein was best man at his brother's wedding. "She Loves You"/"I'll Get You" reached No. 1 in the UK charts, remaining there for four weeks.

15 The band topped the bill at the Great Pop Prom at the Albert Hall.

16 "She Loves You"/"I'll Get You" was released on Swan 4152 in the US. Again it failed to enter the *Billboard* chart listings. Holiday time at last; the Lennons went to Paris and were joined by Brian Epstein.

17 The 14th edition of *Pop Go the Beatles* was broadcast.

19 George and his brother Peter visited their sister, Louise, who had emigrated to Benton, Illinois, in 1954.

20 Paul and Ringo opted to travel to Greece together.

24 The last edition of *Pop Go the Beatles* was broadcast.

27 Reports were published rumouring that Brian planned to move NEMS Enterprises from Liverpool to London in early 1964.

30 In the band's absence an editing, mixing, and overdubbing session was held at Abbey Road with George Martin adding some extra keyboard passages.

The Beatles had neither the time nor the inclination to examine the fine details of deals done in their name. In addition to live performances and guest appearances on numerous radio and TV shows, they hosted their own radio series, *Pop Go the Beatles*, which ran for thirteen weeks over that summer. In the middle of that run, 3 August, they played the Cavern for the final time. Their fee was £300, sixty times greater than the £5 they received for the first Mathew Street gigs, but that was now small change. It was a valedictory set for their hometown fans, whose growing fears over the past nine months had finally crystallized: the Beatles had outgrown Liverpool.

ABOVE LEFT: **Ringo dances with Mrs. Lou Levy, the wife of a music publisher.**

ABOVE: **Paul's new girlfriend, Jane Asher, tries to avoid the spotlight during a date at the theatre. The young actress had first caught the Beatle's attention in April when she was covering his band for *Radio Times*.**

OPPOSITE: **George looks in good humour at John Bloom's party.**

Martin pleads for better EMI deal

Prolific output and phenomenal sales figures prompted George Martin to plead with the EMI bosses for a better deal for the Beatles when their contract came up for renewal. Epstein could be forgiven for signing the original penny-per-record royalty deal, having little bargaining power at his disposal. A year on, it was a different matter completely. A 25 percent increase would automatically apply under the terms of the original contract, but a hefty percentage on a tiny figure still amounted to a derisory offer. Martin stuck his neck out with his bosses, demanding a doubling of the royalty for nothing in return. He got his way, though he would later say it came at a personal cost, with management regarding his actions as akin to corporate treachery.

OCTOBER 1963

2 All the Beatles returned home except George.

3 George returned to England in the afternoon. That morning the other three had attended an overdubbing session at Abbey Road. John and Paul added vocals to "Little Child" while Ringo put new vocals onto "I Wanna Be Your Man". That afternoon all four went to the NEMS Enterprises office in Monmouth Street, London, to record the first of three appearances on *The Public Ear*, a BBC radio programme.

4 The boys made their debut on *Ready, Steady, Go!* when the programme was broadcast live from Television House in London. The band mimed to "Twist and Shout", "I'll Get You", and "She Loves You" while young fans danced around them. They were interviewed by Keith Fordyce, the show host, and also by Dusty Springfield.

5 A three-night tour of Scotland organized by promoter Albert Bonici began at the Concert Hall in Glasgow.

6 The next night was at the Carlton Theatre, Kirkcaldy, where they played to two houses: a total of 3,000 people watched them.

7 Finally to Dundee where they played at the Caird Hall.

9 *The Mersey Sound* was broadcast in the north and in London. Back at the BBC Paris Studio an appearance on *The Ken Dodd Show* was taped when the boys provided the musical slot playing "She Loves You". It was John's 23rd birthday.

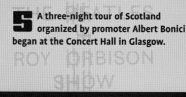

SONG STORY: "I WANNA BE YOUR MAN"

By September 1963 the Lennon–McCartney hallmark was established as the gold standard of popular music. Artists would fall over themselves for one of their cast-offs, including the Rolling Stones, who were looking for a follow-up to their Chuck Berry–penned debut single, "Come On". On 10 September, the day the Beatles picked up their Variety Club award for Top Vocal Group, they bumped into the Stones' co-manager Andrew Loog Oldham, who invited them along to Studio 51 in Soho, where his band was recording. John and Paul said they might have something suitable from their work-in-progress cache, and played a snatch of "I Wanna Be Your Man". Bill Wyman's jaw dropped as Paul hammered out the bass line on a borrowed right-handed instrument. The Stones liked the number, so John and Paul disappeared into a huddle to knock off a middle eight and final verse. The song gave the Stones their first Top 20 hit, and also helped kickstart the Jagger–Richards writing partnership. The next day the Beatles also recorded "I Wanna Be Your Man", but to them it was merely an album filler that provided a vocal spot for Ringo.

ABOVE AND LEFT: **The boys were amazed at the thousands of fans who had waited at London Airport to welcome them home from Sweden. They proved to be a bigger security problem than the prime minister, Alec Douglas-Home, who was passing through the airport at the same time.**

OPPOSITE: **George captures the return from Sweden on film with a cine-camera.**

OPPOSITE INSETS: **Souvenir from the Beatles' three-night minitour of Scotland in October (right). A ticket to one of two performances in Stockholm, where the Beatles were second on the bill after Joey Dee and the Starliters (left).**

continued from previous page

OCTOBER 1963

13 *The Mersey Sound* was broadcast all over the country. The Beatles finally secured their first booking with Associated TeleVision, one of the leading ITV companies. They appeared on *Val Parnell's Sunday Night at the London Palladium*, a peak-time show with audience figures of around 15 million. This was their most prestigious booking to date. The success of the group was well and truly established.

14 Photographs of the performance at the London Palladium were on the front of every London newspaper. The band was invited to perform in the Royal Variety Show due to go out on 4 November.

15 A photographic session with Leslie Bryce. The boys played at the Floral Hall in Southport.

16 Another recording session at the Playhouse Theatre in London when they made the last recording for *Easy Beat*. The fifth recording was cancelled as Brian Epstein had become concerned for the band and the fans' safety. As a result he decided radio shows would only be recorded without an audience and concert halls needed fixed seats, thus ruling out ballrooms as venues.

17 The boys had lunch with the winners from the *Boyfriend* magazine competition at the Old Vienna. Two further recording sessions took place at Abbey Road. The tracks for the new single, "I Want to Hold Your Hand" and "This Boy" were taped using four-track recording for the first time. The A-side had been written at Jane Asher's parents' house in Wimpole Street, London.

18 At the Granada TV Centre in Manchester the boys mimed to "She Loves You" for *Scene at 6.30*.

19 A date at the Pavilion Gardens Ballroom in Buxton.

20 The last recording on *Easy Beat* was broadcast. Another appearance on *Thank Your Lucky Stars* was taped at the Alpha Television Studios in Birmingham. They mimed to "Money (That's What I Want)" and "All My Loving", two tracks from the forthcoming album.

21 George Martin completed more mixing and editing to "This Boy" and "I Want to Hold Your Hand".

23 A final recording session at Abbey Road for the next album. In the afternoon the band flew to Sweden to embark on their first tour abroad.

24 Initially the four recorded a radio appearance at the Karlaplansstudion in Stockholm.

25 The first concert booking was at Nya Aulan, Sundsta Läroverk, a high school hall in Karlsatad. Two houses were played to a screaming audience.

26 Two houses were played at the Kungliga Tennishallen, Stockholm.

27 Three shows were performed at the Cirkus, Göteborg.

28 Half an hour was spent in the afternoon signing records at the Waidele record shop in Boras, followed by a show at the Boråshallen in Boras.

29 Brian Epstein agreed to a deal with United Artists to make a Beatles movie. The last performance of the tour took place at the Sporthallen in Eskilstuna.

30 At Abbey Road, the last track for the album, "Money (That's What I Want)", was mixed and the LP *With the Beatles* was finally ready for production. In Sweden the boys taped an appearance for the Swedish television show *Drop In*.

31 The band flew back to England, arriving at the same time as the prime minister, Miss Universe, and Ed Sullivan. Thousands gathered at London Airport to welcome the band home.

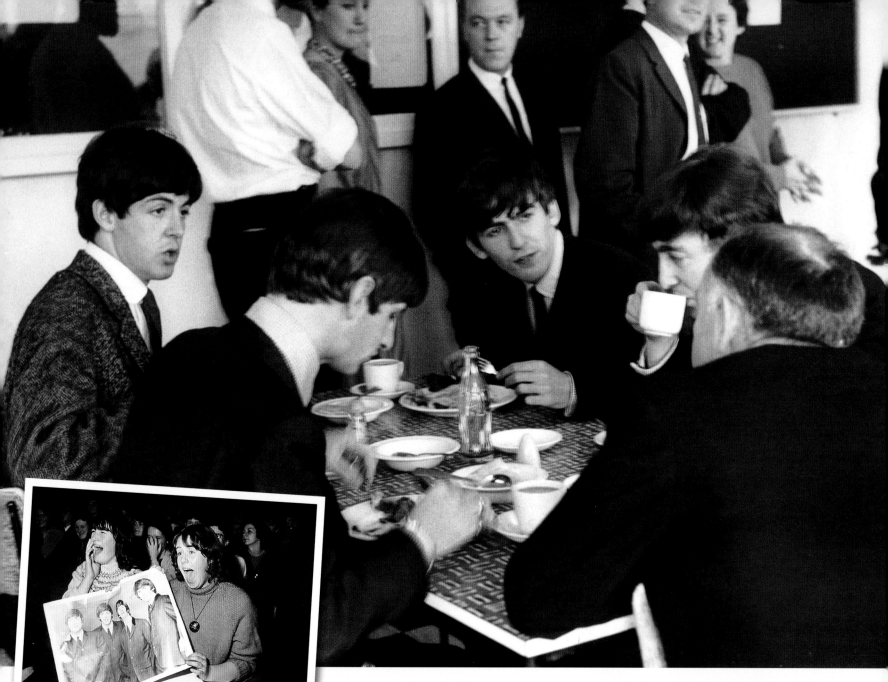

LEFT: **The sight of crazed fans at the concerts caught the attention of American journalists, who recorded scenes from the concert at the Winter Garden Theatre in Bournemouth on 16 November and broadcast them on American television news later that week.**

ABOVE: **The boys take a lunch break during a television recording at the Alpha Studios in Birmingham.**

OPPOSITE: **The Beatles use their newfound fame for good by supporting Oxfam's latest charity drive.**

NOVEMBER 1963

1 The EP *Beatles (No 1)* was released in the UK on Parlophone GEP 8883 (mono only). The A-side featured "From Me to You" and "Thank You Girl" while "Please Please Me" and "Love Me Do" were on the flipside. "The Beatles Autumn Tour" began, for which they were paid £300 a night. It kicked off at the Odeon Cinema in Cheltenham with the band heading a ten-act bill.

2 The tour continued at the City Hall in Sheffield while the *Daily Mirror* coined the phrase "Beatlemania" during a review of the Cheltenham performance.

3 The *Ken Dodd Show* was broadcast from 2:30–3:00 p.m. and was immediately followed by the first *The Public Ear*, a programme that could be heard from 3:00–4:00 p.m. That night the tour played at the Odeon Cinema in Leeds.

4 For the Royal Command Performance the band were seventh on a 19-act bill and played to the Queen Mother, Princess Margaret, and Lord Snowdon.

5 The tour resumed to play two houses at the Adelphi Cinema in Slough. Earlier in the day the boys recorded

interviews for the Associated-Rediffusion show *This Week*, a current affairs programme.

6 On *Scene at 6.30* the footage filmed by Granada Television at the Cavern Club in 1962 was shown. That night they played at the ABC Cinema in Northampton, where two girls climbed onto the roof to see them.

7 *This Week* was broadcast. For the next two nights the Beatles made their only appearances in Ireland. Frank Hall, a reporter for Radio Telefis Eireann, met them at Dublin Airport. The interview

George enters the songwriting race

The group was being pressed to deliver a follow-up album despite the fact that *Please Please Me* had been in the shops for just five months. *With the Beatles* was another fourteen-song offering, with the same 8–6 split as their debut LP's ratio of self-penned songs to covers. "Hold Me Tight" was dusted off, and there were six new Lennon–McCartney numbers. The other Beatles song on the album, "Don't Bother Me", marked George's first credit on vinyl, though a collaboration with John had produced the instrumental "Cry for a Shadow" back in 1961. Creatively speaking, George wouldn't get another look in until *Help!*. At first he was overawed by John and Paul, and the fact that George Martin concentrated his

efforts on the group's two "winners" didn't help. Over the years this would turn to frustration, something that would not be completely exorcized until the release of his acclaimed solo album *All Things Must Pass*, which featured a number of songs that had failed to pass muster for a Beatles record.

There was no such inner seething on Ringo's part. He was sanguine about his role within the band, content with his drumming and the occasional lead vocal. On *Please Please Me* Ringo had sung the cover of the Shirelles number, "Boys". This time John and Paul decided to write something specifically for him. They came up with two possibles that suited Ringo's limited vocal range, "Little Child" and "I Wanna Be Your Man", though at the last minute it was decided that the two frontmen themselves would share the vocals on the former.

SONG STORY: "I WANT TO HOLD YOUR HAND"

"I Want to Hold Your Hand" was the song that cracked America, a graveyard for so many top British artists; the song that turned the group from a British phenomenon into a global brand, selling 15 million copies in the process. John and Paul wrote "I Want to Hold Your Hand" in the autumn of 1963 at the Ashers' Wimpole Street house, Paul's sometime-residence for the next three years. Another domestic smash hit was a given, but Brian Epstein was becoming increasingly irked by Capitol Records' refusal to throw its weight behind Beatles releases, and seeing successive singles farmed out to minor labels in the US. In November 1963 Epstein buttonholed Capitol president Alan Livingston and wrung a deal out of him, including an unprecedented $40,000 promotional budget. The Beatles took the States by storm long before those funds were exhausted. Capitol even had to bring forward the release date by three weeks as import copies hit the airwaves to wild acclaim.

"I Want to Hold Your Hand" hit the top of the Billboard chart on 1 February 1964, and dropped anchor there for seven weeks, when it was supplanted by "She Loves You". Ironically, the Beatles were struggling to win over impassive Parisian audiences when the song that was to become a cultural watershed hit the number one spot in America.

---

he recorded with the band was broadcast that night. Later they played at the Adelphi Cinema in Dublin. That day also marked the first of three days when Alun Owen observed the group's lifestyle. He was a screenwriter chosen by producer Walter Shenson, who was to eventually make the movie *A Hard Day's Night*.

8 The band made its second appearance on *Ready, Steady, Go!* In Ireland the band travelled to Belfast, stopping en route to be interviewed by Jimmy Robinson for Ulster television's *Ulster News*. In Belfast that afternoon an interview with Sally

Ogle from the BBC for the show *Six Ten* was taped. The band then played the Ritz Cinema in the city that night.

9 Back in England they played at the Granada Cinema in East Ham, East London, and then attended a party in London thrown by the millionaire John Bloom.

10 The *Royal Command Performance* was broadcast on television and radio. That Sunday evening they played at the Hippodrome Theatre in Birmingham.

11 In the States Epstein met Ed Sullivan to arrange the band's appearance on his show and also signed a deal giving CBS-TV the exclusive rights to the band's television appearances for a year.

12 The boys were due to play at the Guildhall in Portsmouth but were forced to postpone the date when Paul was hit by gastric flu, with his progress reported regularly during the day.

13 An interview for Westward Television's programme *Move Over, Dad*, was recorded at their studios in

Plymouth. Later that evening they played to two houses at the ABC Cinema.

14 Another performance at an ABC Cinema, this time in Exeter.

15 Moving east to Bristol to play at the Colston Hall.

16 A Saturday night at the Winter Gardens in Bournemouth. It was clear by now that Beatlemania was reaching the US when three different networks came to film the show.

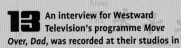

With the Beatles

The Beatles may have been keen to get maximum return for their efforts, and John and Paul were aware that they had the ability to "write a swimming pool" in an hour or two, but for the new album the group made a conscious decision not to bleed the fans by including any new or previous single releases. They held equally firm over the artwork for the cover, the stark, unsmiling, half-light shot captured by photographer Robert Freeman in the corridor of a Bournemouth hotel. EMI condemned it as drab and dour, while even Epstein thought it would be

detrimental to their fun image. The group would be totally vindicated. *With the Beatles* went on to become only the second UK album, following *South Pacific*, to sell a million copies, while the sleeve photograph would take its place among the iconic imagery of the era.

By the time the second album hit the shops, the Beatles had moved on from being merely the hottest pop act around. An extraordinary sea change had taken place, one that propelled them onto the front pages of newspapers. To call it an epiphany, a zeitgeist moment, would be no exaggeration, for it would be difficult to oversell what occurred in the UK in the autumn of 1963.

continued from previous page

NOVEMBER 1963

17 On to perform at the Coventry Theatre in Coventry. When the tickets went on sale the previous month, fans had waited in line through the night.

18 The band was at EMI House in London to receive silver LPs for *Please Please Me* and *With the Beatles* (this in advance of its release on 22 November) from Sir Joseph Lockwood, the company chairman. Gerald Marks, editor of *Disc*, presented a silver EP and a single for "Twist and Shout" while George

Martin also presented a miniature EP for *Twist and Shout*. A formal lunch followed the ceremony.

19 The tour resumed at the Gaumont Cinema in Wolverhampton.

20 That evening they played the ABC Cinema in Manchester and allowed Pathe News to film two of the songs. This formed part of a brief newsreel titled *The Beatles Come to Town*, which was shown in theatres just before Christmas. Granada TV also filmed the band that night

using backstage scenes and interviews with the boys for the programme *Scene at 6.30*. Additionally, BBC Radio was there recording an interview with the band for *Voice of the North* while the reporter Michael Barton interviewed George for a programme entitled *Wacker, Mach Shau*, which discussed the links between rock music in Hamburg and Liverpool.

21 Paul's interview for *A World of Sound* was broadcast in the episode titled "Liverpool: A Swinging City". In the evening they played the ABC Cinema in Carlisle.

WiTH THE BeaTLes

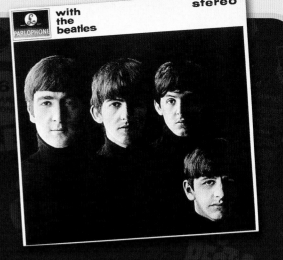

Released
🇬🇧 22 November 1963 (Parlophone)

Side One:
It Won't Be Long
All I've Got to Do
All My Loving
Don't Bother Me (Harrison)
Little Child
Till There Was You (Willson)
Please Mister Postman (Dobbins–Garrett–
    Gorman–Holland–Bateman)

Side Two:
Roll Over Beethoven (Berry)
Hold Me Tight
You Really Got a Hold on Me (Robinson)
I Wanna Be Your Man
Devil in Her Heart (Drapkin)
Not a Second Time
Money (Bradford–Gordy)

Cover Story

After taking pictures of the Beatles' performance at Bournemouth in August 1963, photographer Robert Freeman was invited to shoot the cover for *With the Beatles* at the Palace Hotel. Freeman had previously photographed jazz legends such as John Coltrane and Dizzy Gillespie, and in 1963 he sent some of these pictures to Brian Epstein in the hope of securing a photo shoot with the Beatles.

The resulting black-and-white photograph, shot against a heavy, dark curtain, with a natural sidelight that cast the Beatles' faces in half shadow, was somewhere between Freeman's jazz portraits and the striking early images of the band that were taken by Astrid Kirchherr in Hamburg: exactly what the Beatles were looking for.

Brian Epstein and EMI, however, were initially disappointed, believing that the image was too moody—but eventually the Beatles got their way. Capitol was also persuaded and the same photograph was used for the American release, *Meet the Beatles!*, although there it was given a blue tint.

Although he was never the band's official photographer, Freeman would produce five of their iconic album covers between 1963 and 1965: *With the Beatles*, *A Hard Day's Night*, *Beatles for Sale*, *Help!*, and *Rubber Soul*. He also provided the title sequences for the movies *A Hard Day's Night* and *Help!*, as well as supplying photographs for John's books *In His Own Write* and *A Spaniard in the Works*.

Beatling on . . .

A million copies of the Beatles's latest single record, *I Wanna Hold Your Hand*, have been sold before the record is released today.

An EMI spokesman said: "It is becoming increasingly difficult to find new superlatives for the Beatles, who have been making and breaking records for little over a year. A pre-release sale of a million is absolutely unprecedented."

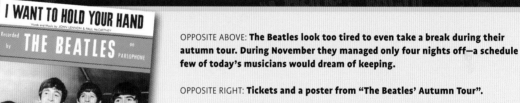

OPPOSITE ABOVE: **The Beatles look too tired to even take a break during their autumn tour. During November they managed only four nights off—a schedule few of today's musicians would dream of keeping.**

OPPOSITE RIGHT: **Tickets and a poster from "The Beatles' Autumn Tour".**

LEFT: **"I Want to Hold Your Hand", the fifth Beatles single, was released in the UK on 29 November. Already a million-seller in the UK, the single went on to be the first Beatles record to reach the No. 1 spot in the American *Billboard* Chart after it was released in December 1963.**

FAR LEFT: **The *Daily Mail* reports record-breaking sales of Beatles discs.**

---

22 The album *With the Beatles* was released in the UK on Parlophone PMC 1206 (mono) and PCS 3045 (stereo) with advance orders of 300,000. It rapidly passed the half-million mark and by 1965 had sold in excess of 1 million. The black-and-white cover photo was taken by Robert Freeman. Staying in the north of England, the Globe Cinema in Durham was that night's venue.

23 Then to a Saturday night performance at the City Hall in Newcastle-Upon-Tyne. Fans had queued for two nights to get tickets and 7,000 fans reportedly broke through the police cordon.

24 Then on to play at the ABC Cinema in Hull.

25 In the afternoon they taped a performance and interview for Granada's *Late Scene Extra* and *Scene at 6.30*. During the interview with Gay Byrne they were joined by infamous ad-libber Ken Dodd.

26 Back on tour at the Regal Cinema in Cambridge.

27 "She Loves You" finally reached 1 million sales. That night they played the Rialto Theatre in York.

28 The tour continued at the ABC Cinema in Lincoln.

29 The fifth single, "I Want to Hold Your Hand"/"This Boy", was released in Britain on Parlophone R5084 and was the first single to receive in excess of 1 million advance orders. That night two houses were played at the ABC Cinema in Huddersfield. Between shows Gorden Kaye interviewed them individually and asked them to read requests for *Music Box*, a show for hospital broadcast.

30 A Saturday night at the Empire Theatre in Sunderland where they met Jeffrey Archer, who asked them to help with an Oxfam appeal—he was at that time hoping to become an MP.

Movie studio spots contract loophole

A spot on *The Ed Sullivan Show* wasn't the only transatlantic deal in its gestation period at this time. United Artists also came wooing, dangling a juicy movie carrot in front of Epstein's nose. The brief from United Artists boss Bud Ornstein was simple: he wanted a cheap movie and a valuable soundtrack album, the studio having learned that the latter wasn't covered in the Beatles' EMI contract. Producer Walter Shenson was tasked with delivering the goods, and he hit it off well with the Beatles camp. United Artists were prepared to offer a modest fee plus 25 percent of the net. Epstein, no doubt still thinking in record-royalty ballpark figures, must have thought he was driving a hard bargain when he informed them that they wouldn't take

less than seven and a half percent. The studio couldn't put pen to paper quickly enough.

As was typical at this stage in their career, the Beatles were more concerned with their art than business dealings. Paul and John had written their next single at the Wimpole Street home of Paul's new girlfriend, Jane Asher, whom he had met at a Royal Albert Hall concert in April. "I Want to Hold Your Hand" was released 29 November, knocking "She Loves You" off the top of the UK singles chart two weeks later.

ABOVE: **The Vernons Girls, one of the support acts in the autumn tour, pictured with their idols on 13 November.**

BELOW: **A ticket for the 7 December edition of *Juke Box Jury*, when the Beatles formed the jury, as well as tickets from their Christmas show and a night in Leicester.**

ABOVE AND LEFT: **The Beatles, costumed in striped blazers and boater hats, pose alongside the legendary British comedy double act, Morecambe and Wise. The occasion was the Beatles Christmastime guest spot on *The Morecambe and Wise Show*, where they joined the hosts in several sketches as well as performing three numbers including "I Want to Hold Your Hand". The reason for boating attire was a short rendition of an old classic, "Moonlight Bay", for which Morecambe and Wise joined them to close the show. The television programme was recorded on 2 December at Elstree Studios in Hertfordshire, near London.**

DECEMBER 1963

1 A tour date at the De Montfort Hall in Leicester.

2 A contract was signed for the group to undertake a tour of Australia in June 1964. During the day they recorded an appearance on *The Morecambe and Wise Show* at Associated TeleVision's studio in Elstree. After performing three songs there followed a fabulous comic sketch with the duo. That evening they played a charity performance at the Grosvenor Hotel with an audience in ball gowns and black ties replacing the usual frenzied crowd.

3 The tour resumed at the Guildhall in Portsmouth, rescheduled from 12 November when Paul was ill.

7 After three rest days the tour continued in Liverpool at the Odeon Cinema. In the afternoon they had played to members of the Northern Area Fan Club at the Empire Theatre, part of which was recorded and played on BBC's *It's the Beatles!* later that evening. That afternoon the BBC had also recorded an edition of *Juke Box Jury*—this time with all four taking part. They also made a brief interview for

Top Pops of 1963 to be broadcast on radio on Christmas Day. *With the Beatles* topped the British album charts, remaining there for 21 weeks.

8 A tour date at the Odeon Cinema in Lewisham, London. Fans again broke through police lines.

9 The BBC interviewed the group in their dressing room prior to a house at the Odeon Cinema in Southend-on-Sea. Queues for tickets began two and a half days before the box office opened.

EMI turns up heat on Capitol

Epstein didn't wait for the new single to reach number one, something that was already assured with advance orders of 1 million. He went to the States in mid-November, in part to finalize arrangements for the appearance on *The Ed Sullivan Show* but primarily to mount a frontal offensive on Capitol Records. Epstein would have been overplaying his hand. He had no clout in that neck of the woods, and he certainly couldn't intimidate Capitol boss Alan Livingston. But L.G. Wood, EMI's managing director, undoubtedly could. EMI had always been loath to pull rank on Capitol, but with company profits soaring on the back of the Beatles, the time for a laissez-faire attitude to its American subsidiary was over. Unknown to Epstein, Wood had also paid Livingston a visit to discuss the release of the new single. And this time he wasn't asking, he was telling.

In December 1963, America remained largely unaware of the pop phenomenon that was sweeping Britain. CBS had carried a news item on Beatlemania, but a teenage craze four thousand miles away cut little ice. There were Capitol Records executives who hadn't heard of the Beatles, so it was hardly surprising that the rest of the country was oblivious. Now, having been leaned on by their UK parent company, Capitol planned to release "I Want to Hold Your Hand" in late January 1964. The company hastily revised its plans when Washington, DC radio station WWDC began playing an import copy and getting rave feedback, rushing the single out on 26 December. Capitol had been dragged kicking and screaming to the Beatles' cause, even agreeing to Epstein's bold request for a staggering $40,000 promotional budget. The label showed its true feelings by initially pressing just five thousand copies of the new single. It would prove to be something of an underestimate. The Beatles were coming.

THE BEATLES CHRISTMAS SHOW

By the autumn of '63 the Beatles had made numerous media appearances, had a movie in the pipeline, and embarked on their latest £300-a-night screamfest round Britain. Predictably, Brian Epstein looked to the tradition of the great British pantomime as a vehicle to keep the Fabs working and the fans happy over the festive season.

The Beatles Christmas Show, which ran from 24 December until 11 January at the Finsbury Park Astoria, was conceived and produced in haste. The sketches and sight gags weren't the slickest in showbiz history, and the Beatles soon realized that revue-style productions weren't their forte. The 100,000 fans who managed to get a ticket didn't agree, though, as Paul drily noted: "They would have laughed if we just sat there reading the Liverpool telephone directory."

Even if the jokes had fallen flat, there was the pulsating 25-minute set that closed the show. The delirious crowd bayed for more, but the Beatles were already out of the theatre under cover of the National Anthem, which kept the audience captive for a few precious seconds while they made good their escape.

continued from previous page

DECEMBER 1963

10 At the Gaumont Cinema in Doncaster, another pre-performance interview, this time for the BBC's Transcription Service for overseas broadcast.

11 Staying north, the boys played the Futurist Theatre in Scarborough.

12 Another Odeon Cinema, this time in Nottingham.

13 The last date of this tour was held at the Gaumont Cinema in Southampton.

14 "I Want to Hold Your Hand" topped the British charts and stayed there for five weeks. It eventually sold 1.5 million copies in the UK and 15 million worldwide. In the afternoon the boys played to the Southern Area Fan Club at the Wimbledon Palais. They were filmed by television and cinema news and had to play behind a metal cage to keep the fans back.

15 A Sunday recording session at the Alpha Studios in Birmingham for *Thank Your Lucky Stars*, featuring only Merseyside acts.

17 Another taping session at the Playhouse Theatre, London, this time for *Saturday Club*.

18 At the BBC Paris Studios in London the lads taped a two-hour special for Boxing Day, eventually called *From Us to You* and hosted by Rolf Harris. The Beatles

OPPOSITE: **The Beatles in costume for their Christmas show at the Finsbury Park Astoria on Christmas Eve 1963. The Beatles took part in comic sketches in the show and "Roll Over Beethoven", "I Want to Hold Your Hand", and "Twist and Shout" were among the numbers they performed.**

ABOVE: **The local press in each town or city the band visited was always keen to take some shots of them before the concert. Often representatives from the national press would be present too.**

joined him in a version of "Tie Me Kangaroo Down Sport". Other guests included Joe Brown and the Bruvvers and Kenny Lynch.

21 *Thank Your Lucky Stars*, taped the previous Sunday, was broadcast. It included a presentation of two more gold discs. The edition of *Saturday Club* taped four days earlier was also transmitted. At the Gaumont Cinema a preview performance of the forthcoming *The Beatles Christmas Show* was held.

22 The second preview, this time at the Empire Theatre, Liverpool. Guest artists included Rolf Harris, Cilla Black, and Billy J. Kramer with the Dakotas.

23 The Radio Luxembourg show, titled *It's the Beatles*, began.

24 The first of the full stage production of *The Beatles Christmas Show* at the Astoria Cinema in Finsbury Park, London.

25 Christmas Day: a day off with their families, having flown home to Liverpool on a specially chartered plane with fellow cast-members. They were heard on the Christmas Day edition of *Top Pops of 1963*, with DJ Alan Freeman.

26 Meanwhile in the States, "I Want to Hold Your Hand"/ "I Saw Her Standing There" was released on Capitol 5112. Sales in the first three days topped a quarter million and less than a month later reached 1 million.

27 The London *Times* critic gave Lennon and McCartney the award of best composers of the year.

31 The band made their third appearance on *Ready, Steady, Go!* broadcast from 11:15 p.m. to 12:15 a.m. to see in the New Year.

THE CAVERN CLUB

Opened in 1957 at 10 Mathew Street, Liverpool's Cavern Club was initially a haven for jazz musicians, but it soon began to open its doors to skiffle, blues, and rock 'n' roll groups and quickly became established as the premier venue for the emerging Merseybeat sound.

The Beatles made their first appearance there on 21 March 1961, although the Quarry Men had already played there. Along with the Searchers and Gerry and the Pacemakers, they rapidly became one of the club's leading attractions.

In November 1961, a curious Brian Epstein attended a lunchtime session at the Cavern in order to see the Beatles perform, and within a month the band had accepted his offer to manage them.

After securing their recording contract in 1962, the Beatles continued to play at the Cavern, but as their fame began to spread beyond Liverpool, their appearances at the venue became more infrequent, and they would take the stage there for the last time on 3 August 1963, having notched up an impressive tally of almost three hundred performances.

The Beatles left the Cavern with a thriving music scene and international reputation, and over the next few years the venue would play host to such names as Sandie Shaw, John Lee Hooker, the Yardbirds, the Rolling Stones, and the Who. Despite this, however, the club fell into financial difficulties and was briefly closed in 1966, before being officially reopened by then–prime minister Harold Wilson.

During the early 1970s, Thin Lizzy, Supertramp, and Judas Priest all performed at the Cavern. However, the halcyon days of the Merseybeat era could not be recaptured and the club closed in May 1973.

Eleven years later, it was decided to reopen the Cavern Club, but structural damage to the site meant that a new venue had to be constructed nearby. Its design remained faithful to that of the original, however, even using reclaimed bricks from the original Cavern, and it continues to be a highly popular music venue to this day, hosting original groups as well as various Beatles tribute bands.

OPPOSITE: **Ringo takes to the cockpit of a plane chartered by Epstein at a cost of £400 to ferry his various acts back to Liverpool for a Christmas Day break from performing** *The Beatles Christmas Show* **in London.**

OPPOSITE BELOW: **Ringo is joined by singer Cilla Black (right) and a view of the cabin with Ringo, Cilla Black, and Brian Epstein (left).**

BELOW LEFT: **Dancers at the original Cavern Club.**

BELOW: **An article from the** *Daily Mail* **of 30 December reports that the stage from the Cavern is to be sold in aid of Oxfam, a charity with which the Beatles themselves were involved.**

ON SALE FOR OXFAM: BOARDS THE BEATLES TROD

By Daily Mail Reporter

THE stage that the Beatles made famous in Liverpool's Cavern Club, birthplace of the Mersey Sound, is to be broken up and sold for Oxfam.

The club's owner, Mr Ray McFall, said last night that pieces of the stage would cost 5s. each.

More money will come from four sections bearing the names of the Beatles—Ringo Starr, Paul McCartney, George Harrison and John Lennon. The sections are to be auctioned.

Mr. McFall said: "The Beatles were unanimous that Oxfam should benefit from the auction.

"Besides bearing one of their names, the four pieces will each have an engraved plate giving details of the group's appearances at The Cavern.

"It hasn't been decided where to hold the auction. I hope Oxfam might be able to arrange it in London."

Big count

A new, bigger stage is to be put up at the club Mr McFall said: "Inquiries for the old stage are coming in from all over Britain and Europe.

"When the cutting up starts I shall have to arrange a guard on the wood. It is about the most sought-after in the world."

1964

Things We Said Today

By any standards 1963 had been a remarkable year for the Beatles: four smash-hit singles, two number-one albums, sell-out concerts, media appearances—even the royal seal of approval.

At the beginning of 1964 the Beatles were ready to launch themselves on the world stage, but this was the fickle world of popular music, where trend and transience ruled. Even Elvis, whom the Beatles held in godlike awe, had been reduced to making low-budget films. If the King could be dethroned, then surely the Beatles could easily be toppled. Or at least that was the accepted wisdom. Already there was talk that the "London Sound" of the Dave Clark Five would bring the Mersey Beat's run of success to a shuddering halt, and if not them, there would be someone else waiting in the wings. The boys were hardly short on self-confidence, but even they were daunted at the prospect of trying to replicate their UK success further afield. Sweden was one thing, the US quite another.

ABOVE: **A membership card for the 1963 season at the Cavern Club. 1964 was to be the year the "Mersey Sound" broke out of Liverpool and went global.**

LEFT: **1964 was also the year that the Beatles were transformed from singing sensations to movie stars. A handful of lucky fans were invited to a US preview of their first film, *A Hard Day's Night*, at the Embassy Theatre, New York.**

SPECIAL PREVIEW · ADMIT ONE
№ 1473
Wed. Aug. 12th at 2:00 p.m.
THE BEATLES
in their First Feature-Length Motion Picture
"A HARD DAY'S NIGHT"
Produced by Walter Shenson/Released Thru United Artists

ALL SEATS $1.00
This Ticket Is Good Only For This Performance
at the

EMBASSY
THEATRE

DO NOT DETACH. Present Entire Ticket To Doorman

THIS TICKET IS GOOD ONLY AT

EMBASSY THEATRE

All Seats $1.00

Triomphe des Beatles as the Mersey sound sweeps Paris

RIGHT: **John and George on their way to Paris on 14 January, just a few days after the final performance of the *Beatles Christmas Show* on 11 January.**

OPPOSITE: **The schedule in Paris was gruelling and the boys had only two days off out of a total of 15. Here a rare window in their timetable allows the Beatles to enjoy a drink on the Champs Elysées. The decision to let them venture 500 yards from the hotel on to the Champs Elysées was not taken lightly by their management because of their experiences of security problems at home. However, they needn't have worried: although crowds gathered to see who was attracting the photographers, only three girls asked the Beatles for their autographs. Beatlemania had not reached France and the boys were able to revel in a last taste of freedom to enjoy the sights without being pursued by thousands of hysterical fans.**

RIGHT: **While in France, the Beatles discovered that "I Want to Hold Your Hand" and its B-side, "I Saw Her Standing There", had rocketed to No. 1 in the *Cash Box* charts.**

FAR RIGHT: **The popularity and influence of the Beatles became the thing of dreams for advertisers. Here they are fittingly used to market music hardware—soon their names would be used to sell everything and anything, no matter how unconnected to the band.**

JANUARY 1964

1 For 11 nights the band continued to play at the Astoria Cinema, Finsbury Park, London. The first edition of *Top of the Pops*, introduced by Jimmy Savile, included the Beatles playing "She Loves You".

5 A rest day from the *Christmas Show*, but the band made a radio recording for the series *The Public Ear*. Two different takes were kept; one broadcast on 12 January and the second left unreleased until 1972, when it was played on *The Beatles Story*, a Radio One documentary.

7 A recording was made at the Playhouse Theatre for *Saturday Club* that was due to be transmitted when they were in the States.

8 Footage of the boys performing in Bournemouth was shown in the States for the first time on the *Jack Paar Show*.

11 The final performance at Finsbury Park.

12 The band made a second appearance on the live show *Val Parnell's Sunday Night at the London Palladium* when they joined Bruce Forsyth, Alma Cogan, and Dave Allen. The first booking three months previously earned the band £250—this time they received £1,000. *The Public Ear* recording was broadcast on BBC Light radio.

A mixed response in Paris

There was little evidence of the famous *entente cordiale* during the Beatles' three-week stint in Paris, which began with a concert at the Cinema Cyrano, Versailles, on 15 January 1964. France was a notoriously difficult market to crack for overseas performers, and the male-dominated audiences found both the music and the winsome charm of the musicians perfectly resistible.

The boys certainly earned their £50-a-night fee for the eighteen-day residency at the Paris Olympia, where they played two, sometimes three, shows daily and had just two days off. They didn't take the place by storm, though there were mitigating circumstances. Paris's smart set filled the seats for the opening night, a stuffed-shirt brigade who took in the proceedings with polite aloofness. Matters weren't helped by the fact that there were teething problems with the amps, and with the press corps in attendance it came as no surprise that the reviews the next day were hardly gushing. It is difficult to imagine that American singer Trini Lopez and French chanteuse Sylvie Vartan wowed the Parisian audiences more than "Les Beatles", but such was the case.

The one dubious advantage to the cool reception was that for once they could actually hear themselves play. The downside could easily have been a blow to their confidence. If they couldn't crack France, what chance the States? If the boys needed a fillip, they got the best imaginable when they arrived back to the George V hotel after their first Olympia show. News came through that "I Want to Hold Your Hand" had rocketed from 43 to No. 1 in America's *Cash Box* chart. The *Billboard* Hot 100, America's other main music industry listing, would follow

suit soon afterwards. The single had hit the top spot just three weeks after its release, a feat no other British act had managed. Brian Epstein's exhortation for John and Paul to write a song that would appeal to the American market had paid off in spades. It also meant that by a whisker the Beatles had made good on their promise that they would go to the States only when they had a number one to their name. Suddenly a little local difficulty in Paris—hardly the epicentre of the rock 'n' roll explosion —didn't seem quite so important.

BOTTOM: **A badge featuring the names and faces of the Fab Four was a rather conservative indicator of the huge variety of merchandise that would hit the stores over the year as Beatlemania swept the globe.**

14 George, Paul, and John flew out to Le Bourget Airport in Paris.

15 The boys played at Versailles, a small town west of Paris, before embarking on a three-week season at the Paris Olympia. Ringo had flown out earlier in the day. In Chicago, Illinois, Capitol Records was granted an injunction that stopped Vee-Jay Records from marketing or distributing any further discs recorded by the band.

16 The first performance at the Olympia Theatre, Boulevard des Capucines, Paris, France. This was followed by 18 days of two houses daily in a nine-act bill.

19 Three shows were performed in Paris. Part of the matinée performance was broadcast live on *Musicorama*, a programme on the French radio station Europe 1. Five songs were

transmitted along with material from some of the other artists in the show.

20 The LP *Meet the Beatles* was released in the US on Capitol T-2047 (mono) and ST-2047 (stereo) and ultimately sold three and a half million copies in two months. A brief interview with the band was heard on Europe 1.

continued from previous page

JANUARY 1964

21 A rest day from the Paris performances.

23 The band went to Alma Cogan's party, held at her flat.

24 A radio interview for the American Forces Network was recorded at a Paris studio for the programme *Weekend World*. At Abbey Road Norman Smith made a tape-to-tape copy of "I Want to Hold Your Hand" to take over to France.

27 The album *Introducing the Beatles* was re-released in the States on VJLP 1062 (mono only).

28 A rest day from the Paris performance. John and George flew back to London briefly.

29 At the EMI Pathe Marconi Studios the band recorded "I Want to Hold Your Hand" and "She Loves You" in German as the West German branch of EMI had insisted the songs be translated for the German market. They also recorded "Can't Buy Me Love" in English.

30 The single "Please Please Me"/"From Me to You" was re-released in the US by Vee-Jay Records on VJ 581. *Billboard* magazine described the record as "a driving rocker with surf-on-the-Thames sound and strong vocal work".

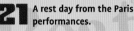

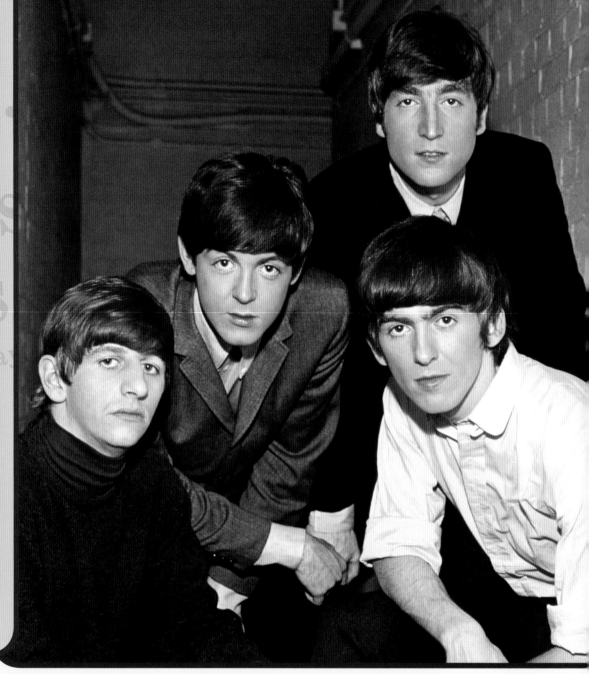

"She Loves You"

John and Paul were well used to fitting in writing sessions between concerts, and during their stay in Paris the pressure was on to come up with material for the forthcoming film and new album, the next single, and some throwaways for some of their NEMS stablemates. The George V hotel offered much more salubrious surroundings for composing than the back of a van, the boys enjoying the luxury of having a piano installed in their suite. The result was a crop of songs that came right out of the top drawer. So prolific was this spell that the original template for the forthcoming soundtrack album—seven new songs to be interwoven with some older numbers used in the film—had to be abandoned. The as-yet-untitled third LP would feature thirteen new songs, the first Beatles album to be filled exclusively with Lennon–McCartney compositions. An entirely self-penned long-player was almost unheard of at the time. Buddy Holly, one of the Beatles' heroes, had carried it off, but for "mortal" bands it was regarded as a high-risk strategy.

George Martin had one further request during the Paris sojourn: to record "I Want to Hold Your Hand" and "She Loves You" in German. EMI's German offshoot insisted that the English versions would not sell as well, and although neither the producer nor the group believed that for a minute, they shrugged their shoulders and relented. The songs were duly translated—"Komm, Gib Mir Deine Hand" (Come, Give Me Your Hand) and "Sie Liebt Dich" (She Loves You)—and the boys were coached on how to deliver the vocals. At the time appointed for recording the new versions, the Beatles mischievously decided to hold a tea party at the hotel, leaving an apoplectic Martin at the Paris studio with the company's German representative. It was the only time Martin found the Beatles unprofessional with regard to a recording commitment, and he stormed round to the hotel to give them a piece of his mind. After some contrite tomfoolery, the boys cut the two tracks, the only foreign-language recordings they ever made.

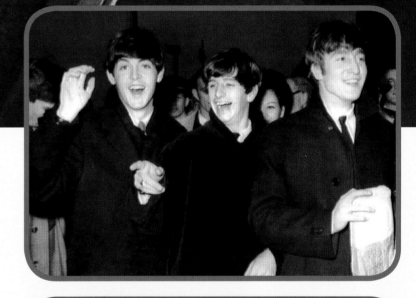

OPPOSITE: **While staying in the George V Hotel in Paris, the boys composed several songs on the grand piano installed in their suite. Chief among this batch was Paul's "Can't Buy Me Love", which was recorded alongside the German version of "She Loves You" at a Paris studio.**

THIS PAGE: **The Beatles enjoy their sojourn in Paris.**

MAIN AND OPPOSITE: **The Beatles returning from their 18-day trip to Paris, where audiences had been staid but amicable: the French press had given the Beatles a decent review. Meanwhile, the Moscow press had been following events in France with interest and made some unflattering remarks.** *Evening Moscow* **disregarded the Beatles' act as little more than "screams, grimaces, and convulsions". This was the first reference to the boys in the Soviet press, and in some sense it was a considerable coup for a British band to have any coverage at all in the tightly controlled world of the Soviet Union.**

BELOW: **Ringo watches Sylvie Vartan try out one of his cameras.**

Reading the Reviews

The boys' first performance in Paris led to a complete dichotomy in French opinion. The morning following the band slept through until lunchtime while the press let rip with their views. The witty but unforgiving critic in *Le Figaro* stated that in his opinion they "dressed like gamekeepers and held their guitars like watering cans". On waking George Harrison dryly commented, "He must write for a gardening journal".

Conversely, *France Soir* focused on the music saying, "These four boys captivated us with their astonishing rhythm", while the *Paris-Presse* sagely commented "If the more important invited guests applauded with more politeness than vigour, the young people in the gods, who had paid for their seats, kept yelling, 'Let's have another'."

Needless to say the Beatles were unperturbed by the reviews. "It's a good thing", stated Ringo Starr. "Now perhaps they won't expect too much." Paul McCartney likened it to a previous performance in Scandinavia, "We thought we'd died the death on our first night in Sweden. But a week after we left, we were top of the hit parade there".

EXTRACTED FROM THE
DAILY MAIL, 16 JANUARY 1964

FEBRUARY 1964

1 The single "I Want to Hold Your Hand" was No. 1 in the US charts, remaining at the top position for seven weeks.

3 The band went to the American Embassy in Paris to collect the visas and work permits required for the US tour. "I Want to Hold Your Hand" and the album *Meet the Beatles!* were awarded a gold disc in the States.

4 The final date in Paris.

5 The boys flew back to England.

6 Beatles wigs went on sale in the United States.

7 The group finally flew to the States. Landing at John F. Kennedy Airport on flight PA 101 at 1:20 p.m., they were greeted by 3,000 screaming fans. An edition of *Saturday Club* broadcast the next day included interviews and special reports from reporters Malcolm Davis and Brian Matthew from the Plaza Hotel. The EP *All My Loving* was released in Britain on Parlophone GEP 8891 (mono only). The A-side featured "All My Loving" and "Ask Me Why" with the B-side playing "Money (That's What I Want)" and "P.S. I Love You".

8 During the two-week tour of the US the band was constantly filmed by Albert and David Maysles to produce a documentary made in association with Granada Television. They regularly flew footage back to England to broadcast the American phenomenon. The band spent the day on studio rehearsals at CBS Television's Studio 50 in Manhattan for *The Ed Sullivan Show*. In the States Epstein asked attorney Walter Hofer to take responsibility for the band's fan mail; the first delivery consisted of 37 sacks. Back in the UK the band was heard on *Saturday Club*.

9 More rehearsals in the morning at the CBS Studios, although George was ill and replaced by Neil Aspinall. In the afternoon George was able to take part in the recording for *The Ed Sullivan Show* due to be broadcast after they left the US. That evening in front of a different audience the band appeared live on *The Ed Sullivan Show*, reaching an estimated audience of 73 million across the US. Before the show they received a telegram of congratulations from Elvis.

11 A train journey from New York to Washington, DC, was followed by a performance at the Washington Coliseum— their first US concert venue held just over 8,000. They played on a central stage so that they could be seen from all four sides of the auditorium. Later the band attended a party at the British Embassy.

12 Back in New York two shows were played at Carnegie Hall; the tickets had sold out within a day. In the UK a documentary titled *Yeah! Yeah! Yeah! The Beatles in New York*, detailing the US tour, was shown on Granada Television.

13 The band flew to Miami Beach. At the airport, doors and windows were broken as 4,000 fans tried to catch a glimpse of the Beatles.

Meet the Beatles!

For Brian Epstein, France and Germany remained a sideshow; events in the US were a different matter entirely. Capitol, having realized that they had dramatically underestimated demand for "I Want to Hold Your Hand", hastily contracted out some of the pressing to RCA and Columbia—ironically, two of the major labels that had decided to pass when offered the Beatles the previous year.

Capitol was quicker off the mark when it came to putting out a long-player. *Meet the Beatles!*, released 20 January 1964, carried the strap line: "The first album by England's phenomenal pop combo". It contained nine of the fourteen songs from *With the Beatles* and used the same monochrome sleeve photograph. But a fourteen-track album was considered too generous for the US market, where royalties were paid per song. Furthermore, Capitol, along with all American labels, believed that album sales were singles driven, so "I Want to Hold Your Hand" was tacked on, plus the B-side "I Saw Her Standing There" and "This Boy". The Beatles were against this kind of duplication, regarding it as a raw deal for the fans, but it was Capitol's call.

Something had to give to accommodate the extra material, and Capitol decided to dispense

OPPOSITE: **George gets a kiss from his number-one fan, his proud mum, Louise Harrison. She had supported his dream from the very beginning, encouraging his early efforts with the guitar and taking him to gigs. The kiss was also to be passed on to George's sister, Louise, who lived in America and whom George would see while on tour.**

BELOW: **The boys are interviewed by a journalist about their feelings ahead of the visit to the US.**

continued from previous page

FEBRUARY 1964

14 A rehearsal for *The Ed Sullivan Show*.

15 *Meet the Beatles!*, subtitled "The First Album by England's Phenomenal Pop Combo", reached the No. 1 position in the US and remained there for 11 weeks. The afternoon was spent rehearsing for their second appearance on *The Ed Sullivan Show*. Another recording of *Saturday Club* was transmitted in England.

16 The group's second live appearance on *The Ed Sullivan Show* was broadcast from the Deauville Hotel in Miami Beach before an audience of 3,500. Mitzi Gaynor topped the bill, with audience figures reaching 70 million.

17 The band had a break from appearances and spent the day fishing and water skiing.

18 The Beatles met Cassius Clay at his Florida training camp just before his fight with Sonny Liston.

19 The first of two more rest days relaxing on Miami Beach.

21 The boys left Miami and made a brief stop in New York.

22 The band returned to London Airport at 8:10 a.m.; the BBC

with five covers of songs originally recorded by American artists. The feeling was that the American public would be disinclined to prefer the Beatles' version of songs such as "Roll Over Beethoven" and "Money" to the originals. That principle would soon be discarded, all five numbers being included on the follow-up album, released three months later.

Meet the Beatles! rewrote the rulebook for album sales. It flew off the shelves as fast as "I Want to Hold Your Hand", fending off Vee-Jay's Introducing the Beatles for top spot in the album charts. Sales eventually topped the five million mark, at a time when shifting five hundred thousand copies was considered hugely successful and a million-seller was a rarity.

ABOVE: **With less than two days between returning from Paris and heading to America, John, Ringo, and Paul remained in London but George rushed back to Liverpool to see his father, Harold Harrison, who was ill with flu. George's parents helped him pack his "BEA-TLES" travel bag for his US voyage. British European Airlines (BEA) had given the boys free flights to Paris in return for prominently displaying the bag.**

meet the Beatles!

Released
🇺🇸 **20 January 1964 (Capitol)**

Side One:
I Want to Hold Your Hand
I Saw Her Standing There
This Boy
It Won't Be Long
All I've Got to Do
All My Loving

Side Two:
Don't Bother Me (Harrison)
Little Child
Till There Was You
Hold Me Tight
I Wanna Be Your Man
Not a Second Time

Cover Story

In the summer of 1963, photographer Robert Freeman was invited by Brian Epstein to shoot some images of the Beatles for the cover of the album With the Beatles. The band was in the middle of a six-day engagement at the Gaumont Cinema in Bournemouth and so the nearby Palace Court hotel was the venue for the shoot on 22 August 1963. Freeman's dark, moody images, which were shot in the hotel corridor, did not please EMI executives but the Beatles pressed to use one. Capitol chose the same image for this album, adding a blue tint to the photograph and some colour to the title lettering.

---

duly filmed the landing and sent sports reporter David Coleman to interview the band. The footage was broadcast during that afternoon's Grandstand. Pathe News also used the material to broadcast Beatles Welcome Home in cinemas, and a telephone interview by Brian Matthew was included in that morning's Saturday Club.

23 At the Teddington Studio Centre, near London, the boys went straight on to record another appearance on Big Night

Out. They joined guests Mike and Bernie Winters in some of their comedy sketches.

24 Ringo visited his family in Liverpool.

25 At Abbey Road the band began to record some new material for the forthcoming film. They also finished the overdubbing needed for the next single, "Can't Buy Me Love". It was George Harrison's 21st birthday.

26 More mixing for "Can't Buy Me Love" and the B-side "You Can't Do That". After the disruption caused by the Beatles' arrival at London Airport, the Ministry of Aviation announced that they would be investigating arrangements for VIPs using the airport.

27 The sessions at Abbey Road continued. "And I Love Her" (a song written about Jane Asher), "Tell Me Why", and "If I Fell" were completed.

28 Another special edition of From Us to You was recorded at the BBC Piccadilly Studios, to be broadcast on Easter Monday. Hosted by Alan Freeman, it included music and sketches with guest appearances from Acker Bilk and Vince Hill. Peter and Gordon released "A World Without Love", written by Lennon–McCartney.

29 Big Night Out was broadcast on ABC Television.

Vee-Jay jump on bandwagon

Capitol's decision to throw its considerable weight behind the Beatles was a beacon to Vee-Jay and Swan, who had gained precious little from their earlier efforts with the group and were keen to get a piece of the action now that they were the hottest ticket around. On 30 January, Vee-Jay issued "Please Please Me"/"From Me to You", the A-sides of the two single releases of the previous year. The latter had sold the better of the two first time round, though not well enough to break into the Hot 100, peaking at 116. The new single reached No. 3, but in trying to guarantee a surefire hit Vee-Jay wasted an opportunity: Had the songs been released separately, Vee-Jay would undoubtedly have had two top-five hits instead of one.

Vee-Jay also issued the Beatles album it had been forced to shelve the previous summer because of the parlous state of the company finances. Vee-Jay mistakenly thought that *Introducing the Beatles* contained essentially the same material as Capitol's album and wanted

to make a quick buck before the inevitable litigation began. In fact, *Introducing the Beatles* mirrored the UK album *Please Please Me*, minus the title track and "Ask Me Why", which Vee-Jay had already put out as a single. Thus, the only song common to both US albums was "I Saw Her Standing There". It was still a minefield, however. Vee-Jay was unsure of the precise legal position, though one thing was clear: the company didn't hold the rights to issue "Love Me Do" or "P.S. I Love You". These were hastily replaced with "Please Please Me" and "Ask Me Why", though not before a number of pressings had been made. *Introducing the Beatles* thus exists in two forms.

Capitol still filed suit, on the grounds that Vee-Jay had defaulted on the royalty payments due for the two singles issued in 1963, resulting in the termination of their contract with EMI in August of that year. Vee-Jay had indeed failed to pay its royalty dues, the gambling predilection of then-company president Ewart Abner having created a financial black hole in the company accounts.

INTRODUCING THE BEATLES

Released
🇺🇸 10 and 27 January 1964 (Vee-Jay)

Side One:
I Saw Her Standing There
Misery
Anna (Go to Him) (Alexander)
Chains (Goffin–King)
Boys (Dixon–Farrell)
Love Me Do
Ask Me Why (on second pressing)

Side Two:
P.S. I Love You
Please Please Me (on second pressing)
Baby It's You (Bacharach–David–Williams)
Do You Want to Know a Secret
A Taste of Honey (Marlow–Scott)
There's a Place
Twist and Shout (Medley–Russell)

BIO: CYNTHIA LENNON

Save for the loss of her father when she was seventeen, Cynthia Powell enjoyed a comfortable middle-class upbringing in a pleasant Liverpool suburb. She showed an artistic bent from an early age, and at eighteen enrolled at Liverpool College of Art, where she was both intimidated and drawn by the disruptive, acerbic Teddy Boy with whom she shared a lettering class. The magnetism won out when John made his play for the shy, bespectacled Cynthia in the summer of 1958. They quickly became inseparable lovers, Cynthia moulding her appearance to accord with John's blonde bombshell fantasy, Brigitte Bardot. Cynthia was pregnant when they married on 23 August 23 1962, John Charles Julian arriving on 8 April the following year. As Beatlemania swept the country, Cynthia was consigned to the background as it was deemed bad for business for a pop star to have a wife and child in tow. The press soon unearthed the truth, and Cynthia took her place in the limelight when the Beatles set out to conquer America in February 1964. The marriage was soon in trouble, and according to Cynthia it was John's drug habit that caused the rot to set in, long before Yoko Ono's arrival on the scene. "We were on different mental planes," she reflected, and the divisions were highlighted when John met the avant-garde artist who was very much on his wavelength. The Lennons divorced in November 1968, with Yoko cited in the proceedings. Cynthia has since married three times: Italian hotelier Roberto Bassanini (1970–73); Lancastrian engineer John Twist (1976–83); and nightclub owner Noel Charles (2002–present).

OPPOSITE: **The Beatles waiting to embark on their debut tour of the United States. It was notoriously difficult for British acts to make it big in America, but billboards across the country had announced that "The Beatles are Coming" long before the boys touched down at John F. Kennedy Airport in the early afternoon on 7 February. They were greeted by thousands of screaming fans and a large police presence ready to take them to the Plaza Hotel for the duration of their stay in New York.**

RIGHT: **John was accompanied on the US tour by his wife, Cynthia. Nosy Fleet Street reporters had only just discovered that John was married with a child, and Cynthia had fast become the envy of many young women.**

The Beatles hit New York

On 7 February 1964 the Beatles steeled themselves for the acid test: could they cut it in America, the land of their musical heroes and graveyard of so many other top British acts? Despite the phenomenal success of "I Want to Hold Your Hand", the boys had serious misgivings. America had everything, they mused; why would it want the Beatles? John and Paul openly admitted to being musical jackdaws who "borrowed" from other composers, most of whom were American. Why go for imports when the original was on your doorstep?

The doubts must have been swept away by the reception they were given at JFK Airport. The kids turned out in force, the chaotic scenes matching any the Beatles had witnessed on their home turf. True, that was partly down to hype. Capitol had run a very slick, very expensive marketing campaign in the weeks leading up to the group's arrival. Truckloads of stickers informed the populace that "The Beatles are coming", while a plethora of gimmicks included an instruction to all sales staff to wear Beatle wigs during business hours.

Radio was the single most important driver in bringing America to a state of fevered anticipation prior to the group's arrival, and here Capitol pulled a masterstroke. An all-purpose Beatles interview was taped, with gaps for the DJ to read the prepared questions. It created the illusion that the boys were in the studio, an "exclusive" for countless minor stations coast to coast. And as airplay was key, naturally the interview segued into a burst of "I Want to Hold Your Hand", which was cued up on the turntable.

On 7 February the New York stations went to town covering the group's arrival, moving the clocks to "Beatle time" and thermometers to "Beatle temperature". Kids were told they could make a quick buck and get a free T-shirt if they accepted a bus ride to the airport and screamed on cue. A few might have succumbed to this modest inducement, but no one could have orchestrated the crowds that packed the terminal, lined the route to the city, and laid siege to New York's Plaza Hotel.

It's Presley x four

IT'S the same all over the world. Wherever the Beatles go the teenagers scream, shriek, shout and shower them with jelly babies.

And at New York's Kennedy Airport yesterday it happened again. Fans pushed aside the police to mob Ringo, George, John and Paul as their plane touched down from London.

They came from hundreds of miles around. One came from Arkansas, 1,500 miles away. A boy, 250 miles from his New Hampshire home, said: "This is worth cutting school for." Many of the 3,000 teenagers were playing truant to welcome their heroes.

An American psychiatrist said: "The Beatles, I think, are perhaps Presley multiplied by four, and represent a manifestation of sexuality among teenagers." He may be right. One thing is certain. Wherever the Beatles go, the girls scream.

ABOVE: **British newspapers report the American reaction to their precious export on 8 February.**

LEFT: **Ringo and Paul hold gold discs for "I Want to Hold Your Hand", presented to them by Capitol.**

OPPOSITE: **The boys look bemused if not altogether unhappy at their reception at JFK Airport in New York and at the brief press conference.**

OPPOSITE BELOW LEFT: **A badge perpetuating the fresh-faced image of the boys amongst the American youth.**

Welcoming The Beatles

B-day arrived in New York as 3,000 screaming fans greeted the band as they stepped off the plane. New York's Kennedy Airport was in pandemonium as the boys ran the gauntlet of shrieking fans that showered them with jelly babies and candy kisses. More than 100 policemen struggled to keep back the fans while one American reporter began dictating his story with "Not since the day General MacArthur returned from Korea."

Nevertheless the boys took it all in their stride. "Just fab...just fab" they chorused, surveying the heaving mass of fans wearing Beatles' T-shirts, waving records and carrying welcome placards.

The boys were still uttering the same words as police escorted them into New York in a siren-wailing cavalcade of Cadillacs. Publicity men had organized teams of cheerleaders for the ten-day visit but could have saved their money. Some members of the teams were at the airport before dawn before the band's plane had even left London.

Police had planned to isolate the fans but they swarmed through turnstiles into the customs area. One girl hung from the third storey with two friends holding her hands as she screamed "Here I am. Here I am" to the group.

Alongside the fans and police presence over 200 reporters and photographers were waiting. Many questions were asked, some often stuffy or hostile but the boys gave as good as they got.

"Can you explain the social significance of the effect your singing has on the teenage element?" asked one American reporter. "How's that?" queried Paul McCartney now labelled by the Americans as the Bouncy Beatle. "Are you part of a social rebellion?" asked the reporter again. "It's a dirty lie," replied John Lennon. Another asked "What's your secret" to which they all chorused, "We wish we knew."

EXTRACTED FROM THE DAILY MAIL, 8 FEBRUARY 1964

Selling the Beatles

The rent-a-crowd crew at JFK had been there at the behest of Nicky Byrne, who would become the latest person to make a fortune hanging on to the Beatles' coattails. Byrne was a small-time operator out to make a big score when a golden goose fell into his lap. He had secured exclusive merchandising rights in the US, forming a company called Seltaeb—Beatles spelled backwards—which issued licences for the manufacture of anything from lunchboxes to bubble bath. Epstein had delegated what he regarded as a petty task to his lawyer, David Jacobs, not realizing that merchandising was a multimillion-dollar industry. Jacobs was equally ignorant of the potential sums involved and agreed to a 90–10 split with Byrne—in the latter's favour. It was a licence to print money, which Byrne recognized immediately and which slowly dawned on the NEMS camp during the Beatles' first trans-Atlantic visit of 1964. Epstein feverishly began trying to renegotiate the deal,

and by the summer the Beatles' end was upped to 46 percent. Even that figure represented woeful maladministration of the group's affairs, and Epstein compounded his mistake by issuing licences direct. That caused confusion among retailers, many of whom backed out, and also precipitated a costly court battle as Byrne sued for breach of contract.

The Beatles were blissfully unaware of the Seltaeb deal when they conducted their first press conference on American soil. The boys were in fine form, firing off a volley of one-liners in response to the journalists' questions. It made great copy and the press corps lapped it up. But witty horseplay and pin-up appeal would count for little if the Beatles couldn't back it up in their two appearances on *The Ed Sullivan Show* and three concert performances.

ABOVE: **Police try to contain fans who have flocked to JFK to greet the Beatles.**

LEFT AND BELOW: **Beatles candy was sold across the United States. Each packet carried the image of just one of the Beatles, encouraging young fans to buy four times as much. Many different lunch boxes were produced over the years, often to coincide with an album release.**

Sullivan fumes over rival show's coup

Part of Brian Epstein's pitch to Ed Sullivan was the kudos that breaking the Beatles on American TV would bring. Both men were left fuming when the *Jack Paar Show*, aired 3 January 1964, featured an extended piece on the group, including concert footage. Paar had purchased the film from the BBC, prompting Epstein to seek redress from that corporation. The BBC was keen to pacify the man who controlled the biggest media draw of the day, but its hands were tied; the deal was done. There was long-standing animosity between Paar and Sullivan, which made matters worse. Sullivan issued instructions to cancel the Beatles' appearance on his show, but relented before the threat was carried out. The loss of exclusivity was annoying, but he wasn't about to cut his nose off to spite his face. After all, he had secured two live Beatles performances plus a taped set at a garage-sale price.

ABOVE AND RIGHT: **The Beatles and Ed Sullivan. Sullivan got the boys at a steal, but Epstein realized the long-term potential of a prime slot on *The Ed Sullivan Show* and agreed to a low fee for the appearance.**

Record-breaking American TV debut

On the afternoon of Sunday, 9 February the Beatles performed live on American soil for the first time. CBS Studio 50 was the venue for the dress rehearsal for that evening's *Ed Sullivan Show*. The boys ran through the five numbers they would perform on the night, then treated the 728 lucky people who had managed to get a ticket to an extra three songs, a set that would be aired after the Beatles had returned to Britain.

Sullivan thought he had done a shrewd piece of business to get two live performances and one recorded set for $10,000, well below the going rate for a headline act on the show. However, unlike the deals he made with Dick James, Walter Shenson, and Nicky Byrne, Epstein had on this occasion pulled off a major coup. This trip was all about maximum exposure, not the bottom line, and NEMS was only too happy to underwrite

any losses in return for the amount of domestic penetration that an appearance on the Sullivan show guaranteed.

Over 70 million people—more than the entire UK population—tuned in to see what all the fuss was about. The boys opened the show with "All My Loving", "Till There Was You", and "She Loves You", then returned in the second half to belt out both sides of their number-one single. There were technical gremlins, notably a problem with John's mike. Earlier the sound console had been marked with chalk to indicate the desired mix, but these levels had been wiped off, apparently by an over-diligent cleaner. The seven hundred-strong audience either didn't notice or didn't care. The confines of the CBS studio meant that the kids didn't quite reach the fever pitch of the UK gigs, but when the moptops shook, they screamed just the same. Sullivan was forced to make a deal with the audience: they could let rip during the Beatles' performance as long as they restrained themselves when the other acts were on.

ABOVE: **Backstage on *The Ed Sullivan Show*, the boys clown around with another guest, Olympic speed skater Terry McDermott. McDermott, who pretends to cut Paul's precious mop, had just won gold at the Winter Olympics in Innsbruck, Austria.**

ABOVE INSET AND OPPOSITE: **The Beatles played five songs during their first *Ed Sullivan Show* appearance. During the second number, "Till There Was You", the camera lingered on each Beatle in sequence. When it came to John's turn, a caption saying, "Sorry Girls, He's Married" flashed on the screen.**

ON THE ED SULLIVAN SHOW

"...their voices are pleasant, they can sing sweetly, and now and then one could actually understand the lyrics."

—*New York Daily News*

"Talentwise the Beatles seems to be 75 percent publicity, 20 percent haircut and 5 percent lilting lament. They're really a magic act that owes less to Britain than to Barnum."

—*New York Herald Tribune*

"Whether it is intentional I can't say, but the Beatles are wildly funny."

—*New York World Telegram and Sun*

"Put away the spray guns. We're safe. The Beatles are harmless."

—*New York Post*

"The Beatles are fun... sartorially they are silly, tonsorially they're wildly sloppy, musically they're not quite hopeless."

—*New York Journal*

"The Beatles appear to be a harmless, youthful fad, like rolling hula hoops and swallowing goldfish."

—*New York World Telegram and Sun*

Critics attack

Amazingly, the reviewers didn't take their cue from the audience. *Newsweek*, which had reported on Beatlemania following the Royal Variety Show triumph in November, described their music as "a near disaster" and their lyrics as "a preposterous farrago of Valentine-card romantic sentiments". New York's *Herald-Tribune* thought the performance signified that the Beatles were little more than a trick that was easy to see through, dismissing them as "75 percent publicity, 20 percent haircut and 5 percent lilting lament". *The Ed Sullivan Show*'s musical director gave them no more than a year.

The boys were mildly irritated at all the trenchant reviews; Epstein was incandescent, and had to be talked out of cancelling the next round of press conferences by way of reprisal for what he saw as a hatchet job. The fact that he relented offered a golden opportunity to answer the critics—quite literally. For the day after their debut appearance on American TV, the Beatles were presented with gold discs for "I Want to Hold Your Hand" and *Meet the Beatles!* by Capitol boss Alan Livingston, with the newshound pack in full attendance. On 12 February, prior to the Beatles' two Carnegie Hall concerts, there was a presentation for another million-seller. "She Loves You" was racing up the singles charts and would eventually knock "I Want to Hold Your Hand" off the top spot.

The Beatles beat Elvis

NEW YORK, Friday
Fifty thousand people have applied for tickets for the Beatles' first appearance on American television. Ed Sullivan, who runs the programme, said today: "I've never seen anything like it and that includes Elvis Presley's three appearances in 1958.

"I'm amazed by the number of executives, banking Goliaths and so on, who have asked me personally for tickets. They always preface their request with the words 'Of course, it's for my daughter.'" —A.P.

LEFT: **The *Daily Mail* of 9 February reports on the popularity of the Beatles in America ahead of their appearance on *The Ed Sullivan Show*.**

THE COPS FIND OUT WHAT **BEATLEMANIA** IS ALL ABOUT

ON CROWD CONTROL

"Not since Castro, Khruschev, and Tito were all in town together in 1960 have the New York police had such a rough time."

—Ian Smith, *Daily Mail*

Beatlemania Hits New York

After the band's arrival in New York on Friday, the city police rapidly discovered exactly what Beatlemania entailed. The Beatles' hotel, the old, staid Plaza on Fifth Avenue, overlooking Central Park, was under siege with the press calling the Beatles the "prisoners of the Plaza".

The harassed police department ordered that the boys give at least one hour's notice before leaving the hotel, warning manager Brian Epstein "Otherwise we can't guarantee their safety". During a brief sightseeing visit to Times Square they were soon mobbed by a sea of fans, which led to any other excursions being conducted from the safety of their cars. During a brief session at a rehearsal studio it took 100 policemen plus assistance from mounted colleagues to hold back the screaming fans.

The New York radio station has played nothing but Beatles records –interspersed with news items and bulletins about them. George Harrison has spent most of the weekend in bed with a sore throat although on Sunday ventured out after being fortified with penicillin, making the last half an hour of rehearsal prior to the television show.

The management of the hotel stated that the Plaza thought the bookings in the name of Paul McCartney, George Harrison, Ringo Starr and John Lennon were just for ordinary businessmen and had been astounded by events. Other guests soon joined in the spirit of the occasion by sporting Beatles' wigs.

The boys did finally manage to escape their fans for a short while by slipping through a side door to enjoy a ride around Central Park in a horse-drawn carriage, albeit surrounded by police also enjoying a moment of peace.

EXTRACTED FROM THE
DAILY MAIL, 8 FEBRUARY 1964

ABOVE: **When the Beatles did leave the hotel, they had to do so under intense police protection. Wherever they went, a large number of officers accompanied them, even when they went to ride in a horse-drawn buggy in Central Park.**

RIGHT AND OPPOSITE TOP LEFT: **Bad weather had forced the Beatles to make the trip from New York to Washington by train, but the band needed the help of the New York Police Department to be able to reach the platform.**

OPPOSITE: **With Beatlemania roaring across New York City, the boys were largely confined to the usually sedate Plaza Hotel, where they could do little but observe the fans besieging the building from their windows. From their suite the Beatles innocently took calls from what turned out to be radio DJs, and many of the calls were put out live on the air. When Brian Epstein discovered what was going on, he was furious about the potentially lucrative interview material the boys had given away for free.**

OPPOSITE: **The boys pose for photographers in Central Park.** BELOW: **Bad weather caused flights from New York to Washington to be cancelled, and the Beatles were forced to take the train. A few thousand people had braved the cold weather and icy roads to turn up to greet the new pop sensation, but the frenzied scenes of John F. Kennedy Airport were not replicated at the station in Washington. The boys were freer to move around the city than they had been in New York, and they enjoyed a tour of the sights with just a handful of photographers and a few fans in tow.**

Washington goes wild

The 8,000-seat Washington Coliseum was the venue for the Beatles' first concert performance on American soil. It was the biggest gig they had ever played, and the fact that the stage was in the centre of the auditorium meant some nifty midset manoeuvring was required to give the entire audience a front-on view for at least some part of the show. Whichever way they faced during the twelve-song, twenty-eight-minute set, there was no respite from the barrage of jelly beans that rained down onto the stage. The fans had picked up on reports of George's weakness for jelly babies—a much softer British sweet—and obliged him and the others with a torrent of their hard-shelled American counterparts. If they weren't stinging the flesh, they were pinging off the instruments, causing the odd rogue note. It mattered not a jot. Many regard this electrifying performance as the apogee of the touring era. The charged atmosphere of the vast auditorium galvanized them on the night of Tuesday, 11 February. The novelty quickly wore off and they would come to loathe the huge impersonal venues where they would be screamed at, not listened to.

LEFT: **The band's first-ever US concert at the Washington Coliseum was a sell-out. Many people were turned away, and crowds in front of the venue numbered more than 7,000.**

OPPOSITE LEFT: **A commemorative booklet issued in Britain to illustrate the Beatles' first New York concerts at Carnegie Hall.**

Beatles play Carnegie Hall

The Beatles returned to Penn Station in New York from Washington on 12 February—President Lincoln's birthday—to play two concerts at Carnegie Hall that evening. The concert had been arranged by Sid Bernstein before he had ever heard any of the Beatles' music. He took a gamble on the band based upon the reviews coming in from Europe and borrowed the money to put down the deposit on Carnegie Hall. They were to be the first popular-music act to perform at the venue, and the ticket office was inundated with requests; the two shows completely sold out and even many high-profile celebrities could not obtain tickets. The spectacular interest in ticket sales was almost certainly created by the appearance on *The Ed Sullivan show* just a few days before, but the Beatles' music also sold itself. Thousands who could not get tickets gathered outside instead and Epstein and Bernstein were fast realizing quite what a sensation the Beatles had become in America. After the show, the two men took a walk to Madison Square Garden, and Bernstein tried to convince Epstein to cash in on the popularity and hold a last-minute show there before returning to Britain. Epstein deferred until their next visit, but admitted he did not think that even Madison Square Garden would be big enough.

ABOVE AND OPPOSITE RIGHT: **For their first concert in North America, the Beatles performed on a stage positioned in the centre of the auditorium. This meant that they had to reposition themselves, and Ringo's drum kit, at regular intervals so that all sections of the audience had an equally good view of the band.**

RIGHT: **The Beatles were guests at a formal reception at the British Embassy in Washington. The boys left the party in a hurry after one of the guests attempted to cut off a lock of Ringo's hair as a souvenir.**

Welcome to Miami

With three triumphant stage shows behind them, the Beatles were able to indulge themselves for much of the second week of their American sojourn. The Miami sunshine was a welcome change from snowbound New York, with the tanned beach babes a particular attraction. Apart from the inevitable stream of media interviews, the only commitment was the second *Ed Sullivan Show* appearance, broadcast live from the Deauville Hotel on Sunday, 16 February. The boys performed four of the five numbers they had sung the previous week, replacing Paul's showpiece ballad "Till There Was You" with the superb "This Boy", whose delicious three-part harmonies had gone down so well in the larger venues. They also added "From Me to You" to the set, which was again split so that the Beatles featured in both halves of the show. While Paul gave Capitol a plug as he informed the audience that "This Boy" was on *Meet the Beatles!*, he didn't extend the same courtesy to Vee-Jay in introducing "From Me to You", no doubt for political reasons. Mitzi Gaynor was nominally the headline turn, but there was no doubt who the 70-plus-million audience had tuned in to see.

BELOW: **After Washington the boys made for Miami, where they were to perform live for a second time on *The Ed Sullivan Show*. Here the Beatles are pictured rehearsing at the Deauville Hotel in Miami Beach ahead of their performance.**

10,000 greet Beatles

MIAMI, Thursday
Nearly 10,000 teenagers mobbed the Beatles when they flew in tonight from New York.
Bands played on the tarmac as the crowds pushed aside police and surrounded the Beatles' car.
—D.M. Reporter.
Beatles and the future—Page 14.

ABOVE: **Ed Sullivan runs through the schedule of the show with Paul.**

RIGHT: **The boys have one last run-through on the set of *The Ed Sullivan Show* at the Deauville Hotel, Miami.**

OPPOSITE INSET: **The *Daily Mail* reports on the chaos that ensued when the Beatles arrived in Florida on 13 February. They were flown into Miami International by a pilot wearing a Beatles wig and were met by the standard fare of thousands of screaming admirers. The scrum of fans was whipped into such a frenzy that events quickly descended into chaos and several thousand dollars' worth of damage was done in the resulting unrest.**

All alone—Mrs Beatle

Sunshine and sand and the beach at Miami . . . for Cynthia it can be lonely. But she says : " I love every minute."

ALONE and ignored, a pretty blonde girl sits on this palm-shaded beach and wiggles her toes in the sand.

A hundred yards away a mob of photographers and fans surround The Beatles as they splash and fool around in the surf.

There was no one to talk to the solitary "Beatlewife," Cynthia Lennon—until I slumped down on the sand beside her.

"Being left alone doesn't worry me a bit. I am enjoying myself," she said.

I am sure she believed what she said, but the fact remains that from the moment The Beatles arrived in America Cynthia Lennon has virtually been the woman who doesn't exist.

The reason? The publicity machine which now dominates The Beatles' lives believes that too much publicity about Mrs. Lennon will destroy The Beatle image.

To see her husband's shows, she had to stand in the shadows at the back of the TV studios, or in the wings, trying not to attract too much attention. But now the tour is nearly over security has relaxed.

What does she feel, watching fans throwing kisses to her husband, screaming in ecstasy when he plucks his guitar and sings? "I don't let it bother me," she said. "I know it's not for real. It's the music. I'm sure that makes them feel that way." In England, more fans are aware John is married than in America. Does this affect his popularity compared with the other members of the group —Paul, George and Ringo?

Mrs. Lennon pondered the question, letting sand trickle through her toes. "It's a funny thing," she said, "the fans, as you say, know we are married, that we have a child. Some write to John about the baby—they call him a 'Baby Beatle'—but they ignore the fact I exist." Surprisingly, this did not alarm her.

"One of the things I have realised now," she said, "is the high price one has to pay for fame in loss of personal freedom."

Said Cynthia, watching the group of which she is part—and yet not—disporting in the water: "I have loved every minute of the trip. It has been tough at times but I think America is great.

"I only hope we can come back."

The next time, it is to be hoped it won't be as the wife who doesn't exist.

LEFT: The *Daily Mail* interviews a content but lonesome Cynthia Lennon in Miami Beach on 17 February 1964.

BELOW AND OPPOSITE: **Miami Beach: the perfect setting for the Beatles to relax as millionaires competed to woo and pamper the latest pop sensation. One wealthy local allowed the Beatles the use of his extravagant yacht and another the use of his pool. The warmer weather in Miami also allowed the Beatles to frolic in the sea—inevitably with the press and a select few lucky ladies in tow. At the Deauville Hotel, the boys caught a show by the American comedian Don Rickles. However, the Beatles proved easy game for him and the boys would later recollect being left distinctly uncomfortable. Less taxing was watching Elvis Presley in *Fun in Acapulco* at a drive-in theater—a way of seeing movies that was alien to Britain.**

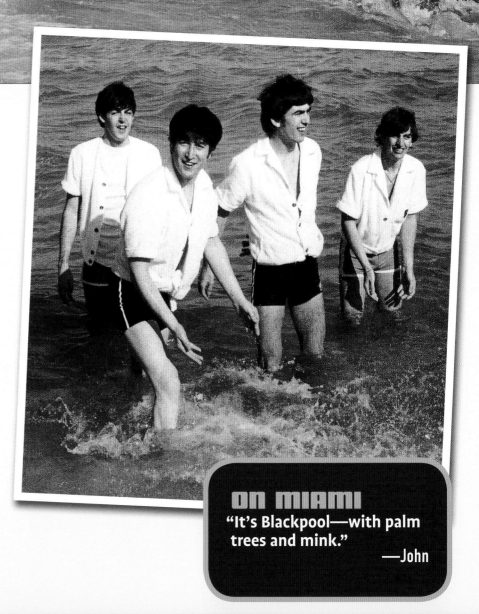

THIS PAGE AND OPPOSITE: **The Beatles cruise along the Florida shoreline aboard the *Southern Trail*. While in Miami, the four Beatles were invited by the Florida detective who was assigned to protect them to visit his home for a "typical American dinner". The detective, Sergeant Buddy Dresner, later said, "Nobody told me to do it. I think they are great kids and I wanted them to see what a typical American home is like. Also some home cooking." On the menu was what Mrs. Dresner described as "a good plain meal: roast beef, baked potatoes, and strawberry cheesecake".**

After the meal the band posed for snapshots for the family album and autographed pictures for Sergeant Dresner's three children.

Daily Mail

BEATLES PLAY STOOGE TO THE LOUISVILLE LIP

Beatles spar with Clay

While in Miami, the Beatles took the opportunity to visit heavyweight-title contender Cassius Clay, who was training locally for his forthcoming bout with champion Sonny Liston. It is said that the group, keen to ally themselves with winners, would have preferred a photo call with red-hot favourite Liston. But the champion, who had been in the audience for the second Sullivan show, was unimpressed. He was particularly disparaging about Ringo, who was actually the most popular Beatle Stateside. The boys thus ended up enjoying some clowning with the Louisville Lip instead. A week later, Clay defied the odds and claimed his place at the top of his profession, which he dominated for the rest of the decade. The parallel is clear. The future Muhammad Ali was being prescient as well as playful when he said the Beatles were "the greatest".

ON THE BEATLES' VISIT

"This is going to make Liston mad, the Beatles coming to see me and not him."

—Cassius Clay

OPPOSITE AND THIS PAGE: **The Beatles turned out to support Cassius Clay, who was in Miami ahead of his title fight with Sonny Liston. Clay towered over the fab foursome, leading the Beatles' publicity assistants to fear he was stealing the show. The band didn't seem to mind: they had a great time with him in the ring.**

RIGHT: **The *Daily Mail* of 19 February 1964 reports on the meeting that had taken place between Clay and the band at the Fifth Street Gym, Miami.**

From JEFFREY BLYTH
Miami Beach, Tuesday

IT was the contest— the publicity contest, that is—of the year.

In one corner stood the Beatles, weighing in at a total of 560lb. and not one over 5ft. 10in.

In the other strutted Cassius Clay, contender for the world heavyweight championship, 6ft. 3in., weighing in at 218lb.

The Beatles had dropped in this afternoon at the gym where Clay is training for his fight next week with champion Sonny Liston.

"Hi, champs," Clay greeted them. "I mean singing champs, of course. Me, I'm the fighting champ."

He invited the Beatles to join him in the ring. Bravely they did. Ringo and Paul tried on boxers' training helmets but wisely declined the offer to spar a round.

As Clay bounced round the ring shadow' boxing he chuckled: "This is going to make Liston mad, the Beatles coming to see me and not him."

He even composed a poem to celebrate the occasion. His fight manager commanded silence as Clay took up a stand in the middle of the ring and began:

When Sonny Liston picks up the papers
And sees the Beatles came to see me
He will be angry.
And I'll knock him out in three.

Fabs top Hot 100 for thirteen weeks

Capitol seriously considered putting out "Roll Over Beethoven" as the follow-up to "I Want to Hold Your Hand". The Chuck Berry number had been released in Canada and was doing a storming trade as an import. In the end the label deferred to George Martin, and "Can't Buy Me Love" followed on the heels of "I Want to Hold Your Hand" and "She Loves You" at the top of the chart, giving the Beatles an aggregate thirteen consecutive weeks at No. 1 in America.

"Roll Over Beethoven" was accorded second prize: the important track-one slot on the follow-up album to *Meet the Beatles!*. *The Beatles' Second Album* was hardly the most imaginative title, though Capitol was no doubt keen to take a sideswipe at Vee-Jay by asserting its status as the official Beatles label. Emblazoned across the sleeve cover, alongside the photo montage, were the words: FEATURING "SHE LOVES YOU" AND "ROLL OVER BEETHOVEN", indicating Capitol's view of the stand-out tracks for marketing purposes. Swan Records had twice issued "She Loves You" as a single, and Capitol lost no time in giving it yet another airing now that it had acquired the rights to the song.

THIS PAGE AND OPPOSITE: **On 22 February the boys departed from the US for Britain. In a visit lasting little more than two weeks, and stopping in only three cities, the boys had managed to take the whole nation by storm. They did not seem fazed by this mighty success; in fact, Paul even viewed it as a "logical progression" from their days in the Cavern Club. They all enjoyed their visit and felt a natural affinity with the cool, relaxed attitude of 1960s America.**

OPPOSITE LEFT INSET: **The *Daily Mail* of Saturday 22 February reports on the large number of fans that turned up at London Airport to greet the returning Beatles.**

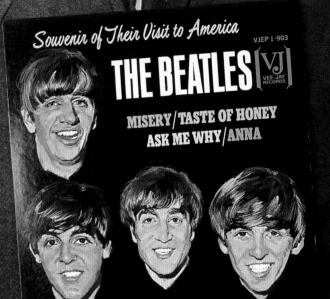

Wait up

Last night Beatle fans wearing Beatle sashes and badges, started to pour in at the airport.

Girls equipped with blankets were ordered by police to a corner of the Continental arrivals building until a dance had ended in the Queen's Building.

Then the floors were swept and they were allowed to pass their all-night vigil in the hall—which the girls called the "Beatles' Lounge."

No conquering army had returned home in such triumph. The Beatles hired a VIP lounge for their arrival—the Kingsford-Smith suite, normally reserved for Very Top People.

Souvenir of Their Visit to America VJEP 1-903

THE BEATLES [VJ] VEE-JAY RECORDS

MISERY / TASTE OF HONEY
ASK ME WHY / ANNA

Back from the US

No sooner had the Beatles arrived home from their triumphant first visit to the US than Brian Epstein was inundated with offers for them to return and virtually name their price. Epstein had pocketed a $253,000 cheque from Capitol for royalties earned from a single month's sales. There was also a less impressive $10,000 from Seltaeb, representing the Beatles' niggardly end of the first $100,000 of merchandising sales.

The boys had a lot of commitments before they could return to the States for a proper concert tour. Even celebrations for George's twenty-first birthday perforce had to be restrained as that very day, 25 February, they had pressing business to attend to at Abbey Road. With a week to go before the start of shooting for the new movie, the priority was to lay down the tracks that would feature in the picture. There was also the small matter of the next single. After putting the finishing touches to "Can't Buy Me Love", the boys quickly laid down a version of John's "You Can't Do That," pencilled in for the B-side. The latter would see George give his newly acquired twelve-string Rickenbacker 360 its first airing. It was only the second instrument of its kind the company had made, and in George's hands it would become a signature Beatles sound, exemplified most famously on the opening chord of the new album's title track. It would influence a generation of guitarists, including Pete Townshend and Roger McGuinn: the latter bought an identical model after seeing *A Hard Day's Night* and would use it to provide the foundation for the Byrds' sound, most memorably on "Mr. Tambourine Man".

ABOVE RIGHT INSET: **In March 1964 Vee-Jay attempted to cash in on the Beatles' visit by releasing a souvenir edition of "Misery" and "Taste of Honey" on the A-side and "Ask Me Why" and "Anna" on the B-side.**

Birthday Beatle

On 25 February the youngest Beatle finally turned twenty-one. George's birthday was marked by thousands of cards and presents that filled fifty-two mail sacks, keeping the local postman very busy. For the most part, fans had sent him jelly babies, which he had confessed were his favourite sweets, but all sorts of gifts were sent, including guitars, cakes, cigarettes, and toys—one fan even sent him a full-sized door to put his twenty-first birthday key in.

The other Beatles did not have the chance to join in the celebrations because they were busy rehearsing their new song "Can't Buy Me Love". George's family was also absent, but his mother, Louise Harrison, called him from Liverpool to sing "Happy Birthday" on the phone.

By Daily Mail Reporter

A BEATLE has a birthday —and in one day an estimated 15,000 cards, letters and parcels arrive. Yesterday Beatle George Harrison was 21. And all those cards, letters and parcels pack the home of George's parents in Liverpool. The biggest haul arrived in a

Beatle birthday . . . and loads of mail are carried in.

Post Office van. Three postmen staggered up with four wicker hampers and two large boxes. All full of many-happy-returnses. Presents . . .

ABOVE: **The *Daily Mail* reports from George's parents' house in Liverpool.**

THIS PAGE AND OPPOSITE: **George opens his cards with the help of a member of the Beatles Fan Club and enjoys a large Cuban cigar that he had been given as a birthday present.**

BIO: JANE ASHER

Jane Asher was born into a well-to-do English family on 5 April 1946, the second of three children of eminent physician Richard Asher and his wife Margaret, an orchestral musician and teacher of oboe at London's Guildhall School of Music. All three children had hallmark red hair and became involved in the performing arts at an early age— Jane's first acting role was at the age of five—with older brother Peter having a short but successful pop career as half of the duo Peter and Gordon (he later became A&R man for Apple and eventually vice president of Sony USA) and younger sister Claire also acting.

Jane attended a top private school, Queen's College, in Harley Street, central London, passing all her exams despite her performing and writing commitments. Writing an article commissioned by *Radio Times* when Jane was only seventeen brought her into contact with the Beatles after a performance at the Royal Albert Hall, London. She got to know the Beatles better as a result of her regular appearance on the TV show *Juke Box Jury*.

With her striking looks, privileged upbringing, and good education she was pretty much everything (and more) an aspiring Paul McCartney could desire as a girlfriend and they became an item, at first in great secrecy until it was made public in 1965, then openly living together as an engaged couple. When the Beatles first made London their home base, their addresses quickly became known to fans who laid siege. Paul had a double benefit in Jane when the motherly Margaret offered him their attic in 57 Wimpole Street as his London residence. He lived there for three years, initially unknown to fans. Paul worked in the family music room and composed a number of Beatles songs there: "Here, There and Everywhere", "We Can Work It Out", and "And I Love Her" are said to be inspired by Jane.

Paul and Jane moved into a house in St. John's Wood in 1966; they also bought a farm together in Scotland soon after. Jane became a member of the Bristol Old Vic, a respected acting company based in the west of England. She celebrated her twenty-first birthday on tour with Paul in the US in 1967 and in December that year they became engaged. When she returned home unexpectedly one night in spring 1968 she found Paul with another woman and this signalled the end of their relationship. Jane continued her acting career, founded an elite cake-making company, and authored numerous books. She married the well-known satirical cartoonist Gerald Scarfe in 1981 with whom she has three children.

ON SUCCESS

"I've had caviar and I like it. But I'd still rather have an egg sandwich."
—George

"I used to think, 'It must be marvellous to be up there, it must be different.' Well, it's great, but it isn't different."
—John

ABOVE : **The Beatles went to university for the first time when they attended a dinner at Brasenose College, Oxford, with the college principal, Sir Noel Hall, tutor David Stockton, and two students, Michael Lloyd and Jeffrey Archer. The dinner was informal and the guests were invited to sit on the floor to create a more relaxed atmosphere. Not all the food was to the Beatles'** liking: George asked the waiter to switch his smoked salmon sandwiches for simple "jam butties" and Paul asked for a glass of milk, which was presented to him in a seventeenth-century tankard. The dinnertime conversation centred around academia, with John discussing Chaucer, whom he had read in school, and with Ringo enquiring into the college's policy on sex.

JANE ASHER, that beguiling 17-year-old actress, is envied by every girl in two continents these days. For she is the regular girl-friend of Beatle Paul McCart-ney.

They met in the Albert Hall, in those dim days before the Beatles had ousted the Election, the weather and the Prime Minister from the headlines.

Since then they've seen as much of each other as work, fans and photographers allowed.

When the Beatles went to Paris, Jane was there to give moral support. And when Jane opened in The Jew of Malta in Canterbury last week, Paul drove her mother there to watch.

Sometimes publicity has been oppressive. Too many of their few evenings out together are spoilt by Paul being recognised, then mobbed.

Jane isn't just a Beatle girl-friend : she's a person and an actress in her own right, and a year ago was rather better known than the Beatles.

She has been in show busi-ness since she was five. First as a deaf mute in Mandy, then she played Alice in Wonderland, Wendy in Peter Pan, the younger sister in Greengage Summer.

She has been in show busi-ness since she was five. First as a deaf mute in Mandy, then she played Alice in Wonderland, Wendy in Peter Pan, the younger sister in Greengage Summer.

Natural

BUT it was on Juke Box Jury that she became known as a personality. Very pretty, with round blue eyes, a mass of red hair and amazingly articulate.

In spite of her show busi-ness success she's not a typical show biz doll.

"She's completely natural," one of her friends told me. "Full of vitality and in-terested in things and people.

"At school she was a dominant character, much admired and everyone liked her. She has lots of interests, painting, reading, films. And she managed to pass all her 'A' and 'O' levels while she was working."

One reason for her natural ease is that she was brought up in a busy, interesting family. Her father is a doctor, mother teaches the oboe, she has a brother at university and a sister at school.

OPPOSITE TOP: **Paul and Jane Asher chatting with Lionel Blair and comedian Dickie Henderson at the Pickwick Club party for Sammy Davis Jr.**

ABOVE: **The *Daily Mail* breaks the hearts of many young Beatles fans when it announces the relationship between Paul and Jane in March.**

ABOVE RIGHT: **Before embarking on filming *A Hard Day's Night*, George, pictured with actress Hayley Mills, was the only Beatle without a steady girlfriend.**

BELOW RIGHT: **George talks to Jane Asher, who is seated with Paul at the Pickwick Club in London.**

ON JANE ASHER

"Paul was obviously as proud as a peacock with his new lady. For Paul, Jane Asher was a great prize."

—Cynthia Lennon

I LOVE the "BEATLES"

I'M A BEATLE FAN In Case of EMERGENCY CALL PAUL OR RINGO

PAUL AND JANE ASHER

To the adolescent Beatles, Brigitte Bardot represented the last word in femininity and sexual allure. At John's behest Cynthia Lennon made a conscious effort to adopt the look of La Bardot, and when Paul became taken with a young actress who was a regular panellist on the TV record-review show *Juke Box Jury*, he saw a dazzling blonde who fitted the bill perfectly. He was undone by monochrome television, for when he finally got to meet Jane Asher, he found that she was a titian-haired beauty.

That first meeting took place in London on 18 April 1963. The Beatles were in town to play the Royal Albert Hall, and Jane introduced herself during their stay at the Royal Court Hotel in Sloane Square. She had been commissioned by *Radio Times* to write a piece on the band, and all four were only too happy to grant an interview—and not merely for PR purposes. Paul won the battle for her attention and they were soon an item, a golden couple among the capital's smart set.

Seventeen-year-old Jane was already a veteran of stage and screen, cultured and intelligent as well as beautiful. Paul undoubtedly saw her initially as a trophy girlfriend, and was hardly less impressed with her family. With a respected physician for a father, a Guildhall School of Music lecturer for a mother, and two other precociously talented children on the scene, the Ashers' home was a hotbed of ideas and debate, the polar opposite of ForthlinRoad. At a time when he was thirsting to complete his education, Paul needed no second invitation when he was offered the use of the Ashers' attic room. Number 57 Wimpole Street would be home for the next three years.

LEFT AND BELOW: **Ringo missed out on the party for Sammy Davis Jr. at the Pickwick Club because he had to be on set very early the next morning. In the movie, Paul's grandfather, John McCartney, played by Wilfred Brambell from the BBC sitcom *Steptoe and Son*, was cast as a scheming old man determined to stir up trouble in the group. Sensing that Ringo is stressed by the demands of a hectic schedule, he presses him until Ringo goes AWOL, walking about the city and eventually getting himself arrested. These scenes, shot largely at Kew in West London, required only Ringo and so George, John, and Paul were able to enjoy a well-deserved break. Ringo's busy filming timetable led him to coin the phrase "a hard day's night".**

OPPOSITE: **The model and actress Pattie Boyd (centre) shooting her scene with Ringo in the "Liverpool Arms", which was in fact a London pub called the Turks Head. A street market was added into the background to give the scene some authenticity.**

Moptops in movie mode

On Monday, 2 March 1964, the cast and crew of the new Beatles feature film convened at Paddington Station. Despite the boys' enormous popularity, it was a project not without risk. Hamming it up in the odd sketch was one thing; carrying a movie was quite another, as director Dick Lester well knew. Lester quickly realized that the Beatles' strength lay in snappy, quick-fire banter, a talent all had displayed in handling hard-bitten press hacks over the previous year. Screenplay writer Alun Owen knew it too. Having spent his formative years in Liverpool, Owen was well versed in the ways of abrasive Liverpudlian wit. A couple of days spent in the Beatles' company during a brief concert tour of Ireland in November '63 was enough to convince Owen of the kind of script required—certainly no long-winded speeches, which the Fabs would have struggled to learn, let alone deliver.

The vehicle initially proved problematic, however. Owen said he had "a couple of false starts trying to write a fantasy film, but swiftly realized that nothing could compare with their own fantastic lives". He had witnessed the events in Paris, noting the extent to which they were trapped by their fame, and set out to capture the kind of pressure that attended pop superstardom. The result was a madcap romp through a typically frenetic forty-eight hours in the lives of the Beatles, shot in *cinéma vérité* style. The mock-documentary approach gave an insight into their goldfish-bowl existence, though without the smoking, drinking, bad language, and groupies, it was hardly an accurate representation of Beatlemania.

The decision not to include any specific love interest was taken early on. Girls wouldn't like to see a Beatle spoken for, something Cynthia Lennon had discovered to her cost when it became public knowledge that she and John had tied the knot. But romance did flourish, on the set if not the screen. George was smitten by model Pattie Boyd, whom Lester had worked with on a Smith's crisps advert and cast as one of the schoolgirls who meet the Beatles on the hectic London-bound train journey.

BIO: PATTIE BOYD

Pattie Boyd left her West Country home for London at eighteen in 1962, hoping to further her modelling and acting career. She paraded Mary Quant designs on the catwalk, but it was an advertising campaign for potato chips that landed her a part in the Beatles' first movie. The ads were directed by Dick Lester, who cast her as one of the schoolgirl fans in *A Hard Day's Night*. George was soon smitten with the twenty-year-old beauty who, of all the Beatles' consorts, came closest to resembling their ultimate sex symbol, Brigitte Bardot. They married on January 21, 1966. It was Pattie who first became interested in Transcendental Meditation, she and George sharing an abiding interest in spirituality. She was George's muse for a number of songs, most famously "Something". By the end of the decade they were drifting apart and Pattie flirted with George's great friend Eric Clapton in a bid to elicit a jealous reaction. Instead she won Clapton's heart, while George appeared indifferent to the situation. One of the final straws came when George professed his love for Maureen Starkey in front of her. In 1974 Pattie moved in with Clapton, who also poured out his feelings on vinyl, in songs such as "Layla" and "Wonderful Tonight". George and his second wife, Olivia, were among the guests when the couple tied the knot in 1979, but Clapton's addiction to alcohol and serial infidelity made it a tempestuous marriage. They divorced in 1988. The former *Vogue* covergirl has since won admiration for her work on the other side of the lens. Pattie has also been an active campaigner in the field of alcohol and drug addiction, most notably through SHARP (Self-Help Addiction Recovery Program), which she and Barbara Bach set up in 1991.

LEFT: The Beatles have their hair styled by their co-stars on the set of *A Hard Day's Night*. Susan Whiteman, Pru Bury, and Tina Williams tend to John, Paul, and Ringo respectively, while Pattie Boyd runs a comb through George's locks. George was initially shy around Pattie, but when she asked for an autograph he obliged, adding lots of kisses to the bottom of his signature. Soon after he asked her out on a date, but she declined because she had a steady, long-term boyfriend. However, George was persistent and Pattie finally relented, ending her relationship so that she could date George.

While trying to keep the new relationship a secret from the press, George and Pattie accompanied John and Cynthia on an Easter break in Ireland. Although the foursome had done well to elude photographers, their hotel was finally discovered and the media moved in. John and George pretended to be alone and, in a move befitting a Hollywood comedy, Pattie and Cynthia had to sneak out dressed as maids, hidden in a laundry basket.

George's contribution

A neat title demanded a top-notch title track, and time was short. It was the first time Lennon and McCartney had been hamstrung by a pre-determined title, but it proved no obstacle. John arrived with the completed song the morning after Dick Lester had thrown down the creative gauntlet. "A Hard Day's Night" was conceived and recorded in barely twenty-four hours, John having the satisfaction of racking up another A-side in the ongoing competitive jousting in which he and Paul engaged. John took the verse, but had to hand over to Paul for the middle eight because it was beyond his range.

George contributed the famous opening chord, which in itself became the source of endless analysis as musicians tried to reconstruct it: a G eleventh with suspended fourth is one of many suggestions. Gary Moore was among the legions of aspiring guitarists who smugly thought they had cracked the code until many years later George showed him the error of his ways. Moore was so nonplussed he asked George if he was sure that's how it was done. But most fans neither knew nor cared about chord sequences. All they were interested in was the result: "A Hard Day's Night" was another instant classic.

United Artists initially may have regarded the movie simply as a means to acquire the soundtrack album, but the studio found itself with a cinematic gem on its hands. *A Hard Day's Night* received two Academy Award nominations, for Best Score and Best Screenplay (losing out to *My Fair Lady* and *Father Goose* respectively). One American critic would hail it as "the *Citizen Kane* of jukebox movies." It also did extraordinary business at the box office, taking well over fifty times what it cost on its initial release. And fifteen years later it proved to be a lucrative addition to producer Walter Shenson's portfolio when the rights to the film reverted to him, as per the terms of the original deal made with Brian Epstein.

RIGHT: **George confirmed his place as lead guitarist in the best band in the world by playing the famous opening chord to "A Hard Day's Night" with the Rickenbacker he had been given during his trip to America**.

ABOVE: **Making a film involved a lot of waiting around. The boys sometimes used the time to develop new songs and rehearse their lines, but here George takes the opportunity to give Ringo a guitar lesson, John has a smoke, and Paul plays the piano (inset).**

The Magazine of the Official National Beatles Fan Club   August, 1964

SPECIAL TO MEMBERS — SCRIPT

A HARD DAY'S NIGHT

starring
THE BEATLES
with WILFRED BRAMBELL
Released by United Artists

A HARD DAY'S NIGHT

Cast List

John Lennon	John
Paul McCartney	Paul
George Harrison	George
Ringo Starr	Ringo
Wilfrid Brambell	Grandfather
Norman Rossington	Norm
John Junkin	Shake
Victor Spinetti	TV director
Anna Quayle	Millie
Deryck Guyler	Police Inspector
Richard Vernon	Man on train
Edward Malin	Hotel Waiter (as Eddie Malin)
Robin Ray	TV Floor Manager
Lionel Blair	TV Choreographer
Alison Seebohm	Secretary

OPPOSITE: **Paul on the set of *A Hard Day's Night*.**

OPPOSITE LEFT INSET AND ABOVE: **The train sequences for the movie were recorded over a six-day period as the train went back and forth between London and Minehead, covering thousands of miles by the end of the shooting.**

OPPOSITE RIGHT INSET: **Members of the Official Beatles Fan Club received the script of *A Hard Day's Night* in their copy of the club's magazine, *The Beatle Bulletin*.**

ABOVE LEFT: **Despite the problems engendered by being recognized everywhere they went, the Beatles did little to try to disguise themselves. However, here George stylishly conceals his moptop haircut.**

MARCH 1964

1 At Abbey Road, "I'm Happy Just to Dance With You", "Long Tall Sally", and "I Call Your Name" were completed in a three-hour session.

2 Joining Equity only minutes before shooting began, the band gathered together at Paddington Station to start the filming for the forthcoming film. Six days' shooting was booked as they headed for the West Country, with much of the filming done on the train. It was during the shooting that George met Pattie Boyd, whom he was to eventually marry. The single "Twist and Shout"/"There's a Place" was released on Tollie 9001 in the US and reached No. 2 on the *Billboard* charts.

3 While filming progressed, George Martin continued the work at the Abbey Road Studios, producing mono mixes of some of the songs including "If I Fell" and "And I Love Her". While filming, the band agreed to meet a four-year-old girl named Alison Clark who suffered from a hole in the heart.

4 George Martin continued with the mixing—this time the turn of "I Call Your Name". George asked Pattie Boyd out.

5 The band had dinner with Jeffrey Archer at Brasenose College, Oxford, as part of their continuing support for the Oxfam campaign.

6 Filming took place between London and Minehead.

RIGHT: **John sets a good example to his younger fans by keeping his milk intake up during filming of *A Hard Day's Night* at the Scala Theatre. The theatre, located in Charlotte Street near Tottenham Court Road in London, was used to film all the concert scenes in the film.**

OPPOSITE RIGHT: **John performing on *Ready, Steady, Go!*, a leading television programme for the British music industry. On the show, the boys received a special award from *Billboard* magazine recognizing the band's occupation of the top three positions on the American chart.**

continued from previous page

MARCH 1964

9 The last day of train filming. The band travelled from London to Newton Abbott, after having covered 2,500 miles in the previous seven days.

10 The sequence when Ringo went to a pub was filmed at the Turks Head in Twickenham. At Abbey Road George Martin was producing stereo mixes for songs including "Long Tall Sally" and "Can't Buy Me Love".

11 The band was at the Twickenham Film Studios to begin its first day of shooting, this time on the guard's van set.

12 More film shooting at Twickenham, this time for the hotel room scenes. George Martin continued to mix at Abbey Road, this time for "Komm, Gib Mir Deine Hand" and "Sie Liebt Dich" for release in West Germany and the US.

13 The filming moved to Gatwick Airport to record the last scenes in the movie when the band takes off in a helicopter.

16 "Can't Buy Me Love"/"You Can't Do That" was released in the States on Capitol 5150. The record company sold two million copies within a week. Back at Twickenham, George recorded the canteen scene with Wilfrid Brambell. George and Brian Epstein watched Cilla Black make a recording for *Saturday Club*.

17 Filming took place at Les Ambassadeurs, a private club in Hamilton Place, London. While there, John was interviewed by Jack de Manio for the Home Service programme *Today*.

Fan club in trouble

Thousands of angry young fans were asked: "Please be patient." The appeal came from the group's fan club which was frantically trying to keep up with the avalanche of 5 shillings-a-head membership applications. Despite 13 members of staff working 13-hour days, the club still has a six-month backlog to clear up and Beatle fans are becoming very impatient. This had led to police visits to the headquarters in Monmouth Street, Soho, London after complaints from fans. Officer manager Michael Crowther-Smith, aged 18, stated, "Apparently they've had complaints about us running a fraud—collecting 5 bob *(shilling)* postal orders as a racket. It's preposterous of course."

The club already has 30,000 signed up members and deals with another 2,500 per day. Joint secretary Anne Collingham, also 18, said, "We daren't think about how many we still have to go through. At one stage we were getting four or five sacks a day—at 2,000 letters to a sack."

While still dealing with last October's mail, November's remains unopened in 25 cardboard boxes while 2 other rooms hold 57 sacks of waiting mail. On George Harrison's 21st birthday over 50 sacks arrived in two days. Tina Rose, aged 20, also joint secretary, simply stated, "We're rushed off our feet." Mr. Crowther-Smith added, "I'm afraid we've been caught napping. Nobody could foresee the really incredible demand."

EXTRACTED FROM THE
DAILY MAIL, MARCH 1964

Beatles raid reveals hideaway

By **BRIAN DEAN**

A BURGLAR ran-sacked a £30-a-week Knightsbridge flat—and revealed a Beatles secret.

The flat was the London hideaway home of George Harrison and Ringo Starr.

The two Beatles were in hiding again last night as scores of teenage girls waited outside the flat in William-mews, near Lowndes-square, Westminster.

Ringo and George moved into the second-floor four-room service flat last month. Early on Sunday morning they arrived home after a party, found a balcony window forced and the flat ransacked.

Missing was £200 in cash that George had left in a dressing-table drawer with a pair of cuff-links.

Mr. Brian Somerville, Beatles' publicity manager, said yesterday : "At first the boys thought some fans had found out the address and broken in to steal souvenirs.

"But when they discovered cash had been stolen George rang the police and reported the burglary."

Mr. Brian Epstein, the Beatles' manager, has a fifth-floor flat in the same block. But it was not touched.

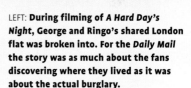

John Lennon broke off filming yesterday and said: "George and Ringo have been given two days off from filming.

"The burglary has really annoyed them. Not so much because the cash was pinched, but because they'll have to find a new place to avoid the fans."

It will be the fourth time in six months that George and Ringo have moved flats.

Twelve-year-old Solveig Turner, who lives in a cottage opposite the William-mews block, was the only Beatles fan to know of the hideaway.

She said: "I saw George and Ringo several times. But Mummy told me not to say a word to anyone. I did not even tell my closest friends."

Mr. Eddie Williams, porter at the flats, moved away teenage fans who tried to get up to the Beatles' flat.

LEFT: **During filming of *A Hard Day's Night*, George and Ringo's shared London flat was broken into. For the *Daily Mail* the story was as much about the fans discovering where they lived as it was about the actual burglary.**

FAR LEFT AND OPPOSITE LEFT: **John at the Scala Theatre during filming of *A Hard Day's Night*.**

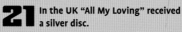

18 Back at Twickenham, the dressing room scenes were filmed. During the day the band also made some recordings for *The Public Ear*. The previous day's recording of *Today* was transmitted.

19 At Twickenham the corridor scenes at the studios were filmed. An interview with Peter Noble was also recorded for *Movie-Go-Round*. At lunchtime the Beatles were at the Dorchester Hotel in Park Lane to be presented with the Variety Club of Great Britain's award for Showbusiness Personalities of 1963 by Harold Wilson (then Leader of the Opposition). In the evening they moved to Shepherd's Bush to record their first proper appearance on *Top of the Pops*, performing "You Can't Do That" and "Can't Buy Me Love".

20 "Can't Buy Me Love"/"You Can't Do That" was released in Britain on Parlophone R 5114. Advance orders had already exceeded one million, with the total international advance orders eventually in excess of two million. Further corridor scenes were made at Twickenham, while Ringo was also interviewed for *Movie-Go-Round*—this time by Lyn Fairhurst. In the evening they appeared live on *Ready, Steady Go!* During the show they were presented with an award from *Billboard* for holding three singles chart positions at the same time. Meanwhile on the BBC, the Variety Club of Great Britain Awards for 1963 was televised.

21 In the UK "All My Loving" received a silver disc.

22 The band interviewed each other on *The Public Ear*.

23 "Do You Want to Know a Secret?"/"Thank You Girl" was released in the US on Vee-Jay VJ 587. Seven days' filming began at the Scala Theatre in Charlotte Street, London. Lennon's first book, *In His Own Write*, was published, and to promote it he appeared on *Tonight*. After reading parts of the book he was interviewed by Kenneth Allsop. In the evening the band were presented with two awards at the Carl-Alan at the Empire Ballroom, Leicester Square, by the Duke of Edinburgh.

THE Beatles, on a tour of the North, said last night that they won't be voting tomorrow.

They will be in Stockton, Co. Durham, and Paul Mc-Cartney explained: "We don't care a lot about politics, so we never bothered to fix a postal vote."

John Lennon said: "We've been away from Liverpool so long that we have forgotten which constituency we are in. It's a lot of rubbish, anyway."

Politicians pay court

It wasn't just the likes of EMI, United Artists, and the merchandising men who knew that the Beatles "sold". Those who inhabited the corridors of power were also cognizant of the fact. There were votes to be had in being "with it", and the leaders of the main political parties in the UK were keen to hitch a ride on the Beatles bandwagon. Conservative Prime Minister Sir Alec Douglas-Home lauded the group's contribution to the country's balance of payments, describing them as a "secret weapon" to roll out against any country with whom Britain had a trade deficit. With an election looming in the spring of 1964, it was said that Conservative candidates were urged to include references to the Beatles in their speeches. Opposition leader Harold Wilson, a northerner whose constituency was in Liverpool, was just as quick off the mark in trying to align himself and his party with the Fabs. Wilson stole a march on his rival when he angled for the job of presenting the boys with their Royal Variety Club Awards for Showbusiness Personalities of 1963. The Dorchester Hotel ceremony provided just the photo opportunity Wilson wanted, though almost inevitably John couldn't resist an impish dig. His acceptance speech began in the traditional manner, thanking the Variety Club president, known as the Chief Barker. He then nodded towards Wilson and added: "And Mr. Dobson". It was a sweet gag—quite literally—as Barker and Dobson was a celebrated confectionery manufacturer based on Merseyside. Not to be

continued from page 115

MARCH 1964

24 Wax models of the band went on show at Madame Tussauds. John took part in a further interview to promote his book, this time with Dibbs Mather for the BBC's Transcription Service.

25 The Beatles mimed "Can't Buy Me Love" on *Top of the Pops*.

26 Pete Best flew to America for an appearance on the television show *I've Got a Secret*.

27 Over Easter weekend John and Cynthia Lennon accompanied George and Pattie Boyd to Dromolan Castle in County Clare, Ireland. Ringo went to Woburn Abbey while Paul remained in London.

28 The band held a new record for having ten songs in the *Billboard* charts in the US at the same time.

29 As the pirate radio station Radio Caroline began broadcasting, its first record was "Can't Buy Me Love".

30 *From Us to You* was broadcast.

31 Filming continued at the Scala Theatre when the band performed to a live, paid audience. In the evening they were at the Playhouse Theatre London to make a recording for *Saturday Club*. Additionally, John was interviewed for two separate BBC Home Service programmes; his book was already a bestseller. "Can't Buy Me Love" was awarded a gold disc in the States.

ON POLITICS

"We don't care a lot about politics..."
—John

"It's a lot of rubbish."
—Paul

MR. HAROLD WILSON met the Beatles yesterday to hand over to them their award as the Show Business Personality (the Beatles have a very singular image) of the Year.

by **DAVID LEWIN**

Mr. Wilson also met the other award winners, Margaret Rutherford, Steptoe and Son, Sir Michael Redgrave, Maggie Smith, and Honor Blackman and Patrick Macnee from *The Avengers*.

At the end of it he probably deserved the show business personality award himself — for when it comes to talking in public in a gathering of professionals, Mr. Wilson can outpoint the "pros."

"Elder Statesmen from Merseyside," was the way he greeted the Beatles: speaking, of course, as a Merseyside M.P. himself.

'Nothing'

Before the award-giving ceremony, organised by the Variety Club of Great Britain, there was a slightly mad reception in which all the artists got pushed to one side while a concerted rush was made on the Beatles and their three "guardsmen" who were there to see that the "boys" got some room and some air.

Someone asked John Lennon: "Have you ever met a politician

before?" Said Lennon: "No—but they're only people, aren't they?"

Paul and George were asked if they would vote for Mr. Wilson. They said: "We'll have to think about it a bit . . . we haven't made up our minds like." So you can put them down as "floating voters."

Ringo, who has a reputation for saying nothing, said nothing.

At lunch Mr. Wilson handed over the awards in the shape of a silver heart. Said George: "It is nice to get one each. We usually have one between us and it's so much trouble cutting it into four."

Paul said: "You should have given one to good old Mr. Wilson." (So maybe he's not floating so much after all.)

John said: "Thanks for the purple heart."

Ringo said nothing.

After that the Beatles left smartly to get back to work on their film and "save the producer money."

Politely

The rest of the artists accepted their honours politely and quietly.

And Margaret Rutherford, rivalling the cheers for the Beatles, accepted her honour for being the Film Actress of 1963 with phrases like this: "This sumptuous assembly . . . this peerless emblem . . . this talisman. I have never been so excited since my wedding day."

James Fox, given the award for the Most Promising Newcomer because of his performance in the film *The Servant*, provided the most ironic laugh of the day.

He opened this week in a new musical (*All in Love*) which the critics did not love at all. James Fox told how Robert Morley phoned him and said: "I hope they won't take away your award now."

outdone, George quipped: "We're grateful for being given four separate awards; normally we have to cut them into quarters". It was a good line, and also revealed the extent to which the four lived as one.

Wilson went on to win the general election and remained prime minister until 1970, when he was ousted at the same time that the Beatles were breaking up. It was Wilson who recommended them for their MBEs, and he would also get a name check on "Taxman", along with Conservative politican Edward Heath. It was a desire to improve on "One for you, nineteen for me", a reference to the 90 percent tax rate for high earners in Britain at the time, that led to the foundation of Apple, though that was still four years away.

ABOVE, OPPOSITE, AND RIGHT: **During a break from filming, Labour Party leader Harold Wilson presents the Showbusiness Personality of the Year Award to the Beatles at the Royal Variety Club luncheon at the Dorchester Hotel on 19 March, assuring the audience that he would "refrain from making political capital out of the Beatles".**

OPPOSITE INSET: **Despite their friendly disposition towards Harold Wilson, the *Daily Mail* reports that the band opted not to vote in the general election held in October.**

OPPOSITE: **The boys enjoy coffee after lunch at the Dorchester Hotel and John chats with Mary Wilson, the wife of the future prime minister. Thursday, 19 March was a typically busy day for the Beatles. Both in the morning and after the celebratory lunch they were at Twickenham Studios, working on scenes for *A Hard Day's Night*, and the early evening was spent taping an appearance on the popular TV show *Top of the Pops*.**

THIS PAGE: **The boys proudly display their Variety Club Awards, expressing pleasure in having one each rather than having to share.**

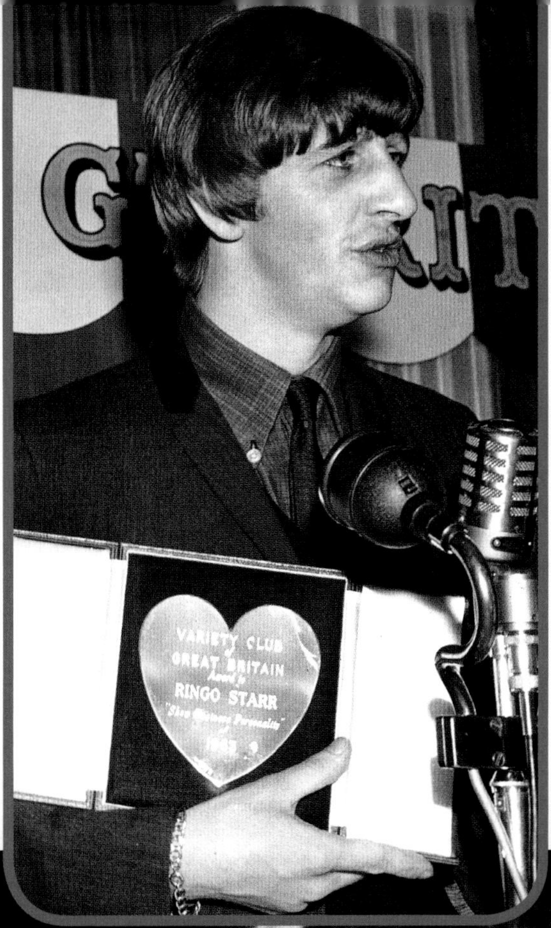

BEATLES IN THE HOT 100

With the release of "Can't Buy Me Love" at the end of March 1964, the Beatles made music history. They became the only band to hold each of the top five slots on the *Billboard* Hot 100—a record they still hold to this day. With almost one million records sold on the first day, "Can't Buy Me Love" inevitably shot straight to number one. "Twist and Shout" was in second place followed by "She Loves You" and "I Want to Hold Your Hand" in third and fourth respectively, while "Please Please Me" held the all-important fifth spot. The Beatles also had another seven songs in the Hot 100 that week, making a total of twelve charting records. The unprecedented domination continued the following week as "Love Me Do" and "There's a Place" charted at 81 and 74 respectively, taking the tally to fourteen—the most songs by one group in the Hot 100 in the history of the chart. That week, 11 April, the chart positions of the fourteen songs in the Hot 100 were "Can't Buy Me Love" in the top spot, "Twist and Shout" at number 2, "She Loves You" at 4, "I Want To Hold Your Hand" in 7th, "Please Please Me" at number 9, "Do You Want to Know a Secret" at 14, "I Saw Her Standing There" at 38, "You Can't Do That" at 48, "All My Loving" at 50, "From Me To You" at 52, "Thank You Girl" at 61, "There's A Place" at 74, "Roll Over Beethoven" at 78, and "Love Me Do" at 81.

Chartbusters supreme

On 23 March 1964, just four days after picking up their Variety Club Awards, the Beatles were suited and booted for another gala occasion where more honours were heaped upon them. The prestigious Carl-Alan Awards were organized by Mecca, a vast leisure group whose famous chain of ballrooms had witnessed a number of Beatles gigs. At the ceremony, staged at London's Empire Ballroom, the Duke of Edinburgh presented the Beatles with two awards: Best Group of 1963, and Best Vocal Record of that year, for "She Loves You". Later in the year they would scoop up five Ivor Novello Awards, including one for the Most Outstanding Contribution to British Music in 1963.

There was inevitably a considerable time lag between the achievement and when it gained recognition in the form of such coveted music industry awards. Not so with the fans, who could vote with their feet and their money as soon as a new Beatles record was released—the results of which could be seen within days. In the week before the Carl-Alan Awards ceremony, "Can't Buy Me Love" hit the shops on both sides of the Atlantic. Advance sales of a million were now the norm in the UK, but even that figure was dwarfed in the US, where Beatlemania was in full swing. When "Can't Buy Me Love" went to No. 1 in the

States on 4 April, the Beatles occupied the top five spots on the *Billboard* chart. The boys had seven other numbers in the listing, and when "Love Me Do" and "There's a Place" broke through a week later, it gave the boys fourteen songs in the Hot 100. Several of those, such as "All My Loving" and "Do You Want to Know a Secret", were designated good enough only for album material in the UK, but in the States it seemed that Capitol and Vee-Jay could issue almost anything from the Beatles back catalogue and watch the sales figures rocket. For good measure, *Meet the Beatles!* and *Introducing the Beatles* were still riding high at the top of the album chart, creating a dominant position unlikely ever to be equalled.

RIGHT: **"Can't Buy Me Love" was released in America on 16 March and in the UK on 20 March. Advance sales topped one million on both sides of the Atlantic. At the beginning of April, the new single replaced "She Loves You" at the top of the *Billboard* chart, which in turn had displaced "I Want to Hold Your Hand" from the No. 1 spot in March. The Beatles had held the top position with three consecutive singles for a period spanning some two months.**

BELOW AND OPPOSITE: **The boys enjoy the relaxed atmosphere of the Variety Club, where amongst the other celebrities they attract less attention than usual.**

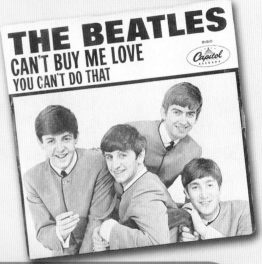

OPPOSITE: **As some of the most prominent ambassadors for Great Britain, the Beatles and the Royal Family crossed paths on numerous occasions. Here they are introduced to Prince Philip at the Carl-Alan Awards at the Empire Ballroom in Leicester Square, where they won two awards. The boys' introduction to royalty was at the Royal Variety Show, where they met the Queen Mother, who readily sang their praises. The band was also popular with a young Prince Charles, who wrote to them requesting their autographs.**

OPPOSITE BELOW RIGHT: **The envy of young girls across the world was heaped on an unlikely candidate when Liverpool Member of Parliament Bessie Braddock stole a dance with her famous constituent at the Carl-Alan Awards at the Empire Ballroom in Leicester Square.**

ABOVE: **George and Ringo celebrate success at the Carl-Alan awards with a cigar.**

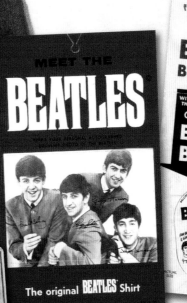

ABOVE: **Fame meant that the Beatles were able to rub shoulders with royalty, but it also meant that their names and faces were used to sell all kinds of products, such as shirts, greeting cards, candy, and even hairbrushes.**

A ghost from the past

During the filming of the concert scenes for *A Hard Day's Night* at the Scala Theatre, the NEMS offices in Argyll Street received a visit from a ghost. It had been nineteen years since John had seen his father, and Freddie Lennon chose this moment to seek a reconciliation. To John, resentment had given way to indifference; instead of wondering what had become of his feckless father, he preferred to think of himself as an orphan. Desultory paternal visits during the first five years of his life were a distant memory, though the pain of abandonment still burned deep.

The war accounted for some of Freddie Lennon's protracted absences, though not all. He maintained that he planned to emigrate to New Zealand in the summer of 1946, and take his son with him. As Freddie's relationship with John's mother, Julia, had irretrievably broken down, a choice had to be made. John chose an antipodean adventure with his father—at least according to Freddie. But when it came to the crunch, five-year-old John raced after his mother.

At Brian Epstein's suggestion, John gave Freddie £30 and suggested a modest weekly allowance. Epstein was concerned about bad publicity—the press had a field day over the fact that a Beatle's father was washing dishes in a London hotel. If Epstein thought this might persuade Lennon Senior not to sell his story, he was soon disabused of the notion. A year later fifty-three-year-old Freddie cashed in further as he made his own bid for pop stardom. In his youth Freddie had been an entertainer with grand showbiz ambitions; now, in a fanfare of publicity, he cut a single. "That's My Life" was bubbling

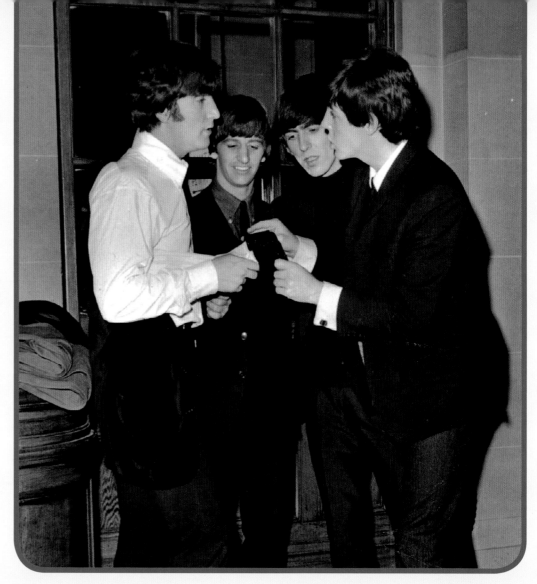

under in the charts when it suddenly disappeared without a trace, courtesy of the pull Epstein had in the record business.

Relations between the two men thawed when John learned that his party-loving mother had had a child by another man when Freddie was away at sea. Freddie had forgiven her and offered to bring up the child as his own. It seemed that he wasn't as black as Aunt Mimi

had painted him. It proved to be a temporary lull in hostilities though, the uneasy truce breaking down after Freddie took himself a teenage bride and presented John with two half brothers. It was only when Freddie was terminally ill with stomach cancer in 1976 that there was a further reconciliation of sorts. There were lengthy phone calls, John sent flowers and a "Get well soon" message, but the two men never met again.

APRIL 1964

1 John met his estranged father, Freddie, whom he had not seen for nearly 20 years, at the NEMS offices. Filming of *A Hard Day's Night* continued at the Scala Theatre for a further two days, with fans forcing their way into the building at one point.

2 The scene at the press party was filmed, recalling the events at the British Embassy in Washington, DC.

3 The band held the top six positions in the singles chart in Sydney. The

trailer for the movie showing the boys in prams was made.

4 "Can't Buy Me Love"/"You Can't Do That" went to the top of the UK charts, remaining there for three weeks. "Can't Buy Me Love" also reached the top of the US charts, holding the position for five weeks. The Beatles held the top five positions in the *Billboard* charts. *Saturday Club* was transmitted.

5 At Marylebone Station the opening scenes of the movie were made because the station was always closed on a Sunday. Some recording was also done in nearby Boston Place, showing the band being chased by fans.

6 At Twickenham Studios the makeup-room scenes were shot.

7 Scenes inside the police station were filmed at Twickenham.

OPPOSITE: **1 April 1964: The Fab Four make adjustments to the sleeve of John's jacket at the Scala Theatre.**

LEFT AND RIGHT: **Paul reads a magazine during a break in the filming. There was a lot of sitting around while making a movie, and at one stage everybody was idle as a dispute over unpaid extras** derailed the filming. Eventually the extras, who were used for the audience scenes, were given £3 15 shillings and a free lunch. Among these 350 extras was a young Phil Collins, who would later go on to make his own mark on popular music.

ABOVE RIGHT AND LEFT: **The Beatles filmed these nightclub scenes for** *A Hard Day's Night* **in the middle of the afternoon at the exclusive Les Ambassadeurs nightclub in London.**

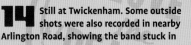

Teenage Extras

HUNDREDS of teenage girls who paid 2s. 6d. for a day out with the Beatles screamed in anger outside a theatre yesterday after being told : " It's all off."

Police chased some off the roof and gatecrashers had to be ejected from the Scala Theatre, London, where scenes for the Beatles' film were being shot.

But inside the theatre 350 girls screamed with delight.

Not only were they with the Beatles, but:

It had not cost them 2s. 6d. ; They were paid £3 15s. for the day's screaming ;

And they were each given a free packed lunch.

The big teenage mix-up that had the hundreds of girls sieging the theatre began with a union dispute.

New forms

The film production manager, Mr. Denis O'Dell, wanted girls to play the audience in scenes for the film. So he invited fans to send for a yellow form to give them admission to the theatre. It cost them 2s. 6d. because the invitation was in a film magazine.

Then in stepped the Film Artistes Association — the film extras' union. Officials insisted : " You must pay the audience girls £3 15s. a day each, the agreed rate."

So the company signed on

350 new girls and gave them white forms—the new passport to a day with the Beatles.

Enter the union again. Officials said : " We've got 350 teenagers on our books. You must use them first."

So the angry clamour raged in the streets yesterday when the girls with yellow forms, the girls with white forms and 300 union teenagers all demanded entry to the theatre.

Inside technicians downed their equipment. Union leaders and film chiefs talked. The four Beatles waited.

Then in scenes of pandemonium 300 white form girls and 55 union girls were let in, and filming began.

The disconsolate yellow forms stayed outside until the Beatles left at 6.30 p.m. chanting in the cold : " It's a swindle."

Francesca Lee, 16, of Hayes, Middlesex, told me : " I have taken the day off to come here.

I had to get up at five this morning to be here and I haven't even seen the Beatles."

Francesca's job : Testing records at the E.M.I. factory where the Beatles records are pressed.

Her friend, Linda Palmer, 15, said : " I reckon she ought to sling out their next one after the way we have been treated."

One theatrical agent told me : " This is an almighty shambles. Many of my girls paid 1s. 6d. for the film magazine.

" Then there was 6d. for postage and another 6d., which I charged for services. When the original plan was scrapped, I tried to contact all these youngsters. It was a hopeless task."

Mr. Denis O'Dell said : " I just wanted to give these kids a chance to see the Beatles. We were not trying to find cheap labour."

9 Only Ringo was needed as he filmed the solo scenes along the River Thames near Kew Bridge. The band appeared on *Star Parade* for Tyne Tees.

10 Filming continued at Twickenham—this time for the production-office scene. *The Beatles Second Album* was released in the US on Capitol T-2080 (mono) and ST-2080 (stereo).

11 Further filming at the Twickenham Studios.

12 A return to filming at Marylebone Station. On the radio the boys could be heard on *Movie-Go-Round*.

13 Back to Twickenham, where the morning was spent filming George's solo spot at the clothing company. Later that afternoon he and John filmed the sequence in the bathroom. In the US *The Beatles Second Album* received a gold disc.

14 Still at Twickenham. Some outside shots were also recorded in nearby Arlington Road, showing the band stuck in

a traffic jam. Frank Thornton played the chauffeur.

15 Further exterior filming—this time outside the Scala Theatre, in Charlotte Mews, and in Tottenham Street. In the evening Paul was interviewed by David Frost for the BBC1 programme *A Degree of Frost*. It was recorded at the Television Centre in Wood Lane in front of an audience.

16 The Notting Hill Gate scenes were shot. The local high school was used as a mock police station while the

chasing scenes with policemen were filmed. The song "A Hard Day's Night" was recorded in three hours at Abbey Road.

17 The press announced that the film would be called *A Hard Day's Night*. Back at Les Ambassadeurs the dancing scene was filmed. The boys were also interviewed by Ed Sullivan, who had flown into Britain two days earlier. The result was a brief interview lasting just over one and a half minutes that would be shown on *The Ed Sullivan Show* on 24 May.

THIS PAGE: **Paul enjoys a moment of tranquility (right), but the eight-week shoot for *A Hard Day's Night* was action packed (above). The helicopter sequences (left) were filmed at Gatwick Airport and augmented with footage shot at Thornbury playing fields in West London.**

continued from previous page

APRIL 1964

18 The morning was spent filming at Twickenham, while in the afternoon the band was at the Hall of Remembrance in Flood Street, London, rehearsing for Rediffusion's show *Around the Beatles*. In the evening the *Morecambe and Wise Show*, recorded in December, was broadcast.

19 Further rehearsals for *Around the Beatles* at the BBC Studios in Portland Place.

20 Paul's turn to film his solo sequence—this time at the Jack Billings TV School of Dancing, where he acted with Isla Blair, a scene that was ultimately cut from the movie. George Martin was at Abbey Road in the afternoon making stereo and mono mixes of "A Hard Day's Night". George and Ringo's flat was ransacked by intruders.

21 Paul continued filming at the dancing school. In *Melody Maker* Petula Clark stated that the French did not like the Beatles.

22 Exterior filming at the Odeon Cinema in Hammersmith and more police chases in Notting Hill Gate. Ringo and Paul also filmed some more solo spots.

23 The band met early in the morning at the Thornbury Playing Fields in Isleworth, London, for

THIS PAGE: **Paul and Ringo on the set of *A Hard Day's Night*. While Ringo and Maggie London dance to "Twist and Shout" (right), Merrill Colebrook cosies up to Paul on the sofas (below right).**

BELOW: **An official pictorial souvenir book for the film *A Hard Day's Night*.**

EXCLUSIVE !   2968

THE BEATLES
STARRING IN
A HARD DAY'S NIGHT

With a special foreword by The BEATLES themselves

THE OFFICIAL UNITED ARTISTS' PICTORIAL SOUVENIR BOOK
★ Candid cameras behind the scenes
★ Stories you won't see on the screen
THE WHOLE CRAZY MAKING-OF-THE-FILM STORY – FROM START TO FINISH   Whitman

further filming on a fake helicopter pad. John had to leave early to attend a Foyle's literary lunch at the Dorchester Hotel. Another mono version of "A Hard Day's Night" was made at Abbey Road that afternoon.

24 The last movie sequences were filmed in West Ealing: Ringo laid his coat over a puddle that was actually a hole in the road. The end-of-film party was held that afternoon in the private hall behind the Turks Head pub.

25 Rehearsals for *Around the Beatles* continued at the Hall of Remembrance.

26 The band returned to the stage for the first time in 15 weeks to play at the Empire Pool in Wembley. The occasion was the *New Musical Express* 1963–64 Annual Poll Winners' All-Star Concert. They topped the bill in front of an audience of 10,000 and received their award from actor Roger Moore. In the evening they went to Roy Orbison's 28th birthday party.

27 A dress rehearsal for *Around the Beatles* at the Wembley Studios. "Love Me Do"/"P.S. I Love You" was released in the US on Tollie 9008.

28 *Around the Beatles* was finally taped at the Wembley Studios. It was broadcast by Rediffusion, but Brian Epstein also sold it to ABC for the American market.

29 The first of two Scottish concerts at the ABC Cinema in Edinburgh.

The boys were interviewed in their dressing room for *Scottish News*, a radio show. At a press conference the Lord Provost, Duncan Weatherstone, asked them for a donation of £100,000 to the Edinburgh Festival Fund.

30 Two houses at the Odeon Cinema in Glasgow. In the morning they were interviewed at their hotel for the local BBC show *Six Ten*, and in the afternoon they recorded an item for *Roundup* at the Theatre Royal Studios, Glasgow.

John's "Thurberesque" literary debut

John was an inveterate scribbler with a passion for wordplay, quirky turns of phrase, nonsense verse, and anarchic humour. "It won't be long till I belong to you" was typical of the kind of verbal trick he and Paul played in their lyrics, though John by no means confined himself to musings that might be used in his songwriting. On the road he would jot down his flights of fancy on scraps of paper, and, unsurprisingly, "Ringoisms" were assiduously recorded.

Fellow students—and sometimes staff—at Quarry Bank in Liverpool provided the readership for John's early literary efforts, which circulated under the *Daily Howl* banner.

When the Beatles took off in Liverpool, the local music publication *Mersey Beat* published doodles, poems, and anecdotes penned by one of the city's most famous sons under the

BELOW AND LEFT (BOTTOM): **Cynthia and John at a Foyle's literary luncheon held at the Dorchester Hotel, London, to celebrate the publication of John's new book, *In His Own Write*. The night before, his fellow band members had celebrated John's newfound success as a writer with a late-night party, leaving John and Cynthia the worse for wear at the lunch the next day.**

BELOW LEFT (TOP): **The reception at the Dorchester Hotel was a star-studded event. Here John chats with Lionel Bart, the composer of the musical *Oliver*.**

byline "Beatcomber". Worldwide celebrity meant there was a ready market for the "witty" Beatle's outpourings, and on 23 March 1964, a slim seventy-eight-page volume reached the bookshops. The first edition of *In His Own Write* sold out immediately, and the critics were equally impressed. The *Times Literary Supplement* saw elements of Lewis Carroll and James Thurber in a "remarkable" book that was "worth the attention

of anyone who fears for the impoverishment of the English language and British imagination".

A month after publication, 23 April, John slipped away from filming *A Hard Day's Night* to attend a Foyle's literary luncheon held at London's Dorchester Hotel. The assembled luminaries were less than impressed with the brief contribution made by the guest of honour: "Thank you all very much; you've got a lucky face".

His attendance at the luncheon also had implications for the film. In John's absence Richard Lester completed the sequence accompanying "Can't Buy Me Love", the end of which thus features only the other three Beatles.

ABOVE: **The boys pose with Walter Shenson, producer of *A Hard Day's Night*.**

Around the Beatles

There was no time to draw breath following the completion of *A Hard Day's Night*. In fact, rehearsals for their next project began even before the film was in the can. Brian Epstein signed the boys to an hour-long television special, *Around the Beatles*, which aired in the UK in early May and America later that year. For their performance part of the show the Beatles mimed to a specially recorded set that included their most recent number one, "Can't Buy Me Love", and a medley of early hits. Then it was into costume for their other contribution, a scene from *A Midsummer Night's Dream* in which Paul played Pyramus to John's Thisbe. This camped-up sketch wouldn't be the Beatles only connection with the Bard: In 1965 Peter Sellers had a Top 20 hit with his Shakespearian spoof, "Richard III Meets A Hard Day's Night".

It was back to live performance for the *New Musical Express* Poll Winners' Concert, staged at Wembley's Empire Pool on 26 April. The Beatles gave a barnstorming rendition of "She Loves You", "You Can't Do That", "Twist and Shout", "Long Tall Sally", and "Can't Buy Me Love". At the same show the previous year the Beatles hadn't picked up any awards, the votes having been cast before "Please Please Me" sent them into outer orbit. This time things were very different, the boys taking a clean sweep of Best UK Vocal Group, Best World Vocal Group, and Best Single of 1963, for "She Loves You". They would go on to dominate the *New Musical Express* Awards for the rest of the decade, winning "Best UK Vocal Group" category eight years running. Post-break up only Paul would take any of that publication's prestigious honours, and those were for Bass Guitarist of the Year, which he won four times in the 70s.

RIGHT: **In addition to the skit, the boys performed a number of their songs including their latest hit, "Can't Buy Me Love". The Beatles were joined by several guest artists who performed on the show; most notable were Cilla Black and Sounds Incorporated, who were both managed by Brian Epstein.**

RIGHT INSET: **Having been fully occupied by their filming commitments, the show at the *New Musical Express* Poll Winners' Concert at the Empire Pool in Wembley on 26 April was the first performance the Beatles had given in fifteen weeks.**

OPPOSITE: **John's Thisbe discovers Paul's dead Pyramus in their own spoof version of *A Midsummer Night's Dream*, performed as a segment on their TV show *Around the Beatles*. George stands over Paul in his role as Moonshine (bottom right); Ringo also had a part as the Lion, although he messed up his lines. To make up numbers, the boys were joined by Trevor Peacock, who played the part of Wall. The sketch was produced by Jack Good, who had flown in from Hollywood specially for the occasion. The *Daily Mail* reports on the occasion (bottom left).**

And now the Beatles pay their tribute

IT had to happen. The Beatles last night provided their own, inimitable tribute to the Bard.

And if Shakespeare never before turned in his grave, Wacks, he probably has now.

It began at Rediffusion's studios in Wembley with Ringo, in 16th - century doublet, firing a cannon.

It went on to a shot of Paul, George and John, similarly clad, playing heraldic trumpets.

And then, finally, there were the four of them, full of joy and mirth, hamming it up in *A Midsummer Night's Dream*, with Paul as Pyramus, George as Moonshine, Ringo as Lion, and John, looking heavily pregnant, as Thisbe.

I don't know how the National Theatre would have handled this scene. All I know is that at one glorious moment Ringo forgot his lines, the prompter called them out, and Ringo hollered back " Pardon ? "

All this went on, naturally, to the twittering of 500 near-hysterical and largely leather-clad " birds " who wouldn't have swapped one of their heroes for a dozen Oliviers.

Producer Jack Good told the audience to " behave like ordinary people and not like teenage monsters."

They behaved like teenage monsters.

Mr. Good had come all the way from Hollywood to do this show and he had arranged the set like the original Globe Theatre, apron stage and all.

HAIRCUT NOTE: Demetrius, in *Midsummer Night's Dream*, might have had trouble finding the Beatles. When he was looking for Lysander, he said: " Speak ! In some bush ? Where dost thou hide thy head ? "

LEFT AND ABOVE: **After eight weeks of shooting, the Beatles work on *A Hard Day's Night* was completed on the morning of 24 April. However, filming was immediately followed by rehearsals and the recording of the TV special *Around the Beatles*. The next engagement on the busy schedule was a short visit to Scotland, the band arriving in Edinburgh on 29 April. These sell-out events had been promoted by Albert Bonici with the support of Brian Epstein. A young Beatles fan, Linda McLean, had the good fortune to present the band with a lucky mascot upon their arrival at a windswept Turnhouse Airport (left above).**

OPPOSITE: **Crowds gather outside the ABC in Edinburgh.**

BELOW, OPPOSITE INSET, AND LEFT: **The band take time to sign autographs and chat with the young people who have come to see them. However, during the course of the year, as the demand for signed pictures grew, the Beatles often enlisted members of their entourage to help in the task.**

WEDNESDAY AT 6.30 AND 8.50
IN PERSON
THE BEATLES

A.B.C. CINEMA
EDINBURGH

2nd Performance 8-50
WEDNESDAY
APRIL 29
2
Centre Stalls (Front)
12/6

N39

No Tickets exchanged nor
money refunded
TO BE GIVEN UP

THIS PAGE: **The Beatles pose in Edinburgh before their show.**

LEFT AND ABOVE: At the stage door, the Beatles make one last play for the cameras (left) before getting ready to give their show in Edinburgh (above).

ABOVE INSET: Beatlemania Scottish style, as the fans in Edinburgh go wild for the Beatles.

ABOVE: A ticket stub for the show in Glasgow, Scotland. Although they only visited Glasgow and Edinburgh, the Beatles were brought to the rest of Scotland over the airwaves. A BBC Scotland interview conducted by Bill Aitkenhead was broadcast on the same evening as the Edinburgh performance.

THE ODEON THEATRE
GLASGOW
THE BEATLES
1st Performance 6-15 p.m.
THURSDAY
APRIL **30**
STALLS 15/-
S 3
No ticket exchanged nor money refunded
THIS PORTION TO BE RETAINED

Beatles take a break while record sales soar

In May 1964 the Beatles were finally able to draw breath. They spent most of that month on vacation, recharging their batteries before embarking on their first world tour. Privacy was the main requirement, and to that end far-flung exotic locations were chosen. John and George went to Tahiti, Paul and Ringo to the Virgin Islands, all with their respective partners. In an effort to prevent the arrangements from reaching the public domain the boys were given code names in what amounted to a military-style operation. The plan wasn't quite foolproof. By the time John and George reached their stopover in Honolulu,

American radio stations were tracking their progress and there were the usual tumultuous scenes that accompanied a Beatle's presence.

Not that it required the Beatles to be around in person for their influence to be felt—and heard. The day they left the UK, 2 May, *The Beatles' Second Album* replaced *Meet the Beatles!* at the top of the US chart. It was yet another first, as no other artist had ever unseated one of his or her previous releases in reaching the number one spot.

The new long-player included "She Loves You", Capitol quick to start making capital out of the smash-hit song to which they had just acquired the rights. Swan had a neat trick up its sleeve, however. It may have lost that song but it had the rights to "Sie Liebt Dich", and promptly issued it

on 21 May. Even that broke into the Hot 100, an indication that the American public's thirst for Beatles music was unquenchable.

A glance at the track list for *The Beatles' Second Album* showed that America still had some catching up to do. "She Loves You" had rocked Britain the previous summer, and there were five tracks from *With the Beatles*, released six months earlier in the UK. But America did have one coup: the new album included "Long Tall Sally" and "I Call Your Name", neither of which had yet been featured on a UK release. The Beatles recorded both on 1 March, but they wouldn't see the light of day in Britain until June, when they appeared on an EP along with covers of Carl Perkins's "Matchbox" and "Slow Down", a Little Richard number.

RIGHT AND BELOW: **Pattie and George return to the UK after their Pacific break. They had flown with John and Cynthia via Honolulu under the strictest of secrecy; the boys had even changed their names to elude the press. However, the media, like the *Daily Mail*, was not to be beaten and were lying in wait when the couples landed in Hawaii. The press pursued the boys on their stopover until they found a remote area to lie low before flying on to Tahiti. The island was a paradise, and John, with George's help, found time to write *A Spaniard in the Works*. However, four weeks of the same setting, no matter how idyllic, began to bore the boys, who had become accustomed to the busy lifestyles of pop stars.**

A rest for

The Beatles are having a month's holiday in May before they tour Australia. George Harrison, John Lennon and his wife, Cynthia, are in Honolulu, while Paul McCartney and Ringo Starr have left Lisbon for Puerto Rico.

MAY 1964

1 Another bank-holiday special due to be broadcast at Whitsun was recorded, still with the title *From Us to You*. Eight numbers were taped at the Paris Studio, with Alan Freeman again the host.

2 Holiday time as they all flew off for an extended break. Meanwhile the band could be heard on *A Slice of Life* on the radio. *The Beatles' Second Album* was at the top of the US charts for five weeks.

3 John and George spent their break together in Hawaii and Tahiti.

4 In Honolulu John and George were forced to retreat to their hotel after being besieged by fans on the beach.

5 In the UK the first pictures of baby Julian Lennon were featured in the press. The band appeared on *Roundup*, a local Scottish programme.

6 ITV broadcast *Around the Beatles*.

9 Paul and Ringo were on holiday in the Virgin Islands.

10 The Beatles were featured on Radio Luxembourg's Sunday night programme *This Is Their Life*. Their performance on the *New Musical Express* Poll Winners' concert was broadcast on ITV.

THE BEATLES' SECOND ALBUM

featuring SHE LOVES YOU and ROLL OVER BEETHOVEN

ELECTRIFYING BIG-BEAT PERFORMANCES BY ENGLAND'S Paul McCartney, John Lennon, George Harrison and Ringo Starr

THE BEATLES' SECOND ALBUM

Released
🇺🇸 **10 April 1964 (Capitol)**

Side One:
Roll Over Beethoven (Berry)
Thank You Girl
You Really Got a Hold on Me (Robinson)
Devil in Her Heart (Drapkin)
Money (That's What I Want) (Bradford–Gordy)
You Can't Do That

Side Two:
Long Tall Sally (Blackwell–Johnson–Little Richard)
I Call Your Name
Please Mister Postman (Bateman–Dobbins–Garrett–Gorman–Holland)
I'll Get You
She Loves You

ABOVE RIGHT: **Paul signing autographs after his return from the Virgin Islands, where he and Jane Asher had spent the holiday with Ringo and Maureen Cox.**

RIGHT: **Julian Lennon around the time of his first birthday. When the British press realized that John was married with a child, they snapped pictures of Julian despite Cynthia claiming to be her own twin sister in a desperate, if improbable, plan to elude them.**

FAR RIGHT: **John and Cynthia Lennon return from their vacation in Hawaii and Tahiti.**

17 The Beatles were again featured on Radio Luxembourg's *This Is Their Life*.

18 *From Us to You* was broadcast on BBC radio while *A Degree of Frost* was featured on BBC television.

21 "Sie Liebt Dich"/"I'll Get You" was released in the US on Swan 4182 but didn't make much of an impression on the charts.

24 A previously recorded interview with the band was broadcast on *The Ed Sullivan Show*.

26 John and George returned from their holiday.

27 Paul and Ringo returned from their trip. *Roundabout* was transmitted on the radio.

31 Fresh from their respective breaks, the boys performed to two houses at the Prince of Wales Theatre in London. Along with six support acts, the Beatles played in the fifth *Pops Alive Show!*—a series of seven Sunday night pop shows at the theatre that were promoted by Brian Epstein. "Love Me Do" reached the top of the US charts for one week.

LEFT AND BELOW: **The boys on a visit to Madame Tussauds. They were honoured by the famous London museum with their own waxwork effigies to be introduced that summer. The waxwork models proved an incredible draw for Madame Tussauds, especially after they were borrowed by the Beatles in 1967 to use on the cover of** *Sgt. Pepper's Lonely Hearts Club Band.*

LEFT INSET: **Ringo adds a cigarette as the finishing touch.**

OPPOSITE LEFT: **George plays with a spare pair of eyes at Madame Tussauds.**

RIGHT: **The boys pause for a cigarette while setting up for a show at the Prince of Wales Theatre to celebrate the beginning of the world tour that would begin with several dates in north Europe. After a concert in Holland, the Beatles planned to make for Australia, stopping off for a show in Hong Kong on the way. On returning from Australia the band played a handful of dates in England and one in Sweden before beginning the long-awaited tour of America.**

ABOVE: *Four by the Beatles* **was released by Capitol on 11 May 1964.**

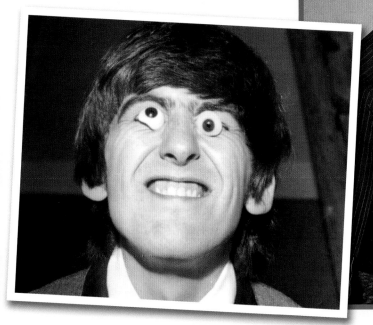

Beatlemania meets academia

By 1964 the mass hysteria caused by the merest sighting of a Beatle had attracted the interest of a number of academics, who were more interested in analyzing a social and cultural phenomenon than chord progressions and middle eights. Renowned American psychologist Dr. Joyce Brothers noted that the Beatles brought out a natural rebellious streak in all teenagers, glossing over the fact that many of their parents were equally taken with the group's clean-cut image and cheery banter. Indeed, sociologist Vance Packard, also writing in 1964, predicted that the Beatles' bubble would soon burst precisely because the mums and dads warmed to them

too. In short, kids wanted heroes who did a much better job of antagonizing the older generation.

Brothers took up the theme of alienation, comparing the boys' image to that of Oliver Twist. By associating them with an orphaned waif, the teenagers were subconsciously removing any parental influence from the equation. It also provided a focus for their own angst; their heroes reflected how "neglected and misunderstood" they felt themselves to be.

Both Brothers and Packard highlighted the fact that the Beatles' boyish charm fulfilled the need for an emotional release in pubescent girls. In the herd of a concert hall they could abandon themselves completely—hence the regular fainting episodes—yet it was in a safe environment. The Beatles' image was crucial in this respect. More than one commentator

remarked on their perceived androgynous look, and mannerisms such as tossing their hair and singing in a falsetto voice were "a shade on the feminine side", according to Brothers. Girls in their early teens were attracted to this "less manly" persona, which was seen as less threatening at a time when they were becoming aware of their sexuality. The implication was that had they maintained their Teddy-boy look and surlier expressions, the Beatles would have scared off quite a few fans.

Attempting to deconstruct Beatlemania was one thing; analyzing the Beatles' appeal was another. The essential ingredient in the latter was the music, which will endure long after Beatlemania has passed from living memory.

A writing partnership

As the boys were returning from their island idylls, Peter and Gordon released their latest Lennon–McCartney number, "Nobody I Know". Paul's relationship with Jane Asher had quickly raised the profile of her brother Peter and his school friend Gordon Waller, who had been trying to get a break in the music business for some considerable time. Paul was only too glad to be of assistance. "Nobody I Know" was a giveaway, written to order and never conceived as a Beatles song. The same can't be said for the duo's debut single, "A World Without Love", which had toppled "Can't Buy Me Love" from the UK chart a month earlier and would also reach number one in America. Paul wrote it at ForthlinRoad when he was sixteen, a song that would become a huge transatlantic hit but that wasn't considered up to scratch for the Beatles to record.

Paul had no illusions about his extraordinary talent, but nevertheless wondered whether his name on a songwriting credit was now enough to guarantee a hit. He put that to the test in one of his other offerings to Peter and Gordon. Their 1966 song "Woman", penned by the unknown "Bernard Webb", still made the charts and did respectable business.

TOP RIGHT AND LEFT AND OPPOSITE: **Paul and George tuning their guitars ahead of the two shows at the Prince of Wales Theatre on Sunday, 31 May. The Beatles headlined this, the fifth concert in a series of seven organized by Brian Epstein.**

ABOVE : **Ringo puts in less preparation. While sitting at his drum kit, he has time for a cigarette.**

RIGHT: **The Beatles are the main feature in *Chicago's Sunday American Magazine*.**

THIS PAGE AND OPPOSITE: **The boys fix themselves drinks after a press conference at the Prince of Wales Theatre. Free bars became a normal feature of the Beatles' lives. The slightly unusual combination of whisky and Coke was one of their favourite tipples. Ever playing up to the camera, Paul pretends to down a whole bottle (opposite inset).**

SONG STORY: "IF I FELL"

While the Beatles and Parlophone had a policy of issuing up-tempo numbers for the UK singles market, Capitol had no such qualms about releasing ballads on 45 rpm. In July 1964 the US company paired two achingly beautiful songs, "And I Love Her" and "If I Fell", both culled from *A Hard Days Night*. The A-side, penned by Paul, was further proof of the master tunesmith and sweet lyricist in top form. "If I Fell", which John called his "first attempt at a proper ballad", ought to have dispelled the myth that his metier was hard-edge rock songs, yet the pigeon-holing of their compositional talents persisted. Lennon's song featured in the film, but as there was no love interest—deliberately so—he sang it to a sulking Ringo in a TV studio scene.

ABOVE AND RIGHT: **The Beatles seemed to find themselves behind the bar on a regular basis.**

OPPOSITE: **Paul is interviewed by Cathy McGowan, presenter of *Ready, Steady, Go!***

RINGO VS. PETE

"Pete Best is a great drummer but Ringo's a great Beatle."

—John

RIGHT: **Ringo pictured just as the Beatles were preparing to embark on their world tour, and shortly before he fell ill with a bout of tonsillitis that caused him to miss the performances in Denmark, the Netherlands, and Hong Kong. George in particular was keen to cancel the tour, not wishing to depart without Ringo, but Brian Epstein pressed the band to honour its commitments.**

OPPOSITE RIGHT AND LEFT: **Fans were obviously concerned about Ringo's health. These images of him sitting up eating in his bed at University College Hospital, London, were released to reassure them.**

OPPOSITE RIGHT ABOVE: ***Daily Mail*, 18 June: While the boys were in Sydney, EMI announced the good news concerning the band's incredible average record sales.**

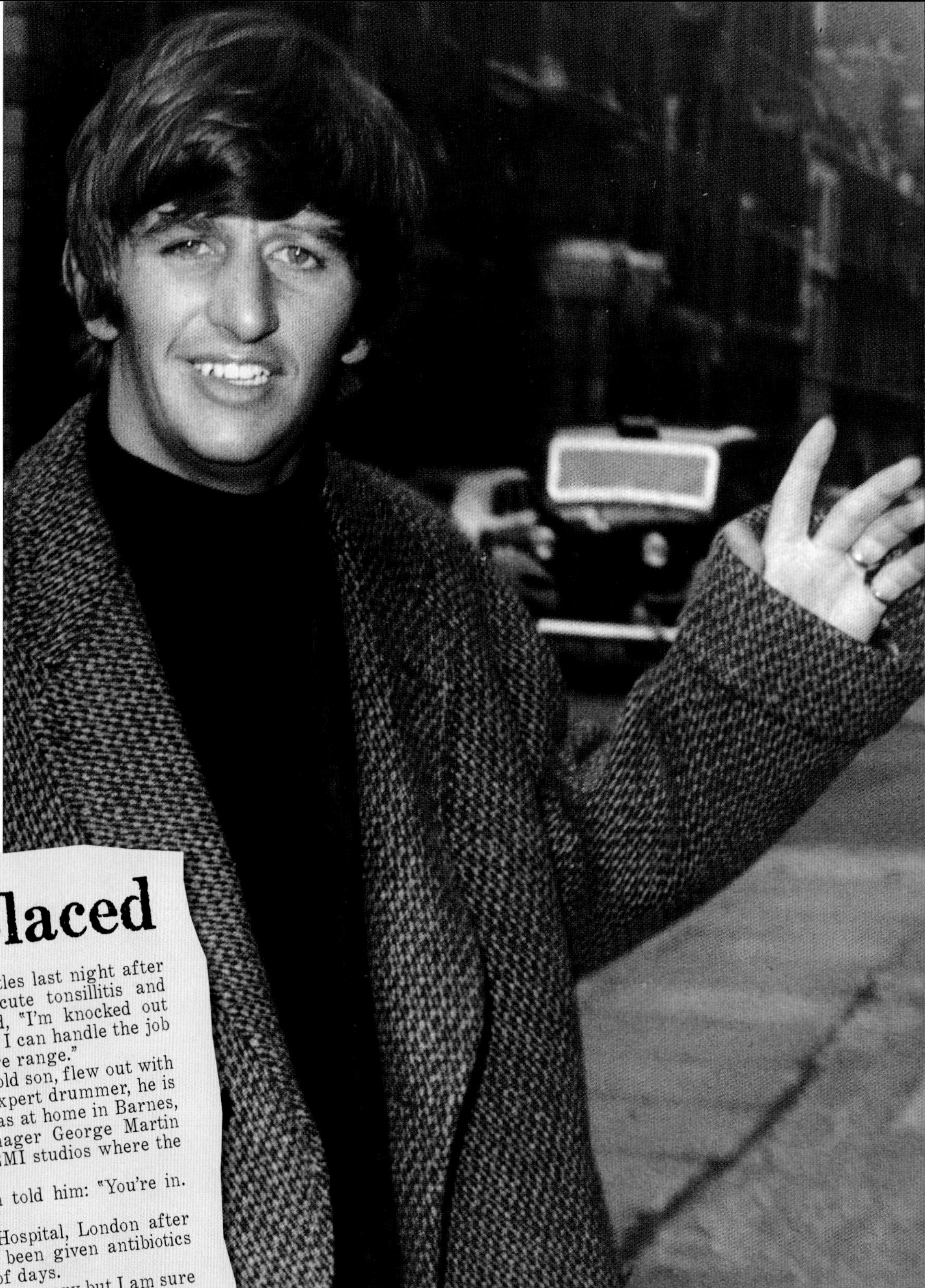

Ringo Is Replaced

Cockney drummer Jimmy Nicol joined the Beatles last night after Ringo Starr was taken into hospital with acute tonsillitis and pharyngitis. He told reporter Robert Bickford, "I'm knocked out man. It's quite a laugh being one of the Beatles. I can handle the job OK. Ringo can swing all right, but I've got more range."

Jimmy, who is married and has a five-year-old son, flew out with the band for a three-day European tour. An expert drummer, he is highly regarded by the record industry and was at home in Barnes, Middlesex when the Beatles' recording manager George Martin phoned and asked him to go straight to the EMI studios where the other three band members were recording.

After a two-hour rehearsal John Lennon told him: "You're in. This should be worth a couple of quid to you."

Ringo was taken to University College Hospital, London after collapsing at a photographic studio. He has been given antibiotics and told he will need to stay in for a couple of days.

He said, "I'm not too bad really. I feel pretty groggy but I am sure I'll be well enough to go with the boys on Sunday to Hong Kong. It's pretty nice in here. I'm surrounded by hot water bottles but I am still shivering. It's a terrible drag not being able to go with the boys to Europe." His girlfriend Maureen Cox was seen taking in a bunch of red roses.

EXTRACTED FROM THE *DAILY MAIL* 4 JUNE 1964

Ringo forced to stay at home

Almost as soon as the boys returned from their vacation they were back in the studio to record the non-soundtrack side of *A Hard Day's Night*. The Abbey Road session on 3 June was to have been their last before heading off to Denmark, the first leg of their world tour. At a photo shoot that morning Ringo collapsed and was rushed to hospital, where he was diagnosed as suffering from tonsillitis and pharyngitis. Cancelling the early tour dates was considered. The Beatles were a foursome, and George was particularly vociferous that it should be the full complement of Fabs or none. John had once opined: "Pete Best is a great drummer, but Ringo's a great Beatle." In the end management held sway. Brian Epstein was caught between a rock and a hard place: to risk antagonizing his boys or disappointing hordes of fans. He came down on the side of honouring the contract; three Beatles would have to do.

A meeting was called to discuss the possibility of a replacement. Jimmy Nicol emerged as the obvious choice. Twenty-four-year-old Nicol was an accomplished session drummer who had played with Georgie Fame and also fronted his own band, the Shubdubs. He looked the part, was well known to George Martin, and, in a neat twist, had even played on an ersatz Beatles album and so was familiar with the material. Martin made the phone call: How would he like to become a Beatle, albeit temporarily?

Beatles' sales £½m a month

SYDNEY, Tuesday The retail sales of Beatles records all over the world is now £500,000 a month. E.M.I. recording company managing director Mr. John Wall said in Sydney today. "I don't know how much they get, but it would be only a small portion of that figure," he said.—D.M. Cable.

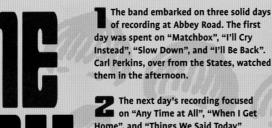

JUNE 1964

1 The band embarked on three solid days of recording at Abbey Road. The first day was spent on "Matchbox", "I'll Cry Instead", "Slow Down", and "I'll Be Back". Carl Perkins, over from the States, watched them in the afternoon.

2 The next day's recording focused on "Any Time at All", "When I Get Home", and "Things We Said Today" (written by Paul when he was on holiday with Jane Asher in the Bahamas).

3 Ringo was taken ill with violent tonsillitis and pharyngitis and was hospitalized at the University College,

London. Session drummer Jimmy Nicol (of the Shubdubs) was swiftly recruited in his place. Instead of the original recording session planned, the group took him through their stage routine so he could play in the concert in Copenhagen the next day. During the evening the remaining three recorded some demos and overdubbed onto "Any Time at All" and "Things We Said Today".

4 A total of nearly 9,000 fans watched the band play two houses at KB Hallen in Copenhagen as they began a world tour that was to last 27 days. Jimmy Nicol played in place of Ringo for the first five dates. During that afternoon George

Martin and Norman Smith completed some mono mixing on "Matchbox", "I Call Your Name", and "Long Tall Sally". Martin also overdubbed some piano onto "Slow Down" and then finished the mono mixing. These four songs made up the EP *Long Tall Sally* that was for release in Britain. The two then continued to work on songs for the forthcoming album *A Hard Day's Night*.

5 The Beatles arrived in Holland at 1 p.m. and immediately went into a press conference at Schiphol Airport. They then drove to Hillegom to rehearse and tape a programme for VARA-TV. At the Café-Restaurant Treslong they initially answered

LEFT AND OPPOSITE: With a little help from his new friends, Jimmy Nicol was expected to hit the ground running. Luckily, he was a seasoned drummer and had very little problem with the songs.

BELOW: Paul displays a pair of wooden clogs, a souvenir from his visit to Holland.

LEFT INSET: Danish audiences got the Beatles tour off to a typical start. Fans stormed the stage and hundreds gathered outside the venue in Copenhagen, reports the *Daily Mail* on 5 June.

OPPOSITE RIGHT: A programme printed for the 6 June performance at Blokker in the Netherlands.

Bonk ! To Paul, with love

COPENHAGEN, Thursday

GIRLS tried to storm the stage at the first of two concerts by the Beatles here tonight. It took 12 hefty ushers to get them back to their seats.

Paul McCartney was hit on the head by a piece of paper thrown by a girl who screamed: "It was a love letter."

Outside the hall police used dogs to help disperse fans who were unable to get into the hall.

Inside the hall the audience gave a special ovation to Jimmy Nicol, the stand-in for Ringo Starr.

In London, Ringo, who is suffering from acute tonsillitis and pharyngitis, was improving.

continued from previous page

JUNE 1964

questions from the audience before playing. By the sixth song the boys were completely surrounded by the audience and, as officials were unable to clear the stage, the band was ordered to leave. Only Jimmy Nicol continued to play along with the backing track they had been miming to.

6 Two performances at Veilinghal Op Hoop Van Zegen in Blokker, the Netherlands, when they appeared with eight other support acts. The evening house was recorded for television and newsreel.

7 The band left the Netherlands to fly back to London before taking a flight to Hong Kong.

8 In Hong Kong John visited the President Hotel Kowloon to attend the Miss Hong Kong pageant. *The Beatles in Nederland* was broadcast using the recording at Hillegom along with some filming made the following day on a boat trip around Amsterdam.

9 On to Hong Kong. Two houses were played to at the Princess Theatre in Kowloon. Although the Beatles were very popular, neither show was a sell-out as the ticket price of HK $75 was equivalent to a week's wages for the average working man. In England George Martin continued with the mono mixing for "Things We Said Today" and "A Hard Day's Night". Some mono mixes

were also copied for Capitol Records and United Artists Records for the American market. *The Teen Scene* was broadcast.

10 A mono mix was made at Abbey Road for "I'll Be Back".

11 The Beatles arrived in Darwin, Australia, at 2:35 in the morning. They then flew on to Sydney, where they were trapped in their hotel due to the number of fans surrounding the building. Ringo was discharged from hospital.

12 They flew to Adelaide, where an estimated 100,000 fans lined the route from the airport to the town

Theaterproducties
DICK VAN GELDER
Amsterdam

BEN ESSING
Blokker

N.V. NED.THEATERBUREAU
s-Gravenhage

presenteren in
samenwerking met
STIBBE/PARLOPHONE

THE BEATLES

THE BEATLES UITSLUITEND
OP PARLOPHONE

**programma
festival
blokker
1964**

6 juni

aanvang
middagvoorstelling 14.30 uur
avondvoorstelling 20.00 uur

prijs 50 ct.

medewerking van

THE BEATLES

Wanda
Ciska Peters
Jack and Bill
The Torero's
Herman van Keeken
Don Mercedes and his Improvers
The Fancy Five
Karin Kent
Candy Kids
Hotjumpers
Kwintet Dominique
John Rassel and his Clan

Jimmy Nicol stands in for Ringo

Barely twenty-four hours and one run-through later, Nicol took to the stage in Copenhagen. There was no time for bespoke tailoring; Jimmy had to pull on Ringo's stage gear and get on with it. Ringo's set-piece vocal turn, "I Wanna Be Your Man", was dropped from the set, but otherwise there were few glitches.

After eleven days, during which time Nicol also wielded the sticks in Holland, Hong Kong, and Australia, Ringo was well enough to join the tour. Nicol found himself on a plane home, £500 and a gold watch to the good. It was back to earth with a bump. A month later, 12 July 1964, the Shubdubs were one of the support acts when the Beatles headlined at Brighton Hippodrome, but there was no pally reunion. John, Paul, and George had been welcoming enough, but Nicol said he felt like an interloper in "the most exclusive club in the world". He would be neither the first nor last to discover that when it came to music, the Beatles didn't embrace outsiders.

The latest candidate for the "Fifth Beatle" tag found it difficult to readjust to life out of the spotlight. Within a year Nicol was declared bankrupt, and he eventually swapped his drumsticks for a paintbrush as he turned to decorating to earn his living. Nicol got slightly more than his fifteen minutes of fame, however, thanks to a Paul-inspired composition for *Sgt. Pepper*. "Getting better" became Jimmy's catchphrase during his brief stint as a Beatle, one he used when the other group members asked him how he was faring learning Ringo's rolls and fills. When Paul came up with an idea for an "optimistic song" three years later, Nicol's refrain handed him a ready-made title.

centre. They performed two houses at the Centennial Hall Showgrounds, one of which was recorded for radio.

13 Two more houses at the Centennial Hall. A total of 54,000 fans tried to get the 12,000 tickets on sale, and police were eventually called to break up fights between fans.

14 The band flew into Melbourne to be met by an estimated 300,000 fans; 50 were injured in the crush. Ringo had recovered sufficiently to join them.

15 The recording from 12 June was broadcast as the *Beatles Show*.

That night the boys—now rejoined by Ringo began the first of three nights at the Festival Hall, playing two houses each evening. An acoustics expert measured the screams at 112 decibels.

16 Performances at the Festival Hall continued.

17 At the last performance the concert was taped by Australian Channel 9. The result was a programme called *The Beatles Sing for Shell* (the sponsors), broadcast on 1 July.

18 Returning to Sydney, they embarked on another three-night

run of two houses a night at the stadium in Rushcutter's Bay. There were 12,000 fans watching each performance, and Paul complained about the number of jelly babies thrown at them (fans had found out that George liked them). On the outside of the eighth floor of their hotel a 13-year-old girl was caught by police trying to reach the band. It was Paul's 22nd birthday.

19 The EP *Long Tall Sally* was released in Britain on Parlophone GEP 8913 (mono only). The A-side featured "Long Tall Sally" and "I Call Your Name", with "Slowdown" and "Matchbox" on the B-side.

20 As they continued to play in Sydney, a telephone interview was recorded for *Roundabout* that would be played in England the following Saturday.

21 The band flew down to New Zealand.

22 Two houses were held at the Town Hall in Wellington, with Ringo able to resume a vocal contribution at last. George Martin, along with Norman Smith and Geoff Emerick, spent the whole day at Abbey Road working on mono and stereo mixing.

THIS PAGE: **After touching down briefly in Darwin and Sydney, the Beatles and Jimmy Nicol arrived in Adelaide on 12 June. Fans lined the six-mile route from the airport to the city centre in the hope of catching a glimpse of the band.**

LEFT INSET: **The *Daily Mail* estimates 250,000 fans turned out to welcome the Beatles (including Ringo) to Melbourne on 14 June, but subsequent estimates have suggested that the figure might have been as high as 300,000 people. When put in this context, 50 injuries doesn't sound so bad.**

BELOW INSETS: **Programmes for the Hong Kong and Australian dates, along with a ticket for the Melbourne concert.**

Beatles welcome injures 50

MELBOURNE, Sunday Fifty people were taken to hospital today during Melbourne's frenzied welcome to the Beatles. Police called in soldiers and sailors to help control the crowds, estimated at about 250,000.—B.U.P.

The Beatles Show

OFFICIAL SOUVENIR

THE BEATLES

ESTIVAL HALL.
DLEY STREET, MELBOURNE
STADIUMS & AZTEC Presents
The BEATLES
MONDAY 15th JUNE
8.15 p.m. STALLS
Sec.7 F 28
TURN LEFT

Wizards of Oz

Prior to June 1964, no major recording artist had ever visited Australia's shores. Then the biggest act in the world descended and it was party time. Three weeks of the Beatles' 27-day world tour in June 1964 were spent in Australia and New Zealand, where they caused a furor that made what happened in America look like a tea dance. Months of pent-up anticipation were unleashed as soon as John, Paul, George, and Jimmy Nicol touched down in Sydney. It was as if the fans realized that they weren't going to get many chances to see the Beatles live—their only opportunity, as it turned out—and they were going to make the most of it.

An estimated 300,000 thronged the route along Anzac Highway into the centre of Adelaide, around half of the city's population turning out to welcome the boys to the city that hosted their first concert on the continent. It was

Friday, 12 June, but workplaces and schools saw little industry in what became a de facto public holiday. Some educational establishments demanded business as usual and became virtual internment camps. At one the students made their feelings known by inserting "Yeah, yeah, yeah" into the school hymn.

It was in Melbourne two days later that Ringo joined the party. He had set off from Britain minus his passport, but special dispensation was granted; after all, it wouldn't do to impede a Beatle's travel plans. Ringo was first to arrive at Melbourne's Southern Cross Hotel, where a sizeable crowd had already gathered. The burly police inspector responsible for getting Ringo inside unscathed decided to hoist the drummer onto his shoulders and make a dash for it, a plan that went well until he stumbled and spilled his valuable cargo into any number of gleeful hands. Ringo was badly shaken by the mauling he received.

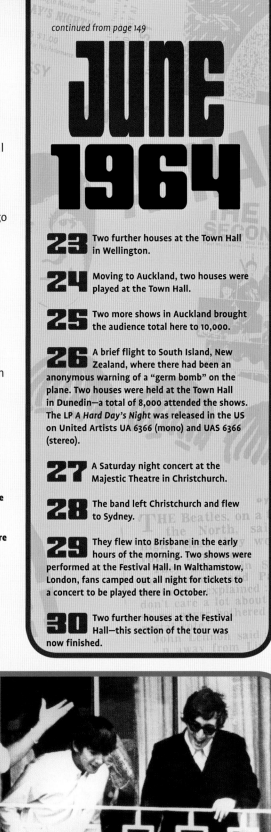

continued from page 149

JUNE 1964

23 Two further houses at the Town Hall in Wellington.

24 Moving to Auckland, two houses were played at the Town Hall.

25 Two more shows in Auckland brought the audience total here to 10,000.

26 A brief flight to South Island, New Zealand, where there had been an anonymous warning of a "germ bomb" on the plane. Two houses were held at the Town Hall in Dunedin—a total of 8,000 attended the shows. The LP *A Hard Day's Night* was released in the US on United Artists UA 6366 (mono) and UAS 6366 (stereo).

27 A Saturday night concert at the Majestic Theatre in Christchurch.

28 The band left Christchurch and flew to Sydney.

29 They flew into Brisbane in the early hours of the morning. Two shows were performed at the Festival Hall. In Walthamstow, London, fans camped out all night for tickets to a concert to be played there in October.

30 Two further houses at the Festival Hall—this section of the tour was now finished.

Being A Beatle Nearly Drove Me Potty...

The redundant Beatle came home from Australia yesterday and said "I nearly went potty". Jimmy Nicol, the 24-year old drummer who took Ringo Starr's place when Ringo was ill, said: "It was a marvellous experience but I wouldn't want to be a Beatle full-time.

They live in boxes, in cars, aeroplanes, hotel rooms. They're all shut in. I couldn't stand it. I like to walk about free. On my last night with them in Australia when Ringo came back, I just wanted to go out and walk about. I wasn't allowed to. Brian Epstein didn't think it was a good idea. I suppose he was right. He runs an infallible organization. It's incredible. He says 'Jump' and everybody jumps. But that night I nearly went potty. They said there had to be a security guard with me. I said, 'But I'm finished with them now'. It was ridiculous. But they insisted so I went to bed."

Later, once at home, he added: "I never went out with the Beatles in our spare time, what little there was. I always felt like an intruder. The boys were very kind, they accepted me. They treated me marvellously, but you can't just get into a group like that. They have their own atmosphere, their own sense of humour. It's a little clique and outsiders just can't break in."

EXTRACTED FROM THE
DAILY MAIL, JUNE 1964

BELOW: **Ringo was finally well enough to join the boys in Melbourne, and the Fab Four were reunited with much of the Australasian tour still to go. The scenes in Melbourne and Adelaide were replicated across the continent, and the boys usually found themselves prisoners in their hotel. Here they wave to the crowds amassed below.**

Army assist the police

Shortly after Ringo reached the band's Melbourne hotel on 14 June, the rest of the group stole in after a slick piece of decoy work. For the one and only time the Fab Five paraded themselves on the first-floor balcony in an attempt to quell the volatile crowd. The hysteria had a more menacing edge than in Adelaide. One sleek Italian sports car found itself in the wrong place at the wrong time and looked as if it had been through a crusher after the fans had used it as a thoroughfare. There were broken bones as fans fell from vantage points. If someone's view was blocked, a fight invariably broke out. The army had been brought in to assist the police but it made little difference. John saw an obvious comparison and couldn't resist treating the assembled masses to a Hitler impression and a "Sieg Heil" salute.

The first leg of the world tour had been a triumph, though there was one disturbing trend: sick or disabled people angling to get within touching distance of a Beatle. In some cases it was nothing more than subterfuge, but some genuinely thought the hands that worked such magic on Rickenbackers and Hofners had even greater powers.

RIGHT: **Death threats made against the Beatles ahead of their concert in Wellington, New Zealand, were discussed in the *Daily Mail* on 22 June.**

BELOW: **Ringo with Vivien Leigh, who happened to be catching the same flight as the boys back from Australia and was delighted to have the opportunity of meeting them.**

I'll blow up the Beatles...

WELLINGTON, Tuesday

ANONYMOUS telephone caller tonight threatened to blow up the hotel where the Beatles are staying here, blow up the town hall where they are appearing — and cut off their hair.

Police Inspector T. J. Kyle, who heads the Beatles' protection force, said police had received several calls, one of them threatening that a bomb would go off in the Town Hall during tonight's Beatle show.

But no search was made in the hall and the Mersey group's final show ended with-

out any explosion—other than that of thousands of hysterical teenagers.

Police had yet another "Beatle battle" on their hands as wave after wave of screaming fans surged forward and overpowered the police cordon separating the audience from the stage.

Several teenagers reached the stage and Paul McCartney was almost pulled off it as policemen were knocked to the floor.

A 20-year-old girl was found with her wrists slashed in the Beatles' sixth floor hotel suite here today but was discharged from hospital after treatment.

ABOVE AND OPPOSITE: **The Beatles returned to Britain on 2 July. The crowds that came to greet them were even larger than those in February when the boys returned from America.**

OPPOSITE BELOW RIGHT: **John and Cynthia rush to escape the crowds of pressmen who hounded their every move.**

A Family Affair

The Beatles have asked their parents and an aunt to accompany them on their Australian tour. George Harrison and Ringo Starr have invited their parents, Paul McCartney has asked his father and John Lennon will take along his Aunt Mimi. Mrs. Mimi Smith, who brought up John after his mother died, said last night "John gave me no excuse for turning the trip down. He's a pet for giving me such a treat. I've never travelled so far from home before."

Bus driver Mr. Harold Harrison, who has been given a year's leave from Liverpool Corporation so he can help his wife, Louise, handle their son's personal affairs said: "I think it will be good for George that we are going along. We will probably be able to take a load off his shoulders by dealing with the fans out there."

Ringo's mother, Mrs. Elsie Graves-Starkey, added: The only snag is that my husband is not keen on flying. I hope he will change his mind before the weekend so we'll not hold up their plans."

Paul's father, ex-musician Mr. James McCartney, turned the invitation down fearing that the 30 hours flying would be too much for him saying, "But I'll be going with the lads to America in August instead."

EXTRACTED FROM THE
DAILY MAIL, 27 MAY 1964

JULY 1964

1 The band left Brisbane, changing planes at Sydney.

2 They flew into London Airport at 11:10 a.m.

3 The Pete Best Four released "I'm Gonna Knock on Your Door". *From Us to You* was transmitted.

4 The Beatles attended the preview of *A Hard Day's Night*.

6 The royal world charity premiere of *A Hard Day's Night* was held at the London Pavilion cinema where the boys were introduced to Princess Margaret and Lord Snowdon.

7 Back in the studio at Lime Grove they mimed to "Things We Said Today", "A Hard Day's Night", and "Long Tall Sally" for future appearances on *Top of the Pops*. Afterwards they recorded an interview at Television House for a *Scene at 6.30*

broadcast that evening. During the day John was interviewed by Chris Hutchins for the BBC radio show *The Teen Scene*. Again the theme of the interview was the forthcoming film. It was broadcast two days later. Ringo celebrated his 24th birthday.

8 The edition of *Top of the Pops* featuring the Beatles was transmitted.

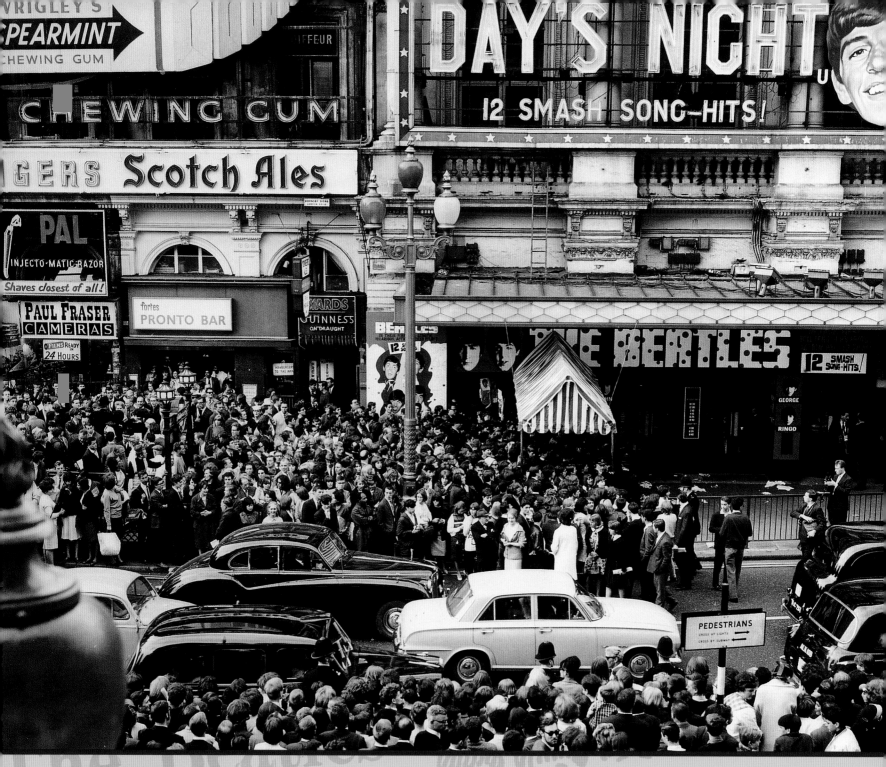

continued from previous page

JULY 1964

10 The album *A Hard Day's Night* was released in the UK on Parlophone PMC 1230 (mono) and PCS 3058 (stereo). It was the first Beatles album to have all its songs written by Lennon and McCartney. "A Hard Day's Night"/"Things We Said Today", the single, was also released in the UK on Parlophone R 5160. The band flew to Liverpool for a press conference. Remarkable scenes were witnessed as fans cheered them through the city centre on their journey to the town hall for a civic reception. The same scenario took place in the evening for the northern premiere of the film at the Odeon Cinema. Footage from the day was broadcast on the news all over the world.

11 A live performance on *Lucky Stars* (Summer Spin) at the Teddington Studios. They had travelled there by boat along the River Thames.

12 The first of five concerts at seaside resorts took place at the Hippodrome Theatre in Brighton.

13 "A Hard Day's Night"/"Should Have Known Better" was released in the US on Capitol 5222. In Broadcasting House the band recorded a session for the new BBC Radio show *Top Gear*. It included seven songs along with conversation with presenter Brian Matthew. Prior to this Paul was interviewed by Michael Smee for BBC General Overseas Programmes.

14 A live session for *Top Gear* was recorded.

15 John bought his house in Kenwood for £20,000 and spent a further £40,000 on renovations.

17 At the BBC Paris Studio another bank-holiday special *From Us to You* was recorded for broadcast on 3 August. Hosted by Don Wardell, it included eight songs along with requests from listeners and conversation with Wardell.

PRINCESS MARGARET learned a new word last night when she and the Earl of Snowdon attended the premiere of the Beatles' first film, A Hard Day's Night.

The Mersey pop stars were lined up in the foyer of the London Pavilion when Lord Snowdon asked : "What in the world is a grotty shirt ?"

The Princess looked at the Beatles. Then she shook her head.

Beatle John Lennon said : "It means simply, grotesque—just a word we used to describe a shirt in the film."

Princess Margaret and Lord Snowdon had seen the word quoted in a review of the film.

What did the Beatles think of A Hard Day's Night ? "We're not very good, but we had a very good producer," Paul McCartney told the Princess.

This was Ringo's night—the eve of his 24th birthday—and the screams and whistles as the Beatles took their seats in the royal row changed to a loud "Happy birthday to you."

Earlier there had been a tremendous reception as 6,000 fans jammed Piccadilly Circus. Nearly 100 people were treated for exhaustion and minor injuries.

While the show was on there was a scuffle outside between Beatle fans and supporters of their rivals, the Rolling Stones. Girls scratched and pulled each other's hair.

There were more screams from the crowd when the royal party left the theatre—and the Princess's car was stopped in the Haymarket by fans who thought it was carrying the Beatles.

But the Beatles were whisked away under police guard to a celebration party in Park-lane.

Police arrested two men who will appear at Bow-street court today.

ABOVE: **The Beatles were presented to Princess Margaret and the Earl of Snowdon, who attended the London premiere of** A Hard Day's Night.

OPPOSITE: **Thousands of fans gathered outside the London Pavilion to see their idols arrive at the premiere of** A Hard Day's Night **on 6 July. The next day's newspapers carried reports of the evening (far left).**

LEFT: **A programme from the premiere.**

18 The band flew to Blackpool to begin rehearsals for the live show the next day.

19 The band appeared live at the ABC Theatre in Blackpool for *Blackpool Night Out*, which was broadcast to all ITV stations. Mike and Bernie Winters hosted the lineup that included Lionel Blair and Jimmy Edwards.

20 In the US "I'll Cry Instead"/"I'm Happy Just to Dance With You" was released on Capitol 5234 while "And I Love Her"/"If I Fell" was released on

Capitol 5235. The LP *Something New* was also released in the States on Capitol T-2108 (mono) and Capitol ST-2108 (stereo).

23 At the London Palladium, The Night of a Hundred Stars was held in aid of the Combined Theatrical Charities Appeals Council. The boys were suspended from the ceiling to take part in a flying ballet sketch.

25 "A Hard Day's Night"/"Things We Said Today" reached the top of the UK charts, remaining there for three weeks. The album *A Hard Day's Night*

reached the top of the UK charts, remaining there for 21 weeks. In the States the album also topped the charts, holding the slot for 14 weeks. George and Ringo took part in *Juke Box Jury*. Recorded at the Television Centre, the two Beatles rehearsed independently, then appeared with other personalities including Reg Varney and Katie Boyle.

26 A Sunday night summer show at the Opera House in Blackpool.

28 The band flew to Sweden. They played two shows that evening at the Johanneshovs Isstadion in

Stockholm. In the first show, both John and Paul received a mild electric shock from faulty equipment.

29 Two further shows at Johanneshovs Isstadion.

30 The boys flew back to England.

LEFT: **Following the London premiere, the first Beatles movie was given the Liverpudlian seal of approval with a northern premiere at the Liverpool Odeon. The boys were treated like homecoming heroes. The Beatles wave to a crowd of 6,000 from the town hall, with thousands of hysterical fans fighting to get to the front. In the ensuing pushing and shoving 400 people fainted and were taken away for medical treatment. Paramedics reported that as soon as patients were revived, they would get up and try to fight their way back to the front.**

BELOW LEFT AND OPPOSITE ABOVE: **The Beatles were the guests of honour at a reception at the town hall in Liverpool hosted by Lord Mayor Alderman Louis Caplan. The Earl of Derby was just one of the 650 guests who attended the reception to toast to the success of *A Hard Day's Night*.**

BELOW: **Paul accompanied by entertainer Lionel Blair.**

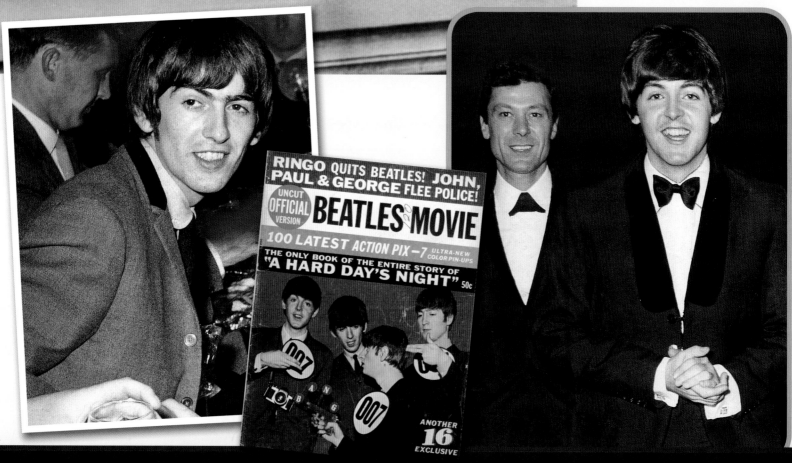

A Hard Day's Night

Released
🇬🇧 **10 July 1964**

Side One:

A Hard Day's Night (SAMPLE)
I Should Have Known Better
If I Fell
I'm Happy Just to Dance With You
And I Love Her (SAMPLE)
Tell Me Why
Can't Buy Me Love (SAMPLE)

Side Two:

Any Time at All
I'll Cry Instead
Things We Said Today
When I Get Home
You Can't Do That
I'll Be Back

Released
🇺🇸 **26 January 1964**

Side One:

A Hard Day's Night (SAMPLE)
Tell Me Why
I'll Cry Instead
I Should Have Known Better (instrumental:
   George Martin & His Orchestra)
I'm Happy Just to Dance With You
And I Love Her (instrumental: George
   Martin & His Orchestra)

Side Two:

I Should Have Known Better
If I Fell
And I Love Her (SAMPLE)
Ringo's Theme (This Boy) (instrumental:
   George Martin & His Orchestra)
Can't Buy Me Love (SAMPLE)
A Hard Day's Night (instrumental:
   George Martin & His Orchestra)

Cover Story

When Robert Freeman was enlisted to produce the sleeve artwork for the Beatles' third album, *A Hard Day's Night*, he decided upon a concept that would suggest movement: Arranging five small head shots of each Beatle across the cover in four rows, resulting in an arrangement of twenty photographs that is reminiscent of a series of movie frames. The effect was enhanced by each member of the group making a different facial expression in each shot. The same pictures were included at the end of the movie.

In the UK, the album photography was bordered in blue, but the US version was red. The US sleeve also differed in using only four, rather than twenty images, somewhat lessening the impact of the original concept.

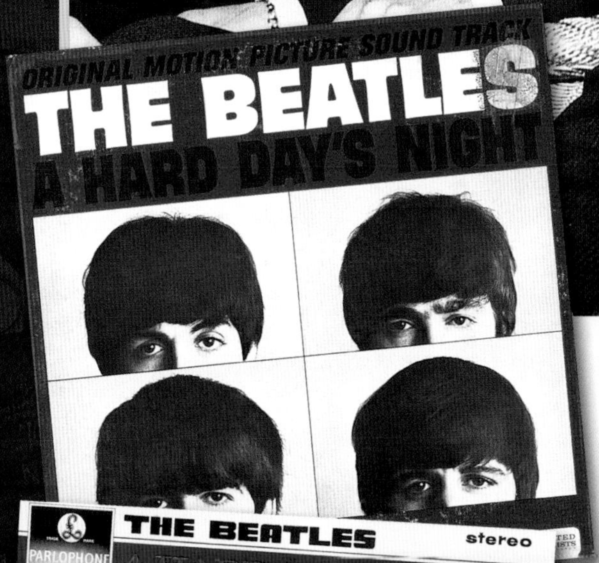

JOHANNESHOVS ISSTADION **1**

THE BEATLES

Tisdagen den 28 juli 1964 kl. 18.45

Sektion **C-2**
LÄKTAREN HÖGER

Bänk 8   Plats 34   Pris kr
                                   12:—

HAROLD FIELDING'S
"SUNDAY NIGHT AT THE
BLACKPOOL OPERA HOUSE"

something new

Released

🇺🇸 **20 July 1964** (Capitol)

Side One:

I'll Cry Instead

Things We Said Today

Any Time At All

When I Get Home

Slow Down (Williams)

Matchbox (Perkins)

Side Two:

Tell Me Why

And I Love Her

I'm Happy Just to Dance
  With You

IF I Fell

Komm, Gib Mir Deine Hand

Cover Story

Despite its title, the album contained no new material, largely consisting of versions of songs already issued on the British and American versions of the soundtrack of *A Hard Day's Night*. Cover images were taken by Joe Covello when the band performed on *The Ed Sullivan Show*.

LEFT, ABOVE, AND OPPOSITE: The Beatles appeared in the variety show *Blackpool Night Out*, hosted by Mike and Bernie Winters. They took part in some comic sketches and performed five numbers including "A Hard Day's Night" and "Long Tall Sally".

BELOW: **The Beatles join the other artists onstage for the finale of *Blackpool Night Out*.**

OPPOSITE INSET LEFT: **An appearance in Blackpool was followed by two nights in Sweden at the end of July.**

OPPOSITE INSET RIGHT: **A programme from 16 August, when the Beatles returned to perform in Blackpool.**

Beatles tour America

When the Beatles departed London Airport on 18 August for their twenty-five-date tour of America, there was no need for a publicity budget, much less any of the apprehension that had beset the boys in the run-up to their first Stateside trip six months earlier. All the shows sold out as soon as tickets went on sale, prompting one of the more enterprising unlucky ones, Charles Finley, to offer Brian Epstein $150,000 to put on an additional performance in Kansas City. As the boys did a stock twelve-number set— with the odd permutation—it worked out at around $5,000 per minute. Initially even that astronomical sum wasn't going to tempt the Beatles to give up one of their precious free days in a demanding four-week schedule, though in the end Epstein relented and the boys shrugged their shoulders and did the extra gig. They even added "Kansas City" to the set, a Little Richard number that would feature on their next album, *Beatles for Sale*.

In that month the Beatles did roughly the equivalent of circumnavigating the globe twice. A chartered plane was not so much a luxury as a necessity. Often they would go straight to the airport from a concert to avoid the worst excesses of the fans' behaviour. There was a fine dividing line between adulation and intimidation, one that was crossed on numerous occasions.

Being cooped up in a plane was much the same as being incarcerated in a hotel. They were rich but couldn't go shopping, so they made their own entertainment. Poker and Monopoly games ran ad nauseam, while pillow and food fights let off steam and relieved the boredom.

BELOW: **Fans wave goodbye in London, but in America every city on the tour laid on an hysterial welcome for the British imports, even when the Beatles arrived in the middle of the night. When the Beatles landed in San Francisco for the first date of the tour, an estimated 9,000 people turned out to greet them.**

RIGHT: **The Beatles were no longer playing the small venues they were used to in the UK; they had traded theatres for sports stadiums. By the time the boys left the country a month later, they had played in front of more than 100,000 people.**

OPPOSITE INSET: **"I'll Cry Instead" and "I'm Happy Just to Dance With You" were both featured on *A Hard Day's Night* but were released as a single by Capitol on 20 August. "Matchbox", a cover of a 1950s Carl Perkins song, was released with "Slow Down" by Capitol on 24 August 1964.**

AUGUST 1964

1 The single "A Hard Day's Night" was at the top of the US charts, and would remain there for two weeks. It was at this point that the band topped the US and UK album and singles charts simultaneously.

2 The next Sunday summer show was at the Gaumont Cinema in Bournemouth. On this occasion the Kinks were on the bill with the Beatles and described as a "new" band.

3 George Martin released *Off the Beatle Track*, an instrumental interpretation of their songs. *Follow the Beatles* was broadcast on BBC1 along with *From Us to You* on the radio.

7 In America, *Time* magazine described the movie *A Hard Day's Night* as "rubbish to be avoided at all costs".

9 This time the summer show was at the Futurist Theatre in Scarborough.

11 Back to Abbey Road to begin recording the next album, which was to eventually be called *Beatles for Sale*. At this session John's "Baby's in Black" was taped.

12 The movie *A Hard Day's Night* was released in the US. On the first night the takings were $75,000. Brian Epstein had a party at his house in William Mews, London; guests included Judy Garland and Mick Jagger as well as the Beatles. During the evening Chris Hutchins

A Hard Day's Month

The most arduous, intensive and improbable adventure this side of science fiction is launched in a four-engined Lockheed Electra early next week in San Francisco. The meticulous timing and security of a manned space-shot could scarcely compare with the tremulous countdown here which culminates when the Beatles, with their Cokes, ciggies and cornflakes, stagger off the ground for the great American tour.

The bald object is to bring Beatlemania to every corner of the United States. Even toughened impresarios at the mighty General Artists Corporation, agents for the tour, trembled at the immensity of the undertaking.

The tour starts in San Franscisco on 19 August and ends in New York on 20 September, taking in 24 cities. That in anybody's rite adds up to a hard day's month. The route involves shunting back and forth across America with the monotony of the Mersey Ferry. In 25 working days, the Beatles make 26 separate appearances in 18 American states and two separate trips to Canada. That means Paul, Ringo, George and John will jog through the North American continent at an average of 650 miles a working day. The strain of travelling by air alone will be considerable. Add the tension of performing before fervid fans, dodging them at airports and hotels–and you begin to get the picture.

Painstaking arrangements have been made to keep the foursome comfortable on the flights. Massive supplies of Coke and cornflakes–their staple diet–are being stowed aboard the Electra. A partition can be dropped if they want to sleep on special couches.

The Beatles will not be separated from the rest of the show. About 20 artists will travel in the Lockheed. Looking after the mammoth problem of the charter flight and the limousine convoys and the hotel bookings is Miss Cappy Ditson of Red Carpet Travel Service.

She told me: "We have moved Broadway shows to the West Coast: casts, scenery, families, kids, dogs, cats and all–but we've never handled anything like this. It's the most stimulating task I've ever tackled. We've had some difficulty persuading caterers from coast to coast that we must have fresh supplies of cornflakes or the tour will collapse. It is amazing how many hotels have refused the Beatles–not because they don't want them but they didn't have the machinery to cope with the necessary security."

The plane is chartered from American Fliers, who have promised to provide their "three prettiest stewardesses". There is no shortage of volunteers.

To avoid violent fans, helicopters will be used in towns that have them at the airports, and standby coaches to sell the dummy on short runs.

EXTRACTED FROM THE
DAILY MAIL, 18 AUGUST 1964

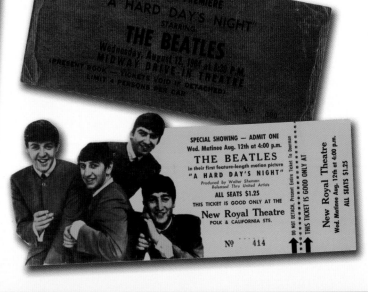

LEFT: **The moptopped official tour map of the United States and Canada. The tour started in San Francisco on the West Coast on 19 August, then crisscrossed the continent before ending at the Paramount Theater in New York on 20 September.**

BELOW: **With Beatlemania preceding the band wherever they went, the Beatles' freedom was severely curtailed. They were confined to hotel rooms for much of their time.**

BELOW INSET: **Ticket stubs for the concert at the Convention Hall in Atlantic City, New Jersey, and for the penultimate show of the tour at the Memorial Coliseum in Dallas on 18 September. The show followed a performance in Kansas City, Missouri, where the boys had added the Little Richard cover "Kansas City" to the set. The song went down so well with the audience that the Beatles had to leave the stage temporarily while the crowd calmed down.**

OPPOSITE LEFT: **The Beatles onstage in Las Vegas on the second date of the tour.**

OPPOSITE RIGHT: **Tickets for local premieres of *A Hard Day's Night*, which took place in August.**

At the Hollywood Bowl

On 23 August they played LA's Hollywood Bowl, a show that was earmarked for a live recording. Live albums were then a relative rarity, but the virtuosity and electric atmosphere of a Beatles performance persuaded Capitol to think it would do good business. A union dispute had stymied plans to record the Carnegie Hall show in February; now George Martin was ready with all his electronic paraphernalia. But even he couldn't figure a way to block out the screams of the 18,000 fans in the arena and probably as many again outside. The VU metres went haywire; it was "like putting a microphone at the tail of a 747", as the producer himself put it. It was no better for the boys, who couldn't hear their output. It was especially difficult for Ringo, who said: "I used to have to follow their three bums to see where we were in the song."

The idea for a live album was shelved, though the tapes were dusted off thirteen years later. Even an imperfect Beatles recording was a jewel, particularly after they had disbanded. Martin and Geoff Emerick worked their magic, skilfully stitching together half of that LA concert with its counterpart on the 1965 summer tour. The result was *The Beatles at the Hollywood Bowl*, which gave the group yet another number one album.

The tour witnessed the usual hairy moments caused by the fans' overexuberance, notably in Cleveland, where a crash barrier broke and the police stopped the show on safety grounds. The boys were virtually frog-marched off the stage until order was restored.

A more incendiary situation arose when the Beatles hurtled headlong into the civil rights issue. President Lyndon Johnson had just steered through Congress the bill championed by John F. Kennedy that outlawed discrimination. But segregation was still a way of life in some parts of the country, though not one that met with the Beatles' approval, and more to the point, not one they would countenance at one of their concerts. Epstein was vehemently against the boys entering into any political debate, but before playing Jacksonville's Gator Bowl they demanded assurances that the audience would not be segregated.

OPPOSITE: **After performing in San Francisco, the boys headed immediately for Las Vegas and arrived in the middle of the night. After some sleep, they performed two shows at the Convention Center.**

OPPOSITE INSET: **A ticket stub for the Beatles' first-ever concert in Canada at the Empire Stadium in Vancouver (bottom). The boys didn't stay in Canada long, making straight for Los Angeles in the middle of the night to prepare for their show at the Hollywood Bowl the next day (top).**

BELOW: **The Beatles onstage again as the US tour carried on relentlessly. The boys had just seven days off during the monthlong trip.**

continued from page 161

AUGUST 1964

interviewed Ringo for *The Teen Scene*, broadcast the next evening. This time the theme was the North American tour, due to take place later in the month.

13 *The Teen Scene* was transmitted.

14 Further recording at Abbey Road for the new album. This session taped "I'm a Loser", "Mr. Moonlight", and "Leave My Kitten Alone"; the latter was never actually used.

16 At the Sunday summer concert at the Opera House in Blackpool, one of the support bands, the High Numbers, was soon to change its name to the Who.

18 The band left London to fly to the US. They were greeted at San Francisco Airport by 9,000 fans.

19 The Beatles' North American tour began with a show at Cow Palace in San Francisco with just over 17,000 watching. Support acts included the Righteous Brothers. They then immediately flew to Las Vegas.

20 Arriving in Las Vegas in the early hours, they went on to play two houses at the Convention Center.

21 Then on to Washington to play to the Coliseum in Seattle.

22 At their first show in Canada, they performed at the Empire Stadium in Vancouver, watched by over 20,000, while the show was also broadcast live on CKNW, the local radio station. They then immediately flew back to Los Angeles.

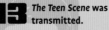

Hollywood cordoned off for the Beatles

Beatles Provoke Hysteria

In a fantastic security operation two square miles around the 23,000-seat Hollywood Bowl have been cordoned off for tonight's Beatles show. Special parking permits have been issued so that residents can have access to their homes. At the Hollywood Bowl management said: "We are taking no chances. It is inconvenient for the residents, but it's safer than if their grounds and gardens were invaded by hordes of fans trying to gain access to the Bowl." Earlier in Vancouver, Canada, a human battering ram of 1,000 teenagers shattered a 20 ft. gateway at a stadium where the group was performing at that weekend. Police threatened to cut off electricity if gathering hysteria among the 20,000-strong audience was not abated. After that show, hundreds of sobbing swooning girls—many of them wandering helplessly or lying rigid as if pole-axed—littered the area near the Beatles' changing caravan behind the stage.

Several American psychologists and social workers have pleaded for the tour to be cut because of the level of hysteria during the performances. The supervisor of Washington State's child guidance centre today urged that no more performances be allowed and blasted parents for "allowing children a mad, erotic world of their own". Already there has been a suggestion that drummer Ringo Starr's singing solo be dropped because of its fantastic effect on girls.

It was Ringo's drums which nearly prevented the group from landing at Vancouver. As the Beatles' special plane neared Canadian air space, they were told "You may not land as the musical instruments on the plane have not been Customs cleared." One stamp promising that Ringo's drums and the group's guitars would not be sold in Canada was missing. The aircraft returned to Seattle for the stamp. Ringo said later: "It's a long way to come to sell me drums."

EXTRACTED FROM THE
DAILY MAIL, 23 AUGUST 1964

23 The boys arrived just before 4 a.m. Later that day the concert held at the Hollywood Bowl was recorded by Capitol Records, who were planning an album for the American market. However, it was not actually used due to poor sound quality, although three songs were eventually used for a live album produced 13 years later.

24 "Matchbox"/"Slow Down" was released in the US on Capitol 5255. The boys had two days of rest in Bel Air, although they did attend a private party in aid of charity in the afternoon. In the States the album *Something New* was given a gold disc.

25 The evening was spent at the nightclub Whiskey A Go-Go on Sunset Boulevard. The single "A Hard Day's Night" was certified gold in the States.

26 A performance at the Red Rocks Amphitheatre in Denver, Colorado.

27 On to Cincinnati, where they played the Cincinnati Gardens before 14,000 fans, then straight onto a plane bound for New York.

28 At the New York airport, 2,000 fans greeted them despite it being 3 a.m. when they landed. The first of two nights at the Forest Hills Tennis Stadium in New York. The band first sampled marijuana, supplied by Bob Dylan.

29 At each show they performed in front of 16,000 people.

30 In Atlantic City, New Jersey, the venue was the Convention Hall, packed with 18,000 fans.

31 Paul spoke to Elvis Presley on the telephone.

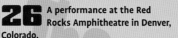

An introduction to Bob Dylan

The final leg of the tour took them back to New York, where the Plaza Hotel politely declined to accommodate the group, obviously feeling that the headaches outweighed the benefits. Instead the entourage put up at the Delmonico Hotel, Ed Sullivan's year-round residence. The Beatles headlined at a glitzy $100-a-ticket charity affair at Paramount Theater, their last public performance of the tour.

It was in New York that they also played host to a visit from Bob Dylan. Elvis might have made them rock 'n' rollers, but they would develop a special reverence for Dylan. *Freewheelin'*, had been played on a loop in Paris, the boys blown away by songs such as "Don't Think Twice, It's All Right" and "A Hard Rain's Gonna Fall" as well as the anthemic "Blowin' in the Wind". Born in 1941, between John and Paul, Dylan was producing songs that stood up as poetry, in a different league from the sad-glad boy-girl spectrum. Dylan thought there were layers of meaning in John and Paul's music, too. He famously misinterpreted the chorus of "I Want to Hold Your Hand", thinking they were singing "I get high". John was forced to reveal the actual words, which had nothing to do with drugs. The four were habitual pill poppers but had never smoked marijuana. They accepted Dylan's offer of an immediate induction course, though John briefly deferred to Ringo, whom he dubbed his "official taster". Dylan's exhortation for them to "Listen to the words, man", played a major part in turning John and Paul from writers of great tunes to writers of great songs.

TOP: **The Beatles were in demand across the country; everywhere they went, local journalists and broadcasters wished to meet them. Often they gave large press conferences to save time.**

ABOVE: **Fans surge forward to try to touch the Beatles when they arrive in Dallas.**

Battle of the Ball Park

Thousands of Beatlemaniacs fought the police in a brutal "Battle of the Ball Park"—by far the worst of this terrible tour. Kicking, biting, clawing, screaming, and sobbing, these fans invaded the field at the football stadium and played a grotesque game of "catch-as-catch-can" with panting, swearing policemen under the floodlights in an attempt to reach their idols.

The police kept the fans in the stands but this posed a challenge to win the game of "get at a Beatle". Slowly at first, in ones and twos, fans began to leap the crush barrier in the front of the stands. As police were drawn from their positions to stop the few, more and more poured through the gaps. A 40-minute running battle commenced. I saw helmeted mounted policemen carry out cavalry charges in attempts to rout the teenagers.

I saw girls brought to the ground by policemen, but struggle to their feet again and continue to dart and weave towards their goal.

When police reinforcements arrived they lassoed and bound together with hundreds of feet of rope a tearful, howling group of 200 fans whom they had cornered on the pitch. And it was all happening in a temperature of 90 degrees and a sticky 79 percent humidity.

Between numbers John Lennon asked regularly: "Who's winning now?" Announcing "She Loves You" he said "We would like you to join in—those of you that are still alive".

By this time the ground was littered with police hats and lost truncheons, the shoes of fleeting fans—and bodies.

ACCOUNT OF THE NEW ORLEANS CONCERT
EXTRACTED FROM THE
DAILY MAIL, 23 AUGUST 1964

ABOVE: **Desperate fans lined the route everywhere the Beatles went, and many camped outside their hotel. Hosting the boys became a nightmare for the local authorities, who had to guarantee the safety not just of the band but of the fans as well.**

BELOW: **The Beatles in performance in front of 8,000 people at the Las Vegas Convention Center. They had been brought to the city by Stan Irwin and the Hotel Sahara. After the show in Vegas, the boys made for the Pacific Northwest, giving a show at the Coliseum in Seattle in front of an audience of 5,000.**

RIGHT: **The Beatles in their dressing room at the Paramount Theater in New York ahead of their final concert of the US tour. The show, called An Evening with the Beatles, was unlike any other on the trip because it was much smaller in scale and was in aid of United Cerebral Palsy and Retarded Infant Services. Newpapers reported on the tour's finale (opposite inset).**

OPPOSITE: **New York City police officers do their best to hold back a crowd of frenzied Beatles fans hoping to catch a glimpse of their heartthrobs outside the Delmonico Hotel.**

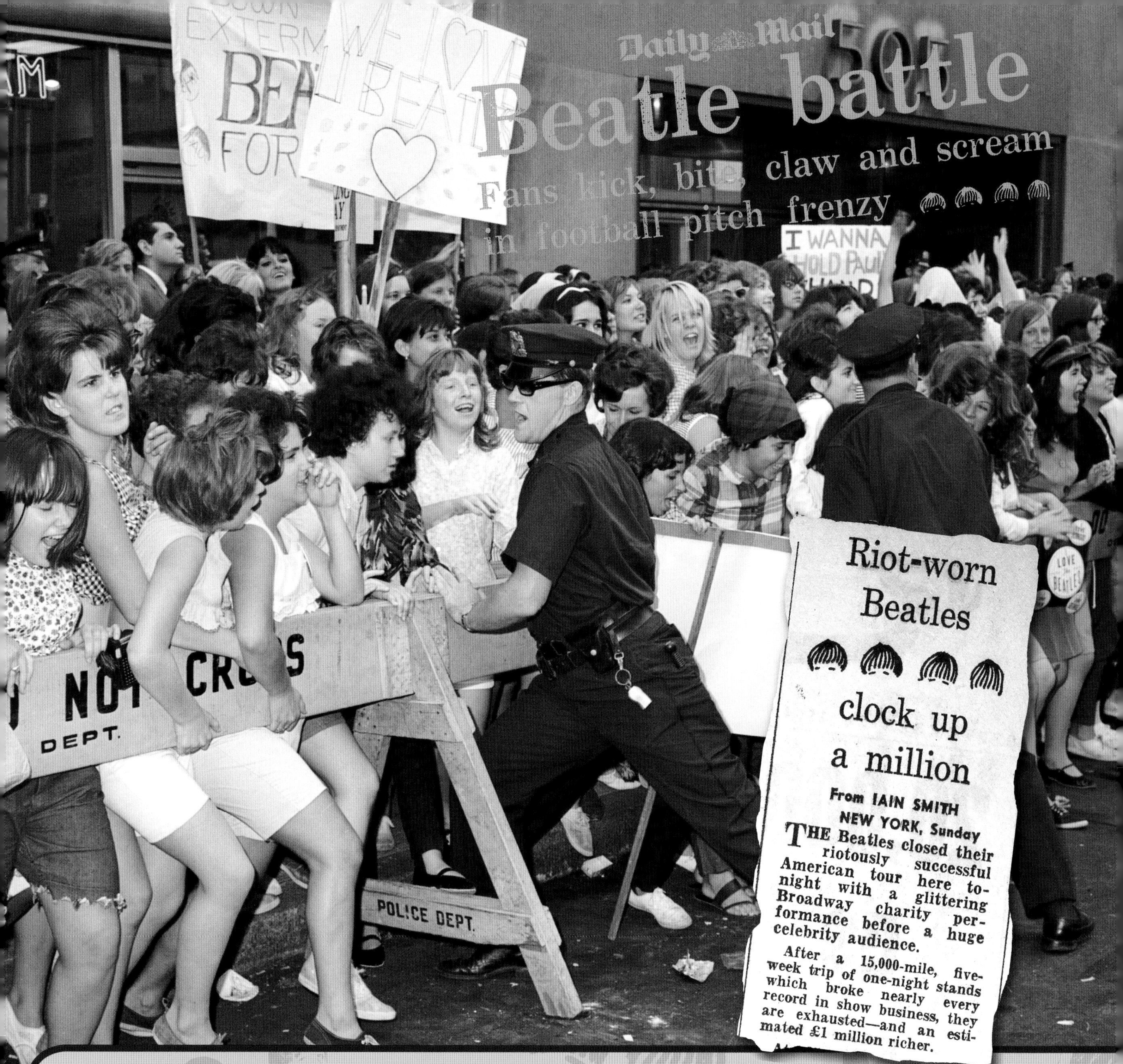

Daily Mail

Beatle battle

Fans kick, bite, claw and scream
in football pitch frenzy

DOWN
EXTERM...
BEA...
FOR

WE LOVE BEAT...

I WANNA HOLD PAUL HAND

NOT CROSS
DEPT.

POLICE DEPT.

Riot-worn Beatles

clock up a million

From IAIN SMITH
NEW YORK, Sunday

THE Beatles closed their riotously successful American tour here tonight with a glittering Broadway charity performance before a huge celebrity audience.

After a 15,000-mile, five-week trip of one-night stands which broke nearly every record in show business, they are exhausted—and an estimated £1 million richer.

SEPTEMBER 1964

1 In the States, the first edition of *The Beatles' Monthly Book* was published.

2 A performance at the Convention Hall, this time in Philadelphia. A live broadcast was transmitted on local radio.

3 In Indianapolis, two houses were held at the Indiana State Fair Coliseum.

4 Then one performance at the Milwaukee Arena in Wisconsin. In Indonesia, the government banned Beatles-type haircuts.

5 Next to the International Amphitheater in Chicago.

6 Two Sunday evening performances at the Olympia Stadium in Detroit.

7 Back into Canada to play two houses at the Maple Leaf Gardens in Toronto.

8 The Forum in Montreal was the venue for two houses; a total of 21,000 people saw the shows. They were then due to fly straight on to Jacksonville, Florida, but were diverted owing to Hurricane Dora, ultimately landing in Key West.

A hard night's wait

BELOW: **The tour was undoubtedly a success, but the Beatles had faced a few problems—chiefly at the show in Jacksonville, Florida, which was given in the wake of Hurricane Dora. After leaving Montreal on 8 September, the Beatles were diverted to Key West, where they remained until the storm had passed. It was decided that the show should go ahead and the boys headed for the city. President Johnson had been touring the disaster zone and the Beatles' plane had to circle the airport until Air Force One had taken off. The devastation meant that many of the ticketholders were unable to get to the stadium, and about 9,000 people, a quarter of the audience, ended up missing out.**

OPPOSITE: **John, Cynthia, and a young Julian send up the suburban stereotype that they had bought into by purchasing a new mansion in the heart of the stockbroker belt in Surrey, England. Their home might have been about as far from rock 'n' roll as you could get, but their lifestyle was not one of perfect domestic bliss.**

LEFT: **The *Daily Mail* of 22 September captures the scene at London Airport where fans spent the night waiting for the boys to return.**

BELOW INSET: **After 32 concerts in 24 cities over just 32 days, the Beatles finally waved goodbye to their American fans, while their British fans gathered at London Airport to welcome them back.**

continued from previous page

SEPTEMBER 1964

11 The band finally reached Jacksonville where they played the Gator Bowl. It was a unique evening: More than a quarter of the spectators didn't make it owing to the hurricane, and the band refused to play until they received guarantees that fans would not be segregated by colour.

12 A Saturday night house at the Boston Garden in Boston, Massachusetts.

13 Two houses at the Civic Center in Baltimore, Maryland.

14 Next to Pittsburgh, Pennsylvania.

15 At the Public Auditorium in Cleveland the show stopped temporarily when fans gained access to the stage.

16 Next to New Orleans to play at the City Park Stadium.

17 For the bonus of being paid $150,000 (about $5,000 a minute), they added an extra show to the schedule at the Municipal Stadium in Kansas City, Missouri. Again, the concert had to stop temporarily while order was restored.

18 A Friday night house at the Dallas Memorial Auditorium.

19 A rest day at a ranch in the Ozark Hills in Missouri. It was Brian Epstein's 30th birthday.

20 The final tour date was the Paramount Theater in New York City, a charity performance for United Cerebral Palsy of New York City and Retarded Infant Services entitled An Evening with the Beatles. They were visited backstage by Bob Dylan.

21 The boys flew back to London.

24 Ringo created the "Brickey Building Company"—a building and decorating firm.

25 Brian Epstein was offered $3.5 million from an American for his managerial position with the band. He refused.

27 Ringo took part in the final of the National Beat Group Competition at the Prince of Wales Theatre, London. He was on the jury for the competition, which was screened live on BBC2 in the program called *It's Beat Time*.

29 Back in the studio they began to complete the recordings for the next album. "Every Little Thing," "I Don't Want to Spoil the Party", and "What You're Doing" were taped.

30 Continuing on the album, more takes of "Every Little Thing" were recorded, along with "What You're Doing" and "No Reply".

Starting work on *Beatles for Sale*

A mere nineteen days after the end of the US tour, the Beatles were on the road again, this time another whistle-stop dash round the provinces of Britain. The cinemas and theatres were tiny in comparison with the huge sporting arenas they had played in the States, with much-reduced fees to match. It might have seemed like a comedown, but if Epstein agreed to terms for his boys to appear, the deal was always honoured.

And then there was the small matter of a new album and single, both of which had to be in the stores by Christmas. Even John and Paul were being stretched to the limit, but they still came up with eight new songs to savour. If they hadn't been working "eight days a week"—a line from Paul's overstretched chauffeur that provided the inspiration for one of the new numbers— then there would have been no need to include any covers.

OCTOBER 1964

2 At the Granville Studio in Fulham Broadway, London, the band began rehearsals for the American show *Shindig*, broadcast by ABC. Jack Good produced the programme and was making an all-British edition that included Sandie Shaw and Tommy Quickly.

3 The Beatles returned to the Granville Studio for the recording of the show. They were taped performing live in front of fans invited from the Beatles Fan Club.

4 Brian Epstein's biography *A Cellarful of Noise* was published in the UK by Souvenir Press. The ghostwriter was Derek Taylor.

6 Back at Abbey Road, "Eight Days a Week" was recorded.

7 The all-British edition of *Shindig* was broadcast in America.

8 Ringo Starr passed his driving test on the third attempt. Paul's song "She's a Woman" was recorded at Abbey Road.

On one day alone, 18 October, the group took advantage of a window in their touring schedule to record seven songs. Six were for the album, the other was "I Feel Fine", which John wrote around a riff he was dabbling with during an Abbey Road session. He and Paul often took a particular song or sound and used it as a springboard. On this occasion, John's source was Bobby Parker's 1961 R&B classic "Watch Your Step", whose influence would also be heard in the catchy riffs that underpinned "Ticket to Ride" and "Day Tripper".

The feedback that gives the song its distinctive intro was the result of serendipity. While George Martin was discussing the effect of placing a guitar too close to an amplifier, the Beatles were more concerned with the possibility of incorporating a new sound into their music. It was another recording milestone. From then on, nothing was labelled extraneous noise or sonic gremlin; if they liked the sound, it was in.

OPPOSITE LEFT: **Kenwood, the mansion that John had purchased as a family home near Weybridge in the affluent, leafy suburbs of Surrey. In late 1964, Cynthia and Julian were the principal residents because John spent much of his time on tour.**

OPPOSITE: **John poses for a photo shoot in his garden at Kenwood wearing a hat of dead ferns.**

ABOVE RIGHT: **The Beatles onstage in Dundee, Scotland, during the Scottish leg of their UK tour and (below) a ticket stub from the concert.**

BELOW RIGHT: **Brian Epstein's autobiography, *A Cellarful of Noise*. John had quipped that it should have been titled "*A Cellarful of Boys*", on account of Epstein's homosexuality, a remark that is said to have deeply wounded Epstein.**

BELOW FAR RIGHT: **The *Daily Mail* reports on Mary Wells, who supported the Beatles on their UK tour.**

9 The band began its British tour at the Gaumont Cinema in Bradford. John was 24. They were to play two houses at each venue and were supported by Mary Wells.

10 A Saturday night at the De Montfort Hall, Leicester.

11 Then on to the Odeon Cinema in Birmingham.

12 In the press, reports came out that the Duke of Edinburgh had claimed that the band were "on the wane". During a one-day break from the tour George Martin and Norman Smith made mono and stereo mixes of "She's a Woman" and "Eight Days a Week".

13 The Duke of Edinburgh sent a telegram to Brian Epstein stating that he actually said that the band was "away at the moment". At Wigan they played at the ABC Cinema.

14 In the afternoon they made a recording for *Scene at 6.30* at the Granada TV Centre in Manchester before playing at the ABC Cinema in the city. During the evening they were interviewed by David Tindall for BBC1's programme *Look North*.

15 The tour date at the Globe Cinema in Stockton-on-Tees coincided with the general election when Harold Wilson was voted into office.

16 A Friday night performance at the ABC Cinema in Hull.

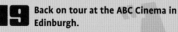

continued from previous page

OCTOBER 1964

17 The first of two rest days from the tour. Despite this the band were at Abbey Road for nine hours completing some album tracks and the A-side of their next single, "I Feel Fine".

18 Further recording at Abbey Road for the next album.

19 Back on tour at the ABC Cinema in Edinburgh.

20 Another Scottish date, this time at the Caird Hall in Dundee. Beforehand Grampian TV had interviewed the band in their dressing room for the programme *Grampian Week*, broadcast the following Friday.

21 The last show north of the border at the Odeon Cinema in Glasgow. Afterwards nine fans were arrested after they rioted, causing severe damage to cars and windows. Back at Abbey Road George Martin was preparing some final mono masters to send to Capitol Records in the States.

22 Back in England to play at the Odeon Cinema in Leeds. George Martin continued with mono mixes at Abbey Road.

THIS PAGE: **The Beatles take a break during their autumn tour of the UK. The tour included 27 venues, beginning in Bournemouth on 9 October and ending in Bristol on 10 November, taking in Ipswich, Kilburn, and a second performance at Bournemouth on 30 October (inset below).**

INSET LEFT: **The Daily Mail of 7 November reports huge advance orders for "I Feel Fine".**

OPPOSITE: **The Beatles and Brian Epstein have come far from their Liverpool roots. The band is pictured taking tea with the Countess of Strathmore and Brian Epstein is shown with his new Bentley (inset).**

Orders for latest Beatles discs top million

By Daily Mail Reporter

ADVANCE orders for I Feel Fine, the new single disc by the Beatles, have already topped the half-million mark.

This means the Beatles have won a Silver Disc three weeks before the record's release on November 27.

The group's next LP, Beatles For Sale, has an advance order of 550,000 copies — a month before its official appearance in the shops on December 4.

Both titles were announced only a week ago.

The sales of the LP With the Beatles have now exceeded 970,000 copies in Britain alone. It may become the first British LP to top the million mark here.

GAUMONT THEATRE
IPSWICH

ARTHUR HOWES & BRIAN EPSTEIN present
THE BEATLES
2nd Performance 8-45 p.m.
SATURDAY
OCTOBER **31**
CIRCLE 15/-
B19
No ticket exchanged nor money refunded
THIS PORTION TO BE RETAINED

Gaumont STATE Kilburn
N.W.6.
ARTHUR HOWES & BRIAN EPSTEIN present
THE BEATLES
2nd Performance 9-0 p.m.
FRIDAY
OCTOBER **23**
CIRCLE 5/-
W60
No ticket exchanged nor money refunded
THIS PORTION TO BE RETAINED

Gaumont Theatre
BOURNEMOUTH
2nd Part. 8-30
FRIDAY
OCTOBER **30**
STALLS
17/6
A25
TO BE GIVEN UP

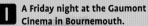

GAUMONT THEATRE
BOURNEMOUTH
Arthur Howes & Brian Epstein present
THE BEATLES SHOW
2nd Performance 8-30 p.m.
FRIDAY
OCTOBER **30**
STALLS 17/6
A25
No ticket exchanged nor money refunded
THIS PORTION TO BE RETAINED

23 Moving south they played at the Gaumont State Cinema in Kilburn, London. The band appeared on the local television programme, Grampian Week.

24 Still in the capital, they performed at the Granada Cinema in Walthamstow.

25 The band won five UK Ivor Novello Awards including Most Outstanding Contribution to Music. Down to the coast to play at the Hippodrome Theatre in Brighton.

26 The band then had two rest days. Again, despite this break from the tour they could be found at Abbey Road producing more mono mixes. The session included the recordings of "Honey Don't" and "What You're Doing." They were also able to complete the work necessary for Another Beatles Christmas Record that was to go out to the Official Fan Club members.

27 More mixing and editing at Abbey Road.

28 The tour resumed at the ABC Cinema in Exeter.

29 It continued in the West Country at the ABC Cinema in Plymouth.

30 A Friday night at the Gaumont Cinema in Bournemouth.

31 Then Saturday night at the Gaumont Cinema in Ipswich.

The best of friends

By ROSALIE MACRAE

THE world can relax. The Beatles are still good friends, and this is official.

So said their guide and mentor, Mr. Brian Epstein, last night after nasty rumours had come from across the Atlantic that there was trouble in the charmed little circle.

"Nonsense, nonsense, nonsense," said Mr. Epstein. "People keep saying these things, ridiculous things," and he sighed deeply—the sigh of a truly injured man.

The rumours came from the American magazine *Newsweek*, which said yesterday that all was not harmonious within the Beatle camp.

Tours

The article says: "The singers admit to friends that they are tired of one-night stands, world tours and each other. They have already agreed that if one quits, the group will disband.

The best gu...

ABOVE: **John filming a cameo for Dudley Moore's new television series, *Not Only...But Also* in the early morning on Wimbledon Common on 20 November. The scene was to accompany the reading of a section of *In His Own Write* on the show.**

ABOVE INSET: **Ringo looking every inch the English country gentleman on 1 December.**

LEFT: **An edition of *The True Story of the Beatles*, written by one of the staff writers of Beat Books, Sean O'Mahoney's publishing company responsible for the long-running monthly fanzine, *The Beatles Book*.**

OPPOSITE: **While the band continued to tour the UK despite rumours of discontent among the band members (above inset), George Martin remained at Abbey Road producing the all-important music.**

NOVEMBER 1964

1 Back to the capital to play at the Astoria Cinema in Finsbury Park.

2 A show at the King's Hall in Belfast, and a return to London the next day.

4 More mixing and editing at Abbey Road. In Luton that evening they played at the Ritz Cinema.

5 On to Nottingham to the Odeon Cinema.

6 The EP *Extracts from the Film A Hard Day's Night* was released in Britain on Parlophone GEP 8920 (mono only). The A-side featured "I Should Have Known Better" and "If I Fell" while the B-side contained "Tell Me Why" and "And I Love Her". Also released on the same day was the EP *Extracts from the Album A Hard Day's Night* on Parlophone GEP 8924 (mono only) featuring "Any Time at All" and "I'll Cry Instead" on the A-side and "Things We Said Today" and "When I Get Home" on the B-side. Back south to the Gaumont Cinema in Southampton. In the dressing room Tony Bilbow interviewed them for Southern Television's *Day by Day*.

7 In Wales for a show at the Capitol Cinema, Cardiff.

8 The Empire Theatre in Liverpool—their first concert there in nearly a year.

9 Sheffield at the City Hall.

10 Finally the last date of the tour at the Colston Hall, Bristol.

13 A documentary about the US tour was broadcast by CBS-TV.

BIO: GEORGE MARTIN

A keen musician from an early age, George Martin studied composition at London's Guildhall School of Music before finding work as a producer with EMI, where he became head of Parlophone in 1955.

Although his foundation was in classical music, Martin also had a keen ear for jazz and pop: Having auditioned the Beatles in 1962, he contracted them to the label, beginning a working relationship as their producer that would contribute significantly to their sound and musical direction. He scored instrumental arrangements for them, and translated their ideas into sound as the group began to experiment with psychedleia.

Martin also released orchestrated albums of the Beatles' music and worked on the scores for their films, including *A Hard Day's Night*, *Help!*, and *Yellow Submarine*, and although he retired as head of Parlophone in 1965, he continued to work with the group on their recordings—with the exception of the proposed *Let It Be* album.

In addition to working with the Beatles, Martin signed and produced many other artists, including several that were discovered by Brian Epstein, and after leaving EMI he went on to found his own production company, AIR (Associated Independent Recording), continuing his highly successful career long after the Beatles split in 1970.

In 1996 he received a knighthood, becoming Sir George Martin, and was inducted into the Rock and Roll Hall of Fame three years later. In 2006, Sir George was inducted into the UK Music Hall of Fame, and today is widely regarded as one of the most influential and successful record producers of all time.

ON MEETING THE BEATLES

"It was love at first sight. That may seem exaggerated but the fact is we hit it off straight away...the most impressive thing was their engaging personalities."

—George Martin

14 At the Teddington Studios the recording was completed for the following week's edition of *Thank Your Lucky Stars*.

16 The songs "I Feel Fine" and "She's a Woman" were recorded at the Riverside Studios for an edition of *Top of the Pops*.

17 At the Playhouse Theatre, London, a session was recorded for *Top Gear*. Six songs and an interview were included.

20 John was filmed on Wimbledon Common with Dudley Moore and Norman Rossington for the first edition of *Not Only...But Also*.

21 An appearance on *Lucky Stars*, broadcast by ABC.

23 "I Feel Fine"/"She's a Woman" was released in the US on Capitol 5327. The LP *The Beatles' Story* was also released in the US on Capitol TBO-2222 (mono) and STBO-2222 (stereo). The boys recorded a session for *Ready, Steady, Go!* at the Wembley Studios.

24 Paul attended his father's second marriage, to Angela Williams.

25 At the Aeolian Hall the last session for *Saturday Club* was taped, the programme due to be broadcast on Boxing Day. Although six songs were featured on this edition, four were used from the recording session on 17 November.

26 *Top Gear* was broadcast.

27 "I Feel Fine"/"She's a Woman" was released in the UK on Parlophone R 5200. The appearance on *Ready, Steady, Go!* was broadcast.

28 Chris Hutchins interviewed John for *The Teen Scene* and a feature on his house, included in the *New Musical Express* edition published on 4 December.

29 John finished filming the piece for *Not Only...But Also*. At TV Centre he read pieces from his book *In His Own Write*, along with Dudley Moore and Norman Rossington. *The Teen Scene* was transmitted.

BeaTLes For SaLe

Released
🇬🇧 **4 December 1964** (Parlophone)

Side One:
No Reply
I'm a Loser
Baby's in Black
Rock and Roll Music (Berry)
I'll Follow the Sun
Mr. Moonlight (Johnson)
Medley:
Kansas City (Leiber–Stoller)
Hey, Hey, Hey, Hey (Little Richard)

Side Two:
Eight Days a Week
Words of Love (Holly)
Honey Don't (Perkins)
Every Little Thing
I Don't Want to Spoil the Party
What You're Doing
Everybody's Trying to Be My Baby
(Perkins)

cover story

In the autumn of 1964, Robert Freeman was again chosen to provide the sleeve photography for the Beatles' next album, *Beatles for Sale*. It would be amongst the first albums with a gatefold sleeve, which provided the opportunity to use images on the interior folds as well as on the front and back.

For the cover shots Freeman and the Beatles decided upon an outdoor shoot, rather than work in the studio. The chosen location was London's Hyde Park, and so on a chilly autumn evening with the light fading, Freeman and the group briefly assembled in the park for the session.

The resulting pictures show the somewhat tired-looking Beatles against the rich colours of autumn leaves, providing a slightly melancholic feel that seemed to complement the album's music. It also hinted at the Beatles' exhausting lifestyle, as did the two black-and-white interior shots, which showed the Beatles at Twickenham Film Studios and performing at the Washington Coliseum earlier in the year.

OPPOSITE AND BELOW: **The Beatles during rehearsals for** *Another Beatles Christmas Show* **at the Hammersmith Odeon. Rehearsals began on 21 November, but the show didn't start until Christmas Eve. Over the festive period, the boys gave a total of 38 concerts before ending the show on 16 January 1965. The proceeds from the show on 29 December were given to charity (opposite inset).**

BOTTOM: **A review of** *Beatles for Sale* **from the** *Daily Mail* **from 7 December 1964.**

Beatles for Sale

Not (dare I say it) as good as the last three, though the first side has some great Lennon-McCartney compositions, including the slow and haunting *Baby's in Black*.

Worth buying, not only because it's *them*, but because Robert Freeman has taken two of the most stunning colour photographs of the Beatles for the cover. (Parlophone.)

DECEMBER 1964

1 Ringo held a press conference about his imminent tonsillectomy.

2 Ringo was admitted to hospital to have his tonsils removed. On the BBC Radio News that morning it was announced that the operation had been successful.

3 *Top of the Pops* was broadcast with the boys playing "I Feel Fine".

4 The LP *Beatles for Sale* was released in the UK on Parlophone PMC 1240 (mono) and PCS 3062 (stereo).

10 Ringo left hospital.

12 "I Feel Fine"/"She's a Woman" reached the top of the UK charts, remaining there for five weeks.

15 The LP *Beatles '65* was released in the US on Capitol T-2228 (mono) and Capitol ST-2228 (stereo).

18 *Another Beatles Christmas Record* (Fan Club Disc) was released.

19 *Beatles for Sale* reached the top of the UK charts, occupying the slot for seven weeks.

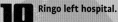

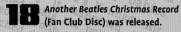

BEATLES '65

Released

🇺🇸 15 December 1964 (Capitol)

Side One:
No Reply
I'm a Loser
Baby's in Black
Rock and Roll Music (Berry)
I'll Follow the Sun
Mr. Moonlight (Johnson)

Side Two:
Honey Don't (Perkins)
I'll Be Back
She's a Woman
I Feel Fine
Everybody's Trying to Be My Baby
  (Perkins)

COVER STORY

Australian photographer Robert Whitaker took the photographs used on the sleeve of Capitol's *Beatles '65*.

The first side of the album mirrored Parlophone's *Beatles for Sale*, only omitting "Kansas City". Side two consists of two songs from *Beatles for Sale*, along with "I'll Be Back", from the British version of *Hard Day's Night*, and "I Feel Fine" and "She's a Woman".

Beatles charity show

The Beatles will give the money from their performance at the Odeon, Hammersmith, London, on December 29, to the Brady Clubs and Settlement, which cater for more than 1,000 children from London's East End.

---

21 Rehearsals began at the Odeon Cinema in Hammersmith for the forthcoming Christmas Show.

22 During rehearsals, the Beatles were briefly filmed in an interview with Jimmy Savile; he was due to appear in *Another Beatles Christmas Show*. This was ordered by *Top of the Pops* producer Johnnie Stewart to be included in the Christmas Eve edition.

24 *Another Beatles Christmas Show* began its first house at the Odeon Cinema in Hammersmith. As before, it included songs, interviews, and comedy. It ran until 16 January with a total of 38 houses. George met Eric Clapton for the first time, as the Yardbirds were on the bill. The boys appeared on *Top of the Pops '64*.

25 Christmas Day—a break!

26 A *Saturday Club* recording was transmitted. "I Feel Fine" reached the top of the US charts, remaining there for three weeks.

31 "I Feel Fine", *the Beatles' Story*, and *Beatles '65* were certified gold in the United States.

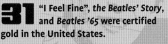

JOHN, PAUL, GEORGE & RINGO

OPPOSITE: **The Beatles appropriately kitted out for the Christmas show at the Hammersmith Odeon. As in 1963, the show comprised a mixture of sketches and music.**

LEFT AND BELOW RIGHT: **After tonsillitis forced him to miss part of the world tour earlier in the year, Ringo checked back into University College hospital in December to have his tonsils removed.**

BELOW LEFT: **George helps Ringo pass the time in hospital with a Chinese version of the game of Solitaire.**

BELOW: **A *Daily Mail* article from December reports that Beatlemania had pervaded every aspect of British life.**

BEATLE fans all over the country are stripping posters of their idols from the walls of school clinics and dentists' surgeries.

But the dentists don't mind, for the posters, which reappear on the fans' bedroom walls, carry an important message — that munching applies helps to fight tooth decay.

The Beatles are backing a General Dental Council campaign to encourage youngsters to eat apples after meals.

The posters showing Ringo, George, Paul and John munching are disappearing as fast as they are put up.

Mr. Oliver Lawson Dick, organiser of the campaign, said last night: " We started sending out these posters only a month ago. More than 100,000 have gone to youth clubs, schools, clinics, dentists and shops. Now the requests for more are flooding in."

1965

In My Life

In 1965 the Beatles both consolidated their position as the world's premier group and took the pop idiom to another level.

The peaks of the previous year were effortlessly scaled again: three more chart-topping singles and a brace of No. 1 albums, a second movie feature—this time a fantasy romp—and another sell-out American tour. As the venues got bigger, the group's musicianship and enthusiasm waned. They had left the "yeah, yeah, yeah" era behind, but the fans were struggling to keep up. Fifty-five thousand screamed Shea Stadium down, hardly the place for Paul to showcase "Yesterday". They were "bigger than Elvis", and even got to jam with the King. They met the Queen, too, as the British Establishment conferred its seal of approval on the Fabs. Musically, it was a transition period. *Rubber Soul* raised the bar and blew the opposition away, a signpost to the studio years that lay ahead. By the end of '65 Beatlemania wasn't over, but it was definitely on the slide. As far as the Fabs were concerned, the screaming couldn't stop quickly enough.

LEFT: **London Airport: in 1965 there were still thousands of screaming fans waiting to welcome the boys wherever they went.**

RIGHT: **Even when the Beatles cartoon was first aired by ABC in the autumn of 1965, the band had left the moptop image behind.**

Fame loses its sparkle

The cover photograph of *Beatles for Sale* told its own story. By the end of 1964 the boys were exhausted and jaded, beginning to recognize that achieving their goal of being "toppermost of the poppermost" had come at a cost. The quest for fame and recognition had lost its sparkle. They were being dragged from pillar to post at a dizzying speed, and resentment gradually built up, not least when they were tied to projects over which they had no control. The Christmas show of 1964–65 was just one example of the fans voting with their feet to pack out a flimsy theatrical production that found little favour with the critics. The follow-up movie to *A Hard Day's Night* would illustrate the same point. Not that the promoters were bothered; the Beatles sold, period.

The year 1965 offered more of the same, a treadmill that they were determined to get off. But first they were committed to another film, more touring, two more albums, and the usual quota of singles. The boys had already had enough of Beatlemania and during 1965 there were also signs of a decline on the part of the fans. One concert in Italy in June was just 20 percent full, though that was by no means the norm. America in particular couldn't wait for its next Fab Four fix. When the boys reconvened for the first of the new year's recording sessions on 15 February, "Eight Days a Week"—about which John was very disparaging even as an album filler—was on its way to the top of the *Billboard* chart.

If they had produced more of the same musically, the future could have looked bleak. Even Brian Epstein at the beginning of 1965 predicted that the Beatles would have only "two or three years more at the top". But the boys were itching to progress, and far from being worried that the screaming was subsiding or that there were fewer fans to wave them off at the airports, they were actually relieved. They could move on, and the fans were ready and waiting to hitch a ride. The critical acclaim for their core business—the music—would continue its upward curve, and 1965 would be a key transition year in which the Beatles would move effortlessly through the gears. The days of the cheeky Fabs were numbered, as were the guitar-drums, boy-girl, three-minute pop song. On its way was something far more sophisticated and substantial, both musically and lyrically.

ABOVE: **This seemingly candid image was in fact staged. John proved to be a natural skier, but hoped that this pose would be enough to get the media off his back for a while so he could enjoy the slopes in peace.**

RIGHT: **Taking a break from skiing, John tries tobogganing in St. Moritz.**

OPPOSITE: **After completing the Christmas show, John and Cynthia accompanied George Martin and his wife on a skiing trip to St. Moritz.**

OPPOSITE INSET: **The *Daily Mail* of 5 February reports on the Beatles' success in America. In 1965, an executive at EMI quipped that the Beatles had sold more records in two years than Bing Crosby had in 40 years.**

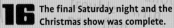

total four million.

THE BEATLES, with "I Want to Hold Your Hand" and "A Hard Day's Night," won two of seven 1964 Gold Record awards for selling a million copies made by the Record Industry Association of America. With "Meet The Beatles" they won 28 record album awards.

PRESIDENT Johnson's former

JANUARY 1965

1 *Another Beatles Christmas Show* continued at the Hammersmith Odeon.

3 A break from the show. It was announced by Brian Epstein that there would be no further visits to the US due to issues with the US tax authorities. The previous year the Beatles earned nearly $3 million, and the income was being blocked by Treasury officials. This was apparently due to an Anglo-American tax treaty that ruled that artists had to pay taxes on earnings to both countries.

9 *Beatles '65* reached No. 1 in the US album charts, remaining there for nine weeks. John's appearance on *Not Only...But Also* was broadcast on BBC2.

10 Another well-earned break from the Christmas show. In New York, promoter Sid Bernstein made an offer to book the band at Shea Stadium, which had a capacity of 55,600.

16 The final Saturday night and the Christmas show was complete.

20 Ringo proposed to Maureen Cox at the Ad Lib Club.

25 John and Cynthia went skiing with George Martin and his wife in St. Moritz.

27 The band had a brief break when Paul travelled to Tunisia. George went back to Liverpool to stand as a witness at his brother Peter's wedding.

John and Paul's talent goes public

Two years after the formation of Northern Songs, the company was floated on the stock market. Neither John nor Paul was keen to go public, but they were persuaded of the case to mitigate the punitive impact of capital-gains tax. In any event, as minor shareholders they were arguing with one hand tied behind their back. Lennon and McCartney each had a 15 percent stake, well short

of the 37.5 percent holding of Northern Songs' chairman Dick James and his partner Charles Silver. George and Ringo shared a modest 1.6 percent interest.

The shares went to market on 18 February 1965 at an issue price of seven shillings and ninepence. It soon fell to six shillings and sixpence, prompting reports in the financial pages that this was one of the stock-exchange flops of the year. That was but a temporary blip, possibly because investors were unused to holding shares in an enterprise based on two men churning

out hit songs. When the figures for 1964 were released—Northern Songs making a profit of over £600,000—investors piled in, and before long the stock had doubled in value.

The flotation brought a handsome dividend to investors, but as far as John and Paul were concerned the status quo had been maintained: they still didn't own their songs, something that irked them not only for the next four years but long after the Beatles would disband.

New American trip planned

Following the triumphant Carnegie Hall concerts of February 1964, American promoter Sid Bernstein immediately raised his sights. The screams had barely stopped ringing round the auditorium when Bernstein entered into talks with Brian Epstein to put on a much bigger show. He initially had in mind Madison Square Garden, whose capacity was six times greater than the 2,800-seat Carnegie Hall. By the time the deal was done, early in 1965, Bernstein's plans were even more ambitious. He wanted the Beatles to play Shea Stadium, New York's 55,600-seat home to the Mets. No act had ever performed before so vast an audience, but could Bernstein sell it out? Epstein wasn't sure, and he was concerned that the Beatles might play to a half-empty house. Bernstein reassured him, even guaranteeing ten dollars for every unsold seat. A reassured Epstein demanded $100,000 against 60 percent of the gross, half of the guaranteed minimum up-front.

It couldn't have come at a worse time for Bernstein. He had lost a fortune putting on a stage version of the US TV show *Shindig*. Ironically, the Beatles had recently headlined a special edition of *Shindig* dedicated to British acts. The promoter must have wished his touring show had boasted the Fab Four on the bill. In short, he didn't have the required $50,000, and his credit rating was so low that the prospects of raising it in the three-month window granted him by Epstein looked bleak. Bernstein's problems would have been solved in an instant had he been able to advertise a Beatles concert, but Epstein stymied that, insisting there be no publicity until the deposit was paid and the show was definitely going ahead.

Word of mouth got the promoter out of a thorny catch-22 situation. He was used to kids approaching him and asking what his next big promotion was, and the news spread like wildfire. Bernstein set up a P.O. box number for ticket applications, hoping to receive enough cheques to buy him some leverage with the banks. In fact, applications poured in by the sackful, some from behind the Iron Curtain at the height of the Cold War! When Epstein came to New York for the appointed meeting in April '65, Bernstein was able to hand over a cheque for the full $100,000 instead of the required minimum fee.

ABOVE: **A second EP, *4 By the Beatles*, featuring two songs written by Carl Perkins, was released by Capitol in February 1965.**

OPPOSITE: **John and Cynthia return from Switzerland.**

TOP: **John finally obtained his driving licence at the age of 24.**

BIO: MAUREEN COX

In 1962 Maureen Cox was one of a long line of teenage Cavernites hoping to catch a Beatle's eye. Sixteen-year-old Maureen—she changed her name from Mary after swapping the classroom for a hairdresser's salon—knew of Ringo from his time with Rory Storm & the Hurricanes, though back then she dated one of the other band members. Within weeks of Ringo's joining the Beatles in August 1962, he and Maureen were an item. She accepted a dare to plant a kiss on the Fabs' new drummer, and he asked her out shortly afterwards. Maureen was expecting their first child, Zak, when the couple married on 11 February 1965. A second son, Jason, was born in 1967, and daughter Lee followed three years later. Maureen sang backup vocals on "The Continuing Story of Bungalow Bill" and received the famous "Thanks, Mo" acknowledgment from Paul at the Apple rooftop concert in 1969. The Starkeys' marriage began to unravel in the early 1970s. Ringo's extramarital dalliances and alcohol consumption were issues, while Maureen's brief affair with George didn't help. They divorced in 1975 but remained close. In 1989 Maureen married long-term partner Isaac Tigrett, the Hard Rock Café co-founder who went on to open the House of Blues chain. They had one daughter, Augusta, born in 1987. In 1994 Maureen was diagnosed with a rare form of leukaemia, which claimed her life on 30 December that year, despite a bone marrow transplant from Zak. She was forty-eight years old. The Paul McCartney song "Little Willow", which featured on his 1997 album *Flaming Pie*, was written as a tribute to "Mo".

LEFT: **Ringo and Maureen pose for cameras while on their honeymoon at the Sussex home of David Jacobs, the Beatles lawyer.**

ON GIRLS

"It's never interested me to go out with a different girl every night. I like to go with girls for weeks or months. Then you know what's happening and you can have your laughs."

—Ringo

FEBRUARY 1965

2 In Portugal, after months of consideration, the censors finally released the movie *A Hard Day's Night*, but gave it an "adult only" rating.

8 A news release in *The Times* reported that 1,250,000 shares in the publishing company Northern Songs would soon go on sale. Dick James took out life insurance for John and Paul.

9 Again in *The Times* it was announced that Eleanor Bron would play the lead in the forthcoming Beatles film.

10 A new fan club for Cynthia Lennon was formed, sending out a magazine every month.

11 Ringo Starr married Maureen Cox at Caxton Hall in London. She was a hairdresser and his long-standing girlfriend.

15 Back into the recording studios at Abbey Road. The session began at 2:30 p.m., and just over three hours later "Ticket to Ride" was finished. This was to be the A-side of the next single, due for

release in April, and would also be used for the forthcoming film. The boys then taped "Another Girl" followed by "I Need You". In the US "Eight Days a Week"/"I Don't Want to Spoil the Party" was released on Capitol 5371. John passed his driving test.

16 Overdubs for "Another Girl" and "I Need You" were completed. They then recorded "Yes It Is" for the B-side of the forthcoming single.

17 "The Night Before" and "You Like Me Too Much" were taped for the

Ringo's turn to marry

11 February 1965 was another dark day for female fans as their hopes of tying the knot with a Beatle were reduced by a further 25 percent. Ringo married his sweetheart from the Cavern era, eighteen-year-old Maureen Cox, in a low-key ceremony at Caxton Hall Register Office, London. It was a hastily arranged affair—the fact that Maureen was already pregnant accounted for that—and the other members of the group were given barely twenty-four hours' notice. Paul missed the big day completely as he was on holiday in Tunisia, but John and George attended with their respective partners, while Brian did the best-man honours, as he had at John's nuptials.

Maureen had suffered the same kind of vitriol from jealous rivals that had befallen Cynthia, the Cavern girls taking none too kindly to anyone lucky enough to catch a Beatle's eye, let alone secure a date with one of the Fabs. She left Liverpool—and hairdressing—behind her but the road ahead wasn't to be filled with milk and honey.

The material advantages were certainly there. On returning from a brief honeymoon in Brighton, Maureen soon found herself installed as lady of Sunny Heights, a mansion not far from the Lennons' property in Surrey, which came complete with its own "pub", the Flying Cow. Son Zak arrived on 13 September, and the couple would have two more children over the next five years.

THIS PAGE: **Ringo and Maureen were married at Caxton Hall Register Office on 11 January 1965. It was a very early start for the pair, who were married at 8 a.m. to avoid thousands of fans turning up. Ringo proposed to his girlfriend at the Ad Lib Club in mid-January, just a few weeks before the ceremony.**

forthcoming film soundtrack. (Although "You Like Me Too Much" was eventually used for the *Help!* album instead.)

18 A whole day in the studio producing mono mixes of previously recorded work after "You've Got to Hide Your Love Away" was finished, with additional overdubs by flautist Johnnie Scott. Later in the day "If You've Got Trouble" was recorded (but never used), followed by "Tell Me What You See".

19 During the afternoon, "You're Going to Lose That Girl" was taped.

20 "That Means a Lot" was recorded but never used; the rights were given to P.J. Proby. Then more mono mixing was undertaken.

22 The boys flew to the Bahamas to begin shooting their new film, eventually to be called *Help!*. They stayed at the Balmoral Club, Cable Beach, for the duration of the shoot.

23 Norman Smith made stereo mixes of all the songs recorded that week. Filming began in the Bahamas, with the boys swimming in the Nassau Beach Hotel pool fully clothed.

24 A full day's filming schedule for *Help!* took place, mainly on the Interfield Road.

25 Filming included footage of Paul at caves in a lime quarry and John and Ringo at a softball stadium.

26 John was filmed running out of the library, Ringo was at a yacht basin, and then he and George were in the grounds of the Royal Victoria Hotel.

27 *Beatles for Sale* went back to the top of the UK charts for one further week. Filming took place on Balmoral Island.

28 Scenes were shot on Cabbage Beach.

MARCH 1965

1 Back to film at Cabbage Beach, this time at the Café Martinique.

2 The next three days were spent filming on Victoria and Cabbage Beach.

5 Filming at various sites around the island.

6 Back at Nassau Airport, the scenes on the aeroplane steps were shot.

7 Filming for the next two days was at a disused army camp that was actually a hospital for the handicapped and elderly. Its state shocked the band.

8 At the Empire Ballroom, Leicester Square, London, Brian Epstein attended the Mecca Carl-Alan Awards where, on behalf of the band, he received the Best Group Award from Princess Margaret.

9 Final shots were taken on Paradise Island.

10 The boys flew back to London, arriving at 7 a.m. the following day.

13 The band and film crew then flew out to Austria. They were met by crowds of fans at Salzburg Airport. After a brief press conference they then drove to the Hotel Edelweiss in Obertauern, their home for the next week. In the States, "Eight Days a Week" reached No. 1, staying there for two weeks.

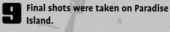

Help!

The Beatles' second movie had a £400,000 budget, three times that of *A Hard Day's Night*, much of which went toward exotic location shooting in glorious colour. Marc Behm wrote the story, originally conceived as a vehicle for Peter Sellers and reworked for the Beatles. Even the stars were hazy about the plot—a fantasy romp involving a ring imbued with magical powers—though this was partly down to a pot-induced fog. Dick Lester again directed, and he was well aware that he had to make best use of the morning's footage, while the stars were reasonably compos mentis.

When the entourage decamped to the Bahamas in late February to begin shooting, the mood was optimistic. The boys were more than happy to trade an English winter for sun and sand, and it also gave the moneymen the opportunity to investigate the possibilities of the island tax haven as a means of shielding the four from a punitive domestic tax regime. Sunbathing was off limits, though, for the scenes shot in the Caribbean appeared at the end of the movie.

The plot involved the boys surviving various scrapes and managing to prevent Ringo from falling victim to the Eastern cult's henchmen, who were determined to part the drummer from the precious sacrificial ring. Some neat set pieces provided the opportunity for slapstick, which again drew comparisons with the Marx Brothers. But overall the glamorous locations couldn't mask the fact that the four weren't trained thespians, and the top-notch supporting cast merely highlighted the fact.

Paul's verdict was that they felt as though they were "guest stars in our own movie", while John dismissed it as "crap". The critics were generally unimpressed, though *Help!* did scoop first prize at the Rio de Janeiro International Film Festival in September. The celebrated critic Kenneth Tynan also found merit in the piece: "To sum up *Help!* I must go to Coleridge, who said that whereas a scientist investigates a thing for the sheer pleasure of knowing, the non-scientist only wants to find out whether it will 'furnish him with food, or shelter, or weapons, or tools, or ornaments, or play-withs.' *Help!* is a shiny, forgettable toy; an ideal play-with."

The cartoon-style fantasy may have been ahead of its time—John certainly thought so. And even if it had its shortcomings as a movie, *Help!* boasted another terrific soundtrack.

ABOVE: **The boys look enthusiastic about the prospect of beginning the new movie.**

OPPOSITE: **The Beatles wave goodbye to the fans at London Airport on 22 February before leaving for the Bahamas, where filming was to begin on their second movie, *Help!*.**

BELOW: **Twenty-year-old comedy actress Eleanor Bron is not sure what to make of her first brush with Beatlemania. She was accompanying the boys on the flight to the Bahamas, where she was to co-star in *Help!*.**

14 Filming began, using doubles at times, for the sleigh-ride sequences.

15 For the next two days doubles were also used on the slopes and ski lifts. At Abbey Road, Norman Smith made a new mono mix of "Ticket to Ride" for Capitol Records.

17 After filming at the curling rink, it was announced that the movie would be called *Eight Arms to Hold You*.

18 The location that day was an Olympic ski jump.

19 More sequences taken in the snow. The band made a telephone interview with Brian Matthew for the BBC that would be used on *Saturday Club*.

20 In the evening Chris Denning from Radio Luxembourg interviewed Ringo and John by telephone for his radio programme *The Beatles*. The band appeared on *Saturday Club*.

21 The film crew left Obertauern.

22 The band also left for London. In the US the album *The Early Beatles* was released on Capitol T-2309 (mono) and ST-2309 (stereo).

24 Shooting on home soil—in and around the Twickenham Film Studios—for three consecutive days.

27 John and George took LSD for the first time.

28 The band recorded its last appearance on *Thank Your Lucky Stars* (the show was to finish the following June) at the Alpha Studios in Birmingham.

29 Filming resumed at Twickenham that week, shooting the railway station and laboratory scenes.

30 After spending the day filming, the boys were at Abbey Road in the evening.

Beatles in the shade

THEY MUSN'T HAVE RED FACES IN THEIR FILM

THE Beatles stayed in the shade on sunshine isle yesterday — by order.

This morning they put on jeans and sports shirts—" our flopping-about kit " — and strolled on to the seafront near their villa.

They were quickly chased back to the shade of a palm tree by one of the team producing their new film.

George Harrison explained : " We aren't allowed any sunshine because it would make our faces red and it would show."

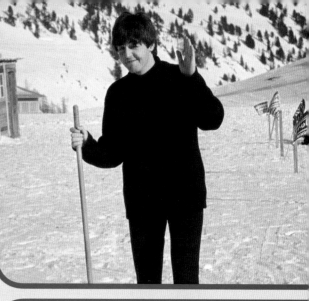

LEFT AND TOP: **The skiing scenes for *Help!* were shot at Obertauern, near Salzburg in the Austrian Alps. The Beatles arrived on 13 March and the weeklong shoot began the following day. Body doubles were used to make the boys appear better at skiing and also to save them from standing around in the cold.**

ABOVE: **During a break in filming in Austria, Paul decided to give skiing a try. His instructor is the niece of the Duke of Norfolk, Harriet Davidson.**

OPPOSITE: **Paul on location in the Bahamas, where the boys were filmed cycling across New Providence Island.**

Concert. ABC Television featured two specials from the show and included the award presented to the band by Tony Bennett. In the evening they were at the Teddington Studio Centre to take part in *The Eamonn Andrews Show* that went out live.

12 Further filming at Twickenham of the "Buckingham Palace" scene for the new movie.

13 At the Grammy Awards the band won Best New Artist and Best Performance by a Vocal Group (for "A Hard Day's Night"). Further filming and a live interview for the lunchtime show *Pop Inn* took place. "Help!" was recorded that evening at Abbey Road. Paul bought a house in Cavendish Avenue in St. John's Wood, North London.

14 Film scenes were shot in Ailsa Avenue, Twickenham.

15 There was a break from shooting for the Easter weekend. The band appeared on *Top of the Pops* performing "Ticket to Ride" for the first time.

16 John and George were interviewed live by Cathy McGowan at Wembley Studios for *Ready, Steady, Goes Live!*

18 The band appeared on *Pop Gear*, which also featured the Animals, Billy J. Kramer, Herman's Hermits, and the Spencer Davis Group. The Poll Winners' Concert was broadcast on ABC Television.

19 In the US "Ticket to Ride"/"Yes It Is" was released on Capitol 5407.

20 Filming resumed. George had set up the publishing company Harrisongs Limited, and Brian Epstein was appointed as a director.

21 The Scotland Yard scenes were filmed.

22 The Beatles began shooting the scenes with Frankie Howerd and Wendy Richard.

23 Further filming with Wendy Richard and Frankie Howerd.

Help, I need somebody...

It was seven weeks into the shoot before the title of the Beatles second feature film was decided upon. *Eight Days a Week* had been an early contender, and that morphed into *Eight Arms to Hold You*, which remained the working title until it became clear that John and Paul didn't relish the prospect of writing a song around such an unwieldy heading. Director Dick Lester came up with the more user-friendly *Help!*, and once again John and Paul withdrew separately to come up with a suitable song. And as had been the case with *A Hard Day's Night*, it was John who produced the goods.

The title track for the new film and album was a genuine cry on John's part. *Help!* may have been written to order under extreme pressure, yet John still managed to lay himself bare more than ever

before. It was a watershed moment in the career of the maturing songwriter, who years later would single out "Help!" and "Strawberry Fields" as the only songs he wrote "from experience and not projecting myself into a situation and writing a nice story about it, which I always found phony".

To most people dissatisfaction and a plea for assistance would have seemed odd themes for one of the leading lights in the world's greatest group, but John's misgivings and insecurities ran deep. He had never totally come to terms with allowing Epstein to smooth out the rough edges and package the Beatles for the marketplace; it still smacked of selling out to climb the greasy pole of pop stardom. Later, the awarding of the MBE brought all those feelings back to the fore. He was also far from content with his domestic set-up: the free-spirited enfant terrible was

cooped up in Surrey's leafy stockbroker belt, hamstrung by his commitments as a husband and father. There were also body-image issues. John's weight had ballooned through excessive drinking and bingeing, an unhappy time he would describe as his "fat Elvis period".

He was self-conscious about his short-sightedness but too vain to wear glasses, preferring to be led by the arm when he needed to find a seat in a dingy nightclub. When the "somebody" whose help he needed appeared on the horizon, life suddenly made sense. Then he would even don unprepossessing National Health spectacles and make them a must-have fashion accessory. But that was still eighteen months away.

John remained justifiably proud of "Help!", though he had reservations over the up-tempo treatment that inevitably had to accompany a Beatles single. Post-breakup he harboured thoughts of rerecording the song with an arrangement more to his liking, but it was an idea that remained unfulfilled.

HELP!

Cast List

John Lennon	John
Paul McCartney	Paul
George Harrison	George
Ringo Star	Ringo
Leo McKern	Clang
Eleanor Bron	Ahme
Victor Spinett	Prof. Foot
Roy Kinnear	Algernon
John Bluthal	Bhuta
Patrick Cargill	Superintendent
Alfie Bass	Doorman
Warren Mitchell	Abdul
Peter Copley	Jeweller
Bruce Lacey	Lawnmower

LEFT: **Radio Caroline DJ Simon Dee presents the station's first Birthday Bell award to the Beatles during shooting at Twickenham Studios.**

OPPOSITE: **John and Eleanor Bron shoot *Help!* on location in Ailsa Avenue in Twickenham, West London.**

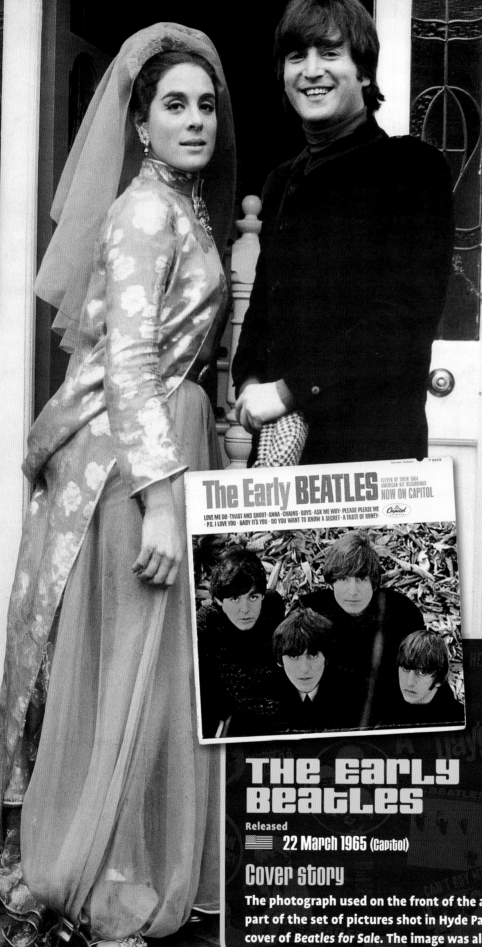

continued from page 195

APRIL 1965

24 Filming was on location in Chiswick, West London. In *The Times* a report stated that the shares issued by Northern Songs had been a "flop sans pareil". They had been released at 7s 9d but were now at 6s 6d.

25 "Ticket to Ride" reached the top of the British charts, remaining there for three weeks.

26 A break from filming.

27 At Twickenham the scenes with the band in disguise were shot.

28 Scenes with Frankie Howerd and Wendy Richard, although they were later deleted, were completed. At the studio the Beatles were presented with a Grammy Award by Peter Sellers for the Best Performance by a Vocal Group for "A Hard Day's Night". This was taped for broadcast in the US by NBC the following month.

29 During filming the Beatles were interviewed by Chris Denning from Radio Luxembourg. Jimmy Nicol was declared bankrupt.

30 Filming continued at Twickenham.

THE EARLY BEATLES

Released
🇺🇸 22 March 1965 (Capitol)

Cover story

The photograph used on the front of the album was taken by Robert Freeman and is part of the set of pictures shot in Hyde Park, London, in the autumn of 1964 for the cover of *Beatles for Sale*. The image was also used on the back cover of *Beatles for Sale*.

Side One:
Love Me Do
Twist and Shout (Russell)
Anna (Go to Him) (Alexander)
Chains (Goffin–King)
Boys (Dixon–Farrell)
Ask Me Why

Side Two:
Please Please Me
P.S. I Love You
Baby, It's You (Bacharach–David–Williams)
A Taste of Honey (Marlow–Scott)
Do You Want to Know a Secret

Ludwig

THE BEATLES

MAY 1965

OPPOSITE AND ABOVE: **Beginning on 3 May, the Beatles spent three days shooting *Help!* at Knighton Down, Larkhill, on Salisbury Plain, where they seek the protection of the British Army to escape the clutches of Clang. During the scene, the boys mimed to "I Need You", while the army conducted manoeuvres in the background. Real army officers were used as the extras for the scene, drawn mostly from the Third Division, which used Larkhill as a training base.**

ABOVE RIGHT: **The Beatles, on the run from murderers, seek protection amongst a handful of friendly policemen in the film.**

RIGHT: **Ringo gets to stay on the drums, but George has to forgo his guitar in favour of the cymbals as the boys join a marching band to disguise themselves in a scene from *Help!*.**

2 The band travelled to Wiltshire.

3 Three days of filming on location on Salisbury Plain. The boys stayed at the Antrobus Arms in Amesbury.

6 The band left to travel back to London.

7 Filming continued at the studio.

9 Filming at various locations in the capital including New Bond Street, Blandford Street, and St. Margaret's near the studio. Later the band watched Bob Dylan perform at the Royal Albert Hall in London.

10 Two days filming at Cliveden House, Berkshire. An evening recording session back at Abbey Road to tape "Dizzy Miss Lizzy" and "Bad Boy", where they were watched by Larry Wiliams.

11 The final day of filming for the band.

12 The last day of filming for the crew, completing shots on location where the boys were not required.

16 John went to a party held for Johnny Mathis.

18 The publishers of *Who's Who in America* confirmed that the boys would be included in the 1966–67 edition. Overdubbing speech for the film at Twickenham. The Grammy Awards were broadcast in the US by NBC and included the recording of Peter Sellers presenting the band with their award.

22 In the US "Ticket to Ride" reached the top of the charts, remaining there for a week.

25 During a visit to the Cannes Film Festival by John and Cynthia, John was interviewed by a US television reporter named Martin Ogronsky.

26 The band's last recording made specifically for BBC radio. At the Piccadilly Studios a bank-holiday special titled *The Beatles (Invite You to Take a Ticket to Ride)* was rehearsed and taped.

The Beatles stay at No. 1

The Beatles are still on top of the Hit Parade after six weeks with their *Ticket To Ride*.

The Seekers move up to No. 2 with *A World of Our Own*, while Roger Miller's *King of the Road* slips to No. 3.

OPPOSITE INSET: **While the Beatles are concentrating on filming, the *Daily Mail* of 11 May reports that "Ticket to Ride" is still riding high in the UK charts.**

THIS PAGE AND OPPOSITE: **The boys at Cliveden House, the country estate in Buckinghamshire, England, that was used to shoot the interior scenes set in Buckingham Palace in the film. While there, the Beatles challenged the cameramen, electricians, and carpenters to a relay race around the grounds, which the boys managed to win.**

A nod to the past, a signpost to the future

Help! is sometimes regarded as the Beatles least-inspired album, and the new crop of twelve original songs, including an unprecedented two from George, certainly included some workaday fillers. John was particularly scathing about "It's Only Love", which he regarded as a low-watermark in his catalogue. His opinion can be seen in the working title: "That's a Nice Hat". But Beatles throwaways were still a cut above most groups' finest efforts, and an album that included "Yesterday", "Ticket to Ride", and "I've Just Seen a Face", as well as the excellent title track, could scarcely be deemed a dud.

Other points of interest in what was undoubtedly a transitional album included John's Dylanesque "You've Got to Hide Your Love Away", the first all-acoustic song recorded by the Beatles. This track was notable for the introduction of a fifth musician, flautist John Scott becoming the first non-Beatle to feature on a recording since Andy White at the "Love Me Do" sessions. George introduced the wah-wah pedal to give one of his new numbers, "I Need You", a suitably mournful quality, using the same effect on "Yes It Is", which went out on the B-side to "Ticket to Ride". This wasn't new: Chet Atkins, one of George's all-time heroes, had pioneered the use of the wah-wah, but from now on the Beatles would be open to the possibilities of any instrument, any gizmo—indeed any object from which they could extract a sound.

"Ticket to Ride" also broke new ground, John describing it as "one of the earliest heavy metal records". The title is said to be a pun on the Isle of Wight town of Ryde, where Paul's cousin ran a pub, though John naughtily suggested it referred to the bill of health the Hamburg hookers needed to ply their trade.

Notwithstanding its weaknesses, *Help!* still spent a healthy nine weeks at the top of the UK chart. Capitol used only the songs featured in the movie, padding out the rest of the album with orchestral pieces, yet sales still comfortably passed the million mark.

Ringo song proves costly for Normal engineer

The *Help!* sessions were noteworthy for spawning two Lennon–McCartney numbers where the group was forced to hoist the white flag. "That Means a Lot" started out as a soundtrack hopeful but was soon relegated to a giveaway, in this instance to a grateful P.J. Proby, who must have wished he hadn't bothered as his version sank without trace. The other failure was "If You've Got Trouble", a rocker written with Ringo's vocal spot in mind. It too was abandoned after several unsuccessful takes.

They needed one final song to complete the set and Abbey Road engineer Norman Smith—nicknamed "Normal" by the band—tentatively suggested he might have something that would fit the bill. Smith had been an accomplished, if somewhat unsuccessful, musician in his own right before turning to production, so the proposal was not that far-fetched. Indeed, the boys liked the song—so much so that Dick James offered Smith £15,000 for it on the spot. He stalled to consider the offer, something he must have regretted when the boys had second thoughts the next day because they needed a showcase for Ringo, not for themselves. A cover of the Buck Owens number

"Act Naturally" was selected instead, and Smith was left to count the cost.

Smith was to have his moment of glory, however, as a performer as well as writer. His involvement with Beatles recordings ended later that year with *Rubber Soul*, when EMI rewarded him with a promotion. He went on to produce the burgeoning supergroup Pink Floyd, though he still fancied that he might cut it in front of the microphone. Smith finally got his big break in the early '70s, when he was turning fifty. He took to the stage as Hurricane Smith and enjoyed a spell in the limelight with hits including "Oh Babe, What Would You Say?" and "Don't Let It Die".

Beatles VI

Released

🇺🇸 14 June 1965 (Capitol)

Side One:

Kansas City (Leiber–Stoller)
Hey, Hey, Hey, Hey (Penniman)
Eight Days a Week
You Like Me Too Much (Harrison)
Bad Boy (Williams)
I Don't Want to Spoil the Party
Words of Love (Holly)

Side Two:

What You're Doing
Yes It Is
Dizzy Miss Lizzy (Williams)
Tell Me What You See
Every Little Thing

Cover Story

Having been introduced to the Beatles during their trip to Australia in the summer of 1964, photographer Robert Whitaker accepted Brian Epstein's invitation to become the NEMS official photographer and moved to London. During the next two years Whitaker travelled with the Beatles in America and on their tour to the Far East and took many intimate portraits of the band. He was also responsible for a number of quirky studio pictures of the group, often involving unusual props. Capitol chose an image of the Beatles holding a knife for the sleeve of *Beatles VI* (although it is not obvious that this is what the object is), part of a sequence of pictures of the Beatles cutting a giant cake.

OPPOSITE AND RIGHT: **Paul and John filming a promotion for the latest release, "Ticket to Ride". "Ticket to Ride" and its B-side "Yes It Is" (right inset), was released by Capitol on 19 April and peaked at No. 1 in the *Billboard* Hot 100. It was released ten days earlier in the UK, where it also reached the top of the charts.**

FAR RIGHT: **After completing filming on *Help!*, John and Cynthia flew out to the Cannes Film Festival.**

ABOVE LEFT: **Paul rejoices at the news that the band are to become MBEs (Members of the British Empire). The honour had been conferred at the personal recommendation of the prime minister, Harold Wilson, a self-confessed Beatles fan with a Liverpool constituency. Traditionalists were angered about the appointment and many of the Establishment agreed with Bernard Levin, who could not understand why four men would be rewarded for putting such "ephemeral rubbish" into the public domain.**

BELOW INSET: **Jane Asher certainly looks pleased with the award as she and Paul read the news in the *Daily Mail* after returning from a break in Albufeira, Portugal.**

OPPOSITE ABOVE: **Speculation was rife that Paul and Jane were going to marry imminently, or that they had already done so in secret.**

OPPOSITE INSET: **The sheet music to the song "Yesterday". The song is thought to be the most covered song of all time.**

JUNE 1965

1 The interview with John in Cannes was broadcast on *The Merv Griffin Show* in the US.

2 Paul and Jane Asher flew to Albufeira in Portugal for a holiday.

4 The EP *Beatles for Sale (No. 2)* was released in the UK on Parlophone GEP 8938 (mono only). "I'll Follow the Sun"/"Baby's in Black" were on the A-side, with the B-side featuring "Words of Love"/"I Don't Want to Spoil the Party".

"Yesterday": like a piece of lost property

If the quality of the music that flowed from John and Paul was extraordinary, it was all the more remarkable for the rate at which the pop masterpieces rolled off the production line. By now they were generally writing individually instead of bouncing musical phrases off each other or trading lyrical blows. But one thing that hadn't changed was the speed at which they composed. This pattern was broken with a new McCartney song that had an inordinately long gestation period. The exact date on which Paul woke with the melody of "Yesterday" swirling round in his head, fully formed, is unclear, though George Martin maintained that Paul played him the tune during the Beatles stay at Paris's George V Hotel in January 1964.

Convinced it was a steal, Paul assiduously ran it by a host of show business luminaries, including Lionel Bart, who assured him it was an original—and marvellous. Paul remained cautious, as though he were in possession of a piece of lost property. "Eventually it became like handing something in to the police. I thought if no one claimed it after a few weeks, then I could have it."

After that hurdle was cleared, another obstacle arose. Paul had blocked in some lyrics—"Scrambled eggs,/Oh, my baby, how I love your legs..."—that proved extremely difficult to displace. He was still wrestling with the problem when he and Jane Asher went on holiday to Portugal in late May. On the journey to Shadows guitarist Bruce Welch's villa, where they were staying, the breakthrough finally came.

7 The Beatles (Invite You to Take a Ticket to Ride) was broadcast.

8 Norman Smith produced a new stereo mix of "I Want to Hold Your Hand" specifically for overseas compilation albums.

11 Paul and Jane flew home amid reports that they had married—which they denied. The band was featured on Late Night Extra, a BBC radio show.

12 News of the boys' MBE awards on the Queen's birthday honours list swept through the media. An ex-squadron leader named Paul Pearson returned his medal in protest. A press conference was hastily convened at the Twickenham Studios where the boys were viewing a rough cut of Help!.

13 A report was issued by Northern Songs saying that so far 1,337 cover versions of Beatles songs had been made.

14 At Abbey Road the recording of Paul's "Yesterday" began. This song was to ultimately produce the record for the most cover versions made (approaching 3,000 to date). Although issued as a single in the US later in the year, it was not released as a single in Britain until 1976. In the States, the album Beatles VI was released on Capitol T-2358 (mono) and ST-2358 (stereo).

15 The band recorded "It's Only Love" for the Help! album.

16 Final postfilming work at Twickenham, and the movie was finished. John began publicising his forthcoming book, A Spaniard in the Works. He was interviewed at the NEMS office by Wilfred De'Ath for the BBC Home Service programme The World of Books.

" 'Yesterday': the most complete thing I've ever written"

On 14 June 1965 Paul was finally ready to take "Yesterday" into the studio. When he played it through, the other Beatles felt they could contribute nothing, and at George Martin's suggestion a string quartet was brought in. Paul didn't want it to be "too Mantovani" and insisted that the musicians rein in the vibrato. The result was magical. "Yesterday" naturally enhanced Pauls's reputation as the balladeer supreme, though he was quick to point out that the larynx-shredding rocker "I'm Down" was recorded on the same day.

The billing issue then arose. It was a sure-fire smash-hit single, but with no contribution from the other three, could it be released under the Beatles banner? Epstein was adamant that it couldn't go out as a solo release, which would have smacked of division in the ranks, something he wouldn't countenance. The most-recorded song in history—some 3,000 cover versions to date—was thus tucked away on the non-soundtrack side of *Help!*. Capitol did release it later in the year in the US, under the Beatles name, and unsurprisingly it topped the *Billboard* chart for four weeks and gave the group yet another million-seller.

"Yesterday" won the Ivor Novello Award for Outstanding Song of the Year, and more than forty years on it still justifies Paul's contention "that it was the most complete thing I've ever written". After John's death, Paul asked Yoko Ono if a compilation album featuring "Yesterday" could carry a McCartney–Lennon credit for that one song, harking back to the brief early period when the names appeared in reverse order. She refused.

LEFT: **John and George lift Paul aloft on his 23rd birthday. Ringo puts in a little less effort, making sure he has a hand free for a cigarette.**

ABOVE: **"Yesterday" was released by Capitol as a single with the B-side "Act Naturally" in September 1965 and went straight to the top of the charts. However, it did not get its UK release as a single for another ten years because Brian Epstein feared that the work was too much of a solo project by Paul (top).**

OPPOSITE: **John strikes a matador pose as the Beatles return from Barcelona, the last date on their short European tour, which began in Paris on 20 June.**

continued from previous page

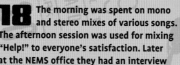

JUNE 1965

17 For the first time the band used a string quartet, added to "Yesterday" before finally mixing to mono. "If You've Got Trouble" was then taped with Ringo singing the lead vocals for the album. "Wait" was also recorded, although it was not used until *Rubber Soul* was released in November.

18 The morning was spent on mono and stereo mixes of various songs. The afternoon session was used for mixing "Help!" to everyone's satisfaction. Later at the NEMS office they had an interview with the BBC Italian-language service to promote the forthcoming European tour. John then appeared on the last edition of *Tonight* to promote *A Spaniard in the Works*.

19 A letter from Charles de Houghton was printed in *The Times* defending the band's MBE awards. He pointed out that they had salvaged the British corduroy industry and were also important earners of foreign exchange.

20 Flying into Orly Airport that morning, the band began its European tour with two shows at the Palais des Sports in Paris. The evening show was broadcast live on Europe 1.

21 In New Guinea, a government official named Richard Pope also protested at the MBEs by returning his Military Medal. The band appeared on *Today*.

22 The Beatles flew to Lyon. Two shows were performed at the Palais d'Hiver de Lyon.

A SPANIARD IN THE WORKS
JOHN LENNON

A SPANIARD IN THE WORKS

After the publication of *In His Own Write* in March 1964, John was given just over a year to come up with a follow-up book. This would be no easy feat: *In His Own Write* was the culmination of a lifetime of musings, but the new book would have to be written with great haste.

John's second book, *A Spaniard in the Works*, was published on 24 June 1965, the title being a play on the phrase "a spanner in the works". The book was similar in character to his first book, and John admitted during an interview on the BBC Radio's *World of Books* that it was an equally undisciplined process. Some of the book had been written with the support of George during their trip to Tahiti in May 1964.

23 The boys' interview taped earlier in the week could be heard on *Londra Iltima Ora* in Italy. During the evening they travelled to Milan by train. They played two houses at the Veodromo Vigorelli.

24 John's second book, *A Spaniard in the Works*, was published.

25 Two further shows at the Palazzo dello Sport in Genoa, Italy. They then flew immediately to Rome.

26 While they were in Italy, Brian Epstein suddenly disappeared and did not return until the tour reached Madrid.

27 Over the next two days, four performances were held at the Teatro Adriano in Rome.

29 In the morning the band flew to Nice, France. In Jakarta the leaders of a dance band called Koes Bersaudara were arrested after playing Beatles music.

30 One performance at the Palais des Expositions in Nice, France.

LEFT ABOVE AND BELOW: **The Beatles with Cynthia and Maureen at the black-tie, royal charity premiere of *Help!* at the London Pavilion. George remarked that the band would be "much happier in jeans and T-shirts".**

OPPPOSITE: **Princess Margaret and Lord Snowdon at the premiere of *Help!*. The Princess remarked that she had enjoyed *A Hard Day's Night* and that she had been looking forward to the latest release.**

BELOW AND LEFT INSET: **Newspapers report the success of the *Help!* album but their reaction to the movie is not as positive.**

To some ears, one Beatle song may sound very much like another. But the trouble with the Beatles' new film — in colour this time—is that they have tried too hard to make it bigger and better than the first.

In other words, where *A Hard Day's Night* was just enough of a good thing *Help!* is much too much.

Where the first film was a highly-personalised piece of surrealism woven around their special talents, the second one reduces them to robots— agreeable as ever, but robots all the same—in a great beanfeast of gimmickry and gadgetry.

Inevitably...

HELP! 360,000 sales shoot Beatles to the top

By Daily Mail Reporter

THE Beatles bounced back to the top of the hit parade yesterday when their latest single, *Help!* went to Number One only 48 hours after its release.

Help! is the title song of the Beatles' new film which has its premiere in London on Thursday in the presence of Princess Margaret and Lord Snowdon.

According to manager Brian Epstein's office, *Help!* had an advance order for 360,000 copies and its success puts a brake on rumours that the beat group boom is in decline.

JULY 1965

1 A midafternoon flight to Madrid, Spain. *Beatles VI* went gold in the States.

2 One show was played at the Plaza de Toros de Las Ventas in the Spanish capital.

3 The Beatles flew to Barcelona during the afternoon. That Saturday night they played the last date of the European tour at the Plaza de Toros Monumental in Barcelona. John's previously recorded interview was featured on *A World of Books*.

10 *Beatles VI* topped the US album charts and remained there for six weeks.

12 Paul, Jane Asher, George, and Pattie Boyd went to a Moody Blues party in Roehampton, also attended by Rod Stewart.

13 Paul arrived at the Savoy Hotel at lunchtime to collect five Ivor Novello awards from Sir Billy Butlin. "Can't Buy Me Love" was awarded Most Performed Work of 1964 and also the Highest Certified British Sales.

14 Paul watched Jane Asher perform at the Palace Theatre in Watford.

15 Filmed by Rediffusion, the Ivor Novello Awards ceremony was broadcast on *Pick of the Songs*.

16 Brian Epstein had been planning to build a new venue called the Pilgrim Theatre in Bromley, but his scheme came to a halt when planning permission was turned down.

19 "Help!"/"I'm Down" was released in the US on Capitol 5476.

ORIGINAL MOTION PICTURE SOUNDTRACK

HELP! · THE NIGHT BEFORE · YOU'VE GOT TO HIDE YOUR LOVE AWAY
ANOTHER GIRL · TICKET TO RIDE · YOU'RE GONNA LOSE THAT GIRL
I NEED YOU
And Exclusive Instrumental Music From the Picture's Soundtrack

HELP!

Released
🇬🇧 6 August 1965 (Parlophone)

Side One:
Help!
The Night Before
You've Got to Hide Your Love Away
I Need You (Harrison)
Another Girl
You're Going to Lose That Girl
Ticket to Ride

Side Two:
Act Naturally (Morrison–Russell)
It's Only Love
You Like Me Too Much (Harrison)
Tell Me What You See
I've Just Seen a Face
Yesterday
Dizzy Miss Lizzy (Williams)

Released
🇺🇸 13 August 1965 (Capitol)

Side One:
James Bond Theme (Instrumental)
Help!
The Night Before
From Me to You Fantasy (Instrumental)
You've Got to Hide Your Love Away
I Need You
In the Tyrol (Instrumental)

Side Two:
Another Girl
Another Hard Day's Night (Instrumental)
Ticket to Ride
The Bitter End/You Can't Do That
  (Instrumental)
You're Going to Lose That Girl
The Chase (Instrumental)

cover story

Robert Freeman once again was the man charged with producing the artwork that would adorn the two album releases of 1965. *The Help!* photograph—the ski-clad quartet shot against a stark white background—conjured up the crisp Alpine scenes that the film contained. It was actually shot in the car park at Twickenham on 7 May, the boys standing on a raised platform against a painted white backdrop. Freeman's original idea was for the semaphore arrangement to spell out the film and album's title, but he rejected it on aesthetic grounds: it actually reads NUJV. A slightly different configuration was used for the Capitol release. George remained on the left but the other three were transposed, such that the US version spelled out the equally enigmatic NVUJ instead.

 23 "Help!"/"I'm Down" was released in the UK on Parlophone R 5305.

24 Ringo Starr paid £37,000 for a house named Sunny Heights in Weybridge, Surrey.

 29 The royal world premiere of *Help!* was screened at the London Pavilion cinema in Piccadilly Circus.

30 At the Saville Theatre in Shaftesbury Avenue the boys rehearsed for *Blackpool Night Out*.

31 The band was featured on the BBC radio programme *Lance a Gogo*.

Back to the USA

The US tour of 1965 was half the length of the gruelling 1964 marathon, but by concentrating on bigger venues the second visit was even more profitable. Seventeen days, ten cities, sixteen shows—and more than 300,000 satisfied customers. The satisfaction didn't extend to the performers, however.

On Saturday, 14 August, the day after their arrival in the US, the Beatles taped what was to be their final appearance on *The Ed Sullivan Show*. Paul performed "Yesterday", a song that would have been unthinkable to include in the set list of the succession of vast sporting arenas that was about to pass before their eyes.

An armoured car was the group's usual means of ingress and egress, which summed up the level of detachment that had been reached. By the time they launched into the final song, the engine was already running. Logistically, it was a demanding exercise; artistically, it was futile. There were also a number of hairy moments when the four feared for their lives. If a firecracker exploded, they would look around to see if any member of the group had been shot.

George was the first to become frustrated, bored, and unnerved by touring. He had railed against their being touted around as "performing fleas" after the first tour of the States. Now the cracks had widened significantly. If they played badly—and they often did—no one knew or cared; if they stopped playing completely, nobody noticed. Sometimes John shouted obscenities into the microphone, but it made no difference. They were riding an unstoppable wave of emotion, something that increasingly discomfited all four. And even if they had been happy to trade unrewarding stage shows for a bulging bank balance, the IRS denied them that solace by slapping a million dollar order on them. The Beatles would carry on performing for another year, but the seeds that would end their days as a touring band had already been sown.

ABOVE AND RIGHT: **The Beatles receive a rapturous send-off from the hundreds of fans who had gathered to see them leave London Airport for their US tour on 13 August 1965.**

OPPOSITE: **The boys arrived in New York on the afternoon of 13 August and stayed at the Warwick Hotel until flying on to Toronto on 17 August.**

AUGUST 1965

1 The band appeared on ABC's *Blackpool Night Out*, their first live television appearance for more than a year.

2 Paul and Jane spent the evening at the Scotch of St. James with the Byrds. Brian Epstein declared there would be no more tours that year, although he later changed that decision.

3 In Poole, Dorset, John purchased a house for his Aunt Mimi.

5 John and George saw the Byrds at Blaises, Knightsbridge.

6 *Help!* the album was released in the UK on Parlophone PMC 1255 (mono) and PCS 3071 (stereo) and was to be the first LP to go straight to No. 1 in the album charts in its seven-year history. Paul saw the Byrds at the Flamingo in London.

7 "Help!"/"I'm Down" was at No. 1 in the UK singles chart and remained there for three weeks.

8 John and George went to the Fifth Annual National Jazz and Blues Festival in Richmond together.

9 At the IBC Studios, John produced The Silkies' rendition of "You've Got to Hide Your Love Away", with George playing the tambourine and Paul on guitar.

11 The premiere of *Help!* was held in New York.

12 At the IBC Studios, John tried using a Mellotron for the first time.

13 The band left London Airport for their North American tour, arriving in New York in the early afternoon. The album *Help!* was released in the US on Capitol MAS-2386 (mono) and SMAS-2386 (stereo) with slightly different tracks used.

14 At Studio 50 they rehearsed and taped their appearance on *The Ed Sullivan Show*. Cilla Black was also featured

on the show. *Help!* went to the top of the UK album charts, staying there for nine weeks.

15 At Shea Stadium, they performed to an audience of 55,600, setting a new record for attendance at a pop concert. They flew by helicopter from the hotel onto the roof of the World Fair building, then travelled the short distance to the stadium by armoured truck before sprinting through the tunnel onto the stage. The show was filmed by Sullivan Productions for a one-hour special. The band then spent

the evening with Bob Dylan at the Warwick Hotel.

16 Brian Matthew, who had been invited to spend some of the tour with the boys on behalf of the BBC Transcription Service, made his first report on *Today and Roundabout '65*. Eventually the material gathered was put together in a documentary called *The Beatles Abroad*. Visitors to the band at the Warwick Hotel included the Supremes, the Exciters, the Ronettes, and Bob Dylan.

17 The band flew into Toronto to give two performances at Maple Leaf Gardens.

18 Back in the US where one show, watched by 30,000, was held at Atlanta Stadium in Atlanta, Georgia.

19 In Houston, Texas, two shows were held at Sam Houston Coliseum.

20 Two performances at White Sox Park in Chicago, Illinois.

ABOVE INSET: **The boys returned to the scene of their groundbreaking American debut: Studio 50 at CBS Studios on Broadway. They were there to record another stint for *The Ed Sullivan Show*, 18 months after their first appearance. This time they performed six numbers, including the latest sensations "Help!", "Yesterday", and "Ticket to Ride". Epstein's other talent, Cilla Black, was also featured on the show, broadcast across America on 12 September.**

RIGHT: **One of the 55,600 tickets for the concert at Shea Stadium on 15 August.**

FAR RIGHT: **A ticket stub for the Beatles concert on 17 August at Maple Leaf Gardens in Toronto, Canada. The Beatles gave two half-hour performances to 18,000 people after flying in from New York earlier in the day.**

SHEA STADIUM **A**
ENTER GATE
MEZZ. RESERVED $5.65
20 G 12
SEC. ROW SEAT
SUN., AUG. 15, 1965-8 P.M.

SID BERNSTEIN Presents

RAIN CHECK—SEE REVERSE SIDE

SEC. ROW SEAT
53 A 6
EAST
Retain Stub — Good Only
SERIES 57
TUES. AUG. 17th
Davis Printing Limited
4.00 P.M.
THE "BEATLES"
PRICE $5.50
ADMIT ONE. Entrance by Main
Door or by Church Street Doors

continued from previous page

AUGUST 1965

21 A Saturday evening show at Metropolitan Stadium in Minneapolis. George was given a Rickenbacker 12-string guitar by Ron Butwin and Randy Resnick from B-Sharp Music, a local shop.

22 Two shows at Memorial Coliseum in Portland, Oregon. In the dressing room they were visited by Carl Wilson and Mike Love from the Beach Boys.

23 The band flew into Los Angeles and had a break from the tour, staying in Benedict Canyon, Hollywood. In the US *Help!* reached gold.

24 The Beatles went to a party also attended by Peter Fonda and the Byrds.

25 In *The Times*, a report on the financial success of Northern Songs stated that the previous year's profit was £621,000 rather than the £550,000 anticipated.

27 In the evening they met Elvis Presley at his home in Perugia Way in Hollywood. It was reported that the band spent the evening jamming with Presley while the two managers played pool.

28 The Balboa Stadium in San Diego was the next venue on the US tour.

29 The first concert at the Hollywood Bowl in Los Angeles.

30 *The Beatles Abroad* was broadcast on BBC radio. A second show at the Bowl.

31 The last two shows of the tour were held at Cow Palace in San Francisco.

"LIVE" CONCERT GIVEN MAJOR SURGERY

The Shea Stadium concert was filmed for posterity, Ed Sullivan's production company collaborating with NEMS to make a TV special of the record-breaking extravaganza. The Beatles standard eleven-song set wouldn't have filled the fifty-minute programme, especially since a couple of numbers, "She's a Woman" and "Everybody's Trying to Be My Baby", were omitted. The performance footage was padded out with backstage shots, setting up, and snippets of other acts on the bill. But there was a trickier problem. The wall of unrelenting adulatory noise meant that the group's singing and playing were patchy, to say the least. Major surgery was needed, and five months later the Beatles went to the studio to iron out the imperfections. Some songs needed just a little sweetening. Paul added new bass lines on several tracks, while John tagged an organ piece onto "I'm Down". "Help!" and "I Feel Fine" were deemed beyond salvation and were re-recorded in toto. The boys studied the film to get the lip-sync as close as possible, and tried to give the new recording a live feel rather than a polished studio performance. Ringo's "Act Naturally" was swapped for the disc version that appeared on *Help!*, leaving obvious rough edges for the sharp-eyed viewer.

The Beatles at Shea Stadium aired in the UK on 1 March 1966, and early the following year in America. The sound may have been cleaned up to bring it to broadcast standard, but there was certainly no need to crank up the fans' fervour in post-production. As a performance it had understandable failings; as an experience it was unrivalled.

The Beatles at Shea Stadium

The Shea Stadium concert of 15 August 1965 has gone down in the annals of entertainment history. The sell-out crowd paid a world-record $304,000 for the privilege of watching—as opposed to listening to—the eleven-song set. Over five kilowatts worth of amplification was employed, specially manufactured by Vox, but it was no match for 55,600 delirious fans even with the stadium PA system thrown in. The first chord was enough to identify the song; that was enough to crank up the decibel level. The fans, including future Beatle wives Linda Eastman and Barbara Bach, left the stadium with the illusion that they had heard a concert. A heartbroken twelve-year-old Cyndi Lauper missed out, having to make do with hearing the screams from the nearby World's Fair, where the Beatles helicopter

had landed. As an event—if not a performance—this was, arguably, the pinnacle of the Beatles' era as a touring band. But it also added further weight to the argument that the future lay in the unfettered realms of the recording studio.

The concert hardly put promoter Sid Bernstein back on sound financial footing, either. The Beatles were due a further $80,000 to cover their end of the deal. Once all the overhead was taken care of—more than a thousand policeman and a $25,000 insurance policy took a hefty slice of the cake—Bernstein cleared just $6,500. The Beatles, by contrast, each collected $33,000 for their twenty-eight minutes' work, while Epstein's 25 percent cut amounted to $45,000.

ABOVE AND OPPOSITE: **The Beatles record-breaking performance at Shea Stadium in Queens, New York. A record audience of 55,600 fans crammed into the stadium, and a record $304,000 was taken at the box office.**

US TOUR DATES:

August 15	Shea Stadium, New York
August 17	Maple Leaf Gardens, Toronto
August 18	Atlanta Stadium, Atlanta
August 19	Sam Houston Coliseum, Houston
August 20	White Sox Park, Chicago
August 21	Metropolitan Stadium, Minneapolis
August 22	Memorial Coliseum, Portland
August 28	Balboa Stadium, San Diego
August 29	Hollywood Bowl, Los Angeles
August 30	Hollywood Bowl, Los Angeles
August 31	Cow Palace, San Francisco

ABOVE, RIGHT, AND OPPOSITE BOTTOM: **The Beatles performed two shows at White Sox Park, Chicago, on 20 August. The size of the combined audience for the afternoon and evening shows was more than 60,000 people.**

OPPOSITE TOP: **One of the 30,000 tickets issued to fans for the show in Georgia at Atlanta Stadium, on 18 August.**

RAIN OR SHINE — FAMOUS ARTISTS
— PRESENTS —

THE BEATLES

ATLANTA
STADIUM
ATLANTA, GEORGIA

WEDNESDAY
AUGUST 18, 1965
8:15 P. M.

EST. PRICE 4.95
FEDERAL TAX .40
STATE TAX .15

TOTAL $5.50
NO REFUNDS

Gate F Aisle 113 SEAT 102 ROW 24

Attendance at the performance for which this ticket is sold shall be at ticket holders sole risk and by use of this ticket to gain admission to the performance, holder shall be deemed to have waived and released any and all claims against seller on account of any injury or damage to personal property suffered by holder from any cause while within the Stadium where performance is to be held.

Beatles at the court of the King

"Nothing affected me until Elvis", John once said. Presley's music career may have stalled by the mid-sixties, and the Beatles may have hated the movies he was now making, but he was still "the King". 27 August 1965 witnessed the historic meeting between the Beatles and the rock 'n' roller who had blown them away with "Heartbreak Hotel" a decade earlier.

The visit to Elvis's Bel Air home was anything but a love-in between pop music legends. Initially the Beatles were overawed and tongue-tied, and Elvis was so discomfited at being stared at that he was ready to pull the plug on the evening and retire to bed. John did some Inspector Clouseau-style clowning, which eased the tension, while Paul seized on the fact that Elvis was strumming a bass guitar and offered to show him a riff or two. They jammed together quite contentedly, but found they had little else in common and the atmosphere was strained at best. There were some barbed exchanges between Lennon and Presley, the latter's support for America's involvement in Vietnam inevitably raising the hackles of the man who would pen "Give Peace a Chance". The visit affirmed John's belief that his idol had been emasculated by his stint in the army. "Long live ze King!" was his official verdict, but in private he expressed his true sentiments: "It was a load of rubbish. It was just like meeting Engelbert Humperdinck."

The Beatles made a half-hearted effort to reciprocate the hospitality they had been shown by inviting Elvis to their Hollywood Bowl concert, but Presley didn't attend. Eighteen months later, when the Beatles would list their icons and heroes for the *Sgt. Pepper* cover, Elvis would be a glaring omission.

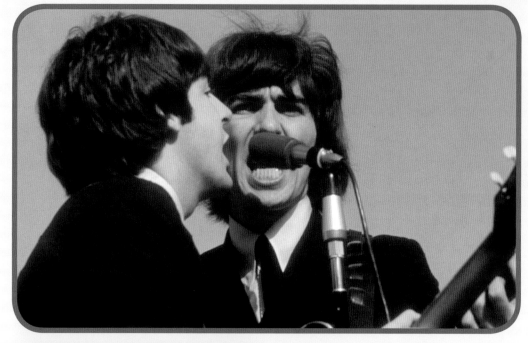

"I know what it's like to be dead."

The only real respite on the frenetic '65 US tour was a four-day stopover in Los Angeles, where the group rented a house in Benedict Canyon, off Mulholland Drive. This was their base for the Hollywood Bowl shows of 29 and 30 August, a slack schedule by Beatles standards, that left plenty of downtime.

George and John were ready for another acid trip, this time of their own volition. They hoped Paul and Ringo would also take the plunge, for they felt LSD had opened up new horizons that had put them on a different level of consciousness. George sensed that his and John's shared experience had drawn them closer together and put distance between them and the other two Beatles. Ringo was game to rectify that, and celebrity guests David Crosby and Roger McGuinn of the Byrds were more than willing, as was young actor Peter Fonda, who had yet to become a global star with *Easy Rider*. Not Paul, though; he would hold off for more than a year.

What transpired that day would furnish John with a linguistic germ that he would work into a standout track during the *Revolver* sessions the following year. He and George already knew that an acid trip was a balancing act between euphoria and terror. When he was unwittingly initiated earlier that year, John had experienced the high of passing through the doors of perception, and the low of a panic attack when he was convinced the building was ablaze. He wasn't very pleased when Fonda emphasized the negative by repeatedly droning, "I know what it's like to be dead", a reference to the fact that he had once accidentally shot himself and had a near-death experience. "She Said She Said" begins and ends with the line "I know what it's like to be dead", the lyric undergoing a gender transformation for the final cut.

ABOVE, LEFT, AND OPPOSITE: **The Beatles opened their set at White Sox Park with "Twist and Shout".**

BELOW: **A ticket for the show at Sam Houston Coliseum, Houston, Texas.**

Radio Station KILT
Presents
The Sixth Annual Back-To-School Show
Sponsored By
THE VARIETY BOYS CLUB OF HOUSTON
STARRING THE BEATLES
(IN PERSON)
AND ALL-STAR SUPPORTING CAST
Master of Ceremonies: RUSS KNIGHT—The Weird Beard
GENERAL ADMISSION TICKET: $5.00
SAM HOUSTON COLISEUM — 3:30 P.M.
THURSDAY, AUGUST 19, 1965 • HOUSTON
KILT N.º 10888 KILT

BELOW FAR LEFT: **A stub from the first of two performances at the last venue on the trip, the San Francisco Cow Palace. Following the performance the boys flew home for more than a month of rest and relaxation.**

BELOW: **Avid fans who wanted to be the first to see the Beatles new movie would have had to take the morning off school or work to attend this 10 a.m. showing of *Help!*.**

Paul R. Catalana
Presents
THE BEAT[
AUG.
31
Tuesday Eve.
COW DALA
SAN [FRANCISCO]
Elevated Main
1965 Admission Tax
$6.45 55c
No Refund
NN K 2
NN K 2

THE BEATLES
HELP!
PREMIERE SHOWING
ADMIT ONE
10:00 A.M. ONLY
WEDNESDAY SEPT. 1st
PORT THEATRE
Corona Del Mar
A UNITED ARTISTS RELEASE
Nº 531
$1.25
THIS TICKET GOOD ONLY AT 10:00 A.M. WEDNESDAY, SEPT. 1st
PORT THEATRE
531

ABOVE: **Scores of photographers and journalists descended to see Ringo at Queen Charlotte's Hospital in Hammersmith, where his wife, Maureen, had given birth to a baby boy on 13 September. The proud father announced the new arrival would be called Zak. Ringo gives a crude estimation of the size of the new baby (left), but follows it up with a more reliable statistic, 8 lbs.**

OPPOSITE: **Paul and Ringo on the steps of Ringo's home in Montagu Square. Ringo and Maureen were to leave the flat for a larger house shortly after the birth of Zak.**

SEPTEMBER 1965

1 After spending the day with the Byrds, the band left the US.

2 They landed at London Airport in the morning and then had a clear six-week break. The single "Help!" went gold in the States.

4 "Help!" reached No. 1 in the US singles charts and remained there for three weeks.

A step on the road to becoming a studio band

The cupboard was somewhat bare when the Beatles repaired to Abbey Road on 12 October to set to work on their sixth album. The only song in the can was "Wait", which had been held over from the *Help!* sessions. And yet just a month later they had completed what some regard as their finest work, or at least a turning point during which the group converted pop wizardry into timeless genius. That autumn they extended their musical horizon; just as the drugs had expanded their minds, the music had a wider palette and richer texture. The recent US tour had highlighted the constraints and frustrations of grand-scale live performance. Abbey Road, by contrast, was a liberating sanctuary. The Beatles were on the road to becoming a studio band, and not merely by inclination: Soon their music would be difficult—in some cases impossible—to reproduce live.

Brian Wilson of the Beach Boys gave a widespread view of *Rubber Soul* among music aficionados when he said it "blew my mind because it was a whole album with all good stuff". The Beatles were indeed now thinking of albums in the round, not merely collections of songs. The path to *Revolver* was clearly signed, and many think its predecessor bettered it in a lot of ways. Rather than compare them, George said they were like volumes one and two of the same album.

10 Reports claimed that Brian Epstein was trying to make a UK deal to show *The Beatles*, a US TV cartoon series.

11 *Help!* the album made the top of the US album charts, holding the spot for nine weeks.

12 *The Ed Sullivan Show* featuring the band was broadcast.

13 "Yesterday"/"Act Naturally" was released in the US on Capitol 5498. Ringo and Maureen's first son, Zak, was born.

15 Paul watched Ben E. King perform at the Scotch of St. James, London.

16 "Eight Days a Week" made gold in the States.

20 In the States, Pete Best released "Kansas City" and "I Can't Do Without You Now".

21 At the Royal Festival Hall, Brian Epstein's *Evening of Popular Music* took place.

25 In the States, *The Beatles* cartoon show began on Saturday mornings.

26 The film *Help!* won the Grand Prix at the International Film Festival in Rio.

Honoured by the Queen

The Beatles were told while shooting *Help!* that they were being awarded the MBE, though the official announcement wasn't made until 11 June, for the convention was that Buckingham Palace had to be certain that the honour would be accepted. That was by no means certain. The boys hardly knew what the initials stood for; such honours were far removed from their roots.

John in particular had reservations about selling out to get to the top, and all had experienced meeting dignitaries at civic functions, which they loathed. Thus an Establishment honour, even though it was the lowest order, was never going to sit easily on their shoulders. Indeed, they decided initially not to accept an award more associated with industrialists, public servants, and military men. Then they thought, why not? They certainly merited recognition for their contribution to the nation's finances in overseas earnings, not to mention the fact that the Beatles had almost single-handedly secured the future of Britain's corduroy industry. Prime Minister Harold Wilson's effort to align himself and his party with the biggest phenomenon in youth culture seemed to have paid off.

There was a backlash, though. Even parts of the tabloid press—never mind the highbrow broadsheets—thought it a perverse decision to honour a mere pop group in such a way. Some war veterans who had received the same award thought their honour had been debased. Many returned them in protest. One objected to being equated with "a bunch of vulgar numbskulls". Acerbic as ever, John pointed out that a lot of recipients from the armed services had got their medals for killing people, whereas theirs was for

entertaining people, concluding: "On balance I'd say we deserve ours more". And many of the good and the great agreed, as well as the adoring legions of fans. The furor helped persuade the recalcitrant, bloody-minded John to accept.

The investiture ceremony took place on 26 October, the boys taking a brief time-out from putting the final touches to *Rubber Soul*. There was one notable absentee from the august proceedings. Brian Epstein, who had urged the boys to accept their awards and to whom it meant most, was not accorded the same honour, which he took to be a pointed snub of his Jewish faith and homosexuality. More likely it was simply a case of Wilson wanting to bask in reflected glory, and that didn't require the

presence of the man who had guided them to the top. The Beatles mentor received his credit when George is said to have quipped that the award stood for Mr. Brian Epstein.

Sharp-eyed fans spotted that eighteen months later, George and Paul wore their MBEs for the *Sgt. Pepper* cover shoot. John's award had pride of place in the home of his beloved Aunt Mimi, but in November 1969 he would "borrow" it to make a political protest. He sent it to the Palace with a note saying: "I am returning this MBE in protest against Britain's involvement in the Nigeria-Biafra thing, against our support of America in Vietnam, and against 'Cold Turkey' slipping down the charts."

OCTOBER 1965

2 At the Grand Gala du Disques in Amsterdam, Brian Epstein accepted an Edison Award for *Beatles for Sale*.

3 The band decided to turn down a script for another movie entitled *A Talent for Loving*.

4 Paul and John watched Alma Cogan record "Eight Days a Week".

7 At his home in Esher, Surrey, George was photographed for an article to be included in the *Beatles Book* magazine.

9 "Yesterday" reached No. 1 in the States, remaining there for four weeks. The band went to a party hosted by Lionel Bart to celebrate his musical *Twang!*.

11 At the Decca Studios in London, Paul watched Marianne Faithfull record "Yesterday".

12 Recording began for the forthcoming album *Rubber Soul*. They taped "Run for Your Life" and "Norwegian Wood (This Bird Has Flown)". George used his sitar on a record for the first time.

13 In a recording session that lasted until after midnight, "Drive My Car" was taped.

14 In New York, Brian Epstein gave his approval to the film made from the Shea Stadium concert.

OPPOSITE: **Paul McCartney MBE, George Harrison MBE, John Winston Lennon MBE, and Richard Starkey MBE.**

LEFT: **Ringo carefully examines his award.**

ABOVE TOP: **Brian Epstein was notably absent from the honours list, and the reason for this is unclear. Epstein was not happy about being overlooked, but was placated by the widespread press reporting on George's comment that the "MBE" after the name of each Beatle really should stand for "Mr. Brian Epstein". The Beatles were each allowed to take two guests to the ceremony, but all agreed that they would go as a foursome and ask Brian to accompany them.**

ABOVE: **Thousands of fans gathered at the Palace in the hope of catching a glimpse of their idols.**

16 "Day Tripper" was recorded for the next single, with some work done on "If I Needed Someone" afterwards.

18 Further work continued on "If I Needed Someone", followed by "In My Life".

19 The Beatles third Christmas Record was taped.

20 "We Can Work It Out" was completed to form the flip-side for the next single, destined to be a double A-side. In the States, "Yesterday" went gold.

21 "Norwegian Wood (This Bird Has Flown)" was finished, and work then began on "Nowhere Man".

22 George Martin completed some piano pieces for "In My Life". During the afternoon the band then finished the work for "Nowhere Man".

24 The whole day was spent on "I'm Looking Through You".

25 George Martin spent the morning on mono mixes.

26 The band went to Buckingham Palace to collect their MBEs, then held a press conference at the Saville Theatre. George Martin spent the morning on stereo mixes.

28 A mono version of "We Can Work It Out" was mixed specifically for a television show called *The Music of Lennon and McCartney*.

29 The previous day's results made the band realize they needed extra vocals, so more were added to "We Can Work It Out" and "Day Tripper".

Writing together

John and Paul may not have been writing "in each other's faces" by this time, but each saw the merit of having an idea tweaked by the other to good effect. Paul's "Drive My Car" was a typical example, John rejecting the original idea of a chorus that ran: "You can buy me golden rings". John saw the inherent weakness in an idea they had already visited twice, in "Can't Buy Me Love" ("I'll buy you diamond rings, my friend...") and "I Feel Fine" ("Her baby buys her things, you know/ he buys her diamond rings, you know..."). As soon as John came up with the suggestive motoring metaphor to tell the story of the wannabe star, the song practically wrote itself, complete with a neat payoff line at the end. An example of Paul repaying the compliment came on "Norwegian Wood", in which the house where the tale unfolds burns down at his suggestion.

This reciprocal outbidding process, where the stronger bid was happily accepted, didn't extend to George. He may have got two songs onto the set list for *Rubber Soul*—"Think for Yourself" and "If I Needed Someone"—but on John and Paul's songs he was hardly given his creative head. Paul in particular was prescriptive regarding George's guitar work, and was more than prepared to take over on lead to show what was required. It created a resentment that would fester right through to the infamous "Get Back" sessions of 1969. George felt overshadowed by the two big egos—and talents—when it came to putting forward his compositions. The balance between Paul and John would also change as John began to drop increasing quantities of acid, leaving Paul to become the band's driving force and creative director.

NOVEMBER 1965

1 *The Music of Lennon and McCartney* was recorded at the Granada TV Centre in Manchester over the next two days. They were backed up by other artists including Lulu, Cilla Black, Marianne Faithfull, and Peter and Gordon.

3 At Abbey Road, "Michelle" was recorded.

4 Back at Abbey Road with only a month before the album was due to be released, the band began to look at songs previously written and as yet unused. Recording sessions that lasted well into the early hours of the morning became a regular feature. "What Goes On" was taped and also "12-Bar Original", a purely instrumental number.

6 "I'm Looking Through You" was worked on.

8 Rehearsal of "Think for Yourself", which was recorded in one take. They also recorded their Christmas message at the end of the session.

9 More mixing work—probably done without the boys being present.

10 Some afternoon mixing work done without the band, who did not begin a session until 9 p.m. They then taped "The Word" and "I'm Looking Through You".

"In My Life"

Rubber Soul saw the Beatles offering not only different perspectives on romance, but new themes entirely. "In My Life" began as an homage to the city of John's birth, the lyric name-checking all the places that a bus ride from Menlove Avenue to the city centre would take in, a list that included Penny Lane. He abandoned the idea—for now—and it turned into an exquisite song of reminiscence and reflection. Or rather, a poem, for in this instance John completed the lyrics before turning his thoughts to the music. The writing of "In My Life" would become one of the main bones of contention between John and Paul. Paul recalled writing the tune around John's lyrics, while John insisted that Paul merely contributed the middle eight melody line and the harmonies. However the cake was divided, the world had another Lennon–McCartney masterwork.

When the group recorded the song, the middle eight was left blank, and it was several days before its distinctive instrumental break was added. George Martin supplied the piano solo, recorded at half speed as he couldn't play it fast enough. None of the Beatles had the training to tell Martin what they wanted in technical language, and the producer became proficient at interpreting their metaphorical shorthand. In this case John requested that he play the piano break "like Bach". Fortuitously, at playback speed the piano resembled an Elizabethan-style harpsichord, which exactly fitted the bill.

LEFT AND OPPOSITE: **During 1965 the Beatles had obviously matured, and their music and image were slowly undergoing transformation. Rather than trading on their boyish charm, the Beatles began to exhibit a more serious, artistic side.**

11 "The Word" was mixed for mono and stereo. Then the last three tracks for the LP were completed: "Wait", "You Won't See Me", and "Girl".

12 An album called *The Beatles in Italy*, produced only for the Italian market, was released.

15 Mixing for the LP was completed by George Martin.

23 The band decided to produce its own promotional material. NEMS Enterprises financed the work and appointed Joe McGrath as director. The set was constructed in two days, and the band worked into the night to produce ten different clips, promoting "We Can Work It Out", "Day Tripper", "Help!", "Ticket to Ride", and "I Feel Fine". The material was distributed immediately.

25 The department store Harrods was closed for three hours so the band could complete their Christmas shopping.

27 In East Ham, London, Paul watched the Yardbirds, Manfred Mann, and the Scaffold (which featured Paul's brother Mike).

29 At Studio One at the Aolian Hall, London, the band was interviewed by Brian Matthew for the Christmas Day edition of *Saturday Club*.

30 At the NEMS offices, George and John were interviewed by Brian Matthew for *Pop Profile*. At Abbey Road Norman Smith mono-mixed "12-Bar Original", the last piece of work he did for the band, as he was destined for promotion.

 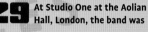

RUBBER SOUL

Released

🇬🇧 **3 December 1965 (Parlophone)**

Side One:
Drive My Car
Norwegian Wood (This Bird Has Flown)
You Won't See Me
Nowhere Man
Think for Yourself (Harrison)
The Word
Michelle

Side Two:
What Goes On (Lennon–McCartney–Starkey)
Girl
I'm Looking Through You
In My Life
Wait
If I Needed Someone (Harrison)
Run for Your Life

Released

🇺🇸 **6 December 1965 (Capitol)**

Side One:
I've Just Seen a Face
Norwegian Wood (This Bird Has Flown)
You Won't See Me
Think for Yourself (Harrison)
The Word
Michelle

Side Two:
It's Only Love
Girl
I'm Looking Through You
In My Life
Wait
Run for Your Life

Cover story

Just as the *Rubber Soul* album marked something of a musical departure for the Beatles, the sleeve design and photography reflected a group in transition; the familiar suits had been replaced by more fashionable suede attire, and the album would also be the first not to bear the Beatles' name on the front. In addition, it would be the last sleeve produced by Robert Freeman, who had photographed the band for the previous four album covers.

The shot of the band, positioned in front of a large rhododendron bush, was selected from a session that had taken place in John's garden in Weybridge, and, although he used colour, Freeman had attempted to create a more monochromatic impression.

Later, when the group was gathered to select an image for the sleeve, the card onto which the pictures were being projected was accidentally tipped backwards, producing a distorted, stretched effect. Taken by the slightly hallucinogenic quality, the Beatles asked Freeman if he could produce a similar result when printing the photograph, and he duly obliged.

DECEMBER 1965

2 The new promotion films for "Day Tripper"/"We Can Work It Out" were shown on *Top of the Pops*.

3 The band began a brief British tour starting at the Odeon Cinema in Glasgow. Two houses were played at each venue. "Day Tripper"/"We Can Work It Out" was released in the UK on Parlophone R 5389 along with the album *Rubber Soul* on Parlophone PMC 1267 (mono) and PCS 3075 (stereo).

4 The next tour venue was the City Hall in Newcastle-Upon-Tyne for the Saturday night shows.

5 Two houses at the Empire Theatre in Liverpool were to be the band's last concerts in Liverpool.

6 "Day Tripper"/"We Can Work It Out" was released in the US on Capitol 5555. The album *Rubber Soul* was also released on Capitol T-2442 (mono) and ST-2442 (stereo). In the UK the EP *The Beatles'*

Million Sellers was released on Parlophone GEP 8946 (mono only). "She Loves You"/"I Want to Hold Your Hand" were featured on the A-side with "Can't Buy Me Love"/"I Feel Fine" on the flip side.

7 The tour continued in Manchester at the ABC Cinema.

8 Staying in the north, they appeared at the Gaumont Cinema in Sheffield.

Lennon–McCartney— and Starkey

Rubber Soul provided Ringo with his first composing credit. He had tried his hand at penning a tune before, but unlike John and Paul, who were able to "lift" selectively from other songs and take a borrowed trifle to a new and exciting place, Ringo had a tendency to make unconscious wholesale duplications of existing tunes. In which case, it seems most likely that he contributed a snatch of the lyric to "What Goes On", a Lennon rockabilly number dating back to the late '50s that was given a fresh lick of paint for inclusion on the group's sixth album. If he came up with a melody line for the song that provided his vocal showcase this time round, then at least he had Paul on hand to assist. Whatever the case, Ringo's contribution was undoubtedly modest. It wasn't until the *White Album* that the drummer would have a completely self-penned song included on a Beatles release—"Don't Pass Me By"—though his most celebrated Beatles composition remains his second offering, *Abbey Road*'s "Octopus's Garden".

Despite Ringo's enormous popularity in the States, "What Goes On" was one of four tracks omitted from Capitol's version of *Rubber Soul*, issued 6 December 1965, three days after the British release. "Drive My Car", "Nowhere Man", and "If I Needed Someone" were also left off, with two *Help!* songs—"I've Just Seen a Face" and "It's Only Love"—added to bring the American release up to the standard tweve-track format. The alterations seem to have been a deliberate move to position the album in the folk-rock genre championed by the Byrds and much in vogue. John doubtless would have preferred to see "It's Only Love" buried without trace, though the fans Stateside obviously disagreed. *Rubber Soul* held the number one spot for six weeks and remained in the US charts for more than a year.

ABOVE: **At the end of a photo shoot, the boys are allowed to tear down the set as the photographer continues to snap.**

OPPOSITE: **George is reflected in John's sunglasses.**

---

9 That evening performances were at the Odeon Cinema in Birmingham.

10 Friday night's venue was the Odeon Cinema in Hammersmith.

11 Staying in London, the group's next night was at the Astoria Cinema in Finsbury Park.

12 The last date was at the Capitol Cinema in Cardiff. This was to be the band's last British tour.

15 The band appeared on television on *Here Come the Pops*.

16 *The Music of Lennon and McCartney* was shown in the London area only.

17 *The Music of Lennon and McCartney* was shown nationally.

21 John received a three-day visit from his father, Freddie.

24 John asked his Aunt Mimi to look after his MBE. *Rubber Soul* received a gold disc in the US.

25 George proposed to Pattie Boyd who immediately accepted. The band appeared on *Top of the Pops* and *Saturday Club*. The album *Rubber Soul* reached the top of the UK charts, staying there for nine weeks.

26 While spending Christmas with his father, Paul fell off a moped, resulting in a large cut on his mouth.

30 Paul had produced a limited edition of four copies of a record called *Paul's Christmas Record*—he gave them to John, George, Ringo, and Jane Asher.

31 In the States, *Beatles '65* received a gold disc.

First double A-side

With the deadline for the completion of *Rubber Soul* looming, John and Paul also had to come up with a new single to catch the Christmas market. They shared the load. John came up with "Day Tripper", a song based around the same riff as "Ticket to Ride". The lyric poured scorn on the "Sunday driver" drug dabblers, those who took the mind-altering experience and counterculture somewhat less seriously than he did. It may also have been a veiled sideswipe at Paul, who was still showing himself to be wary of taking his first acid trip.

"We Can Work It Out" took some eleven hours of studio time to complete, the longest session thus far to perfect one number. The entire debut album had been reeled off in the same time two years earlier. Another dazzling offering from Paul saw him articulating his hopes for a relationship with Jane Asher that was beset by difficulties.

Unlike the other Beatle wives, who were content to take a backseat, Jane was a celebrity in her own right and had aspirations and professional commitments that caused Paul a degree of consternation. The song showed John and Paul in microcosm, the upbeat optimism of Paul's verse reined in by John's edgy middle eight.

The only remaining issue was to decide which of these two gems should get the A-side tag. EMI wanted "We Can Work It Out", but John was determined his song should get top billing, and the compromise of a double A-side was reached. In America "We Can Work It Out" was promoted more heavily and proved more popular, topping both the *Billboard* Hot 100 and *Cash Box* chart, while "Day Tripper" reached only No. 5 and No. 10 respectively. It signalled a return to singles ascendancy for Paul, the first time since "Can't Buy Me Love" eighteen months earlier that a McCartney song had prevailed in the 45-rpm stakes.

BELOW: **John and Paul surrounded by showgirls as they prepare for the Granada special television show celebrating the songs of Lennon and McCartney. A string of guests were invited to cover Beatles songs on the show, including Lulu, who sang "I Saw Him Standing There".**

THIS PAGE : **John and Paul on the set at Granada Studios, where the showcase of their songs was being filmed.**

OPPOSITE TOP: **Ticket stubs from the short UK tour the Beatles embarked on 3 December.**

THE MUSIC OF LENNON AND MCCARTNEY

By the middle of 1965 Brian Epstein was worried that the Beatles were in danger of spreading themselves too thin and diluting the magic; or else they were becoming overexposed. But Epstein could hardly have refused an invitation for the boys to appear in a TV special celebrating the music of Lennon–McCartney. Filmed in early November, the show was first broadcast on 16 December.

A host of stars lined up to perform cover versions or songs specially written for them by John and Paul. Cilla Black sang "It's For You", Billy J. Kramer did "Bad to Me", Peter and Gordon performed their chart-topping "World Without Love", and Marianne Faithfull gave her rendition of "Yesterday". Faithfull had enjoyed a Top 40 hit with her version of Paul's classic ballad, but it didn't do quite as well as Peter Sellers's novelty record, "Richard III Meets A Hard Day's Night", which reached No. 14 in the UK chart.

JOHN, PAUL, GEORGE & RINGO

1966

I Want to Tell You

1966 was a year of crisis management as the Beatles fell victim to tall-poppy syndrome, with a long line of people wanting to cut them down to size.

They came under fire for an album cover that affronted too many sensibilities, a concert given in a hallowed arena, a snub to a dictator's wife, and a throwaway remark by John on the relative popularity of the Beatles and the Almighty. In each case they were guilty till proven innocent, salutary experiences they vowed never to repeat. Concerts had become tribal rituals rather than musical events, and the Beatles had had enough. On 29 August at Candlestick Park, they bade farewell to touring. The Beatles were going to be masters of their own destiny. They put out just two singles and hopped off the two-album-per-year treadmill, concentrating instead on multilayered perfection in the studio. The result was the breathtaking soundscape of *Revolver*, a masterwork that saw all four Beatles at the top of their game.

LEFT: **The Beatles had earned their spurs as a live act, but in 1966 they turned their backs on touring and became a studio band. What turned out to be their final concert performance in the UK was a 15-minute set at the Empire Pool, Wembley, London, on 1 May.**

RIGHT: **An advertisement for Beatles pendants. The demand for Beatles merchandise began to die down in 1966, but the market was still lucrative.**

LEFT AND BELOW: Ringo and Maureen leave for a mid-January break with John and Cynthia in Trinidad. Ringo took the break as an opportunity to forgo the Beatles' clean-cut image for a while and grow a beard. "I hate shaving," he admitted, "and while we're on holiday there's no need to".

OPPOSITE: George and his new wife, Pattie, at Epsom Register Office on their wedding day. George said he was was initally attracted to Pattie because she resembled Brigitte Bardot.

OPPOSITE INSETS: George and Pattie on the way to their reception. In the cool January weather, Pattie kept warm in a red-fox fur coat, designed by Mary Quant. It had been a wedding present from George. Pattie had chosen a set of George III wine goblets for the groom.

JANUARY 1966

1 "We Can Work It Out"/"Day Tripper" was at the top of the UK charts. Parlophone released *Sing a Song of Beatles* featuring Dick James, the music publisher, singing various Beatles songs.

3 Los Angeles rock 'n' roll club Hullabaloo showed promotional clips of the Beatles songs "Day Tripper" and "We Can Work It Out".

4 Brian Epstein flew to the States to start the negotiations and arrangements for the forthcoming tour.

5 The band arrived at CTS Studios, Kensington Square Gardens, to overdub the soundtrack of their TV film *The Beatles at Shea Stadium*.

6 In the States "Day Tripper" was awarded a gold disc.

7 "We Can Work It Out" reached the top of the charts in the US, holding that position for two weeks, while the flip side "Day Tripper" was at No. 5 in its own right. Ringo, George, and John went to Mick Jagger's party at his house in Bryanston Mews East in London.

8 The album *Rubber Soul* reached No. 1 in the States, remaining there for six weeks.

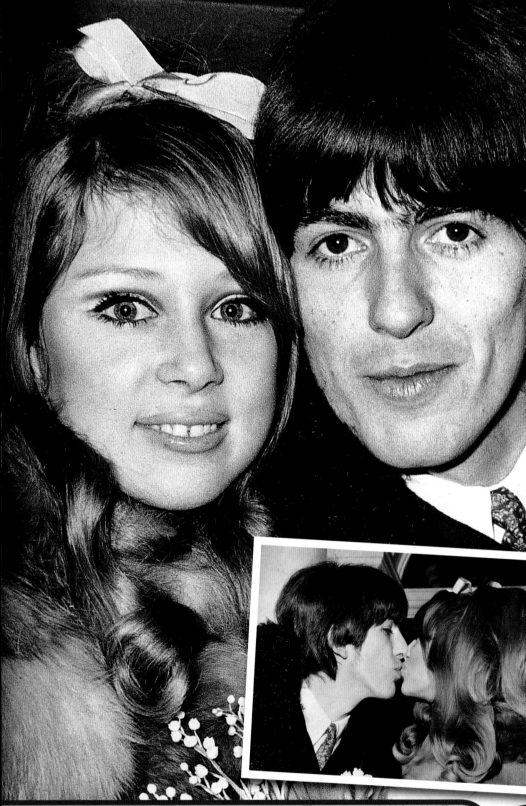

George and Pattie tie the knot

With no Christmas show commitment to fulfil, the Beatles enjoyed an unusually leisurely start to the new year. It was an indication of the shape of things to come. No longer were they prepared to dance to the tune of record companies, promoters, TV and radio producers—not even Brian Epstein.

Of the four, George was the most disillusioned with the grind of Beatledom. He put that aside on 21 January when he and Pattie tied the knot in a low-key ceremony at Epsom Register Office. It was hardly a shock considering the fact that they'd been living together for two years, but the timing caught a lot of people out—not least the Lennons and the Starrs, who had skipped off to Trinidad for a holiday. Paul and Brian shared the best man duties. There was much wailing and gnashing of girls' teeth when it emerged that a third Beatle had entered the realms of connubial bliss.

The newlyweds honeymooned in Barbados, but in 1966 George would find his true spiritual home.

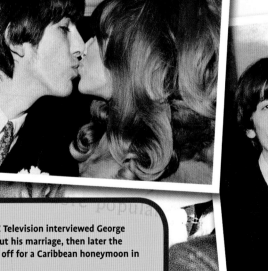

10 Lennon Books Ltd appointed Brian Epstein as a director.

12 Ringo flew to Port of Spain, Trinidad, with his wife, Maureen.

14 The British exhibition rights were acquired by BBC TV for the film of *The Beatles at Shea Stadium*.

21 George married Patricia (Pattie) Ann Boyd at Epsom Register Office.

22 ABC Television interviewed George about his marriage, then later the newlyweds set off for a Caribbean honeymoon in Barbados.

29 "We Can Work It Out" returned to the top of the US charts for one final week.

31 Paul and Jane went to the premiere of *How's the World Treating You* at the Wyndham Theatre in London.

PATTIE, GEORGE, AND ERIC

It is said that George Harrison popped the question to Brian Epstein before Pattie Boyd to ensure that the Beatles' punishing schedule could accommodate a wedding early in 1966. After almost two years as a Beatle's consort, Pattie was all too aware of the attendant pressures, including a willingness to accept a supporting role. The *Vogue* covergirl withdrew from the media spotlight and set about finding an outlet that would offer fulfilment. She launched into charity work and looked eastwards for spiritual growth long before any of the Beatles. Ironically, when George immersed himself in Indian culture, the couple began to drift apart.

In an attempt to save her ailing marriage, Pattie flirted with regular houseguest Eric Clapton, but instead of rekindling a dying flame she ignited a new one. Clapton became infatuated, laying bare his obsessive love in "Layla" and numbing the pain in a self-destructive drug binge.

Pattie's resolve to fight for her marriage weakened; George's declaration of love for Maureen Starkey—later consummated—was, perhaps, an infidelity too far. In 1973 she returned to modelling and had a brief affair with Ronnie Wood. When that ended, the Faces axeman joined the list of those for whom Pattie had been a muse, pouring out his angst in songs such as "Mystifies Me".

The Harrisons divorced in 1977, by which time Clapton had claimed the prize he had long coveted. Two years later George, Paul, and Ringo shared a stage at Eric and Pattie's wedding, yet another near-miss for those who harboured hopes of a Beatles reunion, and one of the last before speculation ceased with an assassin's bullet outside the Dakota building.

ABOVE: **Aside from the groom, only one Beatle was present at the wedding: Paul, the band's only remaining bachelor, played best man. John and Ringo sent a telegram of congratulations from Trinidad.**

LEFT: **Without John and Ringo at the wedding, Brian Epstein (centre) played a prominent role, sharing best man duties with Paul.**

ABOVE AND LEFT: **Two weeks after their wedding, George and Pattie headed for Barbados: "More of a holiday than a honeymoon", according to George. Before marrying George, Pattie had already cleared a major hurdle: winning over her mother-in-law. Louise Harrison, George's mother, praised Pattie's cooking, and Pattie admitted that she loved to cook and enjoyed working out what to prepare for George's dinner. Newlywed Pattie announced she intended to cut down on her modelling career but not stop altogether.**

FEBRUARY 1966

3 During a visit to Britain, Stevie Wonder performed at the Scotch of St. James nightclub in Mason's Yard, London. Paul was in the audience and met him after the show.

11 Peter and Gordon released "Woman", composed by Paul McCartney. He had used the pseudonym Bernard Webb to see how the song would fare without the Lennon–McCartney name.

13 Paul and Peter Asher, Cilla Black, Gerry and the Pacemakers, Ringo and Maureen, and John and Cynthia were among the guests at a party held by Brian Epstein at his London home at 34 Chapel Street.

21 The single "Nowhere Man"/"What Goes On" was released on Capitol 5587 in the US.

23 At the Italian Institute in London, Paul attended a performance by composer Luciano Berio.

28 The Cavern Club's manager, Ray McFall, filed for bankruptcy. A group of fans barricaded themselves inside the club until the police were called to remove them.

Revolver: "trying to create magic"

The spring of 1966 should have seen the Beatles working on their third film, but with no acceptable script forthcoming, the group instead repaired to the studio to cut their seventh album and came up with thirty-five minutes of magic that made the proposed title, *Abracadabra*, eminently suitable. That was dropped when it was found that someone else had got there first, but *Revolver* fitted the bill just as well, for here was indeed a revolution in which the rule book of musical form was torn up. Instruments were distorted to take them to new sonic places; backwards guitar became almost de rigueur; and access to varispeed taping equipment opened up new vistas for both recording and playback. As Paul put it, "The aim is to change it from what it is and to see what it could be. To see the potential in it. To take a note and wreck the note and see what else there is in it... It's all trying to create magic."

For loose definition purposes, *Rubber Soul* has been described as the pot album, *Revolver* its acid counterpart. In order to transfer the kaleidoscopic vision onto vinyl, sounds were daubed on, sometimes with a randomness that rendered the recordings unique. Nothing was off-limits save for their desire to have the tracks glide seamlessly into one another, which the conservative record company regarded as pushing the boundaries a little too far.

Revolver is regarded as the last album on which the group worked as a cohesive unit. A year later, Paul would be the architect and driving force behind *Sgt. Pepper*, and thereafter a chill wind of discontent would blow all too frequently through Abbey Road. Here all four were at the top of their game. Paul's quota included the masterly "Eleanor Rigby", "For No One", and "Here, There and Everywhere", while John supplied "I'm Only Sleeping", "And Your Bird Can Sing", and the stunning finale "Tomorrow Never Knows". George contributed an unprecedented three songs, with the acerbically witty "Taxman" taking the prime side-one, track-one slot. And Ringo came to the party with drumming that he rightly regarded as his finest work, plus a lead-vocal spot that became a number-one single and not just the usual album filler. Little wonder that *Mojo, Rolling Stone,* and *Q Magazine* have all placed *Revolver* not just above *Sgt. Pepper,* but number one in the all-time album list.

ABOVE: **Ringo, George, Paul, and John pose in front of mirrors on rolls of coloured papers in a London photographer's studio.**

OPPOSITE: **The Beatles take a staged sandwich break during a photo shoot.**

BELOW: **"Nowhere Man", from the album *Rubber Soul*, was released as a single by Capitol on 21 February and reached No. 3 in the *Billboard* charts.**

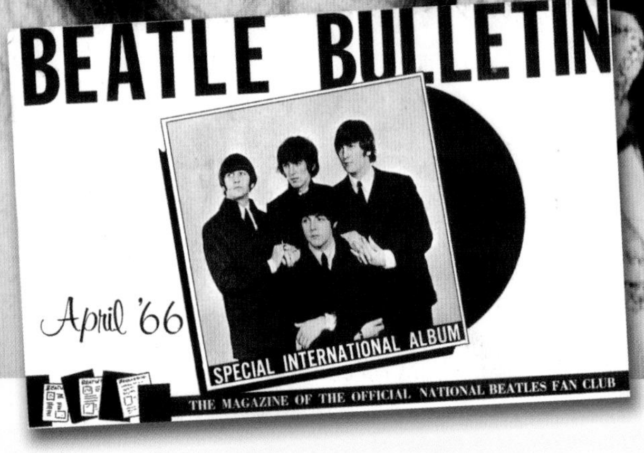

BEATLE BULLETIN

April '66

SPECIAL INTERNATIONAL ALBUM

THE MAGAZINE OF THE OFFICIAL NATIONAL BEATLES FAN CLUB

UP

THE BEATLES' FAMILY TREE

5s.

TOP: **Paul and Jane Asher arrive at the premiere of her latest film, *Alfie*.**

ABOVE INSET: **A special international version of the *Beatle Bulletin*, the magazine for the official Beatles Fan Club. The edition contained a large feature on ABC's *Beatles* cartoon, which was at the height of its popularity in 1966. None of the boys performed the voices for their animated counterparts; instead Paul Frees provided the voices of John and George, while Lance Percival took on Paul and Ringo.**

RIGHT: **Up the Beatles Family Tree: A Canterbury-based company specializing in genealogy published this collection of each Beatle's family tree as a small booklet.**

FAR RIGHT: **Paul on a night out with Jane Asher and her brother, Peter.**

"Eleanor Rigby"

"Eleanor Rigby" started out as a snatch of melody and an image: Paul pictured a woman cleaning up after a wedding. He soon decided that his protagonist was dealing with the shattered remains of her own unfulfilled marital ambitions, as well as the detritus of the present joyous occasion. This juxtaposition gave the song its theme, though the storyline wasn't fleshed out until some time later at a brainstorming session involving the other members of the group and Quarry Man Pete Shotton.

In the meantime, Paul played around with various name combinations for his lonely spinster. Miss Daisy Hawkins was an early contender that was ditched. The choice of "Eleanor Rigby" has been the source of endless comment and speculation. Subconscious may have played a part; even Paul himself may not have been able to supply the definitive answer.

The perfect surname emerged from a trip to Bristol in January 1966. Paul was in town to see Jane Asher, who was appearing at the Old Vic Theatre, when he lighted upon a local wine merchant: Rigby & Evens. Paul had a name for his rice-gathering spinster.

It was at the Lennons' home, Kenwood, that Paul played through what he had and laid the song open to suggestion. Pete Shotton suggested that Father McCartney—as the priest was then called—might be too close to home, which brought forth a trawl through the telephone directory and a suitable three-syllable alternative. Ringo said that the priest might be "darning his socks in the night", while George suggested the "lonely people" refrain. Shotton came up with the idea of Father McKenzie presiding over Eleanor's funeral, thus bringing the two protagonists centre stage at the end of the song.

A family gravestone at Woolton Cemetery does include a 44-year-old Eleanor Rigby, and a John McKenzie lies at rest nearby. As Paul and John used to hang out at the cemetery, it is possible that these names lay dormant in the recesses of Paul's mind. Or it might be pure coincidence.

John seemed to have contributed little—"about half a line" was Paul's estimate—yet he later laid claim to just about the entire lyric apart from the opening verse. The duo often disagreed at the margins over who had written what, but with "Eleanor Rigby" they remained wildly at odds over their respective contributions.

TOP LEFT: **Paul listens to composer Luciano Berio discuss his latest work, "Un Omaggio a Dante" (An Homage to Dante), at the Italian Institute in Belgravia, London. Paul attended to hear Berio's thoughts on electronic music, with which the Beatles were experimenting on their new album, *Revolver*.**

MARCH 1966

1 The BBC showed an edited version of *The Beatles at Shea Stadium* on TV. The film had to be overdubbed due to the poor quality of the original tape.

2 The *Radio Times* review of the Shea Stadium concert commented on the mass hysteria that took place.

4 London's *Evening Standard* published an interview with Maureen Cleave in which John Lennon announced that the Beatles were "more popular than Jesus now". The EP *Yesterday* was released in the UK on Parlophone GEP 8948 (mono only) with the tracks "Yesterday" and "Act Naturally" on the A-side with "You Like Me Too Much" and "It's Only Love" on the flip side.

6 Prime Minister Harold Wilson received a petition with 6,000 signatures complaining about the closure of the Cavern Club.

15 *Help!* was one of the nominees for the Best Original Score for a Motion Picture or Television Show at the Grammy Awards held at the Beverly Hilton Hotel, Los Angeles.

24 George and Paul attended the London premiere of *Alfie*, starring Jane Asher and Michael Caine, at the Plaza Cinema, Haymarket, London.

25 The band recorded a contribution to *Sound of the Stars*—a flexi-disc containing interviews

with other singers and groups including Cliff Richard, Cilla Black, Sandie Shaw, and the Walker Brothers. They were interviewed by Radio Caroline DJ Tom Lodge. Following the interview there was a photo session with photographer Bob Whitaker when the controversial "butcher" photographs were taken.

28 George and Ringo went to see Roy Orbison's concert at the Granada Cinema, Tooting, London.

31 Brian Epstein was in Tokyo making arrangements with Tatsuji Nagashima for the forthcoming tour.

Into the void

Revolver is suffused with drug references, not all of them immediately obvious. The inspiration for John's "She Said She Said" was a haunting remark uttered by a stoned Peter Fonda during the previous summer's US tour. At the time John hadn't welcomed Fonda's disturbing recollection of a near-death experience, but it provided him with a lyrical hook on which to peg his burgeoning interest in LSD as the gateway to a quasi-religious experience. Fonda had been describing a self-inflicted gunshot wound when he repeatedly clamoured, "I know what it's like to be dead". John transmuted this to the death of ego, the feeling of depersonalization said to accompany the acid-fuelled trip to a higher level of consciousness. The song's working title was "He Said He Said," but it underwent a gender transformation for the final cut.

Paul, the last of the four to try LSD, responded with: "I was alone, I took a ride, I didn't know what I would find there"; it wasn't a girl that he had to get into his life. Dr. Robert was a reference to the celebrated "Dr. Feelgood" physician Robert Freymann, who kept New York's smart set supplied with their happy pill of choice. In "I'm Only Sleeping" John gave us the dreamy, contemplative "Stay in bed, float upstream", a "trip" image that would be repeated in the album's tour de force climax.

"Tomorrow Never Knows" was in fact the first of the fourteen new songs to be recorded, though when John turned up at the studio on 6 April it was untitled, initially pencilled in as "Mark 1" and later "The Void" before a quirky Ringoism once again came to the titular rescue. The lyric was

inspired by Timothy Leary's instructional volume *The Psychedelic Experience*, a copy of which John had picked up at Indica Bookshop in London. Leary sought to guide the reader through the mind-expanding trip, using the *Tibetan Book of the Dead* as a rudder. The trip took a different direction this time—"Turn off your mind, relax, and float downstream"—perhaps reflecting John's own conversion from pot to acid, but the sentiment was much the same: a desire to attain a state of heightened perception and enlightenment by abandoning the corporeal world.

"Tomorrow Never Knows" is seen as the first great psychedelic song, a bravura attempt to capture the disconnected unreality of an acid trip on vinyl. It employed several innovative recording techniques. Backroom boffin Ken Townsend came up with artificial double tracking, an electronic means of thickening the vocal, forerunner of the now-ubiquitous chorus effect. This in particular pleased John, who hated double-tracking the long-winded way.

On "Tomorrow Never Knows" they went even further. John's vocal was fed through a

1 In Italy the band were on the cover of the magazine *Ciao Amici*. In the States "Nowhere Man"/"What Goes On" was awarded a gold disc.

5 It was Jane Asher's 20th birthday, so Paul gave her 20 dresses.

6 The first recording session for the album *Revolver* began at Abbey Road with "Tomorrow Never Knows" recorded in just three takes. Twenty-year-old Geoff Emerick had now replaced Norman Smith, and the partnership with George Martin and the band instantly gelled. The album

incorporated significant new technology such as artificial double tracking, tape loops, and the use of a Leslie speaker.

7 The afternoon was spent overlaying "Tomorrow Never Knows", and work began on Paul's "Got to Get You into My Life".

8 Further work to fine-tune the rhythm track on "Got to Get You into My Life".

11 Further overdubs to "Got to Get You into My Life"; then work began on

George's composition "Love You To", which clearly demonstrated his Indian influences. The song included the use of the tabla and sitar.

13 Final work was completed on "Love You To", then recording began of "Paperback Writer", the A-side of the new single to be released in June.

14 "Paperback Writer" was finished, then work commenced on "Rain"— the B-side of the single.

Hammond organ's rotating Leslie speaker to give it the desired ethereal, disembodied quality. Rigging the circuitry to achieve that effect was much easier than John's suggestion: that he be suspended from the ceiling by a rope and deliver the vocal while circumnavigating the room.

Tape loops were also used extensively. Paul had dabbled with feeding a loop of tape through a recorder that had had its erase head removed. The recorded sound replicated itself until saturation point was reached. A multitude of these loops were made, creating a plethora of surreal effects

including a seagull-like cawing— actually a speeded-up guitar. The whole was such a spontaneous, random event that George Martin said it was the only Beatles track that would be impossible to re-create.

ABOVE: **While the Beatles were in the studio working on the forthcoming album,** *Revolver*, **they took some time out between 13 April and 16 April to record a new single, "Paperback Writer"/"Rain". Here they are filming a promotional clip for the single.**

16 "Rain" was completed in a studio session lasting 11 hours, first superimposing tambourine, bass, and vocals, and then adding more overdubs.

17 The start of recording of John's new composition, "Dr. Robert". This was written about a New York doctor who it was believed gave hallucinogenic drugs to his friends.

18 Joe Davey, a café proprietor, purchased the Cavern Club. At the Marquee in London, Eric Clapton, George, and John watched the Lovin' Spoonful play.

19 "Dr. Robert" was completed.

20 Recordings began for "And Your Bird Can Sing" and "Taxman" in another long 12-hour studio session.

21 Eleven takes of the rhythm track for "Taxman" were recorded.

22 The "Mister Wilson, Mister Heath" refrain was added to the final version of "Taxman", a perfect promotion for the UK's two main political leaders.

23 In the UK *Disc and Music Echo*, a new pop paper, was published. It was part of a merger including the Brian Epstein owned *Disc with Music Echo*. He therefore owned half the stakes in the new paper.

25 Two rough mono mixes of "Got to Get You into My Life" were made.

26 Another long session resulted in 11 more takes of the rhythm track of "And Your Bird Can Sing".

27 An evening recording session as the band began work on John's new song, "I'm Only Sleeping", along with further work on "Taxman", "Tomorrow Never Knows", and "And Your Bird Can Sing".

28 The string section of "Eleanor Rigby" was recorded using a double string quartet.

29 The main focus of this session was the vocal overdubbing on "Eleanor Rigby", with some additional work on "I'm Only Sleeping".

The Beatles' final UK concert performance

On Sunday, 1 May, the Beatles came hotfoot from working on "Eleanor Rigby" to turn out at Wembley's Empire Pool for their fourth appearance at the *New Musical Express* Poll Winners' Concert. It was the group's first live engagement since 12 December, the biggest gap in their performing history since the days when the Quarry Men were scratching round trying to drum up trade.

The Beatles did a fifteen-minute set comprising "I Feel Fine", "Nowhere Man", "Day Tripper", "If I Needed Someone", and "I'm Down". The fans would have relished a selection that included two tracks from *Rubber Soul*—which had been top of the album chart until mid-February—and a couple of singles from the previous year, with "I Feel Fine" representing Beatles '64 vintage. As yet there had been no 1966 release, so the set would have seemed pretty much up to date. Of course, they weren't privy to the material that was emerging from the *Revolver* sessions.

Politics played a part in what turned out to be the Beatles' final concert performance on home soil. They and the Rolling Stones were the biggest names on the bill, the clean-cut crew going head-to-head with the bad boys to see who would steal the show. It was all media invention. In fact, the members of the two supergroups were quite friendly. John and Paul sang along quite happily on "We Love You", Brian Jones chipped

LEFT: **Paul at Abbey Road studios during the 11-hour session to record "Rain".**

MAY 1966

1 The last live Beatles performance in Britain at the Empire Pool Wembley for the *NME* Annual Poll Winners' All-Star Concert. They performed five songs in a brief 15-minute set. The concert was filmed but the cameras were switched off for the Beatles and Rolling Stones sets as there was a dispute running between the bands' managers and ABC Television. However, the bands were taped receiving their awards.

2 Brian Matthew interviewed the group for the 400th edition of *Saturday Club* at the Playhouse Theatre, London. Matthew then interviewed Paul and Ringo separately for *Pop Profile*, an overseas

programme. Bob Dylan flew into London to begin a UK tour. He met Keith Richards, Brian Jones, and Paul at the Mayfair Hotel, where he was staying.

4 In Japan the Finance Minister allowed the band to play in the country, permitting each of them to receive £10,000 from their earnings.

5 George Harrison spent many hours recording the sound of guitars playing backwards for the track "I'm Only Sleeping" at Abbey Road.

6 There was more overdubbing of vocals before the recording of "I'm Only Sleeping" was mixed into mono.

9 Ten takes of Paul's ballad "For No One" took up most of the session, which included the overdubbing of a clavichord.

12 Mono mixes and edits of "Dr. Robert", "I'm Only Sleeping", and "And Your Bird Can Sing" were recorded for an album to be released in the US the following month.

15 The *New Musical Express* Annual Poll Winners' All-Star Concert was

in on "Yellow Submarine", and they were forever crossing each other's paths at the Bag O' Nails or Ad Lib clubs.

Their respective managers weren't quite so accommodating. Brian Epstein and Andrew Loog Oldham each wanted his act to get the star spot, which, traditionally, meant closing the show. But on this occasion a contractual dispute with ABC, the TV company filming the event, meant that the last act was in danger of being edited out of the broadcast. That left Epstein and Oldham vying for the penultimate spot on the day, which they believed would be the top-of-the-bill slot as far as the millions watching on television were concerned.

Epstein had to concede. The promoter was never going to entertain the idea of the Beatles appearing anywhere on the bill other than as the grand finale. In the end, neither the Beatles nor the Stones featured in the TV special, though with another forty years—and counting—on the road, it was hardly significant for the latter. It was an epoch for the Beatles, whose adieu to their home fans was restricted to those lucky enough to be in the Wembley audience that day.

RIGHT: **Paul and George perform in what was to be the Beatles' last British concert, which took place at Empire Pool, Wembley, London, on 1 May. The 15-minute set was part of the *New Musical Express* Poll Winners' concert.**

transmitted by ABC on British television. As the Beatles and the Rolling Stones were omitted, several television companies did not broadcast the programme.

16 A long day of overdubbing, mixing, and copying for the album *Revolver* took place at Abbey Road.

18 "Got to Get You into My Life" was finalized in a long 12-hour studio session. Eddie Thornton and Peter Coe (from the band Georgie Fame and the Blue Flames) were two of the instrumentalists recruited for the brass section.

19 The first of a two-day shoot to produce four promotional films for "Paperback Writer" and three for its B-side, "Rain". The French horn solo, played by Alan Civil, was added to "For No One".

20 Director Michael Lindsay-Hogg took the band on location to the 18th-century gardens of Chiswick House, London, for the second day of the shoot.

21 John and Cynthia went out partying with Mick Jagger and Chrissie Shrimpton.

26 Due to food poisoning, George Martin missed the taping of the initial tracks of "Yellow Submarine". Geoff Emerick directed the session in George's absence.

27 Bob Dylan and John Lennon were filmed in the back of a limousine driving from John's house in Surrey to the Mayfair Hotel in Stratton Street. Much of their conversation was incoherent due to the strong influence of drugs on Dylan and possibly John. Later that evening, Dylan appeared at the Royal Albert Hall in London.

30 The single "Paperback Writer"/ "Rain" was released in the US on Capitol 5651.

31 At his home, Sunny Heights, Ringo was photographed for *The Beatles Book*'s "At Home" feature.

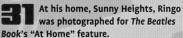

BIO: MAL EVANS

A former doorman at the Cavern Club, Mal Evans, who became known as "the gentle giant", was invited by Brian Epstein to shift equipment for the Beatles in 1963. He went on to become their road manager, driver, and personal assistant, and later an executive at Apple Corps.

Evans also appeared in the Beatles' films *Help!* and *Magical Mystery Tour*, and contributed vocal and instrumental parts to several song recordings, apparently including lyrics to "Fixing a Hole".

In 1968 Evans discovered the band the Iveys, who were later signed to Apple as Badfinger, and as well as producing some of their recordings he worked as a producer on *Two Sides of the Moon*, Keith Moon's solo album.

Following the breakup of his marriage in 1973, Mal Evans relocated to Los Angeles, and it was there, three years later, that a drugged and despondent Evans was shot dead by police after brandishing an air gun.

Musical mayhem

In both style and substance *Revolver* represented a move away from pop music convention. Mere guitars, drums, keyboard, and vocals seemed like something out of the Dark Ages as the Beatles looked to classical instruments—and even the EMI props cupboard—to extend their range.

String accompaniment was nothing new: "Yesterday" had featured a quartet, "Eleanor Rigby" an octet. On "For No One", which captured with elegant poignancy the death throes of "a love that should have lasted years", Paul wanted a French horn solo. George Martin hired Royal Philharmonia Orchestra player Alan Civil, who was about to get the defining credit of his illustrious career.

ABOVE AND RIGHT: **George (right) and Paul with Mal Evans (above), filming promotional material for "Paperback Writer" and "Rain" at Chiswick House. A total of seven films were made, four for "Paperback Writer" and three for "Rain". Most of the material was shot in the studio on 19 May, but scenes of the boys in the gardens of the 18th-century estate were added the following day.**

OPPOSITE: **The Beatles rehearsing for their first and only live performance on *Top of the Pops* on 16 June.**

Paul hummed what he envisioned, and Martin transcribed it into sheet form. Paul's suggested piece included a high F, a note outside the French horn's normal range. Civil immediately queried it, but with wry smiles all round, and some extemporization on the soloist's part, another memorable instrumental break was soon in the can.

"Yellow Submarine", a charming McCartney children's song with a nod to psychedelia, provided the Beatles, their entourage, studio staff, and the odd passerby with the chance to let their hair down in one of the most chaotic, fun-filled sessions ever seen at Abbey Road. On top of the rhythm track and Ringo's vocal, the group plus an ad hoc supporting cast blew, rattled, clanged, and whooped, using an assortment of effects equipment that probably hadn't seen the light of day for years. Long-time chauffeur Alf Bicknell provided the sound of the dropping anchor, achieved by rattling a chain round a tin bath, while the Stones' Brian Jones clinked glasses together. John spouted, "Full speed ahead, Mister Captain" from inside the echo chamber adjoining Studio Two, and stayed there to answer Ringo's lyric in the last verse. The zany effects embellished the whole song, but appeared only selectively on the released version. A wacky spoken introduction was also dropped.

This rollicking fantasy was paired with the spare, hauntingly poetic "Eleanor Rigby" for the singles market, yet another testament to the fact that the Beatles really were a group for all seasons.

JUNE 1966

1 In a madcap session at Abbey Road, Brian Jones, Marianne Faithfull, Pattie Boyd, and many Abbey Road staff members helped to add the sound effects to the *Yellow Submarine* soundtrack. As John blew bubbles into a bucket and shouted out "Full speed ahead, Mister Captain", the others all joined in, making as much noise as they could. In the evening George watched Ravi Shankar play at the Royal Albert Hall.

2 The majority of this session at Abbey Road was spent recording George's song, which had the working title of "I Don't Know" but was later changed to "I Want to Tell You".

3 Further work was completed for "I Want to Tell You" and "Yellow Submarine".

4 The band appeared on the 400th edition of *Saturday Club*.

5 Promotional films shot in May for "Rain" and "Paperback Writer" were screened on *The Ed Sullivan Show* in America.

6 The final overdub for "Eleanor Rigby" was recorded by Paul.

8 Recording began for Paul's "Good Day Sunshine", while Geoff Emerick finished some editing on "And Your Bird Can Sing".

9 "Good Day Sunshine" was completed in two days.

10 "Paperback Writer"/"Rain" was released in the UK on Parlophone R 5452.

13 Brian Epstein received a letter from BBC producer Johnnie Stewart asking the band to appear live on *Top of the Pops*.

Latest single signals a new direction

By 1966 it wasn't just touring that had lost its lustre. The Beatles broke with the old template of two albums and four singles per annum, halving that prodigious output as they opted for intensive bursts of creativity in the studio and long periods away from it. The greater complexity of their material, plus the freedom to redo anything that to their ears fell short of perfection, meant there were no quick fixes. The *Revolver* sessions lasted ten weeks, far longer than any of the previous six LPs had taken to record. It was well worth the wait, for these sessions yielded sixteen top-drawer songs, a stunning new single as well as an album packed with gems.

Four months had passed since the last 45 release when the group started work on *Revolver*, and even though they were working under a more relaxed regimen, a new single was a matter of pressing importance. The Beatles decided that of their completed songs "Paperback Writer" and "Rain" were the most commercial.

The single had a tepid reception by Beatles standards, though in truth it hadn't been written with the 45 market in mind. They could hardly have put out "Tomorrow Never Knows".

The latest single was a signpost offering, giving a number of clues to a new direction. The A-side allowed Paul to showcase his new

Rickenbacker bass, which he used instead of his trusty old Hofner. The Beatles were constantly nagging the Abbey Road engineers to crank up the bottom end, and here they got their wish as a bass speaker was used as a microphone to boost the signal. It incurred a ticking-off from upstairs, for EMI set strict limits on the bass levels to forestall the possibility of

ABOVE: **"Paperback Writer"/"Rain" eventually reached No. 1 on both sides of the Atlantic, replacing "Paint It Black" by the Rolling Stones in America and "Strangers in the Night" by Frank Sinatra in Britain.**

LEFT: **John and George perform on *Top of the Pops* on 16 June. Brian Epstein had decided to go ahead with the appearance after "Paperback Writer"/"Rain" entered the British charts at No. 2 rather than going straight to No. 1. The appearance did the trick: the track hit the top spot the following week and remained there for two weeks.**

continued from previous page

JUNE 1966

14 "Here, There and Everywhere" was started and four rhythm tracks were recorded. The song was perfected in sessions spread over three days. In the US, Ron Tepper at Capitol announced the decision to change the cover of the new LP *Yesterday and Today*. It had originally showed the band smiling amongst dolls that had been decapitated and covered in blood. The original photographs had been designed as pop-art satire, but Capitol was unhappy with it. This became known as the "butcher" cover.

16 DJ Pete Murray was the host for the Beatles' only live appearance on *Top of the Pops*; they appeared as the final act of the show, miming to "Paperback Writer" and "Rain". After a long session at the BBC Television Centre they returned to Abbey Road for a recording session that went on until 3:30 a.m., to complete "Here, There and Everywhere".

17 An additional overdub was added to Paul's ballad "Here, There and Everywhere", with another guitar piece added to "Got to Get You into My Life". In *The Times* it was revealed that Paul had purchased a farm in Scotland on the Mull of Kintyre.

20 An additional mono mix of "Got to Get You into My Life" was recorded, increasing the brass section. *Yesterday and Today* was released in the US on Capitol T-2553 (mono) and ST-2553 (stereo) with a new sleeve.

21 John's new song, "She Said, She Said", was recorded from start to finish in one session lasting seven hours. The lyrics told the story of John and Peter Fonda (who was experiencing an LSD trip) talking while the band was on tour in North America.

22 The final mixing session of mono and stereo versions for

the stylus jumping. It was yet another example of the Beatles acknowledging a rule and then deliberately flouting it.

Paul's jokey, aspirational lyrics had a zeitgeist feel for the classless mid-'60s youth, while the "Frère Jacques" refrain revealed an interest in kids' songs and childhood reminiscence that would be reprised on a number of occasions.

John's "Rain", the "trippy" antidote to "Good Day Sunshine", was a cut above B-side fare. The pounding, saturated sound was achieved by slowing down the rhythm track. Backwards instrumentation wasn't enough; the outro vocals are a line lifted from earlier in the song and played backwards. John claimed he discovered this by accident when he spooled a rough take the wrong way round on his tape machine at home. George Martin recollects that the idea was his, sparked by the group's obsession for breaking with convention.

"Paperback Writer"/"Rain" raised an eyebrow as it reached only No. 2 in the week of its release, the first time since "She Loves You" that a Beatles single hadn't gone straight to the top of the UK chart. Sinatra's "Strangers in the Night" held them up, an obstacle Epstein determined to remove by reconsidering the decision to concentrate on self-made promotional films instead of appearing on *Top of the Pops*. The Beatles made a hastily arranged, triumphant return to the flagship show—their one and only live appearance—and regained their rightful chart position a week later.

yesterday and today

Released

🇺🇸 **15 June 1966** (Capitol)
20 June 1966 (Capitol)

Side One:
Drive My Car
I'm Only Sleeping
Nowhere Man
Dr. Robert
Yesterday
Act Naturally
 (Morrison–Russell)

Side Two:
And Your Bird Can Sing
If I Needed Someone
 (Harrison)
We Can Work It Out
What Goes On (Lennon–
 McCartney–Starkey)
Day Tripper

cover story

Yesterday and Today, due to be issued by Capitol on 15 June, was a real mongrel: songs left over from *Help!* and *Rubber Soul*, plus three tracks culled from the yet-to-be-released *Revolver*. If they had no say over the content, at least the Beatles were going to leave their mark on the artwork.

When Australian photographer Bob Whitaker posed them with mutilated dolls and slabs of raw meat, they weren't at all sure what message was being conveyed, but pictorially it certainly drew a line under the cheeky Fabs era, just as *Rubber Soul* and *Revolver* had done in musical terms. Whitaker insisted the "butcher" shot was only ever intended to be a small inset in a multi-image gatefold sleeve that was conceived as a comment on icons and hagiography. Had Capitol boss Alan Livingston received the complete set, all would have been well. It wasn't. Livingston was horrified, but backed off when he was informed that the Beatles wouldn't budge. The pressing went ahead, but when his sales team reported uniformly negative feedback from the retailers, Livingston pulled the plug and an anodyne shot of the Beatles posing around a steamer trunk was used instead.

Capitol wasn't about to waste the sleeves already produced, so the new image was simply pasted over the offending shot. A little steam and gentle coaxing brought some lucky fans a much-sought-after collector's item.

---

the *Revolver* album before its release in August. George opened a new disco called Sybilla's, which he part owned with Sir William Piggott-Brown.

23 The band flew into Munich to start a short tour covering Germany, Japan, and the Philippines.

24 The live act at Circus Krone, Munich, reflected their lack of rehearsals prior to the tour. The band had to interrupt "I'm Down" to discuss the lyrics. The second concert was filmed by Zweites Deutsches Fernsehen for a programme called *Die Beatles* to be broadcast the following month.

25 The group travelled from Munich to Essen in a unique train that had been used by Queen Elizabeth II the previous year, before performing two shows at the Grugahalle, then returning straight back to the railway station. "Paperback Writer" leapt to the top of the UK charts, remaining there for two weeks. In the States it was at the top of the charts for one week.

26 The first time the band had returned to Hamburg since their visit to the Star-Club at Christmas 1962. Arriving at the station at 6 a.m., they travelled in a motorcade made up of eight cars and 12 police motorcycles before

playing to two houses, totalling 11,000 spectators, at the Ernst Merck Halle.

27 The band flew back to London before flying on to Japan.

28 Their plane had to stop unexpectedly in Anchorage, Alaska, for 24 hours due to a warning about Typhoon Kit.

29 The band flew into Haneda Airport, Tokyo. They were greeted by 1,500 fans who had turned out to see them—some of whom were roughly handled by riot police. Despite trying to quietly hide in an entire floor of a local

hotel, the band was soon found by the local radio station, who recorded their movements throughout their stay.

30 The first of five shows was performed later that day at Nippon Budokan Hall, Tokyo. Many Japanese considered the Budokan a sacred building, as it housed sumo wrestlers, and were horrified it was to be used for a pop concert.

On the road again

Anyone plotting the course of events that culminated in George's declaration, "That's it, I'm not a Beatle anymore" in August 1966 would have to give considerable weight to the woes of the Far East trip two months earlier. Things ran less than smoothly from the outset. The group's plane had to divert to Anchorage to avoid flying into a Southeast Asian storm, a suitable portent for what was to come.

After playing three venues in Germany, the next port of call was Tokyo, where the local police took security to new levels of precision. Touring always brought with it claustrophobic confinement in hotel rooms, but the officiousness of the security personnel made the Hilton Hotel experience more oppressive than ever. Paul and George did manage a fleeting escape, but to all intents and purposes they were captive guests, occupying themselves with a spot of home shopping and a collaborative effort on a piece of abstract artwork. They may have felt trapped and bored, but that was soon to be the least of their troubles.

Beatlemania was alive and well in Japan—in the ballot for tickets, demand outstripped supply by seven to one—but there was a rump of fanatical opposition, at the forefront of which was a militant student faction who resented the fact that a sacred martial-arts venue was about to be defiled in the name of decadent Western pop music. It is doubtful that the Beatles had ever heard of the Budokan Hall, where they were to play five concerts over three days. Even without death threats, the boys were wont to race through the songs at a far greater lick than would be found on studio recordings, and no doubt they employed that tactic here so that they could get off the stage as quickly as possible. In the event, a security ratio of one policemen for every three fans kept a tight lid on the proceedings, though an unusual level of restraint during the numbers exposed how sloppy the group's performance had become.

At least the concerts went off without a hitch. The same couldn't be said for the next stop: the Philippines.

JULY 1966

1 The second and third shows in Japan. Each performance was in front of a crowd of 10,000—with 3,000 policemen carefully scattered throughout the Hall to keep order. In Munich, West Germany, the authorities began to initiate plans to introduce an "entertainment tax".

2 The fourth and fifth performances in Tokyo. Highlights from the performances were videoed in colour and later were amalgamated into a one-hour programme, *The Beatles Recital, from Nippon Budokan* screened by NTV Channel 4.

3 Departure for the Philippines with a brief stopover at Kaitak Airport, Hong Kong.

4 Two performances in front of a total of 80,000 fans at the Rizai Memorial Football Stadium, Manila.

5 The band departed Manila International Airport at 4:45 p.m. after controversy: they had been accused of snubbing Imelda Marcos, the president's wife.

6 After briefly refuelling at Bangkok, the band stopped off at New Delhi, India, on their way home. They were hoping for a break and some quiet, but were yet again surrounded by screaming fans.

8 They finally landed at London Airport at 6 a.m. George and Ringo were interviewed for the radio programme *Today*. The EP *Nowhere Man* was released in the UK on Parlophone GEP 8952 (mono only) with tracks "Nowhere Man" and "You Won't See Me" on the A-side and "Drive My Car" and "Michelle" on the B-side. In the States

OPPOSITE AND THIS PAGE: **Another summer of touring got underway on 24 June when the Beatles flew to Munich, West Germany. After giving two performances in both Munich and Essen the boys arrived in Hamburg on 26 June, the first time they had been back since Christmas 1962. They performed two shows at the Ernst Merck Halle before paying a visit to old haunts on the Reeperbahn, Hamburg's nightlife district. The Beatles had come a long way since the early Hamburg days when they barely scratched a living; in 1966 they travelled from Munich to Essen in a special train that had carried Queen Elizabeth II on her recent visit to West Germany.**

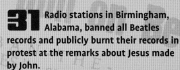

"Paperback Writer" spent another week at the top of the charts and *Yesterday and Today* was certified gold.

12 In the Ivor Novello Awards, "Yesterday" was awarded "Outstanding Song of 1965" while "We Can Work It Out" received Highest Certified British Sales. Cliff Bennett and the Rebel Rousers began to tape Paul's "Got to Get You into My Life". He was present at the recording session.

13 "Got to Get You into My Life" was completed.

14 In the States the show *Where the Action Is* featured three singers all performing cover versions of Beatles songs. "Paperback Writer"/"Rain" was certified gold in the States.

23 The Cavern Club reopened under new management. The opening was attended by Prime Minister Harold Wilson and Ken Dodd. The Beatles sent a telegram with wishes of good luck.

29 American teen magazine *Datebook* published John's *Evening Standard* interview including his comment that "We are more popular than Jesus". This caused a huge furor in the US. The band refused to sign a contract that would include touring South Africa, as the apartheid policy would have stopped black people from attending the shows.

30 *Yesterday and Today* topped the US charts and remained there for five weeks.

31 Radio stations in Birmingham, Alabama, banned all Beatles records and publicly burnt their records in protest at the remarks about Jesus made by John.

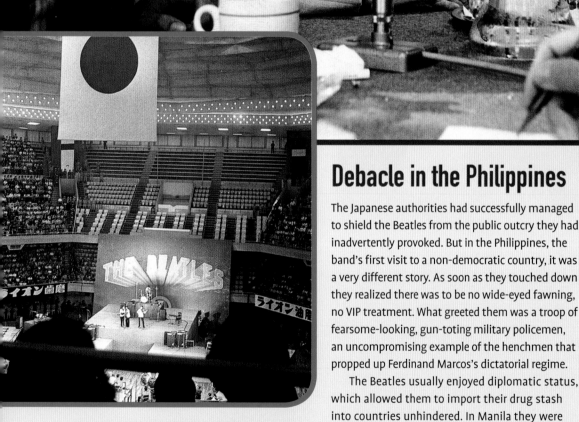

Crowd boos as the Beatles fly out

MANILA, Tuesday
THE BEATLES were jostled, booed and jeered when they flew out today after Philippines newspapers accused them of snubbing the President's family by not turning up for lunch yesterday.

Screwed up pieces of paper were thrown at them at the airport and adults shouted: "Beatles go home," "Go to hell," and "We don't want you here."

An angry...

ABOVE: **The Beatles perform to one of the most orderly audiences they ever encountered. The fans in Budokan Hall, Tokyo, were strictly marshalled and the Beatles' music was, unusually, not drowned out by screams.**

Debacle in the Philippines

The Japanese authorities had successfully managed to shield the Beatles from the public outcry they had inadvertently provoked. But in the Philippines, the band's first visit to a non-democratic country, it was a very different story. As soon as they touched down they realized there was to be no wide-eyed fawning, no VIP treatment. What greeted them was a troop of fearsome-looking, gun-toting military policemen, an uncompromising example of the henchmen that propped up Ferdinand Marcos's dictatorial regime.

The Beatles usually enjoyed diplomatic status, which allowed them to import their drug stash into countries unhindered. In Manila they were separated both from their personal luggage and from Brian Epstein, Mal Evans, and Neil Aspinall as they were herded onto a boat for several hours

with no explanation. Apprehension quickly turned to fear as they realized that their reputation and standing counted for nothing here.

All hell broke loose the following day when they were informed they were late for a function at the presidential palace. There was a collective shrug. It was the first they'd heard of a reception organized by the country's first lady, Imelda Marcos, and they assumed it was a mistake. Ever

asked the boys to give his love to his wife. It was another example of being given the bureaucratic runaround, the authorities claiming there was no record of their arrival in the country, ergo they had to be illegal aliens. A shell-shocked Epstein handed over a substantial fee, a trumped-up "Beatles tax" in all but name.

The forthcoming American tour would bring more trials and controversy, but this weeklong trip was one of the final nails in the touring coffin. It was also a turning point in the Beatles' relationship with Epstein, who took a lot of flak for the whole sorry debacle.

LEFT: **Trying to blend in in Japan; John reads a book while Ringo looks on. Both are wearing kimonos they received as gifts during their stay in Japan.**

OPPOSITE TOP: **The Beatles giving a press conference in London after returning from the Far East. The chief topic of conversation was the trip to the Philippines, where the band had missed a meeting with the first lady, Imelda Marcos, and had come under intense attack as a result. The state press wildly criticized the band and the boys were forced to make a quick exit.**

OPPOSITE INSET: **The *Daily Mail* of 5 July reports on the Beatles' difficulties in Manila.**

BELOW: **The Beatles and Brian Epstein are glad to be on friendly soil after a harrowing trip to the Philippines. The experience was instrumental in the band's decision to discontinue touring.**

since the Washington Embassy fiasco in 1964 they had made their views clear to Brian on the subject of being paraded in front of dignitaries. Epstein indeed knew their feelings, and thought he had politely but firmly declined the invitation. But there was the evidence before their eyes on TV, live pictures from the palace assuring viewers that the Beatles were on their way. There were lingering shots of disappointed children as it became clear that the superstars were not going to show.

A record 80,000 people attended the two concerts, but the Beatles had no time to reflect on that phenomenal statistic. BEATLES SNUB FIRST FAMILY ran the headlines the next day. The group found that to offend the rulers in an autocratic regime carried severe consequences. Epstein tried to calm the waters, but his media apology was drowned out by carefully orchestrated static. It wasn't just a question of having room service curtailed; protection was withdrawn completely, and they were left to run the gauntlet of an angry populace as they fled for their lives.

At Manila Airport the officials stood by as the hostile crowd was allowed to assault the entourage. The power to the escalators was turned off, leaving them to negotiate stairs with heavy equipment. "You treat like ordinary passenger" was the officials' cry, prompting John to wryly comment that he hoped getting kicked, punched, and spat upon wasn't the lot of the ordinary visitor passing through the country's airport.

When they were on the plane, the call came for Mal Evans and press officer Tony Barrow to alight. Evans thought his number was up and

An unholy row

For more than two years the Beatles PR machine had worked perfectly in America. To all intents and purposes they were the group that bucked the trend of rock 'n' roll excess. Ed Sullivan had bestowed the ultimate seal of approval. It was all rot, of course, but it made the perceived fall from grace, when it came, the more dramatic.

On 29 July, two weeks before the Beatles were due to arrive in the States, the teen magazine *Datebook* reprinted a Maureen Cleave article about John that had appeared in the London *Evening Standard* four months earlier. The article had spanned a wide range of lifestyle topics, from the number of cars and TV sets he owned to his interest in natural history and ownership of a gorilla suit. But in America one segment was extracted for banner-headline treatment: "Christianity will go. It will vanish and shrink. I needn't argue about that. I'm right and I will be proved right. We're more popular than Jesus now. I don't know which will go first, rock 'n' roll or Christianity."

Remarks that passed almost without comment the first time round sent the US into a ferment, particularly the Bible Belt. Christian fundamentalists had a long history of equating rock 'n' roll with moral turpitude, and this was grist to their mill.

Other Beatles outpourings were trawled through in search of corroborative evidence to support the view that they were, after all, subversive undesirables. A Lennon story from *A Spaniard in the Works* titled "Father, Sock and Mickey Most" was one of the exhibits used to show that his comments to Cleave were not an unfortunate aberration. Radio stations banned Beatles music—primarily, but not exclusively, in the South. Public burnings of Beatles records invoked the nightmare vision of Bradbury's *Fahrenheit 451*. The Ku Klux Klan let it be known it wasn't merely going to wave a placard to show its Christian credentials. They may have misunderstood the message, but shooting the messenger seemed a real possibility.

Epstein flies to probe ban on Beatles

A "BAN-THE-BEATLES" campaign is spreading across America after John Lennon's comments on Christianity.

Dozens of radio stations say they will no longer play the group's records.

Even the Ku Klux Klan has joined the campaign with a planned "Beatle bonfire."

The cause of the trouble: An interview Beatle Lennon gave to a London newspaper. It was published this week in the American teenage magazine *Date Book*.

In it he is quoted as saying: "Christianity will go. . . . We (the Beatles) are more popular than Jesus.

"Jesus was all right, but his disciples were quick and ordinary."

Beatles manager, Mr. Brian Epstein, left London for New York last night to "assess the situation" before the group arrive in America next week to begin a tour of 13 American and one Canadian cities.

The first radio station to announce a Beatle ban was WAQY, at Birmingham, Alabama, in the heart of the American "Bible Belt."

'An affront'

Listeners were invited to send Beatle records and photographs to a public bonfire.

In Mobile, Alabama, Station WTUF described Lennon's remarks as "not only deplorable but an outright sacrilegious affront to Almighty God."

Several stations polled listeners asking whether the group should be banned. One at Longview, Texas, claimed that it received 1,000 calls—97 p.c. of them for a ban.

Some stations said the ban could be lifted by a public apology, but in San Angelo, Texas, Station KTEO said: "We don't care if they come out with a thousand apologies—we will not play the Beatles again."

Many stations, however, refused to join the ban. In Salt Lake City an official of Station KCPX said: "I'm playing their records not their religious ideals."

ABOVE: **Brian Epstein has his work cut out for him as he arrives in the United States to assess the damage done by John's comment that the Beatles were more popular than Jesus (top). The *Daily Mail* of 5 August (above) reports on the situation.**

LEFT: **The band take a tour of the airport when their flight is delayed.**

OPPOSITE: **Fans gathered to say goodbye to the boys when they flew to Boston on 11 August.**

OPPOSITE INSET (LEFT AND CENTRE): **After playing five American cities, the band flew to Toronto to perform at Maple Leaf Gardens.**

OPPOSITE INSET (RIGHT): **The double A-side single "Eleanor Rigby"/ "Yellow Submarine" was released by Capitol on 8 August in the US.**

AUGUST 1966

1 Paul recorded an editon of *David Frost at the Phonograph*, a BBC Light Programme radio show, when David Frost would interview a famous person while playing a variety of records.

3 It was announced that John Lennon would be playing the part of Private Gripweed in the movie *How I Won the War*, directed by Richard Lester. In South Africa, the sale of Beatles records was banned, supporting the demonstrations in America.

4 Several US radio stations declared they would not play Beatles music.

5 "Eleanor Rigby"/"Yellow Submarine" was released in the UK on Parlophone R5493. The LP *Revolver* was released in the UK on Parlophone PMC 7009 (mono) and PCS 7009 (stereo).

6 A one-hour programme entitled *The Lennon and McCartney Songbook* was recorded at Paul's house in St. John's Wood. *David Frost at the Phonograph* was broadcast. Brian Epstein flew to the US ahead of the Beatles' tour to try to calm the volatile situation following John's remarks.

7 US Senator Robert Fleming revealed a campaign to stop the band from playing in Pennsylvania.

8 "Eleanor Rigby"/"Yellow Submarine" was released in the US on Capitol 5715 while the album *Revolver* was also released in the States on Capitol T-2576 (mono) and ST-2576 (stereo). The South African Broadcasting Corporation banned Beatles records.

9 In the UK, fans petitioned the band not to go to the States for fears of reprisals.

1966 PRESS CONFERENCE PASS for the BEATLES
6:30 pm – Aug. 17

*** CONDITIONS FOR ADMISSION
— Pass good for press conference ONLY.
— NO ONE UNDER 18 YEARS WILL BE ADMITTED.
— Only full-time reporters to be admitted.
— No autographs to be requested.
— No one allowed backstage.
— Photographers should fly their lapel photo pass besides this general pass.

(IMPORTANT — Gather in the EAST lobby for instructions as to location of press conference.)
(Admission by this card ONLY. ONE admission per card. Carry in hand or, preferably, tie to button-hole.)
No. 038

SEC. ROW SEAT
73 D 4
EAST
SERIES R2
THE "BEATLES"
8.30 P.M. PRICE $5.00
ADMIT ONE. Entrance by Male Door or by Church Street Door.
Maple Leaf Gardens LIMITED

THE BEATLES
YELLOW SUBMARINE
ELEANOR RIGBY

ABOVE: **The band arrive at a press conference at the Warwick Hotel in New York.**

RIGHT: **The Beatles onstage at Shea Stadium in front of 45,000 fans.**

RIGHT INSET: **Tickets from the Beatles' final US tour that took in 14 cities, beginning in Chicago and ending in San Francisco.**

OPPOSITE ABOVE: **Newspapers follow the reaction to John's remark.**

OPPOSITE BELOW: **Fans are removed from the stage at Suffolk Downs, Boston.**

ON JOHN'S COMMENT ABOUT JESUS

"I agree with what John said, but that doesn't mean I'm against religion. He was making a serious point, but his remarks were taken out of context..."

—George

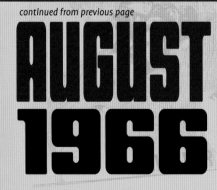

continued from previous page

AUGUST 1966

10 In the States, the share price of Capitol Records fell in direct response to the ban on the band's music.

11 The band flew to the States, travelling via Boston to land at Chicago at 4:55 p.m. In Chicago John made a public apology at a swiftly organized press conference to try to calm the situation.

12 The band began its last concert tour in America, supported by the Remains, Bobby Hebb, the Cyrkle, and the Ronettes. At another press conference at the Astor Tower in Chicago, John was grilled by the American press about his "blasphemous remarks". They then performed two shows at the International Amphitheater, Chicago—each seen by about 13,000 fans.

13 Another two shows at the Olympia Stadium, Detroit, to a total audience of 28,000. Afterwards they departed for Cleveland, travelling on a Greyhound bus. The album *Revolver* went straight into the UK charts at No. 1 and remained in the top position for seven weeks.

14 The band arrived in Cleveland at 2:30 a.m. They performed one concert in front of 20,000 fans. At one point the show was suspended as 2,500 fans got onto the Cleveland Indians' baseball field, where the band was playing. In Italy the paper *L'Observatore Romano* printed an apology from John about his remarks.

15 Five members of the Ku Klux Klan paraded outside the DC Stadium, Washington, before the show when the band played to 32,000 fans.

16 21,000 people watched the performance at John F. Kennedy Stadium, Philadelphia, despite the constant

THE APOLOGY

"I wasn't saying whatever they are saying I was saying. I was sort of deploring the attitude towards Christianity. I'm sorry. I'm sorry I said it really. I never meant it as a religious thing."

—John

The voice of reason was not quashed entirely. Some church leaders pointed out that John's remarks had an unshakable ring of truth, while one university student urged those affronted to consider the possibility "that everything that enters Memphis not wearing a cross is not evil". Radio station WSAC, which had never before placed a Beatles record on the turntable, did so now, pointing out that if the Beatles were indeed more popular than Jesus Christ, then the very people burning the merchandise were the ones who had elevated them to that position.

John, Epstein, and press officer Tony Barrow held a damage-limitation meeting to decide how to deal with the fallout. Epstein considered pulling the plug on the tour and taking a six-figure hit, and although that was ruled out, meeting the issue head-on at a press conference was unavoidable. At Chicago's Astor Towers hotel on 11 August, John made a long-winded defence of his position, but it was too waffly and imprecise to completely appease those who wanted an unconditional apology and side order of humble pie.

There were demonstrations during the tour, but what was essentially a nonstory soon slipped from the news agenda, and no doubt the Beatles' coffers were amply swelled as temporarily irate fans replaced their incinerated records.

Beatle fans back as Lennon says 'I'm sorry'

From JEFFREY BLYTH
NEW YORK, Friday

AMERICAN teenagers, at least in Chicago, have forgiven the Beatles.

Twenty-six thousand fans are expected at the first two concerts of their new American tour. Both concerts are a sell-out.

Today several hundred fans, mostly girls, gathered outside the Beatles' hotel waiting for a glimpse of them leaving for their concerts. There were no anti-Beatle demonstrations.

On their arrival in Chicago late last night John Lennon gave a semi-apology for his remarks on the comparative popularity of the Beatles and Christianity.

Ku-Klux-Klan will picket the Beatles

WASHINGTON, Monday (Reuter)

THE Ku-Klux-Klan plans to picket Washington's huge football stadium tonight—an hour before the Beatles are due to give a concert there.

A police official said Klansmen intended to come out into the open to protest about John Lennon's remarks about Christianity. They plan a "peaceful demonstration."

Police met the Klan last week to make sure that there would be no violence. Its members promised not to carry any posters proclaiming racial hatred and not to infiltrate the stadium itself.

About 400 police and special security forces will be on duty.

Last night 2,500 teenage fans broke through police lines at Cleveland, Ohio, and stormed on to a baseball pitch to mob the Beatles in the middle of a concert.

● The Beatles' new record *Yellow Submarine / Eleanor Rigby* is top of the *New Musical Express* pop chart.

John Lennon right

BOSTON: Cardinal Cushing, Roman Catholic Archbishop of Boston, said Beatle John Lennon was right—the Beatles "are more popular than Christ."

threat of lightning and torrential rain. Then back on the bus to travel to the airport, bound for Canada.

17 On to Maple Leaf Gardens, Toronto, where the band performed two more shows in front of a total of 32,000 fans before flying back to the US.

18 This concert took place in the middle of a racecourse at the Suffolk Down Racetrack in Massachusetts. "Eleanor Rigby" and "Yellow Submarine" went to the top of the British charts, remaining there for four weeks.

19 Before two concerts at the Mid-South Coliseum, Memphis, an anonymous phone call had been received warning that one or all of the band would be assassinated during their performance. Despite this the Beatles still played, but received a huge shock when a firecracker exploded onstage during the second half.

20 Arriving at Ohio at 1:35 a.m. The open-air performance at Crosley Field, Cincinnati, due to be played that day was postponed for 24 hours due to torrential rain; the concert promoters hadn't built a canopy.

21 Due to the postponement, the band had to give two concerts in two different cities—340 miles apart. Following the show in Cincinnati, they travelled to Busch Stadium in St. Louis and performed for 23,000 fans under a tarpaulin cover; it was still raining.

22 The group arrived in New York early in the morning and went to the Warwick Hotel. They stayed for two days, remaining inside the hotel for most of the time. *Revolver* was certified gold in the States.

23 11,000 of the 55,600 seats remained unsold for the concert at the William A. Shea Municipal Stadium, New York City. This was in marked contrast to the concerts in 1965, which had all sold out within hours. After the performance they flew to Beverly Hills.

24 A rest day in Beverly Hills, Los Angeles.

25 Two shows at the Coliseum, Seattle. Only 8,000 tickets were sold for the afternoon performance, the evening show was fully booked, with 15,000 fans.

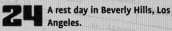

JOHN, PAUL, GEORGE & RINGO

The show's over, folks

After the "butcher" cover row, the unnerving events in the Far East, and the invective that John's *Evening Standard* interview had provoked, the Beatles had little enthusiasm for their third US tour. Even if the run-up to the eighteen-day American blitz had been headache-free, it would still have been a hard slog for the group that had just made "Tomorrow Never Knows" to go back to belting out classics from the Fab era. Tellingly, there were no songs from *Revolver* on the set list. Today it would be unthinkable for an artist to go on the road and completely ignore an album released just days earlier. But the Beatles had neither the wherewithal nor the inclination to even try to reproduce their recent material. The only taste of the 1966 vintage the fans were going to be treated to was "Paperback Writer".

USA '66 was successful, though by no means a sell-out smash. Had Sid Bernstein underwritten any void seats at Shea Stadium this time around, he would have been left with a very large bill as it was only 80 percent full. The fans who turned out were just as loyal and passionate—and loud— but there weren't quite so many of them this time around.

The thought that someone incensed by the "more popular than Jesus" comment might take a potshot at them wasn't their only concern. In Cleveland thousands of fans broke ranks and threatened to swamp the stage. The security cordon looked as if it might be breached, and the boys dropped their instruments midsong and fled for their lives. In Cincinnati Paul was physically sick at the prospect of playing in a rainstorm beneath a flimsy canvas canopy. That gig was cancelled—the only performance they ever missed—and rescheduled for lunchtime the following day. After that show it was on to St. Louis for the evening date. The inclement weather followed them and sparks flew—quite literally.

By the time they got to Candlestick Park on Monday, 29 August, they had had enough of being mannequins rather than musicians. Even Paul, the group's most natural showman and committed performer, had finally conceded that he could live without the smell of the greasepaint and roar of a Fab-loving crowd, for now at least. No official footage was shot, though one member of the 25,000-strong audience caught a flavour of the Beatles' final concert performance. The group themselves took to the stage armed with still cameras to record the valedictory moment, and Paul asked one of the crew to run an audio tape to capture for posterity the Fabs' final outing.

When the amps were packed away for the last time, George made his oft-quoted declaration, "That's it, I'm not a Beatle anymore". The relief was palpable. A quick calculation revealed that they had done around 1,400 gigs. At the beginning it had been fun, notwithstanding the straitened circumstances and gruelling schedules. They had often played intimate venues where they could crack jokes and pass notes or drinks to members of the audience. They had earned their spurs as a tight working band, chasing success, recognition, fame, and fortune. None of those were factors now; Candlestick Park closed the book on touring, but it wasn't the beginning of the end, merely the end of the beginning. The Beatles were now a studio band.

continued from page 253

AUGUST 1966

26 The Beatles returned to Los Angeles for further rest days.

28 45,000 fans watched the group in Dodger Stadium, Los Angeles, before the band flew to San Francisco.

29 After nine years and more than 1,400 live appearances, the Beatles gave their last concert performance at Candlestick Park, San Francisco, in front of a crowd of 25,000. Onstage John and Paul took photographs and Tony Barrow, the NEMS Enterprises press officer, was asked to make a recording on audio cassette. The *Lennon and McCartney Songbook* was broadcast.

30 The band left California to fly back to London, arriving at London Airport the following morning.

OPPOSITE AND BELOW: **The Beatles return home to the standard greeting of desperate fans waving banners. The fans don't yet realize it, but as far as the boys are concerned, their touring days are over.**

ON HEARING TRACKS FROM REVOLVER

"I get it: you don't want to be cute anymore."

—Bob Dylan

REVOLVER

Released
🇬🇧 **5 August 1966** (Parlophone)

Side One:
Taxman (Harrison)
Eleanor Rigby
I'm Only Sleeping
Love You To (Harrison)
Here, There and
  Everywhere
Yellow Submarine
She Said She Said

Side Two:
Good Day Sunshine
And Your Bird Can Sing
For No One
Dr. Robert
I Want to Tell You
  (Harrison)
Got to Get You into My
  Life
Tomorrow Never Knows

Released
🇺🇸 **8 August 1966** (Capitol)

Side One:
Taxman (Harrison)
Eleanor Rigby
Love You To (Harrison)
Here, There and
  Everywhere
Yellow Submarine
She Said She Said

Side Two:
Good Day Sunshine
For No One
I Want to Tell You
  (Harrison)
Got to Get You into My
  Life
Tomorrow Never Knows

Cover story

It would have been all too obvious for the Beatles' drug-inspired new album to advertise itself with the bold, swirling arcs of colour that were already a cliché in psychedelic art circles. John had a Rolls-Royce that you couldn't help but view through "kaleidoscope eyes", while the Fool—Dutch artists Simon Postuma and Marijke Koger—were hard at work obliterating the mahogany case of the Bechstein piano he kept at Kenwood.

Long-time friend from their Hamburg days Klaus Voormann was asked to come up with a cover design for *Revolver*, and he opted for part line drawing, part collage in monochrome. The collage included pictures by Bob Whitaker, of "butcher" cover fame, who also took the studio shot that adorned the back cover. Voormann worked his own photograph and name into the artwork—woven into George's hair on the right-hand side of the sleeve, just below John's mouth. He became the first non-Beatle to appear on an album cover, a year ahead of the *Sgt. Pepper* stampede.

This brilliantly original design, which earned Voormann the princely sum of £50, won a Grammy Award for Best Album Cover in 1966. He subsequently produced sleeve artwork for other bands including the Bee Gees, in addition to his day job as bass player with Manfred Mann.

Epstein struggling to manage

The end of the touring era had a profound effect on Brian Epstein. At a stroke he saw a substantial part of his management role with the Beatles disappear, and although he could have allocated more time to his multifarious interests, it wasn't simply a question of occupying himself with other ventures. Epstein's attachment to "his boys" went far beyond a business arrangement or contractual remit. In short, the group's decision threatened to leave a deep emotional void in his life. Worse, he was worried that he might find himself surplus to requirements completely when the management contract next came up for renewal. A catalogue of miscalculations had been laid at Epstein's door, from the disastrous Seltaeb merchandising deal to the recent life-threatening Far East trip. Epstein was so shattered by the latter experience that he developed a skin complaint requiring hospital treatment. He suffered mood swings that were exacerbated by his own drug dependency and a string of sexual liaisons that brought only fleeting happiness.

When the existing EMI contract expired in mid-1966, Epstein did manage to secure substantially better terms, though that wouldn't have been difficult. The Beatles were to receive a 10 percent royalty on sales, a nine-year deal that thus spanned the demise of the group and the birth of their solo careers. Epstein insisted on negotiating with the American market direct. He had talks with the major labels, but not all welcomed him with open arms and a blank cheque. Columbia, maybe with an eye on recent half-empty concert venues, thought they were on the slide. Capitol boss Alan Livingston didn't. He matched the EMI percentage and threw in a $2 million bonus for good measure. Even EMI chairman Sir Joseph Lockwood thought the subsidiary would struggle to recoup that outlay. Livingston told him not to worry. "I'll get it back on the first album, Joe."

For EMI and Capitol, *Sgt. Pepper* lay just round the corner. For Brian Epstein, there was merely increasing trepidation over his own contract with the Beatles, due to expire in September 1967. The favourable terms would surely have been adjusted to reflect a decreased workload, but there was no suggestion that Epstein might have been frozen out completely. The Beatles' mentor couldn't see that; he was already on a downward spiral, and would be dead before the contract renewal date arrived.

ABOVE: **The decision to stop touring might have been a relief to the boys, but for Brian Epstein it was a bad omen. Without tours to arrange and promote, his position was becoming ever less certain.**

RIGHT: **Paul and Ringo with two other British greats, Dusty Springfield and Tom Jones, at the *Melody Maker* awards held at the GPO Tower in London.**

OPPOSITE: **John and Cynthia pictured shortly before Yoko moved into his life.**

WHO? It is Beatle John Lennon, playing a soldier in the film, *How I Won the War*, which he is making near Hanover, Germany. In fact, John is now even less recognisable than in the picture above. Yesterday he had his hair cut to regulation short back and sides for his role. After nine hours' filming, he decided to go to bed early. But he complained that young guests at his hotel were preventing him from getting to sleep. They were playing Beatle records.

THIS PAGE: **John pretends to cut the hair of his costar Ronald Lacey in *How I Won the War*. Cloistered out in Spain, where the film was shot, John used the time to write "Strawberry Fields Forever". The *Daily Mail* of 7 September comments on his new image (left inset).**

John, was rather lost without the skeleton of the hectic Beatles schedule to prop him up; but Ringo was bored rather than scared.

It was less than a week after Candlestick Park when John embarked on what was, literary musings apart, his first solo project. Predictably, his billing in Dick Lester's antiwar satire was bigger than the minor role warranted. He played oily fascist Private Gripweed, a part specially written for him by screenwriter Charles Wood, who had also worked on *Help!*. The plot, which revolved around the efforts of a ragtag bunch of squaddies and their inept commander to construct a cricket pitch behind enemy lines, no doubt appealed to John's sense of the absurd.

One of the new recruit's first orders was to report for a makeover. John had his hair cropped to regulation length while the glasses, which would become a Lennon trademark, made their first appearance. With the new look came new depths of introspection as he pondered an uncertain future. The madness of war was an apposite backdrop for the inner turmoil that spawned "Strawberry Fields Forever".

How I Won the War opened to lukewarm reviews in October 1967. It was hardly *A Hard Day's Night*, but United Artists wasn't going to let that stand in their way when there was a Beatle angle to exploit. An eponymous single was issued, credited to "Musketeer Gripweed and the Third Troop", but a line of dialogue culled from the film was the sum total of his contribution to the song.

Private practice

"I was always waiting for a reason to get out of the Beatles from the day I made *How I Won the War* in 1966. I just didn't have the guts to do it, you see. Because I didn't know where to go. I did it because the Beatles had stopped touring and I didn't know what to do."

John's reflections on the events of 1966 show that, of all the Beatles, he was the most disturbed by the newfound liberation of the post-touring era. There were scarcely enough hours in the day to contain the flow of Paul's creative juices, and he immediately took off in a new direction, collaborating on the score for the Boulting Brothers film *The Family Way*. Inwardly, George had been heading eastwards for some time, and now he was able to follow that path. Ringo, like

ABOVE: **Kitted out in army fatigues and glasses, John spent two months away from his bandmates trying his hand at acting.**

SEPTEMBER 1966

5 John flew to Hanover in West Germany in preparation for his role in the film *How I Won the War*. He played Private Gripweed.

6 John had a haircut to prepare for his part in the movie and started wearing his famous "granny glasses". The hairdresser burnt his hair clippings to stop them being sold off as souvenirs.

10 The album *Revolver* reached the top of the US charts, remaining there for six weeks.

12 "Eleanor Rigby"/"Yellow Submarine" was awarded a gold disc in the States.

14 George and Pattie flew to India to study the sitar, yoga, and Indian philosophy and culture. They stayed at the Taj Mahal Hotel in Bombay using the pseudonym Sam Wells. George was to receive sitar lessons from Ravi Shankar.

15 John and road manager Neil Aspinall took a train to meet Paul and Brian Epstein in Paris, where they spent the weekend.

18 John and Neil Aspinall moved on to Spain, the main location for the film *How I Won the War*, where he remained until 7 November. It was during this time that he wrote "Strawberry Fields Forever".

20 In India George met Maharashi Mahesh Yogi. Later that day he granted an exclusive interview to BBC's radio correspondent, Donald Milner, and talked about his Indian interests and Eastern beliefs.

27 Brian Epstein was admitted to the Priory hospital in Roehampton, London, for "an overdose of prescribed drugs".

George heads east

If the prospect of life without the Beatles was a double-edged sword for John—attractive and disturbing in equal measure—George was far less ambivalent. His interest in India's culture and religion had been growing alongside his disenchantment with the trappings of pop superstardom. There had been time for a brief stop-off en route home from the fraught Far East tour that summer, and now there was the opportunity for a lengthy sojourn.

On 14 September Mr. and Mrs. Sam Wells took a flight from Britain to Bombay. Mr. Wells sported a fine new moustache, but subcontinent Beatle fans weren't fooled for long.

George studied the sitar under the tutelage of Ravi Shankar, whom he had met socially a couple of times earlier in the year, including at a party at Peter Sellers's house. His broadened horizons would have major implications for the Beatles. As his sitar playing improved, his guitar work suffered; hardly surprising as over the next couple of years he barely picked up the instrument that had made him famous. More importantly, he found himself as a musician and began producing songs he felt stood up next to those of Lennon and McCartney. A quart wouldn't fit into a pint pot, however, and the struggle to get his songs recorded would continue, creating no small amount of resentment. It was little wonder that by the time the Beatles disbanded he had stockpiled material enough for a triple album, the acclaimed *All Things Must Pass*.

LEFT AND INSET: **George goes personally to pick up Ravi Shankar at the airport. Shankar, a highly accomplished sitar player, had been mentoring George in the instrument during George's recent five-week stay in India. George returned the favour by hosting Shankar in London in the hope that sitar music could work its way onto more Beatles records following its use on *Rubber Soul* and *Revolver*.**

McCartney almost goes too far

The pigeonholing of John as the intellectual cynic and Paul the sweet balladeer was a myth that proved difficult to dislodge. It was a perception that crumbled under close inspection. Songs such as "If I Fell" showed that John was capable of writing beautiful love songs: the thick carapace hid a soft and insecure centre. Witness the fact that he broke down in tears before being thrown to American press hounds scenting blood over the "more popular than Jesus" row.

Paul, meanwhile, could rock with the best of them. His showstopping "Long Tall Sally" was a hardy perennial, the song that brought the curtain down on the Beatles' last-ever concert performance. And while he was always the one with the cheery smile, ever ready for a thumbs-up photo opportunity, behind the scenes the image-conscious conciliator was the uncompromising taskmaster who would issue prescriptions for George and Ringo's playing.

Moreover, while John and the other Beatles were rubbing shoulders with the golf-club set, Paul was at the hub of the metropolis, soaking up every cultural experience London had to offer. When he wasn't racing from cinema to theatre to gallery, he was making Warhol-inspired home movies or tape loops. Paul was keen for Joe Orton to script the new Beatles film, but the ever-conservative Brian Epstein nipped that in the bud when he saw a draft script that included seduction, murder, and cross-dressing.

John once self-deprecatingly joked that his songs used the same few chords. Paul's palette was far wider. He was fascinated by the work of avant-garde musicians such as Karlheinz

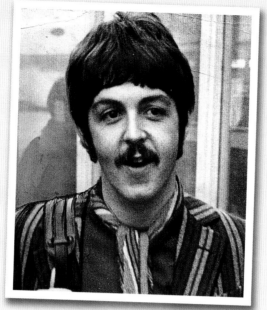

ABOVE: **Paul returns from a trip sporting a new look, the "Viva Zapata" moustache, as the press called it.**

Stockhausen and John Cage, the latter famous for his piece entitled "4'33", which was silent save for audience noise. In 1966 Paul attended a workshop run by Cornelius Cardew, who had worked with Stockhausen. The session required the participants to contribute random sounds that they felt fitted the rhythm and flow of a background wall of noise. Paul scratched a coin across a radiator and used a beer mug as a percussive instrument.

Overall the master tunesmith found the experience too free to be unconditionally rewarding, and it was clear that to include such experimental material on a Beatles album was a nonstarter. However, the free-form approach undoubtedly informed his thinking with his tape-loop experiments and, memorably, in the orchestral crescendo in "A Day in the Life". He considered making a solo album titled *Paul McCartney Goes Too Far*, where he could give free rein to such off-the-wall ideas, but it never materialized.

OCTOBER 1966

8 Ringo and Maureen flew out to Malaga in Spain for a holiday.

11 At the Scotch of St. James, John and Cynthia watched Ben E. King.

14 The press revealed that Paul was writing the musical score for a film starring Hayley Mills that was eventually given the title *The Family Way*.

15 Paul attended the launch of the new London underground paper the *International Times*. Soft Machine and Pink Floyd performed.

22 *Revolver* was awarded a gold disc in the UK.

26 George was at the airport to meet Ravi Shankar when he flew in from India.

28 Brian revealed to Sid Bernstein that the band was not planning to tour the States again.

31 The first of a series of mix sessions at Abbey Road. Several Beatles hits were remodelled to be included in the first British greatest-hits compilation, *A Collection of Beatles Oldies*. The back cover included the phrase "But Goldies!"

John meets Yoko

John had endured weeks of boredom filming *How I Won the War*, and thoughts of home should have been appealing. Yet no sooner had he returned than he was looking to escape the family seat and a wife with whom he could no longer connect. These days even when he and Cynthia were under the same roof it was purely geographical proximity. Julian couldn't bridge the divide; John had hardly been a hands-on father. He would be lost in music, spaced out on drugs, staring at static on the TV, barely exchanging a word with Cynthia for days on end. One door was all but shut; another was about to swing open.

John was invited to an exhibition at Indica Gallery, the focal point of London's counterculture, the capital's very own Haight-Ashbury. It was a magnet for conceptual artists such as Yoko Ono, who had already gained a degree of notoriety for a live exhibition that involved her thrashing around inside a black sack. When Indica's owner, John Dunbar, informed John that this same woman had a new show opening at Indica—Unfinished Objects and Paintings—John was mildly intrigued. If it was anything like the black-sack event, it might even provide a sexual frisson.

John was accorded the luxury of attending a special preview the day before the 10 November opening. Initially he felt a little cheated. It was certainly not the hoped-for sexual happening, plus he was disposed to think a lot of modern art was so much pretentious baloney. He wasn't sure what to make of a card inviting him to "Breathe" or an apple on a stand with a £200 price tag, but when he climbed a ladder and read another card that simply said "Yes", he warmed to the theme and decided to engage. Yoko offered him the opportunity to hammer a nail into a virgin exhibit at a cost of five shillings. John said he would knock an imaginary nail in for an imaginary five shillings.

Although it would be some time before they would renew their acquaintance, the connection was made. And it was a connection the twice-married Yoko appears to have angled for, as several reports suggest that she targeted the Beatles in general as a means of enhancing her career, and John in particular for more personal attention.

ABOVE AND LEFT: **Yoko pictured with various pieces from her exhibition, including a timeless clock and a bag for hiding in. In later years John and Yoko would use the idea of the bag again when they developed the concept of "bagism".**

OPPOSITE: **Born in Tokyo in 1933, Yoko was raised mostly in America, only returning periodically to Japan. By the time she met John in 1966, Yoko had been married twice, first to a Japanese musician named Toshi Ichiyanagi and then to an American film director, Antony Cox, with whom she had a daughter, Kyoko, in 1963.**

NOVEMBER 1966

6 Paul and Jane flew out to Kenya for a holiday, stopping in France and Spain on the way.

7 A new stereo mix of "I Want to Hold Your Hand" was made at Abbey Road. John flew back from Spain.

8 Geoff Emerick produced a mix of "She Loves You".

9 John met Yoko Ono for the first time when he attended a private viewing of her art exhibition Unfinished Paintings and Objects at London's Indica Gallery.

10 New stereo mixes of "Day Tripper" and "We Can Work It Out" were made by balance engineer Peter Brown. Photographs printed for the first time showed the band sporting new moustaches and beards.

11 After the Aberfan disaster, the band and Brian Epstein donated £1,000 to the appeal.

12 The final day of Yoko's exhibition Unfinished Paintings and Objects.

13 A report in the *Sunday Telegraph* stated that "Mr. Allen Klein, the American impresario, has been approached by two of the Beatles over their future management".

15 Brian Epstein denied rumours that the Beatles had split up.

19 Paul and Jane returned from Kenya.

24 The first session to begin recording for the next album, starting with "Strawberry Fields Forever".

SONG STORY: "STRAWBERRY FIELDS FOREVER"

Even as a child John had felt he was different. Beatlemania had given him ample opportunity to ponder the theme of reality versus illusion, and through an increasingly rapacious intake of LSD he strove to reach a heightened state of perception. Add in the uncertainties surrounding the Beatles' future following the Candlestick Park finale, heaped on top of his deep insecurities, and the ingredients were in place for what many regard as the apogee of John's output during the Beatle era.

While filming on location in Spain, John worked on a new song, provisionally titled "It's Not Too Bad". A few revisions later, "Strawberry Fields" made its first appearance in the lyric; John had found the perfect metaphor for the shifting sands of reality that he was trying to encapsulate.

Strawberry Field was real enough, a Salvation Army-run children's home a stone's throw from Menlove Avenue. John had idyllic memories of attending summer fetes in its grounds with Aunt Mimi, and yet even the concrete past became nebulous as nostalgia was refracted through psychedelia, the age of innocence clashing head-on with acid-fuelled perspicacity.

"Strawberry Fields Forever" was several weeks in the making, and even when John finally unveiled his latest creation at Abbey Road, it would take some fifty hours' studio time to perfect. The famous mellotron opening was there right from the start, but John was dissatisfied with the "best" take first time round. A new faster version was recorded a week later, with brass and string accompaniment. Still John wasn't happy, for he liked the first half of the earlier recording and the latter half of the second attempt. George Martin was tasked with knitting the two together, something he initially thought impossible as the versions were a semitone apart as well as in a different tempo. But by slowing one down and speeding the other up, Martin managed a seamless join. Or at least, seamless to the layman's ears. The producer maintained that the weld, which occurs one minute into the song, "sticks out like a sore thumb", though most fans regard "Strawberry Fields Forever" as a tour de force of the Beatles canon.

Strawberry Field was a Salvation Army home in Liverpool near where John was brought up.

25 The band got together at Dick James House, New Oxford Street, to record "Pantomime: Everywhere It's Christmas"—an annual gift for their fan club members.

27 John filmed a sequence for Peter Cook and Dudley Moore's BBC programme, *Not Only...But Also* at the underground men's lavatories in Broadwick Street, where he played an attendant.

28 The band had another session working on "Strawberry Fields Forever".

29 Recording continued on "Strawberry Fields Forever"; there was no recording deadline, so they were able to take their time producing this album.

ON DISCONTINUING THE BEATLES LIVE SHOWS

"Our stage act hasn't improved one bit since we started touring four years ago. The days when three guitarists and a drummer can stand up and sing and do nothing else onstage are over. Many of our tracks these days have big backings. We couldn't produce the sound onstage without an orchestra. We feel that people only really listen to us through our recordings, so that is our most important form of communication now."

—Paul

DECEMBER 1966

2 Final mixing and editing of "Pantomime: Everywhere It's Christmas".

6 The band recorded Christmas and New Year's greetings to be played on the "pirate" stations, Radio London and Radio Caroline.

8 The group worked in the studio on Paul's vaudeville song "When I'm Sixty-Four".

10 *A Collection of Beatles Oldies* was released on Parlophone PMC 7016 (mono) and PCS 7016 (stereo). The only new track for the British public was "Bad Boy", which had originally been issued in the US. In the UK the *NME* annual readers' poll revealed that the Beatles had won the British Vocal Group award.

11 George's interview, recorded in India, was broadcast on the BBC Home Service in the series *The Lively Arts*.

13 An interview with John was printed in *Look* magazine with his photograph on the front cover.

15 After adding strings and brass to "Strawberry Fields Forever", the song was ready to be mixed into mono. In London the Speakeasy Club was opened. It was to become a favourite with the band.

16 An extract from George's interview of 20 September was repeated on the BBC Home Service in the series *Pick of the Week*. The Beatles' fourth Christmas record, "Pantomime: Everywhere It's Christmas", was released for fan-club members only.

 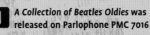

Beatles vs. Beach Boys

In December 1966 the Beatles ceded their throne as World's Top Vocal Group to the Beach Boys in the annual *New Musical Express* poll. The Fab Four had won both the Top British and Top International Group awards three years running, but this time around they retained only their domestic crown. John also lost his title of Best British Male Singer to Cliff Richard.

If large swaths of the record-buying public were placing the Beach Boys above the Beatles, their number didn't include Brian Wilson. The creative genius behind songs such as "Good Vibrations" and "Wouldn't It Be Nice"—both huge hits that year—was himself in awe of the Beatles'

prodigious output. *Rubber Soul* had spurred Wilson into trying to make a Beach Boys album of the same quality. The result was his own masterwork, *Pet Sounds*, released in July 1966. Paul in particular was hugely impressed. It is said that he wrote "Here, There and Everywhere" after hearing the gorgeously mellifluous "God Only Knows". And now, in turn, Wilson was galvanized to turn up the heat in a spirit of creative rivalry.

The release of "Strawberry Fields Forever"/ "Penny Lane" in February 1967, followed by *Sgt. Pepper* in June, derailed Wilson completely. He abandoned his latest project, *Smile*, reportedly commenting that there was no point in continuing; the Beatles had "got there first".

OPPOSITE: **John made a cameo appearance on the Peter Cook and Dudley Moore comedy show *Not Only...But Also* when he played the part of the doorman of a members-only gentlemen's lavatory. The scenes were filmed in Broadwick Street, London. The sketch was a welcome break for John from recording "Strawberry Fields Forever".**

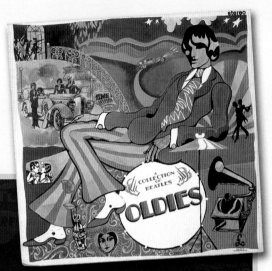

A COLLECTION OF BEATLES OLDIES

Released
🇬🇧 **10 December 1966** (Parlophone)

Side One:
She Loves You
From Me to You
We Can Work It Out
Help!
Michelle
Yesterday
I Feel Fine
Yellow Submarine

Side Two:
Can't Buy Me Love
Bad Boy (Williams)
Day Tripper
A Hard Day's Night
Ticket to Ride
Paperback Writer
Eleanor Rigby
I Want to Hold Your Hand

Cover Story

A Collection of Beatles Oldies was released in the UK to provide a new Beatles album for Christmas. The title continued on the back cover with "But Goldies!". Although the album, as the title suggests, was a compilation of previously released hits, it did feature one new number, "Bad Boy". The track, written by Larry Williams, had not been released in Britain before, despite being put out on the *Beatles VI* album in the US in 1965. The psychedelic artwork on the front cover was by David Christian and the photograph on the back cover was by Robert Whitaker. One part of the artwork shows a car on a road driving towards the head of the Paul look-alike. This was one of a number of "clues" that later fed the rumour of Paul's death.

18 Tara Browne, a friend of the band, was killed in a car crash. The lyric "He blew his mind out in a car" in "A Day in the Life" came from this tragedy. The premiere of *The Family Way* was held at Warren Theatre, London: Paul received his first credit as a solo composer.

20 Each member of the group was interviewed by ITN reporter John Edwards to stop speculation about the Beatles breaking up. The interviews went out on *Reporting '66* later that month. Further overdubs to "When I'm Sixty-Four" were added at Abbey Road.

21 In another studio session the band continued to work on "When I'm Sixty-Four", adding clarinets to the track. John added more vocals and another piano track to "Strawberry Fields Forever".

22 "Strawberry Fields Forever" was finally completed, with George Martin and Geoff Emerick mixing and editing the two different versions.

23 The soundtrack album for the film *The Family Way* was released in the UK.

26 John appeared on Peter Cook and Dudley Moore's BBC TV programme *Not Only...But Also*.

28 Over the next two days the interviews with John Edwards were transmitted in various regions in *Reporting '66*, together with library footage of the group and interviews with fans.

29 The basic track of "Penny Lane" was recorded by Paul on his own at Abbey Road.

30 Further mixes of "When I'm Sixty-Four" and some takes of "Penny Lane" were made.

31 At Annabel's nightclub in Berkeley Square, London, George was refused entry for not wearing a tie and so, accompanied by Pattie, Brian Epstein, and Eric Clapton, he went to Lyons' Corner House in Coventry Street to celebrate the New Year.

1967

I Read the News Today

In 1967 the Beatles changed the face of popular music with the release of *Sgt. Pepper*, the breadth of the album's palette leaving fans, critics, and peers alike in awe of the inventiveness and virtuosity on show.

However, for good measure they also recorded the Summer of Love's enduring anthem and performed it to a global audience. The stellar highs were tempered by tragedy and criticism. Brian Epstein's instability finally cost him his life, leaving a vacuum that the Beatles themselves tried to fill. Paul led the way by inviting us along on a Magical Mystery Tour. The critics demanded a refund, but the band remained unbowed by their bold experiment. They set up Apple and went into the retail business, quickly finding that a benevolent corporation attracted many takers. The Beatles had been at the epicentre of the kaleidoscopic counterculture and had set the trend for concept albums, gatefold sleeves, and printed lyrics. As ever, having scaled one peak, it was time to move on and conquer another.

LEFT: **The Beatles celebrate at a party to launch *Sgt. Pepper*. The image of the band had altered substantially since 1963, but so had its music. In 1963 *Please Please Me* had been churned out in just 13 hours, but *Sgt. Pepper* was the fruit of more than 700 hours in the studio.**

RIGHT: **The second edition of *Beatwave*, issued around the time of the release of *Sgt. Pepper*, featured a stylized self-portrait of Paul on its cover.**

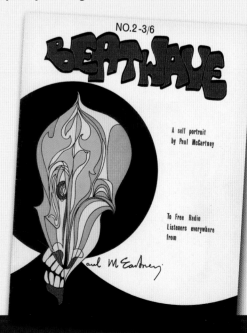

NO.2-3/6

A self portrait by Paul McCartney

To Free Radio Listeners everywhere from

Paul McCartney

A relative failure

"To this day I cannot imagine why that single was beaten to the number one spot, because for my money it was the best we ever issued. But there it was, and now we were left with 'When I'm Sixty-Four' on its own for the new album." George Martin's bemused reflection on the "failure" of "Strawberry Fields Forever"/"Penny Lane" was shared by hordes of adoring fans, though, curiously, not the Beatles themselves. They were remarkably sanguine about being pipped to a twelfth straight UK number one by "Humperbert Engeldinck", as John dubbed the cabaret crooner. The Beatles had unburdened themselves over the touring issue; now they could breathe another collective sigh of relief over a statistical blip that had to happen sooner or later. Some no doubt saw it as evidence of decline; to the Beatles it was, if anything, a relief.

The ascendancy of "Release Me" over the definitive Beatles double A-side would become a regular on the pop-trivia circuit, but of much greater moment was the way it affected the group's latest album project. When "Penny Lane" and "Strawberry Fields Forever" were hived off for the singles market, it derailed the idea that had been mooted for an album taking the group's roots and childhood experiences as its theme. It isn't overstating the case to suggest that Brian Epstein's urgent request for a top-drawer single changed the course of pop music history. For it allowed another seed to germinate, one that would flower in the Summer of Love and forever after be synonymous with that epoch of heady optimism.

RIGHT: **Paul brings stripes and moustaches back into fashion.**

INSETS: **In February, the *Daily Mail* carried news of the success of "Strawberry Fields Forever" in the US and the cementing of the Beatles' relationship with EMI.**

Golden Beatles

Prerelease sales in America of the latest Beatles single have already topped a million and earned a golden disc. Titles: *Strawberry Fields Forever* and *Penny Lane.*

Beatles sign

The Beatles have renewed their contract with EMI Records for nine years.

JANUARY 1967

3 "When I'm Sixty-Four" and "Strawberry Fields Forever'" were copied for the US market.

4 Recording continued on "Penny Lane" at Abbey Road with additional guitar, vocal, and piano overdubs.

5 A studio session to record a tape for the Carnival of Light Rave that was to take place at the Roundhouse in London. It was made in only one take and, by the time overdubs were added, made up a distorted track lasting nearly 14 minutes; the longest single piece recorded by the band.

6 More overdubbing on "Penny Lane" in a six-hour studio session.

8 John and Paul went to the Cromwellian Club in London wearing fancy dress. It was Georgie Fame's fiancée's 21st birthday.

9 Flutes, trumpets, piccolos, and a flügelhorn were added to "Penny Lane".

10 During the ninth take of "Penny Lane" a handbell and harmonies were added as part of the sound effects.

11 Trumpets, oboes, cor anglais, and a double bass were then added to the forthcoming single.

12 Brian Epstein decided to merge his business interest in NEMS with the Robert Stigwood Organization. Epstein remained as chairman, and Australian impresario Robert Stigwood became Joint Managing Director with Vic Lewis.

14 Paul and George attended Donovan's concert at the Royal Albert Hall.

Creating a new identity

In the fall of 1966 Paul had taken his Aston Martin DB6 for a spin through France, donning a false beard so that he could indulge his bohemian spirit unhindered. He shot a lot of arty cine footage, revelling in the role of free-spirited poet alone on the open road. He then hooked up with stalwart roadie-cum-minder Mal Evans for an impromptu safari trip to Kenya, but thoughts of image and disguise were still whirling round in his head. An idea began to form. How better to show that the cheeky Fabs era was really over than to give the group a completely new persona? How better to cast off the slough of Beatlemania than to create a band of alter egos? During the plane trip home, legend has it that Mal enquired about the initials S and P on the sachets provided with the in-flight meal. Salt and Pepper became Dr. Pepper—which was rejected when it was discovered it was a soft-drink brand name in the US—and that morphed into Sergeant Pepper. The fictional band now had a name.

Sgt. Pepper's Lonely Hearts Club Band—the name extended to fit the trend for long-winded group nomenclature—was seven hundred hours' studio time in the making, at a cost of £25,000. These were mind-boggling figures for the ephemeral pop industry. Four years earlier the Beatles had knocked out the fourteen tracks of *Please Please Me* in a single thirteen-hour session. But this was a different era. Indeed, the Beatles were out of contract when the *Pepper* sessions began, and had only themselves to please. As Paul put it: "Instead of looking for catchy singles, it was more like writing your novel." It was a nice analogy for a project that would be regarded as the Beatles' magnum opus, arguably the most influential album in recording history.

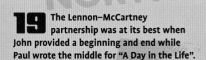

ABOVE: **In January Brian surprised many people by deciding to merge NEMS with the Robert Stigwood Organization, despite having been offered a lot more money by other businessmen. The deal meant Brian could keep control of the Beatles and Cilla Black and hand the remainder of his clients over to Stigwood.**

TOP: **Paul is pictured with his Aston Martin.**

ON THE BEATLES' NEW IDENTITY

"It was my idea to say to the guys, 'Hey, how about disguising ourselves and getting an alter ego, because we're the Beatles and we're fed up? Every time you write a song, John, you gotta sing it like John would. Every time I approach a ballad, it's gotta be like Paul would.' And it freed us. It was a very liberating thing to do."

—Paul

---

16 Inspired after watching Masterworks, Paul asked David Mason from the New Philharmonia to play the B-flat piccolo trumpet on "Penny Lane".

17 Jo Durden Smith interviewed Paul for Granada's *Scene Special*. The objective was to discuss the London "underground" culture in which Paul was involved.

18 This was the first studio session working on "A Day in the Life".

19 The Lennon–McCartney partnership was at its best when John provided a beginning and end while Paul wrote the middle for "A Day in the Life".

22 "Penny Lane" was sent to Capitol records for production for the American market.

24 At Brian's home, playwright Joe Orton met Paul to discuss the possibility of Orton writing the script for a future Beatles film.

25 Paul felt that "Penny Lane" could still be improved and continued

to remix until a new master was finalized for the UK market.

27 The four band members signed a new contract, binding them to EMI until January 1976 with immediate effect. A deal was also signed with Hunter Davies, a journalist with the *Sunday Times*, to write a biography about the band.

28 Paul and George attended a concert by the Four Tops at the Royal Albert Hall. The first Carnival of Light Rave was held.

29 The band joined Brian Epstein in a box at the Saville Theatre, London, to watch Soundarama, a concert that featured the Who, the Jimi Hendrix Experience, the Koobas, and the Thoughts.

30 The first shoot at Knole Park, near Sevenoaks, Kent, to produce promotional films for "Strawberry Fields Forever" and "Penny Lane". Produced by Tony Bramwell, the films were directed by Peter Goldmann from Swedish television.

31 The band continued to film in Sevenoaks and finished the "Strawberry Fields Forever" piece.

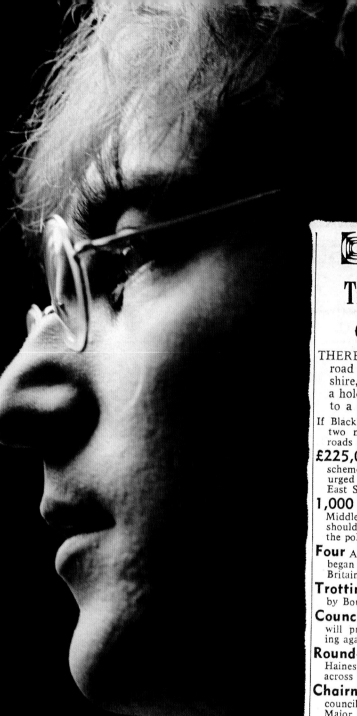

FAR&NEAR

The holes in our roads

THERE are 4,000 holes in the road in Blackburn, Lancashire, or one twenty-sixth of a hole per person, according to a council survey.

If Blackburn is typical there are two million holes in Britain's roads and 300,000 in London.

£225,0000 sea defence scheme for Felixstowe is being urged on the Government by East Suffolk River Board.

1,000 ratepayers in Harrow, Middlesex, said the Exchequer should pay for education and the police.

Four Australian State Ministers began a three-week tour of Britain.

Trotting ground will be opened by Bournemouth council.

Council tenants in Ipswich will protest at a public meeting against a 25 p.c. rent rise.

Round-Britain walker Frank Haines, 23, of Rugby, is to walk across the U.S.A.

Chairman of Petworth rural council, Sussex, for 20 years, Major George Mant, 71, died.

British Red Cross has sent £1,000 to Malaysian flood victims.

"A Day in the Life"

Even John, so often hypercritical about his achievements, thought "A Day in the Life" was "a damn good piece of work". Just as "Tomorrow Never Knows" was the only possible candidate to close *Revolver*, this Lennon-inspired tour de force had to be *Sgt. Pepper*'s grand finale. Or, more precisely, its rousing encore, for the reprise of the title song had already completed the regular concert performance.

The 17 January issue of the *Daily Mail* featured the stories of human tragedy and banal absurdity, the juxtaposition of which gave John his theme of spiritual decline. A song that referenced the death of socialite Tara Browne in a crumpled Lotus in one verse and the observation that Blackburn had 4,000 potholes in another, with a victory for the English army sandwiched between, was pop music's equivalent of "April is the cruellest month...". At least *Newsweek* saw echoes of T. S. Eliot's "The Wasteland", one of the most important poetic works of the twentieth century. The mood was not irredeemably defeatist, though. Paul's "beautiful little lick" rescued the disenchantment of the verses, though the authorities wouldn't countenance the antidote. "I'd love to turn you on" earned the song a BBC ban.

When they laid down the basic rhythm/vocal track, two 24-bar gaps were left, an alarm clock signalling the end of the first, where a middle eight was required. Paul had just the thing. "Woke up, fell out of bed..." was a fragment he had salted away, an old party piece that had finally found the perfect home. It was perfect Lennon–McCartney synergy: The former had a beginning and an end, the latter had a middle. But how to

FEBRUARY 1967

1 The first studio session recording the title song for the *Sgt. Pepper's Lonely Hearts Club Band* album.

2 Further overdubbing of the song "Sgt. Pepper's Lonely Hearts Club Band".

3 "A Day in the Life" was the focus of this session. Ringo taped his contribution on the tom-toms.

4 The second Carnival of Light Rave event.

6 To produce the promotional film for "Penny Lane", Goldmann chose

Stratford in the East End of London. This footage was mixed with film taken in Liverpool.

7 Back in Knole Park, further filming completed the work for the "Penny Lane" film.

8 Eight takes for John's song "Good Morning Good Morning"—it was the TV commercial for Kellogg's Corn Flakes that initiated the song.

9 It was the first time they recorded at a different studio. Regent Sound Studio, Tottenham Court Road, was owned

independently, so George Martin could attend, but others still employed by EMI were prevented from doing so.

10 Forty musicians were used for the orchestral piece in "A Day in the Life". The band had asked the musicians to wear evening dress and include some kind of novelty item. It was filmed by Tony Bramwell for NEMS Enterprises.

11 Part of the "Penny Lane" promotional film was shown on *Juke Box Jury*.

join them together? Paul serendipitously "fell out of bed" just after the alarm rang, so they decided to leave the latter sound in. There were still the two 24-bar blanks to fill, and these provided Paul with the opportunity to employ an avant-garde idea that complemented the theme. A discordant orchestral glissando resolving into a unified chord affirmed that it was possible to find meaning amid the chaos and fragmentation of the physical world.

Paul wanted a full symphony orchestra for what George Martin described as "orchestral orgasm". The producer balked at that, insisting that the idea would work just as effectively with half that number. Even forty musicians attracted a hefty £367 price tag, though they were recorded four times, so it was tantamount to a 160-piece orchestra. Paul's brief was simple: They were to progress from the lowest note in their instrument's range to the highest. How they did it was up to them; only the parameters were fixed.

It was an alien concept for an assembly of some of the country's finest musicians. Some harrumphed at being asked to turn out in evening-dress regalia, only to have an assortment of novelty items attached to them or their instruments. The first violinist had surely never been called upon to play whilst wearing a gorilla's paw. It was party time at Abbey Road, with the Beatles playing the role of court jesters.

The Beatles toyed with the idea of using overdubs to create the illusion of a mantra chanted by a cast of thousands. In the end that was rejected in favour of a single, sustained piano chord. Almost two weeks later, Paul, John, Ringo, and Mal Evans all hammered down on an E major. They made nine attempts, for they had to hit the keys exactly in concert. Onto the best take George Martin overdubbed three pounding harmonium chords to thicken the sound still further. As it died away, Geoff Emerick opened up the faders to squeeze every last ounce of sound into the mix. It came in at just over fifty seconds, faded earlier on the vinyl release.

Still they weren't finished. Homo sapien might have had his aural fill, but what about the animal kingdom? A high-pitched whistle audible only to dogs was duly added. Surely now they had thought of everything? Not quite. They hated the scratchy sound as the stylus hit the run-out groove, so they decided a bit of gibberish would fit the bill nicely if the listener was too stoned to get to the record player and remove the needle. "Couldn't really be any other" was selected, looped ad nauseam until it was unrecognizable. Knowing the Beatles' penchant for tape inversion, fans played it backwards and thought they had discovered a naughty message, yet another example of not letting the truth get in the way of a good Beatles story.

RIGHT: **Paul and Jane at the premiere of *Here We Go Round the Mulberry Bush*. Paul had considered writing the score for the film, but later declined the offer.**

OPPOSITE: **When John claims to have "read the news today" in the song "A Day in the Life", it was the *Daily Mail* of 17 January that he had in mind. This article on page seven provided the famous lyrics about counting all the small holes in the road in Blackburn, Lancashire.**

ON SGT. PEPPER

"*Sgt. Pepper* is called the first concept album, but it doesn't go anywhere. All my contributions to the album have absolutely nothing to do with this idea of Sgt. Pepper and his band; but it works, because we said it worked...when you get down to it, it was nothing more than an album called *Sgt. Pepper* with the tracks stuck together."

—John

12 Throughout February and the beginning of March postproduction work was done at the Twickenham Film Studios for *How I Won the War*. John was to attend on various occasions.

13 "Strawberry Fields Forever"/"Penny Lane" was released in the US on Capitol 5810. A studio session was spent preparing George's "Only a Northern Song".

14 Another session on George's song. This was to be part of his contribution to *Sgt. Pepper's Lonely Hearts*

Club Band, but it wasn't actually published until January 1969, when the *Yellow Submarine* album was released.

16 Promotional films for "Penny Lane" and "Strawberry Fields Forever" were broadcast on *Top of the Pops*. Overdubs were added to "Good Morning Good Morning".

17 "Strawberry Fields Forever"/"Penny Lane" was released in the UK on Parlophone R 5570. In the studio the band embarked on "Being for the Benefit of Mr Kite!".

20 Continuing to record "Being for the Benefit of Mr Kite!", Geoff Emerick mixed up the sounds of old Sousa marches to emulate a circus sound and mimic a steam organ.

21 "Fixing a Hole" was completed.

22 "A Day in the Life" was recorded, using three pianos.

23 Geoff Emerick made the stereo master for "A Day in the Life",

then the band began to record "Lovely Rita". The "Penny Lane" clip was again screened on *Top of the Pops*.

24 More work at Abbey Road on "Lovely Rita".

25 In America the clips for "Penny Lane" and "Strawberry Fields Forever" were screened on ABC's *The Hollywood Palace*. "Penny Lane" entered the British charts, staying there for 11 weeks. It ultimately reached No. 2.

THIS PAGE: **Paul and Jane had begun dating in 1964, but by the beginning of 1967 there was a gulf growing between them. Jane was to spend the early part of the year touring the US with a theatre company, and she would later comment that Paul had changed considerably during their separation—a result of his experiences with the "heaven and hell" drug LSD.**

George and Ringo have reservations

For George, fresh from his six-week stay in India searching for truth and enlightenment, a return to the studio to work on a project based on pretence was hardly going to set his pulse racing. India had liberated him from Beatledom, and he struggled with the idea of returning to the group's confines, even without the pressures of public engagements. "My heart was still out there", he said, and he didn't relish the prospect of being put back in harness.

While most were eulogizing about the great leap forward *Sgt. Pepper* represented, George regarded it as a retrograde step. Because the songs were constructed in layers, with numerous overdubs, there was little opportunity for whole-group performance. Ringo had similar reservations. With brass and strings to the fore, he said he felt like a session musician much of the time. There were long periods when Ringo wasn't required at all, and he used them to master the rudiments of chess, or else kicked his heels at home waiting for a call. *Sgt. Pepper* wasn't to go down as his favourite album.

Ringo was less intense, more easily mollified than George. The latter felt his "day job" was more tedious during the *Pepper* sessions than it had been during the making of the previous two albums. "I felt we were just in the studio to make the next record, and Paul was going on about this idea of some fictitious band. That side of it didn't really interest me, other than the title song and the album cover… It was becoming difficult to me because I wasn't really into it".

It was easy to see why George was frustrated. Guitars didn't feature heavily, and after the

breakthrough with *Revolver* he was again struggling to get any of his material included. "Only a Northern Song" was George's first contribution to the *Pepper* sessions, but when it was decided that it wouldn't make the final cut, he wrote "Within You Without You", the fruit of a session dabbling on a harmonium at Klaus Voormann's house. None of the other Beatles performed on the song, which has often been

unfairly derided as the seminal album's weak link. In fact, with lines such as "We were talking about the love that's gone so cold/and the people who gain the world and lose their soul", "Within You Without You" stands as *Sgt. Pepper*'s spiritual core.

BELOW: **While Paul relished the thought of beginning work on a new album, for George the prospect of returning to the studio was unappealing.**

MARCH 1967

1 Recording for "Lucy in the Sky with Diamonds" began. The song was named after a painting brought home from nursery school by John's three-year-old son, Julian.

2 At the ninth annual Grammy Awards Lennon and McCartney's "Michelle" won Song of the Year. Klaus Voormann also won an award for his artwork on the *Revolver* album cover and Paul won in the category of best performance for "Eleanor Rigby". The "Strawberry Fields Forever" promotional film was shown on *Top of the Pops*. Another late-night session at Abbey

Road as work continued on "Lucy in the Sky with Diamonds".

3 The French horns on the title track of *Sgt. Pepper* were recorded, after which George added guitar before more work on "Lucy in the Sky with Diamonds".

6 Clapping and laughing were also recorded to add to the illusion that Sgt. Pepper was a real band. From the archives, extracts from "Volume 28: Audience Applause and Atmosphere, Royal Albert Hall and Queen Elizabeth Hall" gave

the illusion of an audience talking before the start of the song.

7 Harmony and vocal effects were added to "Lovely Rita". The band was featured on *Scene Special* on Granada.

9 The session at Abbey Road began the work for Paul's "Getting Better".

10 A droning tamboura, bass guitar, and drums were added to the day before's takes.

"A Little Help From My Friends"

It was nearing the end of March, almost four months since the Beatles had begun work on "When I'm Sixty-Four", and the new album was still lacking a Ringo vehicle. Paul and John put that right with a fascinating brainstorming session in which they bounced ideas off each other to fit suitable lyrics to a McCartney melody. The final track to be recorded—not counting the "Sgt. Pepper" reprise—was originally titled "Bad Finger Boogie". That soon became "With a Little Help from My Friends", though Paul would recall the working title of the song the following year when the Iveys were signed to Apple. They would have three UK top ten hits as Badfinger.

It was always planned that this song would occupy the track-two slot, running straight

on from the introduction "Billy Shears" had been given by the Sgt. Pepper Band. Instead of being an obligatory filler, "With a Little Help from My Friends" became one of the most popular *Sgt. Pepper* tracks and a perennial Beatles favourite. The Beatles didn't issue any *Sgt. Pepper* tracks as singles, but "With a Little Help from My Friends" was covered by a great number of artists, notably Joe Cocker, who had a UK number one with the song in the autumn of 1968.

Ringo demurred at one line John and Paul came up with: "Would you stand up and throw tomatoes at me?" was a hostage to fortune if the Beatles went back on the road and he "sang out of tune". Memories of the jelly bean bombardment were all too vivid, and painful.

ABOVE: **Paul conducts a 41-piece orchestra (top) and Ringo films John waving a scarf (above) during recordings for *Sgt. Pepper*. The orchestra had been brought in to fill in a 24-bar gap in "A Day in the Life", which had emerged when John and Paul's separate contributions to the song had been brought together.**

OPPOSITE: **While at the wheel of his Aston Martin, Paul is accosted by autograph hunters.**

continued from previous page

MARCH 1967

11 ITV showed the clips of "Penny Lane" on the first edition of *As You Like It*, presented by Pete Murray. Northern Songs revealed that a total of 446 cover versions of Paul's "Yesterday" had been recorded since the song's release.

13 Six members of Sounds Inc joined the group to add brass effects to "Good Morning Good Morning". They had been signed up by Brian Epstein the previous year and had played on some of the Beatles' tours.

14 The clips for "Penny Lane" and "Strawberry Fields Forever" were screened on the American show *Where the Action Is*.

15 George wrote another song for the *Sgt. Pepper* album, "Within You, Without You". It had very strong Indian influences and used the tabla, dilruba, swordmandel, and a droning tamboura, all played by external musicians.

17 The orchestral section for Paul's "She's Leaving Home" was recorded. The score was written

by Mike Leander, as George Martin had been working with another artist at the time. The musicians included the first woman to be engaged to perform on a Beatles track: Sheila Bromberg on harp.

18 "Penny Lane" reached the top of the US charts, staying there for one week.

20 Brian Matthew interviewed John and Paul for BBC's *Top of the Pops*. The footage was to be used by the Transcription Service that sold to overseas stations, so it would not be seen at home. He also recorded

A smaller contribution from John

The Beatles' first seven albums had been shared triumphs for the group's two stellar talents, but during the making of *Sgt. Pepper* John was undoubtedly playing catch-up. Paul hit the ground running with the new project, while John spent a lot of time in a torpid haze. John was the sole or chief contributor on just four of the twelve tracks, and two of those he later dismissed somewhat peremptorily. "Good Morning Good Morning" and "Being for the Benefit of Mr. Kite!" might have been throwaways to John, quickfire fillers to fulfil a quota, but simply in terms of soundwash and texture, these two offerings were integral to the iconic set.

John was an inveterate TV consumer, as happy to let banal advertisements or static wash over him as formal programmes. In the case of "Good Morning Good Morning" it was a Kellogg's Corn Flakes jingle that gave him the start he needed. In John's hands, however, the chirpy, top-of-the-morning sentiment took on a very different hue. Instead we were given trenchant dissatisfaction, a goldfish-bowl view of a mundane relationship in a deep rut. "It's time for tea and meet the wife" was a reference to a popular sitcom of the day revolving round the travails of a put-upon husband. The male protagonist might have "nothing to say" to his partner, but in the final verse he is "watching the skirts you start to flirt, now you're in gear", a thinly disguised comment on his own domestic setup.

John is said to have insisted that the farmyard sounds at the end of the song be placed in "food chain" order, such that each animal was prey to its successor. Fortuitously, the final hen's cluck married nicely with the opening guitar note of the "Sgt. Pepper" reprise, and they were stitched together to create one of the cleverest segues to appear on record.

The lyrics of "Being for the Benefit of Mr. Kite!" were lifted wholesale from an 1843 circus poster, acquired by John at an antiques shop in Sevenoaks during the making of the "Strawberry Fields Forever"/"Penny Lane" promotional film on 31 January. If the words were a gift from the past, creating the effects that would bring Pablo Fanque's Circus Royal to life proved trickier.

George Martin knew just the instrument for the job: a traditional hand-cranked steam organ. Unfortunately, to acquire one of those and set it up would have been prohibitively expensive, even for the Beatles. The punch-card automatic alternative simply wouldn't do, so they manufactured the required sound using a combination of harmonium, bass harmonica, and organ plus various keyboard overdubs. It still wasn't quite right, so Martin dug into the sound archives and found some steam-organ tapes, which he instructed engineer Geoff Emerick to cut up, fling into the air, and splice together randomly. It wasn't random enough, the sections landing in just about the same order, but with a little judicious manual rearrangement, Martin met John's demand that he be able to "smell the sawdust".

Paul and John accepting three Ivor Novello awards. "Yellow Submarine" won "The A-Side of the Record Issued in 1966 Which Achieved the Highest Certified British Sales in the Period 1 January 1966 to 31 December 1966" while "Michelle" won "The Most Performed Work of the Year" and "Yesterday" won "Runner-Up to the Most Performed Work of the Year". It was the first time Abbey Road had been used for an interview. Afterwards work continued on "She's Leaving Home".

21 More studio recordings of "Getting Better" and "Lovely Rita". John was on an LSD trip at the time and went up to the roof for some air. He was quickly fetched back by Paul and George as there was a 30-foot drop and no rails.

22 Further overdubs of the dilruba and swordmandel parts on "Within You Without You".

23 The Ivor Novello Awards for 1966 were recorded live at the Playhouse Theatre in London. John and Paul did not attend, so the awards were collected by Tony Barrow from NEMS and Ron White from EMI while their previously recorded speeches were played. In the studio more work was done on the vocals for "Getting Better".

24 An edited version of the "Strawberry Fields Forever" promotional film was used on The Best on Record Grammy Awards special.

27 The Ivor Novello Awards for 1966 were broadcast by the BBC Light Programme on Easter Monday. Paul watched Fats Domino play in the UK for the first time at the Saville Theatre.

28 John recorded the lead vocals for "Good Morning Good Morning". Again archive material was used when the animal noises were recorded.

29 The sound effects previously recorded were added to "Being for the Benefit of Mr. Kite!" along with extra harmonica and organ. Ringo's vocal contribution to *Sgt. Pepper* was recorded, using the song "With a Little Help from My Friends".

30 A photo shoot at Chelsea Manor Photographic Studios in Chelsea. Michael Cooper took the pictures that would supplement Peter Blake's design for the sleeve of *Sgt. Pepper*.

31 A studio session working on "With a Little Help from My Friends" and "Being for the Benefit of Mr. Kite!".

SGT. PEPPER'S LONELY HEARTS CLUB BAND

Released

🇬🇧 1 June 1967 (Parlophone)   🇺🇸 2 June 1967 (Capitol)

Side One:
Sgt. Pepper's Lonely Hearts Club Band
With a Little Help from My Friends
Lucy in the Sky with Diamonds
Getting Better
Fixing a Hole
She's Leaving Home
Being for the Benefit of Mr. Kite!

Side Two:
Within You, Without You (Harrison)
When I'm Sixty-Four
Lovely Rita
Good Morning, Good Morning
Sgt. Pepper's Lonely Hearts Club Band (Reprise)
A Day in the Life

Cover Story

Long before the completion of *Sgt. Pepper*, it was clear to all that here was a groundbreaking album that required special packaging. Art dealer Robert Fraser suggested they employ a fine artist and put them in touch with Peter Blake. Paul sketched out his ideas to Blake. The floral clock motif, creating a distinctive "northern" feel, was there from the start and the idea quickly emerged for a tableau, Sgt. Pepper's Lonely Hearts Club Band surrounded by their heroes after putting on an open-air performance.

Blake made life-size cut-outs of an eclectic cast of characters. John was in mischievous mode: As well as Edgar Allan Poe, Lewis Carroll, and Oscar Wilde, he wanted the Marquis de Sade, Jesus, and Hitler. George

chose gurus and mystics, while Ringo was quite happy to rubber-stamp the selections of the others. Surprisingly, musical influences were thin on the ground. Dylan was there, and Dion—apparently at Blake's behest—but none of the heroes of their formative years: no Carl Perkins, Little Richard, or Chuck Berry. Not even Elvis.

Blake spent two weeks arranging the cut-outs and waxwork models at the Chelsea studio of photographer Michael Cooper, whose work Fraser had exhibited at Indica Gallery. The shoot took place on 30 March, though not everyone was happy with the result. Brian Epstein, no doubt with thoughts of another "butcher" cover row in the making, was wrestling with the issue during a flight home from the States. He scribbled a note to his American lawyer, Nat Weiss, suggesting that the new album should be concealed in brown paper wrapping.

EMI chairman Sir Joseph Lockwood also had misgivings. First, there was a bill tipping the scales at over £2,800 when record companies might typically budget less than £100 for sleeve artwork. However, he was worried that this astronomical figure might be a drop in the ocean if lawsuits from people seeking to protect their image rights came flooding in. Lockwood had the art department prepare an alternative cover—minus the crowd. Paul, who wouldn't budge, opined that those still living would be flattered to be included on a Beatles album cover and in the end Lockwood relented—Gandhi and Hitler were removed, consents were obtained, and EMI was indemnified against any action that might arise. Mae West initially took umbrage at the idea that she might be associated with a lonely hearts club, but was soon talked round.

Still the Beatles weren't finished. *Sgt. Pepper* would have a gatefold sleeve and printed lyrics. Both were pop firsts. A goodie bag of *Pepper* paraphernalia was also included, though the giveaways were reined in as even the Beatles realized that they had to balance a value package for the fans with worrying cost overruns.

The Grammy Award-winning *Sgt. Pepper* cover perfectly complemented the musical content. It, too, was innovative, elaborate, a dazzling kaleidoscope on a grand scale.

APRIL 1967

1 A reprise of the album's title track was swiftly recorded before Paul left for the US.

3 George was the only Beatle present to work on "Within You Without You". Three cellists and eight violinists recorded George Martin's score before George added the vocals, the sitar, and acoustic guitar to the piece. Paul flew to the US.

4 "Within You Without You", the final song for the album, was finished.

5 Paul flew to Denver, Colorado, to celebrate Jane Asher's 21st birthday.

6 After further mixing, the master tape was compiled for the album.

7 George Martin, Geoff Emerick, and Richard Lush produced stereo mixes of "With a Little Help from My Friends", "Being for the Benefit of Mr. Kite!", "Fixing a Hole", and "Lucy in the Sky with Diamonds".

8 In the band's absence stereo mixes of the title track were made.

9 Paul flew on to Los Angeles in Frank Sinatra's Lear Jet. The advisory board responsible for planning the Monterey Pop Festival asked him to join them; his initial advice was to book Jimi Hendrix.

10 Paul attended a recording session with the Beach Boys.

11 Flying home from Los Angeles, Paul jotted down some ideas for a TV

ABOVE: **The Beatles pose at Brian Epstein's launch party for the *Sgt. Pepper* album.**

LEFT: **The new album and image direction allowed for a whole host of merchandise such as this button and patch.**

RIGHT: **This poster advertising a circus in Rochdale, Lancashire, in 1843 was purchased by John at an antiques shop in Sevenoakes, Kent, in January 1967 and provided the inspiration for the song "Being for the Benefit of Mr. Kite!".**

PABLO FANQUE'S CIRCUS ROYAL.
TOWN-MEADOWS, ROCHDALE.

Grandest Night of the Season!
AND POSITIVELY THE
LAST NIGHT BUT THREE!
BEING FOR THE
BENEFIT OF MR. KITE,
(LATE OF WELL'S CIRCUS) AND
MR. J. HENDERSON,
THE CELEBRATED SOMERSET THROWER!
WIRE DANCER, VAULTER, RIDER etc
On TUESDAY Evening, February 14th 1843

Messrs. KITE & HENDERSON, in announcing the following Entertainment to the Public that they have engaged and gone to a great expense Mr. Town, having been some days in preparation.

Mr. KITE it, ill, but this night only, introduce the

CELEBRATED
HORSE, ZANTHUS!
Well Known to be one of the best Broke Horses
IN THE WORLD!!!
Mr. HENDERSON will undertake the arduous Task of
THROWING TWENTY ONE SOMERSETS
ON THE SOLID GROUND

Mr KITE will appear for the first time this season
On the Tight Rope.
When two Gentlemen Amateurs of this Town will
perform with him.

Mr HENDERSON's gift, for the first time in Rochdale, introduces his extraordinary:
TRAMPOLINE LEAPS
AND
SOMERSETS!
Over Men & Horses, through Hoops, over Garters, and lastly, through a Hogshead of REAL FIRE! In this branch of the profession, Mr H. challenges THE WORLD!

For particulars, see letter of the day

---

film about a mystery tour on a coach—later to be named *Magical Mystery Tour*.

13 Richard Lush made his debut as the Beatles' tape operator, working on *Sgt. Pepper's Lonely Hearts Club Band*.

17 More stereo mixing of some of the *Sgt. Pepper* songs.

19 A legal business partnership, The Beatles and Co., was formed to bind the group together until 1977. In the

studio, "Good Morning Good Morning" was remixed.

20 A stereo mix was made of the reprise to "Sgt. Pepper's Lonely Hearts Club Band" before adding overdubs to "Only a Northern Song".

21 *Sgt. Pepper's Lonely Hearts Club Band* was finished after a total of 700 studio hours and a budget of £25,000.

24 The band went to watch Donovan on the opening night

of his engagement at the Saville Theatre, London. In the US, George Martin and His Orchestra released "Love in the Open Air", written by John and Paul.

25 The first session working on the title song of *Magical Mystery Tour*, using "Volume 36: Traffic Noise Stereo" from the Abbey Road archives as sound effects.

26 Bass, maracas, cowbells, tambourines, and backing vocals were all added to "Magical Mystery Tour".

27 The vocal parts were then added to "Magical Mystery Tour".

29 The 14-Hour Technicolor Dream Event took place at Alexandra Palace and included Yoko Ono as one of the performers. John was filmed there while watching.

30 John went to visit the Isle of Dornish off the coast of County Mayo in Ireland. He had bought it six weeks earlier.

BIO: LINDA EASTMAN

Linda Eastman was born into a wealthy New York family on 24 September 1941. Her father, Lee, was an attorney specializing in show business copyright law, while her mother Louise's family had made a fortune in the retail sector. After high school, Linda attended Sarah Lawrence School in Bronxville, whose alumni included Yoko Ono. After hearing that her mother had been killed in a plane crash, a grief-stricken Linda rushed into marriage with fellow student Melvin See. She soon realized her mistake and negotiated an amicable end to a union that produced a daughter, Heather, born 31 December 1962. Music and photography were twin passions, the latter fired by a course she took at the University of Arizona. Her big break into professional photography came when she covered a reception for the Rolling Stones on a yacht on the Hudson River. Rock star portraits became her métier, and her pictures of subjects including Jimi Hendrix and Bob Dylan won many accolades. Linda saw the Beatles at Shea Stadium and photographed them in Austria in 1965, during location shooting for *Help!*, but it was another two years before she made their acquaintance. On 15 May 1967 Linda was in the Bag O' Nails club with members of the Animals, having crossed the Pond on an assignment to photograph the cream of swinging London's musical talent. Paul was there, and she met him again four days later, as part of the press entourage covering the *Sgt. Pepper* launch party at Brian Epstein's Chapel Street home. It was a year before they met again, during Paul and John's visit to America to promote Apple. Three months later, in September 1968, Paul invited her to stay. They married on 12 March 1969, when Linda was pregnant with Mary. Stella was born in 1971, and James—Paul's given name—arrived six years later. Linda was subjected to jibes when she took to the stage alongside Paul as keyboard player with Wings. But it was she who led the way on environmental and animal rights issues, and the couple championed the cause of vegetarianism. Her cookbooks and vegetarian food products were hugely successful and added to her personal fortune. She was diagnosed with breast cancer in 1995 and died in Tucson on 17 April 1998, aged 56. Paul's knighthood in 1997 meant that she became Lady Linda McCartney for the last year of her life.

MAY 1967

3 Four musicians attended the sessions to add trumpets to "Magical Mystery Tour".

4 Mono mixing of "Magical Mystery Tour".

5 Paul decided to shave off his moustache.

7 Ringo went to see the Jimi Hendrix Experience at the Saville Theatre, London.

9 A seven-hour studio session resulted in only 16 minutes of final recording. Mick Jagger was in the studio at the time.

11 At the Olympic Sound Studios, Barnes, London, the band finalized "Baby You're a Rich Man"—the first song to be recorded for the forthcoming film *Yellow Submarine*.

12 Back at Abbey Road, another new song for the *Yellow Submarine* soundtrack was completed in a single session: "All Together Now". *Sgt. Pepper's Lonely Hearts Club Band* was first played on the pirate station Radio London.

15 Paul met Linda Eastman at the Bag O' Nails Club in London when he was watching Georgie Fame and the Blue Flames.

17 This was the first of several sessions working on John's "You Know My Name (Look Up the Number)"; this song was not issued until March 1970. The band was featured on *Man Alive* on BBC2.

ABOVE AND LEFT: **Two weeks ahead of the release of *Sgt. Pepper*, the boys turned up at Brian Epstein's house for a launch party and press conference. The album spent 15 weeks at the top of the US *Billboard* chart and an incredible 23 weeks in the No. 1 spot in the UK.**

OPPOSITE: **While Jane Asher was in America with a touring theatre company, at the *Pepper* party Paul was captivated by Linda Eastman whom he had met for the first time four days earlier.**

18 Paul and John added vocals to a Rolling Stones recording of "We Love You" at Olympic Studios. It was announced that the Beatles were to be one of two British representatives in a TV programme set up for live broadcasting worldwide on Sunday, 25 June—the first-ever global satellite link-up. They agreed to be filmed recording a song written specially for the occasion.

19 Brian Epstein held a party for the launch of *Sgt. Pepper's Lonely Hearts Club Band* at his Belgravia home in London.

20 Kenny Everett's interviews with the four Beatles were included in the BBC's Light Programme's *Where It's At* broadcast. He had recorded them in private and the programme focused on the forthcoming album. However, the BBC had just imposed a radio and TV ban on "A Day in the Life" due to the song's drug references.

24 At the annual NBC-TV Grammy Awards, Liberace introduced an excerpt from the "Strawberry Fields Forever" promotional film. During the same evening the band watched Procol Harum play at the Speakeasy Club.

25 Another number from *Yellow Submarine*, "It's All Too Much", was recorded at De Lane Lea Recording Studios, London. John bought a Rolls-Royce Phantom V.

29 *The Times* published an article called "The Beatles Revive Hope of Progress in Pop Music". Written by music critic William Mann, it was an analysis of *Sgt. Pepper's Lonely Hearts Club Band*. Paul met

Jane Asher at Heathrow Airport—she had been on tour in the US with the Bristol Old Vic Company.

31 Another session at De Lane Lea, overdubbing "It's All Too Much" with percussion and handclaps along with extra vocals.

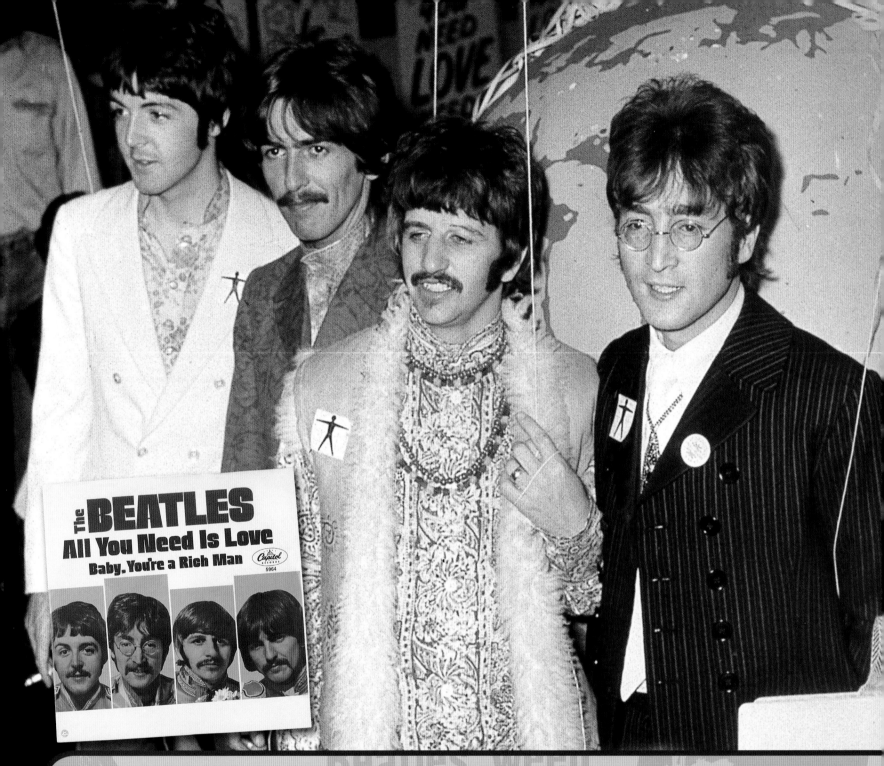

JUNE 1967

1 The official UK release of *Sgt. Pepper's Lonely Hearts Club Band* on Parlophone PMC 7027 (mono) and PCS 7027 (stereo). It sold 250,000 copies in the first week. At De Lane Lea Studios the band recorded an informal jam session.

2 When *Sgt. Pepper's Lonely Hearts Club Band* was released in the US on Capitol MAS-2653 (mono) and SMAS-2653 (stereo) it had advance orders of more than a million copies. Back at the De Lane Lea Studios, four trumpeters and a bass clarinetist worked with the band until the small hours of the morning.

4 George, Pattie, Paul, and Jane attended a concert at the Saville Theatre, London, featuring the Jimi Hendrix Experience, Denny Laine and his Electric String Band, Procol Harum, and the Chiffons. Paul held a party at his home after the event.

7 More recordings of "You Know My Name (Look Up the Number)" at Abbey Road.

8 Brian Jones of the Rolling Stones joined in this session, playing alto saxophone on "You Know My Name (Look Up the Number)".

9 "You Know My Name (Look Up the Number)" was almost finished. No further work was done on this song until April 1969.

10 *Sgt. Pepper's Lonely Hearts Club Band* reached the top of the UK charts, remaining there for 23 weeks.

12 Paul and John provided backing vocals on the song "We Love You", recorded by the Rolling Stones at the Olympic Studio in Barnes.

"All You Need Is Love"

Not content with producing the album synonymous with the Summer of Love, the Beatles also came up with the single most identified with that epochal period. Epstein was approached to see if the Beatles would appear in a live TV extravaganza called *Our World*, a twenty-four-country satellite link-up across five continents. Beatlemania might have passed, but there was still only one contender to represent popular culture in the UK. The deal wasn't signed until 18 May, just five weeks before the historic broadcast to an estimated audience of 300 million-plus across the globe.

Each participating country had a five-minute slot to showcase itself "bringing man face to face with mankind", as the BBC billed it. The Beatles left it alarmingly late to come up with a suitable song, one with a catchy melody and simple lyric that would work for a worldwide audience. As had been the case with the title songs for *A Hard Day's Night* and *Help!*, John and Paul each went away and tried to come up with an idea. And once again it was John who delivered the goods.

"All You Need Is Love" was recorded over a ten-day period in the run-up to the day of the broadcast. "The Marseillaise" intro set the perfect tone for a supranational composition, and the sense of fun shone through in the wacky ending, where the Beatles invited George Martin to use snatches of anything that took his fancy. There were bursts of "Greensleeves" and Bach, though the producer got into a spot of bother when he included "In the Mood", which he thought—wrongly—was in the public domain and freely available. The publishers did eventually receive their fee. Paul had the idea to reprise the Fabs era with "She Loves You". In the studio this "simple" song was a fifty-take behemoth. The question was, could they create the impression of a live recording session on the big day?

George Martin knew that the Beatles' track record in live performance suggested that the event could be a spectacular failure. These days they were used to the comfort zone of retakes, delivering multilayered perfection in the studio. There would be no screams to drown out the rough edges either, so he insisted on the safety net of a backing track. This provoked a row with the BBC, who thought it was against the spirit of the link, but as it had already been trailed that the Beatles would be performing, the organization backed down.

After the final rehearsal on Saturday—the day before transmission—it was decided that an audience would work well to make it into a carnival atmosphere. A quick trawl round some of the Beatles' favourite local haunts threw up a host of celebrities who came to the party and made the sing-along chorus go with a bang. Mick Jagger, Keith Richards, Keith Moon, Eric Clapton, Marianne Faithfull, and Graham Nash were among the Beatles' backing group that day. It wasn't party time in the control room. George Martin and Geoff Emerick took the live vocals and orchestra and mixed them with the backing track on the fly before feeding the signal to the BBC's outside broadcast van for transmission.

Belatedly, it was announced that "All You Need Is Love" would be the Beatles' new single.

This was partly down to the fact that it would have been against the spirit of the programme to use it as a platform for a worldwide plug. The "live" version wasn't the one that was pressed: The Beatles tweaked the vocals and instrumentals for the 45 release two weeks later. After the unfathomable "Penny Lane"/"Strawberry Fields" blip, "All You Need Is Love" put the Beatles back on top of the UK charts and became the enduring anthem for the flower-power generation.

ABOVE: **"All You Need Is Love"**, spelled out on sandwich boards in French, German, Spanish, and English, was a fitting message to broadcast around the world—and it set the tone for the forthcoming Summer of Love.

OPPOSITE: **The Beatles prepare to perform to their largest audience to date—some 400 million people. The spectacular feat was Britain's contribution to** *Our World*, **a global satellite broadcast involving more than 20 different nations.**

OPPOSITE INSET: **"All You Need Is Love" was destined for success. It topped the charts on both sides of the Atlantic when it was released in July 1967 with "Baby You're a Rich Man" on the B-side.**

---

13 The second day recording "We Love You", produced by Andrew Loog Oldham.

14 The band was filmed at the Olympic Sound Studios working on "All You Need Is Love", in readiness for the *Our World* broadcast of 25 June, the first global satellite link-up.

15 *Sgt. Pepper's Lonely Hearts Club Band* was certified gold in the States.

16 The band was on the cover of *Life* magazine, while inside Paul admitted that he had taken acid.

19 In the *Daily Mirror*, Paul again admitted to taking acid. The vocals, drums, piano, and banjo were added to "All You Need Is Love".

20 Paul was criticized by Billy Graham following his revelations that he had taken LSD and that the experience had brought him closer to God.

21 Mono versions of "All You Need Is Love" were mixed.

23 An orchestra joined in the studio session to make the recording for "All You Need Is Love".

24 Before the big event of 25 June, more than 100 journalists and photographers answered the press call at Abbey Road Studios. In the afternoon there was a full television rehearsal before taping further overdubs to the song that evening.

25 The band performed "All You Need Is Love" on BBC's *Our World*, watched by an estimated 400 million viewers over five continents. The band was shown sitting on stools in the studio in full evening dress. On the floor sat many friends including Keith Richards, Keith Moon, Mick Jagger, Eric Clapton, and Marianne Faithfull. It was to be the Beatles' last live TV performance. In Battersea Park, London, John entered his Rolls-Royce into a Concours d'Elegance competition at an Oxfam rally.

26 Back to Abbey Road for another session, perfecting "All You Need Is Love".

28 George was caught speeding in his Mini Cooper and fined £6.

JOHN, PAUL, GEORGE & RINGO

A slow start on the *Magical Mystery Tour*

Just four days after the side-two groove-run-out fun and games had put the final flourish to *Sgt. Pepper*, the Beatles were back in the studio working on Paul's new pet project. He didn't have much: a snatch of the opening for a title track, a few chords, and an idea. The idea had formed during the return flight from his recent trip to the States: a free-form film of sketches and musical interludes based around a coach trip. The template for the madcap bus romp was Ken Kesey's Merry Pranksters, who had acquired cult status for their psychedelic jaunt across America. Paul's anglicized vision of that celebrated road trip was a mystery coach tour of the kind that had become part of the fabric of the English leisure scene, the working classes at play. They would produce and direct it themselves, and so put an end to all the speculation about the Beatles' long-awaited third movie project.

The plan may have been sketchy, but from the outset the title was emblazoned across the top of the scrap of paper on which Paul mapped out the concept: *Magical Mystery Tour*. The Beatles soon had the title song in the can, but when they convened at Abbey Road in the second week in May they had a long, unproductive session, unsure where to go with the idea next. The project threatened to stall before it had really got off the ground.

To move things along they left Abbey Road for only the second time in their careers, repairing to Olympic Studio, Barnes, where the boss Keith Grant had a reputation for taking things at a sprightly lick. That was appealing to the Beatles, who had no wish to become embroiled in another *Pepper*-style marathon. The song they recorded there was "Baby You're a Rich Man", which was done and dusted in six hours, including mixing, the first time that the entire process had been completed away from Abbey Road.

The new song wasn't slated to appear in *Magical Mystery Tour*, which slipped off the agenda somewhat during the Summer of Love. It would take Brian Epstein's death to kick-start the idea and get the bus rolling on its surreal journey.

OPPOSITE AND ABOVE: **After the launch of *Sgt. Pepper*, Pattie, George, Ringo, and new friend Alexis Mardas head for a break in Greece, where they looked into buying an island. The idea was to have a sanctuary where the band and their entourage could relax without the constant invasions of privacy. However, the authoritarian Greek government tried to make political capital out of the Beatles, and the boys decided to pull out of negotiations.**

Island retreat

The Beatles were ever receptive to new ideas, both musically and in the search for extracting greater meaning from their daily existence. With *Sgt. Pepper* the group had pushed back the boundaries of popular music, and that summer the road to greater spiritual fulfilment led to Greece. John's latest brainchild was for the four and their inner circle to set up an island commune, and a likely location was suggested by his new "guru", electronics wizard Yanni "John" Alexis Mardas.

The two had met through a mutual friend who had exhibited at the Indica Gallery, and John was immediately taken with the young Greek's surreal ideas, many of which would have been perfectly at home in the pages of a science-fiction novel. The other members of the group were somewhat less impressed by "Magic Alex", as John dubbed him, but went along for the ride when it was suggested that Mardas's homeland would be the perfect place to realize John's dream of an idyllic island haven.

Negotiations reached an advanced stage to buy the island of Leslo for £90,000—they even got special dispensation from Chancellor of the Exchequer James Callaghan, allowing them to take the required funds out of the country. But the warm glow of drug-fuelled days on sun-kissed beaches quickly cooled. It didn't help that Mardas was tipping off the authorities regarding the group's itinerary, the junta looking to score PR points via a Beatle seal of approval, in return for which the entourage would be given diplomatic immunity. It meant that hordes of fans and journalists appeared wherever they went, the antithesis of what had underpinned the whole idea.

JULY 1967

1 The BBC Light Programme, *Where It's At*, included an interview with Paul by Kenny Everett discussing "All You Need Is Love".

2 Pattie met Eric Clapton at a party held at Brian Epstein's house.

3 John, Paul, George, Jane, and Pattie were guests at a party in honour of the Monkees, held at the Speakeasy.

7 The single "All You Need Is Love" backed by "Baby You're a Rich Man" was released in the UK on Parlophone R 5620.

17 "All You Need Is Love"/"Baby You're a Rich Man" was released in the US on Capitol 5964. Brian Epstein's father, Harry, died when convalescing in Bournemouth following a heart attack the previous year.

20 Chris Barber & His Jazz Band recorded Paul's song "Catcall". Paul and Jane attended the recording session and added their voices to the finale. George, Pattie, Ringo, and Neil Aspinall flew to Athens—there had been rumours that the band had bought a Greek island for £150,000.

The Beatles had flirted with the idea of a laissez-faire sanctuary; what they got was a new military junta trying to exploit their presence for propaganda purposes while at the same time slapping a ban on rock 'n' roll music. They returned home disillusioned by the experience, though when the purchase principal was converted back to Sterling they found they had made over £11,000 on the deal. The search for imbuing their lives with greater meaning went on, however. The following month they would meet the Maharishi Mahesh Yogi; Indian mysticism would be the next source of inspiration.

ABOVE AND OPPOSITE: **John and Paul joined Ringo and George in Greece in the search for the island getaway, although soon after they arrived Ringo returned to the UK to be with his wife, Maureen, who was in the late stages of pregnancy. Although the deal collapsed, British newspapers reported information from the Greek government that the boys had indeed bought an island in the Aegean Sea for £150,000. In reality, the remaining three Beatles returned to Britain at the end of July empty-handed.**

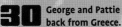

22 "All You Need Is Love" topped the UK charts and remained there for three weeks. Paul, Jane, John, Cynthia, and Julian flew to Athens.

24 John, Paul, George, Ringo, and Brian Epstein lent their names to a petition published in *The Times* calling for the legalization of marijuana.

26 Ringo returned to the UK as Maureen was pregnant, while the rest of the party cruised around the Greek islands. They visited the island of Leslo, and although plans were made to take money out of Britain for its purchase, the deal never went through.

30 George and Pattie flew back from Greece.

31 As the end of pirate radio approached, Ringo recorded a farewell message on behalf of all the Beatles to be broadcast on Radio London's last day: It closed down on 5 August 1967. Paul and John returned from Greece.

Coming clean about a drug habit

In June 1967, barely two weeks after the release of *Sgt. Pepper*, Paul gave an interview during which he was put on the spot about his drug habit. Instead of stonewalling, he decided that honesty was the best policy and admitted to having taken LSD, dubbed the "heaven and hell" drug in media circles. Paul sought to give a rational response, generating light instead of heat on a sensitive issue. "After I took it, it opened my eyes... [it made me] a better, more honest, more tolerant member of society. This was an experience I wanted for myself, and it has made me a better person, I think."

He made it clear that this was a personal view, and he wasn't advocating that anyone should follow his example. If the reporter chose to broadcast his remarks, then any culpability rested with the network. Paul himself was more than willing to keep the subject off the record. It was naïve to expect a news crew to sit on a story of such magnitude, and it duly exploded in Paul's face.

John and George in particular were somewhat irked that Paul had taken the spotlight when he had been the most hesitant and last of the four to experiment with acid. Dr. Billy Graham was more annoyed at the suggestion that LSD could bring about a quasi-religious experience, while in a House of Commons debate on the issue one government minister said: "What sort of society are we going to create if everyone wants to escape from reality into a dream world"?

The following month, 24 July, all four Beatles were signatories to a full-page *Times* advertisement advocating the legalization of marijuana. At least this time they were in illustrious company, as celebrities from all walks of life subscribed to the view that "The law against marijuana is immoral in principle and unworkable in practice".

Against this backdrop, it was inevitable that *Sgt. Pepper* would be put under the microscope and examined in minute detail for drug references. "Fixing a Hole" was seized upon as an obvious candidate, though Paul made it clear that the lyric was a simple "repair" analogy: about "the hole in your makeup which lets the rain in and stops your mind from going where it will"; Ringo, in his Billy

Beatles song ban by BBC

The BBC has banned a song from the Beatles' new LP, *Sergeant Pepper's Lonely Hearts Club Band*. The song, *A Day in the Life*, was written by John Lennon who sings it on the LP.

It refers to "catching a bus," having a "smoke," and going off in a "dream." An official said: "We listened to this song several times and decided that it goes a little too far and could encourage a permissive attitude to drug-taking."

Shears incarnation, got high with a little help from his friends; and in "A Day in the Life" the composers expressed a desire to turn the listener on.

The BBC didn't wait for the Beatles' interpretation of "Lucy in the Sky with Diamonds"; a glance at the song's initials was enough for the Corporation to impose a ban posthaste. It mattered not that three-year-old Julian Lennon handed his father the title when he brought home from school a picture of school friend Lucy O'Donnell; nor that Lennon Senior and Paul took that title as a springboard, trading psychedelic, *Alice in Wonderland*–inspired imagery to flesh out the lyric. True, John was taking prodigious quantities of LSD at the time, and he and Paul daubed the song with extraordinary "trippy" images that led George Martin to describe its chief contributor as an "aural Salvador Dali". And yet on this occasion, at least, it was a case of coincidence, not conspiracy.

ABOVE: **Ringo arrives at Queen Charlotte's Hospital with a camera to take pictures of his new son, whom Maureen had chosen to name Jason after the character in Greek mythology.**

LEFT: **Ringo poses with his mother-in-law, Florence Cox.**

OPPOSITE: **Paul and Jane babysit Julian Lennon at the airport after returning from Greece with his parents.**

OPPOSITE INSET: **The *Daily Mail* reports on the BBC's banning of the song "A Day in the Life" because of its perceived permissive attitude to drugs. However, Paul always held that there was no intentional underlying message about drugs; rather it was simply a nostalgic lyric about school days.**

ABOVE AND LEFT: **The Beatles became interested in Transcendental Meditation and attend a lecture given by the Maharishi Mahesh Yogi at the Park Lane Hilton Hotel in London. After the lecture, the Beatles were granted a private meeting with the Maharishi when he invited them to come and join a ten-day course he was giving at University College in Bangor, Wales.**

AUGUST 1967

1 In Sunset Strip, Los Angeles, George and Pattie rented a house on Blue Jay Way. *Sgt. Pepper's Lonely Hearts Club Band* spent 15 weeks at the top of the US album charts.

4 George watched Ravi Shankar play at the Hollywood Bowl in Los Angeles.

5 Ringo's message was played on Radio London's last day of transmission.

7 George met with Ravi Shankar.

8 George visited Haight-Ashbury in San Francisco.

9 Playwright Joe Orton was found murdered in his bedsit in Islington, London. Paul was one of many who backed the original stage production of his play *Loot*. George flew back to London.

19 "All You Need Is Love" reached the top of the US charts, staying there for one week. The second son of Ringo and Maureen, Jason, was born at Queen Charlotte's Hospital, London. In Denver KNOW radio banned all Beatles songs, claiming they encouraged drug taking.

22 After a long break away from the studio, the band met at Chappell Recording Studios to work on "Your Mother Should Know".

All aboard the mystical special

George spoke of the Beatles having a "collective consciousness". They gravitated towards the same position, were invariably on the same wavelength. Someone would lead on an issue, and the others would naturally follow. Of the *Sgt. Pepper* era, Paul said: "We were all opening our minds to different areas, and then we'd come together and share it all with each other. It was exciting because there was a lot of cross-fertilization."

The collective spirit came to the fore in August 1967, following George's uncomfortable visit to Haight-Ashbury. Instead of a thriving counterculture he saw a lot of vagrancy, which unnerved and depressed him. It convinced George that drugs weren't the gateway to enlightenment; he needed something new to show him the way. Or someone.

Pattie Harrison was just as eager to imbue her life with greater spiritual meaning, and to that end she had attended a lecture on Spiritual Regeneration at Caxton Hall in February of that year. A disciple of Maharishi Mahesh Yogi had led the meeting, and Pattie discovered that the guru himself was delivering a lecture at the London Hilton on 24 August. Tickets were also obtained for John and Paul, but Ringo was otherwise engaged, Maureen having just given birth to their second son, Jason.

The Maharishi—or "great sage"—had founded the International Meditation Society in 1959. He effectively packaged Eastern mysticism for Western culture, including a Western-style price tag. Spiritual cleansing was available to anyone who stumped up the membership fee. The Summer of Love was the perfect time for the Maharishi to draw in converts; his message of love, peace, and spiritual fulfilment hit all the right notes, and he had already acquired celebrity status on the media circuit. Long before the Beatles came within the charismatic guru's orbit, he had built up a worldwide following—and a sizeable bank balance.

On the strength of what they heard, the Beatles were enthused to attend a seminar in Bangor, Wales, that weekend, where they would learn the principles and practice of Transcendental Meditation. George in particular was hooked. He fervently believed that it was through reaching a pure level of consciousness that the power of prayer came into its own. "Meditation is only a means to an end. You do it to release all the clutter out of your system, so that when it's gone you become that which you are anyway. That's the joke: we already are whatever it is we would like to be. All we have to do is undo it."

Euston Station on Friday, 25 August wasn't quite a throwback to *A Hard Day's Night*, but it was chaotic enough for Cynthia Lennon to find herself embroiled in a platform melee and left behind—in more ways than one. The Beatles were safely aboard what the press pack dubbed the Mystical Special.

RIGHT: **John unveils an outlandish paint-job on his Rolls-Royce Phantom V. The makeover cost £1,000 and took six weeks to complete.**

23 Another session at Chappell Studios. Overdubs for "Your Mother Should Know" were made. Brian Epstein was present at a studio session for the last time before his death a few days later.

24 The group met Maharishi Mahesh Yogi at the Hilton Hotel, London.

25 In Bangor, Wales, the band attended a weekend seminar on Transcendental Meditation led by Maharishi Mahesh Yogi.

26 Brian Epstein was at his East Sussex home.

27 The following day Brian was found dead in bed at his London home from a drug overdose. He had been suffering with depression for a long time and was only 32. In the *Sunday Express* an article about Pete Best revealed that he was now working in a bakery earning £18 a week.

28 The death of Brian Epstein was featured on the front of most of the daily newspapers.

29 Brian Epstein's funeral was held in Liverpool. It was a family affair and none of the Beatles attended.

More than £250,000 was initially lost on the value of the shares in Northern Songs, but they had recovered by the close of trading.

30 The inquest on Brian's death was opened at Westminster Coroner's Court but immediately adjourned.

31 In *The Times* an article reported that the band now planned to manage themselves.

Brian Epstein is found dead

Brian Epstein was invited to join the Beatles in Bangor and be inducted into the mysteries of Transcendental Meditation, but he had other things on his mind. His father had died the previous month and he had been playing the dutiful son for his mother, Queenie, who had been staying at his Chapel Street home. It was a sobering experience, quite literally: Epstein kept normal office hours and had early nights. Revelling was off the agenda. But he was off the leash that weekend, and he was in no mood for a spiritual uplift: he wanted to party.

Brian invited Geoffrey Ellis and Peter Brown to Kingsley Hill, his Sussex retreat, where he hoped they would be joined by some young blood. A weekend of fun and frolics lay ahead, but when the other guests failed to arrive, the prospects for entertainment and diversion nosedived. The thought of being cooped up with two long-standing NEMS friends and colleagues held little appeal, and Epstein announced that he was returning to London for the night. After he left a taxiload of friends did turn up, but the tragic sequence of events had already been set in motion.

By Sunday lunchtime, concerns were being raised. Epstein's housekeeper couple, Antonio and Marcia, called his secretary, Joanne Newfield, and informed her that their employer had been in his room for twenty-four hours. Newfield wasn't fazed; she was used to seeing notes instructing her to wake him with breakfast at 3 p.m. Epstein was probably sleeping off the effects of too much booze and some sleeping pills. But she decided to check on her boss anyway, and made her way to Chapel Street.

ON BRIAN EPSTEIN

"We were working in the studio. We'd make a record and the record would come out. What was there left for him to do? Book the studio—one phone call. That was the extent of it at that time."

—Ringo

ABOVE: **Brian Epstein pictured with his mother, Queenie, who had been widowed only a few weeks before the death of her son.**

OPPOSITE TOP AND BOTTOM: **George and Paul attend the memorial service for Brian Epstein at the New London Synagogue on Abbey Road.**

OPPOSITE LEFT: **Like most other British newspapers, the *Daily Mail* carried the news of Brian Epstein's death on the front page on 28 August.**

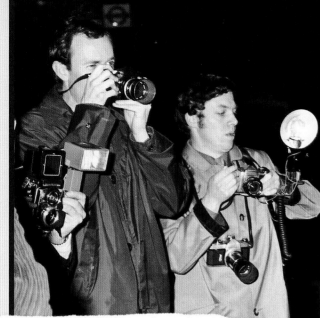

Beatles weep as Brian Epstein dies

BRIAN EPSTEIN, millionaire boss of the Beatles, was found dead in bed in his London home yesterday.

Thirty-two-year-old Mr. Epstein was found when his housekeeper called for help because his door was locked and she could get no reply.

He had been suffering from recurring glandular fever and had been taking tablets prescribed for him.

Mr. Don Black, a business associate, said: "I understand his death was an accident."

Scotland Yard said early today that bottles of tablets were taken from the house.

An officer said: "This is a normal procedure. So far as we are concerned death was due to natural causes."

A phone call gave the news to the Beatles, who had gone to Bangor in North Wales to join an Indian mystic cult. Mr. Epstein himself was to have gone there today to be initiated into the cult.

The Beatles were meditating in their rooms at Normal College after studying with a Himalayan mystic, Maharishi Yogi, of the International Meditation Society.

A messenger hurried along a corridor to the room of Paul McCartney and said there was an urgent phone call from London.

Paul ran in bare feet downstairs to a telephone kiosk.

A minute later, shocked and pale, he staggered back calling for John, George and Ringo, who ran into the corridor.

"Brian is dead," he said. Then he burst into tears.

Miss Jane Asher, his girl friend, Mrs. Cynthia Lennon, model Patti Boyd (Mrs. Harrison) and her sister Jennie were also told.

Later Paul and Miss Asher returned to London in a friend's car. The others followed in two more cars.

In London last night a crowd gathered outside Mr. Epstein's £31,500 home in Chapel Street, Belgravia, and his theatre, the Saville, in Shaftesbury Avenue.

Assistant Commissioner J. Lawlor, of Scotland Yard, said after leaving the house: "It was a sudden death. There will probably be a

BRIAN EPSTEIN . . . ill but he went on working.

The stars that Epstein made — Page THREE.

An astonishing conversation with the Beatles—Page SIX.

post-mortem. It is a matter for the coroner."

Later Mr. David Jacobs, Mr. Epstein's solicitor, left after spending several hours at the house.

He said a statement would be issued by Mr. Epstein's company, NEMS Enterprises.

At the Saville Theatre the news was announced half an hour after the start of a Sunday night pop concert.

Mr. Epstein was to have taken his usual box seat for the second performance.

As the cheering and clapping died down for the star of the show, Jimi Hendrix, the curtains were dropped and manager Michael Bullock said: "It is with deep regret that I have to tell you that Mr. Brian Epstein was found dead this afternoon."

Then, in silence, the packed house walked out. The second performance was cancelled.

Mr. Epstein's mother, Mrs. Queenie Epstein, arrived in London from her home in

When she got no response from the intercom, Newfield became uneasy and decided to force entry into Epstein's room. She called Kingsley Hill first, and Peter Brown advised caution. Epstein had a nasty temper if roused for no good reason. Newfield was determined, but wanted someone other than the housekeeping staff present. Epstein's own doctor wasn't contactable, so Brown suggested his own physician, John Galway. She called him in, and also Alastair Taylor, a friend and NEMS man from the Liverpool days.

When the two men arrived, they forced entry into Epstein's room and found his body. A number of pill bottles lay on the bedside table, but none had been emptied and all had their lids on, suggesting a tragic accident. That didn't prevent speculation that Epstein had committed suicide. He was prone to fits of depression and was at a low ebb over a number of personal and professional issues: the death of his father; the callousness of the opportunistic Diz Gillespie, who had blown hot and cold in their relationship as the mood took him; and then there was the formation of Apple, which had left him unsure as to whether he had a future with the Beatles when his contract expired that autumn.

Some time later Joanne Newfield did find suicide notes, written to Queenie and his brother Clive, but these were dated several weeks before. Epstein undoubtedly had suicidal tendencies—he had overdosed before—but it seems clear that he didn't intend to take his life on the weekend of 26–27 August 1967. The coroner reached the same conclusion: accidental death.

Understanding Epstein's affairs

A merger between NEMS and Robert Stigwood's organization was made public in mid-January 1967, six months before Brian's death. Epstein was in no state to manage a large stable, nor did he have the appetite to do so. He would have been happy to retrench, perhaps paring the artist roster down to the Beatles, Gerry and the Pacemakers, Cilla Black, and Billy J. Kramer. Epstein wanted to devote more time to his Saville Theatre productions, and harboured a dream to move to Spain and manage bullfighters.

He had delegated to Stigwood the day-to-day running of NEMS, apart from dealings with the Beatles—not that they needed much management during this period, ensconced in the studio making *Sgt. Pepper*. The top two executives were on a collision course, however, for Stigwood wanted growth. He already managed Cream, one of the hottest bands on the circuit, and he had a new group he wanted to break, a trio of Australian brothers whose unsolicited letter and demo had been dismissed by Epstein. Stigwood loved the Bee Gees' sound, dubbing them "the most significant talent since the Beatles", which was guaranteed to antagonize Epstein still further.

Stigwood signed Barry, Robin, and Maurice Gibb and set in motion plans to launch their career in America. He chartered a yacht and threw a lavish New York launch party. Far from warming to the buccaneering showmanship and bold PR, Epstein was livid. As far as he was concerned, the Bee Gees could have that kind of money spent on promoting them once they had done some gigs, shifted a few records, and established a following.

Epstein started to get cold feet about bringing Stigwood on board, and in particular he was regretting the offer of an option for his new partner to buy a controlling interest in NEMS for £500,000. It was a pittance compared to what he had been offered for the company at the height of

ABOVE: **John and George's appearance on *The Frost Programme* was so popular that they were invited back the following week, when the entire show was devoted to a question-and-answer session with them.**

OPPOSITE: **George and John discuss Transcendental Meditation and LSD with David Frost on *The Frost Programme*. The show also featured a brief interview with the Maharishi Mahesh Yogi that had been pre-recorded at London Airport earlier in the day.**

Beatlemania, but it reflected the fact that the touring and merchandising bonanza was over. In fact, apart from the Beatles, only Cilla Black's career was still on an upward curve; neither Billy J. nor Gerry had had a UK hit since '65. Most seams of the Merseybeat goldmine had by now been worked out. And even the Beatles—the jewel in the crown—were thought to have peaked by some of the major labels, as Epstein found when he had been looking to negotiate a new contract the previous year.

Epstein is said to have consulted lawyers in a bid to extricate himself from the deal that allowed Stigwood to buy a 51 percent stake in NEMS. Also preying on his mind in the spring of 1967 was the fact that he still hadn't told the Beatles that NEMS had a new man at the helm, soon to be the major shareholder.

Before the fateful events of 27 August, Stigwood made it clear that he wished to exercise his option. But after Epstein's death, the Beatles made it clear that they weren't going to have a new boss foisted upon them. Stigwood might have owned NEMS, but all he would get from the Beatles was out-of-tune renditions of "God Save the Queen". Stigwood realized that he was pushing at a bolted door and he and NEMS parted company. As for the Beatles, with Epstein gone they decided they would manage themselves.

Magical Mystery Tour

For all Brian Epstein's shortcomings, he had cemented the band together for more than five years. Epstein's role had diminished—more so following the establishment of The Beatles & Co. in April 1967—but his death did create a potential vacuum. Ever the pragmatist, Paul was quickest to realize that Beatle life could proceed as normal—and should do so as soon as possible.

Thus, when the band met to discuss their immediate future in the first week of September, Paul thought it was time to move ahead with the stalled *Magical Mystery Tour* project, deferring until the new year the proposed trip to India to further their study of Transcendental Meditation.

Three cameramen and a soundman were recruited along with a thirty-three-strong cast list made up of jobbing actors sourced from the thespians' directory, *Spotlight*. The principals included Scottish comedian Ivor Cutler, who played Buster Bloodvessel; actress Jessie Robins, who took the role of Ringo's aunt; and music hall veteran Nat Jackley as Happy Nat the Rubber Man. The bus departed from central London on the morning of 11 September, pursued by the inevitable posse of journalists, intrigued—quite literally—to see where all this was leading.

The answer was the West Country. There were frayed tempers on day two as the bus got stuck on a narrow bridge at Widecombe, forcing the entire caravan to undertake a lengthy reversing manoeuvre and the abandonment of plans to shoot some sequences at the famous annual fair held at the Dartmoor town. It encapsulated the haphazard nature of the entire project. The five-day trip didn't produce anywhere near enough usable material. No linking shots had been filmed—those had to be cobbled together later. There was no footage to accompany "Fool on the Hill", an oversight that was rectified by a hasty trip to the South of France in late October. Paul had made a virtue of back-of-an-envelope planning, but it was badly exposed when the Beatles learned that film studios could not be booked at a week's notice. When location filming was finished, they would have to find somewhere other than Shepperton to shoot the studio scenes.

An old US air base at West Malling, Maidstone, came to the rescue. "Blue Jay Way" and "I Am the Walrus" were shot there, as was the Busby Berkeley–inspired finale "Your Mother Should Know". This featured the Beatles in white tie and tails, the world famous Peggy Spencer Formation Dancing team, and a huge sweeping staircase that had been quickly cobbled together and was far less secure than it looked.

The editing process took eleven weeks, in which ten hours' worth of material was reduced to fifty-two minutes. The technician employed to do the cutting found himself caught between two masters, Paul and John often countermanding each other's instructions. Unsurprisingly, the finished print was disjointed, though the mere

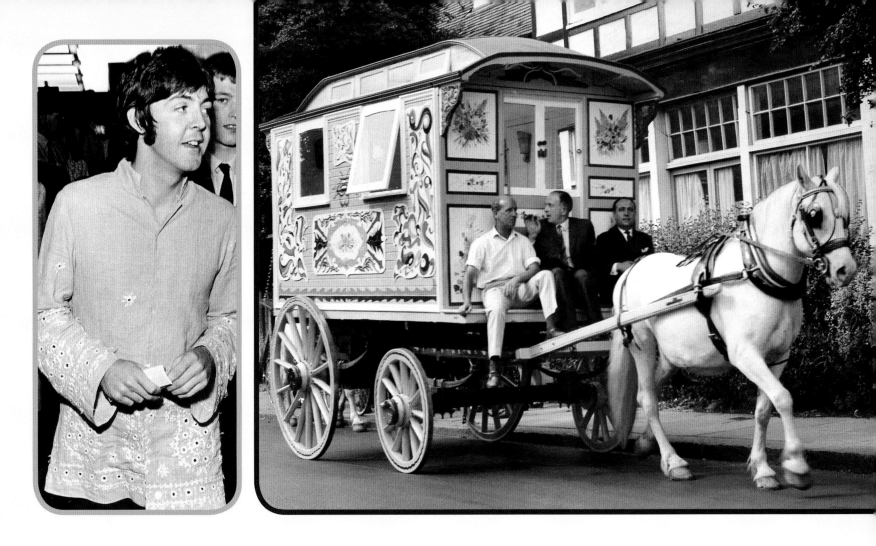

ABOVE LEFT: **Paul developed the idea for a new, improvised Beatles film. Shooting began in September, just weeks after Brian's death.**

ABOVE RIGHT: **The painted caravan was a gift from John to his son, Julian.**

OPPOSITE ABOVE: **One of the inspirations for the film was Ken Kesey and the Merry Pranksters, who toured California in a bus freely distributing LSD during 1965. Filming of *Magical Mystery Tour* got off to an inauspicious start when the tour bus got stuck on a narrow bridge.**

OPPOSITE BELOW: **The sheet music for "I Am the Walrus", John's biggest contribution to the project.**

fact that it contained six new Beatles numbers rendered *Magical Mystery Tour* a significant event in the show business calendar.

Unfortunately, it had to work as a film, not merely a music promo. ITV decided that it didn't and pulled out of the bidding war to screen it. Paul Fox at BBC1 also thought it was flawed, but felt it had merit as a freewheeling art-house road movie. And after all, it was the Beatles, available at a knockdown price of £10,000 for the Christmas schedule.

Magical Mystery Tour got a critical mauling, and even the consensus of the NEMS coterie was that it was a £40,000 home movie, albeit punctuated by some fine songs. It didn't help that the film was initially screened in black and white, which drained it of its visual impact. Aspiring young filmmaker Steven Spielberg was among those who greatly admired *Magical Mystery Tour*'s surreal set pieces, and over time the Beatles' first solo venture following Epstein's death came to be seen in a much more favourable light.

SEPTEMBER 1967

1 Four days after Brian's death, the four met at Paul's house to discuss their future. They decided to continue with *Magical Mystery Tour* while also postponing a proposed visit to India.

5 Recording sessions for *Magical Mystery Tour* resumed at Abbey Road, beginning with "I Am the Walrus".

6 Paul recorded a demo for his song "The Fool on the Hill" prior to a recording session later that month. Further work was completed on "I Am the Walrus",

then initial recordings for George's "Blue Jay Way" were made.

7 "Blue Jay Way" was the focus of the session.

8 Initial recording on "Flying", the first composition by all four band members, began.

11 The band, with a number of crew members and passengers, set off in a coach from Baker Street for the first of an initial five-day shoot for *Magical*

Mystery Tour. Paul was the first band member on board—the other three were collected in Virginia Water, Surrey. Scenes were shot inside the bus and at the Pied Piper Restaurant in Basingstoke, the venue for lunch on the first day. That night they stayed at the Royal Hotel in Teignmouth, where a press conference was held.

12 The *Magical Mystery Tour* party left Teignmouth, aiming for Widecombe Fair. However, due to a diversion by the driver, the bus got stuck on a narrow bridge, and thus the plans

magical mystery tour

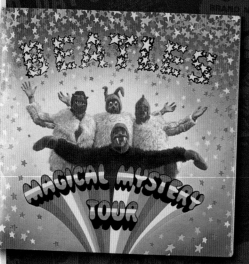

Released

🇺🇸 **27 November 1967 (Capitol)**

Side One:
Magical Mystery Tour
The Fool on the Hill
Flying (The Beatles)
Blue Jay Way (Harrison)
Your Mother Should
  Know
I Am the Walrus

Side Two:
Hello Goodbye
Strawberry Fields
  Forever
Penny Lane
Baby You're a Rich Man
All You Need Is Love

🇬🇧 **EP Released 8 December 1967 (EMI)**

Magical Mystery Tour
Your Mother Should Know
I Am the Walrus

The Fool on the Hill
Flying (The Beatles)
Blue Jay Way (Harrison)

Cover story

The batch of new Beatles recordings available to EMI and Capitol in the autumn of 1967 presented the two labels with a poser: In what format should the latest material be released? The six songs that provided the soundtrack to *Magical Mystery Tour* fell between the standard EP and album quotas. With *Sgt. Pepper* it seemed that EMI and Capitol had at long last begun to synchronize their Beatles output, but six months on the two companies diverged once again.

EMI opted to put out an extended EP, while Capitol beefed up *Magical Mystery Tour* into a stunning album package by adding five cuts from the three singles issued that year: "Strawberry Fields Forever" and "Penny Lane"; "All You Need Is Love" and its flip side, "Baby You're a Rich Man"; plus the new single, "Hello Goodbye". Since "I Am the Walrus" was tagged on as the B-side to "Hello Goodbye"—much to

John's chagrin—it meant that the American market offered two albums that represented the entirety of the Beatles' output over a twelve-month period. As *Sgt. Pepper* was originally conceived as a double album, the US release can be regarded as its lost sibling. For once it was game, set, and match to Capitol.

EMI's two three-track EPs were advertised as being complete with "A 32-page full colour book packed with exclusive pictures, a strip cartoon of the original story, plus the words to the songs in the show!" Its original cost was 19s 6d.

The cover art was commissioned from pop artist John Van Hamersfeld and shows the Beatles dressed up as animals with Paul as a walrus—John's mischievous reference to this in "Glass Onion" from the *White Album*, combined with Paul being the only one of the Beatles in black, fed later rumours of Paul's death.

"Organized chaos"

From 1966 through the final split, McCartney compositions dominated the Beatles' singles releases. He had been the prime mover behind *Sgt. Pepper* and *Magical Mystery Tour*, the unopposed key player in determining the group's direction. To all intents and purposes John had abdicated his role as leader, though he was still capable of stepping up to the mark with a gem that had his unmistakable signature.

"I Am the Walrus" was John's sole substantial contribution to *Magical Mystery Tour*, but what an offering he served up. The unlikely combination of a police siren and Lewis Carroll's "The Walrus and the Carpenter" provided the inspiration for some of the most memorable and evocative imagery in the Lennon soundscape. He was also using deliberately impressionistic nonsense to take a sideswipe at pretentious intellectuals who read into lyrics' meaning never intended by the composer. "Let them work that one out", he is

---

continued from previous page

SEPTEMBER 1967

were abandoned. Instead they went on to Plymouth, had lunch at the Grand Hotel, then agreed to have photographs taken by the press on the Hoe. John and Paul then gave an interview to Hugh Scully for *Spotlight South West*, broadcast the following day. They then travelled on to Newquay via Liskeard and Bodmin. After staying at the Atlantic Hotel, they decided to use it as a base for the next three nights.

13 Filming was carried out at Watergate Bay, Holywell, and Porth as well as the hotel. George gave

Miranda Ward an interview for BBC's *Scene and Heard*. The band was featured on *Spotlight South-West* on local BBC1 television. The Beatles formed Fiftyshapes Ltd, an electronics company.

14 Miranda Ward then interviewed Ringo for another edition of *Scene and Heard*. In the evening some of the group went to a pub in Perranporth to meet Spencer Davis. A memorable sing-along was led by Paul until the small hours.

15 The entourage headed back to London, stopping at a fish and

chip shop in Taunton, Somerset, and a country pub to continue filming.

16 Back at Abbey Road to work on "Your Mother Should Know", "Blue Jay Way", and "I Am the Walrus".

18 The film crew moved to the Raymond Revue Bar, a striptease club in Soho, London.

19 Filming continued for the next five days at West Malling Air Station in Kent, a base used by the American Air Force during World War II.

 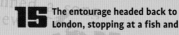

reported to have said after writing the line that had Semolina Pilchard climbing up the Eiffel Tower.

Middle-of-the-road backing group the Mike Sammes Singers were brought in for what was surely their most unusual assignment, chanting "oompah, oompah, stick it up your jumper" and assorted bits of gobbledegook. John wanted a random snatch of a radio broadcast—a technique borrowed from the John Cage school of composition—and lighted upon a BBC production of *King Lear* with John Gielgud in the title role.

George Martin described "I Am the Walrus" as "organized chaos", one of the finer fruits of a hit-and-miss period in which randomness was celebrated for its own sake. John said it was his favourite Beatles song. He was no doubt amused at the thought of his bizarre lyrics leading at least some misguided intellectuals on a wild goose chase.

"There has been more said about Dylan's wonderful lyrics than was ever in the lyrics at all. Mine too. But it was the intellectuals who read all this into Dylan or the Beatles. Dylan got away with murder. I thought, 'I can write this crap too. You just stick a few images together, thread them together, and you call it poetry'."

THIS PAGE AND OPPOSITE: **John and Paul on location in Devon, England, during filming of** *Magical Mystery Tour.*

20 Filming took place inside and outside the base, with everyone staying at a local hotel. Dick James from Northern Songs revealed that the band had earned between £25m and £30m for Britain over the previous five years.

22 Ringo was filmed entering a store in Maidstone High Street and buying tickets for the Mystery Tour from John.

24 On the last day the massive ballroom set was built in a hangar for "Your Mother Should Know", the film's finale. The scene included 24 cadets from the local Women's Air Force Cadets and 160 members of Peggy Spencer's famous formation-dance troupe.

25 At Norman's Film Studios, Old Compton Street, London, the editing of the film began. Roy Benson was contracted to do a job expected to take a week but ultimately taking 11, as John and Paul often had different ideas. Later that evening work on "The Fool on the Hill" was resumed at Abbey Road.

26 Balance engineer Ken Scott worked with the band on "The Fool on the Hill".

27 Orchestral and vocal overdubs were produced for "I Am the Walrus", while in another studio the Mike Sammes Singers recorded some separate vocals for the song. Apple Music Publishing Ltd was formed; their offices were at 94 Baker Street, London.

28 Work continued on "Magical Mystery Tour" and "Flying".

29 At the Wembley Studios, John and George recorded an interview with David Frost that went out on *The Frost Programme* later that evening. The main subject discussed was Transcendental Meditation. Paul and John then worked through the night on "I Am the Walrus" and "Your Mother Should Know".

30 George's radio interview with Miranda Ward was broadcast on BBC Radio 1's *Scene and Heard*. It marked an important day in BBC radio, as the Light Programmes were to be divided between Radio 1 and 2 while Radio 3 was developed for classical music and Radio 4 for the spoken word.

RIGHT, BELOW, AND OPPOSITE: **On 18 October the Beatles and their partners gathered at the London Pavilion to celebrate John's debut solo big screen appearance at the premiere of** *How I Won the War*. **John played Private Gripweed in the movie directed by Richard Lester, the man who directed** *Help!*. **The previous day the boys had been at an altogether more sombre** occasion: **Brian Epstein's memorial service at the New London Synagogue on Abbey Road.**

INSETS: **John Lennon, aka Private Gripweed, takes centre stage in the advertising campaign for the movie and is also mentioned prominently on the cover of the book and the premiere ticket (below inset).**

LONDON PAVILION PICCADILLY CIRCUS W.1

GALA PREMIERE
WEDNESDAY, 18th OCTOBER, 1967 at 8.0 for 8.30 p.m.

MICHAEL CRAWFORD   JOHN LENNON

HOW I WON THE WAR

ROY KINNEAR   LEE MONTAGUE   JACK MacGOWRAN
MICHAEL HORDERN   JACK HEDLEY   KARL MICHAEL VOGLER

EASTMAN COLOUR

DRESS CIRCLE   ROW A   SEAT No. 13

OCTOBER 1967

1 Back at West Malling, they filmed further scenes with the bus.

2 Work started on Paul's song "Hello Goodbye", destined to be the next single. The final mono mix of "Your Mother Should Know" was also finished.

3 John and George recorded a follow-up interview about Transcendental Meditation for the next edition of *The Frost Programme*. It was broadcast that evening.

4 Another showing of John and George's interview with David Frost went out on *The Frost Programme*.

6 The song "Blue Jay Way" was completed with overdubs of a cello and tambourine.

7 George's interview on *Scene and Heard* was repeated on Radio 1. Sid Bernstein offered the Beatles the chance to earn $1 million to once again perform

live. It was just one of many similar offers; all were refused.

11 At the Lisson gallery an exhibition entitled Yoko Plus Me opened. It was financed by John, who was also the "Me" in the title.

12 At De Lane Lea Studios, the mono version of "It's All Too Much" was mixed. John then produced the next session for *Magical Mystery Tour*. Work

Apple launches a new enterprise

Even prior to Brian Epstein's death, the Beatles had taken their first faltering steps toward self-management and an entrée into the world of corporate responsibility. In the spring of '67 their accountants had advised that the Beatles set up a new company as a hedge against crippling tax liabilities. At that point it was a paper exercise, but in the months following Epstein's death the Beatles were called upon to make serious business decisions regarding serious amounts of money.

Apple was the perfect logo for the new enterprise. Kids starting out with the alphabet began with "A is for Apple", which conveyed purity and simplicity. The Beatles would create a new business model, one that would open doors to people with bright ideas. They would be benign facilitators, not obsessed with the bottom line. Creativity would be liberated, not stifled. There would be profit-sharing so that "everyone who needs a Rolls-Royce can have one". It was a commendable philosophy, though perhaps someone should have pointed out that "A is for Apple" conjured up another trait: naïveté.

But what form should the venture take? Real estate? A chain of record shops? Greeting cards? These and many other ideas were kicked and rejected before a corporate picture emerged. One obvious arm of the new organization was a music division, which could nurture new talent as well as putting out Beatles records. John had had literary success, so there would be a publishing offshoot. Another branch could allow their in-house electronics wizard "Magic Alex" Mardas

to get his outlandish ideas off the drawing board. But the first foray into the world of commerce was Apple Boutique, "a beautiful place where beautiful people can buy beautiful things".

The Beatles already owned suitable premises, 94 Baker Street. And they had a design team at the ready. The Fool's efforts might not have passed muster for the *Sgt. Pepper* cover, but they were handed the task of coming up with the goods that would fill the shop's racks and shelves. Against the accountant's wishes, the Fool received an up-front payment of £40,000, much of which was spent sourcing expensive fabrics in Morocco. They let their imaginations run riot: style was not to be reined in by practicality. Even the labels had to be of pure silk, which raised the eyebrows of Pete Shotton, John's oldest childhood friend, who had been brought in to oversee the project. He voiced his concerns, but John was happy to give the designers their head.

The next blunder occurred over the weekend of 10–12 November, when the Fool painted a psychedelic mural over the entire four-storey edifice of the premises. It was an arresting sight, and certainly grabbed the attention of Westminster Council, who instituted proceedings

requiring them to delete what they regarded as a blot on the landscape.

Apple Boutique opened its doors on 7 December 1967, more than a month late. Hordes turned up and took the egalitarian principle to its extremes by making off with a lot of the stock. The retail experiment would fold after just eight months, the store holding a jamboree giveaway the following July. The boutique fiasco showed the flaw in the Apple concept: It was all well and good giving talented people a break, but there was no mileage in throwing wads of cash at people who were at best averagely talented and at worst inept. With the exception of Apple Music, all the company's offshoots haemorrhaged money over the next year. One by one they folded as it became clear that they weren't viable businesses, and that not even the Beatles could afford to bankroll them indefinitely.

OPPOSITE AND THIS PAGE : **The Harrisons and the Lennons were present at the opening of the Apple Boutique. Ringo was away filming *Candy* in Rome and Paul was taking a break in Scotland. The boutique was to be a "psychedelic Garden of Eden". The Beatles were keen to sell things that they themselves would buy, not simply items that could turn profit.**

---

was carried out on "Blue Jay Way", then accordionist Shirley Evans, accompanied by percussionist Reg Wale, recorded "Shirley's Wild Accordion". This was written by Paul and John and arranged by Mike Leander. Unfortunately, it was not used in the film, but shots of Shirley playing on the coach tour were.

14 Ringo's interview with Miranda Ward was broadcast on *Scene and Heard*, transmitted on Radio 1.

17 A memorial service was held for Brian Epstein at the London Synagogue in St. John's Wood—the whole band attended.

18 All four attended the premiere of *How I Won the War* at the London Palladium.

19 A further session working on "Hello Goodbye".

20 Three flautists added the final touch to "Fool on the Hill", and a viola was added to "Hello Goodbye".

25 An eight-hour session on "The Fool on the Hill" and "Hello Goodbye".

29 Additional scenes were shot in Battersea for *Magical Mystery Tour*.

30 Paul flew to Nice in France with cameraman Aubrey Dewar to film scenes to accompany the song "The Fool on the Hill".

31 Another day of filming for Paul in Nice.

THIS PAGE: **A clown fails to induce John to laugh during the opening of the new shop (above), and (left) John and George take a moment to try out the latest design in chairs.**

NOVEMBER 1967

1 Paul and Aubrey flew back to London. At Abbey Road "All You Need Is Love" and "Lucy in the Sky with Diamonds" were mixed for the *Yellow Submarine* movie. Additional work then continued on "Hello Goodbye" and "The Fool on the Hill".

2 "Hello Goodbye" was completed.

3 Final shots for *Magical Mystery Tour* were filmed in Ringo's garden at Weybridge, Surrey.

6 "Hello Goodbye", "I Am the Walrus", "Your Mother Should Know", and "Magical Mystery Tour" were mixed into stereo.

7 A mixing session for the *Magical Mystery Tour* album at Abbey Road. As there were only six songs, EMI decided to market a double EP that would include a booklet of lyrics and some colour pages. However, Capitol chose to sell it as an album, adding five additional songs.

8 In the US the premiere was held for *How I Won the War*.

9 The first edition of new US music magazine, *Rolling Stone*, featured a photograph of John from the film *How I Won the War* on its cover.

10 The band filmed promotional clips at the Saville Theatre, London, for the forthcoming single "Hello Goodbye". However, due to a ruling the previous year banning miming on television broadcasts, it could not be screened in Britain.

13 John and George attended a concert by the Four Tops at the Saville Theatre. The backdrop to their stage

Promo falls foul of union rule

"Hello Goodbye"—or "Hello Hello", as it was titled when the song received its first Abbey Road airing—was recorded during the *Magical Mystery Tour* sessions, but from the outset it was earmarked as the next 45. For the promotional film to accompany the new single the Beatles donned their *Sgt. Pepper* outfits and strutted their stuff to an empty Saville Road Theatre. This was shipped to the States and shown for the first time on 26 November, *The Ed Sullivan Show* once again breaking a new Beatles record to the American market.

In the UK this "performance" film fell foul of a new Musicians' Union ruling forbidding miming on TV. George Martin tried to circumvent the problem by making a fresh recording of "Hello Goodbye" without violas. As there were no such instruments shot in the movie, it could hardly have fooled anyone into believing it was a live performance. The ploy didn't work; it was still obvious that the Beatles were miming, so the film was never shown.

When "Hello Goodbye" shot to the top of the UK chart, where it remained for seven weeks, *Top of the Pops* dredged up some footage from *A Hard Day's Night* as a backdrop for the song. The Beatles were unimpressed at having their latest single played over moptop-era visuals, and for the remainder of "Hello Goodbye's" chart run they arranged for the programme to use a clip of them editing *Magical Mystery Tour*, along with a new batch of still photographs.

"Hello Goodbye" gave the Beatles their fourth Christmas No. 1 in five years in their home market. On this occasion they also had the No. 2 record with *Magical Mystery Tour*, which gave "I Am the Walrus" the distinction of occupying the top two spots over Christmas 1967.

ABOVE AND BELOW: **John and George circulate at the Apple Boutique party.**

---

act had been designed by Paul, who was unable to attend because he was on holiday in Kenya.

17 Road manager Neil Aspinall flew to the US, taking the promotional films of "Hello Goodbye." In the studio further stereo mixes of "I Am the Walrus" were made.

19 Paul watched the Bee Gees play at the Saville Theatre, London.

21 The band allowed the BBC to film them in the cutting room at Norman's Film Productions in London, hoping this could be used to replace the miming sequence on "Hello Goodbye" and that the promotional film could be broadcast on *Top of the Pops*.

22 In the studio George embarked on tracks for the movie *Wonderwall*.

23 "Hello Goodbye" was broadcast on *Top of The Pops*. Despite the special filming that took place two days earlier, the producers still used footage from *A Hard Day's Night* to play during the track.

24 The single "Hello Goodbye" backed with "I Am the Walrus" was released in the UK on Parlophone R 5655. John started work in the studio on his forthcoming stage play.

25 Kenny Everett and Chris Denning hosted *Where It's At* on Radio 1 and included a feature about the *Magical Mystery Tour* double EP. *Sgt. Pepper's Lonely Hearts Club Band* spent another week at the top of the UK album charts.

26 Ed Sullivan read out a short telegram from the Beatles on his show, *The Ed Sullivan Show*, before screening a clip from "Hello Goodbye".

27 In the US the single "Hello Goodbye"/"I Am the Walrus" was released on Capitol 2056 and the album *Magical Mystery Tour* on Capitol MAL-2835 (mono) and SMAL-2835 (stereo).

28 "Christmas Time (Is Here Again)" was recorded for the fan club. John then used the studio time to gather sound effects for his play *The Lennon Play: In His Own Write*, to be based on his two books.

29 The Christmas record was edited by George Martin and Geoff Emerick.

Candy man

By the end of 1967 all four Beatles had embarked on solo projects. A year after Paul had written the score for *The Family Way*, George also accepted a soundtrack commission. In the spring he was asked to write the music for the film *Wonderwall* after Robert Stigwood's protégés the Bee Gees had turned the job down. It would be the first Beatles solo album, although George didn't play on any of the tracks. *Wonderwall Music* also became the first long-player to be released on the Apple label, on 1 November 1968.

Ringo, meanwhile, followed in Private Gripweed's footsteps and went the thespian route. He had been the most natural performer in the Beatles' films and jumped at the chance to appear in a bawdy romp based on a novel cowritten by Terry Southern. Ringo had his hair dyed black and was given voice coaching for the role of Emmanuel, the Mexican gardener who was one of many to fall for the charms of Candy, played by Swedish beauty queen Ewa Aulin. Like *Magical Mystery Tour*, the film was a critical flop despite boasting the talents of Matthau, Brando, and Burton. Ringo's cameo was neither going to make or break the movie, and the starstruck drummer was elated simply to have appeared on the credits alongside some of the greatest names in cinematic history.

DECEMBER 1967

3 Ringo flew to Rome to begin filming his part in *Candy*, written by Buck Henry.

4 Ringo was fitted for his costume and had his hair dyed black for his role as Emmanuel, a Mexican gardener.

5 John and George attended a party to celebrate the opening of the Beatles' Apple Boutique at 94 Baker Street. Cilla Black and John gave interviews to the BBC for that evening's *Late Night Extra* radio show.

7 The sound stage at the Incom Film Studios in Rome was used for further scenes involving Ringo On *Top of the Pops*. Producers finally used the scenes taken in the cutting-room combined with stills provided by NEMS.

8 The double EP *Magical Mystery Tour* was released on Parlophone MMT-1 (mono) and SMMT-1 (stereo). The A-side featured the title track and "Your Mother Should Know" with "I Am the Walrus" on the B-side, "The Fool on the Hill" and "Flying" on the C-side, and finally "Blue Jay Way" on the D-side.

9 The sound stage was used for further scenes involving Ringo at the Studios. "Hello Goodbye"/"I Am the Walrus" topped the British charts, holding the position for seven weeks.

11 Ringo filmed a scene in the basement of Candy's house at the studios. Apple Music Publishing signed its first group, Grapefruit.

12 Ringo continued with the filming of the same scenes.

ON MAGICAL MYSTERY TOUR

"It was a mistake because we thought people would understand that it was 'magical' and a 'mystery tour'. We thought the title was explanation enough. There was no plot and it was formless, deliberately so. We enjoy fantasy and were trying to create this. The trouble is if people don't understand, they say 'A load of rubbish' and switch off. Our problem is that we are prisoners of our own fame. We could put on a moptop show, but we don't really like that sort of entertainment anymore. And we don't work for the bread now... Was the film really so bad compared with the rest of the Christmas TV? I mean, you could hardly call the Queen's speech a gasser."

—Paul

RIGHT AND INSET: **Following the screening of** *Magical Mystery Tour* **on the BBC on 26 December, Paul appeared on** *The David Frost Show* **to defend his project. The film had been panned by critics as a self-indulgent home movie.**

ABOVE: **John arrives in fancy dress for the launch party of** *Magical Mystery Tour* **at the Lancaster Hotel just before Christmas.**

OPPOSITE: **Ringo on the set of the movie** *Candy* **in Rome in December with Ewa Aulin (above) and Christian Marquand (inset right). Acting was perhaps an inevitable progression for Ringo once the Beatles had begun solo projects: He had shown the most potential as an actor in the** *Help!* **and** *A Hard Day's Night* **films.**

---

13 "Hello Goodbye" was certified gold in the US.

14 Another broadcast on *Top of the Pops* of "Hello Goodbye" using the cutting-room footage. A scene was filmed in Rome with Ringo riding a motorbike.

15 The "love-in" scene for the movie was shot with Ringo and 80 hippies in a field. "Christmas Time (Is Here Again)" was released. *Magical Mystery Tour* was certified gold in the States.

16 The final day of filming for Ringo was held at Rome Airport. Paul and John flew to Paris to participate in a UNICEF gala.

17 John and George attended a special Christmas party at the Hanover Grand Banqueting Suite, Mayfair, for 40 of the band's fan-club secretaries. Ringo flew back to London. Beatles & Co. was renamed Apple Corps Ltd.

21 Another broadcast on *Top of the Pops* of "Hello Goodbye" using the cutting-room footage.

23 *Sgt. Pepper's Lonely Hearts Club Band* spent another two weeks at the top of the UK album charts.

25 Paul and Jane Asher announced their engagement, but only to family and friends. The band appeared on the Christmas Day edition of *Top of the Pops.*

26 *Magical Mystery Tour* was screened in black and white for the first time on BBC1. *The Times* review by Henry Raynor stated, "This was a programme to experience rather than to understand: I was unfortunate—I lacked the necessary key."

27 Paul appeared live on *The David Frost Show* to defend *Magical Mystery Tour.*

28 Extracts from *Magical Mystery Tour* were shown on *Top of the Pops* to accompany "The Fool on the Hill".

30 "Hello Goodbye" reached the top of the US charts, remaining there for three weeks.

We Don't Want to Change the World

1968 saw the beginning of the long, slow fragmentation process, the early skirmishes of what would become a bitter courtroom battle.

The year began harmoniously enough as all four trooped off to India to see whether the Maharishi and meditation could imbue their lives with greater meaning. He couldn't for long, though George's commitment to Eastern culture remained steadfast. The ashram sojourn produced an impressive musical yield, but that proved to be a mixed blessing as egos clashed when they repaired to the studio to make the *White Album*. It became too much for Ringo, who put down his drumsticks, feeling unloved. Yoko and Linda's roles changed from walk-on parts in the Beatles' story to star turns. Yoko became a fixture in the studio and convinced John that his genius could flourish outside the confines of the group.

The Beatles guested in their own cartoon movie, while "Hey Jude" launched Apple Music with a fanfare and showed that at least one division of the chaotic organization could turn a healthy profit.

OPPOSITE AND ABOVE: **1968 was to be the year that John declared his love for Yoko, while Paul would split from his long-term girlfriend, Jane Asher.**

RIGHT: **The playing-card covers for the collector's edition of facsimile birth certificates of each band member, which went on sale in 1968.**

"Lady Madonna"

The first release of the new year signalled an emphatic end to the Beatles' yearlong dalliance with psychedelia. With the bluesy, rocking "Lady Madonna" they drew a line under the '67 vintage, which had come to such an inauspicious end with *Magical Mystery Tour*. Paul's paean to motherhood was completed in just two sessions, putting down a marker for the back-to-basics approach that would inform the next phase in the group's career.

This Fats Domino–style number presaged the Beatles' monster album offering later in the year, in which they would cover just about the entire gamut of musical genres. However, this particular boogie-woogie piano riff had its roots somewhat closer to home. It was a lift from Humphrey Lyttelton's "Bad Penny Blues", a minor 1956 hit that had been produced by none other than George Martin. If the Beatles were trying to return to the kind of stripped-down music they used to make, then a little petty pilfering was somehow apposite.

The contender from John that lost out to "Lady Madonna" in the single stakes was the wistful, hauntingly beautiful "Across the Universe", while George contributed the B-side with "The Inner Light", the first time one of his compositions had featured on a 45. These songs were crafted by men hoping to find "The Answer" in the forthcoming trip to India, but it was Paul's A-side that mapped out the Beatles' new direction.

Mumblings by Cynthia as she was trying to get to sleep are said to have moved John to write "Across the Universe". He was more irritated than inspired when he was forced from his bed to jot down a few lines, but the words kept flowing and the lyrics themselves turned into a celebration of the creative process, distilled through cosmic consciousness.

During recording John realized that something was missing: a falsetto harmony. The problem was solved with the recruitment of a couple of "Apple Scruffs", the fanatical followers who hung around the studio and camped outside the Beatles' homes at all hours of the day, hoping for a glimpse of their idols. Lizzie Bravo and Gayleen Pease got a lot more than they bargained for, ushered into Studio Three to lay down a vocal on a Beatles track. Ironically, the line they were required to sing was, "Nothing's gonna change my world". For these two teenagers, this moment must have come very close.

The harmony was in place, but John was dissatisfied with the end result. He would accuse Paul of deliberately sabotaging the production with his indifference. In any event, he was happy to put the song in abeyance, leaving the way clear for a McCartney–Harrison combination for the new release. The Beatles' seventeenth UK single was the first that had no contribution from Lennon.

"Across the Universe" appeared twice on vinyl, though on neither occasion was it in the original February '68 form. It first saw the light of day on a 1969 compilation album in aid of the World Wildlife Fund, when it was "doctored" with appropriate animal sound effects. The following year it turned up on *Let It Be*, where it was slowed down and given the "Wall of Sound" treatment by Phil Spector. Unlike Paul, who famously hated the treatment "The Long and Winding Road" was given on the same album, John must have been content with the result, as he would invite Spector to produce his next three LPs.

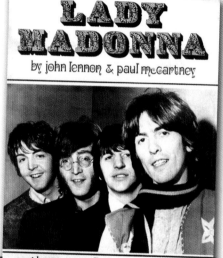

JANUARY 1968

1 Paul gave Jane Asher a diamond-and-emerald engagement ring while they were visiting his family in Liverpool.

5 The first colour screening of *Magical Mystery Tour* was broadcast on BBC2. John's father visited him in Weybridge. He planned to marry 19-year-old Pauline Jones and wanted John's blessing.

6 *Magical Mystery Tour* went to the top of the US charts, staying there for eight weeks.

Ringo and Maureen lasted barely a week. He found neither the spicy vegetarian fare nor the climate palatable; she couldn't bear the flies. Paul and Jane were next to decamp, after five weeks. "We made a mistake", said Paul. "We thought there was more to him than there was, but he's human, and for a while we thought he wasn't". However, he insisted it had been a positive, worthwhile experience. Jane had never wanted to go halfway round the world to find

herself, and soon she would have no need to stand by her man in pursuit of causes that didn't interest her.

John and George carried on, assiduously imbibing the Maharishi's twice-daily lectures, exulting in the simplicity of existence. The ashram overlooked the Ganges, a magical setting that John found equally inspiring. Like Paul, he soon had a stockpile of new songs, but was in no hurry to commit them to vinyl.

ABOVE: **Mike Love of the Beach Boys accompanied the band to the ashram in Rishikesh, where he is thought to have assisted in the writing of "Back in the USSR". Dating from when the Beatles had first toured America in 1964, they had a relationship of friends-cum-rivals with the Californian band. Although the Beach Boys, and especially their frontman, Brian Wilson, always sought to outperform the latest offering from the Beatles, over the years the two bands had developed a warm relationship. It was the Beatles who played an important role in bringing the Beach Boys to the attention of the British public.**

8 George Martin invited Spike Milligan to a studio session. Most of the time was spent developing "Across the Universe". Milligan asked to include the song on a charity album for the World Wildlife Fund, which would ultimately be released in 1969.

9 A series of advertisements began to publicize the Apple enterprise.

10 The *Magical Mystery Tour* was screened on Dutch television. After transferring all their affairs from NEMS to Apple, Peter Asher, Jane's brother, became head of A&R.

11 Just before leaving for India, the band shot promotional film for "Lady Madonna" while working on the song "Hey Bulldog". The scenes filmed by NEMS Enterprises were distributed to the British and US television stations.

15 John and George flew to Rishikesh, India, to study Transcendental Meditation. At Abbey Road the mono master for "Lady Madonna" was made.

19 Paul and Ringo flew out to join the other two Beatles.

24 An interview with Paul was published in the London *Evening Standard*. In it he declared that the band now had all the money they required.

25 George's 25th birthday was celebrated in India. He was presented with a cake with the greeting "Jai Guru" written in gold letters.

29 At the tenth Grammy Awards *Sgt. Pepper's Lonely Hearts Club Band* won four awards, picking up the prizes for Album of the Year, Best Contemporary Album, Best Engineered Album, and Best Album Cover. Yoko Ono split from her husband, Antony Cox.

Disillusioned with the Maharishi

The spell was broken two months into the stay. Rumours began to circulate that the Maharishi had more worldly designs on some of the female students. The allegation was never proved or disproved. Had there been an inappropriate approach, or was it a sign of affection from a mentor that had been misinterpreted?

The question was left hanging; the seed of doubt had been sown. "Magic Alex" nurtured its growth, no doubt fearful of losing his sponsor to a new guru. If that didn't sway John, then the fact that even George was beginning to waver did the trick.

A group led by John confronted the Maharishi and informed him of their imminent departure. A bewildered Maharishi asked the reason. "If you're so cosmic, you'll know why," replied John, the eight-week idyll failing to dull the cynical wit or blunt the sharp-edged tongue.

Thus none of the Beatles completed the course and acquired accredited Transcendental Meditation teacher status; it was a parting of the ways for them and the Maharishi. After a fleeting apostasy, George recovered his faith in the guru. "Although I have not been with him physically, I never left him", he said in 1992. John delivered a harsher and more immediate postscript. Disillusionment brought forth vitriol as he took retribution in the way he knew best: by denouncing the Maharishi in song. The first draft contained ferocious invective, a personal attack full of expletives. Even when the swearing was removed, lines such as "Maharishi, what have you done, you made a fool of everyone" would have induced a panic attack in EMI's legal representatives. Finally John "copped out"—by his own admission—and found a four-syllable substitute for Maharishi: Sexy Sadie.

> ### ON MEDITATION
> "I believe I have already extended my life by twenty years. I believe there are bods up here in the Himalayas who have lived for centuries."
> —George

TOP: **George and actress Rita Tushingham listen while Michael York strums on the sitar.**

RIGHT: **George returning from India, where he had been working on the music for the movie *Wonderwall*. The soundtrack, released by Apple in November 1968, was the first solo album by a Beatle.**

OPPOSITE BOTTOM: **Alexis Mardas with Cynthia, John, and George at a party at Revolution nightclub in Mayfair. He became part of the Beatles' entourage and a favourite of John in particular. John asked him to join them in India, but "Magic Alex" despised the Maharishi and his influence on the Beatles. Alex became intent on exposing the fraudulent behaviour of the Maharishi, with considerable success.**

OPPOSITE TOP: **"Lady Madonna" was the last single to be issued with a Capitol label, and reached No. 4 on the *Billboard* chart in the US.**

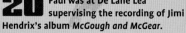

9 Sessions on the *Wonderwall* soundtrack started in Bombay and continued for four further days.

11 *Top of the Pops* broadcast a short silent extract from *Magical Mystery Tour* to accompany the music performance of "Hello Goodbye".

12 George flew to India to produce the *Wonderwall* soundtrack at the EMI studio in Bombay.

17 John, Paul, and Ringo attended an RCA reception for one of Apple's signings, Grapefruit, prior to the release of their single "Dear Delilah".

20 Paul was at De Lane Lea supervising the recording of Jimi Hendrix's album *McGough and McGear*.

22 The Beatles bought 34 Boston Place to house their Apple Electronics laboratory, while the Apple offices were opened at 95 Wigmore Street in London. Paul watched the Supremes at the Talk of the Town.

25 The band was at the Twickenham Film Studios to record their one brief appearance on *Yellow Submarine*.

27 At Kenwood, Kenny Everett recorded an interview with John for his Radio 1 series *The Kenny Everett Show*.

28 Paul was involved in rehearsals with Cilla Black for "Step Inside Love".

30 George finished the recording for *Wonderwall*.

A sojourn in India

Brian Epstein's death had put on hold the Beatles' planned trip to India to further their Transcendental Meditation studies under the tutelage of Maharishi Mahesh Yogi. By mid-February 1968 the diary was clear; they were free to go on spiritual retreat for up to three months, leaving "Lady Madonna" to keep the commercial pot boiling while they were away.

The Beatles and their partners made their way to the Maharishi's International Academy of Transcendental Meditation in Rishikesh in two separate convoys. This spoke volumes for the enthusiasm with which they embraced the eastward quest for wisdom and enlightenment. In the advance party were George and John. The latter was convinced Transcendental Meditation was the real spiritual deal, and for a time he became as intense an advocate, as dedicated a disciple, as George. "We want to learn meditation properly so we can propagate it and sell it to

everyone...This is the biggest thing in my life now and it's come at the time when I need it most. It's nothing to do with mysticism. It's about understanding."

Paul and Ringo brought up the rear, open-minded but never as committed, pragmatism anchoring down any lofty ambitions. For Ringo that meant taking along a consignment of baked beans in case the food disagreed with his delicate constitution. For Paul it was more to do with the creative flux. Meditation couldn't stem the tide of melodies ebbing and flowing in his head, and before long he began formulating ideas for the next Beatles project and setting a timetable for getting back to work. That earned him a reproof from George, who wanted the trip to be an antidote to Beatle life, not a brainstorming session for a new album.

ABOVE: **The stragglers off to visit the Maharishi. The Beatles went to India in two waves. John and George, who were the most enthusiastic, led the way, followed later by Ringo and Paul with Maureen and Jane. Ringo hated the food and Maureen hated the flies—they left India after less than two weeks. Paul and Jane stayed on a few weeks longer, but Paul used much of the time to compose new music.**

BELOW: **At the Hanover Grand, the Beatles, Brian Jones, Donovan, and Cilla Black attend the single launch of Apple's first music signing, a four-piece band called Grapefruit. They were signed to Apple Publishing in the days before Apple Records. The single, "Dear Delilah", charted at No. 21, but the band fizzled out.**

FEBRUARY 1968

1 Ringo attended rehearsals at the Television Rehearsal Rooms, London, for his guest slot on Cilla Black's TV series, *Cilla*.

2 George Martin was at Abbey Road copying the vocal soundtrack to "Only a Northern Song" for the *Yellow Submarine* album.

3 The first of a series of studio sessions before travelling to India. The initial recordings of Paul's "Lady

Madonna" were made. *Sgt. Pepper's Lonely Hearts Club Band* spent another week at the top of the UK album charts.

4 *The Kenny Everett Show* featuring the interview with John was broadcast. Recording began on John's "Across the Universe". Urgently needing two females to provide high falsetto harmonies, they plucked two fans from the ever-present crowd outside: the only two to ever be involved in a recording.

5 Ringo's rehearsals for Cilla's show took place at the BBC's Television Theatre, Shepherd's Bush. Paul was at a press conference at the Royal Garden Hotel, London, to help support the Leicester Community Arts Festival.

6 Ringo appeared on *Cilla* in the second episode of her new series. Paul had written the signature tune, "Step Inside Love". Meanwhile the other members of the band were working on "Lady Madonna" and "The Inner Light" at Abbey Road.

ABOVE: **Paul and Jane give their verdict on the Maharishi after returning from a month in India (left). Paul intended to stay only a fixed amount of time and never found enlightenment, but he learned to meditate, a skill he would later encourage others to try.**

OPPOSITE: **Ringo, dancing with Mia Farrow, wasted no time getting back into the old lifestyle after his return from India.**

OPPOSITE INSET: **Writer Hunter Davis was given access to the Beatles and their entourage to produce an official biography of the band, which was published in 1968.**

MARCH 1968

1 Ringo and Maureen left India to return to Britain, landing at Heathrow on 3 March.

9 Cilla Black released "Step Inside Love", written for her by Paul.

15 The single "Lady Madonna"/ "The Inner Light" was released in the UK on Parlophone R 5675.

18 The single "Lady Madonna"/ "The Inner Light" was released in the US on Capitol.

26 Paul and Jane returned to England.

30 "Lady Madonna"/"The Inner Light" reached the top of the UK charts, remaining there for two weeks.

31 The Beach Boys announced that they would embark on a concert tour with the Maharishi called World Peace 1 and hinted that the Beatles would be involved.

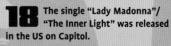

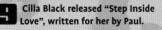
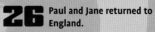

JOHN, PAUL, GEORGE & RINGO

A New Perspective

"When we first started we were 18 and wanted to get rich. And if there was a possibility of getting rich by singing we were willing to forget everything. Well, let's face it, that's what swinging London is really about.

But now we don't have to do things for ourselves so much any more. Instead of trying to amass money for the sake of it we're setting up a business concern at Apple – rather like a Western Communism. A lot of people think that it is just a shop. But we want to make it a complete business organization along the lines of ICI – not just for us, but for the general good. Apple could be a social and cultural environment, as well as a business environment.

We've got all the money we need. I've got the house and the cars and all the things that money can buy. So now we want to start directing this money into a business. Not as a charity. No one likes charity, it makes them wince. Too sickly. We want to get something going where the underwriters will get a decent share of the profits, not $4.00 a week, while we make a million.

We had to do it for ourselves. When Brian died we had to take a look at what we consisted of, and who owned bits of us, and then we got the idea of not only doing it for ourselves, but for everyone.

Now we're really looking for someone like Brian, not in the managerial sense, but someone we could respect and be able to listen to and take advice from. We meet lots of people who are good at business, but they're not necessarily nice people. Still, every big company has the sort of person we want – the trouble is that they all have good jobs already."

– PAUL MCCARTNEY,
EXTRACTED FROM THE *DAILY MAIL*,
24 SEPTEMBER 1968

THIS PAGE AND OPPOSITE: **John and Paul unveil Apple Corps in the Big Apple with "Magic Alex" at their side. The two had flown to New York as businessmen, not musicians. It was the first time either had been to America since the concert tour in 1966. Although they primarily attended press** conferences related to the new venture, they appeared on *The Tonight Show*, hosted by the former baseball player Joe Garagiola. Apple Records was created in the summer of 1968 and James Taylor was the first artist to be signed to the label after being "discovered" by Peter Asher.

APRIL 1968

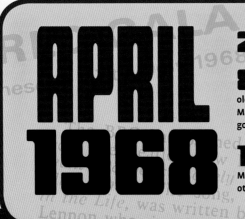

2 The band initiated Python Music Ltd, a new publishing company.

8 Derek Taylor started work as Apple's Press Officer and hired 23-year-old Richard DiLello to assist him. "Lady Madonna"/"The Inner Light" was awarded a gold disc in the States.

12 John, Cynthia, George, and Pattie left Rishikesh. George travelled to Madras to film with Ravi Shankar and the others retuned to London.

13 The most important day of the festival of Ard Khumb in India. The Maharishi Mahesh Yogi had planned to take John and George on a procession through Hardwar on the Ganges; the idea was abandoned because of fears of a possible stampede of people rushing to see the pair.

16 The band set up Apple Publicity.

19 The US record company Bell Records was launched in London, with John and Ringo included on the guest list.

20 In the press Apple Records asked new pop hopefuls to send in demo tapes.

21 George returned to London from Madras.

30 Paul travelled to Yorkshire to record the single "Thingumybob" with the Black Dyke Blues Band.

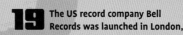

Creating "Revolution"

Sedition was in the air in spring of 1968. With the Vietnam War at its height, idealistic youth rose up around the world to demonstrate against governments perceived as oppressive and authoritarian. John caught the mood of the times with "Revolution", written in India and the first song to be recorded when the Beatles took their stockpile of new material to Abbey Road at the end of May.

At John's insistence, no fewer than three different versions of the same song were committed to vinyl. The original version, "Revolution 9", meandered on for some ten minutes, the latter half of which comprised a lot of wild jamming and off-the-wall ranting from John and Yoko. The two got to work with tape loops, one of which was a male voice repeating the words "Number nine". That was lopped off but not discarded, as the other Beatles might have wished. More than a year earlier Paul had made an avant-garde recording titled "Carnival of Light", which remained securely deposited in the EMI vaults. Paul had been keen to experiment, but instinctively knew that such material wasn't for public consumption—certainly not with the Beatles name attached to it. Relations had worsened since then. Lone furrows were being ploughed. John blithely continued, with Yoko in the role of collaborator as well as partner.

John's shortened attempt to capture in sonic form the turmoil of a fractured society now had a title, distinguishing it from the longer original, and was reclassified as "Revolution 1".

MAY 1968

3 Peter Asher met James Taylor and heard his demo tapes for the first time.

5 Mary Hopkin appeared on the talent show *Opportunity Knocks*—the model Twiggy was to recommend her to Paul.

6 "Step Inside Love" was released on Bell in the US. It did not, however, make any impact on the US charts.

9 At the Apple offices the possibility of opening an Apple School for children was discussed.

11 John and Paul flew to New York for five days, where they announced their Apple business venture.

12 A Chinese junk was the venue for a business meeting when they sailed round the harbour.

13 John and Paul gave a press interview at the St. Regis Hotel.

14 An interview at the Americana Hotel. John and Paul then appeared on NBC-TV's *The Tonight Show*, hosted by baseball player Joe Garagiola. Paul met up again with Linda Eastman—this time she gave him her phone number.

15 Another interview with reporter Mitchell Krause was broadcast on the programme *Newsfront*.

John was wildly enthusiastic about his latest creation. "This is the music of the future. You can forget about all the rest of the shit we've done. Everybody will be making this stuff one day. You don't even have to know how to play a musical instrument to do it."

Not even he thought "Revolution 9" was suitable for release as a single, but the now-truncated "Revolution 1" was a different matter. John had been forced to give way with "Lady Madonna" and was pushing hard this time around. Both Paul and George Martin were aghast at the prospect of "Revolution 9" appearing on the new album, and were about to be wrong-footed again. The Beatles had always favoured upbeat songs when it came to issuing singles, which counted against "Revolution 1", at that point a slow-tempo song. John headed off that objection by recording a speeded-up version, and it was this third incarnation of "Revolution" that appeared on the flip side to "Hey Jude".

The man who had told us that love was all we needed wrestled with the form political struggle should take. John's ambivalence about destruction as a means to an end surfaced in the lyric, which alternated between wanting to be counted both "in" and "out". That equivocation, along with what was seen as the bland assurance that "It's gonna be all right", made John the target of much opprobrium from radicals seeking a new world order.

OPPOSITE: **The Harrisons head for Nice and the Cannes Film Festival to support the movie *Wonderwall*, for which George had composed the soundtrack.**

RIGHT: **Ringo and Maureen lend their support to George in Cannes while John and Paul were in the US.**

ON "REVOLUTION"
"I thought I was painting in sound a picture of revolution but I made a mistake—the mistake was that it was anti-revolution."
—John

16 John and Paul flew back to London.

17 George, Ringo, Maureen, and Pattie were present when *Wonderwall* was first shown at the Cannes Film Festival.

19 John and Yoko made some recordings together at John's Kenwood home when Cynthia was away on holiday. They were eventually released on an album entitled *Unfinished Music No. 1: Two Virgins*, with the famous pictures of the couple naked on the cover. This was generally believed to be when their relationship was consummated.

21 In Esher, Surrey, the band gathered at George's bungalow to begin work on some new pieces, with many eventually appearing on the album *The Beatles* (the *White Album*).

22 John and Yoko appeared together in public for the first time at a launch party and press conference for another Apple Boutique. George also attended.

23 Paul and Ringo were interviewed by Tony Palmer for his Omnibus arts series *All My Loving*, which was to be screened later in the year.

26 Paul directed a promotional film for Grapefruit's "Elevator" single.

On return from her holiday, Cynthia found that Yoko Ono had moved into Kenwood.

30 A studio session working on "Revolution 1" and "Revolution 9"—this was to be the first of many recording sessions attended by Yoko, which was not popular with the rest of the band.

31 Further work on "Revolution 1" was completed.

Becoming "johnandyoko"

Cynthia Lennon was well aware of the existence of Yoko Ono long before the trip to Rishikesh. On one occasion the artist had brazenly invited herself into John's car for a ride home, even though John had his wife in tow. It was part of a protracted pursuit on Yoko's part, involving sending him letters and even turning up in person at John's home, Kenwood. At first John insisted that she was just another besotted fan, or that her interest in him began and ended as a potential sponsor. Cynthia may not have believed that completely, but it was what she wanted to hear. She also wanted India to mark a new beginning in their relationship. In fact, it was the beginning of the end.

John had angled to try and bring Yoko along on the sojourn to India. That was unworkable, but they were in regular correspondence during the two-month period. Yoko's missives were along the same enigmatic lines as the instructions that accompanied her artwork, the kind that had amused and intrigued him when they first met at Indica Gallery fourteen months earlier. "I'm a cloud. Watch for me." He watched the heavens, and also kept an eye out for incoming mail at the post office. Only much later did Cynthia learn that John's early-morning sorties and increasingly distant manner had nothing to do with meditation.

It was around this time that fascination turned to infatuation. The Maharishi turned out not to be the fount of all knowledge, which left a vacuum waiting to be filled. John was beguiled by the elfin creature who seemed to be an enigma wrapped inside a riddle. She was as creative as he, an intellectual equal. Now it dawned on him that she could also fulfil his carnal desires. John was used

JUNE 1968

4 A session of rather unusual overdubs for "Revolution 1", with Peter Brown as engineer.

5 The band began work on Ringo's song "Don't Pass Me By".

6 Kenny Everett visited the studio to record an interview for his weekly BBC Radio 1 series, *The Kenny Everett Show*, as further work took place by Paul and Ringo on "Don't Pass Me By". John, meanwhile, was being interviewed by Peter Lewis for the arts programme *Release*. With the producer Victor Spinetti they discussed the production of *In His Own Write*.

7 George and Ringo flew to the US. George was to take part in a documentary film about the life of Ravi Shankar, eventually titled *Raga*. Paul and Jane attended Mike McCartney's wedding in North Wales.

9 Kenny Everett's interview from earlier in the week was transmitted on his BBC Radio 1 series, *The Kenny Everett Show*.

10 In the absence of George and Ringo, Paul recorded and mixed "Blackbird" while John recorded further sound effects for "Revolution 9". George's scenes for *Raga* were filmed.

11 For the first time recording sessions took place simultaneously in separate studios, with John developing "Revolution 9" and Paul working separately on "Blackbird". During the day Paul was also filmed with Mary Hopkin, a new recruit to Apple. It was George's final day of filming in America.

13 In the States, George and Ringo took part in a jamming session with Peter Asher and David Crosby.

15 John and Yoko took part in the National Sculpture Exhibition and planted two acorns outside Coventry Cathedral.

BIO: YOKO ONO

Yoko Ono was born into a prosperous Tokyo banking family on 18 February 1933. Her formative years were spent commuting between Japan and America, where her father worked, and at the end of World War II the family relocated to the US. They settled in the well-heeled Scarsdale district of New York, and Yoko attended Harvard and Sarah Lawrence School, where Linda Eastman would also study. Against her family's wishes she married Japanese musician Toshi Ichyanagi, an ill-starred match that foundered long before the couple's 1962 divorce. By then she had already met her second husband, New York musician and film producer Antony Cox, with whom she had a daughter, Kyoko, born 8 August 1963. Over the next three years Yoko made a name for herself as an avant-garde artist. She published *Grapefruit*, a book filled with Zen-like instructions, and her conceptual artwork included a forerunner to bagism. In September 1966 Yoko and Cox came to London to further her career, which needed new sponsorship. She attended a symposium called The Destruction of Art, and naturally fell into the orbit of Barry Miles, Peter Asher, and John Dunbar, who ran Indica Gallery and were acquainted with the Beatles. John met Yoko on 9 November 1966, when he attended her Indica exhibition titled Unfinished Paintings and Objects. Exhibits such as a card inviting the reader to "Breathe" appealed to John's wry sense of humour. Eighteen months passed before Yoko's tenacious pursuit of John bore fruit. In that time the self-styled "High Priestess of the Happening" featured regularly in the newspaper columns, which reported on events such as wrapping the Trafalgar Square lions with paper. Yoko regularly turned up uninvited at Kenwood, and in May 1968, with Cynthia out of the country, John yielded to her enigmatic charms. The pair made experimental tapes that would eventually be released as *Two Virgins*. They also became lovers. The couple collaborated on a number of projects, while Yoko's attendance at Abbey Road during Beatles recording sessions caused resentment, exacerbating existing tensions. John and Yoko married in Gibraltar on 20 March 1969, inviting the world's press to their honeymoon "Bed-In for Peace". They moved to New York after the Beatles disbanded, and, following an eighteen-month estrangement, when John co-habited with personal assistant May Pang, the couple reconciled in 1975. Sean Taro Ono Lennon was born on 9 October that year. Over the next five years Yoko showed considerable business acumen, quadrupling their fortune while John took on the role of house-husband. He had just returned to the creative arena with *Double Fantasy* when he was gunned down on 8 December 1980. Since then, Yoko has released a number of John's works, and many others in her own right. She has attended countless dedication ceremonies, including the inauguration of the Strawberry Fields memorial in Central Park, near the Dakota building apartment they shared.

ABOVE AND OPPOSITE: **John returns to his art-college roots by staging an exhibition at the Robert Fraser Gallery in Mayfair, London, called You Are Here. John publicly declared his love for Yoko at the gallery, where her own work was on display. Yoko was still married to the American film director Antony Cox at the time.**

to different people taking these roles; here was someone who could occupy all three. First there had been a meeting of minds, and in May 1968 John and Yoko consummated their love for each other.

Cynthia Lennon had been on vacation in Greece, still harbouring thoughts that the marriage could be saved. Those disappeared when she returned to Kenwood to find she had been supplanted by Yoko. John made no effort to conceal the liaison with a woman he would describe as "the ultimate trip". From that moment nothing could separate them, not even the English language; henceforth they considered themselves johnandyoko.

ON JOHN AND YOKO

"I knew there was no way I could ever fight the unity of mind and body they had with each other...Yoko did not take John away from me because he had never really been mine."

—Cynthia Lennon

---

16 At Stonebridge House, Wembley, Paul recorded an interview for *David Frost Presents...Frankie Howerd*. The show planned for broadcast in the States featured Paul, Frankie Howerd, and Mary Hopkin.

18 John and Yoko attended the opening night of John's play, *In His Own Write*, at The National Theatre.

20 With Paul flying to the US, John continued to work on the sound effects for "Revolution 9".

21 Apple Corps bought new premises at 3 Savile Row, London. "Revolution 1" was completed after trumpets, trombones, and a lead guitar were added. In the States Paul was at a Capitol Records conference explaining that future records would appear on the Apple label although they were still under EMI and Capitol.

22 An interview with John, recorded on 6 June, was shown on the BBC2 programme *Release*.

24 In Los Angeles Paul busked several Beatles songs outside his hotel.

25 Paul flew back from the US while "Revolution 1" and "Revolution 9" were mixed. At the time George was in a separate studio working with Jackie Lomax.

26 The band was together again to start recording John's "Everybody's Got Something to Hide Except Me and My Monkey".

27 Further work on "Everybody's Got Something to Hide Except Me and My Monkey".

28 Recording began for John's "Good Night"—he wrote it especially for Julian, his five-year-old son.

30 Paul was interviewed by BBC reporter Tony Cliff in Saltaire, Yorkshire, for a short piece to be broadcast on the BBC 1 programme *Look North*. On the way back he stopped in Harrold, Bedfordshire, to join a pub sing-along.

With more than twenty songs ready to go into production immediately and several more simmering away, there was no shortage of material. When the tally hit thirty, George Martin thought they had reached overload, that some of the songs were simply not up to the mark. He argued the case for major surgery and a slimmed-down single album that he felt could rival its predecessors. It has been suggested that the Beatles stuck to their guns in order to take a double-sized bite out of the album quota they owed EMI. More significant is the fact that shelving half of the material would have required conciliation and compromise, neither of which was in abundant supply during the four and a half months it took to complete the Beatles' ninth LP. A mood of ill feeling pervaded many of the sessions, and even if resentment didn't boil over, the tensions bubbling beneath the surface were easily discernible.

The problems started on day one, when the doors to what had been a closed shop were thrown open. Yoko Ono's presence at that recording session broke the unwritten exclusivity rule regarding wives and girlfriends, and put a large hole in the collegiate spirit that galvanized and sustained the Beatles when they entered the studio. If the other group members thought it was the manifestation of new love in its infancy, they were disabused of the notion when a bed was imported into the studio. Yoko was here to stay. A microphone was set up in case she wanted to comment on the proceedings, criticize, even. The group dynamics had changed, and for the better as far as John was concerned.

The *White Album*: Son of *Sgt. Pepper*

The Beatles convened at Abbey Road on 30 May to start work on the album John would dub "Son of *Sgt. Pepper*". The group had just been awarded four Grammy Awards for their magnificent 1967 opus: Best Album, Best Contemporary Album, Best Album Cover, and Best Engineered Album. The question was, how to follow that? Certainly not with a Mark Two version. "Lady Madonna" had signposted the way: the new album would be a back-to-basics set, a deliberate move away from the elaborate production methods that had adorned *Pepper*. On occasion the Beatles were happy to sacrifice perfection for spontaneity, and there was even a place for extemporization, unthinkable a year earlier. "The Continuing Story of Bungalow Bill" and "Birthday" were just two examples of the group in glorious carefree recording mode.

ABOVE AND LEFT: **Much of the summer was spent in the recording studio working on the *White Album*. However, recording was frequently interrupted by various members of the band, as well as George Martin, ducking out on holiday or personal business trips. George headed to the US to play a cameo role in *Raga*, a film about Ravi Shankar. Ringo, Pattie, and Maureen joined him for the trip.**

OPPOSITE: **Having enjoyed the experience of working with classical musicians on *Sgt. Pepper*, Paul set himself a new challenge of working with a brass band. He produced one of the first recordings for the Apple label in Saltaire, Yorkshire, leading the Black Dyke Mills Band of Shipley in a recording of the theme music, which he had composed, for a new television sitcom called *Thingumybob*.**

Working together but separately

Up to now, even if a band member unveiled a complete song, running it by the others often resulted in the addition of a little polish, maybe a new lick, a tweaking of the lyric, an idea for a middle eight. During this period it was more common for the composer to present a new work as a fait accompli and use the other three as virtual session musicians. Sometimes they worked in separate studios, a situation that left George Martin feeling more like an executive producer, flitting between stations instead of having a firm hand on a single tiller. Several McCartney songs, including "Blackbird", "Mother Nature's Son", and "Martha My Dear", had zero contribution from any of the other Beatles. John

replied in kind with "Julia", nominally a tribute to his mother, though he slipped "ocean child" into the lyric, a translation of Yoko's name. It was the only Beatles song performed entirely by John. It required no great leap of the imagination to see why George pointed to the *White Album* sessions as the period when "the rot began to set in".

The peace may have been fragile, and the output may have been the fruit of individual contributions rather than collaborative effort, but the yield was still impressive. The Beatles covered just about every musical genre on the *White Album*: rock, blues, reggae, country and western, folk, electronic, ballads, and lullabies. There were undoubtedly flaws. The *New Musical Express* review echoed George Martin's thoughts

in concluding that the collection gave us "the brilliant, the bad, and the ugly", but nevertheless the album flew off the shelves. It topped the UK chart for eight weeks, the *Billboard* chart for nine. Within weeks of its release, Capitol announced that it was the biggest-selling album in the company's history. In Sweden it made the Top Ten in the singles chart.

Despite its weaknesses, the *White Album* remains a bravura display of the band's range and virtuosity. And if the quality did occasionally dip below par, there was more than adequate compensation in the panache and sheer exuberance with which they revealed a breathtaking aural vista.

World premiere of *Yellow Submarine*

The salutary experience of *Help!* and *Magical Mystery Tour* had shown that the Beatles' Midas touch wasn't an all-encompassing gift. In particular, it had left them extremely wary about accepting another film project. None of the many ideas pitched to them over the previous two years had met their stringent quality-control standard, so they were not too enamoured with a long-standing contractual arrangement that meant that the Beatles were coming to the big screen in 1968 whether they liked it or not.

At the height of Beatlemania, when no stone was left unturned in the quest to turn a profit from the band's extraordinary popularity, Brian Epstein had cut a deal assigning the animated image rights of the Fab Four to an American company, King Features. After bringing a successful cartoon series to the small screen, the makers wanted to produce a full-length animated feature, taking up an option that had been part of the agreement.

King Features brought on board George Dunning, head of the London-based studio that had worked on the TV programme. An informal production meeting took place around the time of the release of *Sgt. Pepper*, and a vision for a fantasy adventure quickly emerged. The story line was simple and charming enough: our heroes are called upon to save the undersea inhabitants of Pepperland from the dastardly, music-hating Blue Meanies. Fleshing out the idea proved more difficult, and far more writers than those credited on screen contributed to the script. The team

THIS PAGE: **The Beatles attend the premiere of *Yellow Submarine* at the London Pavilion on 17 July. Because it was a feature-length animation, the boys had minimal involvement in the production of the movie, not even performing the voices for their own animations. In the movie, cartoon versions of the boys help to liberate the inhabitants of Pepperland from the Blue Meanies.**

included Erich Segal, who would go on to enjoy worldwide fame with the saccharine tearjerker *Love Story*. Liverpudlian poet Roger McGough was brought in to ensure the screenplay had the requisite "Scouse" flavour. McGough was also a sometime pop star with Scaffold, a group that featured in its lineup one Mike McGear—né McCartney. Scaffold's biggest hit, "Lily the Pink", would top the UK chart in December 1968, the fifth time in six years that the McCartney clan were able to celebrate having a Christmas No. 1.

The Beatles were consulted in the early days of the *Yellow Submarine* project, but they had minimal input and took little interest. When they filmed a live-action sequence for the film at Twickenham in January, it was a duty more than a pleasure.

That they wanted to fulfil their obligation at the least possible inconvenience to themselves can be seen in the choice of material they put forward for the soundtrack. Even the most ardent fan would concede that "All Together Now", "Only a Northern Song", "It's All Too Much", and "Hey Bulldog" were not among the first rank of Beatles songs. Indeed, the last of those, written by John specifically for the film, was dashed off when they found they had some spare studio time after recording "Lady Madonna". It was originally titled "Hey Bullfrog"—which is mentioned in the song—but after embellishing the fade-out with some nonsense barking, it was changed to "Bulldog"—which didn't appear in the lyrics. There was further confusion as the slapstick sequence accompanying the song ended up on the cutting-room floor, but only after it had premiered in the UK. American movie theatres showed the truncated version, leaving fans with a minor conundrum when they listened to the soundtrack album.

Yellow Submarine stands as a classic creation of the psychedelic era. The Beatles were hugely impressed, belatedly wishing they had taken a more active role in the production process. Their hands-off approach gave rise to the tag that it was "the best film the Beatles never made".

The soundtrack album was something of a hodgepodge: two old No. 1s—the title song and "All You Need Is Love"—plus the four new tracks, padded out with a swath of George Martin orchestral pieces. Release was put back to January 1969, but on both sides of the Atlantic the *White Album* still ruled the charts. *Yellow Submarine* thus became the first—and only—Beatles long-player not to reach No. 1 in the UK. It still sold a healthy million copies worldwide, demonstrating that the Beatles name still had a cachet unmatched by any other artist—and that any new vinyl offering was much coveted by the group's loyal fans.

ABOVE RIGHT: **Adrienne Kennedy, a dramatist from Detroit, first had the idea of adapting John's book *In His Own Write* to create a stage play. She sought the help of Victor Spinetti, who had appeared in all the Beatles' films to date, and together they wrote the play.**

ABOVE: **John and Yoko with Victor Spinetti, the co-producer who played a vital role in getting John to agree to the play. In the end, John loved the piece because it gave him the opportunity to have an objective view on his book. John and Yoko made one of their first public outings as a couple when they attended the opening night of the play at the Old Vic Theatre.**

JULY 1968

1 Paul's interview was broadcast on *Look North*. John's first art exhibition, You Are Here, opened in London. A long studio session developing "Everybody's Got Something to Hide Except Me and My Monkey".

2 Ringo added further vocals to "Good Night". Paul met with EMI chairman Joseph Lockwood to discuss Apple finances.

3 The first of many sessions taping Paul's "Ob-La-Di, Ob-La-Da".

4 Overdubs were put onto "Ob-La-Di, Ob-La-Da".

5 Saxophones and conga drums were added to "Ob-La-Di, Ob-La-Da".

8 A session ending at 3 a.m. was spent working on "Ob-La-Di, Ob-La-Da" and included John's piano introduction.

9 As well as further work for "Ob-La-Di, Ob-La-Da", the band spent time rehearsing "Revolution". This was a slightly different version from "Revolution 1" and was to be the B-side of the next single.

10 Rhythm tracks for "Revolution" were recorded.

11 Another session on "Ob-La-Di, Ob-La-Da" and "Revolution".

An end for Paul and Jane

On 20 July Jane Asher appeared on the BBC's popular Saturday-evening magazine programme *Dee Time* and announced that her engagement to Paul was off. There was no bitterness or rancour as she articulated her thoughts on the split. "I know it sounds corny but we still see each other and love each other, but it hasn't worked out. Perhaps we'll be childhood sweethearts and meet again and get married when we're about seventy."

To the inner circle this was anything but earth-shattering news. The job description of a Beatle consort called for patience and sacrifice. Pattie had given up her modelling career; Cynthia tiptoed round the house in the morning so as not to disturb John's lie-ins after a late night; Maureen would cook a roast dinner for Ringo when he arrived home, even if it was four in the morning. Only Jane had a work and social diary to rival the Beatles', and of the four she was the least suited to the role of subservient appendage to a pop superstar.

From Paul's point of view, when he and Jane first got together he had been in awe of the circles she and her family moved in and the breadth of knowledge they displayed. It was a world he wanted to inhabit, and he set about completing his education with alacrity. By 1968 he had caught up, and in some fields he had overtaken the Ashers' milieu, leading the dinner-table conversation instead of following.

The fact that Jane had never been interested in the drug scene was another long-standing wedge between her and Paul. Even when they announced their engagement over the Christmas period, insiders thought it was a case of going through the motions. The break was almost inevitable; it was just a question of when and under what circumstances.

The final straw for Jane came in the shape of a rival. In the spring of 1968 Paul began an affair with twenty-four-year-old American Francie Schwartz after the latter approached Apple for funding for a movie idea. Paul took Francie to some of the early *White Album* sessions, suggesting that if John had seen fit to allow Yoko into the exclusion zone, then he might as well reply in kind.

It could also have been a deliberate attempt to provoke the end of his faltering relationship with Jane. He hardly seemed put out when she arrived home unexpectedly from her latest theatre tour and found the couple in flagrante delicto at Cavendish Avenue.

Francie was soon out of the picture; the field was now clear for a much more serious liaison. Paul had renewed his acquaintance with Linda Eastman during the trip to New York to launch Apple in mid-May. A month later they met again in Los Angeles when Paul was in town to attend the annual Capitol convention. He

invited Linda to London as the finishing touches were being put to the *White Album*, and soon became as besotted as John with his new love. Before the year was out he had asked Linda and daughter Heather to move to England lock, stock, and barrel.

ABOVE: **Paul and Jane in happier times.**

LEFT: **Despite Beatlemania cooling off, the American fan club magazine was still in operation in 1968.**

OPPOSITE INSET: **Lobby cards for *Yellow Submarine*.**

OPPOSITE: **Paul speaks to the press outside his father's home in the Wirral after news breaks that he and Jane had split up.**

continued from previous page

JULY 1968

12 "Don't Pass Me By" was almost completed in one session, then more overdubs to "Revolution".

13 John took Yoko to Poole to meet his Aunt Mimi.

15 In addition to further work on "Ob-La-Di, Ob-La-Da" and "Revolution", the band rehearsed John's "Cry Baby Cry". Apple staff began to move into the building at 3 Savile Row, London.

16 Work continued on "Cry Baby Cry". Due to the increase in tension among the band members, balance engineer Geoff Emerick stopped working with them.

17 The world premiere of *Yellow Submarine* took place at the London Pavilion. All four Beatles attended, then partied afterwards at the Royal Lancaster Hotel.

18 After yesterday's "day off", work resumed in the studio on "Cry Baby Cry" and Paul's "Helter Skelter".

19 Recording for John's "Sexy Sadie" (originally titled "Maharishi") began.

20 Jane Asher announced on *The Simon Dee Show* that her relationship with Paul was over.

22 "Don't Pass Me By" was finished, then a 26-piece orchestra and members of the Mike Sammes Singers were used to complete "Good Night".

23 The final version of "Everybody's Got Something to Hide Except Me and My Monkey" was finished. The Iveys were signed up to the Apple label.

24 Further takes of "Sexy Sadie".

25 George introduced his composition "While My Guitar Gently Weeps" at this session.

26 John worked at Paul's house to help him finish "Hey Jude". Paul had written it for John's son, Julian.

28 All the band spent the day in London for a photo shoot at various locations with photographer Don McCullin.

29 Balance engineer Ken Scott was in the control room for this session when "Hey Jude" was recorded; the record was eventually to last seven minutes, eleven seconds.

30 Rehearsals continued for "Hey Jude". They were then filmed working for a documentary, *Music!*. It was produced by James Archibald for the National Music Council of Great Britain and aimed to feature different types of British music.

31 The Beatles Apple Boutique on Baker Street closed down because it was losing money. All the final items were given away, including the female dummy that had a label marked FOR THE ATTENTION OF JOHN LENNON. For the first time the band recorded at Trident Studios in London.

"Hey Jude"

Over the years Paul had pulled many a rabbit out of the hat during the drive from central London to Kenwood. More often than not, by the time he arrived he would have an idea he could run by John, and within a couple of hours a song bearing the Lennon–McCartney hallmark was invariably ready to take to the studio.

A visit by Paul in June 1968 was unexceptional from his point of view: another car ride, another germ of an idea. The difference was that his collaborator-in-chief had moved out of Kenwood, and Paul wanted to show his support for the newly estranged Cynthia. He had even greater sympathy for the innocent five-year-old caught in the crossfire of a foundering marriage. "Hey Jules", ran the comforting appeal of the opening line, "don't make it bad, take a sad song and make it better". Paul decided "Jude" was a better-sounding name, which opened up more than one can of worms when it came to interpreting the lyrics. But the plain fact was that the fallout from a marital breakdown spawned the Beatles' most

successful single and launched Apple Records with a glorious fanfare.

Paul immediately realized he had something special on his hands. With John ensconced in his new all-consuming relationship, he demoed the song to a number of other musicians, including the Iveys, who had just signed to Apple and were yet to be rebranded as Badfinger. When Paul finally played it to John he was particularly defensive about the line "The movement you need is on your shoulder", which he had blocked in as a stopgap and was intent on changing. John declared it the best line in the song. His sole contribution to the Beatles' 15th UK No. 1 was thus a passive one, urging that a line not be taken out.

"Hey Jude" was recorded in the middle of the *White Album* sessions, but from the outset it was marked out as the A-side of the next Beatles single—though not without a fight from John, who wanted that honour to go to "Revolution". The only potential handicap to Paul's offering was its length: seven minutes eleven seconds, including a four-minute coda. It was the second-longest single in the annals of pop music, just short of Richard Harris's "Macarthur Park", also a 1968 hit. To the Beatles barriers were for circumventing or knocking down, and at the recording session they let rip. There were a couple of minor hiccups in what was a classic recording. There is an expletive on the vocal track around the three-minute mark that was buried in the mix but never totally eliminated, and a curmudgeonly member of the orchestra drew the line at hand-clapping and singing along with the protracted fade-out refrain.

John thought "Hey Jude" was Paul's best song. He homed in on the line "You have found her, now go and get her", which he interpreted as a former partner contentedly letting go and giving his blessing to a new relationship. There was more confusion as an idea of Paul's to promote the single misfired badly. The title was inscribed in large lettering on the windows of the empty Apple Boutique premises, the composer failing to realize the unfortunate connotations of 1930s Germany.

Paul pulled a neater promotional trick to give the song its first public airing. It was at a twenty-fifth birthday party for Mick Jagger, held at the Vesuvio Club in Tottenham Court Road.

HEY JUDE
BY JOHN LENNON & PAUL McCARTNEY

Photograph by John Kelly / Stephen Goldblatt

NORTHERN SONGS LTD / MUSIC SALES LTD., 78 Newman Street, London W.1.   20p

AUGUST 1968

1 Making use of Trident's eight-track recorder, a 36-piece orchestra was engaged to play George Martin's arrangement for "Hey Jude".

2 "Hey Jude" was finished.

3 Paul was at the Revolution Club, London, escorted by new girlfriend Francie Schwartz.

4 *Yellow Submarine*, the movie, was released in Britain.

6 "Hey Jude" was mixed into mono at Trident. During a fashion show at the Mayfair discotheque Revolution, John was interviewed by BBC Radio reporter

Matthew Robinson. This was broadcast in the evening edition of *Late Night Extra* by Radio 1 and Radio 2.

7 Back to Abbey Road for the first of more than 100 takes of George's "Not Guilty".

8 Further work on "Not Guilty" took up most of the session. Tape copies of "Hey Jude" and "Revolution" mono masters were also made. John and Paul were at Mick Jagger's 25th birthday party at the Vesuvio Club in Tottenham Court Road.

9 Further work on "Not Guilty". Paul then remained behind to record his new song, "Mother Nature's Son".

10 Joe Cocker sang his cover of "With a Little Help from My Friends" at the National Jazz and Blues Festival. Alan Smith from *New Musical Express* interviewed Paul.

11 Apple Records was launched along with a declaration for National Apple Week.

12 "Not Guilty" was completed but never actually used. It only surfaced in 1979 when another version was used on George's album.

13 Work on two songs in this session—"Sexy Sadie" and "Yer Blues".

The Stones were unveiling their own long-awaited new album, *Beggars Banquet*, but an acetate of the new Beatles single effectively stole their thunder.

"Hey Jude" took the American charts by storm. It entered the chart in the *Billboard* Top 10, hardly unusual in the UK but unprecedented in the US. It held the No. 1 spot for nine weeks, outpacing "I Want to Hold Your Hand", until then the group's most successful single Stateside. It topped the charts in eleven countries round the globe, sales exceeding 5 million that year alone. Strangely, in the home market "Hey Jude" was toppled after just two weeks, though from Apple's point of view there was compensation in that the song that deposed it was Mary Hopkin's "Those Were the Days". Her six-week encampment at the top was the best UK chart performance of the year. Joe Cocker's version of "With a Little Help from My Friends" took over the No. 1 position in the first week of November, which meant that as performers, composers, or producers the Beatles racked up almost three months on top of the domestic pile in 1968.

OPPOSITE: **"Hey Jude" shot into the UK charts at No. 1, only to be replaced by Apple's "Those Were the Days" by Mary Hopkin (playing the guitar above). The record was produced by Paul and spent six weeks at the top of the UK chart.**

RIGHT: **John and Yoko were becoming increasingly inseparable. John had broken a taboo by inviting Yoko into the studio while the Beatles were recording the *White Album*. She was even allowed a microphone to make comments.**

14 "Yer Blues" was finished. Work then began on "What's the New Mary Jane" which featured only George and John.

15 Recording began on Paul's "Rocky Racoon", which had originally been titled "Rocky Sassoon".

16 In the studio, George used an electric guitar on "While My Guitar Gently Weeps".

17 George left Britain for a spontaneous visit to Greece.

20 In George's absence, Ringo and John worked with "Yer Blues" while in a later session Paul developed "Mother Nature's Son".

21 George returned from Greece. "Sexy Sadie" was finished in the studio.

22 Following some tense studio sessions attended by Yoko, Ringo announced to the band that he was leaving and went on holiday. However, the other three Beatles started work on "Back in the USSR". Cynthia sued John for divorce, citing his adultery with Yoko Ono.

23 John, Paul, and George continued to work in the studio, and "Back in the USSR" was completed.

24 John and Yoko recorded an interview at Wembley Studios with David Frost. The interview was

broadcast that same night on the London Weekend Television programme *Frost on Saturday*.

26 Ken Scott continued to work on several of the recently recorded songs. "Hey Jude" backed by "Revolution" was released in the US on Apple (Capitol) 2276.

27 During a visit home, Paul watched Liverpool play a match against Everton.

28 The band, still with Ringo absent, began to record John's "Dear Prudence" with George and John on guitars and Paul on the drums. This was a new composition by John dedicated to Prudence Farrow, sister of actress Mia Farrow. Both

women had studied Transcendental Meditation with the band in India.

29 Handclaps, tambourines, and vocals were added to "Dear Prudence".

30 "Hey Jude" backed by "Revolution" was released in the UK on Apple (Parlophone) R5722. Paul, Ringo, and Maureen attended Neil Aspinall's wedding to Suzy Ornstein. "Those Were the Days" by Mary Hopkin was released in Britain on Apple 2.

LEFT: On 29 July the Beatles and their friends picked out their favourite items from the Apple Boutique in Baker Street. The shop had proved a financial catastrophe and it was to be closed down. The following morning, shoppers arrived to discover that the remaining stock, estimated to have been worth more than £10,000, was to be given away. There had been no publicity about the giveaway, but the news quickly spread by word of mouth. Eventually the police had to be called to control the crowds trying to get in.

ABOVE: Madame Tussauds tried hard to keep up with the Beatles style. Juliet Simpkins gives the boys their fifth wardrobe change since they first appeared at the museum in 1964.

OPPOSITE: One of the attractions of Ringo's home in Surrey was a room that had been decorated to look exactly like a traditional English pub.

SEPTEMBER 1968

3 Ringo rejoined the band for a studio session at Abbey Road led by Ken Scott. It was at this session that they managed to track down EMI's as-yet-unused eight-track recorder and take it from the office of the company's technical expert.

4 The band was at Twickenham Studios to shoot promotional films for "Hey Jude" and "Revolution". Working with director Michael Lindsay-Hogg, two clips were made for each song. A 36-piece orchestra played and 300 singers were used for the chorus—the singers were members of the public recruited from a leaflet drop in the local area.

5 More overdubbing onto "While My Guitar Gently Weeps".

6 Paul accompanied Mary Hopkin on the piano in a short film made at Apple Corps, Savile Row in London. In the evening Eric Clapton played his Les Paul guitar on an overdub of "While My Guitar Gently Weeps" at Abbey Road. In the UK Black Dyke Mills Band released "Thingumybob", written by Paul and John. Jackie Lomax's single "Sour Milk Sea" was released in the UK. It was written by George with him, Ringo, and Eric Clapton playing on the backing track.

8 The first showing of the promotional film for "Hey Jude" appeared on LWT's *Frost on Saturday*. David Frost had been involved with the filming at Twickenham, so this showing gave the impression that the band was actually appearing on the programme.

9 Chris Thomas took over as producer from George Martin while he was on holiday for three weeks. In the studio that evening, the band began to rerecord "Helter Skelter".

10 Final overdubs to "Helter Skelter" produced a very different version from the original. The film with Paul and Mary Hopkin was shown on ITV's new children's series *Magpie*.

11 Work began on John's "Glass Onion".

12 The screening of the "Hey Jude" promotional film was broadcast on BBC's *Top of the Pops*.

Ringo quits

Abbey Road Studios might have considered installing a revolving door in the summer of 1968, so numerous were the comings and goings during the *White Album* recording sessions. Some of those were planned, others most definitely not.

In early June, George and Ringo headed to America, where the former made a cameo appearance in *Raga*, an Apple-financed documentary about Ravi Shankar. Shortly after their return Paul also went to the States on Apple business. George disappeared again, this time on an impromptu trip to Greece. Sometimes work on the new album was suspended if one or more members of the group were absent, but often it was business as usual, indicative of the malaise that was setting in. And the strained atmosphere took its toll on the backroom team as well as the Beatles themselves. Sound engineer Geoff Emerick, who had worked with the Beatles for five years, jumped ship before the album was completed. And in September George Martin upped and went on holiday, leaving twenty-one-year-old rookie producer Chris Thomas to hold the fort. The most serious rupture was kept under wraps and came to light only much later. On 22 August, Ringo put down his drumsticks and walked out.

Ringo had been feeling increasingly marginalized, disconnected from the other three, surplus to requirements, unappreciated. He spent a lot of time kicking his heels, waiting to be called into action, and even then his efforts occasionally counted for naught. For Paul sometimes redid his drum parts, Ringo affecting not to notice when the tapes were played back.

The crunch came during the recording of "Back in the USSR", the drum pattern of which he couldn't get right. Paul snapped, and this time Ringo bit back. He spent the next two weeks sunning himself in the Mediterranean aboard Peter Sellers's yacht, where he wrote his best known song, "Octopus's Garden". It was the first time a disgruntled Beatle had voted with his feet, and the fact that it was the accommodating percussionist, the group member with the smallest ego, was a harbinger for the future.

Ringo returned to find his drum kit festooned with flowers. All was well again, though it was but a temporary balm, a sticking plaster on a gaping, infected wound. And his disappearing act hadn't brought the others up sharp. Paul took up the sticks on "Back in the USSR", which was completed during Ringo's brief sabbatical.

13 An additional drum and piano track were overdubbed onto "Glass Onion", "Hey Jude" was awarded a gold disc in the States.

14 "Hey Jude"/"Revolution" reached the top of the UK charts, remaining there for two weeks.

16 Paul's new ballad, "I Will", took up the majority of this studio session. It featured only three members of the band: George was not involved.

17 Final overdubbing to "I Will" and a mono mix of "Helter Skelter".

18 George was interviewed by *NME* journalist Alan Smith for broadcast on Radio 1 and the BBC World Service. The band, after watching *The Girl Can't Help It* at Paul's house, then went to Abbey Road to record "Birthday".

19 The only British showing of the "Revolution" promotional film was broadcast on *Top of the Pops*. They began to record George's "Piggies", which included Chris Thomas playing the harpsichord.

20 "Piggies" was completed, using Abbey Road archives to re-create the pigs grunting.

22 Apple Records announced that the band's next album would be a double LP.

23 Work began on John's "Happiness Is a Warm Gun".

24 They continued to develop "Happiness Is a Warm Gun".

25 Organ, piano parts, a tuba, a snare drum, bass, and tambourine were overdubbed onto "Happiness Is a Warm Gun".

26 Further mixing of recent recordings in preparation for George Martin's return. John continued to add sound effects to "Glass Onion" that were never actually used. The "Hey Jude" promotional film was repeated on BBC's *Top of the Pops*.

27 "Hey Jude" reached No. 1 in the US charts, where it remained for nine weeks.

28 George's interview with Alan Smith was broadcast on the BBC Radio series *Scene and Heard* and repeated in an edited form the next day on the BBC World Service.

30 McGraw-Hill published Hunter Davies's biography *The Beatles*.

Two virgins uncovered

"She makes music like you've never heard on earth... it's as important as anything we ever did." Fans got to test John's assessment of Yoko's musical ability in November 1968, with the release of *Unfinished Music No. 1: Two Virgins*. The thirty-minute sound collage was recorded days before John launched into "Revolution 9" at Abbey Road. It was one thing to have an experimental piece in the midst of a Beatles LP, quite another to have a complete album of random noise, sound effects, and snatches of dialogue.

John's first solo album would barely have raised a ripple had it not been for the infamous nude cover shot. EMI's Sir Joseph Lockwood, replying to Yoko's contention that it was art, commented: "In that case why not show Paul in the nude—he's much better looking." It was too much for EMI or Capitol; Track Records and Tetragrammaton took over distribution in the UK and US respectively.

Two Virgins sold just 5,000 copies on its UK release, and peaked outside the *Billboard* Hot 100, despite the publicity coup of having 30,000 copies impounded in New Jersey. The other Beatles thought the album irredeemably bad and were concerned that they would be found guilty by association. Not that John cared. It was but another step along the diverging road. He had been moving away from the Beatles for some time; now he had something to go to.

ON TWO VIRGINS

"Our minds met on the music on the record, and our bodies met on the cover of the record."
—John

OCTOBER 1968

1 Back at Trident Studios, the band worked on Paul's "Honey Pie". Jimmy Webb, the American songwriter, called in to see them. George Martin was now back working with them again.

2 Paul overdubbed lead vocal and lead guitar onto "Honey Pie".

3 Still at Trident, they embarked on George's new composition, "Savoy Truffle".

4 Only Paul, assisted by 14 professional musicians, worked on his song "Martha My Dear". Some of the musicians

were also involved with the overdubs to "Honey Pie".

5 The final session of this series at Trident Studios was spent working on "Savoy Truffle", "Honey Pie", "Martha My Dear", and "Dear Prudence".

6 The "Hey Jude" promotional film was screened in the US in colour on several editions of the CBS series *The Smothers Brothers Comedy Hour*.

7 Back at Abbey Road, work began on George's "Long, Long, Long" —John was absent.

8 John's songs "I'm So Tired" and "The Continuing Story of Bungalow Bill" were started and finished in a session that lasted for 16 hours.

9 Paul recorded the basis of "Why Don't We Do It in the Road" composition. Other songs worked on included "The Continuing Story of Bungalow Bill" and "Long, Long, Long".

10 Three more songs were completed in a 12-hour session that ran through the night: "Piggies", "Glass Onion", and "Why Don't We Do It in the Road".

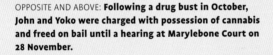

OPPOSITE AND ABOVE: **Following a drug bust in October, John and Yoko were charged with possession of cannabis and freed on bail until a hearing at Marylebone Court on 28 November.**

ON MEETING YOKO

"When I met Yoko is when you meet your first woman and you leave the guys at the bar, and you don't play football any more... Once I found *the* woman, the boys became of no interest whatsoever, other than they were like old friends."

—John

11 Six saxophonists added their piece to "Savoy Truffle", followed by further mixing of other tracks for the forthcoming double album. "The Urban Spaceman" was released in the UK by the Bonzo Dog Doo-Dah Band. Paul had produced the record, albeit under a pseudonym.

12 Further mono and stereo mixing for the album.

13 In one session, John recorded "Julia". The "Revolution" promotional film was also shown on the CBS series *The Smothers Brothers Comedy Hour*.

14 This was the last recording session for the album. John, Paul, and George finished the overdubs for "Savoy Truffle"; Ringo had flown out to Sardinia for a two-week holiday.

15 "Happiness Is a Warm Gun" and "Cry Baby Cry" were mixed.

16 This one and only 24-hour recording session was done without George Martin, who had flown to Los Angeles earlier in the day. The Beatles needed to agree on the running order for the album.

18 John and Yoko were charged with possession of cannabis and obstructing the police.

19 John and Yoko were remanded on bail after an appearance at Marylebone Magistrates' Court.

20 Paul flew to the States with Linda Eastman, now his girlfriend, so she could be reunited with her daughter.

25 John and Yoko announced that Yoko was pregnant, with their child due in February 1969.

28 Ringo returned from Sardinia.

29 Stereo mixes for "Hey Bulldog", "All Together Now", "All You Need Is Love", and "Only a Northern Song" were made by Geoff Emerick for the *Yellow Submarine* soundtrack album.

31 Linda Eastman moved in with Paul.

Clapton takes session-man role on George's song

Ringo may have beaten George to the punch by a few months in terms of walking out on the Beatles, but the latter felt a similar lack of regard during the making of the *White Album*. It wasn't until two months into the sessions that a Harrison song got a look in. Even Ringo had had his self-penned number "Don't Pass Me By" recorded by then. Paul pulled composer's rank during the making of "Hey Jude", vetoing a riff George had wanted to play. It left George determined to have the last word on the arrangement when he finally got the group to give one of his numbers an airing.

The song in question was "While My Guitar Gently Weeps". George had become interested in I Ching philosophy, and in particular the concept of randomness. *The Chinese Book of Changes* taught that events were interrelated rather than coincidental. Accordingly, George decided to write a song based on the first words his eyes lighted upon when opening a book at random. They happened to be "gently weeps", and the song was constructed around that phrase.

George felt the others were apathetic, disdainful almost, when he unveiled the song in the studio in late July. It didn't help matters that he couldn't get the sound he wanted. After numerous remakes over a six-week period, it finally came together. Then, on a whim, he decided on the boldest of finishing touches.

The following day, 6 September, George happened to share a car ride into London with his near neighbour Eric Clapton. Their friendship dated back to the Yardbirds' appearance as a support act on the 1964–65 Beatles *Christmas Show*. Since then, Clapton had been catapulted into the rock stratosphere, having enhanced his reputation with John Mayall's Bluesbreakers and sealed it in supergroup Cream. George was an outstanding guitarist, but Clapton's virtuosity put him on a different plane altogether; he wasn't just revered by his fans, he was deified. And on that early September morning, George invited "God" to come to Abbey Road to play lead guitar on "While My Guitar Gently Weeps".

Far from jumping at the chance, Clapton was extremely apprehensive about intruding on a Beatles session. He was well aware that the group might have imported top-notch brass or wind instrumentalists as needed, but never a guitarist. George assured him that it was his song, and therefore his call.

In previous overdubs George had tried and failed to capture the plangent quality he wanted for the solo. Clapton made his Gibson Les Paul "gently weep" to perfection, and his presence also had a pacifying effect. Peace broke out in the studio the day the Beatles employed their most illustrious session musician.

ON THE WHITE ALBUM

"If there is still any doubt that Lennon and McCartney are the greatest songwriters since Schubert, then...[the album, *The Beatles*]...should surely see the last vestiges of cultural snobbery and bourgeois prejudice swept away in a deluge of joyful music making..."

—Tony Palmer, *The Observer*

LEFT: **George and Pattie dressed up for an evening out.**

NOVEMBER 1968

1 George's soundtrack for the film *Wonderwall* was released on the Apple label.

3 *All My Loving* (with interviews from Paul and Ringo) was shown in black and white on BBC1 as part of the *Omnibus* arts series. While in the States, George recorded an electronic piece with Bernie Krause called "No Time Or Space".

4 Yoko was admitted to Queen Charlotte's Hospital, as her pregnancy was in danger.

5 Paul and Linda travelled to Paul's farm in Scotland.

8 John and Cynthia were divorced. George's songwriting contract with Northern Songs expired and was not renewed.

11 John and Yoko's album *Unfinished Music No. 1: Two Virgins* was released in the US.

13 The film *Yellow Submarine* opened in New York.

15 George took part in a recording for *The Smothers Brothers Comedy Hour* at the CBS TV Studio in Hollywood.

THE BEATLES (THE WHITE ALBUM)

Released

🇬🇧 **22 November 1968** Apple (Parlophone)

🇺🇸 **25 November 1968** Apple (Capitol)

Disc One, Side One:
Back in the USSR
Dear Prudence
Glass Onion
Ob-La-Di, Ob-La-Da
Wild Honey Pie
The Continuing Story of Bungalow Bill
While My Guitar Gently Weeps
Happiness Is a Warm Gun

Disc One, Side Two:
Martha My Dear
I'm So Tired
Blackbird
Piggies
Rocky Racoon
Don't Pass Me By
Why Don't We Do It in the Road
I Will
Julia

Disc Two, Side One:
Birthday
Yer Blues
Mother Nature's Son
Everybody's Got Something to Hide
  Except Me and My Monkey
Sexy Sadie
Helter Skelter
Long, Long, Long

Disc Two, Side Two:
Revolution 1
Honey Pie
Savoy Truffle
Cry Baby Cry
Revolution 9
Good Night

Cover story

Had the Beatles stuck with *"Umbrella"* or *"A Doll's House"*—two of the titles considered for their ninth album—pop artist Richard Hamilton might well have reached a different decision over the cover design.

"Umbrella" was an early suggestion by Paul for the eclectic mix housed under a single canopy. The doll's house idea stuck much longer. Ibsen's play was the obvious reference point, though Doll may have been a madame whose house of ill repute served as a meeting place for the cast of characters found in the songs. The playhouse motif would have fitted well, particularly since the Beatles took pains to place songs of a similar hue on each of the album's four sides. But the idea was dropped when rock group Family released their debut album, *Music In The Doll's House*, while the Beatles were hard at work in the studio.

The fans had been *With the Beatles* and offered *Beatles For Sale*, but never presented with *The Beatles*, pure and simple. That decision left Hamilton a blank canvas, which he and Paul between them made into an artistic virtue, the perfect contrast to *Sgt. Pepper's* blaze of pychedelic colour. The minimalist theme was maintained by having the band's name in embossed lettering, rendering to the whole a starkness that would give the album its popular name.

The cover bridged the gap between music and fine art by having each of the first 2 million copies pressed with its own number, like a limited edition print. Paul considered taking the idea a stage further and holding a lottery, with a prize for the holder of the "winning" album, but it was dismissed as a cheap stunt unworthy of the group. The low numbers of the first pressing became highly prized collectors' items, though most of those were given to the members of Apple's inner circle.

The album's interior packaging included a poster, the lyrics to the songs, and a set of photographs taken by John Kelley during the autumn of 1968 that have themselves become iconic. This is the only sleeve of a Beatles' studio album not to show the members of the band on the front.

---

17 George's appearance on *The Smothers Brothers Comedy Hour* was broadcast; the programme also included Dion and Donovan.

19 Ringo moved to a new house in Elstead called Brookfields.

20 Paul was interviewed at home by former Australian DJ Tony Macarthur for Radio Luxembourg.

21 Paul's interview from the previous day was broadcast in a special programme featuring the forthcoming album. Yoko miscarried their child; John stayed with her at Queen Charlotte's Maternity Hospital, London.

22 The double LP *The Beatles* (known as the *White Album*) was released in the UK on Apple (Parlophone) PMC 7067-7068 (mono) and PCS 7067-7068 (stereo).

25 The LP *The Beatles* (the *White Album*) was released in the US on Apple (Capitol) SWBO-101 (stereo only).

28 John admitted to possessing cannabis, resulting in a fine of £159 with 20 guineas' costs.

29 The album, *Unfinished Music No. 1: Two Virgins* was issued in the UK, while John and Yoko were filming *Rape*.

30 It was reported that "Hey Jude" had sold nearly six million copies around the world.

Beatles to play live again?

In the summer of 1966 the Beatles toured fourteen North American cities, ending with a performance at Candlestick Park, San Francisco, on 29 August, which was to have been their last-ever live concert. From that time the fans had pressed to see the Beatles live again.

On 4 September the Beatles repaired to Twickenham Studios to film the promo for their latest single. It was a "semilive" performance, Paul and John singing over a backing track to "Hey Jude" and "Revolution", and the amps were there just for show. But with a three-hundred-strong audience hauled in off the street to join in with the A-side's extended coda, it was the nearest thing to a Beatles concert performance for two years.

The *White Album* was still a month away from completion, and shooting the promo was a welcome distraction from the fractiousness that blighted so many of the recording sessions. It wasn't all gloom and doom, however. They had been in rocking good form on John's "Yer Blues", a tight recording not subjected to ad nauseam overdubs. Paul felt it was no coincidence that when the four played together and simplicity ruled, a lot of their problems melted away. It was he who suggested they put petty squabbles and business dealings to one side and go back to what they did best.

In early November it was announced that the Beatles would put on three shows at London's Roundhouse the following month. Those plans quickly evaporated, though one Beatle did take to the stage in the run-up to Christmas. John filmed a sequence for a proposed Rolling Stones TV special, *Rock and Roll Circus*, singing "Yer Blues" with an all-star backing group comprising Eric Clapton, Keith Richards, and Jimi Hendrix Experience drummer Mitch Mitchell. Though the show was never broadcast, it was a watershed moment, the first time John had performed in public without any of the other Beatles. And the rehearsal tapes show that he was clearly enjoying himself, which didn't augur well for Paul's pet project.

Missing the December deadline didn't dent Paul's enthusiasm for a return to concert mode. There was talk of a one-off performance early in the new year, and then the idea of a television special emerged. No dates were set, but rehearsals would begin in January, and the cameras would be allowed in to film the proceedings. Again, that was Paul's idea. Pablo Picasso had recently been filmed working on a canvas, and it struck a chord with Paul: Why not show the artistic process as well as the result? Instead of providing a fly-on-the-wall insight into genius at work, the documentary would show a band disintegrating in front of the viewers' eyes.

RIGHT: **A cinema lobby card for the movie *Candy*. The picture was released in December 1968, one whole year after Ringo had filmed his cameo role as a Mexican gardener in Rome.**

DECEMBER 1968

1 The soundtrack for *Wonderwall* was released in the States.

4 Marmalade's cover of "Ob-La-Di, Ob-La-Da" was released.

6 Apple Records released James Taylor's first album. *The Beatles* (the *White Album*) was awarded a gold disc in the States.

7 The Beatles (the *White Album*) topped the UK charts, remaining there for eight weeks.

9 In *Newsweek* it was announced that the *White Album* had sold 1.1 million copies in the States within five days of release.

10 Rehearsals and filming for the Rolling Stones' television special *Rock and Roll Circus* took place at Stonebridge House in Wembley; it included a musical guest appearance by John. Kenwood, John and Cynthia's home, was put up for sale.

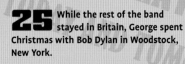

THIS PAGE: **Five-year-old Julian Lennon with his father, Yoko, Eric Clapton, and Brian Jones at the Rolling Stones' *Rock and Roll Circus* in December. The young Julian, trapped in the middle of his parents' divorce, was the inspiration for "Hey Jude".**

11 Further filming at Stonebridge House after which John and Yoko took part in the show *Night Ride*, transmitted just after midnight. They discussed their album *Two Virgins* with John Peel.

17 The film *Candy*, which included Ringo playing a Mexican gardener, was released in the US.

18 John and Yoko appeared together inside a white bag at the Royal Albert Hall.

20 The Beatles' sixth Christmas record, *Christmas 1968*, was released for fan-club members.

23 At the Apple Christmas party for the children of its employees, John and Yoko went as Father and Mother Christmas.

25 While the rest of the band stayed in Britain, George spent Christmas with Bob Dylan in Woodstock, New York.

26 The "Hey Jude" promotional film was repeated on BBC's *Top of the Pops*.

28 The *White Album* reached No. 1 in the States, holding the spot for six weeks.

JOHN, PAUL, GEORGE & RINGO

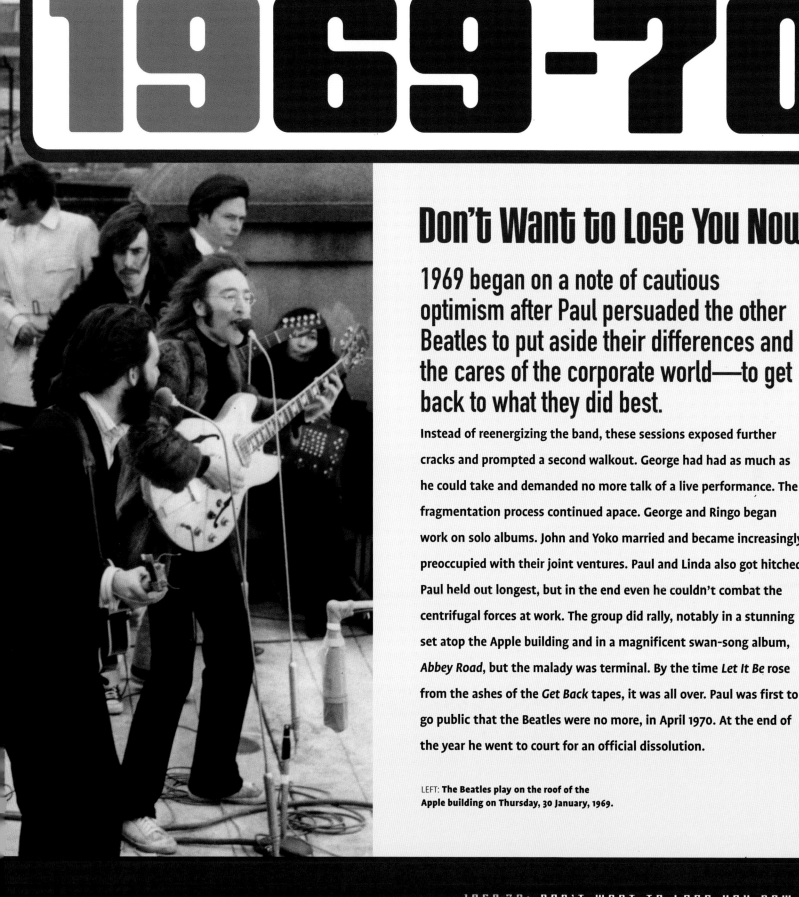

1969-70

Don't Want to Lose You Now

1969 began on a note of cautious optimism after Paul persuaded the other Beatles to put aside their differences and the cares of the corporate world—to get back to what they did best.

Instead of reenergizing the band, these sessions exposed further cracks and prompted a second walkout. George had had as much as he could take and demanded no more talk of a live performance. The fragmentation process continued apace. George and Ringo began work on solo albums. John and Yoko married and became increasingly preoccupied with their joint ventures. Paul and Linda also got hitched. Paul held out longest, but in the end even he couldn't combat the centrifugal forces at work. The group did rally, notably in a stunning set atop the Apple building and in a magnificent swan-song album, *Abbey Road*, but the malady was terminal. By the time *Let It Be* rose from the ashes of the *Get Back* tapes, it was all over. Paul was first to go public that the Beatles were no more, in April 1970. At the end of the year he went to court for an official dissolution.

LEFT: **The Beatles play on the roof of the Apple building on Thursday, 30 January, 1969.**

Getting back to where they belong

When the cameras started rolling for rehearsals at Twickenham Studios on 2 January 1969, none of the Beatles were entirely sure what they were rehearsing for. A televised performance in front of a live audience, but where? There had been many an exotic suggestion for a venue: an ocean liner, a Roman amphitheatre, the middle of the Sahara desert. Any of those would have made a bold statement and broken new ground, which always appealed. But the plan to ease the tensions between the four and reenergize the Beatles by "getting back to where they once belonged" was fraught with danger. Instead of breathing new life into the band, there was always the risk of a suffocating expiration. In the event, the patient rallied more than once in 1969, most memorably on the roof of the Apple building at the end of January. But overall the *Get Back* sessions showed a group that was mortally wounded.

Ringo, notwithstanding his foot-stamping display of the previous summer, remained the most amenable of the four, yet it was he who steadfastly refused to entertain the idea of performing overseas. The Bedouin Arabs wouldn't get to see a Beatles show after all. George had reservations about the whole idea and still harboured resentment about being ticked off for his guitar work and having his compositions overlooked. John's fixations were shared between Yoko and heroin. It was his least creative period, and one that completed the abdication process that had been taking place since Epstein's death. Paul had donned the crown, though it was as much by default as through any natural assertiveness on his part.

Paul was undoubtedly the most passionate about keeping the group together, and that meant biting his lip on occasions. But the sessions were a powder keg waiting for a spark, and it came on 10 January, when George fell out with both John and Paul. Patronized once too often, George packed up his guitar and left, the second Beatle in six months to walk away midsession. Yoko, obviously feeling she was next in the pecking order, moved into George's seat and began wailing into the microphone. John shrugged off the incident and said that if George

wasn't back by the start of the following week, they should invite Eric Clapton to take his place.

A few days later, at a clear-the-air meeting, George laid down terms for his return: abandon all the grand schemes for a concert and find somewhere new to rehearse. Neither stipulation grated with the others. The Twickenham soundstage was cold and damp with poor acoustics, while the concert idea had begun to pall. But where to relocate to at such short notice? Not Abbey Road; the *White Album* sessions were too raw and recent. The answer was under their noses. Hadn't "Magic Alex" promised to build a state-of-the-art seventy-two-track studio in the Apple basement? As with so many of Mardas's technological flights of fancy, the delivery failed to match the rhetoric. George Martin had to ship some equipment over from EMI before recording could recommence.

A new studio heralded a change of direction. Instead of filming rehearsals for a TV special, the cameras would record the Beatles at work on a new album. It would make fascinating viewing, though it was inevitably a watered-down proposal. The release of a new Beatles record, significant though that was, couldn't match the immediacy and impact of a live performance. Belatedly, the Beatles realized this and decided to give the monthlong session a focal point after all, a glorious forty-two-minute impromptu set that turned out to be their final public performance.

RIGHT AND OPPOSITE INSET: **The Beatles in the studio during filming of *Let It Be*. Under the contract signed with United Artists, the Beatles were obliged to make three movies. *A Hard Day's Night* and *Help!* were the first two, but the animated *Yellow Submarine* hadn't fulfilled the band's quota. The answer was to put out footage of the band recording songs at Twickenham and Apple studios during January 1969. Tensions were running high between the band members, and the resentment felt by each meant that the sessions were less than productive.**

RIGHT INSET: ***Yellow Submarine*, the soundtrack album for the animated film of the same name, was issued on both sides of the Atlantic in January 1969. For most Beatles fans the album was a disappointment since it contained only six tracks performed by the band, two of which, "Yellow Submarine" and "All You Need Is Love" had already been released. Four new songs made up the contents of side one: "Only a Northern Song", "Hey Bulldog", "It's All Too Much", and "All Together Now" and side two of the album consisted of orchestral music provided by George Martin and His orchestra.**

The final public performance

Three weeks into the *Get Back* sessions, a new candidate for the "Fifth Beatle" tag entered the frame. Billy Preston had been a callow fifteen-year-old when he played in Little Richard's backing group at the Star-Club in 1962. All the Beatles had befriended him, though a special bond had developed with George, who knew what it felt like to be the barely-tolerated junior member of a band. Their paths hadn't crossed for seven years, until George approached the keyboard virtuoso after seeing him supporting Ray Charles at a Royal Festival Hall concert.

Whether it was inspiration or desperation that made George invite Billy Preston to join the fray, the move had a hugely beneficial effect. Just as Eric Clapton's presence had brought an oasis of calm to the troubled *White Album* sessions, so Preston in his ten-day stint as an honorary Beatle lifted the gloom that shrouded Apple's basement. "Straightaway there was 100 percent improvement in the vibe in the room", George recalled. It showed in the music, too, which became much tighter. Within days "Get Back" and "Don't Let Me Down" had been buffed up and ready for release as the

next single, Preston becoming the only musician to get joint billing on a Beatles record.

The sessions had to be wound up at the end of January, not least because Ringo was required on set for *The Magic Christian*, which was about to start shooting. Paul hadn't given up hope of a live performance to provide a final flourish, though perforce it had to be a low-key affair if George and Ringo were to be persuaded. Someone mentioned the rooftop space, and as soon as it was investigated it had obvious appeal: all the joys of a concert performance without any of the hassle. And it was as much a first as any of the grander schemes that had been floated.

The strains of "Get Back" emanating from atop the Apple building on Thursday, 30 January had passersby craning their necks and peering into the lunchtime sky. The news spread like wildfire: The Beatles were giving an impromptu free concert. Over the next forty-two minutes they ran through assorted versions of five numbers: "I've Got a Feeling", "One After 909", "Dig a Pony", and both sides of the new single.

Not everyone was delighted at hearing the Beatles play live for the first time in two and a half years. By the time Paul launched into "Get Back" for a third time, the police had arrived. The Beatles would have preferred the long arm of the law to wrench them off stage, which would have made for a dramatic finale in front of the cameras, but it was all rather tame, as if they were being asked by an apologetic neighbour to keep the noise down. It was left to John to bring the curtain down on the Beatles' final public performance: "I'd like to say thanks on behalf of the group and ourselves, and I hope we passed the audition."

JANUARY 1969

1 George flew back into London from the States.

2 At Twickenham Film Studios, the band embarked on rehearsals and filming for the *Get Back* documentary. Eventually titled *Let It Be*, it was directed by Michael Lindsay-Hogg.

3 In Newark, New Jersey, a shipment of 30,000 copies of the *Two Virgins* album was confiscated by police, the cover having been deemed to be pornographic. Rehearsals continued at Twickenham.

4 Derek Taylor announced to the media that the next album was to be a live recording. London's Roundhouse or Liverpool's Cavern were quoted as possible venues.

6 The first of four further days of filming of *Get Back*.

10 George announced that he was going to leave the band, but went back on the decision later in the evening.

12 *Wonderwall* premiered in Britain at the Cinecenta, London.

13 The *Yellow Submarine* LP was released in the States on Apple (Capitol) SW-153 (stereo only).

14 Filming continued.

 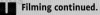

continued from *previous page*

JANUARY 1969

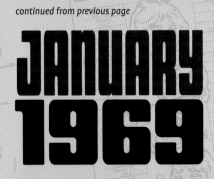

15 George returned to Twickenham Studios for a meeting to discuss the future of the band. An interview with John and Yoko, recorded in November 1968, was broadcast on the Dutch youth-interest series *Rood Wit Blauw*.

17 *Yellow Submarine*, the LP, was released in the UK on Apple (Parlophone) PMC 7070 (mono) and PCS 7070 (stereo). Beatles songs were featured on the A-side, with George Martin's original film score on the B-side.

18 An interview with journalist Ray Coleman appeared in the *Disc & Music Echo*, in which John revealed that Apple was losing money rapidly.

20 The recording sessions for *Get Back* were scheduled to start, but due to technical problems did not begin for a further two days.

21 *Daily Express* reporter David Wigg recorded an interview with Ringo in the back of his car.

22 Glyn Johns (balance engineer) and Billy Preston (an American organist) joined the band for one of many sessions working on the *Get Back* recordings at the Apple Studios.

23 Alan Parsons made his debut as the tape operator for the band; he was later to become a successful producer.

24 Several songs were worked on, including Paul's "On Our

The album that never was

The joyous rooftop concert had vindicated Paul's belief that the magic was still there when the four rolled back the years and took to the stage together. Unfortunately, it was more pejorative adjectives that best described most of the January sessions, and the euphoria of the 30 January concert quickly ebbed away. John summed up the prevailing mood: "Even the biggest Beatles fan couldn't have sat through those six weeks of misery. It was the most miserable session on earth."

The Beatles headed off to work on separate projects, scarcely able to contemplate the prospect of trying to make a viable album out of the tapes. They passed the buck to a producer, though for once it wasn't George Martin. Paul had invited Glyn Johns to work on the project back in December, when it was still envisaged as a TV spectacular. That idea fell by the wayside but Johns remained on board, nominally as assistant engineer to Martin but in practice taking over the producer's role on many of the sessions. Where the balance of production power lay was unclear, to the extent that the single "Get Back" was released without a producer's credit.

Johns was a top producer in his own right, and his presence could only be seen as undermining Martin's position. The Beatles, it seems, were asserting themselves. John was irked by reports that inflated Martin's contribution to the Beatles' work. In a *Rolling Stone* interview he railed against people "who think they made us", and included their long-time producer in that group. Martin's orchestral padding for the *Yellow Submarine* album, released mid-January, incensed John still further.

Martin's loss was Johns's gain, though given the fiendishly difficult task at hand it was a moot point as to who got the better end of the deal. Johns waded through the tapes, bypassing the aimless jamming in search of a coherent set of songs that would fulfil the brief. The Beatles had wanted it raw, not refined; warts and all, not whitewashed by lavish production and endless overdubs. They needn't have worried: a shortage of imperfections wasn't going to be a major concern.

By the end of May Johns did produce a master for a forty-four-minute album that reached the pressing stage before the plug was pulled. The Beatles had lost interest in the *Get Back* project, and perhaps there were just too many rough edges. John was all for putting it out in its dishevelled state—to show the Beatles "with no trousers on" as a means of hastening the group's demise. He was overruled. In March John was still under the impression that they were patching up the *Get Back* album, but around that time—the dividing line is indistinct—a fresh idea evolved. Paul began talking animatedly about a new studio album, a polished collection this time, with George Martin back at the helm.

The *Get Back* tapes would lie dormant for the best part of a year. It was even longer before the sleeve photograph for the aborted album saw the light of day. On 13 May the Beatles posed in the stairwell at EMI House as Angus McBean re-created the shot used on the cover of their debut LP, *Please Please Me*. It was the perfect image to accompany a back-to-the-roots album, the wheel coming full circle. The shot was overlooked the following year, when Phil Spector got to work and *Get Back* morphed into *Let It Be*. By then the game was up, and individual photographs framed in a black border was more fitting.

The two McBean photographs, taken six years apart, were used on EMI's compilation double albums released in 1973, the fresh-faced Fabs on the cover of the 1962–66 set, with the more hirsute, maturer visages adorning its 1967–70 counterpart.

BELOW: **During filming, George, feeling unappreciated, stormed out after arguing with Paul. He was eventually coaxed back to the studio, but a perilous gulf had already opened between the members of the band.**

OPPOSITE: **An intimate scene in the studio from takes for *Let It Be*.**

Way Home", "Teddy Boy", "Maggie Mae" (written about a Liverpool prostitute), then John's "Dig It" and "Dig a Pony", and the joint composition "I've Got a Feeling".

25 "Let It Be" (inspired by Paul's dream about his mother, Mary) and "For You Blue" (written by George and dedicated to his wife, Pattie) were developed in the studio. Ringo's interview was broadcast on the Radio 1 news programme *Scene and Heard*.

26 Six-year-old Heather Eastman (Linda's daughter) was in the studio and sang some backing vocals for "Dig It". The band then embarked on a rock 'n' roll medley and concluded the session with "The Long and Winding Road".

27 Most of this session was spent developing "Get Back". John asked Allen Klein to take care of his finances.

28 "Get Back" and "Don't Let Me Down" were recorded for the forthcoming single. Ringo's *Scene and Heard* interview was repeated. Ringo and George also requested that Allen Klein look after their financial interests.

29 "Teddy Boy", "The One After 909" (written mainly by John at Paul's house in 1957), and "I Want You" were taped.

30 The famous last live performance from the Beatles took place on the roof of the Apple Studios in London. The show lasted for 42 minutes before the police forced them to stop, as they had brought the surrounding area to a complete standstill.

31 The band recorded "The Long and Winding Road" and "Let It Be" as the final songs for the *Get Back* documentary. They were reportedly written on the same day.

The naked truth

The *Get Back* sessions saw the Beatles under the microscope for a more sustained period than any other in their career. It was unfortunate that the best-documented period in the group's history had dissolution as its theme, and that the music—the scorching rooftop set excepted—was somewhat patchy.

John maintained that Phil Spector did a fine job with the material available to him; Paul, George Martin, and a fair number of fans begged to differ. Paul felt the original concept had been subverted, which is undeniably true. More than thirty years on, Spector's "doctoring" of the tapes still rankled with Paul, who wanted to remix them and achieve the visceral sound originally intended. In 2003 three Abbey Road engineers attempted to do just that, the remastered album issued as *Let It Be...Naked*.

The tracks were cleaned up, mistakes patched over, and extraneous noise removed. The banter between the songs was taken out, which riled some fans. "Maggie Mae" and "Dig It" were dropped, as they were thought too lightweight. To compensate for the cuts, the engineers included an excellent new version of "Don't Let Me Down", which had been omitted from the 1970 collection, and a bonus disc titled *Fly on the Wall*, a mixed bag of music outtakes and snippets of conversation from the *Get Back* sessions.

1 *Yellow Submarine* entered the British album charts. It remained there for ten weeks and peaked at No. 3.

2 Yoko divorced Antony Cox and was given custody of their daughter, Kyoko. Allen Klein officially took over the band's finances, albeit against Paul's wishes—he was in favour of using Linda's father's firm, Eastman and Eastman.

3 Ringo began his next film role as Youngman Grand, son to Peter Sellers'

Sir Guy Grand, in *The Magic Christian*. This was filmed at Twickenham Film Studios and various London-area locations for the next three months. Allen Klein became the band's business manager.

4 Paul appointed Eastman and Eastman as general counsel to Apple Corps in direct response to Klein's appointment.

5 A session in the Apple Studios, when the songs recorded on the rooftop on

30 January were mixed and taped. *Yellow Submarine* went gold in the US.

7 George was taken to London's University College Hospital with an infected back molar that had subsequently infected his tonsils.

8 George's tonsils were immediately removed.

11 Further studio work on some of John and Yoko's recordings.

RIGHT: **Paul and Mary Hopkin in the studio working on her debut album, *Postcard*. Paul not only produced the album but played guitar on several tracks.**

BELOW RIGHT: **Paul and Linda attend the launch of *Postcard* at the Post Office Tower in London. Jimi Hendrix and Donovan were among the guests that evening.**

BELOW: **Paul meets a group of female fans as he leaves the Apple Studios on the day of the announcement of his engagement to Linda.**

OPPOSITE: **Paul and Linda at the premiere of *Isadora* at the Odeon on St. Martin's Lane, London.**

OPPOSITE INSET: **Paul and Linda leave Apple Studios in Paul's Mini. Filming had just concluded on *Let It Be*, but new fissures were opening over the band's legal representation. Paul wanted Linda's father to counsel the band, but John questioned the firm's impartiality, fearing it would focus on Paul's best interests.**

13 Paul and Linda attended the launch of Mary Hopkin's debut album on the Apple label, *Postcard*, at the restaurant at the top of the Post Office Tower, London.

15 George left hospital.

19 Following John's conviction for possessing cannabis at Ringo's Montagu Square apartment, a writ was issued by the landlords for "misuse of property". They used civil proceedings to try to ban John and "other undesirables" from the property.

20 The London premiere of Ringo's film *Candy* at the Odeon, Kensington, London.

21 Mary Hopkin's debut LP, *Postcard*, was released in Britain. Paul had produced the album and designed the cover.

22 The main recording for the *Abbey Road* album did not begin until July, some compositions were started prior to that, including John's "I Want You (She's So Heavy)", recorded in a session at Trident Studios.

23 *David Frost Presents...Frankie Howerd* was transmitted in the US and included Paul's interview from the previous June. Editing and mixing for "I Want You" took place.

24 At Trident Studios a copy of the final master of "I Want You (She's So Heavy)" was made.

25 On his 26th birthday, George worked alone in the studio with Ken Scott recording new compositions "Old Brown Shoe", "Something", and "All Things Must Pass".

28 After receiving the writ, Ringo sold the leasehold to his apartment in Montagu Square.

ABOVE AND OPPOSITE BOTTOM: **George and Pattie arrive at Esher and Walton Magistrates Court charged with drug possession after the police had discovered cannabis resin when they raided George's home on the same day as Paul's wedding. They were remanded on bail until the end of March and eventually fined £250 each (opposite bottom). On the evening of the raid, the couple had shocked Princess Margaret when they bumped into her at a party in Chelsea and suggested she use her influence to help them.**

BIO: BILLY PRESTON

Of all the claimants to the "fifth Beatle" title, keyboard virtuoso Billy Preston is the only one who can boast equal billing on vinyl. Texas-born William Everett Preston was just fifteen when he first met the Beatles, during their third Hamburg tour in the spring of 1962. Preston was above them on that Star-Club bill, backing headliner Little Richard, with the Beatles firmly in the support camp.

The list of artists with whom Preston collaborated reads like a Who's Who of popular music—such luminaries as Ray Charles, Sam Cooke, Eric Clapton, and the Rolling Stones. His writing credits include "You Are So Beautiful", which provided Joe Cocker with a huge 1975 hit some seven years after the blues legend had taken "With a Little Help from My Friends" to No. 1. But Preston's chief claim to fame remains his brief stint as an honorary Beatle in January 1969.

George's main aim in inviting Preston to join the *Get Back* sessions may have been to pour oil on troubled waters, but the latter made an unforgettable contribution on a number of *Let It Be* and *Abbey Road* tracks, as well as making the Beatles' final concert a five-piece rooftop extravaganza.

Preston earned £500 and an Apple contract for his efforts. He had a UK Top 20 hit with "That's the Way God Planned It" and made a couple of albums for the label. He would guest on a number of solo Beatle projects, but it was with George whom he developed the closest bond. Preston's roots were in gospel music, a musical form George was keen to explore when the two found themselves on tour with Delaney and Bonnie in December 1969. Preston gave George an impromptu master class in how to write a gospel song—a fragment that George took away and worked on. The result was "My Sweet Lord", which Preston himself recorded before it gave George the honour of being the first Beatle to have a UK No. 1 after the four went their separate ways. Preston died in 2006 from kidney disease.

ABOVE: **Paul is seen leaving Olympic Studios in the early hours of the morning after a session with Jackie Lomax.**

ABOVE RIGHT: **Billy Preston, the keyboard master, was drafted by George to help defuse tensions in the studio.**

BELOW: **Paul and Linda use a back alley to slip into Marylebone Register Office on 12 March. The wedding was held up for almost an hour by the late arrival of the best man, Paul's brother, Mike McGear, of Scaffold fame, after his train from Birmingham had been delayed. The decision to marry had been last-minute. Paul and Linda claimed to have decided upon it only a week earlier. The wedding ring was also a last-minute affair as Paul admitted it cost him £12 and he bought it just before the shop closed. During the festivities, the couple slipped out to have the marriage blessed by the local reverend, Noel Perry-Gore of St. John's Wood Parish Church.**

MARCH 1969

1 Mary Hopkin recorded "Goodbye" at Morgan studios, London. The song was written specially for her by Paul, who also produced the record.

2 John supported Yoko in a concert performance at Lady Mitchell Hall, Cambridge, watched by an audience of 500. A series of screams and guitar feedback was recorded and constituted one side of the album *Unfinished Music No 2: Life with the Lions* to be released later in the year.

4 David Wigg interviewed George for the weekly programme *Scene and Heard*,

broadcast on 8 March. Paul invited Glyn Johns to prepare the *Get Back* album, which at that time was merely a pile of tapes.

7 Mary Hopkin released her single "Lontano Dagli Occhi"/"The Game" in Italy on Apple 7.

10 At the Olympic Sound Studio, Barnes, Glyn Johns began assembling the *Get Back* album.

11 Part of George's interview was broadcast on a repeat of *Scene and Heard*.

12 Paul married Linda Louise Eastman at Marylebone Register Office while John and Yoko were working at the Abbey Road Studios. George and Pattie were arrested for possessing cannabis just before the ceremony.

13 On Chobham Common in Surrey, Ringo filmed the grouse-shooting scene for the film *The Magic Christian*.

14 *Yellow Submarine* was certified gold in the States.

Both Paul and John marry——within eight days

In March 1969 John and Paul each set the seal on the enduring relationship of his adult life. Yoko Ono's divorce from second husband Antony Cox came through during the *Get Back* sessions, and although John believed they existed on a higher plane of "total communication", he was content to go through the legal niceties for a second time.

Paul and Linda beat them to the punch by eight days. Despite mounting press speculation that the last bachelor Beatle was about to marry, the couple had managed to keep their plans under wraps. It was anything but a superstar's wedding. Paul and Linda slipped into Marylebone Register Office through a side door, past the dustbins. There was a blessing at St. John's Church followed by a reception at the Ritz Hotel. Paul's brother Mike did the best man honours, while the Beatles' coterie was represented by Mal Evans and Peter Brown. Paul said he couldn't recall whether he invited the rest of the group, though it is clear that by now relations were at an all-time low.

George had a more pressing concern that day, as he took a call from a distressed Pattie informing him that the police were ransacking their house looking for drugs. It was further confirmation that the gloves were off, or, as George himself put it, that "the Cromwell figures in the Establishment were trying to get their own back on us".

While distraught females were weeping at Paul's passage into the realms of connubial bliss, it was business as usual for John, who spent the day working with Yoko at Abbey Road. Their own marriage eight days later was not so much an event as a saga. Holland couldn't offer the quickie, no-frills ceremony they wanted, as there was a two-week residency requirement. An idea to get hitched aboard a cross-Channel ferry foundered. Then Peter Brown discovered that as a UK citizen, John could marry without hindrance in Gibraltar, a British protectorate.

ABOVE, LEFT AND OPPOSITE: **Paul and Linda accompanied by Linda's daughter, Heather, on their wedding day.**

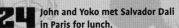

15 At the Thorenson Ferry Passenger Terminal in Southampton, John and Yoko were stopped from taking a boat to France because of issues with their passports.

16 Instead of taking the boat, they flew to Paris the next day.

18 Ringo's scene with Spike Milligan, playing a traffic warden, was filmed outside the Star and Garter pub on the Thames Embankment.

19 George and Pattie were at Esher and Walton Magistrates' Court to face their drug charges.

20 John and Yoko were married at the British Consulate in the British protectorate of Gibraltar.

22 The newlyweds spent their honeymoon by the Seine in Paris.

24 John and Yoko met Salvador Dali in Paris for lunch.

25 Room 902 at the Amsterdam Hilton was the scene for John and Yoko's famous seven-day "bed-in" in the name of world peace.

26 George Martin worked at Abbey Road to produce four mixes of "Get Back".

27 Ringo announced that the band would never play in front of an audience again.

28 Mary Hopkin released her single "Goodbye"/"Sparrow" in the UK. It reached No. 2 in the British charts. Written by Paul, it also featured a guitar track played by him.

31 John and Yoko left Amsterdam for Vienna to promote the world premiere of their movie *Rape*. At a press conference in the Hotel Sacher they appeared enclosed in a white-sheet bag. After pleading guilty to their drug charge, George and Pattie were fined £250 each with 10 guineas' costs.

APRIL 1969

1 John and Yoko appeared live on Thames Television's *Today*. As part of their peace message they again appeared inside a white bag. Ringo took part in a filming session at the Theatre Royal, Stratford, East London.

3 Sue McGregor interviewed George for the Radio 4's *The World at One*, where he discussed Ravi Shankar's music. John and Yoko took part in *The Eamonn Andrews Show*. Apple signed Billy Preston.

4 Further mixing on "Get Back" and "Don't Let Me Down" by Glyn Johns in the Olympic Sound Studio.

5 Paul and John refused an offer of £9 million from ATV for their Northern Songs shares.

6 Alan Freeman and John Peel announced that "Get Back" would be released on 11 April. Paul however, was still not happy with the final version and went back to the studio with Glyn Johns.

7 Radio 1 DJs Kenny Everett and John Peel both played "Get Back" on their radio shows before the official release date of 11 April.

9 Ringo was present for the boat-race scene filmed at the Barclays Bank rowing club on the Embankment.

11 "Get Back" with "Don't Let Me Down" on the B-side was released in the UK on Apple (Parlophone) R 5777. Some shops were late in receiving copies due to the extra mixing session.

12 A further extract of George's interview with David Wigg was broadcast on *Scene and Heard*. John and Yoko were at the offices of Henry Ansbacher & Co to attend a financial meeting.

By Beatle standards, a quiet affair

IT was, by Beatle standards, a quiet affair. Only a handful of fans turned up to sob in the rain as Paul McCartney wed yesterday.

They were vastly outnumbered outside Marylebone Register Office by more than 200 photographers.

Paul's marriage to 27-year-old New Yorker Linda Eastman was held up for 45 minutes by the late arrival of his brother, Mike McGear, of the Scaffold group.

The train from Birmingham, explained Mr McGear, had broken down.

Miss Eastman, whose first marriage was dissolved, wore a bright yellow coat over a fawn dress. Her six - year - old daughter, Heather, carried a posy of freesias.

Paul, 26, wore a formal black suit, a white shirt and a wide yellow tie.

After the ceremony the newlyweds returned to Paul's home in St. John's Wood. Two hours later they slipped out, unnoticed, to be blessed by the local rector.

The Rev. Noel Perry-Gore, of St. John's Wood Parish Church, explained : 'Paul rang last week and asked me to bless the marriage. It was a very simple ceremony.'

Back home, Paul and his bride talked for the first time about their love and their life together.

Paul said : 'We decided about a week ago to get married. We thought : "Instead of talking about it, let's do it".'

Miss Eastman, who has worked as a photographer, killed rumours that she was an Eastman-Kodak photographic company heiress. 'I have nothing to do with them,' she said.

At which Paul protested, jokingly : 'I've been done. Where's the money ?'

How did the couple meet ?

Paul explained : 'I saw her fleetingly at Press conferences and I couldn't help noticing her. One night we went out on the thrash.'

Did they want a family ? Yes, said Paul.

How large ? 'Six foot six inches.'

Paul said he invited his father, who lives at Wirral, Cheshire, to the wedding, but he had flu.

Miss Eastman wore a £12 wedding ring which Paul bought on Tuesday 'just before the shop shut.'

There will be no honeymoon. Last night Paul attended a recording session.

Words: DOUGLAS MARLBOROUGH and PHILIP WHITFIELD

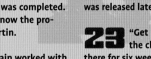

Paul, how COULD you . . . fans lament the loss of the last unwed Beatle

ABOVE AND OPPOSITE: **The crowds outside the register office comprised mostly photographers and the most die-hard fans. Newspapers wrongly reported Linda as the "Kodak girl", referring to the widespread belief that she was the wealthy heiress to the Eastman-Kodak photography company. Paul laughed about this mistake after the wedding. "I've been done", he joked. "Where's the money?"**

13 The *Sunday Times* published an article criticizing Allen Klein.

14 Paul and John recorded "The Ballad of John and Yoko". They were joined by George Martin and Geoff Emerick and had a very successful day in the studio, which was now becoming a rare event.

15 George's interview with David Wigg was broadcast on a repeat of *Scene and Heard*. John and Yoko were again at the offices of Henry Ansbacher & Co, this time taking Allen Klein with them.

16 George's "Old Brown Shoe" was recorded with vocal, guitar, and drum overdubs, and the first takes of "Something" were taped.

18 "Old Brown Shoe" was completed. Chris Thomas was now the producer instead of George Martin.

20 Chris Thomas again worked with the band on "I Want You" and "Oh! Darling".

21 John and Yoko's company, Bag Productions, was formed to publish books and release films.

22 John formally changed his middle name to Ono in a ceremony conducted by the Commissioner of Oaths, Señor Bueno de Mesquita, on the roof of the Apple building. John and Yoko recorded their heartbeats for *The Wedding Album*, which was released later in the year.

23 "Get Back" reached the top of the charts in the UK, remaining there for six weeks.

24 Paul and John, aiming to gain full control of Northern Songs, made a counteroffer against ATV.

25 *Rape* premiered at the Montreux Film Festival.

26 Initial work on Ringo's "Octopus's Garden". He had written the song the previous summer when he temporarily left the band and took his family to Sardinia. While chatting to fishermen there, he found out how the octopuses picked up stones and objects from the seabed to build gardens. "Get Back"/"Don't Let Me Down" reached the top of the British charts, staying there for six weeks.

27 John remixed his and Yoko's heartbeats.

29 Chris Thomas and Ringo added vocals to "Octopus's Garden".

30 John and Paul worked together on "You Know My Name (Look Up the Number)", last taped a year earlier.

"Honeymooning down by the Seine"

John and Yoko travelled to Gibraltar via Paris on 20 March. Both were dressed from head to toe in white, making it difficult for the locals and tourists to miss the Rock's illustrious visitors. They had to be quick to catch a glimpse, however, for the couple were on the island barely an hour, just long enough for the registrar at the British Consulate to perform the ceremony.

After a traditional spot of "honeymooning down by the Seine", it was on to Amsterdam. Far from seeking privacy during their weeklong stay at the Hilton, they invited the media into the Presidential Suite, gaining worldwide publicity for their peace "bed-in".

Naturally, John wanted to put his artistic stamp on what he described as "a fantastic happening". In fact, the event was marked in two ways, one an avant-garde offering with Yoko as collaborator, the other a barnstorming pop song, a brilliant John and Paul two-hander.

The Wedding Album was a souvenir box set that included all manner of memorabilia, including a photocopy of their marriage certificate, press cuttings, and a plastic bag to promote "Bagism"—communicating from within a sack in order to focus on the message rather than the messenger. The A-side of the accompanying disc consisted of John and Yoko calling out each other's names in a variety of registers.

MAY 1969

1 Stereo mixing for "Oh! Darling" and "The Ballad of John and Yoko". A new label, Zapple, was created to focus on more experimental music.

2 John and Yoko were interviewed for *How Late It Is* at Lime Grove Studios in London and discussed their film, *Rape*, with Michael Wale. The band continued to work on "Something". ATV declared that their share offer was still on the table, which created a 9-pence-a-share rise in price.

4 John, Paul, and Ringo attended the private end-of-shoot party for *The Magic Christian* at Les Ambassadeurs, London. Some footage filmed at the party was shown in the documentary *Will the Real Mr. Sellers...*, which was to be broadcast in December.

5 "Get Back" with "Don't Let Me Down" on the B-side was released in the US on Apple (Capitol) 2490. Overdubs were recorded for "Something" at Olympic Studios. John purchased Tittenhurst Park, Ascot.

6 Paul's ballad "You Never Give Me Your Money" was recorded for the *Abbey Road* album. The lyrics penned by Paul referred to the band's money issues at the time, and in particular Allen Klein's management of their finances. The US took away John's visa due to his drug charge the previous year.

7 All four were at the stereo-mixing session at Olympic Studios with Glyn Johns. Accompanied by Allen Klein, John and Paul attended a meeting with Sir Joseph Lockwood from EMI. Their request for an increase in royalty payments was refused.

8 It was John and Yoko's turn to be interviewed by David Wigg for *Scene and Heard*. An agreement was signed by George, John, and Ringo with ABKCO, letting Allen Klein take 20 percent of the band's earnings.

9 John and Yoko's album *Unfinished Music No 2: Life with the Lions* was released in Britain. George released his second solo LP, *Electric Sound*, in the UK. During a session with Glyn Johns at Olympic, the rest of the band tried to make Paul sign the agreement with ABKCO; he refused, and after the meeting stayed behind to record "My Dark Hour".

11 An extract of John and Yoko's interview with David Wiggs was broadcast on *Scene and Heard*.

The *Wedding Album* sank without trace in the UK and just made the Top 200 on the US chart. John's 45-rpm commemoration of his nuptials, on the other hand, gave the Beatles their seventeenth and last chart topper in their home market. The group hadn't recorded together for almost two months when John set to music the fraught circumstances surrounding his wedding in "The Ballad of John and Yoko". Neither George nor Ringo was available when he wanted to record the song, and John called a truce with Paul. The song was recorded and mixed in a single session, John and Paul sharing the instrumental and vocal load. At one point, when Paul was on drums and John on lead guitar, the latter cried out: "Go a bit faster, Ringo!", which received the swift riposte, "Okay, George."

The BBC had slapped a ban on the song because of the Christ reference, but it made little difference. Just one week after "Get Back" had been knocked off the No. 1 spot in the UK, "The Ballad of John and Yoko" put them back on top. Restricted air play in the States had a greater effect and the song stalled at No. 8.

OPPOSITE: **After getting married at the British Consulate in Gibraltar on 20 March, John and Yoko left for a brief honeymoon in Paris before heading to Amsterdam, where they staged a weeklong "bed-in" at the Hilton Hotel. The message was to "stay in bed and grow your hair", which was part of their antiwar campaign.**

RIGHT: **Wearing matching attire, John and Yoko return to the UK as a married couple. After the bed-in in Amsterdam they attended the premiere of their new film, *Rape*.**

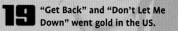

Yoko gets her man in just three minutes

From Daily Mail Correspondent
GIBRALTAR, Thursday

JAPANESE actress Yoko Ono, 34, took Beatle John Lennon, MBE, for her third husband to-day — in three minutes flat.

Their marriage, behind the locked doors of Gibraltar's back - street register office, was sealed just after 9 a.m.

An hour later they were back aboard the chartered jet which had flown them to the Rock from Paris, where they will spend their honeymoon.

Mr Lennon, 28—whose first marriage was dissolved last year—told reporters: 'We want some peace and quiet.'

Miss Ono, previously married to a Japanese composer and then to American film producer Anthony Cox, by whom she has a six-year-old daughter, said nothing.

The build-up to the wedding —the second for a Beatle in eight days—began at Gibraltar Airport at 8.30 when their plane touched down.

With their two witnesses, Peter Brown, the Beatles' personal assistant, and photo-

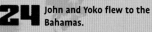

After the wedding—Mr and Mrs Lennon.

grapher David Nutter, they took a car to the register office.

There, the registrar, Mr Cecil Wheeler, performed the special licence ceremony.

The bride and groom both wore white, including white tennis shoes.

Back in Paris, Mr Lennon said that he had not told the other Beatles: 'We never tell each other what we are doing. They are a loud-mouthed lot, like everybody else, you know.'

Before we went to his hotel he told reporters: 'I may have a big surprise for you on Monday.' But he gave no details.

---

13 A repeat of John and Yoko's interview with David Wiggs was broadcast on *Scene and Heard*. A session with photographer Angus McBean was held at the EMI office in Manchester Square, London, to produce cover shots for the *Get Back* album.

15 While back in Liverpool visiting family, Paul was interviewed by Roy Corlett from Radio Merseyside.

16 Several of the personnel from *The Magic Christian*, includ-ing Ringo and Peter Sellers, were given a trip on the *Queen Elizabeth II*, which left Southampton that day. Paul's interview with Roy Corlett was broadcast on the programme *Light and Local*. John was at the US Embassy trying to gain a visa for the US.

17 Paul and Linda announced that she was expecting a baby before they set off for a holiday in France.

18 A colour version of *All My Loving*, featuring interviews with Paul and Ringo, was broadcast on BBC2. This was a repeat of the transmission from November 1968 that was originally broadcast in black and white. The second extract of John and Yoko's interview with David Wiggs was broadcast on *Scene and Heard*. "Get Back" was given a gold disc in the States.

19 "Get Back" and "Don't Let Me Down" went gold in the US.

20 A repeat of the second extract from John and Yoko's interview with David Wiggs was broadcast on *Scene and Heard*.

21 The formal announcement was made that Allen Klein would manage the Beatles' business affairs.

22 The *Queen Elizabeth II*, with Ringo and his party on board, arrived in New York. "Hey Jude" received an award for Best-Selling A-side of 1968 at the 14th Ivor Novello Awards.

23 "Get Back" by the Beatles with Billy Preston went to No. 1 in the US, remaining there for five weeks. Only he and Tony Sheridan ever shared a label billing with the band.

24 John and Yoko flew to the Bahamas.

26 John and Yoko's album *Unfinished Music No 2: Life with*

the Lions was issued in the US on the same day that they began their second "bed-in" for peace in room 1742 at the Queen Elizabeth Hotel in Montreal, Canada. George released his second solo LP, *Electronic Sound*, in the US.

28 Glyn Johns finalized the work on *Get Back*—an album that was never released. A variation, *Let It Be*, was eventually issued.

30 "The Ballad of John and Yoko", backed by George's "Old Brown Shoe", was released in the UK on Apple (Parlophone) R5786.

Eastman vs. Klein

By the end of 1968 the accountants made it clear that not even Apple Music could prop up the company's loss-making divisions indefinitely. It was one of the few things the Beatles could agree on. "Apple wasn't being run, it was being run into the ground", said Ringo. John bemoaned the fact that he was down to his last £50,000 in hard cash and said they would all be broke within six months. That might have been an exaggeration, but the situation was undoubtedly serious. From the start the Beatles had been bankrolling a well-intentioned but ailing concern, and it couldn't go on.

If there was consensus over the diagnosis, there was a schism regarding the treatment. Linda's father, Lee Eastman, was a top lawyer specializing in the entertainment field. He sent his college-graduate son John on a scouting mission to assess the nature and extent of the problem. A major excision exercise was suggested, cutting out the frippery and focusing on the profitable core business. Eastman Jr. also recommended that the Beatles buy out NEMS—which took a mighty 25 percent top slice—and wrest control of their back catalogue. Clive Epstein was keen to sell, and the million-pound cost could be borne by EMI, a loan guaranteed against future earnings. It made sense, but the battle lines were being drawn up. John thought Paul's relationship with Linda would give him an unfair shake of the dice, and besides, he had someone else in mind to fight his corner.

JUNE 1969

Allen Klein had forged an impressive track record in the entertainment business, earning himself the sobriquet "The Robin Hood of Pop" for renegotiating artists' contracts to their advantage or finding discrepancies in existing deals that just happened to be in the record company's favour. John's jaw had dropped when he learned of the $1.25 million advance Klein obtained from Decca on the Rolling Stones' behalf, a deal that cast many of Brian Epstein's efforts in a poor light. Had John been aware that the money found its way into the account of a Klein-owned company and became the subject of a legal wrangle between the Stones and their manager, he might have been less enthusiastic about doing business with him.

For some time Klein had been tracking the Beatles, looking for a way in. And in January 1969 the door swung open invitingly. John's public pronouncement regarding the parlous state of Apple's finances drew him like a moth to a flame.

The two men hit it off immediately. Klein played on the fact that he was an orphan who made good. He was a tough-talking street fighter whose speech was peppered with expletives. His sloppy attire set him apart from the suited clones of the business world, whose number included the suave preppie John Eastman. It all resonated with John, who was also flattered by the fact that Klein had mugged up on the Beatles' history and catalogue. Tactically, the coup de grace was the wooing of Yoko, Klein including support for her projects in his pitch.

The upshot was a memo to the EMI chairman: "Dear Sir Joe, From now on Allen Klein handles all my stuff". John's recollection of the actual wording may have been slightly out, but the thrust was clear. George and Ringo also swung behind Klein, which marked a major turning point. Until now the Beatles had had a Musketeer philosophy: Unanimity was required in decision making, and any one person had the right of veto. Not anymore. The majority vote counted, and Paul was left out on a limb.

OPPOSITE AND BELOW: **John and Yoko discuss their film, *Rape*, on the *Today* show with Eamonn Andrews. The concept of the film was to view media and press intrusion as a form of assault. The film simply consisted of a camera crew relentlessly following a girl but refusing to speak to her.**

1 The Plastic Ono Band recorded the peace anthem "Give Peace a Chance" during their Canadian "bed-in".

2 "New Day"/"Thumbing a Ride" by Jackie Lomax was released as a single in the US. The B-side was produced by Paul the day before he got married. The Lennons flew back to the UK.

4 "The Ballad of John and Yoko" was released in America on Apple (Capitol) 2531.

5 Clips of John and Yoko in various cities were shown on *Top of the Pops* to accompany "The Ballad of John and Yoko".

12 The film clips of John and Yoko were repeated on *Top of The Pops* with "The Ballad of John and Yoko".

14 In front of a studio audience, John and Yoko recorded an interview with David Frost at Stonebridge House, Wembley, for his new weekly US television series *The David Frost Show*. They were also interviewed for a Radio Luxembourg show during the day. "The Ballad of John and Yoko"/"Old Brown Shoe" went to No. 1 in the British charts, holding the position for three weeks.

16 "The Ballad of John and Yoko" was certified gold in the States.

18 Paul celebrated his 27th birthday.

22 John and Yoko's interview was broadcast on Radio Luxembourg as part of *The David Christian Show*.

26 *Top of the Pops* repeated the previous film clips of John and Yoko when playing "The Ballad of John and Yoko".

27 Maureen and Ringo set off for a break in France.

29 John and Yoko travelled to Scotland for a holiday.

Slicing the Beatles cake

Allen Klein cut a deal that gave him 20 percent of any income he generated on the Beatles' behalf, and he set about a lucrative belt-tightening exercise with gusto. He didn't just have the in-house cordon-bleu chefs and gargantuan hospitality bill in his sights, nor the offices decked out with genuine antiques and works of art. He was also gunning for the men who might pose a personal threat. Alistair Taylor, the man who accompanied Epstein on that historic first visit to the Cavern to watch the Beatles perform, was one of the first out the door. Ron Kass, "Magic Alex", Dennis O'Dell, and Derek Taylor all went the same way. Peter Asher jumped

before he was pushed, taking James Taylor with him. Peter Brown lasted until the next annual board meeting. Resignation followed by reappointment was usually a formality, but by no means a certainty, as Brown found to his cost. As each one left, another Apple division closed, another millstone lifted from the corporate shoulders. Only Neil Aspinall was to survive long-term.

Klein stripped away a lot of dead wood and negotiated a much improved royalty deal with EMI—earning grudging praise from Paul—but had less success when it came to acquiring control of NEMS. Clive Epstein wanted to sell but had become exasperated by the delay and infuriated by a letter from John Eastman questioning the

LEFT AND ABOVE: **Pursuing his interest in acting, Ringo costarred in *The Magic Christian* with Peter Sellers, filming taking place in the early part of the year. Ringo's character, Youngman Grand, did not feature in Terry Southern's original novel but was written exclusively for the film. In the comedy, Sellers's character, Sir Guy Grand, shows his son, Youngman Grand, the humiliating lengths people will go to to get their hands on money. Paul wrote the theme song, "Come and Get It", which was performed by Badfinger, a band signed to the Apple label.**

OPPOSITE: **In keeping with the film's message about the acquisition of wealth, money is callously thrown around the room during the party to celebrate the end of filming. The money could be instantly spotted as fake—not least because Sellers and Ringo appeared on the notes. The wrap-up party was held at a Mayfair gaming club, and the money was for exclusive use in the club casino.**

JULY 1969

1 The first day back in the studio to record the *Abbey Road* album, although Paul was the only band member present. John had been in a road accident with Yoko, her daughter Kyoko, and his son Julian while travelling in Golspie, Scotland. They were taken to Lawson Memorial Hospital.

2 Paul, George, and Ringo recorded "Golden Slumbers"/"Carry That Weight".

3 Further work on "Golden Slumbers"/ "Carry That Weight".

4 "Give Peace a Chance" backed with Yoko's "Remember Love" was released by the Plastic Ono Band as a single worldwide—the first solo single by one of the Beatles. Work on "Golden Slumbers"/"Carry That Weight" was combined with listening to the Wimbledon ladies' final, when Ann Jones beat Billie Jean King.

6 John came out of hospital following the car accident earlier in the week.

7 Paul, George, and Ringo spent the day working on George's "Here Comes the Sun" as Ringo celebrated his 29th birthday. A press launch was held at the Chelsea Town Hall for the Plastic Ono Band, but without John and Yoko due to their injuries.

8 Vocals were overdubbed onto "Here Comes the Sun".

9 John returned to the studio after his car accident and worked with the other band members on "Maxwell's Silver Hammer", written about a homicidal maniac.

continued from previous page

JULY 1969

10 John and Yoko's interview with David Frost was broadcast in the US on his new television series, *The David Frost Show*. Guitar and vocal parts were over-dubbed onto "Maxwell's Silver Hammer".

11 Further overdubbing to "Maxwell's Silver Hammer" before moving on to "You Never Give Me Your Money".

12 Several US radio stations banned "The Ballad of John and Yoko" due to lyrics that were considered to be blasphemous.

15 Two studios were used to add further pieces to "You Never Give Me Your Money"—this was a clear indication that differences between the band members continued to intensify.

16 Still using two studios, the band developed "Here Comes the Sun" and "Something". "The Ballad of John and Yoko" was given a gold disc in the States.

17 Paul worked independently on "Oh! Darling", then the rest of the session was assigned to "Octopus's Garden".

18 Still in two studios, Paul continued with "Oh! Darling" and Ringo added takes to "Octopus's Garden". Although stereo and mono mixes of the tracks were being made, the monos were never used: *Abbey Road* was their first album to be produced only in stereo. Carlos Mendez released "La Penina", written by John and Paul.

21 John and Geoff Emerick worked on "Come Together".

22 Paul continued his quest for the best version of "Oh! Darling".

propriety of the deal between NEMS and the Beatles. He didn't have to look far to find another willing buyer to Triumph Investments. Klein tried to put the screws to Triumph: sell, or he would drive a coach and horses through the contract NEMS had with the Beatles and they would pick up the tab. Triumph swatted him aside. The Beatles eventually bought themselves out of the deal with Triumph and freed themselves from NEMS, but they still didn't have ownership of their catalogue.

Since Epstein's death the Beatles had become openly hostile about the lousy deal that had made Dick James inordinately wealthy on their backs. James had had enough of that, and he also didn't like the way the wind was blowing. Nude record covers, drugs, Eastern mysticism, weird music—where would it end? He was thinking along the same lines as the Queen, who, at a Buckingham Palace reception, had remarked to Sir Joseph Lockwood that the Beatles were "turning awfully funny". Her Majesty didn't have a financial stake in them; James did. He wanted out, and on 28 March 1969 he sold his holding to media tycoon Sir Lew Grade of ATV.

Like Klein, Grade had wanted a piece of the Beatles' action for a long time. The piece wasn't big enough for majority control, but he let it be known that was his objective. The Beatles had a long-held antipathy for Grade and were determined to block the bid. When they counted up to see what shares they could muster between them, John discovered that Paul owned 751,000 to his 644,000. It wasn't a big deal now—they had bigger fish to fry—but down the line John would rail against Paul's clandestine activities, which he saw as an act of treachery.

A brutal PR war was waged between the Beatles and Grade's ATV. Both parties were after the crucial 14 percent holding of a City consortium. This group was on the verge of selling to the Beatles but changed their minds at the eleventh hour after a savage outburst by John: "I'm not going to be fucked around by men in suits sitting on their fat arses in the City." Grade won; the Beatles had their catalogue snatched from under their noses.

BELOW: **Yoko began to make her mark on the charts with "Give Peace a Chance", written by her and John (although it was still credited as Lennon–McCartney). The song was performed by an ad hoc group of musicians collectively titled the Plastic Ono Band. It was recorded in Montreal in May, while the couple were staging a bed-in at the Queen Elizabeth Hotel. When it was released in July, the song hit No. 2 in Britain and charted at No. 14 in America.**

OPPOSITE AND BELOW INSET: **Five-year-old Kyoko Cox flies into the UK from New York to be greeted by her mother and her new stepfather.**

23 "The End" was recorded, the last song on the last album that the group would produce.

24 Paul recorded "Come and Get It" as a demo for the Apple group Badfinger. It was to be the theme to *The Magic Christian*. Work on "Sun King"/ "Mean Mr. Mustard" then began.

25 Tracks were recorded for "Sun King"/"Mean Mr. Mustard", "Come Together", John's "Polythene Pam", and Paul's "She Came in Through

the Bathroom Window". The last two songs were penned in 1968, one about an original Cavern Club fan called Polythene Pat and the other about a fan who got into Paul's house and stole a photograph of his father; he had to negotiate with the fans who used to gather outside his house to get it back.

28 Vocals and instrumental parts were overdubbed onto "Polythene Pam" and "She Came in Through the Bathroom Window".

29 "Sun King"/"Mean Mr. Mustard" and "Come Together" continued to be developed.

30 This long session was mainly used to put all the songs for the album together.

31 The drums, timpani, and vocal overdubs were recorded for "Golden Slumbers"/"Carry That Weight".

Abbey Road

By the spring of 1969 it was all too painfully clear that getting back to where they once belonged was no panacea to the Beatles' ills. The prognosis was grim, and yet, in between solo projects and in-fighting about their business interests, there was still just enough goodwill left in the tank for one final hurrah. The *Get Back* tapes were a jumble that none of the Beatles could face unravelling. Much better to draw a line under that and move on, this time to make a well-crafted studio album. It took George Martin by surprise when Paul approached him with the idea. After having his nose put out of joint with the arrival of Glyn Johns on the scene, Martin thought he had produced his last Beatles album.

AUGUST 1969

1 The rhythm track of the harmonies for John's "Because" were taped. He had written the song while under the grip of heroin.

4 Final harmony recordings for "Because" were completed. George stereo-mixed "Here Comes the Sun" and "Something".

5 Using Dr. Robert Moog's synthesiser, they added overdubs to "Because".

6 Paul used the synthesiser to produce various takes of "Maxwell's Silver Hammer", while George worked separately with "Here Comes the Sun".

7 Further work and mixing on "Come Together" and "The End".

8 The familiar photograph by Iain Macmillan with the band walking across the zebra crossing outside the Abbey Road Studios in North London was taken for the *Abbey Road* cover. Afterwards work continued on "The End" and "I Want You" while Paul developed "Oh! Darling"

9 In Los Angeles the Manson "Family" murdered Sharon Tate, the pregnant wife of Roman Polanski, and four friends. Charles Manson believed that the Beatles were sending messages to him through their songs.

11 "I Want You" became "I Want You (She's So Heavy)" during the early part of this recording session.

12 "Maxwell's Silver Hammer" and "Oh! Darling" were mixed to stereo.

By no means was it all smooth sailing. There was enough discontent to indicate that the ultimate destination would be the divorce court. In April John had spoken enthusiastically about the song montage that would fill side two, but three months later, when the recording sessions began in earnest, his interest had waned. By keeping out of each other's way as much as possible, they held it together well enough to produce the dazzling album that, chronologically speaking, was their true swan song.

The majority of the songs featured on the album had surfaced during the *Get Back* sessions: Only "Come Together", "Here Comes the Sun", "Because", "You Never Give Me Your Money", and "The End" were written specifically for the new project. John's gorgeous ballad "Because" was written around the chord structure of Beethoven's *Moonlight Sonata*—played backwards. Its three-part harmony was redolent of "This Boy", though the warming image of John, Paul, and George huddled round a single microphone was a far cry from the truth. After laying down the basic rhythm tracks, the Beatles frequently dispersed to flesh the songs out. In that respect the scenario was similar to that which pertained during the *White Album* sessions. The difference was that the new work had a more unified, coherent feel than its predecessor. It was an illusion that worked only on vinyl. Within weeks of completing the new album, Paul was to discover that the days of having to "Carry That Weight" of keeping the band together were numbered.

THIS PAGE: **Yoko takes to her new estate, Tittenhurst Park, in Ascot, England. She and John moved in during the summer of 1969 after the sale of Kenwood, John and Cynthia's home. John and Yoko customized the house at great expense, building a man-made lake and a recording studio in the grounds. When they moved to America, Ringo bought the property and lived there until the 1980s.**

OPPOSITE LEFT: **Paul and Linda at the premiere of *Alfred the Great*, starring David Hemmings as Alfred.**

OPPOSITE RIGHT: **Feeling increasingly removed from the band, George returns from a break in Sardinia.**

13 Further stereo mixing; this time for "You Never Give Me Your Money".

14 Stereo mixing continued. Kenny Everett visited the studio to interview John for his radio show.

15 Professional musicians were in the studio to record the orchestral parts for the album. For the first time on a Beatles session, CCTV was used to link Studio One to Studio Two.

18 More stereo mixing for "Golden Slumbers"/"Carry That Weight".

19 "Here Comes the Sun" and "Something" were finished.

20 A studio session to finalize the running order of the album. Momentously, it was the last time all four Beatles were together inside Abbey Road.

21 "Sun King"/"Mean Mr. Mustard", "You Never Give Me Your Money", and "The End" were edited and completed.

22 The Beatles were photographed together for the last time at a photo session in the grounds of Tittenhurst Park—John and Yoko's home.

25 Various effects for the start of "Maxwell's Silver Hammer" were made during this session but never used. The final master for *Abbey Road* was produced.

26 George visited Bob Dylan at Forelands Farm, the Isle of Wight.

28 Linda and Paul's daughter, Mary, was born, weighing 6lb 8oz, at the Marie Louise Clinic in London. George attended a press conference for the Radha Krishna Temple in Sydenham, Kent.

29 The closure of Apple Electronics was announced.

31 Ringo, John, and George watched Bob Dylan at the Isle of Wight Festival.

"The greatest love song of the past fifty years"

Ever since the Beatles had signed with EMI, George had found himself squeezed by the gargantuan talents of Lennon and McCartney. The latter pair would invariably turn up for recording sessions with enough material to fill an album, leaving him struggling to get his songs aired. And even when he managed that, the approval rating tended to be low. On the ten album releases up to and including *Yellow Submarine*, George had notched just fourteen songwriting credits, while in the single stakes he had racked up only a couple of B-sides. In creative terms he was still the annoying kid brother who had to be tolerated and tossed the occasional few crumbs.

As a result, by the summer of '69 George had a lot of material in the bank. The stockpile included "All Things Must Pass", unveiled during the *Get Back* sessions but overlooked for both *Abbey Road* and *Let It Be*. George ruefully observed that "at the rate of two or three an album with the group, I'm not even going to get the ones I've already done out for three or four years".

With the cracks in the group growing ever wider, it became clear that he couldn't rely on drip-feeding his songs into the public domain via Beatles albums. George started planning a solo LP in October 1969, by which time he had finally emerged from John and Paul's shadow thanks to two superlative *Abbey Road* tracks. The joyously uplifting "Here Comes the Sun" was written in Eric Clapton's garden, whither George had gone to escape the tensions in the studio and the

ON STARTING OVER

"For me, that was the great thing about splitting up: to be able to go off and make my own record and record all those songs I'd been stockpiling. And also to be able to record with all these new people, which was like a breath of fresh air."

—George

SEPTEMBER 1969

1 Bob Dylan visited John at his home in Ascot.

2 George gave Bob Dylan a lift to Heathrow.

8 Ringo was rushed to the Middlesex Hospital with stomach problems.

10 The New Cinema Club held an evening of John and Yoko's films at the Institute of Contemporary Art, where a couple that might have been John and Yoko sat onstage inside a white bag during the show.

11 Malcolm Davies made a new mix of the "What's the New Mary Jane" tape for John, who was thinking of using it for the Plastic Ono band to record. Ringo was released from hospital with no further treatment needed.

12 John accepted an offer to play at the Toronto Rock 'n' Roll Revival Festival.

13 The Plastic Ono Band made their debut at the Varsity Stadium, Toronto. Together with John and Yoko, the lineup included Eric Clapton, Klaus

Voormann, and Alan White. John had already decided to leave the Beatles, but his news was kept quiet due to legal issues.

17 *The Times-Delphic* published at Drake University carried an article by Tim Harper suggesting that Paul had been killed on 9 November 1966 in a car crash in Scotland and had subsequently been replaced by a look-alike.

19 The late-night arts show *Late Night Line-Up* focused on the forthcoming release of *Abbey Road*. Paul was interviewed by David Wigg for *Scene and*

burdensome responsibilities of the corporate world. But it was "Something" that really made everyone sit up and take notice.

Regarded by Sinatra as "the greatest love song of the past fifty years", "Something" was conceived the previous year during the *White Album* sessions. The opening line may have been a lift from a James Taylor song, but George took it to a place that earned admiration, not censure or litigation. John became embroiled in a legal wrangle over some Chuck Berry lyrics that found their way into "Come Together", whereas Taylor was merely flattered that a few of his words, consciously or unconsciously, had turned up in such a stunning piece of work.

Not that George immediately recognized the quality of his Pattie-inspired love song. His long apprenticeship had rendered him diffident, more needful of approval than the senior songwriting partnership. Stand-in producer Chris Thomas

heaped praise on the song after he heard George tinkering with it at Abbey Road in summer '68, though that didn't stop Harrison from offering it to Joe Cocker.

As well as being the first Harrison A-side, "Something" became the only Beatles single to be released from an album already issued. Allen Klein maintained that decision had more to do with boosting George's career than Apple's coffers, though it sold enough copies to make the top five on both sides of the Atlantic. And it was extremely lucrative on a personal level, for George had just lost his songwriting contract and had set up his own company, Harrisongs, to publish his material. The numerous cover versions earned George plenty of money and an Ivor Novello Award, but doubtless he was most pleased by the fact that John and Paul both regarded "Something" as the stand-out track on *Abbey Road*.

OPPOSITE AND ABOVE: **George discovers new kindred spirits in the shape of a shaven-headed Hindu Sect called the Radha Krishna Temple. Unlike the Maharishi, the sect professed self-purification and shied away from material possession. Instead they preferred to cleanse themselves of all vice, such as drugs and eating meat. George was sympathetic to the cause but discovered he was unable to forgo cigarettes and alcohol. He was nevertheless attracted to the sect's concept of meditation, which emphasized chanting rather than silence. George began recording some of the chants and releasing them to the public. "Hare Krishna Mantra" became an unlikely success, charting in the Top 20 in the UK. John was also interested in the sect and allowed them to stay at his house until George found a home for them.**

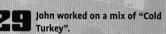

Heard. ATV finally gained a 50 percent share in Northern Songs.

20 The first part of Kenny Everett's interview with John was broadcast on his BBC1 Radio 1 programme *Everett Is Here*. At a meeting with Klein and the band, John announced his intention to leave the group. The band were voted best group in a poll carried out by *Melody Maker*.

21 The first extract of Paul's interview with David Wigg was transmitted on *Scene and Heard*.

22 Clips of John and Yoko in Paris, Amsterdam, Vienna, and at London Airport were shown in the US on the premiere edition of the ABC-TV series *Music Scene*.

25 John returned to the studio to work on tapes of the Plastic Ono band's concert in Toronto. The album was eventually released under the title *Live Peace in Toronto 1969*. Later that evening the band returned to the studio to record "Cold Turkey". John had written the song to describe the agony of trying to break his addiction to heroin. After gaining another

4 percent of shares, ATV took control as the major shareholders of Northern Songs.

26 *Abbey Road* was released in the UK on Apple (Parlophone) PCS 7088 (stereo only). The fact that Paul was dressed in black on the cover strengthened the rumour that he was dead.

27 The second extract from John's interview with Kenny Everett was broadcast on *Everett Is Here*.

28 The second part of Paul's interview to promote *Abbey Road* was

broadcast on *Scene and Heard*. The Plastic Ono band returned from Toronto and went back into the studio to record "Cold Turkey".

29 John worked on a mix of "Cold Turkey".

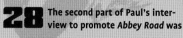

ABBEY ROAD

Released

🇬🇧 26 September 1969 Apple (Parlophone)

🇺🇸 1 October 1969 Apple (Capitol)

Side One:
Come Together
Something (Harrison)
Maxwell's Silver Hammer
Oh! Darling
Octopus's Garden (Starkey)
I Want You (She's So Heavy)

Side Two:
Here Comes the Sun (Harrison)
Because
You Never Give Me Your Money
Sun King
Mean Mr. Mustard
Polythene Pam
She Came in Through the Bathroom Window
Golden Slumbers
Carry That Weight
The End

ON JOHN

"By the time we made *Abbey Road*, John and I were openly critical of each other's music and I felt John wasn't much interested in performing anything he hadn't written himself."

—Paul

Cover story

The new album remained untitled for some considerable time, as was often the case with Beatles long-players. *"Everest"* emerged as a contender. It may have sprung from a prosaic source—the cigarette brand smoked by sound engineer Geoff Emerick—but it had magnitude. After all, the Beatles had scaled the highest peaks of the music industry. The idea was quickly dropped when a Himalayan photo shoot was mentioned, and in the end they opted for simplicity. In January, plans for a performance in an exotic location had given way to a rooftop set, and now they decided on the same tack with the album: call it *Abbey Road*, and do the cover shot on the studio's doorstep.

On the morning of 8 August the local police helpfully stopped the traffic so that photographer Iain Macmillan could mount his stepladder and shoot the Beatles as they filed over what would become the most famous zebra crossing in the world. This iconic image has been replicated by countless fans on pilgrimage to the sites of special significance in the group's career. An effort was made to remove the VW saloon, left of shot, but as there were Beetles before Beatles, it made for a nice visual touch.

OPPOSITE LEFT: **Yoko sports a plaster above her eye following a car crash in the north of Scotland. They were forced to miss a press launch for the Plastic Ono Band, but were lucky to have avoided more serious injuries.**

OPPOSITE ABOVE RIGHT: **John, George, Ringo, and their wives join the 150,000-strong crowd watching Bob Dylan perform at a music festival on the Isle of Wight at the end of August. After the show, Dylan accompanied the band by helicopter to John's house, Tittenhurst Park.**

OCTOBER 1969

1 *Abbey Road* was released in the US on Apple (Capitol) SO-383 (stereo only).

2 George Martin worked in the studio to add wildlife sounds and the noise of children playing to "Across the Universe", recorded the previous year. It was to be the initial track on the wildlife charity album *No One's Gonna Change Our World*.

3 Yoko's "Don't Worry Kyoko (Mummy's Only Looking for Her Hand in the Snow)" was recorded—it was to be the flip side to "Cold Turkey".

4 *Abbey Road* went straight to No. 1 in the UK album charts, staying there for 11 weeks.

5 Apple distributed a colour film to promote "Cold Turkey". It included scenes from John and Yoko's Canadian bed-in and footage shot at the Plastic Ono Band's concert in Toronto. Further mixing for the band's forthcoming single continued in the studio.

6 The single "Something"/"Come Together" was released in the US on Apple (Capitol) 2654.

8 George was interviewed by David Wigg and discussed his single "Hare Krishna Mantra", made by the Radha Krishna Temple.

9 John celebrated his 29th birthday.

10 A repeat of the arts show *Late Night Line-Up* was broadcast on BBC2.

12 The first extract of George's interview with David Wigg was transmitted on the BBC Radio 1 series *Scene and*

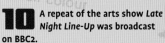

LEFT: **Ringo and Maureen in 1969.** Ringo had come a long way from his humble Liverpool origins. He now had three properties in wealthy suburbs near London, including the latest: a seven-bedroom mansion in Kenwood.

ON THE NEW ALBUM

"I thought it would be good to go out—the shitty version—because it would break the Beatles. It would break the myth: 'That's us with no trousers on and no glossy paint over the cover and no sort of hope'... but that didn't happen. We ended up making *Abbey Road* quickly and putting out something slick to preserve the myth."

—John

Heard. Mary Hopkin held her first concert at the Savoy Theatre, London, with Paul and Ringo there to support her. Yoko suffered another miscarriage.

15 "Golden Slumbers"/"Carry That Weight" was released in America. Ringo and Maureen flew to Los Angeles to attend a Vietnam "Moratorium" in the States.

19 The second part of George's interview was broadcast on *Scene and Heard*.

20 "Cold Turkey"/"Don't Worry Kyoko (Mummy's Only Looking for Her Hand in the Snow)" by the Plastic Ono Band was released in the US. John and Yoko also issued the *Wedding Album* LP in the US. Back in the studio, "Don't Worry Kyoko" was mixed again.

21 Another interview by David Wigg—this time with John.

22 Paul announced publicly that he was very much alive.

23 Vic Lewis issued an orchestral album of Beatles covers called *Beatles My Way* on the NEMS record label.

24 "Cold Turkey"/"Don't Worry Kyoko (Mummy's Only Looking for Her Hand in the Snow)" by the Plastic Ono Band was released in the UK. Journalist Chris Drake travelled to Kintyre for an interview designed to scotch the rumour that Paul was dead.

26 An extract from John's interview with David Wigg was transmitted on *Scene and Heard*. Part of Chris Drake's

interview with Paul was heard on *The World This Weekend* on Radio 4.

27 The interview between Paul and Chris Drake was again broadcast on *The World This Weekend*. Ringo began his own studio album, *Sentimental Journey*. "Something"/"Come Together" and the album *Abbey Road* were certified gold in the States.

31 "Something"/"Come Together" was released in the UK on Apple (Parlophone) R5814.

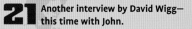

over 300,000 sold
throughout the world

**the gift book
of the season**

A collection of the 100 best Beatles lyrics
excitingly illustrated by Alan Aldridge and
other famous pop artists and photographers.
The Beatles own comments on how and
why they came to write the songs.
156 pages · 10½" x 8½"
Every page illustrated — 76 in full colour
Retail price **25/-**

The
Official
Beatles'
Fan Club

THIS PAGE: **John and Yoko took an increasing interest
in political and social issues. John holds up a copy of
his letter to Prime Minister Harold Wilson detailing
his reasons for returning his MBE. He outlined the
government's stance on the conflicts in Nigeria and
Vietnam as his chief complaints, but also added the poor
performance of his latest single to his list of grievences.
A similar letter was sent to the Queen together with
the medal itself. Although the medal could be returned,
the title itself could not be rescinded. John's Aunt
Mimi was furious with her nephew for returning such
a prestigious accolade.**

ABOVE INSET: **The Official Fan Club continued to operate
in 1969, although it began winding down as the decade
progressed and the fan base matured. The club outlasted
the breakup and continued to function until 1972.**

OPPOSITE: **A nonchalant Paul chats outside Apple's Savile
Row office.**

Speculation over Paul

That autumn the Abbey Road cover was used as prime facie "evidence" to support the theory that Paul was dead. It was a funeral procession, so the bizarre theory ran, and Paul was cast in the role of the departed. It stood to reason: Bare-footedness was a cosa nostra death sign, and the VW number plate was 281F—Paul would be twenty-eight if he were still alive.

The story gathered extraordinary momentum as fans scanned other sleeves, lyrics, and music—especially in reverse gear—looking for corroborating clues. Naturally, it became a self-fulfilling prophecy as the amateur detectives were determined not to disappoint themselves. Personal denials by the "deceased" carried no weight: it was a doppelgänger who had taken the summer stroll over the zebra crossing, and the double had slipped up by holding a cigarette in his right hand, something the left-handed Paul would never do, of course.

If an inconvenient detail came to light—such as the fact that Paul was actually twenty-seven—it was ignored or massaged away. In the case of the VW plate, someone pointed out that in the Hindu tradition the day of delivery was counted as the first birthday, which neatly plugged a mathematical hole in the theory.

The impetus may have come from students with too much time on their hands, but the conspiracy eventually became the subject of serious reportage. It was discussed over the airwaves in Detroit, and a mock trial on the issue was held on primetime TV in America. A journalist from *Life* magazine door-stepped an irate Paul on his Scottish farm to ascertain if this was indeed the real "Macca".

The VW owner discovered that being captured on a Beatles album cover and bound up in a conspiracy theory was a mixed blessing. The celebrated number plate became a regular target for trophy hunters. On the other hand, the eighteen-year-old vehicle would hardly have fetched £2,300 at Sothebys in 1986 had it not been parked near the Abbey Road zebra crossing on 8 August 1969.

ON ABBEY ROAD

"John Lennon has said that *Abbey Road* is an attempt to get away from experimentation and back to genuine rock 'n' roll. When one is as inventive as the Beatles, to try non-experimentation is a forlorn hope."

—William Mann, *The Times*

John goes cold turkey

During 1969 the law of diminishing returns set in regarding John's commitment to the Beatles. With every recording session the urge to break away gathered strength. The music was by now largely unrewarding, mostly irrelevant. Far from seeing side two of *Abbey Road* as some kind of inspired pop symphony, John dismissed Paul's brainchild as a ragbag of incomplete oddments. Far more fulfilling and meaningful were the events and happenings of his non-Beatle existence: the peace campaign, bed-ins, Bagism, art exhibitions, and sound mosaics. In short, his all-consuming passion for Yoko had supplanted his love of being a Beatle. George, who found Yoko's presence in the studio the most stifling, felt that she was steering John away from the band, and it seemed he was only too happy to be led.

In the summer of 1969, two events made John even more certain that when it came to music there was more to life than being "sidemen for Paul". "Give Peace a Chance", recorded on 1 June during the Montreal bed-in, gave John his first solo hit. There was none of the eccentricity or self-indulgence that went into the making of *Two Virgins* or *The Wedding Album*. This was a classic Lennon anthem, a direct descendant of "All You Need Is Love". It reached No. 2 in the UK chart and was a Top 20 hit in the States, further evidence to support Yoko's belief that John's genius would truly flourish outside the restrictive confines of the group. The Plastic Ono Band may have been a notional concept, with no members as such, but it was emblematic. The fact remained that while the Beatles were putting the finishing touches to *Abbey Road*, John was having mainstream success with another group.

LEFT AND ABOVE: **John and Yoko with the parents of James Hanratty. Fellow campaigner Edith Whicher stands to the right (above).**

NOVEMBER 1969

1 *Abbey Road* went to the top of the US charts, remaining there for eight weeks.

6 The promotional film for "Cold Turkey", with scenes from John and Yoko's Canadian bed-in and footage of the Plastic Ono Band's concert in Toronto, was shown on *Top of the Pops*. Ringo continued to work on *Sentimental Journey*.

7 John and Yoko's third experimental LP, *The Wedding Album*, was released in the UK, comprising audio highlights from their bed-in of March 1969. Ringo continued to work on his album in the studio. Paul and Linda were shown on the cover of *Life* magazine.

13 A promotional clip for "Something" was broadcast on *Top of the Pops*. The film showed each member of the band walking round in a beautiful country garden with his respective wife.

14 A further session on Ringo's *Sentimental Journey*.

BRITAIN MURDERED HANRATTY

ABOVE: **John and Yoko practise what they preach by covering themselves completely in a bag. The concept, called Bagism, argued that if everybody lived in a bag, then nobody would be able to make preconceived judgments about a person's physical characteristics.**

LEFT AND BELOW; OPPOSITE TOP: **John and Yoko take up the cause of James Hanratty, who had been hanged in 1962 for the murder of a scientist. Many people believed Hanratty was wrongfully executed, and his murder served to galvanize campaigners for the abolition of the death penalty. Capital punishment was suspended for five years in 1965, and John and Yoko became involved with the movement just as the legislation came up for renewal in 1969.**

25 In a bid to gain more coverage of his peace campaign, John returned his MBE to Buckingham Palace. He gave a succession of interviews to a number of journalists including BBC's David Bellan.

26 John's interview with David Bellan was broadcast on Radio 4's programme *Today*. In the studio,

John worked with Geoff Emerick on "What's the New Mary Jane" and "You Know My Name (Look Up the Number)"—his aim was to issue the two as the Plastic Ono Band's next single. They were finished by the end of the session but never actually released.

28 Further work on Ringo's *Sentimental Journey* album.

29 In the States *Billboard* changed its chart-compilation system by ranking both sides of double-sided hits in the same position. As a result, "Come Together" and "Something" both moved to the top of the chart for one week.

The Plastic Ono Band

On 13 September the Plastic Ono Band performed in public for the first time. At short notice, John had been invited to appear at the Toronto Rock 'n' Roll Revival Festival, on the same bill as a number of the Beatles' heroes: Gene Vincent, Jerry Lee Lewis, Chuck Berry, and Little Richard. Ticket sales had been flagging, and the desperate promoter chanced his arm and approached a Beatle, the ultimate rescue package.

An ad-hoc band comprising Klaus Voormann, Eric Clapton, and top session drummer Alan White was hastily assembled. They cobbled together a set consisting of a few old standards plus a new Lennon song, "Cold Turkey", which they vainly tried to rehearse while crossing the Atlantic. John was out of his comfort zone, gigging for the first time in three years and without the support of his familiar confederates. But the nerves dissipated when he took to the stage. Jamming rock 'n' roll classics gave him renewed thirst for playing live and a buzz that convinced him more than ever that he was finished with the Beatles.

"Cold Turkey", which John had put forward at a Beatles recording session, became the Plastic Ono Band's second single and another UK Top 20 hit. John was trying to get off heroin, and he decided he had had enough of the slow weaning process when it came to kicking the Beatles habit. "I want a divorce, just like the divorce I had from Cyn", he told the others on his return from Canada. Allen Klein had been in delicate contract talks with EMI and persuaded him to keep the lid on it for now. The only thing left to decide was the timing of the split, and who would go public first.

THIS PAGE AND OPPOSITE: **War Is Over. That was the message propounded by John and Yoko at the Plastic Ono Band's Peace for Christmas concert, given at the Lyceum Ballroom in London on 15 December. The hastily assembled band included George as well as Eric Clapton and Keith Moon of the Who. The concert was given in aid of UNICEF and was recorded live by EMI.**

DECEMBER 1969

1 A film documentary about Ringo was shot in various London locations and included footage taken in the back of his car. George watched Delaney and Bonnie at the Royal Albert Hall; also appearing was a group called Friends, led by Eric Clapton.

2 Desmond Morris interviewed John in the grounds of his home at Tittenhurst. Morris had nominated John as the person he felt should be the "man of the decade" for an ATV programme due to

be screened at the end of December. Ironically, during this interview the BBC filmed John for their *24 Hours* documentary *The World of John and Yoko*. Eric Clapton persuaded George to join the Delaney and Bonnie tour and play with the Friends group; it was his chance to play onstage again in virtual anonymity.

3 The BBC continued to film John and Yoko for four more days. Astutely, the couple made a contract with the BBC to return all the footage for their sole use in

the future. George was onstage at the Town Hall in Birmingham.

4 Orchestral pieces were added to "Blue Turning Grey Over You", then Ringo added vocals before it was mixed. George played two houses at the City Hall in Sheffield. The BBC continued to film John and Yoko, this time in a Plastic Ono Band recording session when recordings of laughing and shouting and then whispering were made and mixed together.

"The party's over," says Paul

By the end of 1969 it dawned on Paul that John's decision to quit the Beatles was more than just a brief time-out, a cooling-off period. If it was indeed the end, then McCartney—prolific writer, multi-instrumentalist, great singer, and driven perfectionist—was best equipped to succeed on his own. His desire to keep the Beatles together stopped him from turning his thoughts towards solo projects, and he spent the last weeks of the year in a solemn, reflective mood. Sooner or later, however, his extraordinary creativity would have to be channelled somewhere.

Ringo and George appeared to be finding the transition easier to deal with. In late October Ringo sprinted out of the blocks by starting work on an album of classics from the pre–rock 'n' roll era, an idea that had been fermenting for some time. With the help of George Martin and some of the best arrangers in the business, Ringo crooned his way into the record books with *Sentimental Journey*, becoming the first Beatle to cut a full-blown studio album. George, meanwhile, was busy producing Billy Preston and trying to promote the career of American backing singer Doris Troy, whom he had signed to Apple. Like John and Ringo, he also got a taste of life as

a solo performer when he guested on a Delaney and Bonnie tour at the end of the year.

Which left Paul. His suggestion that the Beatles should go on the road again, playing small venues, had fallen on stony ground. It hit him hard, but around Christmastime he responded to the situation in the way he knew best: by starting work on a solo album of his own. Paul chose not to publicize the venture. He had a four-track recording facility at home, and when he did book an Abbey Road session, he did so under an assumed name. All four were now immersed in their own projects, and even Paul thought it was now time to admit that the

continued from previous page

DECEMBER 1969

5 George played two more shows at the City Hall in Newcastle-upon-Tyne, while John and Yoko were the subject of further filming for the *24 Hours* production. Back in the studio "Revolution" and "Hey Jude" were mixed for the album *Hey Jude* to be released by Capitol.

6 Ringo appeared with Peter Sellers and Spike Milligan on *Frost on Saturday* to advertise *The Magic Christian*, due for release five days later. It was the last day of filming for *The World of John and Yoko*. George returned to Liverpool to play at the Empire Theatre.

7 On the BBC1 religious series *The Question Why*, chaired by Malcolm Muggeridge, John and Yoko took part in

a live debate about evil. George played the last British tour date at the Fairfield Hall, Croydon.

8 *Will the Real Mr. Sellers...* was transmitted. The documentary, produced by Denis O'Dell and directed by Tommy Palmer, was made just after the filming of *The Magic Christian*. Vocal overdubs were added to "Octopus's Garden".

OPPOSITE AND ABOVE: **Filming George Martin's *With a Little Help from My Friends*. Ringo with Lulu, Spike Milligan, Dudley Moore, and the Hollies. Ringo performed the title song.**

RIGHT: **John and Yoko took their antiwar message to Canada just before Christmas. On 23 December the couple were granted a meeting with the Prime Minister, Pierre Trudeau. It was the first time they were able to discuss their pacifist message directly with a world leader.**

10 The documentary filmed earlier in the month with Ringo talking at length to Tony Bilbow took up the whole edition of the BBC2 arts series *Line-Up*. John and Yoko met the parents of James Hanratty; they were planning to make a film that could prove his innocence. George played for three more evenings on the tour at the Falkoner Theatre in Copenhagen, Denmark.

11 The royal world charity premiere of *The Magic Christian* took place at the Odeon Kensington, London. Ringo attended with his wife, Maureen, while John and Yoko protested about James Hanratty's 1962 execution outside the cinema.

12 The World Wildlife Fund charity record, *No One's Gonna Change Our World*, was released. The LP opened with the Beatles song "Across the Universe".

The Plastic Ono Band released the album *Live Peace in Toronto*.

14 George Martin's film *With a Little Help from My Friends* was shot in the studios of Yorkshire Television. John and Yoko protested silently inside a white bag at Speakers' Corner, Marble Arch, over the hanging of James Hanratty.

15 *The World of John and Yoko* documentary, introduced by David Dimbleby, was screened on the BBC series *24 Hours*. The Plastic Ono Band's performance in a live charity concert for UNICEF at the Lyceum Ballroom was taped. Titled Peace For Christmas, the special band line up included George, Billy Preston, and Eric Clapton. Glyn Johns was once again asked to produce a new album. Ringo recorded a radio appeal on behalf of the British Wireless for the Blind Fund.

Beatles were no more. Early in 1970 he called John to inform him that he was leaving the group. "Good", came the reply. "That makes two of us who have accepted it mentally".

Hidebound by business concerns, they couldn't simply shake hands and go their separate ways. In fact, they were on a collision course. During the making of his eponymous debut album, Paul discovered that Phil Spector had been given carte blanche to salvage a record from the wreckage of the *Get Back* sessions. Paul was incandescent at the thought of a third party being given licence to roam over his work, and insult was added to injury when he was told the release date for his album would have to be put back to accommodate the butchery.

continued from previous page

DECEMBER 1969

16 John and Yoko flew to Toronto for a brief holiday.

17 Tapes of the Plastic Ono Band's Lyceum Concert were mixed at Abbey Road by Geoff Emerick, although they were not released until 1972. John announced his intention to hold a peace festival in Toronto.

18 Recordings from the end-of-shoot party for *The Magic Christian* were broadcast on BBC 1's *Will the Real Mr. Sellers....*

19 The flexi-disc for members of the Beatles fan club, *The Beatles Seventh Christmas Record*, was released. The back cover featured a drawing by Ringo's young son Zak.

20 In Canada John was filmed for CBS-TV talking to Marshall McLuhan, author of *The Medium Is the Message*. Afterwards he appeared live on CBC Weekend being interviewed by Lloyd Robertson.

21 A studio session of mixing and editing for *Get Back* by Glyn Johns at the Olympic Sound Studios in Barnes, London.

John and George sent him a note to explain the predicament: "It's stupid for Apple to put out two big albums within seven days of each other, so we sent a letter to EMI telling them to hold your release date. It's nothing personal."

To Paul this was beyond the pale. He insisted that EMI stick to their original agreement with him, neither side showing the slightest inclination to move one inch. Ringo was cast in the role of peacemaking envoy, dispatched to St. John's Wood to try and build bridges. For his conciliatory pains he received a tongue-lashing from Paul.

Paul pulled the rug from under the others by issuing a Q and A insert in the liner notes for his album, which was released three weeks before *Let It Be.* By then the news that Paul was quitting had already been splashed over the front pages. It was the news John in particular wanted to hear, though the other Beatles were exasperated by the timing. The suggestion was that the media-savvy Paul had once again demonstrated his flair for promotion. Paul denied that it was a cynical piece of opportunism on his part, or that he was responsible for the split. "I didn't leave the Beatles. The Beatles have left the Beatles, but no one wants to be the one to say the party's over."

OPPOSITE: **John and Yoko pass through Heathrow Airport on their way to Canada to deliver their peaceful message to the Canadian Prime Minister.**

LEFT: **Ringo was increasingly occupied by solo projects. After completing *The Magic Christian*, he began work on a solo album, *Sentimental Journey*. The album was highly collaborative, a stark contrast with the atmosphere generated when the Beatles were working in the studio. Ringo had asked others to help select suitable tracks, and the songs were arranged by a variety of artists including Paul and Maurice Gibb.**

23 John and Yoko used the opportunity to promote their peace message when they met Prime Minister Pierre Trudeau while on a trip to Canada.

24 George Martin's show *With a Little Help from My Friends* was shown on Yorkshire Television. Charles Manson and his associates were arrested and charged with mass murder.

25 Ringo's appeal on behalf of the British Wireless for the Blind Fund was broadcast on BBC Radio 1.

26 A colour version of the film of John and Yoko in Paris, Amsterdam, Vienna, and at London Airport were shown on *Top of the Pops* to accompany "The Ballad of John and Yoko".

27 *Abbey Road* went back up to No. 1 in the UK album charts, remaining there for another six weeks.

29 John and Yoko flew to Denmark for a holiday, with Kyoko, her father Antony Cox, and his wife, Melinda.

30 The ATV programme *Man of the Decade* was transmitted. John had been the choice of anthropologist Desmond Morris. The other contenders were John F. Kennedy and Ho Chi Minh.

31 Ringo held a New Year's Eve party at his north London home. Kenny Everett, Michael Caine, and singer Lulu were among the guests.

ON PHIL SPECTOR AND LET IT BE

"I felt that what Phil Spector had done was not only uncharacteristic but wrong. I was totally disappointed with what happened to *Let It Be*."
—George Martin

"It was tampered with, or, in the words of the sleeve, 'freshened up'. Some people will say castrated is a better word, because great choirs of falsetto angels have been added to some tracks along with harps, violins, etc. This awful spectre (Spector?), the very idea that John or Paul's songs need slick production is an impertinence."
—*Record Mirror*, 9 May 1970

"*Let It Be* made more money for them than all the other films put together. They wanted it for TV, but I told 'em that was stupid."
—Allen Klein

"Let us attend the funeral when life is pronounced extinct: at the moment the corporate vitality of the Beatles, to judge from *Let It Be*, is pulsating as strongly as ever."
—William Mann, *The Times* 8 May 1970

Spector's wall of sound

Given that the thinking behind the *Get Back* sessions of January 1969 was to bring a live feel to a studio production, Phil Spector was hardly an obvious choice to execute such a brief. His trademark was the lavish, elaborate "Wall of Sound" Wagnerian grandeur that was the antithesis of what the Beatles had in mind. They had been keen to cut out the technical sleight-of-hand and endlessly layered overdubs to present the music in a rough and ready state.

A year on, things were very different. By the time Spector got his hands on the tapes, the Beatles had long since made their final appearance in the studio together, and Paul was about to drop a bombshell regarding the group's future—or lack thereof—in a Q and A appended to his debut solo album. It was clear that no lucrative new Beatles material would be forthcoming, so Klein turned his attention to making commercial hay from the year-old tapes gathering dust in the EMI vaults. If the 16mm footage were blown up to 35mm, it would be suitable for a more profitable cinema release. And if a new single and album were culled from the stockpiled material and issued at the same time, cross-promotion would make it a huge money spinner.

The phoenixlike project couldn't rise from the ashes under the same banner. "Get Back" had been released as a single in April 1969, and the new album had to be presented as fresh product. Paul's outstanding ballad "Let It Be" was selected to be the standard bearer for the revivified project.

If there were lingering suspicions about the Spector treatment being applied to a Beatles album, they were somewhat dissipated by the

production job he did on "Instant Karma", a UK Top 10 hit for John in February 1970. It was tantamount to an audition, and Spector passed with flying colours—at least as far as John and George were concerned, if not Paul.

Spector waded through twenty-four hours' worth of material, which included numerous versions of each song. Strings were added to the title track, "Across the Universe", and "I Me Mine", while a choir gave "The Long and Winding Road" a cloying, glutinous quality that Paul never envisioned. Spector said the embellishment was to cover the tracks of John's dire bass playing, a claim Paul dismissed, as it would have been far easier—and cheaper—to redo the bass line than to hire a fifty-piece orchestra. It was academic: "The Long and Winding Road" went out bearing Spector's signature. Ironically, while the hatchet job was being performed on his work, Paul was in a different Abbey Road studio, working incognito on his debut solo album.

There is some dispute as to whether Paul was accorded the opportunity to sanction the

1970

3 JANUARY Paul, George, and Ringo recorded George's "I Me Mine" at Abbey Road. John was on holiday in Denmark.

4 JANUARY George, Paul, and Linda worked on harmony vocal overdubs for "Let It Be" before brass sections and further guitar pieces were added.

5 JANUARY At the Olympic Sound Studio, Glyn Johns made a master for *Get Back*, but this version of the album has never been released.

8 JANUARY Further mixing to "Let It Be" and "For You Blue".

9 JANUARY The *Magic Christian Music* album by Badfinger was released in Britain.

15 JANUARY Bag One, John's lithograph exhibition, began at the London Arts Gallery.

16 JANUARY After the police took away eight lithographs showing John and Yoko on their honeymoon, the exhibition was closed on the grounds of obscenity.

20 JANUARY John and Yoko had their hair cropped in Denmark.

22 JANUARY John took his lithographs to the States, where they went on show at Detroit's London Gallery.

27 JANUARY At Abbey Road, Geoff Emerick produced a stereo mix for "The Inner Light". Then the Plastic Ono Band recorded John's "Instant Karma" in a session produced by Phil Spector. Ringo taped an appearance for the comedy series *Rowan and Martin's Laugh-In* while he was in Los Angeles for a local premiere of *The Magic Christian*.

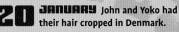

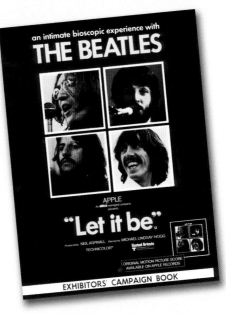

an intimate bioscopic experience with
THE BEATLES

APPLE
An ABKCO managed company
presents

"Let it be" (U)

Produced by NEIL ASPINALL Directed by MICHAEL LINDSAY-HOGG
United Artists TECHNICOLOR®

ORIGINAL MOTION PICTURE SCORE
AVAILABLE ON APPLE RECORDS

EXHIBITORS' CAMPAIGN BOOK

Let It Be

Released

🇬🇧 8 May 1970 Apple (Parlophone)

🇺🇸 18 May 1970 Apple (Capitol)

Side One:
Two of Us
Dig a Pony
Across the Universe
I Me Mine (Harrison)
Dig It (The Beatles)
Let It Be
Maggie Mae (Traditional)

Side Two:
I've Got a Feeling
One After 909
The Long and Winding Road
For You Blue (Harrison)
Get Back

LONDON PAVILION
PICCADILLY CIRCUS W.1.
GALA PREMIERE
WEDNESDAY MAY 20th 1970 at 8.00 for 8.45 p.m.

an intimate bioscopic experience with
THE BEATLES

APPLE
An ABKCO managed company
presents

"Let it be"

Produced by NEIL ASPINALL Directed by MICHAEL LINDSAY-HOGG
United Artists

YOU KNOW MY NAME
(LOOK UP THE NUMBER)
Words & Music by
JOHN LENNON & PAUL McCARTNEY

NORTHERN SONGS LIMITED   20p
4s

Cover story

The *Let It Be* cover, with its four distinctive but very separate and individual images set against a black background, was designed by John Kosh. Kosh had also created the iconic *Abbey Road* cover on which all four Beatles appeared together in one photograph. Whether intentional or not, the sleeve and the promotional material for *Let It Be*, showing four individual musicians, reflected the mindset of the band. For its initial release the album was packaged as a boxed set along with a book, as had been originally planned for *Get Back*.

LET IT BE

LEFT AND OPPOSITE: **The** *Let It Be* **world premiere was in New York on 13 May followed by a UK premiere at the London Pavilion and the Liverpool Gaumont on 20 May. Not one of the foursome chose to attend, strange in retrospect when this film was to win them an Oscar. Shown here are the UK lobby card, UK premiere ticket and UK Exhibitors Campaign Book.**

LEFT BELOW: **Sheet music for "You Know My Name", which was on the B-side of the single "Let It Be".**

release of *Let It Be*. Paul insisted that he wasn't, and in the High Court action to dissolve the Beatles' partnership he would cite "The Long and Winding Road"—the most heinous example of overproduction in his view—as evidence that the other Beatles were out to undermine his reputation.

Let It Be was given a cool reception by the critics, though the fans found much to recommend it. The Beatles' twelfth and final album topped the charts on both sides of the Atlantic, and the title track picked up a Grammy and an Oscar. Even bearing the hand of Spector's "intolerable interference", "The Long and Winding Road" was the other standout track and an obvious choice for a second single. Paul vetoed that idea in the UK, but couldn't prevent Capitol from issuing it. The song followed "Let It Be" to the top of the *Billboard* Hot 100, the Beatles' twentieth No. 1 in America. With an arrangement reviled by its composer, "The Long and Winding Road" sold more than six million copies, more than any other Beatles single released in the States.

29 JANUARY Ringo attended *The Magic Christian* premiere in Los Angeles.

3 FEBRUARY Arranger Quincy Jones and organist Billy Preston help to rerecord Ringo's "Love Is a Many Splendoured Thing".

4 FEBRUARY John and Yoko took part in an event with Michael X, the British Black Power Leader, at his "Black Centre" in London. They swapped pieces of their hair for Muhammad Ali's boxer shorts.

5 FEBRUARY Ringo's vocals were added to "Love Is a Many Splendoured Thing". "Instant Karma" was played on *Top of the Pops*, accompanied by footage of John and Yoko.

6 FEBRUARY John and Yoko recorded an interview with David Bellan at Apple Studios. "Instant Karma"/"Who Has Seen the Wind" was released in Britain; it had taken only ten days to write and release.

7 FEBRUARY Michael X accompanied John and Yoko when they recorded an appearance for *The Simon Dee Show*.

9 FEBRUARY Ringo recorded a demo for "Whispering Grass", then added vocals onto "Have I Told You Lately That I Love You".

10 FEBRUARY Geoff Emerick worked on new mixes of the Plastic Ono Band's "Instant Karma", then in the evening George Martin recorded his orchestral arrangement for "Dream".

11 FEBRUARY The Plastic Ono Band recorded "Instant Karma" for an appearance on *Top of the Pops*. Ringo began to record "I'm a Fool to Care", using an orchestra conducted by Klaus Voormann, before adding vocals and guitar pieces. In New York City, *The Magic Christian* opened.

HEY JUDE

Released

🇺🇸 26 February 1970 Apple (Capitol)
🇬🇧 11 May 1979 Parlophone

Side One:
Can't Buy Me Love
I Should Have Known Better
Paperback Writer
Rain
Lady Madonna
Revolution

Side Two:
Hey Jude
Old Brown Shoe (Harrison)
Don't Let Me Down
The Ballad of John and Yoko

Originally planned to be released as *The Beatles Again*, *Hey Jude* was a compilation album that enabled Capitol to put a mix of numbers from A- and B-sides not previously released on a US album. The title was revised at the last minute to get the benefit of the huge sales of "Hey Jude" the single.

Commercially the album plugged a gap caused by the late running *Let It Be*. The sleeve carried photographs taken at John's new house, Tittenhurst Park on 22 August 1969—the Beatles last photo shoot. Until the UK release in 1979 it was a popular import album for British fans.

ABOVE: **A week before the release of his first solo LP, *McCartney*, in the UK, Paul made a statement publicly announcing the split of the Beatles.**

RIGHT: **An exhibition at the London Arts Gallery of John's "erotic" lithographs, depicting himself and Yoko on honeymoon, opened on 15 January 1970. The exhibition was raided by police and closed the following day, on the grounds of obscenity. Eight pictures were confiscated by the police and returned three months later after a court declared they were not indecent. After their return, fans eagerly snapped them up.**

OPPOSITE: **John and Yoko strike an intimate pose for the camera whilst in Denmark, where they spent Christmas and New Year with Antony Cox, the father of Yoko's daughter, Kyoko. Their freshly cropped hair gives them a new, radical look.**

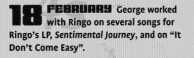

continued from the previous page

1970

12 FEBRUARY John was the first of the Beatles to appear on *Top of the Pops* since the band performed "Paperback Writer" in 1966, playing "Instant Karma". In the studio Les Reed conducted singers and an orchestra to produce "Let the Rest of the World Go By" for Ringo's album. In Morgan Studios, Paul began work on an instrumental called "Kreen-Akore" for his forthcoming debut solo album.

16 FEBRUARY Badfinger's album *Magic Christian Music* was issued in the US.

18 FEBRUARY George worked with Ringo on several songs for Ringo's LP, *Sentimental Journey*, and on "It Don't Come Easy".

19 FEBRUARY Further overdubs were added to "Love Is a Many Splendoured Thing" before continuing with "It Don't Come Easy".

21 FEBRUARY Under his pseudonym of Billy Martin, Paul booked this first session at the Abbey Road Studios to work on his solo album.

24 FEBRUARY Two separate Beatle members were working on individual albums: while Paul was working in Studio Two, Ringo was in Studio One.

26 FEBRUARY *Hey Jude* was released in the US on Apple (Capitol) SW-385.

6 MARCH "Let It Be"/"You Know My Name (Look Up the Number)", the band's last single, was released on Apple (Parlophone) R 5833 and reached No. 2 in the charts. The recording of Ringo's solo album *Sentimental Journey* was finished. *Hey Jude*, the album, was certified gold in the States.

8 MARCH George Harrison played guitar on the second remake of Ringo's "It Don't Come Easy".

11 MARCH Johnny Moran interviewed George at the BBC studios in Aeolian Road for the radio programme *The Beatles Today*. "Let It Be"/"You Know My Name (Look Up the Number)" was released in the US on Apple (Capitol) 2764.

12 MARCH George and Pattie moved into Friar Park at Henley-on-Thames, Oxfordshire.

17 MARCH "Let It Be"/"You Know My Name (Look Up the Number)" was certified gold in the States.

22 MARCH John revealed in an interview with French magazine *L'Express*, that the Beatles smoked cannabis in the toilets at Buckingham Palace in 1965.

23 MARCH John, George, and Allen Klein asked Spector to re-produce the tapes for the *Get Back* album to accompany the movie *Let It Be*. Paul finished the master for the album *McCartney*.

25 MARCH Ringo was interviewed by David Wigg for *Scene and Heard*. Phil Spector mixed "Two of Us" and "For You Blue".

26 MARCH "Let It Be", "Get Back", "Maggie Mae", and "The Long and Winding Road" were developed by Spector.

27 MARCH Ringo's debut album *Sentimental Journey*, was released in Britain (24 April in the US).

1 APRIL The culmination of work on *Let It Be*. Ringo was the only Beatle to participate in this long and eventful session, which included the use of 50 musicians. The tempestuous Spector upset nearly everyone in the studio before Ringo calmed him down.

2 APRIL The last mixing and editing session for the album.

4 APRIL "Let It Be" reached No. 1 in the US, remaining there for two weeks.

"One thing you can't hide is when you're crippled inside"

While Beatles fans were trying to come to terms with their loss, John was engaged in a reconciliation struggle of his own. Over a torturous four-month period he sought to reach a new level of introspection under the guidance of psychotherapist Arthur Janov. It was hardly surprising that the theories Janov expounded in his book *The Primal Scream* resonated strongly with John. They spoke of neurotic adults racked with pain and guilt over traumatic childhood experiences, which had the visceral familiarity of a mirror to John's soul. Deserted by his father, farmed out by a mother to accommodate her new man, John felt that here was someone who could finally rid him of the bitter anguish he had

long repressed. The other Beatles attested to the fact that the caustic wit was a veneer for deep insecurities. The plea to Yoko in "Don't Let Me Down" revealed a man still wrestling with issues of trust and constancy. Perhaps with the help of Janov, the trusty John defence mechanism would now become redundant, as would the search for meaning that had taken in marijuana, "Magic Alex", and the Maharishi along the way: "It was like taking gloves off and feeling your own skin for the first time...facing up to reality instead of always looking for some kind of heaven".

The treatment was not for the faint-hearted. To exorcise the demons of the past, they had first to be confronted. Over numerous sessions with Janov in the spring and summer of 1970 John found himself wailing uncontrollably on the floor of the treatment room. The cost of catharsis was fragility.

John ultimately rejected primal therapy, for its benefits were transient. But the euphoria of that liberating first release produced a crop of songs full of raw emotion. *John Lennon/Plastic Ono Band* witnessed an unprecedented baring of the soul, the intensity of which remained long after the treatment had ended. It was justifiably regarded as his "Sgt. Lennon".

"In the therapy you really feel every painful moment of your life...although we repress it it's still there. The worst pain is that of not being wanted, of realizing your parents do not need you in the way you need them. When I was a child I experienced moments of not wanting to see the ugliness, not wanting to see not being wanted".

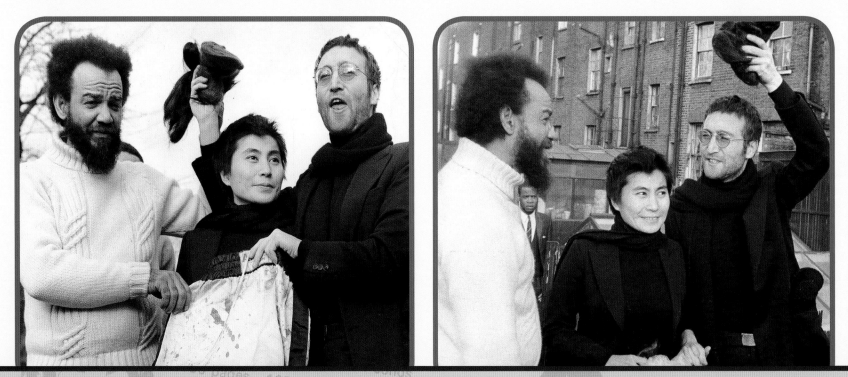

continued from the previous page

1970

9 APRIL John was at the Arthur Janov clinic, getting treatment for heroin addiction, when he received a phone call from Paul. It was believed that this was the time Paul told him he planned to go public about leaving the band.

10 APRIL Newspapers round the world carried Paul's statement that the Beatles would never work together again. George was filmed for the BBC1 programme *Fact or Fantasy?*.

17 APRIL Paul's first solo LP, *McCartney* was released in Britain (20 April in the US) and eventually reached No. 2 in the charts.

27 APRIL The courts returned John's lithographs after deciding that they were not indecent.

30 APRIL John and Yoko returned to Los Angeles, where they planned to start some more Primal Therapy.

1 MAY George and Bob Dylan spent the day jamming at Columbia Studios in New York, producing work for Dylan's *New Morning* album.

8 MAY *Let It Be* was released in the UK on Apple (Parlophone) PCS 7096. It was presented as a boxed package with the glossy book *The Beatles Get Back*.

11 MAY "The Long and Winding Road"/"For You Blue" was released in the US on Apple (Capitol) 2832.

13 MAY The film *Let It Be* opened in New York.

17 MAY Ringo's promotional film for *Sentimental Journey* was shown on *The Ed Sullivan Show*.

18 MAY *Let It Be* was released in the US on Apple (Capitol) AR-34001. It had the highest advance sales on record: a total of 3,700,000.

TOP, LEFT, AND OPPOSITE: **John and Yoko pay a visit to the Black Power organization headquarters in Holloway and meet its leader, Michael X. Their shorn hair is exchanged for a pair of Muhammad Ali's boxing shorts, and both items are shown to the press on the roof of the Holloway building.**

ABOVE: **Cynthia with Julian and new husband, Italian hotelier Robert Bassanini, whom she first met in 1966 and started dating after her breakup with John.**

20 MAY None of the four Beatles attended the showings of *Let It Be* when the film premiered in London and Liverpool.

23 MAY *Let It Be* reached No. 1 in the UK, remaining there for three weeks.

26 MAY George began recording tracks for his solo debut album, *All Things Must Pass*, at Abbey Road with Phil Spector.

28 MAY The whole edition of the BBC World Service programme *Profile* was taken up with extracts from the interview between John and Yoko and David Bellan, recorded at Apple on 6 February.

1 JUNE John announced that he and Yoko planned to live in New York City.

13 JUNE In the US singles charts "The Long and Winding Road" reached No. 1, holding the spot for two weeks, while *Let It Be* was at the top of the album charts, staying there for four weeks.

26 JUNE *Let It Be* was certified gold in the States.

26 JULY At the Primal Therapy Institute in Los Angeles, John started to record a demo of the song "God".

29 JUNE Ringo begins studio sessions for his album *Beaucoups of Blues*.

31 JULY Cynthia Lennon married Roberto Bassanini at Kensington Register Office. Julian was a page boy.

1 AUGUST Yoko Ono had another miscarriage.

29 AUGUST In *Melody Maker* a letter appeared saying, "Dear Mailbag, In order to put out of its misery the limping dog of a news story which has been dragging itself across your pages for the past year, my answer to the question, 'Will The Beatles get together again?'...is no. —Paul McCartney."

The end of a long and winding road

The media were falling over each other to get the other Beatles' reactions to Paul's "unilateral" declaration that he was no longer a member of the group. On one occasion when George was buttonholed on the subject, he flippantly remarked that it would mean getting a new bass player. Though not so far-fetched, as it turned out, for there was talk of bringing Klaus Voormann on board and performing as the Ladders. That ersatz Beatles lineup, plus Billy Preston, did play together on Ringo's eponymous album in 1973.

Of course, the fans wanted no new recruits. Like Paul, they instinctively felt that the Beatles were "four sides of a square". Any newcomer, no matter how gifted, would have rendered the shape of the band asymmetrical. From the moment news of the split broke on 10 April 1970 until John's death a decade later, the fans never gave up hope that the Beatles would re-form, and it was a hardy perennial in the gossip columns.

In fact, the thaw seemed to have set in before 1970 was out. Ringo was positively glowing at the prospect, while George made the odd guarded remark. John and Paul kept their own counsel, but at least they weren't going out of their way to scotch the rumours. By the end of

LEFT: **News of the Beatles' split did not appear to shake the happy, strong relationship Paul and Linda shared.**

OPPOSITE: **With his spiritual home still in the East, George attends the Festival of Arts of India at the Royal Festival Hall, meeting up again with Ravi Shankar (inset and above right). Earlier in the year, George had started work on his solo album, *All Things Must Pass*, recorded at Abbey Road studios and produced by Phil Spector.**

continued from the previous page

1970

4 SEPTEMBER The George Harrison composition "My Sweet Lord", sung by Billy Preston, was released in Britain. It was coproduced by George and Billy.

11 SEPTEMBER Doris Troy's album *Doris Troy* was released in Britain with instrumental contributions from both George and Ringo.

20 SEPTEMBER George attended the opening night of A Festival of Arts of India at the Royal Festival Hall, London.

25 SEPTEMBER Ringo released his album *Beaucoups of Blues* in the UK.

26 SEPTEMBER John and Phil Spector began recording at Abbey Road for the *John Lennon/Plastic Ono Band* album.

28 SEPTEMBER *Beaucoups of Blues* was released in the US.

15 OCTOBER In the States Phil Spector started to mix George's *All Things Must Pass*.

27 OCTOBER Having finished their album, John and Yoko returned to the US.

28 OCTOBER George flew to New York City to finish the album with Phil Spector.

11 NOVEMBER Maureen Starkey gave birth to a daughter, Lee Parkin.

15 NOVEMBER Paul instructed solicitors to begin the legal procedures needed to end the band.

1970 all four had made solo albums that would reach the Top 20, though none climbed to No. 1 in their homeland. Inevitably, their individual releases were compared with the collective magic of the Beatles era. Ringo spoke of a telepathic understanding within the group, something they couldn't hope to re-create elsewhere.

There were plans for an informal meeting early in 1971, but they were torpedoed over the festive period. While most people were gearing up for a harmonious rendition of "Auld Lang Syne", Paul was being advised that he had to take the Beatles to court to protect his interests and prevent Klein from bleeding Apple dry. By taking care of business, Paul had effectively wiped any hope of a Beatles reunion off the agenda. Even if the others hadn't taken umbrage at being dragged into the High Court, relations would have been soured by some of John's comments in a major *Rolling Stone* interview that had just hit the newsstands. He was scathing about Paul's paternalistic manner, and said that his attempts to keep the band together post-Epstein were not so much group altruism as ego trip. Neither John nor Paul's actions were conducive to burying the hatchet, unless, it seemed, it was buried between the other's shoulder blades.

Paul was in a democratic bind, faced with the unappealing prospect of being constantly outvoted and outmanoeuvred by the other three—and therefore by Klein. He felt he had no choice but to formally sever his links with the group. Thus, on New Year's Eve a writ was issued on Paul's behalf, beginning the legal process to dissolve the Beatles' partnership. It pigeonholed Paul as the man who broke up the Beatles, a facile reading of the situation. There were artistic disputes and political differences, but the sticking point for Paul was the appointment of Klein. The events of December 1970 have to be seen in a wider context, including the fact that John, George, and Ringo eventually turned on the sharp New Jersey operator. "Let's say possibly Paul's suspicions were right", John commented in April 1973 when Klein was shown the door.

23 NOVEMBER George released a single, "My Sweet Lord"/"Isn't It a Pity" in the US.

27 NOVEMBER George released his third solo album, *All Things Must Pass*, in the US (30 November in the UK).

8 DECEMBER John gave a major interview to Jann Wenner of *Rolling Stone* magazine, which was later published in two parts the following year and also as a book, *Lennon Remembers*.

11 DECEMBER John released the *John Lennon/Plastic Ono Band* album.

14 DECEMBER John and Yoko began work on a film, *Up Your Legs Forever*, that was completed in three days.

18 DECEMBER *From Them to Us: The Beatles Christmas Album* was issued to members of the Beatles fan clubs in both Britain and America. It contained all the previous seven Christmas flexi-discs that were distributed free each year.

21 DECEMBER John and Yoko started on another film, entitled *Fly*.

26 DECEMBER "My Sweet Lord"/"Isn't It a Pity" became the first solo Beatles single to go to No. 1 in the US charts.

28 DECEMBER "Mother" backed by "Why" was released in America by John and Yoko with the Plastic Ono Band.

31 DECEMBER Paul filed a lawsuit in the London High Court to dissolve the partnership the Beatles & Co. and to appoint a receiver to handle the group's affairs. He also cut the band's links with Allen Klein. Ringo held a New Year's Eve party at Ronnie Scott's Club in London. A jamming session included Eric Clapton, Maurice Gibb, Charlie Watts, Georgie Fame, Klaus Voormann, and Bobby Keys.

JOHN, PAUL, GEORGE & RINGO

After the Beatles

The Ice Is Slowly Melting

The Beatles couldn't "work it out" so they settled their differences in court, embarked on solo careers—and left the fans wanting more.

By the beginning of 1971 the artistic split occurred, though the bitter High Court wrangling lay ahead and legal dissolution would take four more years. Each of the Beatles was enjoying chart success with solo projects and, subsequently, with new bands, but fans never gave up hope of a reconciliation. Fifteen years after an assassin's bullet closed the door on that possibility in 1980, Paul, George, and Ringo embellished some of John's demos to produce the first "Beatles" single in twenty-five years. Since George's tragic demise in 2001, fans continue to harbour hopes that Paul and Ringo—perhaps accompanied by second generation Beatles—might one day take to the stage.

LEFT: **John and Yoko pictured in New York. After more than a decade of working and socializing together, the Beatles not only split as a band but by March 1971 most of their social ties were also broken and it took several years before the relationships improved.**

ABOVE LEFT: **Paul and Linda with their 18-month-old daughter, Mary.**

LEFT INSET: **Paul pictured with Linda during the High Court hearing for the dissolution of the Beatles partnership. He was the only member of the band to appear in person to give evidence.**

ABOVE: **Ringo and Maureen arrive for Peter Sellers's farewell party before he takes refuge in Ireland as a tax exile.**

1971

19 FEBRUARY In the London High Court, Paul's legal case to dissolve the Beatles partnership began. In the UK Paul released his first single, "Another Day"/"Oh Woman, Oh Why".

22 FEBRUARY Paul's "Another Day"/"Oh Woman, Oh Why" was released in the US.

23 FEBRUARY George was fined and then banned from driving for a year for driving "without due care and attention" when driving his Mercedes towards a traffic policeman in Westminster, London.

26 FEBRUARY While Paul gave evidence in court, John, Ringo, and George decided not to appear but sent written affidavits instead.

12 MARCH "Power to the People"/ "Open Your Box" was released by John and Yoko in the UK. In the High Court the judge ruled in favour of Paul.

22 MARCH John and Yoko released "Power to the People"/ "Touch Me" in the US.

9 APRIL Ringo's "It Don't Come Easy"/ "Early 1970" was issued in the UK.

15 APRIL Let It Be won an Oscar for the Best Original Song Score.

16 APRIL "It Don't Come Easy"/ "Early 1970" was released in the US.

26 APRIL John and Yoko appeared on Parkinson. When the host commented that the public perceived Yoko as the woman who broke up the band, John immediately jumped in to defend her.

12 MAY Mick Jagger married Bianca Perez-Mora in St. Tropez. Ringo and Maureen and Paul and his family were among the guests.

15 MAY At the Cannes Film Festival John and Yoko's films Apotheosis (Balloon) and Fly premiered.

17 MAY Ram, Paul's second solo album, was released in the UK.

28 MAY Ram was released in the US.

Some time in New York City

Having visited New York on several occasions in early 1971, John and Yoko left England for the Big Apple in September, essentially at Yoko's behest. Although he could not have known it at the time, John would never again return to Britain.

The couple took up temporary residence at the St. Regis Hotel, Manhattan, before moving to a small apartment in Greenwich Village in November, a month after the release of John's No. 1 album *Imagine* and the opening of Yoko's one-woman show at the Everson Museum, This Is Not Here.

But it was not just avant-garde art and music that interested John: He was soon becoming increasingly interested in radical left wing politics, associating with Jerry Rubin and a host of other activists and participating in the rally at Ann Arbor and demonstrations in support of the IRA and the Attica Prison riot victims. Many of John's political sentiments also found expression in his 1972 album, *Some Time in New York City*. All of this drew increasing attention from the US authorities and, in March of that year, the Immigration and Naturalization Service began moves to have John deported as an undesirable.

Since Allen Klein's contract had come to an end and was not renewed, it was with the help of lawyer Leon Wildes that John and Yoko fought the case, initially on the pretext that John needed to be in the US due to the custody battle for Yoko's daughter, Kyoko, but increasingly on the grounds that John's 1968 drug conviction was not sound, and that he was being unfairly and unreasonably harassed by agents of the government.

Having become increasingly paranoid and exhausted on account of these events, something had to give. Perhaps surprisingly, it would prove to be the Lennons' marriage.

ABOVE: **John and Yoko leaving London for a short break. On his return John began work on *Imagine*, which was released in the UK in October 1971 and was viewed as a startling contrast to Paul's album *Ram* released earlier in the year.**

RIGHT: **John and Yoko left London for New York on 3 September 1971 for what was intended to be a visit but turned into a permanent stay. Following the breakup of the band, neither John's absence nor the hostile relationship between John and Paul was sufficient to quell the constant speculation about the possibility of the Beatles re-forming.**

28 JULY In the US George released "Bangla Desh"/"Deep Blue". The proceeds were sent to famine relief and homeless in Bangladesh.

30 JULY "Bangla Desh"/"Deep Blue" was released in the UK.

1 AUGUST After a request from Ravi Shankar, George put together the Concert for Bangladesh at Madison Square Garden that included Ringo Starr, Bob Dylan, Ravi Shankar, and Eric Clapton. After two houses were played there were legal issues with the proceeds, so George wrote a personal cheque to keep the fund going. The recording was later released as a triple album titled *The Concert for Bangladesh*.

2 AUGUST Paul's "Uncle Albert/ Admiral Halsey"/"Too Many People" was released in the US only.

3 AUGUST Paul announced that he was forming a new band, soon to be called Wings, that included his wife, Linda, Denny Seiwell on drums, and Denny Laine, former guitarist with the Moody Blues.

13 AUGUST Paul's "Back Seat of My Car"/"Heart of the Country" was released in the UK only.

3 SEPTEMBER John and Yoko flew to New York—it was to be the last time he left England.

13 SEPTEMBER Stella Nina McCartney was born.

8 OCTOBER John's album *Imagine* was released in the UK.

8 NOVEMBER At the Empire Ballroom, London, Paul held a fancy-dress party to celebrate the launch of Wings.

9 NOVEMBER *Imagine* was released in the US.

10 NOVEMBER The film *200 Motels* was premiered in New York. Ringo appeared in a cameo role.

15 NOVEMBER The premiere of *Blindman*, in which Ringo played a cameo role, is held in Rome.

1 DECEMBER "Happy Christmas (War Is Over)"/"Listen, the Snow Is Falling" by John and Yoko was released in the US.

4 DECEMBER In *Melody Maker* John publicly attacked Paul.

7 DECEMBER Wings released their first album, *Wild Life*, in the UK.

John's "lost weekend"

In the autumn of 1973 John and Yoko separated, with John leaving Yoko at their recently acquired apartment in the Dakota building, New York, and heading for California, accompanied by their secretary, May Pang.

Yoko had more or less cajoled Pang into having an affair with John (better her, a nice Chinese girl, than a slew of groupies, she reasoned), but nevertheless Yoko remained in constant contact with her husband by telephone and sent various "spies" to check up on him, refusing to allow him back until she thought he had got his drinking and partying out of his system.

Free from his responsibilities, and given the chance to relive his youthful exuberances, John did drink and party. However, lost without Yoko, John became increasingly depressed and hostile to those around him, and what was intended as a temporary separation from his wife mutated into an eighteen-month-long "lost weekend".

John spent his time drinking and hell-raising with, amongst others, Jesse Ed Davis, Derek Taylor, and Phil Spector, to whom he had given over control of his *Rock 'n' Roll* album project. When this fell apart, John's next undertaking was the production of an album for Harry Nilsson, *Pussy Cats*, which provided ample opportunity for the mayhem to continue, with Keith Moon and Ringo Starr thrown into the mix for good measure.

Shortly afterwards, in June 1974, John returned to New York with May Pang, and before the year was out he had recorded and released his *Walls and Bridges* album, much of which appeared to be directed at Yoko by way of an apology. He was also to perform alongside Elton John at his Madison Square Garden Thanksgiving concert in November, partly returning a favour and partly through losing a bet. Elton had played on John's "Whatever Gets You Through the Night", and John had promised to appear live with him if the record went on to top the charts, which it did. Unbeknownst to John, Yoko was in the audience for the concert that night, and after the performance she greeted him backstage. It was their first encounter in a year, and perhaps sparked hopes that they would soon be reunited.

1972

8 JANUARY George's triple album from the Bangladesh benefit concert, *The Concert for Bangladesh*, was released in the UK.

9 FEBRUARY Wings began an impromptu tour of England, starting with an unannounced appearance at Nottingham University.

14 FEBRUARY John and Yoko spent five days as guest hosts on the US talk show *The Mike Douglas Show*. The Lennons provided some of the music with their new band, Elephant's Memory.

20 FEBRUARY *Concert for Bangladesh* was released in the US.

25 FEBRUARY Paul's "Give Ireland Back to the Irish"/"Give Ireland Back to the Irish (version)" was released in the UK.

28 FEBRUARY "Give Ireland Back to the Irish"/"Give Ireland Back to the Irish (version)" was issued in the US.

1 MARCH In the States John risked being deported as his immigration visa had run out. In the ensuing battle with the authorities, the FBI carried out secret investigations on him; the service claimed they were concerned about his 1968 drug conviction.

10 MARCH Allen Klein gave UNICEF a cheque for $1 million, the royalty donation from sales of *The Concert for Bangladesh* album.

16 MARCH John made a formal appeal to the US Immigration and Naturalization Service.

17 MARCH Ringo released "Back Off Boogaloo"/"Blindman" in the UK.

20 MARCH "Back Off Boogaloo"/"Blindman" was released in the US.

 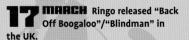

Househusband

Despite John's frequent destructiveness during his "lost weekend", he had also begun to rebuild some bridges in his personal life, notably with his son, Julian, and with Paul, with whom he had jammed in '74 and who had at times acted as something of a go-between with Yoko. In January 1975 the Beatles, as a band, was formally dissolved in the courts, bringing to an end years of financial wrangling and personal disputes, and so it was that the new year found John in a reconciliatory mood. He left May Pang and Yoko welcomed him back to their apartment at the Dakota. Soon Yoko found herself pregnant, and on 9 October, coinciding with John's 35th birthday, she gave birth to their son, Sean.

Having finally extricated the recordings from Spector, Apple had released *Rock 'n' Roll* earlier in the year, and one month after Sean's birth John would release the compilation album *Shaved Fish*. However, he now announced his retirement from the music business in order to devote his time to being a father and househusband.

RIGHT: **John at the Apple Studios holding a copy of "Power to the People", recorded with the Plastic Ono Band, and featuring one of Yoko's songs, "Open Your Box", on the B-side.**

FAR RIGHT: **In September 1971 the Lennons leave for a "short" trip to the US that turned into a permanent stay.**

OPPOSITE AND RIGHT INSET : **John and Yoko pictured in Nice on their way to the premiere of their films *Fly* and *Apotheosis (Balloon)* at the Cannes Film Festival.**

12 MAY In the UK, Wings released their first single, "Mary Had a Little Lamb"/"Little Woman Love".

18 MAY In an article in *The New York Times* it was reported that Paul and the Beatles had reached an out-of-court settlement to release £10 million.

29 MAY "Mary Had a Little Lamb"/"Little Woman Love" was released in the US.

12 JUNE The double album *Some Time in New York City* was released by John and Yoko in the US.

9 JULY The Wings European tour started at Chateauvallon in France.

10 AUGUST The McCartneys were charged with drug possession in Sweden.

30 AUGUST John and Yoko and Elephant's Memory hosted a concert at Madison Square Garden in New York; over $250,000 was raised for children.

15 SEPTEMBER *Some Time in New York City* was released in the UK.

20 SEPTEMBER The police found cannabis plants at the McCartneys' farm in Scotland.

16 OCTOBER Ringo began to film *That'll Be the Day*.

24 NOVEMBER "Happy Christmas (War Is Over)"/"Listen, the Snow Is Falling" by John and Yoko was released in the UK.

1 DECEMBER Wings released "Hi Hi Hi"/"C Moon" in the UK.

4 DECEMBER "Hi Hi Hi"/"C Moon" was released in the US.

14 DECEMBER The world premiere of *Born to Boogie* was held in London. Ringo attended.

23 DECEMBER John and Yoko's film *Imagine* premiered on US television.

Paul goes it alone

Paul's first solo album was followed in May 1971 by the release of *Ram*, which was criticized in certain quarters for its easy-listening quality and lack of musical "bite", a criticism that would continue to be levelled at Paul in respect to much of his solo output. However, the album did contain some biting lyrics aimed at John.

John would later respond in kind with the scathing riposte "How Do You Sleep?" from his *Imagine* album.

1973

9 MARCH Paul received a £100 fine for growing five cannabis plants.

23 MARCH The US Immigration Service ordered John to leave the country within 60 days. He hit back with more litigation and began to apply for a green card that would allow him to remain in the States. Paul and Wings released "My Love"/"The Mess" in the UK.

31 MARCH Allen Klein and ABKCO ended their period as business managers for Apple and the other Beatles companies.

1 APRIL John and Yoko bought an apartment in the Dakota building in New York.

2 APRIL The compilation album *The Beatles 1962–1966* (the *Red Album*) was released in the States, reaching No. 3 and spending a total of 164 weeks in the charts. Also released was *The Beatles 1967–1970* (the *Blue Album*), which reached No. 1 and stayed in the charts for 169 weeks.

9 APRIL "My Love"/"The Mess" was released in the US.

12 APRIL Ringo, Maureen, Paul, and Linda attended the world premiere of *That'll Be the Day* at the ABC Cinema in Shaftesbury Avenue.

13 APRIL In the States both the *Red* and *Blue Albums* were certified gold.

20 APRIL *The Beatles 1962–1966* (the *Red Album*) was released in the UK, reaching No. 3 and spending a total of 172 weeks in the charts. *The Beatles 1967–1970* (the *Blue Album*) was released on the same day, reaching No. 2 in the charts and remaining for 137 weeks.

30 APRIL Paul and Wings released the album *Red Rose Speedway* in the US.

4 MAY *Red Rose Speedway* was released in the UK.

7 MAY George's "Give Me Love (Give Me Peace on Earth)"/"Miss O'Dell" was released in the US.

11 MAY Wings began their first official tour of the UK in Bristol.

26 MAY George's "Give Me Love (Give Me Peace On Earth)"/"Miss O' Dell" was released in the UK.

Against the backdrop of the continuing legal dispute and persistent ill feeling between Paul and the other former Beatles, bitter exchanges between Paul and John were frequently conducted through the press. Despite this, throughout the early 1970s the public and journalists alike were constantly asking the former Beatles when a reunion could be expected, and it seemed that the sustained interest in the conflict, coupled with the eager anticipation of a reconciliation, did nothing to dent record sales. *Ram* was a commercial success, entering the UK chart at No. 1, and reaching that same position in almost twenty countries.

Significantly, it was not only John who would be annoyed by the album. In crediting the work to "Paul and Linda McCartney", Paul also managed to enrage Lew Grade, who stood to miss out on a huge sum for publishing royalties.

A month later, Paul decided to form a new band, and quickly confirmed a lineup that added Danny Seiwell on drums and guitarist Denny Laine, formerly of the Moody Blues. On 13 September a daughter, Stella, was born to the McCartneys, and it was apparently that same night that the name Wings was chosen for Paul's new group.

OPPOSITE ABOVE: **The launch of Paul's new band, Wings. The lineup included ex–Moody Blues singer Denny Laine and drummer Denny Siewell.**

OPPOSITE BELOW: **Paul and Linda, accompanied by Paul's father and stepmother.**

ABOVE: **Ringo and Maureen attended Mick and Bianca Jagger's wedding in St. Tropez. Paul, Linda, and their family were also invited.**

TOP: **John and Yoko in New York, where the children of the Harlem Community Choir joined them to record "Happy Christmas (War Is Over)".**

LEFT: **George, Pattie, Ringo, and Maureen fly to Cannes for the showing of George's *Concert for Bangladesh*.**

LEFT INSET: **Ringo's solo career continued to flourish with the release of "Back Off Boogaloo", a leading part in the film *That'll Be the Day*, and directing T.Rex in *Born to Boogie*. His personal life, however, was suffering—he and Maureen were on the verge of separating.**

30 MAY George released the album *Living in the Material World* in the US.

1 JUNE Paul's "Live and Let Die"/ "I Lie Around", written for the James Bond film, was released.

22 JUNE *Living in the Material World* was released in the UK.

4 JULY At Sheffield, Wings began another brief UK tour.

5 JULY The world premiere of *Live and Let Die*, held at the Odeon, Leicester Square, was attended by all the Wings members.

24 SEPTEMBER Ringo released "Photograph"/"Down and Out" in the US.

OCTOBER John and Yoko separated for 18 months, a period that John later called his "lost weekend". During that time he had an affair with personal assistant May Pang while they lived in Los Angeles. Pang encouraged him to talk to his former wife, Cynthia, and spend time with his son, Julian, now 10 years old.

19 OCTOBER "Photograph"/"Down and Out" was released in the UK.

24 OCTOBER John started further litigation with the US government when he accused them of illegal surveillance and

tapping both his phone and that of his attorney, Leon Wildes. He believed that a fair deportation trial was impossible given the circumstances.

26 OCTOBER Paul released "Helen Wheels"/"Country Dreamer" in the UK.

2 NOVEMBER John, George, and Ringo sued Allen Klein in the High Court for misrepresentation; Klein counter-sued. John released his album *Mind Games* and also the single "Mind Games"/"Meat City" in the US. Ringo released his album *Ringo* in the US.

12 NOVEMBER "Helen Wheels"/ "Country Dreamer" was released in the US.

16 NOVEMBER *Mind Games* and "Mind Games"/"Meat City" were released in the UK.

23 NOVEMBER Ringo released his album *Ringo* in the UK.

3 DECEMBER Ringo then released "You're Sixteen"/"Devil Woman" in the US.

5 DECEMBER Paul and Wings released the album *Band on the Run* in the US.

7 DECEMBER *Band on the Run* was released in the UK.

Wings over America

Wings' first album, *Wild Life*, was released at the end of 1971, and soon afterwards the group would embark on a somewhat spur-of-the-moment and low-key tour of British universities with a new guitarist, Henry McCullough. The live appearances met with a mixed response, but Wings were to enjoy three hit singles in 1972: the controversial "Give Ireland Back to the Irish", which was released in the wake of the "Bloody Sunday" incident, "Mary Had a Little Lamb", and "Hi, Hi, Hi", which was banned by the BBC for apparently alluding to drug taking. In fact Paul made little secret of the fact that he smoked cannabis. In 1973 he was arrested for possession in Sweden during a European tour and again for cultivation of the plant at his isolated Scottish retreat, the perhaps aptly named High Park Farm.

1973 also saw the release of the theme for the Bond film *Live and Let Die* and the Wings album *Red Rose Speedway* as well as a British

tour, but just as the group planned to fly to Lagos, Nigeria, to record their next album, McCullough and Seiwell left the band. Paul, Linda, and Denny Laine went nonetheless and, despite some bad experiences—including the theft and destruction of their demo tape—they returned with the basis of what would prove to be Wings' best album up to that point, *Band on the Run*. The album topped the charts and has been credited by some sources as being one of the first authentic platinum albums.

By the mid-70s and the formal dissolution of the Beatles, Paul's situation had improved dramatically from that in which he had found himself at the start of the decade. He was financially secure, his records were selling well, and in 1975–76 Wings would play a sellout world tour that included their only tour of the US, recordings from which would be released as *Wings Over America*.

Additionally, by this time, Paul's relationship with John was somewhat improved.

1974

JANUARY Pattie began an affair with Eric Clapton, and George met Olivia Trinidad Arias.

8 FEBRUARY Ringo released "You're Sixteen"/"Devil Woman" in the UK.

15 FEBRUARY Paul and Wings' single "Jet"/"Let Me Roll It" was released in the UK. Three days later it was issued in the US.

13 MARCH Ringo released another single, "Oh My My"/"Step Lightly", in the States.

8 APRIL Paul and Wings released "Band on the Run"/"Nineteen Hundred and Eighty Five" in the States only.

28 APRIL Paul and Wings issued "Band on the Run"/"Zoo Gang" in the UK only.

23 SEPTEMBER In the States John released "Whatever Gets You Through the Night"/"Beef Jerky".

26 SEPTEMBER John's album *Walls and Bridges* went on sale in the US.

4 OCTOBER The release of "Whatever Gets You Through the

Night"/"Beef Jerky"and *Walls and Bridges* in the UK.

18 OCTOBER "Walking in the Park with Eloise"/"Bridge over the River Suite" was released in the UK by Country Hams, a pseudonym for Paul and Wings playing with Floyd Cramer and Chet Atkins.

25 OCTOBER Wings' "Junior's Farm"/"Sally G" was released in the UK.

OPPOSITE LEFT: **The phenomenal success of Wings meant a great deal of travelling for the McCartneys and their young family: UK, European, and world tours were interspersed with recording sessions. Work on *Venus and Mars* took them to New Orleans in 1975.**

OPPOSITE RIGHT: **In 1975 John had been served with a deportation order by the US Immigration Service, although this was overturned by the Supreme Court later in the year. It was not until July 1976, after years of uncertainty and legal wrangling with the authorities, that his permanent residency was approved.**

ABOVE LEFT: **Ringo received critical acclaim for his role as Mike in the film *That'll Be the Day*.**

LEFT: **John during his "lost weekend" split of 18 months from Yoko.**

ABOVE: **George was experiencing a difficult time both professionally and personally: His latest album *Dark Horse* had not been well-received, and his marriage to Pattie was about to end.**

28 OCTOBER Allen Klein lost the court case against John, George, and Ringo.

2 NOVEMBER In the US George began a solo tour with a concert at the Pacific Coliseum, Vancouver.

4 NOVEMBER "Junior's Farm"/"Sally G" was released in the States.

11 NOVEMBER Ringo released "Only You"/"Call Me" in the States.

15 NOVEMBER "Only You"/"Call Me" is released in the UK. Ringo also issued the album *Goodnight Vienna* in Britain.

16 NOVEMBER "Whatever Gets You Through the Night" reached the top of the *Billboard* charts, giving John his first solo No. 1 in the US.

18 NOVEMBER *Goodnight Vienna* was released in the States. George's "Dark Horse"/"I Don't Care Anymore" was issued in the US only.

28 NOVEMBER John appeared onstage at Madison Square Garden to join Elton John on his US tour. They performed three songs together; it was to be John's last concert.

2 DECEMBER Paul released "Walking in the Park with Eloise"/"Bridge over the River Suite" in the US.

6 DECEMBER George's "Ding Dong"/"I Don't Care Anymore" was released in the UK only.

9 DECEMBER George's album *Dark Horse* was issued in the US.

16 DECEMBER John's single "#9 Dream"/"What You Got" was released in the States.

20 DECEMBER *Dark Horse* was issued in the UK.

Ringo's sentimental journey

By the time of the Beatles split, Ringo had already enjoyed success with two albums, *Sentimental Journey* and *Beaucoups of Blues,* and, although like John and George he was being represented by lawyer Allen Klein, of all the former Beatles he seemed most able to maintain civil relationships with the rest of his former bandmates. He had worked with both John and George on their solo projects, and his own debut single, "It Don't Come Easy", released in 1971, and its 1972 follow-up, "Back Off Boogaloo", were cowritten with George. Both were highly successful.

In 1971 Ringo also performed at George's Concert for Bangladesh in New York; founded Ringo Or Robin, a design company, with Robin

Cruikshank; and continued to enjoy the acting career that he had begun with the Beatles' movies and carried on with *Candy* and *The Magic Christian*, taking roles in *Blindman* and Frank Zappa's film *200 Motels*.

The following year found him on the other side of the camera, making the T.Rex film *Born to Boogie*, and then in another acting role, in *That'll Be the Day*, which would win him high praise upon its release in 1973. However, the same could not be said of *Son of Dracula*, which he produced and acted in, and which starred Harry Nilsson.

Ringo's third post-Beatles album, *Ringo*, was a much more successful project, making the top ten in 1973, and was notable not just for its robust material but also for including contributions from John, Paul, and George. However, perhaps

not surprisingly considering the climate of ill will between them, Paul would not be found in the studio at the same time as either John or George. Even so, the album represented a musical reunion of sorts. It also spawned two US number one singles: "Photograph" and "You're Sixteen".

Now living at Tittenhurst Park, John's former home, Ringo opened the studios for hire and began his Wobble Music publishing company. In 1974 he released the album *Goodnight Vienna*, which again featured all of the former Beatles. He was also to contribute drums to the Lennon-produced Harry Nilsson album *Pussy Cats*, which was recorded during John's "lost weekend".

By this time, Ringo's own marriage was faltering, and in 1975 he and Maureen would divorce, following which his musical career took a downturn and he adopted something of a playboy lifestyle.

ABOVE: **Ringo with then-girlfriend actress Shelley Duvall on his arm. The couple split up after a short relationship, but their paths crossed again many years later when Ringo narrated her animated series of bedtime stories for television.**

OPPOSITE RIGHT: **Paul and Linda photographed in 1975, shortly before leaving England for New Orleans, where the new album *Venus and Mars* was to be recorded.**

OPPOSITE LEFT: **By 1977 George's fortunes were changing: His album *33¹/₃* had received favourable reviews, and he and Pattie had divorced and he was now living with new love Olivia Arias. Their son, Dhani, was born the following year, and the couple were married a month later.**

1975

2 JANUARY John and Yoko were reunited.

9 JANUARY At a private hearing in the London High Court the Beatles & Co. partnership was officially dissolved. All four band members were still directors of Apple under company law so were still required to attend board meetings.

16 JANUARY Wings began to record their next album *Venus and Mars*.

27 JANUARY Ringo's "No No Song"/"Snookeroo" went on sale in the US only.

31 JANUARY John's "#9 Dream"/"What You Got" was released in the States.

7 FEBRUARY Paul's "Junior's Farm"/"Sally G" was rereleased in the UK. This time the A- and B-sides were swapped over.

17 FEBRUARY John's album *Rock 'n' Roll* was released in the States.

21 FEBRUARY *Rock 'n' Roll* was released in Britain. Ringo's "Snookeroo"/"Oh Wee" was released in Britain only.

28 FEBRUARY George's "Dark Horse"/"Hari's on Tour (Express)" went on sale in the UK only.

1 MARCH John was a guest presenter at the Grammy Awards in the US. It was the first time he and Yoko had been seen together in public since their reunion.

3 MARCH Linda McCartney was arrested in the US and charged with possession of cannabis.

6 MARCH John announced that he and Yoko were back together again.

10 MARCH John released "Stand by Me"/"Move Over Ms. L" in the States.

24 MARCH In the US, Capitol Records held a party for Wings onboard the liner *Queen Mary*, docked at Long Beach.

26 MARCH Ringo and new girlfriend Nancy Andrews attended the premiere of *Tommy* in London.

18 APRIL John appeared on ATV's *A Salute to Lew Grade*. It was to be his last public appearance. "Stand by Me"/"Move Over Ms. L" was released in the UK.

16 MAY Paul and Wings released "Listen to What the Man Said"/"Love in Song" in Britain.

All things must pass

George Harrison began the 1970s in fine form: Freed from the constraints of the Beatles, whose songwriting had been dominated by the Lennon–McCartney partnership, he was now able to release a wealth of accumulated material, starting with the first triple album by a solo artist, *All Things Must Pass*, in December 1970. The album included a composition that he had written with Bob Dylan, and featured musical contributions from Badfinger and Derek and the Dominos amongst others; but more important, it revealed to many George's talents as both a songwriter and musician.

In 1971 George would also contribute to John's *Imagine* album and Ringo's first solo single, "It Don't Come Easy". But perhaps the defining moment of the year for George was the Concert for Bangladesh.

Organized by George, this benefit concert, which was held on 1 August at New York's Madison Square Garden in aid of Bangladeshi refugees, was the largest event of its kind at the time and featured such renowned musicians as Ravi Shankar, Eric Clapton, Bob Dylan, Billy Preston, Leon Russell, Jesse Ed Davis, and Badfinger.

Of the other former Beatles, only Ringo attended and played. Paul declined to appear on account of the acrimony surrounding the Beatles' split, whilst George had requested that John perform without Yoko. John had agreed, but the row that this caused between the couple eventually precluded his participation, in turn causing something of a rift between John and George.

The concert was highly successful, with its two shows being attended by some 40,000 people, and it was also recorded for an album and film release. However, it later became clear that there were financial irregularities relating to expenses, for which Allen Klein would later be indicted.

George's next album, 1973's *Living in the Material World*, was less well received by the critics than his previous material, but it reached the top of the US charts, as did the single "Give Me Love (Give Me Peace on Earth)". The following year saw the foundation of Harrison's Dark Horse record label and the release of an album by the same name. This also fared well in the US, reaching the top five, but it failed to chart in Britain and was accompanied by a disastrous US tour. George was suffering from laryngitis at the time, which severely impaired his voice, and audiences also reacted badly to long performances by the support act Ravi Shankar and Friends. Additionally, Harrison's marriage had broken down, Pattie leaving him for his friend Eric Clapton. Although he began a relationship with Olivia Arias at this time, by the end of the year George was exhausted both physically and mentally.

23 MAY "Listen to What the Man Said"/"Love in Song" was released in the States.

30 MAY *Venus and Mars* was issued by Paul and Wings in the UK.

16 JUNE Back in the US courts, John filed a lawsuit against government officials including former attorney general John Mitchell. The charge was that "deportation actions directed against [him] were improper".

17 JULY Ringo and Maureen divorced.

5 SEPTEMBER Wings released "Letting Go"/"You Gave Me the Answer" in the UK.

9 SEPTEMBER Wings went on a world tour beginning with a date at the Gaumont Cinema, Southampton.

29 SEPTEMBER "Letting Go"/ "You Gave Me the Answer" was released in the States.

3 OCTOBER George released *Extra Texture (Read All About It)* in the UK.

7 OCTOBER In the New York State Supreme Court of Appeals, a two-to-one majority voted to overturn the deportation order served John by the Immigration Department. He finally received his green card the following year.

9 OCTOBER Sean Tara Ono Lennon was born to John and Yoko on John's 35th birthday. John then "retired" to look after his son.

10 OCTOBER The film *Lisztomania* was premiered in New York. Ringo had appeared in a cameo role.

24 OCTOBER In the UK, John's "Imagine"/"Working Class Hero" was released.

1 NOVEMBER The Wings tour continued with a concert in Perth.

21 NOVEMBER In the States Linda's drug charge was dismissed.

25 NOVEMBER Ringo's *Blast from the Past* album was released in the US.

28 NOVEMBER The UK release date for Paul and Wings' "Venus and Mars"/"Rock Show".

8 DECEMBER In the States George released "This Guitar (Can't Keep from Crying"/"Maya Love".

12 DECEMBER *Blast from the Past* was released by Ringo in the UK.

22 DECEMBER George's *Extra Texture (Read All About It)* was released in the States.

The best-selling composer of all time

During the late 1970s, it was almost certainly Paul who remained the most prolific and successful of the former Beatles. Following the success of Wings' US tour, the *Wings Over America* album, which was released in January 1977, became the group's fifth consecutive US number one album and also reached the Top 10 in the UK. In that same month the group was also honoured with an award for their live performances at Wembley the previous year. Soon afterwards Wings released a live recording of "Maybe I'm Amazed"

and Paul continued to work on more avant-garde solo material including an orchestral version of the album *Ram*, titled *Thrillington* and released under the moniker Percy "Thrills" Thrillington.

Wings then began recording sessions for their next album, *London Town*, at Abbey Road Studios, but these were continued in May '77 on a converted boat, the *Fair Carol*, off the Virgin Islands. The sessions generally went well despite some minor mishaps and injuries, but in September, just a few days before a son, James, was born to the McCartneys, Jimmy McCullough left Wings to join the Small Faces, who had recently re-formed for a British tour. The following month also saw the departure of Joe English, but Wings' success continued with the release of the double-A single "Mull of Kintyre"/"Girls School". The latter was essentially promoted as the A-side

in the US, whilst "Mull of Kintyre", an ode to Scotland, featuring the Campbeltown Pipes Band, went on to be a massive hit in the UK. It topped the chart in December, remaining there for nine weeks, and in January 1978 it became the biggest-selling UK single of all time—a record previously held by the Beatles' "She Loves You".

In mid-'78 Laurence Juber and Steve Holly joined Wings, playing guitar and drums respectively, and began work on sessions for the next album, *Back to the Egg*. Paul also began to plan a charity concert in aid of Kampuchean refugees, having been asked by the United Nations if the Beatles would re-form for such an event. He informed them that a re-formation would be out of the question, but at the third annual Buddy Holly Week, which he had inaugurated in 1976, he began assembling the

1976

9 JANUARY Ringo released "Oh My My"/"No No Song" in the UK.

19 JANUARY Using newspaper advertisements, a US promoter offered the Beatles $30 million to join together again and play for one night on July 5 at a venue of the band's choice. The deal was to play together for at least 20 minutes, then the rest of the evening could be made up of solo performances.

25 JANUARY Ringo joined Bob Dylan to perform in a benefit concert for Rubin "Hurricane" Carter.

26 JANUARY The Beatles' nine-year contract with EMI finally ended. While Paul remained with them, Ringo and George signed with other labels. John did not sign with anyone.

6 FEBRUARY "This Guitar (Can't Keep from Crying)"/"Maya Love" was released in the UK.

5 MARCH EMI was free to release any previous Beatles tracks and started with a boxed set of all the original Beatles singles.

8 MARCH EMI released "Yesterday"/ "I Should Have Known Better", which reached No. 8 in the UK charts. It had previously been released only in the US.

20 MARCH The Wings world tour moved to Europe, beginning with a date in Copenhagen, Denmark.

26 MARCH In the UK only, Wings released *Wings at the Speed of Sound*.

1 APRIL Paul and Wings issued "Silly Love Songs/"Cook of the House" in the UK (US April 30).

3 MAY The Wings tour continued in the US and Canada starting at Fort Worth.

7 JUNE The Beatles compilation album *Rock 'n' Roll Music* was released in the States, reaching No. 2 in the charts.

11 JUNE *Rock 'n' Roll Music* was then released in the UK, reaching No. 11 in the charts.

12 JUNE *Rock 'n' Roll Music* was certified both gold and platinum in the States.

14 JUNE "Back in the USSR"/ "Twist and Shout" was issued, reaching No. 19 in the UK charts.

Rockestra supergroup by inviting Dave Gilmour of Pink Floyd and Pete Townshend and Keith Moon of the Who to participate. They agreed, but tragically Moon was later found dead at his Mayfair flat.

Despite this, and amidst rumours that the Beatles were to perform live, the Concerts for the People of Kampuchea went ahead in 1979, featuring Wings, Dave Gilmour, Pete Townshend, and members of Led Zeppelin amongst others. It proved to be Wings' last performance at the end of a year that also saw the release of "Wonderful Christmastime" and Paul being presented with a rhodium-plated disc by the *Guinness Book of Records* as the best-selling composer of all time and most honoured man in music.

Wings had planned to follow their '70s successes with a major world tour, but in January 1980 this was cancelled when Paul, who was finally permitted to perform in Japan, was caught in possession of a large quantity of cannabis at Tokyo Airport. He faced a possible sentence of several years, but after just over a week of imprisonment, he was instead deported.

Paul's actions placed further strain on Wings, as did the subsequent release of his solo album *McCartney II* in May, which to the other members of the band appeared to signal that they had been dumped.

OPPOSITE: **Wings played two concerts at the Empire Pool, Wembley in 1979.**

ABOVE AND RIGHT: **A week before the release of *London Town*, the band held a promotional press conference on a Thames riverboat. The Wings lineup now consisted of Paul, Linda, and Denny Laine.**

23 JUNE The Wings tour concluded with three nights at the Forum in Los Angeles. During the final song of the encore, Ringo made a surprise appearance onstage and presented Paul with a bunch of flowers.

28 JUNE In the States Paul and Wings released "Let 'Em In"/ "Beware My Love".

23 JULY Paul and Wings released "Let 'Em In"/"Beware My Love" in Britain.

27 JULY John finally obtained his green card.

7 SEPTEMBER George was found guilty of plagiarizing the Chiffons' "He's So Fine" in his song "My Sweet Lord". Having bought the rights to Buddy Holly's songs, Paul held a Buddy Holly Week in London that was to become an annual event.

17 SEPTEMBER Ringo's album *Ringo's Rotogravure* was issued in Britain.

19 SEPTEMBER Paul and Wings began a brief European tour in Vienna.

20 SEPTEMBER Ringo's "A Dose of Rock and Roll"/"Cryin'" in the US" was released in the States.

27 SEPTEMBER *Ringo's Rotogravure* was issued in the States.

15 OCTOBER "A Dose of Rock and Roll"/"Cryin' in the US" was released in the UK.

15 NOVEMBER George's single "This Song"/"Learning How to Love You" was released in the US.

19 NOVEMBER The album *Magical Mystery Tour* was released in the UK. "This Song"/ "Learning How to Love You" was issued in the UK.

20 NOVEMBER George's album *33 1/3* was released worldwide. In the States, George appeared on *Saturday Night Live* hosted by Paul Simon. They performed "Homeward Bound" and "Here Comes the Sun" together. Paul and John watched the show from John's New York home.

22 NOVEMBER Ringo's "Hey Baby"/"Lady Gaye" was issued in the States, then one week later in the UK.

10 DECEMBER The triple album *Wings Over America* was released in the UK.

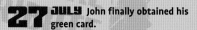

The best of George

Following the poor reception to his 1974 US tour, George returned to his home in England, Friar Park in Henley-on-Thames, where he took up residence with his new girlfriend, Olivia Arias. However, like Ringo he was also spending much of his time in LA, and over the next few years he would frequently travel between England and the US as he attempted to establish his Dark Horse label.

His last album for EMI and Apple was to be *Extra Texture (Read All About It)*, which was followed by the release of 33⅓ on Dark Horse in 1976. The album would prove to be fairly successful, but George had suffered ill health during its recording, delaying its release and resulting in another legal dispute. At the same time, Capitol was to release the compilation album *The Best of George Harrison*, which featured some of his Beatles compositions and solo work, but he was annoyed by his lack of involvement in the project.

The following year, George was divorced from Pattie and essentially took a year off from music, during which he travelled the world to attend that season's Formula One Grand Prix races. Then in September 1978, four weeks after the birth of their son, Dhani, George and Olivia were married at a private ceremony in Henley-on-Thames.

Around this time, George became involved in the production and financing of the Monty Python film *The Life of Brian*, which would lead to the foundation of his production company HandMade Films—a project that he would increasingly devote his time to. However, before the decade was out he would also release the eponymously titled album *George Harrison* and, in May 1979, take part in an impromptu jam with Ringo and Paul at the party that followed Pattie's wedding to Eric Clapton.

BIO: OLIVIA ARIAS

Olivia Arias' roots are Mexican but she was born and raised in California, where her mother worked as a seamstress and her father a dry-cleaner. After finishing her studies Olivia became a secretary, and by 1974 she was working in the administration department at A&M Records. At the time George had a recording contract with A&M, and the two had frequent telephone conversations before meeting at a company party. Romance soon blossomed and Olivia came to work for Dark Horse, the label founded by George that year. They married in 1978, the year after George and Pattie's divorce was finalized. The ceremony took place in London on 2 September, a month after Olivia gave birth to son Dhani. Their twenty-three-year marriage was remarkably low key, save for their efforts in aid of charitable causes such as the Romanian Angel Appeal, when the couple's profile helped raise millions of dollars for orphaned children living in squalor. Olivia was the prime mover, galvanizing the support of Linda McCartney, Yoko Ono, and Barbara Bach to raise funds and increase awareness of the issue. In December 1999 she won plaudits for beating off an intruder who stabbed George after breaking into Friar Park, their Henley-on-Thames home. Since George's death in 2001, Olivia has devoted much of her time to keeping alive the memory of the man and his music.

1977

10 JANUARY The final litigation between the band and Allen Klein was settled.

4 FEBRUARY In the UK Wings released "Maybe I'm Amazed", a live version of Paul's original solo.

11 FEBRUARY In the UK George released "True Love"/"Pure Smokey".

4 APRIL The band appealed to the High Court to prevent the release of an LP recorded live in Hamburg in 1962. The judge ruled against the appeal.

29 APRIL The album *Thrillington* by Percy "Thrills" Thrillington (a pseudonym of Paul McCartney) was released in Britain.

2 MAY In Britain the album *Live! At the Star-Club In Hamburg, Germany 1962* was released.

4 MAY In the States *The Beatles at the Hollywood Bowl* went on sale, reaching No. 2 in the charts.

6 MAY In Britain *The Beatles at the Hollywood Bowl* was also released, reaching No. 1 in the charts.

17 MAY *Thrillington* by Percy "Thrills" Thrillington was released in the US.

31 MAY In the States Linda and Wings released the single "Seaside Woman" under the pseudonym of Suzy and the Red Stripes.

9 JUNE George and Pattie were divorced. He was living in Friar Park, Henley, with Olivia Arias.

GUINNESS
BOOK OF
RECORDS
Salutes
Paul McCartney, MBE
The Most Honoured Man in Music
October 24, 1979

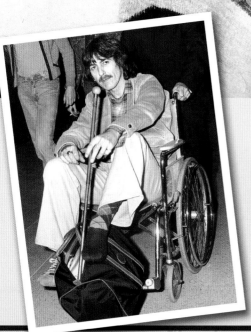

OPPOSITE: **George leaves hospital in Windsor following the birth of his son, Dhani.**

ABOVE: **After his divorce from Maureen, Ringo was seen with many women, one of whom was Nancy Andrews. He and Nancy became engaged but split up shortly afterwards.**

RIGHT: **In 1979 *The Guinness Book of Records* presents Paul with a rhodium disc for being "the most honoured man in music". Sixty gold discs, 100 million albums, and 100 million singles sold worldwide lay testament to this achievement.**

LEFT: **George plus wheelchair after a tractor ran over his foot at his Henley home in 1979.**

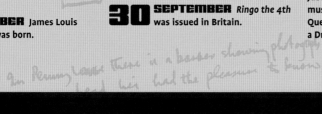

13 JUNE In the States the album *Live! At the Star-Club in Hamburg, Germany 1962* was released.

24 JUNE "Twist and Shout"/ "Falling in Love Again" was released in the UK but did not achieve a chart entry.

12 SEPTEMBER James Louis McCartney was born.

16 SEPTEMBER Ringo's "Drowning in a Sea of Love"/ "Just A Dream" went on release in the UK.

26 SEPTEMBER Ringo's album *Ringo the 4th* was released in the States.

30 SEPTEMBER *Ringo the 4th* was issued in Britain.

18 OCTOBER At the British Record Industry Britannia Awards, held at Wembley Stadium, the Beatles won the Best British Pop Album award for *Sgt. Pepper's Lonely Hearts Club Band* and also the award for Best British Pop Group. The event was held to commemorate the Queen's Silver Jubilee, with the aim of honouring British music since 1952, the year she became Queen. "Drowning in a Sea of Love"/"Just a Dream" went on release in the US.

11 NOVEMBER Paul and Wings released the single "Mull of Kintyre"/"Girl's School" in the UK.

24 NOVEMBER The Beatles compilation album *Love Songs* was released in the States, reaching No. 24 in the charts.

28 NOVEMBER The album *Love Songs* was released in Britain.

Ringo's new love

Ringo, meanwhile, was continuing to enjoy his jet-setting lifestyle, dividing his time between Monte Carlo and LA. Although he was to carry on recording and releasing new material over the next few years and making film appearances, his career seemed to be flagging somewhat around this time. Additionally, Ringo was to endure health problems towards the end of the '70s and collapsed in April 1979, suffering severe intestinal pain—the result of a case of childhood peritonitis. He was hospitalized in Monte Carlo, and an emergency operation was performed to remove part of his intestine. The following month he was well enough to attend Eric Clapton's wedding, but disaster struck again in late November when his Hollywood home, containing a great deal of treasured Beatles memorabilia, was destroyed by fire.

Ringo's fortunes seemed to be improving the following year when he began a relationship with the American actress and model Barbara Bach, whom he met whilst filming *Caveman* in February. However, just months later they were involved in a serious car accident in London, from which they were lucky to escape without severe injury.

RIGHT: **George formed his film production company, HandMade Films, travelling frequently between London and Los Angeles.**

FAR RIGHT: **Ringo's fortunes began to diminish: With no film parts in the pipeline and his records receiving poor reviews, he refused interviews and became more reclusive. In Monte Carlo he was rushed to hospital with severe and life-threatening intestinal problems, but recovered after an emergency operation.**

OPPOSITE: **Paul gives life a thumbs-up while sitting on the gate of his Sussex home shortly after his deportation from Japan. He had been held in prison there for ten days following the discovery of cannabis in his luggage.**

OPPOSITE INSET RIGHT: **Paul and Linda chat with Denny Laine and his wife after playing at a charity concert for Kampuchean refugees and UNICEF at the Hammersmith Odeon.**

OPPOSITE INSET LEFT: **After receiving a special Ivor Novello Award for his services to British music, Paul takes time to sign autographs for waiting fans.**

1978

14 JANUARY The first showing of LWT's *South Bank Show* included an interview with Paul and exclusive footage.

20 MARCH Paul and Wings released "With a Little Luck"/ "Backwards Traveller-Cuff-Link" in the US.

22 MARCH Paul and Wings used a Thames boat trip to hold a press conference for the forthcoming album *London Town*.

24 MARCH "With a Little Luck"/ "Backwards Traveller-Cuff-Link" was released in the UK.

31 MARCH *London Town* went on sale in Britain.

21 APRIL Ringo's album *Bad Boy* was released in the States.

26 APRIL In the States Ringo appeared in his own TV special, *Ringo*, and George made a cameo appearance.

12 JUNE Paul and Wings released "I've Had Enough"/"Deliver Your Children" in the US.

16 JUNE *Bad Boy* was issued in the UK. "I've Had Enough"/"Deliver Your Children" was issued in the UK.

21 JULY In the UK Ringo released "Tonight"/"Old Time Relovin".

1 AUGUST George and Olivia's son, Dhani, was born.

7 AUGUST The medley "Sgt. Pepper's Lonely Hearts Club Band"/"With a Little Help from My Friends" with "A Day in the Life" on the B-side was released in the US.

11 AUGUST In the UK Wings released "London Town"/"I'm Carrying" (21 August in the US).

2 SEPTEMBER George and Olivia Trinidad Arias were married at Henley Register Office, with Joe Brown acting as best man.

30 SEPTEMBER The medley "Sgt. Pepper's Lonely Hearts Club Band"/"With a Little Help from My Friends" with "A Day in the Life" on the B-side was released in the UK, reaching No. 63 in the charts.

15 DECEMBER *The Beatles Collection* was released in Britain; this was also presented as a boxed set.

1979

14 FEBRUARY "Blow Away"/ "Soft Hearted Hana" was released by George in the US. George also released the album *George Harrison* in the States.

16 FEBRUARY George released "Blow Away"/"Soft Touch" in the UK. *George Harrison* was released in Britain.

15 MARCH In the States, Wings issued "Goodnight Tonight"/ "Daytime, Night-time Suffering" (23 March in the UK).

APRIL Ringo had severe intestinal problems and nearly died. His life was saved by an emergency operation in Monte Carlo.

27 APRIL In New York, Allen Klein was found guilty of tax evasion and sent to prison.

9 MAY Ringo, George, and Paul played a jam session to celebrate Eric Clapton and Pattie Boyd's marriage.

11 MAY The album *Hey Jude* was released in Britain. George's "Love Comes to Everyone"/"Soft Touch" was released in the US.

13 JULY George issued "Faster"/ "Your Love Is Forever" in Britain.

10 AUGUST In the UK Linda and Wings released the single "Seaside Woman" under the pseudonym of Suzy and the Red Stripes. Paul and Wings also released "Getting Closer"/"Baby's Request" in Britain.

22 AUGUST George's autobiography, *I. Me. Mine.*, was published, initially as a special limited edition. All 2,000 copies, priced at £148, immediately sold out.

12 OCTOBER The Beatles compilation album *Rarities* was released in the UK.

24 OCTOBER Paul was presented with a rhodium disc by the *Guinness Book of Records*.

16 NOVEMBER "Wonderful Christmastime"/"Rudolph the Red-nosed Reggae" was released in the UK by Paul (20 November in the US).

24 NOVEMBER The Wings UK tour started with three dates in Liverpool.

18 NOVEMBER A fire destroyed Ringo's home in LA and wiped out most of his Beatles memorabilia collection.

7 DECEMBER Wings played at the Empire Pool, Wembley, followed by another date there three days later.

JOHN LENNON'S MURDER WAS A POLITICAL ASSASSINATION!

SUBSTANTIATES THAT LENNON'S KILLER DID NOT ACT ALONE!! *(SEE BELOW)* WAS KILLED ONE WEEK BEFORE A SCHEDULED APPEARANCE IN A LABOR STRIKE!

IT WAS BY NO ACCIDENT OR WHIM THAT JOHN LENNON'S ASSASSINATION CAME AT PRECISELY THE POINT WHEN LENNON RE-EMERGED INTO PUBLIC AND POLITICAL LIFE AFTER 5 YRS. OF SECLUSION FOLLOWING ATTEMPT TO DEPORT HIM!

LENNON ASSASSINATION WAS PART OF A PATTERN WITH CW GARCIA, e PREVENT

JOHN LENNON'S ASSASS
POTENTIAL OPPOSITION AN
WHO IDENTIFIED WITH
ROCKEFELLER-LED U.S.
THE CENTRAL INTELLIGENC
POLITICS IN ORDER TO CO
COMING ON THE HEELS OF
IN ALL MEDIA, THE H
U.S. CAPITALISM-II
WIDESPREAD RECO
FAILURES OF C

"IT'S ALWAYS A LONE NUT-A WACKO!?"

Daily Mail

MONEY MAIL TODAY

Mail Picture Exclusive-The antograph that led to murder

LENNON AND HIS KILLER

1980

16 JANUARY Paul was arrested at Narita International Airport in Tokyo with 7.7 ounces of marijuana in his suitcase found by customs officials. He spent ten days in jail and was then deported, with the Wings tour of Japan cancelled.

26 FEBRUARY At the British Rock and Pop Awards held at the Café Royal, Paul received the award for Outstanding Music Personality.

27 FEBRUARY Paul's "Rockestra Theme" received a Grammy Award.

24 MARCH *Rarities* was issued in the States, reaching No. 21.

11 APRIL Paul released "Coming Up"/ "Coming Up (live)-Lunch Box-Odd Sox" in the UK (15 April in the US).

9 MAY Paul was presented with a Special Ivor Novello Award by Yul Brynner for his services to British music.

16 MAY Paul's *McCartney II* album was released in Britain (21 May in the US).

19 MAY In London Ringo and his new girlfriend, Barbara Bach, were involved in a serious car crash but managed to escape without injury.

13 JUNE Paul released "Waterfalls"/ "Check My Machine" in the UK.

22 JULY "Waterfalls"/"Check My Machine" was issued in the US.

1 AUGUST HandMade Films (productions) Ltd, George's film company, was formed.

9 SEPTEMBER John and Yoko began an interview session with *Playboy* magazine lasting for nearly 19 days.

15 SEPTEMBER Paul's "Temporary Secretary"/"Secret Friend" was released in Britain.

22 SEPTEMBER Yoko signed a record deal with Geffen Records for John and herself.

Grief for John

Although John had effectively retired, claiming that he had literally hung up his guitar for five years, by early 1980 he was showing signs that a return to music might be imminent, and he began working in earnest on demos that he had been recording at home. In June he set sail from Virginia for Bermuda and, having braved severe storms en route, enjoyed a musical outpouring once he arrived, committing several songs to tape on a simple recorder.

Upon his return to New York in July, John and Yoko contacted record producer Jack Douglas, announcing that they were ready to record a new album. Within days Douglas had assembled a group of musicians, and the first rehearsals took place at the Dakota building. Then, on 4 August, John entered the Hit Factory recording studio to begin work on *Double Fantasy*. The name for the album was taken from a flower that John had seen whilst in Bermuda, and which seemed to him to aptly describe his relationship with Yoko.

By September, recordings for the *Double Fantasy* album, which would feature compositions by both John and Yoko, were almost complete, and John signed a contract with Geffen Records. That same month he also gave extensive interviews to *Newsweek* and *Playboy* magazines and would meet up with George at the Monty Python concert at the Hollywood Bowl.

On 9 October, John celebrated his fortieth birthday and Sean his fifth, and it was announced that John would shortly embark on a tour of the US and Europe, including a return to England. Towards the end of the month the first single,

"(Just Like) Starting Over", was released, and the album itself was issued in mid-November. Soon afterwards John met up with Ringo at the Plaza hotel in New York. They talked for several hours and made plans to begin work together on Ringo's next album. But it was not to be. On the night of 8 December, having returned from a recording session at the Record Plant, John and Yoko arrived at the Dakota building, where Mark Chapman, who earlier had a copy of the new album signed for him by John, lay in wait with a .38 revolver. Chapman fired five shots at close range, four of which hit John in the back and shoulder. John managed to stagger inside the building, and within minutes the police had arrived. He was rapidly taken to Roosevelt Hospital in a squad car, but despite the best attempts of hospital staff to revive him, he was pronounced dead as a result of shock and massive blood loss soon after 11 p.m.

RIGHT AND OPPOSITE INSET RIGHT: **The shooting of John on 8 December 1980 outside the Dakota building, New York, caused a worldwide outpouring of shock and grief. Fans poured into the area to set up a vigil outside his apartment immediately following his death. A week later, 100,000 gathered in Central Park to observe a 10-minute silence for John at Yoko's request. Thirty thousand people at St. George's Hall in Liverpool (right) did the same, along with countless others around the world. Five years later, on John's birthday, a memorial garden—Strawberry Fields—dedicated to his memory was inaugurated in Central Park.**

OPPOSITE INSET LEFT: **The *Daily Mail* front page showing the moment that John signed an autograph for his killer.**

OPPOSITE: **Conspiracy theories emerged concerning the circumstances of John's death.**

9 OCTOBER John turned 40 years old.

20 OCTOBER The Beatles Ballads was released in Britain. It made no impression at first, but then rose to No. 17 in the charts after John's death.

24 OCTOBER John released "(Just Like) Starting Over"/"Kiss Kiss Kiss" in the UK (27 October in the US).

3 NOVEMBER The Beatles Box was released in the UK, containing eight albums. It was sold by mail order only.

17 NOVEMBER John and Yoko issued Double Fantasy on both sides of the Atlantic.

26 NOVEMBER Rockshow's world premiere was held in New York. It filmed Wings' 1976 tour of the States.

5 DECEMBER John taped an interview for Rolling Stone magazine.

6 DECEMBER John and Yoko were interviewed for Radio One.

8 DECEMBER John and Yoko recorded an interview for RKO radio. At 10:30 p.m. John was shot dead outside his home in the Dakota building, New York. Mark David Chapman had waited for him and then shot him four times at close range, finally severing his aorta. Despite a patrolman taking him straight to the hospital, John was pronounced dead on arrival due to severe blood loss. Ironically, earlier in the day he had signed a copy of Double Fantasy for Chapman with the inscription "John Lennon 1980". Ringo and Barbara Bach immediately flew to New York to be with Yoko.

10 DECEMBER John was cremated at Ferncliff Mortuary in Hartsdale, New York, with his ashes kept by Yoko. Later Chapman was sentenced for murder and is still in Attica Correctional Facility.

14 DECEMBER Following a request from Yoko, fans held ten minutes' silence at 2 p.m. Eastern Standard Time. In addition to those outside the Dakota building, 30,000 gathered at St. George's Hall on Lime Street, Liverpool, while 100,000 joined together in New York's Central Park.

Give peace a chance

Reports of John's murder quickly began to circulate on television and radio. Just an hour after the shooting Dr. Stephan Lynn, director of the hospital's emergency room, confirmed his death to the press. Two hours later, Chief Detective James T. Sullivan also relayed the news at a press conference. A statement from Yoko was released the following morning by Geffen Records, and Ringo and Barbara Bach immediately travelled from the Bahamas to New York to be with Yoko and Sean.

By this time the newspapers, television, and radio were full of tributes to John, and crowds had begun to gather outside the Dakota building, marking the beginning of a remarkable outpouring of grief around the world. On 14 December, in numerous cities across the globe, a day of mourning was held and, at Yoko's request, ten minutes' silence, were observed at 2 p.m. EST (7 p.m. GMT). Perhaps not surprisingly, Liverpool and New York played host to huge gatherings of mourning fans. For the remainder of the year, and well into the new, the sound of John's "Imagine" filled the airwaves, whilst both

Double Fantasy and "(Just Like) Starting Over" would reach the top of the charts in both Britain and the US.

BELOW: **Police attempt to hold back the crowds at a memorial service in Liverpool.**

OPPOSITE: **Hope, peace, and love: Five-year-old Paula Carney gets the message. In March 1981, 2,000 fans gathered in Mathew Street at the site of the Cavern Club.**

OPPOSITE INSET: **Mourning fans burn black candles in Liverpool.**

1981

12 JANUARY John's "Woman"/ "Beautiful Boy" was released in the States (16 January in the UK).

26 FEBRUARY George had to pay $587,000 damages for his unwitting plagarism of "He's So Fine". The money went to Bright Tunes, owned by Allen Klein.

13 MARCH John's "Watching the Wheels"/"Yes, I'm Your Angel" went on sale in the States.

27 MARCH "Watching the Wheels"/"Yes, I'm Your Angel" was released in the UK.

8 APRIL Paul and Linda were at the UK charity premiere of *Rockshow*, held in London.

10 APRIL In New York the world premiere of Ringo's film *Caveman* was held.

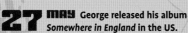

27 APRIL Ringo married Barbara Bach with Paul and George present for the celebrations. Wings officially separated.

11 MAY "All Those Years Ago", George's tribute to John, was released in the US. Paul and Ringo played on the backing track; "Writing on the Wall" featured on the B-side.

15 MAY "All Those Years"/"Writing on the Wall" was released in the UK.

27 MAY George released his album *Somewhere in England* in the US.

5 JUNE *Somewhere in England* was issued in Britain.

31 JULY George's "Teardrops"/ "Save the World" was released in the States.

27 OCTOBER Ringo's "Wrack My Brain"/ "Drumming Is My Madness" was released in the States (13 November in the UK). His album *Stop and Smell the Roses* was also issued in the US.

13 NOVEMBER "Wrack My Brain"/"Drumming Is My Madness" was issued in the UK.

8 DECEMBER From the first anniversary of John's death, and every year thereafter, a memorial is held in front of Capitol Records on Vine Street in Hollywood.

1982

30 JANUARY Paul was the guest on the 40th anniversary edition of *Desert Island Discs*. His selection included John's "Beautiful Boy", and he chose his guitar as a luxury item.

24 FEBRUARY At the Grammy Awards in the US, Yoko and Sean collected the Best Album Award for *Double Fantasy*.

22 MARCH The medley "Magical Mystery Tour"/"All You Need Is Love"/"You've Got to Hide Your Love Away"/"I Should Have Known Better"/"A Hard Day's Night"/"Ticket To Ride"/"Get Back", with "I'm Happy Just To Dance With You" on the B-side, was released in the US, reaching No. 12 in the charts. The album *Reel Music*, featuring songs from Beatles movies, was released in the States, reaching No. 19.

23 MARCH The album *Reel Music* went on sale in Britain.

26 MARCH Paul and Stevie Wonder released "Ebony and Ivory" in the UK. On the flipside was "Rainclouds" by Paul (2 April in the US).

26 APRIL Paul's album *Tug of War* was released simultaneously in the UK and US.

24 MAY The medley "Magical Mystery Tour"/"All You Need Is Love"/"You've Got to Hide Your Love Away"/"I Should Have Known Better"/"A Hard Day's Night"/"Ticket to Ride"/"Get Back", with "I'm Happy Just To Dance With You" on the B-side, was released in the UK, reaching No. 10 in the charts.

31 MAY *Beatles at the Beeb* was broadcast in the States.

21 JUNE Paul's "Take It Away"/"I'll Give You a Ring" goes on release in the UK.

Reunion for Ringo

Although badly affected by John's death, Ringo threw himself back into his work almost immediately, finishing the recording sessions for his next album in January 1981 before flying to Montserrat the following month to record for Paul's album, *Tug of War*. Then on 27 April, Ringo and Barbara Bach were married in London. George and Olivia Harrison and Paul and Linda McCartney were amongst the guests at the wedding, which was followed by a reception and jam session at a London club.

Later in the year Ringo and Barbara moved back to Tittenhurst Park in England, having completed a promotional tour for the album *Stop and Smell the Roses* and the film *Caveman*. Neither was particularly well received, however, and for much of the decade Ringo's career was blighted by an increasing dependence upon alcohol, for which he and his wife would receive treatment in 1988. Despite this, Ringo was to connect with a new audience during the 1980s by providing the narration for the highly successful children's television series *Thomas the Tank Engine* and, in 1989, he made a successful return to music, touring the US and Japan with Ringo's All-Starr Band.

OPPOSITE: **Four months after John's death, Paul, George, and their families are together again for Ringo's marriage to Barbara Bach at Marylebone Register Office.**

ABOVE LEFT: **Paul is honoured as Freeman of the City of Liverpool, an award he received when he returned to his hometown for the premiere of his film *Give My Regards to Broad Street*.**

ABOVE RIGHT: **Policemen are on duty to hold back photographers as Ringo and Barbara Bach leave the building.**

RIGHT: **George and Olivia Arias leave the Register Office after the ceremony.**

BIO: BARBARA BACH

Barbara Goldbach was born on 27 August 1947 in New York, the eldest of her Irish mother and Austrian father's five children. She shortened her name when she entered the modelling world at sixteen. Barbara saw the Beatles perform at Shea Stadium in 1965, though mainly as chaperone to her younger sister; she herself was no great fan of the Fab Four. She married Italian businessman Augusto Gregorini and moved to Rome, the marriage producing two children before the couple separated in the mid-seventies. Barbara was dubbed "Queen of the B-Movies" for the number of second features in which she appeared in Italy, and while she tried to avoid being cast for her looks, her big break came when she played Anya in the 1977 Bond film, *The Spy Who Loved Me*. The following year she appeared alongside Robert Shaw and Harrison Ford in *Force 10 from Navarone*. Barbara and Ringo fell in love while shooting the 1981 film *Caveman*, and married on 27 April that year. The ceremony took place at Marylebone Register Office, where Paul and Linda had married twelve years earlier. She had a cameo role in Paul's 1984 film, *Give My Regards to Broad Street*, but then stepped away from the limelight to devote herself to her family and charity work.

20 SEPTEMBER Paul released "Tug of War"/ "Get It" in Britain.

26 SEPTEMBER "Tug of War"/ "Get It" went out in the States.

27 SEPTEMBER The Complete Silver Beatles was released in the States, reaching No. 2.

29 SEPTEMBER The Complete Silver Beatles was issued in Britain.

5 OCTOBER EMI reissued "Love Me Do" to celebrate the 20th anniversary of the song. It reached No. 4 in the UK charts, and afterwards all other Beatles singles were rereleased on their 20th anniversary dates.

18 OCTOBER 20 Greatest Hits was issued in Britain and in the States, although the album had different track listings in the two countries.

25 OCTOBER A simultaneous release in the UK and US of Paul and Michael Jackson's "The Girl Is Mine" with "Can't Get Outta the Rain" by Michael Jackson on the B-side.

27 OCTOBER Gone Troppo by George was released in the UK.

29 OCTOBER In the UK George issued "Wake Up My Love"/ "Greece".

1 NOVEMBER In Britain The John Lennon Collection was released.

8 NOVEMBER The John Lennon Collection and Gone Troppo went on sale in the States. At Elstree Film Studios, filming began on Paul's film Give My Regards to Broad Street. Paul, Ringo, and Linda starred.

15 NOVEMBER EMI issued John's "Love" for the first time, with "Give Me Some Truth" on the flip side.

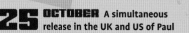

Give my regards

In response to John's death, Paul, like Ringo, busied himself with recording, flying to George Martin's Montserrat studios early in 1981. However, with the exception of Linda, the other members of Wings were sidelined at this time, and by May the group had permanently disbanded, leaving Paul to release *Tug of War* with a solo credit. The album went to number one on both sides of the Atlantic in 1982, as did the single, "Ebony and Ivory"; a duet with Stevie Wonder. Two further duets, "The Girl Is Mine", and "Say Say Say", both recorded with Michael Jackson, would provide further hits, but McCartney and Jackson would later come into conflict after Jackson bought the rights to Northern Songs and the Beatles' back catalogue.

In 1984 Paul was again arrested for possession of cannabis, but this did nothing to slow his

record sales: The album *Give My Regards to Broad Street*, from his film project of the same name, entered the UK charts at No.1. The film itself was savaged by the critics, however, and was a box-office flop. Far more successful was the animated short *Rupert and the Frog Song*, which provided the UK hit single, "We All Stand Together".

In July 1985 Paul performed "Let It Be" at the Live Aid Concert, Wembley, in front of a record estimated television audience of over 1.5 billion people, and he continued to enjoy musical success in the latter part of the decade, with his albums *Press to Play*, the compilation *All the Best* and the album *Flowers in the Dirt*, which was written with Elvis Costello and went on to top the UK charts.

In September 1989, Paul embarked on his record-breaking "Get Back" world tour, which would take in thirteen countries and conclude in Chicago at the end of July 1990.

1983

8 FEBRUARY At the BPI awards Paul was voted Best British Male Solo Artist while the Beatles were awarded Outstanding Contribution to British Music.

16 JUNE Ringo's album *Old Wave* was issued in West Germany. It was subsequently released in Brazil and Canada, but no record company in the UK or US accepted it.

17 OCTOBER Paul's album *Pipes of Peace* went on release in Britain.

26 OCTOBER *Pipes of Peace* went on sale in the States.

5 DECEMBER The single "Pipes of Peace" was released in the UK. In the States *Heart Play: Unfinished Dialogue* was issued, an album containing excerpts from John and Yoko's interview for *Playboy* magazine.

16 DECEMBER *Heart Play: Unfinished Dialogue* was issued in the UK.

1984

5 JANUARY John's "Nobody Told Me"/"O' Sanity" was released in the States (9 January in the UK).

19 JANUARY John and Yoko's *Milk and Honey* was issued in the States.

23 JANUARY The UK release of *Milk and Honey*.

9 MARCH John's "Borrowed Time"/ "Your Hands" was released in the UK.

15 MARCH John's "I'm Stepping Out"/"Sleepless Nights" went on sale in the States.

21 MARCH Strawberry Fields, an area dedicated to John Lennon, was officially opened in Central Park.

11 MAY "Borrowed Time"/"Your Hands" went on release in the States.

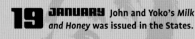

29 JUNE John's Rolls-Royce Phantom V was auctioned by

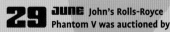

RIGHT: **Paul performing for the camera at his Soho office.**

BELOW: **Paul, Linda, Ringo, Barbara and George's wife, Olivia, attend the pre-screening party for** *Give My Regards to Broad Street* **at the London Hippodrome.**

BELOW RIGHT: **Ringo became the first Beatle grandfather at the age of 50 after the birth of a daughter, Tatia Jayne, to his son Zak and wife Sarah.**

OPPOSITE RIGHT: **At a Chelsea Arts Club masked ball, Ringo and Barbara arrive suitably attired.**

OPPOSITE LEFT: **Sporting the requisite hairstyle, Paul attends the annual Buddy Holly Week with Linda. A lifelong fan, Paul first began organizing the week-long tribute in 1976 on what would have been Buddy's birthday.**

Sotheby's in New York. The existing owner was the Cooper-Hewitt Museum, which had been given the car by John in 1977. The sale set a new record when new owner Jim Pattison from South Carolina paid $2,299,000.

15 JULY "I'm Stepping Out"/ "Sleepless Nights" was issued in Britain.

24 SEPTEMBER Paul released "No More Lonely Nights" in Britain.

5 OCTOBER In Britain John's "Every Man Has a Woman Who Loves Him" was released, with Sean singing "It's Alright" on the B-side.

9 OCTOBER *Thomas the Tank Engine*, narrated by Ringo, was broadcast for the first time on ITV.

16 OCTOBER "Every Man Has a Woman Who Loves Him"/ "It's Alright" went on sale in the States.

22 OCTOBER A soundtrack album from the film *Give My Regards to Broad Street* was issued in the UK and US.

25 OCTOBER In New York the world premiere of *Give My Regards to Broad Street* was held. Both Paul and Linda attended.

12 NOVEMBER In the UK Paul released "We All Stand Together"/ "We All Stand Together (Humming Version)".

28 NOVEMBER Paul attended a ceremony to become a Freeman of the City of Liverpool. That evening the UK premiere of *Give My Regards to Broad Street* was held in the city. *Rupert and the Frog Song* was the supporting film.

29 NOVEMBER The London premiere of *Give My Regards to Broad Street* at the Odeon, Leicester Square, was attended by Barbara, Ringo, Paul, Linda, and Olivia Harrison.

14 DECEMBER George made a surprise appearance with Deep Purple at their concert in Sydney, Australia.

"All Those Years Ago"

Although he would continue working on his album *Somewhere in England*, in the wake of John's murder George retreated further from public life, preferring to focus on his movie projects with HandMade Films. However, he was to attend Ringo and Barbara's wedding in April 1981, and in May would release his tribute to John, "All Those Years Ago", which featured backing from Ringo and Paul. *Somewhere in England* was released soon afterwards, reaching the Top 20 in both the US and UK charts, but George decided not to promote the follow-up, *Gone Troppo*, which subsequently fared poorly in the charts.

HANDMADE FILMS

During the 1980s one of George's most successful projects outside of the music business was his venture into film production with HandMade Films, a company that he founded with business partner Denis O'Brien in 1979 in order to help finance *Monty Python's Life of Brian* after EMI Films withdrew its backing.

Throughout the 1980s HandMade produced several highly acclaimed British films, such as *The Long Good Friday*, *Time Bandits*, *Mona Lisa*, and *Withnail and I*, but during the 1990s the company fell into difficulties due to mismanagement. As a result, George successfully sued O'Brien over the affair and, in 1994, the company was sold to a Canadian business, Paragon Entertainment. Since then HandMade's best-known and most successful release has probably been the British gangster movie *Lock, Stock and Two Smoking Barrels*.

1985

18 JANUARY The world premiere of *Water* was held in London. Made by HandMade Films, it had cameo roles from both George and Ringo.

11 MARCH Ringo had a cameo role in *Willie and the Poor Boys*.

13 JULY Paul took part in the Live Aid concert at Wembley Stadium. Combined with another concert later in the day at JFK Stadium in Philadelphia, the event raised $70 million.

10 AUGUST Michael Jackson paid $47.5 million to purchase the ATV music-publishing catalogue that held the rights to most of the Lennon–McCartney songs. He outbid Paul, who was dismayed by this move.

7 SEPTEMBER Ringo became the first grandfather in the group when his son Zak and his wife Sarah had a daughter, Tatia Jayne.

18 NOVEMBER In the UK Paul released "Spies Like Us". John's "Jealous Guy"/"Going Down on Love" was released in the UK.

9 DECEMBER Ringo played the Mock Turtle in *Alice in Wonderland*, screened in the States.

1986

24 JANUARY The album *John Lennon: Live in New York City* was released in the States (24 February in the UK).

26 JANUARY At the *London Standard* Film Awards, held at the Savoy Hotel, London, George collected several awards for HandMade Films.

27 JANUARY At the American Music Awards, Paul collected an Award of Merit.

15 MARCH George performed at a benefit concert for a local children's hospital held at the National Exhibition Centre in Birmingham, England.

14 JULY Paul's single "Press" was released in the UK (22 August in the US).

29 AUGUST The world premiere of *Shanghai Surprise* was held in New York. The film was made by HandMade Films; George wrote the soundtrack and also had a cameo role.

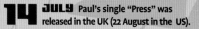

George continued to make musical contributions to some of HandMade Films' movie soundtracks, and in 1984 provided a song for the Greenpeace charity album and appeared onstage with Deep Purple in Australia, but for a number of years he seemed to largely shun both recording and publicity, choosing instead to dedicate much of his time to gardening and attending Formula One races.

In January 1987, however, George returned to the studio to begin work on a new album, *Cloud Nine*, which would be released that November. The album proved to be a commercial success and would provide the hit single "Got My Mind Set on You", which reached No. 1 in the US and No. 2 in the UK charts. The Beatlesque "When We Was Fab" was another hit, and around this time George also made a number of guest appearances with other bands and musicians, including Taj Mahal and Bob Dylan before going on to record with Jeff Lynne, Roy Orbison, Bob Dylan, and Tom Petty as the Traveling Wilburys in 1988. Enjoying his return to public life, George also attended the Beatles' induction into the Rock and Roll Hall of Fame in New York that year, along with Ringo, Yoko Ono, and Sean and Julian Lennon. Paul chose not to appear, however.

OPPOSITE: **George's production company, HandMade Films, reaped a series of awards at the *London Standard* Film Awards in 1986. He is pictured here on the set of his next project, *Shanghai Surprise*, which starred Madonna.**

LEFT: **George, Olivia, and eight-year-old Dhani arrive back from Los Angeles in 1986.**

1 SEPTEMBER Paul's album *Press to Play* went on sale in the UK.

27 OCTOBER Paul's single "Pretty Little Head" was released in Britain. The album *Menlove Avenue* was issued in the States. It contained some unreleased recordings from John.

3 NOVEMBER *Menlove Avenue* was released in the UK.

24 NOVEMBER Paul appeared on the Royal Variety Performance. It was televised on BBC1 five days later.

1 DECEMBER Paul's single "Only Love Remains" was issued in Britain.

1987

26 FEBRUARY EMI released the first official compact discs in the UK: *Please Please Me*, *With the Beatles*, *A Hard Day's Night*, and *Beatles for Sale*.

1 JUNE The documentary *It Was Twenty Years Ago Today* was shown on ITV. It featured the making of *Sgt. Pepper's Lonely Hearts Club Band*. The album, just released on CD, made it to No. 3 in the UK charts.

5-6 JUNE At the Prince's Trust concerts at Wembley George played two concerts alongside guests that included Phil Collins, Eric Clapton, and Ringo.

12 OCTOBER George released "Got My Mind Set on You"/"Lay His Head" in the UK (16 October in the US).

17 OCTOBER At the end of a Bob Dylan concert held at Wembley, George joined him for two songs.

2 NOVEMBER George released *Cloud Nine* as a CD and LP on both sides of the Atlantic.

16 NOVEMBER In the UK Paul released *All the Best*, with a selection of his best post-Beatles work (5 December in the US). On the same day he also issued the single "Once Upon a Long Ago"/"Back on My Feet" in the UK.

1988

20 JANUARY At the Waldorf Astoria in New York the Beatles were inducted into the Rock And Roll Hall of Fame by Mick Jagger. Paul was absent due to his differences with the rest of the group over their business affairs. Yoko, Julian, and Sean attended on behalf of John.

continued from previous page

25 JANUARY A simultaneous release in the UK and US of George's "When We Was Fab"/"Zig Zag".

7 MARCH Release of the albums *Past Masters Volumes One and Two.*

2 MAY George's "This Is Love"/ "Breath Away from Heaven" was issued in the States.

11 JULY John's interview with RKO Radio just before he died was released in the UK on a CD titled *The Last Word.*

19 SEPTEMBER John's "Jealous Guy" with "Give Peace a Chance" went on sale in the States.

30 SEPTEMBER Paul's CD *Choba B CCCP (Back in the USSR)* was released in the UK. It contained many rock 'n' roll classics and was originally intended just for the Russian market.

4 OCTOBER *Imagine: John Lennon* was released in the US.

10 OCTOBER *Imagine: John Lennon* was launched in the UK.

1989

24 FEBRUARY Ringo released *Starrstruck: Best of Vol. 2 (1976– 1983)* in the States (1 March in the UK).

10 MAY Paul's "My Brave Face"/ "Flying to My Home" was issued in the US.

5 JUNE In the UK Paul released the album *Flowers in the Dirt* (6 June in the US).

5 JULY Ringo and Buck Owens released "Act Naturally" with "The Key's in the Mailbox" by Owens on the B-side.

23 JULY Ringo and His All-Starr band played in Dallas at the start of their 1989 world tour.

26 JULY Paul performed at the London Playhouse Theatre and introduced a new backing band.

24 AUGUST In the States, George released "Cheer Down"/"That's What It Takes".

"Free as a Bird"

In 1990, George continued recording with the Traveling Wilburys, who would release their second album, *Traveling Wilburys Vol. 3*, and contribute the song "Nobody's Child" to a charity album of the same name. He also continued to make occasional live appearances with artists such as Gary Moore, Carl Perkins, and Bob Dylan, as well as playing the ukulele at a George Formby convention in Blackpool and featuring on Julian Lennon's *Help Yourself* album.

In 1991 George would return to touring for the first time since 1974, when he embarked on a tour of Japan with Eric Clapton and his band. The following year the group would also perform a one-off concert at the Royal Albert Hall in support of the Natural Law Party.

In the mid-'90s, George then teamed up with producer Jeff Lynne, Paul, and Ringo to work on the Beatles *Anthology* project; recording guitar for the singles "Free as a Bird" and "Real Love", which were based upon John's unfinished demo recordings. Some of these sessions took place at George's home studio, as did work on Ravi Shankar's album, *Chants of India*, which featured George as both a performer and producer.

Around this time George also became embroiled in a verbal conflict with Liam Gallagher of Oasis, having remarked that the singer lacked talent. Gallagher had responded by challenging the former Beatle to a fight, along with Mick Jagger and Keith Richards of the Rolling Stones.

ABOVE AND OPPOSITE RIGHT: **George continued to lend support to worthy causes, playing at a concert in Birmingham in aid of a local children's hospital (above) and in a tribute concert to rock 'n' roll singer Carl Perkins (opposite).**

ABOVE INSETS: **On her first world tour, Yoko returned to the Amsterdam Hilton and talked to journalists whilst sitting on the bed she and John used for their first "bed-in" 17 years previously (inset top). Onstage (inset bottom) she performed some of his best-known songs, including "Imagine".**

OPPOSITE LEFT: **The 20th anniversary of the release of *Sgt. Pepper* is celebrated by Paul and Linda with a slice of cake.**

6 NOVEMBER *The Single Collection* was released in the UK, originally sold only by mail order.

23-29 NOVEMBER Paul was in LA during his world tour. While there he met Michael Jackson backstage.

19 DECEMBER During a show at Madison Square Garden in New York, Paul was given an honour by the Performing Rights Society for a "unique achievement in popular music".

1990

2-26 JANUARY Paul continued his tour, playing the International Arena in Birmingham and 11 further nights at Wembley in London.

1 FEBRUARY Paul released his *World Tour Special Edition* CD.

21 FEBRUARY A lifetime-achievement Grammy Award was presented to Paul.

12 APRIL At the International Astronomical Union Minor Planet Center in Cambridge, Massachusetts, it was announced that asteroids would be named after each of the four Beatles. The asteroids numbered 4147–4150 were discovered by Brian A. Skiff and Dr. Edward Bowell of the Lowell Observatory in Flagstaff, Arizona, in 1983 and 1984.

1 MAY During Eric Clapton's *Journeyman* tour George appeared in LA with him.

5 MAY A John Lennon tribute concert was held at the Pier Head Arena in Merseyside. Ringo took part, and the proceeds went to the Spirit Foundation which had been set up by John and Yoko.

28 JUNE During the world tour Paul performed a concert for charity in Liverpool.

5 OCTOBER George played guitar during a Gary Moore concert.

8 OCTOBER *Ringo Starr and His All-Starr Band* was released in Britain (12 October in the US).

9 OCTOBER It would have been John's 50th birthday; to commemorate his life, "Imagine" was played simultaneously in 130 countries.

All-Starr Band

During the early 1990s, Ringo's talent for narration continued to be in demand, notably for further episodes of *Thomas the Tank Engine*, and the film *Walking After Midnight*, but he was also to lend his voice to his own cartoon depiction in *The Simpsons* in 1991, as would Paul and George in later episodes. In addition, he would feature in various television advertisements throughout the decade, including a pizza advert alongside former members of the Monkees, as well as in commercials for the Japanese soft drink Ringo Suttar.

Musically, Ringo began the 1990s by recording a new album, *Time Takes Time*, which was released in 1992, along with the single "Weight of the World", and that same year he also toured North America and Europe with his new All-Starr Band, which included his son Zak on drums. The tour resulted in a live album, recorded at the Montreux Jazz Festival.

In 1994 Ringo reunited with Paul and George to work on the *Anthology* project and also gave interviews to promote the release of *Live at the BBC* before embarking on another tour; this time taking in Japan and the US, with the third incarnation of his All-Starr Band. The tour was cut short, however, when his daughter, Lee, was rushed to hospital suffering from hydrocephalus.

Work on a new studio album, *Vertical Man*, began in 1997, but despite contributions from Paul, George, Brian Wilson, Aerosmith's Steven Tyler, and Alanis Morissette, sales were disappointing upon its release the following year.

In 2002 Ringo became an inductee of the Percussive Hall of Fame, and since then he has continued to tour regularly with various All-Starr lineups—most recently in 2006. That same year, he appeared on the Jerry Lee Lewis duet album, *Last Man Standing*, and also began work on a new studio album of his own, titled *Liverpool 8* that was released on 15 January 2008.

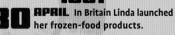
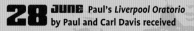

continued from previous page

29 OCTOBER *The Traveling Wilbury's Vol. 3*, their second album, was released in the UK (30 Oct in the US). EMI issued *Lennon*, a boxed set of John's songs, in the UK and the US.

5 NOVEMBER A simultaneous release in Britain and the US for Paul's *Tripping the Live Fantastic*, taken from the 1989–90 world tour.

19 NOVEMBER Another simultaneous release in Britain and the US for Paul's *Tripping the Live Fantastic—Highlights*, this time condensing the music from the 1989–90 world tour.

14 DECEMBER *Testimony* was issued only in the UK, with a longer section of the RKO radio interview with John.

1991

30 APRIL In Britain Linda launched her frozen-food products.

20 MAY A UK release for Paul's *Unplugged: The Official Bootleg*. It was recorded during a show in 1991 and then issued as a limited edition of 250,000 copies (4 June in the US).

28 JUNE Paul's *Liverpool Oratorio* by Paul and Carl Davis received

its world premiere at the Anglican Cathedral in Liverpool.

22 OCTOBER In the States, McCartney's *Liverpool Oratorio* was released.

11 NOVEMBER Paul's single "Save the Child" went on sale in Britain and the States.

1 DECEMBER George toured Japan with Eric Clapton, starting with a date at Yokohama.

26 DECEMBER In the States both the *Red* and *Blue* album were certified platinum.

1992

3 APRIL At the Grammy Awards in the States, Ringo was guest presenter.

6 APRIL At a benefit concert for the Natural Law Party at the Royal Albert Hall, London, George performed and Ringo made a guest appearance.

22 MAY In the States, *Time Takes Time* was released by Ringo (29 June in the UK).

2 JUNE Ringo and His All-Starr Band began a new world tour in Fort Lauderdale, Florida.

ABOVE: **Paul, Linda, and Brian May of the band Queen.**

LEFT AND OPPOSITE: **George's charity concerts continued with one in aid of the Prince's Trust. Guest artists included Eric Clapton, Elton John, and Ringo.**

13 JULY In Britain, George released *Live in Japan*, taped during the previous year's tour (14 July in the US).

16 OCTOBER George performed at the Bob Dylan 30th Anniversary Concert held at Madison Square Garden, New York.

10 NOVEMBER *The Single Collection* was released in the States.

1993

18 JANUARY Paul's "Hope and Deliverance" was issued on both sides of the Atlantic.

2 FEBRUARY Paul issued *Off the Ground* in the UK (9 February in the US).

5 FEBRUARY Paul kicked off another world tour in Docklands, London.

14 SEPTEMBER *Ringo Starr and His All-Starr Band: Live at Montreux* was released. It was taped live at the Jazz Festival in July 1992.

16 NOVEMBER Another simultaneous release for Paul's CD *Paul Is Live*. It included 24 live tracks and two new songs. In the UK it was also issued as an LP.

1994

19 JANUARY Paul inducted John Lennon into the Rock and Roll Hall of Fame.

30 NOVEMBER *Live at the BBC* was released in Britain, selling 350,000 copies in the first week and reaching the top of the charts. Two hundred fans queued outside Tower Records in Piccadilly Circus, London, to purchase the album before anyone else.

6 DECEMBER *Live at the BBC* was released in the States, selling 100,000 copies on the first day and reaching No. 3 in the charts.

30 DECEMBER Ringo's ex-wife, Maureen, died from complications after a bone-marrow transplant.

1995

14 JUNE Ringo and His All-Starr band began the 1995 world tour in Morioka, Japan.

14 SEPTEMBER At Sotheby's in London, Paul's handwritten lyrics for "Getting Better" sold for $249,200.

8 NOVEMBER Paul became a Fellow of the Royal College of Music, the first pop artist to receive this honour.

ABOVE AND RIGHT: **Paul's world tour included concerts in Birmingham and London's Wembley Arena followed by a return to the States.**

continued from previous page

19 NOVEMBER The first part of *The Beatles Anthology* was shown on ABC-TV (the next editions were shown on 22 and 23 November). It documented the band's early years, using new interviews interspersed with archive material. The series was shown in December on British television divided into six one-hour programmes. On this show the Beatles' "new" single "Free as a Bird" was premiered. George had an idea to use a John Lennon demo recorded in 1977, so he, Paul, and Ringo joined with Jeff Lynne to produce the song.

21 NOVEMBER *Anthology 1* was released in Britain and the States, charting at No. 2 in Britain and topping the American charts for three weeks.

4 DECEMBER "Free as a Bird"/ "Christmas Time (Is Here Again)" was released in the UK, reaching No. 2 in the charts.

12 DECEMBER "Free as a Bird"/ "Christmas Time (Is Here Again)" was issued in the States, reaching No. 6 in the charts.

1996

4 MARCH "Real Love"/"Baby's in Black" was released in the UK but didn't make Radio One's playlist. Despite this, it reached No. 4 in the charts. This was the second single released by the three remaining members of the band using an original John Lennon recording.

5 MARCH "Real Love"/"Baby's in Black" was released in the States and sold over half a million copies in four months.

18 MARCH *Anthology 2* was released in Britain and reached No. 1 in the charts (19 March in the US, also topping the charts).

7 JUNE Queen Elizabeth II officially opened the Liverpool Institute of Performing Arts. Paul had purchased his old school building, which had become derelict, to form the Institute, of which he is patron. It was his way of being able to help his hometown.

Hall of Fame

Having completed his highly successful world tour in 1990, Paul then turned his hand to classical composition, collaborating with Carl Davis to produce the *Liverpool Oratorio* in 1991, and later in the decade *A Leaf*, *Standing Stone*, *Working Classical*, and *Ecce Cor Meum*. Paul also created the soundtrack to the 1992 film *Daumier's Law*, and in 1993 would work with dance-music producer Martin Glover, known as Youth on the experimental project *Strawberries Oceans Ships Forest*.

More conventional releases of the early '90s included *Unplugged: The Official Bootleg*, and *Choba B CCCP*, which had initially been recorded in 1987 and released only for the Russian market. Paul's next solo studio album was 1993's *Off the Ground*, the release of which was quickly followed by the start of the New World Tour in February. Encompassing Europe, Australasia, North America, Japan, Mexico, and Brazil, the tour would continue until mid-November.

In January 1994 Paul attended John Lennon's induction into the Rock and Roll Hall of Fame, where Yoko was to provide him with the Lennon demo tapes that would be used for the new singles to accompany the *Anthology* releases.

Sadly, in 1995 amidst the excitement surrounding the release of *Anthology 1*, Linda was found to be suffering with breast cancer, but following an operation, the disease appeared to go into remission the following year.

ABOVE: **Paul, with his new backing band, began a world tour in 1989. Linda continued to be in the lineup, but Paul was the focus onstage.**

8 JULY "Free as a Bird"/"Christmas Time (Is Here Again)" and "Real Love"/"Baby's in Black" were certified gold in the States.

18 SEPTEMBER Part of John's handwritten lyrics for "Being for the Benefit Of Mr. Kite!" were sold at Sotheby's in London for $103,500. During the auction Julian Lennon paid $39,030 for the notes Paul made for the recording of "Hey Jude".

28 OCTOBER *Anthology 3* went on sale in Britain, reaching No. 4 in the charts (29 October in the US, reaching No. 1).

30 OCTOBER It was announced that Paul was to receive a knighthood.

1997
10 JANUARY The album *Love Songs* was certified platinum in the States.

16 JANUARY The album *Rarities* was certified gold in the States.

26 FEBRUARY At the Grammy Awards, the Beatles received three awards, one for *The Beatles Anthology* and two for "Free as a Bird".

11 MARCH Paul received his knighthood at Buckingham Palace.

28 APRIL Ringo and His All-Starr Band began a world tour in Seattle.

6 MAY Paul released "The World Tonight"/ "Looking for You" in the States.

27 MAY Paul's album *Flaming Pie* was issued in the States.

12 AUGUST *Ringo Starr and His Third All-Starr Band*, recorded live in Japan, was issued in the States.

23 SEPTEMBER In the States Paul issued his classical album *Standing Stone*.

THE BEATLES ANTHOLOGY

Ever since the 1970s the Beatles had planned to produce a documentary film in order to provide their own, definitive account of the group's history, but disagreements and legal battles between the former bandmates, and later with EMI, ensured that the project would effectively be shelved for around twenty years.

In the late 1980s, however, Paul began discussing the possibility of reviving the documentary and even reuniting with George and Ringo to produce some new incidental music to accompany it. George was initially dismissive, regarding Paul's comments as self-promotion, but in 1991 he and Neil Aspinall approached Yoko to see if any of John's demo tapes might be used as a starting point for some new recordings. That same year the documentary-production team of Geoff Wonfor, Chips Chipperfield, and Bob Smeaton was assembled and began trawling through the extensive Beatles archive footage and preparing new interviews with Paul, George, and Ringo.

In January '94, at John's posthumous induction into the Rock and Roll Hall of Fame, Yoko Ono passed some of John's tapes on to Paul and, the following month, "the Threatles" assembled to begin recording together at the Mill, Paul's studio, with Jeff Lynne as producer. These sessions focused on John's demo "Free as a Bird", with later sessions taking place in June. A further year passed before work began on the demo "Real Love".

Meanwhile George Martin, who in 1993 had dismissed the idea of releasing an album of studio outtakes and demos, began listening through the Beatles' audio archives with a view to compiling just such an album as part of the project.

So much audio and visual material was unearthed as the project unfolded that *The Beatles Anthology* would eventually be unveiled as a television series, video set, and three double CD albums. Additionally, the completed versions of "Free as a Bird" and "Real Love", would be released as new Beatles singles.

Towards the end of 1995 the documentary series was aired on ABC-TV in the US and ITV in the UK and "Free as a Bird" was issued as a single. Viewing figures for the series were initially high, with estimated audiences of over 48 million and 14 million in America and Britain respectively but, disappointingly, these fell dramatically from each broadcast to the next.

Sales of the album and single releases, however, were huge. "Free as a Bird" reached No. 2 in the UK and No. 4 in the US, whilst "Real Love" made it to No. 4 in Britain and No. 11 in America, and all of the anthology albums went multiplatinum soon after their release. In fact, remarkably, the Beatles were to sell more albums in 1996 than in any other year of their history.

continued from previous page

14 OCTOBER *Standing Stone* received its world premiere.

27 OCTOBER *Lennon Legend: The Very Best of John Lennon* was released in the UK, containing his best solo pieces (23 February in the US).

1998

17 APRIL Linda McCartney died of cancer at the age of 56 at the family farm in Arizona, with Paul by her bedside.

8 JUNE Linda's memorial service was held at St. Martin-in-the-Fields in London, the first time the three remaining band members appeared together in public for 30 years.

16 JUNE Ringo released *Vertical Man* in the States.

20 OCTOBER Ringo released a *VH1 Storytellers* album in the US, telling the story behind each song prior to performing.

2 NOVEMBER In Britain *The John Lennon Anthology* was issued. Spread over four CDs it contained over 100 unreleased tracks. In Britain *Wonsaponatime* was issued, containing a selection from *The John Lennon Anthology*.

3 NOVEMBER *The John Lennon Anthology* and *Wonsaponatime* were released in the States.

1999

15 MARCH Neil Young inducted Paul McCartney into the Rock and Roll Hall of Fame during its 14th annual dinner at the Waldorf Astoria in New York.

10 APRIL Here, There, And Everywhere: A Concert For Linda was held at the Royal Albert Hall. Paul surprised everyone by making his first public appearance since her death when he went onstage to sing "Lonesome Town" and "All My Loving". At the end of the show he led all the performers in a rendition of "Let It Be".

1 MAY Paul exhibited his artwork for the first time in Siegen, Germany; it was met with high acclaim.

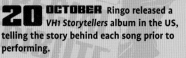

THIS PAGE: **Paul and Linda celebrate his forthcoming world tour at a press conference at the Playhouse Theatre.**

OPPOSITE: **Paul is awarded a small gold guitar by the Performing Rights Society in recognition of his contribution to pop music.**

1 AUGUST In the UK magazine Q, a readers' poll of the 100 Greatest Stars of the 20th Century was issued. John was first, Paul second.

30 AUGUST In the States, the postal service produced a 33-cent Yellow Submarine stamp to celebrate Beatles International Week.

14 SEPTEMBER *Yellow Submarine Songtrack* was released reaching No. 8 in the UK and No. 15 in the US. A restored edition of the film was released at the same time.

4 OCTOBER Paul's *Run Devil Run* went on sale in the UK. It included rock 'n' roll classics and some new songs.

5 OCTOBER *Run Devil Run* was issued in the States.

16 OCTOBER The world premiere for Paul's *Working Classical*, performed by the London Symphony Orchestra, was held in Liverpool.

19 OCTOBER *Working Classical* was issued in the US and the UK. In the States, Ringo released *I Wanna Be Santa Claus.*

2 NOVEMBER *Yellow Submarine Songtrack* was certified gold in the US.

9 NOVEMBER In the States, The Recording Association of America produced its list of Artists of the Century; the Beatles were at the top, having sold 106 million albums in the States.

14 DECEMBER At the new Cavern Club, Paul played a set before an audience of 300 with 15,000 watching on-screen at Chavasse Park in Liverpool and a further 3 million watching through the Internet.

24 DECEMBER George's Hawaiian home was broken into by a woman who was subsequently arrested.

30 DECEMBER George was attacked at home in Henley-on-Thames by an intruder who stabbed him in the chest. His life was saved by Olivia who hit the attacker over the head with a table lamp. Thirty-three-year old Michael Abram from Liverpool was charged with attempted murder.

2000

25 APRIL Paul released the album *A Garland for Linda*, a tribute album to raise money for the Garland Appeal, which supports those suffering from cancer.

7 JULY Ringo turned 60 years old.

25 JULY In the States both the *Red* and *Blue* albums were certified diamond.

13 NOVEMBER The album *1*, containing all the Beatles' number one hits, was released in Britain, selling 59,000 copies in one day and reaching No. 1 in the charts, where it remained for nine consecutive weeks. Worldwide it sold over 23 million copies and topped the charts in 34 countries.

14 NOVEMBER The album *1* was released in the States, selling nearly 600,000 copies in the first week and reaching No. 1 in the charts for a total of seven weeks.

15 NOVEMBER Michael Abram was found not guilty of attempting to murder George on the grounds of insanity (he was a paranoid schizophrenic). He was, however, sent to a psychiatric hospital "without time restriction".

8 DECEMBER On the 20th anniversary of John's death, Fidel Castro unveiled a statue of John in Havana's El Vedado Park.

15 DECEMBER *1* was certified both gold and platinum in the States.

2001

19 JANUARY Ringo's triple-live compilation album *The Anthology... So Far* went on release in the UK.

7 MAY Paul released the album *Wingspan: Hits and History* in the UK (8 May in the US).

2 JULY *The Anthology... So Far* was issued in the States.

Tributes for Linda

In 1997 Paul was knighted, becoming Sir Paul McCartney, and he was to enjoy considerable success with his album *Flaming Pie*, which reached No. 2 in both the US and Britain. In '97 and '98, Paul and Linda also celebrated their daughter Stella's achievements as a fashion designer; but tragically, Linda was to die of cancer in April 1998. Paul was understandably devastated, but urged fans to pay their tributes in supporting one of the many causes that the couple had championed over the years, such as animal welfare and environmental concerns.

Paul largely retreated from public view over the next year, but in 1999 he returned with the album *Run Devil Run* and was inducted into the Rock and Roll Hall of Fame in New York. He also held his first exhibition of paintings and performed at the new Cavern Club in Liverpool.

RIGHT: **Paul met Michael Jackson whilst on the US leg of his tour in 1989, dispelling rumours of a falling-out. Paul had been dismayed when he had been outbid by Jackson for the rights to the Lennon–McCartney songs in 1985, but he insisted that the friendship was strong.**

OPPOSITE RIGHT AND INSET: **Mutual support had been a hallmark of the McCartney marriage, and in 1991, when Linda launched her own brand of precooked vegetarian meals, Paul had backed her all the way.**

FAR RIGHT AND OPPOSITE LEFT: **Paul performs during his world tour in 1989 (opposite left) and four years later, during the 1993 world tour (far right).**

24 JULY Yoko visited the renamed Liverpool John Lennon Airport, which was to carry the motto, "Above Us Only Sky". A statue of John designed by Tom Murphy stands in the entrance.

11 SEPTEMBER When the World Trade Center was attacked, Paul saw the events unfold as he was sitting on a plane in New York City. His anger inspired him to write "Freedom", which was added to *Driving Rain* as an extra track (not listed as the tracks had been printed).

23 SEPTEMBER A full-page advertisement appeared in *The New York Times* reading, "Imagine all the people living in peace". It was anonymously put in the paper by Yoko Ono in response to the 9/11 attacks.

2 OCTOBER *Come Together: A Night for John Lennon's Words and Music* was broadcast on the WB and TNT. It was held at New York's Music Hall and, although initially planned as a one-off tribute, was also used as a benefit event for the relief organizations involved in the aftermath of 9/11.

20 OCTOBER Paul was the lead organizer of The Concert for New York City, a benefit concert held at Madison Square Garden in response to the 9/11 attacks.

29 OCTOBER Paul released "From a Lover to a Friend"/ "Riding to Jaipur".

12 NOVEMBER Paul's album *Driving Rain* was released in the UK (13 November in the US).

29 NOVEMBER George Harrison died of cancer in Los Angeles at the age of 58. His wife Olivia and his son Dhani were with him. He chose to be cremated in a cardboard coffin without any ceremony, with his ashes scattered on the River Yamuna in India.

30 NOVEMBER At Liverpool Town Hall a Book of Condolence for George was opened, with the hall's flags flying at half-mast. During the Changing of the Guard ceremony in London, the Coldstream Guards played a Beatles medley.

Paul remarries

In 1999 Paul became romantically involved with the anti-landmine campaigner Heather Mills, and the couple became engaged in 2001. Shortly afterwards Paul was instrumental in setting up a concert in New York in the wake of the September 11 disaster and also released the album *Driving Rain*.

In June 2002 Paul and Heather were married, and Paul embarked on another extensive world tour, that continued into 2004 and included performances at Red Square in Russia and at the Glastonbury Festival in England. Meanwhile the couple celebrated the birth of a daughter, Beatrice, in 2003.

That same year Paul released the album *Back in the World*, followed two years later by the highly acclaimed *Chaos and Creation in the Backyard*.

BIO: HEATHER MILLS

Heather Mills' life was turned upside down when she was struck by a police motorcyclist in August 1993, sustaining severe injuries which resulted in the loss of her left leg below the knee. Heather's career as a glamour model was over, but the accident allowed her to focus on her entrepreneurial talent. Having already been involved with several successful ventures, she turned her attention to the plight of amputees, especially in the war-torn state of the former Yugoslavia. Heather founded a charity dedicated to ridding the world of landmines, and also became an active campaigner on the issue of animal rights. Her fortitude in the face of adversity and her philanthropic acts have won her numerous awards and honorary titles, including a nomination for a Nobel Prize in 1996. It was at a charity event in May 1999 that Heather met Paul. She had been married once before, to salesman Alfie Karmal, though her second wedding, on 11 June 2002, had a somewhat higher profile. Daughter Beatrice Milly was born the following year. The couple announced their separation in May 2006.

2002

JANUARY George's single "My Sweet Lord" was reissued, reaching No. 1 in the British charts.

3 JUNE At the Party in the Palace, held to celebrate Queen's Elizabeth's 50-year reign, Paul sang "Her Majesty" before leading the climax of the show; all the performers sang "Hey Jude" and "All You Need Is Love".

11 JUNE Paul married model and anti-landmine campaigner Heather Mills at Castle Leslie in the Republic of Ireland.

18 JUNE Paul turned 60 years old.

6 AUGUST Ringo's live album *King Biscuit Flower Hour Presents Ringo & His New All-Starr Band* was released.

21 AUGUST In a poll by the BBC asking the British public to vote for who they thought was the "Greatest Briton" John was polled in eighth place, Paul in 19th and George 62nd.

18 NOVEMBER George's album *Brainwashed* was released. He was still working on it when he died, so coproducers Jeff Lynne and his son, Dhani, completed the work. The single "Marwa Blues" taken from the album won the award for Best Pop Instrumental Performance in the 2004 Grammy Awards.

26 NOVEMBER Paul's album *Back in the USSR, Live 2002* was issued in the States.

29 NOVEMBER Both Paul and Ringo performed at the Concert for George held at the Royal Albert Hall in London on the first anniversary of George's death. The proceeds went to the Material World Charitable Foundation, George's charity.

George dies at 58

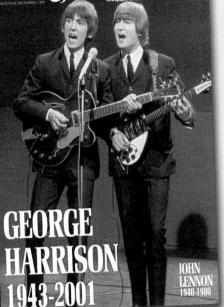

GEORGE HARRISON 1943-2001

In 1997 George discovered a lump on his throat and was treated for suspected throat cancer. He was given the all-clear, but a lengthy battle with the illness ensued, which is thought to have been aggravated by a serious knife attack in late 1999 when an intruder broke into his home and stabbed him, puncturing one of his lungs. George recovered but finally succumbed to the cancer, which had spread to his lungs, in November 2001, passing away at his Hollywood home.

Following his death "My Sweet Lord" was reissued and reached the top of the UK charts in 2002. Later in the year, a posthumous album, *Brainwashed*, which had been completed by his son, Dhani, with Jeff Lynne as producer, was also released, and a concert featuring Paul, Ringo, Eric Clapton, and many others was held at the Albert Hall in his honour.

Two years later, George was inducted into the Rock and Roll Hall of Fame and, in 2006, into the Madison Square Garden Walk of Fame.

LEFT: **Paul is pictured outside his Sussex home after receiving the news of George's death. Having survived a knife attack at his home the previous year, George died of cancer in Los Angeles at the age of 58.**

OPPOSITE LEFT: **A year after Linda's death, Paul met former model Heather Mills through her charity work. The pair became engaged in July 2001 and married the following summer.**

OPPOSITE BELOW LEFT: **Paul returns to Liverpool in July 2002. He and Heather separated and filed for divorce in 2006, blaming constant media intrusion for the damage to their relationship.**

OPPOSITE BELOW RIGHT: **Paul is seen here at the Ivor Novello Awards at the Grosvenor House Hotel, London.**

2003
17 MARCH Paul's album *Back in the World Live* was released in the UK.

24 MARCH Ringo issued the album *Ringo Rama*.

12 MAY Posthumously George's single "Any Road"/"Marwa Blues" was released, with both tracks taken from the album *Brainwashed*.

1 JUNE Ringo issued the promotional live album *Extended Versions*.

28 OCTOBER Paul and Heather's daughter, Beatrice Milly, was born.

17 NOVEMBER *Let It Be... Naked* was released in Britain and the States. The CD and DVD *Concert for George*—a tribute album recorded at the Royal Albert Hall the previous year—went on sale in the States.

2004
15 MARCH George Harrison was inducted into the Rock and Roll Hall of Fame.

23 MARCH Ringo's album *Tour 2003 (Live)* was issued.

26 JUNE Paul played at the Glastonbury Festival for the first time.

2005
7 JUNE Ringo's album *Choose Love* was issued in the US.

2 JULY Paul played "Sgt. Pepper's Lonely Hearts Club Band" with U2 at the Live 8 concert held in Hyde Park.

25 JULY *Choose Love* was released in the UK.

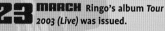

SPREADING THE LOVE

In 2006 the Beatles were heard as they had never been heard before, thanks to the efforts of Sir George Martin and his son, Giles, who remixed some old favourites for a Las Vegas show by Cirque du Soleil. The whole process had emerged from George Harrison's friendship with Guy Laliberté, the founder of the circus. The band's difficult history seemed far away on the opening night of the show on 30 June 2006, which turned out to be one of the greatest Beatles reunions yet seen; Paul and Ringo were joined by Yoko Ono, Olivia Harrison, Cynthia Lennon, and Julian. The soundtrack was released in November 2006 and quickly eclipsed the show, ranking fourth in the *Billboard* charts, taking the No. 3 spot in the UK, topping charts around the world, and winning two Grammy Awards. Featuring twenty-six tracks, the *Love* album was a collage of Beatles songs, often putting well-known sounds in unfamiliar places: Harrison's instantly recognizable opening chord for "A Hard Day's Night" instead introduces "Get Back", and birdsong from "Across the Universe" accompanies "Because". Although the album almost entirely uses existing material, a new score was added for "While My Guitar Gently Weeps".

---

continued from previous page

12 SEPTEMBER Paul's album *Chaos And Creation in the Backyard*, went on sale in the UK (13 September in the US).

29 AUGUST Paul's single "Fine Line"/"Growing Up Falling Down" was released.

OCTOBER *High in the Clouds: An Urban Furry Tail*, Paul's children's book cowritten with Philip Ardagh and illustrated by Geoff Dunbar, was published.

4 OCTOBER Paul released the single "Jenny Wren" and was later nominated for the Grammy Awards 2007 in the Best Male Pop Vocal Performance section.

21 NOVEMBER The album *Working Class Hero: The Definitive Lennon* was released.

8 DECEMBER On the 25th anniversary of John's death, celebrations of his life were held in Britain and the States.

2006

11 APRIL *The Capitol Albums Vol. 2* was released in the States.

17 MAY Paul and Heather announced their separation, saying that media attention had damaged their relationship.

6 JUNE Billy Preston died after being in a coma from kidney disease since November 2005.

18 JUNE True to the words of his song, Paul reached his 64th birthday. He had written it when he was 16.

29 JULY British newspapers announce that Paul had filed for divorce.

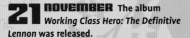

THIS PAGE AND OPPOSITE INSET: **Long queues formed in London when Paul held a signing session to mark the release of** *The Space Within Us* **DVD and his classical album** *Ecce Cor Meum*. **The album and DVD were both released in late 2006, when the** *Love* **compilation also hit the shops.**

15 AUGUST Ringo's album *Ringo Starr and His Friends* was released. Guest performers included David Bowie and Prince.

25 SEPTEMBER *Ecce Cor Meum (Behold My Heart)*, Paul's fourth classical album, was released in the UK and issued in the States the following day.

3 NOVEMBER *Ecce Cor Meum* is premiered at the Royal Albert Hall in London.

14 NOVEMBER *Ecce Cor Meum* received its US premiere at Carnegie Hall.

20 NOVEMBER The *Love* album was issued in both the UK and the US.

7 DECEMBER The DVD of *The Space Within Us* was released, comprising footage from Paul's US tour in autumn 2005. Paul took over Classic FM radio station for 24 hours.

2007

21 MARCH Paul finally left EMI and became the first artist to sign to Starbucks' new record label, Hear Music, based in Los Angeles.

2 APRIL An intruder drove through the security fence at Peasmarsh, Paul's country estate. He was finally arrested after a car chase.

2008

3 FEBRUARY Maharishi Mahesh Yogi died.

10 FEBRUARY *Love* won two Grammy Awards for Best Compilation Soundtrack Album and Best Surround Sound Album.

24 MARCH Neil Aspinall died of lung cancer.

JOHN, PAUL, GEORGE & RINGO

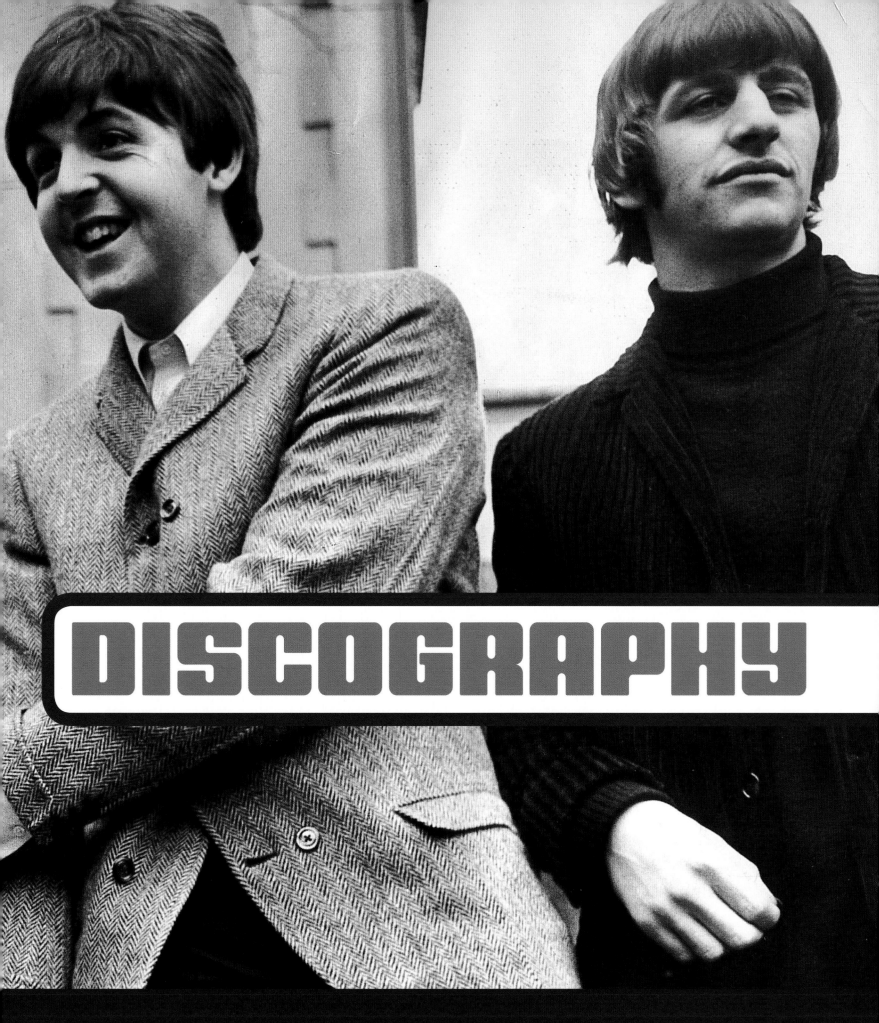

DISCOGRAPHY

170 million albums

In the UK the Beatles released a total of seventeen singles and fifteen albums that reached number one in the Record Retailer charts, while in the US twenty singles and nineteen albums topped the *Billboard* Hot 100 listings. In April 1964 the band held the first five positions in the Hot 100 with another seven singles further down in the charts, a record that still stands today. So far they have sold 170 million albums worldwide, and the number continues to rise.

The discography on the following pages is in chronological order as the records were released. Year-by-year information is provided for the albums, singles, and EPs officially issued by the band and provides track listing, timings, composer, and producer credits from January 1962. From 1976 onwards, catalogue numbers are not included because of the predominance of compilation albums and multiple formats. Where original material is released then catalogue numbers are given.

Details of the band's individual record releases can be found in the chronicle running through the book.

1962-63

5 January 1962 Polydor NH 66-833 (UK)

23 April 1962 Decca 31382 (US)

My Bonnie (2.42) Pratt

The Saints (3.18) Traditional; Arr. Sheridan

(Tony Sheridan and the Beatles) Producer Bert Kaempfert

5 October 1962 Parlophone R 4949 (UK)

Love Me Do (2.19) Lennon–McCartney

P.S. I Love You (2.02) Lennon–McCartney

Producer George Martin

11 January 1963 Parlophone R 4983 (UK)

25 February 1963 Vee-Jay VJ 498 (US)

Please Please Me (2.00) Lennon–McCartney

Ask Me Why (2.28) Lennon–McCartney

Producer George Martin

22 March 1963 Parlophone PMC 1202 (mono) and PCS 3042 (stereo)

Please Please Me

Side One

I Saw Her Standing There (2.50) Lennon–McCartney

Misery (1.43) Lennon–McCartney

Anna (Go To Him) (2.56) Alexander

Chains (2.21) Goffin–King

Boys (2.24) Dixon–Farrell

Ask Me Why (2.24) Lennon–McCartney

Please Please Me (2.00) Lennon–McCartney

Side Two

Love Me Do (2.19) Lennon–McCartney

P.S. I Love You (2.02) Lennon–McCartney

Baby It's You (2.36) David–Williams–Bacharach

Do You Want to Know a Secret (1.55) Lennon–McCartney

A Taste of Honey (2.02) Scott–Marlow

There's a Place (1.44) Lennon–McCartney

Twist and Shout (2.32) Medley–Russell

Producer George Martin

11 April 1963 Parlophone R 5015 (UK)

6 May 1963 Vee-Jay VJ 522 (US)

From Me to You (1.55) Lennon–McCartney

Thank You Girl (2.01) Lennon–McCartney

Producer George Martin

12 July 1963 Parlophone GEP 8882

Twist and Shout

Twist and Shout (2.32) Medley–Russell

A Taste of Honey (2.02) Scott–Marlow

Do You Want to Know a Secret (1.55) Lennon–McCartney

There's a Place (1.44) Lennon–McCartney

Producer George Martin

22 July 1963 Vee-Jay VJLP 1062 (mono) SR 1062 (stereo)
Re-released in January 1964

Introducing the Beatles

Side One

I Saw Her Standing There (2.50) Lennon–McCartney

Misery (1.43) Lennon–McCartney

Anna (Go To Him) (2.56) Alexander

Chains (2.21) Goffin–King

Boys (2.24) Dixon–Farrell

Ask Me Why (2.24) Lennon–McCartney

Side Two

Please Please Me (2.00) Lennon–McCartney

Baby It's You (2.36) David–Williams–Bacharach

Do You Want to Know a Secret (1.55) Lennon–McCartney

A Taste of Honey (2.02) Scott–Marlow

There's a Place (1.44) Lennon–McCartney

Twist and Shout (2.32) Medley–Russell

Producer George Martin

23 August 1963 Parlophone 5055 (UK)

16 September 1963 Swan 4152 (US)

She Loves You (2.18) Lennon–McCartney

I'll Get You (2.04) Lennon–McCartney

Producer George Martin

6 September 1963 Parlophone GEP 8880

The Beatles' Hits

From Me to You (1.55) Lennon–McCartney

Thank You Girl (2.01) Lennon–McCartney

Please Please Me (2.00) Lennon–McCartney

Love Me Do (2.19) Lennon–McCartney

Producer George Martin

1 November 1963 Parlophone GEP 8883

The Beatles No.1

I Saw Her Standing There (2.50) Lennon–McCartney

Misery (1.43) Lennon–McCartney

Anna (Go To Him) (2.56) Alexander

Chains (2.21) Goffin–King

Producer George Martin

22 November 1963 Parlophone PMC 1206 (mono) PCS 3045 (stereo)

With the Beatles

Side One

It Won't Be Long (2.11) Lennon–McCartney

All I've Got to Do (2.05) Lennon–McCartney

All My Loving (2.04) Lennon–McCartney

Don't Bother Me (2.28) Harrison

Little Child (1.46) Lennon–McCartney

Till There Was You (2.12) Willson

Please Mister Postman (2.34) Holland

Side Two

Roll Over Beethoven (2.44) Berry

Hold Me Tight (2.30) Lennon–McCartney

You Really Got a Hold on Me (2.58) Robinson

I Wanna Be Your Man (1.59) Lennon–McCartney

Devil in Her Heart (2.23) Drapkin

Not a Second Time (2.03) Lennon–McCartney

Money (2.47) Bradford–Gordy

Producer George Martin

29 November 1963 Parlophone 5084 (UK)

I Want to Hold Your Hand (2.24) Lennon–McCartney

This Boy (2.11) Lennon–McCartney

26 December 1963 Capitol 5112 (US)

I Want to Hold Your Hand (2.24) Lennon–McCartney

I Saw Her Standing There (2.50) Lennon–McCartney

Producer George Martin

16 March 1964 Capitol 5150 (US)
20 March 1964 Parlophone R 5114 (UK)
Can't Buy Me Love (2.15) Lennon–McCartney
You Can't Do That (2.33) Lennon–McCartney

Producer George Martin

23 March 1964 Vee-Jay VJ 587 (US)
Do You Want to Know a Secret? (1.55) Lennon–McCartney
Thank You Girl (2.01) Lennon–McCartney

Producer George Martin

10 April 1964 Capitol T-2080 (mono) and ST-2080 (stereo)

The Beatles' Second Album

Side One
Roll Over Beethoven (2.44) Berry
Thank You Girl (2.01) Lennon–McCartney
You Really Got a Hold on Me (2.58) Robinson
Devil in Her Heart (2.23) Drapkin
Money (2.47) Bradford–Gordy
You Can't Do That (2.33) Lennon–McCartney

Side Two
Long Tall Sally (1.58) Johnson–Penniman–Blackwell
I Call Your Name (2.02) Lennon–McCartney
Please Mister Postman (2.34) Holland
I'll Get You (2.04) Lennon–McCartney
She Loves You (2.18) Lennon–McCartney

Producer George Martin

20 January 1964 Capitol T-2047 (mono) and ST-2047 (stereo)

Meet the Beatles

Side One
I Want to Hold Your Hand (2.24) Lennon–McCartney
I Saw Her Standing There (2.50) Lennon–McCartney
This Boy (2.11) Lennon–McCartney
It Won't Be Long (2.11) Lennon–McCartney
All I've Got to Do (2.05) Lennon–McCartney
All My Loving (2.04) Lennon–McCartney

Side Two
Don't Bother Me (2.28) Harrison
Little Child (1.46) Lennon–McCartney
Till There Was You (2.12) Willson
Hold Me Tight (2.30) Lennon–McCartney
I Wanna Be Your Man (1.59) Lennon–McCartney
Not a Second Time (2.30) Lennon–McCartney

Producer George Martin

30 January 1964 Vee-Jay VJ 581 (US)
Please Please Me (2.00) Lennon–McCartney
From Me to You (1.55) Lennon–McCartney

Producer George Martin

7 February 1964 Parlophone GEP 8891 (mono only)

All My Loving

All My Loving (2.04) Lennon–McCartney
Ask Me Why (2.24) Lennon–McCartney
Money (2.47) Bradford–Gordy
P.S. I Love You (2.02) Lennon–McCartney

Producer George Martin

2 March 1964 Tollie 9001 (US)
Twist and Shout (2.32) Medley–Russell
There's a Place (1.44) Lennon–McCartney

Producer George Martin

27 April 1964 Tollie 9008 (US)
Love Me Do (2.22) Lennon–McCartney
P.S. I Love You (2.06) Lennon–McCartney

Producer George Martin

21 May 1964 Swan 4182 (US)
Sie Liebt Dich (2.16) Lennon–McCartney
I'll Get You (2.06) Lennon–McCartney

Producer George Martin

19 June 1964 Parlophone GEP 8913 (mono only)

Long Tall Sally

Long Tall Sally (1.50) Johnson–Penniman–Blackwell
I Call Your Name (2.02) Lennon–McCartney
Slow Down (2.54) Williams
Matchbox (1.37) Perkins

Producer George Martin

26 June 1964 United Artists UA 6366 (mono) and UAS 6366 (stereo)

A Hard Day's Night

Side One
A Hard Day's Night (2.28) Lennon–McCartney
Tell Me Why (2.04) Lennon–McCartney
I'll Cry Instead (2.06) Lennon–McCartney
I Should Have Known Better (Instrumental) (2.16) Lennon–McCartney
I'm Happy Just to Dance With You (1.59) Lennon–McCartney
And I Love Her (Instrumental) (3.42) Lennon–McCartney

Side Two
I Should Have Known Better (2.42) Lennon–McCartney
If I Fell (2.16) Lennon–McCartney
And I Love Her (2.27) Lennon–McCartney
Ringo's Theme (This Boy) (Instrumental) (3.06) Lennon–McCartney
Can't Buy Me Love (2.15) Lennon–McCartney
A Hard Day's Night (Instrumental) (2.00) Lennon–McCartney

Producer George Martin

1964

10 JULY 1964 Parlophone PMC 1230 (mono) and PCS 3058 (stereo)

A Hard Day's Night

Side One

A Hard Day's Night (2.28) Lennon–McCartney

I Should Have Known Better (2.42) Lennon–McCartney

If I Fell (2.16) Lennon–McCartney

I'm Happy Just to Dance With You (1.59) Lennon–McCartney

And I Love Her (2.27) Lennon–McCartney

Tell Me Why (2.04) Lennon–McCartney

Can't Buy Me Love (2.15) Lennon–McCartney

Side Two

Any Time at All (2.10) Lennon–McCartney

I'll Cry Instead (1.44) Lennon–McCartney

Things We Said Today (2.35) Lennon–McCartney

When I Get Home (2.14) Lennon–McCartney

You Can't Do That (2.33) Lennon–McCartney

I'll Be Back (2.22) Lennon–McCartney

Producer George Martin

10 JULY 1964 Parlophone R 5160 (UK)

A Hard Day's Night (2.32) Lennon–McCartney

Things We Said Today (2.35) Lennon–McCartney

Producer George Martin

13 JULY 1964 Capitol 5222 (US)

A Hard Day's Night (2.32) Lennon–McCartney

I Should Have Known Better (2.42) Lennon–McCartney

Producer George Martin

20 JULY 1964 Capitol 5234 (US)

I'll Cry Instead (1.44) Lennon–McCartney

I'm Happy Just to Dance With You (1.59) Lennon–McCartney

Producer George Martin

20 JULY 1964 Capitol 5235 (US)

And I Love Her (2.27) Lennon–McCartney

If I Fell (2.16) Lennon–McCartney

Producer George Martin

20 JULY 1964 Capitol T-2018 (mono) ST-2108 (stereo)

Something New

Side One

I'll Cry Instead (1.44) Lennon–McCartney

Things We Said Today (2.35) Lennon–McCartney

Any Time at All (2.10) Lennon–McCartney

When I Get Home (2.14) Lennon–McCartney

Slow Down (2.54) Williams

Matchbox (1.37) Perkins

Side Two

Tell Me Why (2.04) Lennon–McCartney

And I Love Her (2.27) Lennon–McCartney

I'm Happy Just to Dance With You (1.59) Lennon–McCartney

If I Fell (2.16) Lennon–McCartney

Komm, Gib Mir Deine Hand (2.24) Lennon–McCartney–Nicolas–Helimer

Producers Gary Usher and Roger Christian

24 AUGUST 1964 Capitol 5255 (US)

Matchbox (1.37) Williams

Slow Down (2.54) Perkins

Producer George Martin

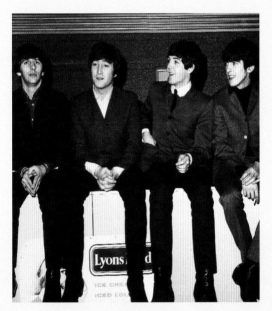

6 NOVEMBER 1964 Parlophone GEP 8920 (mono only)

Extracts from the Film A Hard Day's Night

I Should Have Known Better (2.42) Lennon–McCartney

If I Fell (2.16) Lennon–McCartney

Tell Me Why (2.04) Lennon–McCartney

And I Love Her (2.27) Lennon–McCartney

Producer George Martin

6 NOVEMBER 1964 Parlophone GEP 8924 (mono only)

Extracts from the Album A Hard Day's Night

Any Time at All (2.10) Lennon–McCartney

I'll Cry Instead (1.44) Lennon–McCartney

Things We Said Today (2.35) Lennon–McCartney

When I Get Home (2.14) Lennon–McCartney

Producer George Martin

23 NOVEMBER 1964 Capitol 5327 (US)

27 NOVEMBER 1964 Parlophone R 5200 (UK)

I Feel Fine (2.19) Lennon–McCartney

She's a Woman (2.45) Lennon–McCartney

Producer George Martin

23 NOVEMBER 1964 Capitol TBO-2222 (mono) STBO-2222 (stereo)

The Beatles' Story

Side One

On Stage with the Beatles (1.03)

How Beatlemania Began (1.18)

Beatlemaniain Action (2.24)

Man Behind the Beatles—Brian Epstein (3.01)

John Lennon (4.24)

Who's a Millionaire? (0.43)

Side Two

Beatles Will Be Beatles (7.37)

Man Behind the Music—George Martin (0.47)

George Harrison (4.43)

Side Three

A Hard Day's Night—Their First Movie (3.45)

Paul McCartney (1.55)

Sneaky Haircuts and More About Paul (3.38)

Side Four

The Beatles Look at Life (1.51)

"Victims" of Beatlemania (1.21)

Beatle Medley (3.36)

Ringo Starr (6.19)

Liverpool and All the World! (1.09)

Producers Gary Usher and Roger Christian

4 DECEMBER 1964 Parlophone PMC 1240 (mono) PCS 3062 (stereo)

Beatles for Sale

Side One

No Reply (2.15) Lennon–McCartney

I'm a Loser (2.31) Lennon–McCartney

Baby's in Black (2.02) Lennon–McCartney

Rock and Roll Music (2.02) Berry

I'll Follow the Sun (1.46) Lennon–McCartney

Mr. Moonlight (2.35) Johnson

Kansas City/Hey Hey Hey Hey (2.30) Lieber–Stoller/Penniman

Side Two

Eight Days a Week (2.43) Lennon–McCartney

Words of Love (2.10) Holly

Honey Don't (2.56) Perkins

Every Little Thing (2.01) Lennon–McCartney

I Don't Want to Spoil the Party (2.33) Lennon–McCartney

What You're Doing (2.30) Lennon–McCartney

Everybody's Trying to Be My Baby (2.24) Perkins

Producer George Martin

15 DECEMBER 1964 Capitol ST-2228 (mono) ST-2228 (stereo)

Beatles '65

Side One
No Reply (2.15) Lennon–McCartney
I'm a Loser (2.31) Lennon–McCartney
Baby's in Black (2.02) Lennon–McCartney
Rock and Roll Music (2.02) Berry
I'll Follow the Sun (1.46) Lennon–McCartney
Mr. Moonlight (2.35) Johnson

Side Two
Honey Don't (2.56) Perkins
I'll Be Back (2.22) Lennon–McCartney
She's a Woman (2.57) Lennon–McCartney
I Feel Fine (2.20) Lennon–McCartney
Everybody's Trying to Be My Baby (2.24) Perkins

Producer George Martin

15 FEBRUARY 1965 Capitol 5371 (US)

Eight Days a Week (2.43) Lennon–McCartney
I Don't Want to Spoil the Party (2.23) Lennon–McCartney

Producer George Martin

22 MARCH 1965 Capitol T-2309 (mono) ST-2309 (stereo)

The Early Beatles

Side One
Love Me Do (2.19) Lennon–McCartney
Twist and Shout (2.32) Medley–Russell
Anna (Go To Him) (2.56) Alexander
Chains (2.21) Goffin–King
Boys (2.24) Dixon–Farrell
Ask Me Why (2.24) Lennon–McCartney

Side Two
Please Please Me (2.00) Lennon–McCartney
P.S. I Love You (2.02) Lennon–McCartney
Baby It's You (2.36) David–Williams–Bacharach
A Taste of Honey (2.02) Scott–Marlow
Do You Want to Know a Secret (1.55) Lennon–McCartney

Producer George Martin

6 APRIL 1965 Parlophone GEP 8931

Beatles for Sale

No Reply (2.15) Lennon–McCartney
I'm a Loser (2.31) Lennon–McCartney
Rock and Roll Music (2.02) Berry
Eight Days a Week (2.43) Lennon–McCartney

Producer George Martin

9 APRIL 1965 Parlophone R 5265 (UK)
19 APRIL 1965 Capitol 5407 (US)

Ticket to Ride (3.03) Lennon–McCartney
Yes It Is (2.40) Lennon–McCartney

Producer George Martin

4 JUNE 1965 Parlophone GEP 8938

Beatles for Sale No. 2

I'll Follow the Sun (1.46) Lennon–McCartney
Baby's in Black (2.02) Lennon–McCartney
Words of Love (2.10) Holly
I Don't Want to Spoil the Party (2.23) Lennon–McCartney

Producer George Martin

14 JUNE 1965 Capitol T-2358 (mono) Capitol ST-2358 (stereo)

Beatles VI

Side One
Kansas City/Hey Hey Hey Hey (2.30) Lieber–Stoller/Penniman
Eight Days a Week (2.43) Lennon–McCartney
You Like Me Too Much (2.34) Harrison
Bad Boy (2.17) Williams
I Don't Want to Spoil the Party (2.23) Lennon–McCartney
Words of Love (2.10) Holly

Side Two
What You're Doing (2.30) Lennon–McCartney
Yes It Is (2.40) Lennon–McCartney
Dizzy Miss Lizzy (2.51) Williams
Tell Me What You See (2.35) Lennon–McCartney
Every Little Thing (2.01) Lennon–McCartney

Producer George Martin

19 JULY 1965 Capitol 5476 (US)
23 JULY 1965 Parlophone R 5305 (UK)

Help! (2.16) Lennon–McCartney
I'm Down (2.30) Lennon–McCartney

Producer George Martin

6 AUGUST 1965 Parlophone PMC 1255 (mono) PCS 3071 (stereo)

Help!

Side One
Help! (2.16) Lennon–McCartney
The Night Before (2.33) Lennon–McCartney
You've Got to Hide Your Love Away (2.08) Lennon–McCartney
I Need You (2.28) Harrison
Another Girl (2.02) Lennon–McCartney
You're Going to Lose That Girl (2.18) Lennon–McCartney
Ticket to Ride (3.03) Lennon–McCartney

Side Two
Act Naturally (2.27) Morrison–Russell
It's Only Love (1.53) Lennon–McCartney
You Like Me Too Much (2.34) Harrison
Tell Me What You See (2.35) Lennon–McCartney
I've Just Seen a Face (2.04) Lennon–McCartney
Yesterday (2.04) Lennon–McCartney
Dizzy Miss Lizzy (2.51) Williams

Producer George Martin

13 AUGUST 1965 Capitol MAS 2386 (mono) SMAS 2386 (stereo)

Help!

Side One
The James Bond Theme (0.16) Norman
Help! (2.16) Lennon–McCartney
The Night Before (2.33) Lennon–McCartney
From Me to You Fantasy (Instrumental)* (2.03) Thorne
You've Got to Hide Your Love Away (2.08) Lennon–McCartney
I Need You (2.28) Harrison
In the Tyrol (Instrumental)* (2.21) Wagner; Arr. Thorne

Side Two
Another Girl (2.02) Lennon–McCartney
Another Hard Day's Night (Instrumental)* (2.28) Lennon–McCartney
Ticket to Ride (3.03) Lennon–McCartney
The Bitter End/You Can't Do That (Instrumental)* (2.20) Lennon–McCartney
You're Going to Lose That Girl (2.18) Lennon–McCartney
The Chase (Instrumental)* (2.24) Thorne

*Performed by George Martin and His Orchestra

Producer George Martin

13 September 1965 Capitol 5498 (US)
Yesterday (2.04) Lennon–McCartney
Act Naturally (2.27) Morrison–Russell

Producer George Martin

3 December 1965 Parlophone R 5389 (UK)
6 December 1965 Capitol 5555 (US)
We Can Work It Out (2.10) Lennon–McCartney
Day Tripper (2.37) Lennon–McCartney

Producer George Martin

3 December 1965 Parlophone PMC 1267 (mono) PCS 3075 (stereo)

Rubber Soul

Side One
Drive My Car (2.25) Lennon–McCartney
Norwegian Wood (This Bird Has Flown) (2.00) Lennon–McCartney
You Won't See Me (3.19) Lennon–McCartney
Nowhere Man (2.40) Lennon–McCartney
Think for Yourself (2.16) Harrison
The Word (2.42) Lennon–McCartney
Michelle (2.42) Lennon–McCartney

Side Two
What Goes On (2.44) Lennon–McCartney–Starkey
Girl (2.26) Lennon–McCartney
I'm Looking Through You (2.27) Lennon–McCartney
In My Life (2.23) Lennon–McCartney
Wait (2.13) Lennon–McCartney
If I Needed Someone (2.19) Harrison
Run for Your Life (2.21) Lennon–McCartney

Producer George Martin

6 December 1965 Capitol T-2442 (mono) ST-2442 (stereo)

Rubber Soul

Side One
I've Just Seen a Face (2.04) Lennon–McCartney
Norwegian Wood (This Bird Has Flown) (2.00) Lennon–McCartney
You Won't See Me (3.19) Lennon–McCartney
Think for Yourself (2.16) Harrison
The Word (2.42) Lennon–McCartney
Michelle (2.42) Lennon–McCartney

Side Two
It's Only Love (1.53) Lennon–McCartney
Girl (2.26) Lennon–McCartney
I'm Looking Through You (2.27) Lennon–McCartney
In My Life (2.23) Lennon–McCartney
Wait (2.13) Lennon–McCartney
Run for Your Life (2.21) Lennon–McCartney

Producer George Martin

6 December 1965 Parlophone GEP 8946

The Beatles Million Sellers

She Loves You (2.18) Lennon–McCartney
I Want to Hold Your Hand (2.24) Lennon–McCartney
Can't Buy Me Love (2.15) Lennon–McCartney
I Feel Fine (2.19) Lennon–McCartney

Producer George Martin

21 February 1966 Capitol 5587 (US)
Nowhere Man (2.40) Lennon–McCartney
What Goes On (2.44) Lennon–McCartney–Starkey

Producer George Martin

4 March 1966 Parlophone GEP 8948

Yesterday

Yesterday (2.04) Lennon–McCartney
Act Naturally (2.27) Morrison–Russell
You Like Me Too Much (2.34) Harrison
It's Only Love (1.53) Lennon–McCartney

Producer George Martin

30 May 1966 Capitol 5651 (US)
10 June 1966 Parlophone R 5452 (UK)
Paperback Writer (2.25) Lennon–McCartney
Rain (2.59) Lennon–McCartney

Producer George Martin

20 June 1966 Capitol T-2553 (mono) ST-2553 (stereo)

Yesterday and Today

Side One
Drive My Car (2.24) Lennon–McCartney
I'm Only Sleeping (2.58) Lennon–McCartney
Nowhere Man (2.40) Lennon–McCartney
Dr. Robert (2.14) Lennon–McCartney
Yesterday (2.04) Lennon–McCartney
Act Naturally (2.27) Morrison–Russell

Side Two
And Your Bird Can Sing (2.02) Lennon–McCartney
If I Needed Someone (2.19) Harrison
We Can Work It Out (2.10) Lennon–McCartney
What Goes On (2.44) Lennon–McCartney–Starkey
Day Tripper (2.37) Lennon–McCartney

Producer George Martin

8 July 1966 Parlophone GEP 8952

Nowhere Man

Nowhere Man (2.40) Lennon–McCartney
Drive My Car (2.24) Lennon–McCartney
Michelle (2.42) Lennon–McCartney
You Won't See Me (3.19) Lennon–McCartney

Producer George Martin

5 August 1966 Parlophone R 5493 (UK)
8 August 1966 Capitol 5715 (US)
Yellow Submarine (2.40) Lennon–McCartney
Eleanor Rigby (2.11) Lennon–McCartney

Producer George Martin

5 August 1966 Parlophone PMC 7009 (mono) PCS 7009 (stereo) (UK)
8 August 1966 Capitol T-2576 (mono) ST-2576 (stereo) (US)

Revolver

Side One
Taxman (2.36) Harrison
Eleanor Rigby (2.11) Lennon–McCartney
I'm Only Sleeping (2.58) Lennon–McCartney
Love You To (3.00) Harrison
Here, There and Everywhere (2.29) Lennon–McCartney
Yellow Submarine (2.40) Lennon–McCartney
She Said She Said (2.39) Lennon–McCartney

Side Two
Good Day Sunshine (2.08) Lennon–McCartney
And Your Bird Can Sing (2.02) Lennon–McCartney
For No One (2.03) Lennon–McCartney
Dr. Robert (2.14) Lennon–McCartney
I Want To Tell You (2.30) Harrison
Got to Get You into My Life (2.31) Lennon–McCartney
Tomorrow Never Knows (3.00) Lennon–McCartney

Producer George Martin

1966-68

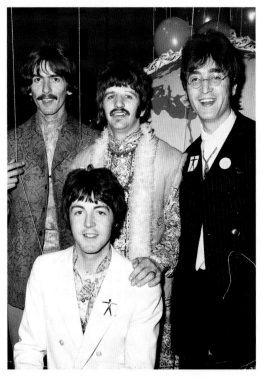

10 December 1966 Parlophone PMC 7016 (mono)
Parlophone PCS 7016 (stereo)

A Collection of Beatles Oldies

Side One

She Loves You (2.18) Lennon–McCartney
From Me to You (1.55) Lennon–McCartney
We Can Work It Out (2.10) Lennon–McCartney
Help! (2.16) Lennon–McCartney
Michelle (2.42) Lennon–McCartney
Yesterday (2.04) Lennon–McCartney
I Feel Fine (2.19) Lennon–McCartney
Yellow Submarine (2.40) Lennon–McCartney

Side Two

Can't Buy Me Love (2.15) Lennon–McCartney
Bad Boy (2.17) Williams–McCartney
Day Tripper (2.37) Lennon–McCartney
A Hard Day's Night (2.23) Lennon–McCartney
Ticket to Ride (3.03) Lennon–McCartney
Paperback Writer (2.25) Lennon–McCartney
Eleanor Rigby (2.11) Lennon–McCartney
I Want to Hold Your Hand (2.24) Lennon–McCartney

Producer George Martin

13 February 1967 Capitol 5810 (US)
17 February 1967 Parlophone R 5570 (UK)
Penny Lane (3.00) Lennon–McCartney
Strawberry Fields Forever (4.05) Lennon–McCartney

Producer George Martin

1 June 1967 Parlophone PMC 7027 (mono) PCS 7027 (stereo) (UK)
2 June 1967 Capitol MAS 2653 (mono) SMAS 2653 (stereo) (US)

Sgt. Pepper's Lonely Hearts Club Band

Side One

Sgt. Pepper's Lonely Hearts Club Band (1.59) Lennon–McCartney
With a Little Help from My Friends (2.46) Lennon–McCartney
Lucy in the Sky with Diamonds (3.25) Lennon–McCartney
Getting Better (2.47) Lennon–McCartney
Fixing a Hole (2.33) Lennon–McCartney
She's Leaving Home (3.24) Lennon–McCartney
Being for the Benefit of Mr. Kite! (2.36) Lennon–McCartney

Side Two

Within You, Without You (5.03) Harrison
When I'm Sixty-Four (2.38) Lennon–McCartney
Lovely Rita (2.43) Lennon–McCartney
Good Morning, Good Morning (2.35) Lennon–McCartney
Sgt. Pepper's Lonely Hearts Club Band (Reprise) (1.20) Lennon–McCartney
A Day in the Life (5.03) Lennon–McCartney

Producer George Martin

7 July 1967 Parlophone R 5620 (UK)
17 July 1967 Capitol 5964 (US)
All You Need Is Love (3.57) Lennon–McCartney
Baby You're a Rich Man (3.07) Lennon–McCartney

Producer George Martin

27 November 1967 Capitol MAL 2835 (mono) SMAL 2835 (stereo) (US)
19 November 1976 Parlophone PCTC 255 (UK)

Magical Mystery Tour

Side One

Magical Mystery Tour (2.48) Lennon–McCartney
The Fool on the Hill (3.00) Lennon–McCartney
Flying (2.16) Lennon–McCartney–Harrison–Starkey
Blue Jay Way (3.50) Harrison
Your Mother Should Know (2.33) Lennon–McCartney
I Am the Walrus (4.35) Lennon–McCartney

Side Two

Hello Goodbye (3.24) Lennon–McCartney
Strawberry Fields Forever (4.05) Lennon–McCartney
Penny Lane (3.00) Lennon–McCartney
Baby You're a Rich Man (3.07) Lennon–McCartney
All You Need Is Love (3.57) Lennon–McCartney

Producer George Martin

24 November 1967 Parlophone R 5655 (UK)
27 November 1967 Capitol 2056 (US)
Hello Goodbye (3.24) Lennon–McCartney
I Am the Walrus (4.35) Lennon–McCartney

Producer George Martin

8 December 1967 Parlophone MMT/SMMT 1 (UK)

Magical Mystery Tour

Side One

Magical Mystery Tour (2.52) Lennon–McCartney
Your Mother Should Know (2.29) Lennon–McCartney

Side Two

I Am the Walrus (4.37) Lennon–McCartney

Side Three

The Fool on the Hill (3.00) Lennon–McCartney
Flying (2.17) Lennon–McCartney–Harrison–Starkey

Side Four

Blue Jay Way (3.57) Harrison

Producer George Martin

15 March 1968 Parlophone R 5675 (UK)
18 March 1968 Capitol 2138 (US)
Lady Madonna (2.17) Lennon–McCartney
The Inner Light (2.36) Harrison

Producer George Martin

26 August 1968 Apple 2276 (US)
30 August 1968 Apple R 5722 (UK)
Hey Jude (7.11) Lennon–McCartney
Revolution (3.22) Lennon–McCartney

Producer George Martin

22 November 1968 Apple PMC 7067-7068 (mono)
PCS 7067-7068 (stereo) (UK)
25 November 1968 Apple SWBO-101 (stereo only) (US)

The Beatles (The White Album)

Side One

Back in the USSR (2.45) Lennon–McCartney
Dear Prudence (4.00) Lennon–McCartney
Glass Onion (2.10) Lennon–McCartney
Ob-La-Di, Ob-La-Da (3.10) Lennon–McCartney
Wild Honey Pie (1.02) Lennon–McCartney
The Continuing Story of Bungalow Bill (3.05) Lennon–McCartney
While My Guitar Gently Weeps (4.46) Harrison
Happiness Is a Warm Gun (2.47) Lennon–McCartney

Side Two

Martha My Dear (2.28) Lennon–McCartney
I'm So Tired (2.01) Lennon–McCartney
Blackbird (2.20) Lennon–McCartney
Piggies (2.04) Harrison
Rocky Racoon (3.33) Lennon–McCartney
Don't Pass Me By (3.52) Starkey
Why Don't We Do It in the Road? (1.42) Lennon–McCartney
I Will (1.46) Lennon–McCartney
Julia (2.57) Lennon–McCartney

1968-73

Side Three
Birthday (2.40) Lennon-McCartney
Yer Blues (4.01) Lennon-McCartney
Mother Nature's Son (2.46) Lennon-McCartney
Everybody's Got Something to Hide Except Me and My Monkey (2.25) Lennon-McCartney
Sexy Sadie (3.15) Lennon-McCartney
Helter Skelter (4.30) Lennon-McCartney
Long, Long, Long (3.08) Harrison

Side Four
Revolution 1 (4.13) Lennon-McCartney
Honey Pie (2.42) Lennon-McCartney
Savoy Truffle (2.55) Harrison
Cry Baby Cry (2.34) Lennon-McCartney
Can You Take Me Back (0.27) Lennon-McCartney
Revolution 9 (8.15) Lennon-McCartney
Good Night (3.14) Lennon-McCartney

Producer George Martin

JANUARY 13 1969 Apple SW 153 (stereo only) (US)
JANUARY 17 1969 Apple PMC 7070 (mono) and PCS 7070 (stereo) (UK)

Yellow Submarine

Side One
Yellow Submarine (2.40) Lennon-McCartney
Only a Northern Song (3.23) Harrison
All Together Now (2.08) Lennon-McCartney
Hey Bulldog (3.09) Lennon-McCartney
It's All Too Much (6.27) Harrison
All You Need Is Love (3.47) Lennon-McCartney

Side Two
(George Martin and His Orchestra)
Pepperland (2.18) Martin
Sea of Time (2.58) Martin
Sea of Holes (2.14) Martin
Sea of Monsters (3.35) Martin
March of the Meanies (2.16) Martin
Pepperland Laid Waste (2.09) Martin
Yellow Submarine in Pepperland (2.10) Lennon-McCartney; Arr. Martin

Producer George Martin

APRIL 11 1969 Apple R 5777 (UK)
MAY 5 1969 Apple 2490 (US)
Get Back (3.11) Lennon-McCartney
Don't Let Me Down (3.35) Lennon-McCartney

Producers George Martin and Phil Spector

MAY 30 1969 Apple R 5786 (UK)
JUNE 4 1969 Apple 2531 (US)
The Ballad of John and Yoko (2.28) Lennon-McCartney
Old Brown Shoe (3.16) Harrison

Producer George Martin

26 SEPTEMBER 1969 Apple PCS 7088 (stereo only) (UK)
1 OCTOBER 1969 Apple SO 383 (stereo only) (US)

Abbey Road

Side One
Come Together (4.16) Lennon-McCartney
Something (2.59) Harrison
Maxwell's Silver Hammer (3.24) Lennon-McCartney
Oh! Darling (3.28) Lennon-McCartney
Octopus's Garden (2.49) Starkey
I Want You (She's So Heavy) (7.49) Lennon-McCartney

Side Two
Here Comes the Sun (3.40) Harrison
Because (2.45) Lennon-McCartney
You Never Give Me Your Money (3.57) Lennon-McCartney
Sun King (2.31) Lennon-McCartney
Mean Mr. Mustard (1.06) Lennon-McCartney
Polythene Pam (1.13) Lennon-McCartney
She Came in Through the Bathroom Window (1.58) Lennon-McCartney
Golden Slumbers (1.31) Lennon-McCartney
Carry That Weight (1.37) Lennon-McCartney
The End (2.04) Lennon-McCartney
Her Majesty (0.23) Lennon-McCartney

Producer George Martin

6 OCTOBER 1969 Apple 2654(US)
31 OCTOBER 1969 Apple R 5814 (UK)
Something (2.59) Harrison
Come Together (4.16) Lennon-McCartney

Producer George Martin

26 FEBRUARY 1970 Apple SW 385 (stereo only) (US)
11 MAY 1979 Parlophone PCS 7184 (stereo only) (UK)

Hey Jude

Side One
Can't Buy Me Love (2.15) Lennon-McCartney
I Should Have Known Better (2.42) Lennon-McCartney
Paperback Writer (2.25) Lennon-McCartney
Rain (2.59) Lennon-McCartney
Lady Madonna (2.17) Lennon-McCartney
Revolution (3.22) Lennon-McCartney

Side Two
Hey Jude (7.11) Lennon-McCartney
Old Brown Shoe (3.16) Harrison
Don't Let Me Down (3.34) Lennon-McCartney
The Ballad of John and Yoko (2.58) Lennon-McCartney

Producer George Martin

6 MARCH 1970 Apple R 5833 (UK)
11 MARCH 1970 Apple 2764 (US)
Let It Be (4.01) Lennon-McCartney
You Know My Name (Look Up the Number) (4.20) Lennon-McCartney

Producers George Martin and Chris Thomas

8 MAY 1970 Apple PCS 7096 (UK)
18 MAY 1970 Apple AR 34001 (US)

Let It Be

Side One
Two of Us (3.33) Lennon-McCartney
Dig a Pony (3.55) Lennon-McCartney
Across the Universe (3.51) Lennon-McCartney
I Me Mine (2.25) Harrison
Dig It (0.51) Lennon-McCartney-Harrison-Starkey
Let It Be (4.01) Lennon-McCartney
Maggie Mae (0.39) Lennon-McCartney

Side Two
I've Got a Feeling (3.38) Lennon-McCartney
One After 909 (2.52) Lennon-McCartney
The Long and Winding Road (3.40) Lennon-McCartney
For You Blue (2.33) Harrison
Get Back (3.09) Lennon-McCartney

Producers George Martin and Phil Spector

11 MAY 1970 Apple (Capitol) 2832 (US)
The Long and Winding Road (3.40) Lennon-McCartney
For You Blue (2.33) Harrison

Producers George Martin and Phil Spector

2 APRIL 1973 Apple SKBO 3403 (US)
20 APRIL 1973 Apple PCSP 717 (UK)

The Beatles 1962-1966

Side One
Love Me Do (2.01) Lennon-McCartney
Please Please Me (2.00) Lennon-McCartney
From Me to You (1.55) Lennon-McCartney
She Loves You (2.18) Lennon-McCartney
I Want to Hold Your Hand (2.24) Lennon-McCartney
All My Loving (2.04) Lennon-McCartney
Can't Buy Me Love (2.15) Lennon-McCartney

Side Two
A Hard Day's Night (2.32) Lennon–McCartney
And I Love Her (2.27) Lennon–McCartney
Eight Days a Week (2.43) Lennon–McCartney
I Feel Fine (2.19) Lennon–McCartney
Ticket to Ride (3.03) Lennon–McCartney
Yesterday (2.04) Lennon–McCartney

Side Three
The James Bond Theme (0.16) Norman (on US version only)
Help! (2.16) Lennon–McCartney
You've Got to Hide Your Love Away (2.08) Lennon–McCartney
We Can Work It Out (2.10) Lennon–McCartney
Day Tripper (2.17) Lennon–McCartney
Drive My Car (2.25) Lennon–McCartney
Norwegian Wood (This Bird Has Flown) (2.00) Lennon–McCartney

Side Four
Nowhere Man (2.40) Lennon–McCartney
Michelle (2.42) Lennon–McCartney
In My Life (2.23) Lennon–McCartney
Girl (2.26) Lennon–McCartney
Paperback Writer (2.25) Lennon–McCartney
Eleanor Rigby (2.11) Lennon–McCartney
Yellow Submarine (2.40) Lennon–McCartney

Producer George Martin

2 APRIL 1973 Apple SKBO 3404 (US)
20 APRIL 1973 Apple PCSP 718 (UK)

The Beatles 1967–1970
Side One
Strawberry Fields Forever (4.05) Lennon–McCartney
Penny Lane (3.00) Lennon–McCartney
Sgt. Pepper's Lonely Hearts Club Band (1.59) Lennon–McCartney
With a Little Help from My Friends (2.46) Lennon–McCartney
Lucy in the Sky with Diamonds (3.25) Lennon–McCartney
A Day in the Life (5.03) Lennon–McCartney
All You Need Is Love (3.57) Lennon–McCartney

Side Two
I Am the Walrus (4.35) Lennon–McCartney
Hello Goodbye (3.24) Lennon–McCartney
The Fool on the Hill (3.00) Lennon–McCartney
Magical Mystery Tour (2.48) Lennon–McCartney
Lady Madonna (2.17) Lennon–McCartney
Hey Jude (7.11) Lennon–McCartney
Revolution (3.22) Lennon–McCartney

Side Three
Back in the USSR (2.45) Lennon–McCartney
While My Guitar Gently Weeps (4.46) Harrison
Ob-La-Di, Ob-La-Da (3.10) Lennon–McCartney
Get Back (3.11) Lennon–McCartney
Don't Let Me Down (3.34) Lennon–McCartney
The Ballad of John and Yoko (2.58) Lennon–McCartney
Old Brown Shoe (3.16) Harrison

Side Four
Here Comes the Sun (3.04) Harrison
Come Together (4.16) Lennon–McCartney
Something (2.59) Harrison
Octopus's Garden (2.49) Starkey
Let It Be (3.50) Lennon–McCartney
Across the Universe (3.51) Lennon–McCartney
The Long and Winding Road (3.40) Lennon–McCartney

Producers George Martin and Phil Spector

7 JUNE 1976 Capitol (US)
11 JUNE 1976 Parlophone (UK)

Rock and Roll Music
Side One
Twist and Shout (2.32) Medley–Russell
I Saw Her Standing There (2.50) Lennon–McCartney
You Can't Do That (2.33) Lennon–McCartney
I Wanna Be Your Man (1.59) Lennon–McCartney
I Call Your Name (2.02) Lennon–McCartney
Boys (2.24) Dixon–Farrell
Long Tall Sally (1.58) Johnson–Penniman–Blackwell

Side Two
Rock and Roll Music (2.02) Berry
Slow Down (2.54) Williams
Kansas City/Hey Hey Hey Hey (2.30) Lieber–Stoller/Penniman
Money (2.47) Bradford–Gordy
Bad Boy (2.17) Williams
Matchbox (1.37) Perkins
Roll Over Beethoven (2.44) Berry

Side Three
Dizzy Miss Lizzy (2.51) Williams
Any Time at All (2.10) Lennon–McCartney
Drive My Car (2.25) Lennon–McCartney
Everybody's Trying to Be My Baby (2.24) Perkins
The Night Before (2.33) Lennon–McCartney
I'm Down (2.30) Lennon–McCartney
Revolution (3.22) Lennon–McCartney

Side Four
Back in the USSR (2.45) Lennon–McCartney
Helter Skelter (4.30) Lennon–McCartney
Taxman (2.36) Harrison
Got to Get You into My Life (2.31) Lennon–McCartney
Hey Bulldog (3.09) Lennon–McCartney
Birthday (2.40) Lennon–McCartney
Get Back (3.09) Lennon–McCartney

Producers George Martin and Phil Spector

2 MAY 1977 Lingasong LNL 1 (UK)
13 JUNE 1977 Lingasong LS-2-7001 (US)

Live! at the Star-Club in Hamburg, Germany, 1962
Side One
I'm Gonna Sit Right Down and Cry(Over You) (2.30) Thomas–Biggs
Roll Over Beethoven (2.17) Berry
Hippy Hippy Shake (1.42) Romero
Sweet Little Sixteen (2.50) Berry
Lend Me Your Comb (1.45) Wise–Weisman–Tworney
Your Feet's Too Big (2.21) Benson–Fisher

Side Two
Where Have You Been All My Life (1.45) Mann–Weill
Mr. Moonlight (2.10) Johnson
A Taste of Honey (1.55) Marlow–Scott
Besame Mucho (2.40) Velázquez–Skylar
Till There Was You (1.55) Willson
Kansas City/Hey Hey Hey Hey (2.30) Lieber–Stoller/Penniman

Side Three

Hallelujah I Love Her So (2.07) Charles
Ain't Nothing Shakin' (1.15) Colocrai–Fontaine–Lampert–Cleveland
To Know Her Is to Love Her (3.05) Spector
Little Queenie (3.57) Berry
Falling in Love Again (1.58) Hollander–Lerner
Be-Bop-a-Lula (2.28) Vincent–Davis

Side Four

Red Sails in the Sunset (2.00) Kennedy–Williams
Everybody's Trying to Be My Baby (2.25) Perkins
Matchbox (2.35) Perkins
Talkin' 'Bout You (1:50) Berry
Shimmy Shake (2.18) South–Land
Long Tall Sally (1.50) Johnson–Penniman–Blackwell
I Remember You (1.51) Schertzinger–Metter

Producer Larry Grossberg

4 MAY 1977 Capitol (US)
6 MAY 1977 Parlophone (UK)

The Beatles at the Hollywood Bowl

Side One

Twist and Shout (1.20) Medley–Russell
She's a Woman (2.45) Lennon–McCartney
Dizzy Miss Lizzy (3.00) Williams
Ticket to Ride (2.18) Lennon–McCartney
Can't Buy Me Love (2.08) Lennon–McCartney
Things We Said Today (2.07) Lennon–McCartney
Roll Over Beethoven (2.10) Berry

Side Two

Boys (1.57) Dixon–Farrell
A Hard Day's Night (2.30) Lennon–McCartney
Help! (2.16) Lennon–McCartney
All My Loving (1.55) Lennon–McCartney
She Loves You (2.10) Lennon–McCartney
Long Tall Sally (1.54) Johnson–Penniman–Blackwell

Producers George Martin and Voyle Gilmore

24 NOVEMBER 1977 Capitol (US)
28 NOVEMBER 1977 Parlophone (UK)

Love Songs

Side One

Yesterday (2.04) Lennon–McCartney
I'll Follow the Sun (1.46) Lennon–McCartney
I Need You (2.28) Harrison
Girl (2.26) Lennon–McCartney
In My Life (2.23) Lennon–McCartney
Words of Love (2.10) Holly
Here, There and Everywhere (2.29) Lennon–McCartney

Side Two

Something (2.59) Harrison
And I Love Her (2.27) Lennon–McCartney
If I Fell (2.16) Lennon–McCartney
I'll Be Back (2.22) Lennon–McCartney
Tell Me What You See (2.35) Lennon–McCartney
Yes It Is (2.40) Lennon–McCartney

Side Three

Michelle (2.42) Lennon–McCartney
It's Only Love (1.53) Lennon–McCartney
You're Going to Lose That Girl (2.18) Lennon–McCartney
Every Little Thing (2.01) Lennon–McCartney
For No One (2.03) Lennon–McCartney
She's Leaving Home (3.24) Lennon–McCartney

Side Four

The Long and Winding Road (3.40) Lennon–McCartney
This Boy (2.11) Lennon–McCartney
Norwegian Wood (This Bird Has Flown) (2.00) Lennon–McCartney
You've Got to Hide Your Love Away (2.08) Lennon–McCartney
I Will (1.46) Lennon–McCartney
P.S. I Love You (2.02) Lennon–McCartney

Producers George Martin and Phil Spector

15 DECEMBER 1978 Parlophone (UK)
1 DECEMBER 1979 Capitol (US)

The Beatles Collection

(boxed set of the following albums):
Please Please Me (22 March 1963) PCS 3042
With the Beatles (22 November 1963) PCS 3045
A Hard Day's Night (10 July 1964) PCS 3058
Beatles for Sale (4 December 1964) PCS 3062
Help! (6 August 1965) PCS 3071
Rubber Soul (3 December 1965) PCS 3075
Revolver (5 August 1966) PCS 7009
Sgt. Pepper's Lonely Hearts Club Band (1 June 1967) PCS 7027
The Beatles (22 November 1968) PCS 7067/8
Yellow Submarine (17 January 1969) PCS 7070
Abbey Road (26 September 1969) PCS 7088
Let It Be (8 May 1970) PCS 7096
Rarities (12 October 1979) PSLP 261

Producers George Martin and Phil Spector

12 OCTOBER 1979 Parlophone (UK)

The Beatles "Rarities"

Side One

Across the Universe (3.41) Lennon–McCartney
Yes It Is (2.40) Lennon–McCartney
This Boy (2.11) Lennon–McCartney
The Inner Light (2.36) Harrison
I'll Get You (2.04) Lennon–McCartney
Thank You Girl (2.01) Lennon–McCartney
Komm, Gib Mir Deine Hand (2.24) Lennon–McCartney–Nicolas–Heilmer
You Know My Name (Look Up the Number) (4.20) Lennon–McCartney
Sie Liebt Dich (2.18) Lennon–McCartney–Nicolas–Montague

Side Two

Rain (2.59) Lennon–McCartney
She's a Woman (2.57) Lennon–McCartney
Matchbox (1.37) Perkins
I Call Your Name (2.02) Lennon–McCartney
Bad Boy (2.17) Williams
Slow Down (2.54) Williams
I'm Down (2.30) Lennon–McCartney
Long Tall Sally (1.58) Johnson–Penniman–Blackwell

Producer George Martin

24 MARCH 1980 Capitol (US)

The Beatles "Rarities"

Side One

Love Me Do (2.22) Lennon–McCartney
Misery (1.43) Lennon–McCartney
There's a Place (1.44) Lennon–McCartney
Sie Liebt Dich (2.18) Lennon–McCartney–Nicolas–Montague
And I Love Her (2.36) Lennon–McCartney
Help! (2.16) Lennon–McCartney
I'm Only Sleeping (2.58) Lennon–McCartney
I Am the Walrus (4.35) Lennon–McCartney

1980

Side Two
Penny Lane (3.00) Lennon–McCartney
Helter Skelter Lennon–McCartney
Don't Pass Me By (3.45) Starkey
The Inner Light (2.36) Harrison
Across the Universe (3.41) Lennon–McCartney
You Know My Name (Look Up the Number) (4.20)
Lennon–McCartney
Sgt. Pepper Inner Groove (0.02) Lennon–McCartney

Producer George Martin

20 October 1980 Parlophone (UK)
The Beatles Ballads

Side One
Yesterday (2.04) Lennon–McCartney
Norwegian Wood (This Bird Has Flown) (2.00) Lennon–
McCartney
Do You Want to Know a Secret (1.55) Lennon–McCartney
For No One (2.03) Lennon–McCartney
Michelle (2.42) Lennon–McCartney
Nowhere Man (2.40) Lennon–McCartney
You've Got to Hide Your Love Away (2.08) Lennon–
McCartney
Across the Universe (3.41) Lennon–McCartney
All My Loving (2.04) Lennon–McCartney
Hey Jude (7.11) Lennon–McCartney

Side Two
Something (2.59) Harrison
The Fool on the Hill (3.00) Lennon–McCartney
Till There Was You (2.12) Willson
The Long and Winding Road (3.40) Lennon–McCartney
Here Comes the Sun (3.40) Harrison
Blackbird (2.20) Lennon–McCartney
And I Love Her (2.27) Lennon–McCartney
She's Leaving Home (3.24) Lennon–McCartney
Here, There and Everywhere (2.29) Lennon–McCartney
Let It Be (3.50) Lennon–McCartney

Producers George Martin and Phil Spector

november 3 1980 Parlophone/World Records (UK)
The Beatles Box

Disc 1, Side A
Love Me Do (2.22) Lennon–McCartney
P.S. I Love You (2.02) Lennon–McCartney
I Saw Her Standing There (2.50) Lennon–McCartney
Please Please Me (2.00) Lennon–McCartney
Misery (1.43) Lennon–McCartney
Do You Want to Know a Secret (1.55) Lennon–McCartney
A Taste of Honey (2.02) Scott–Marlow
Twist and Shout (2.32) Medley–Russell

Disc 1, Side B
From Me to You (1.55) Lennon–McCartney
Thank You Girl (2.01) Lennon–McCartney
She Loves You (2.18) Lennon–McCartney
It Won't Be Long (2.11) Lennon–McCartney
Please Mr. Postman (2.34) Holland
All My Loving (2.07) Lennon–McCartney
Roll Over Beethoven (2.44) Berry
Money (2.47) Bradford–Gordy

Disc 2, Side A
I Want to Hold Your Hand (2.24) Lennon–McCartney
This Boy (2.11) Lennon–McCartney
Can't Buy Me Love (2.15) Lennon–McCartney
You Can't Do That (2.33) Lennon–McCartney
A Hard Day's Night (2.32) Lennon–McCartney
I Should Have Known Better (2.42) Lennon–McCartney
If I Fell (2.16) Lennon–McCartney
And I Love Her (2.36) Lennon–McCartney

Disc 2, Side B
Things We Said Today (2.35) Lennon–McCartney
I'll Be Back (2.22) Lennon–McCartney
Long Tall Sally (1.58) Johnson–Penniman–Blackwell
I Call Your Name (2.02) Lennon–McCartney
Matchbox (1.37) Perkins
Slow Down (2.54) Williams
She's a Woman (2.57) Lennon–McCartney
I Feel Fine (2.19) Lennon–McCartney

Disc 3, Side A
Eight Days a Week (2.43) Lennon–McCartney
No Reply (2.15) Lennon–McCartney
I'm a Loser (2.31) Lennon–McCartney
I'll Follow the Sun (1.46) Lennon–McCartney
Mr. Moonlight (2.35) Johnson
Every Little Thing (2.01) Lennon–McCartney
I Don't Want to Spoil the Party (2.33) Lennon–McCartney
Kansas City/Hey Hey Hey Hey (2.30) Lieber–Stoller/Penniman

Disc 3, Side B
Ticket to Ride (3.03) Lennon–McCartney
I'm Down (2.30) Lennon–McCartney
Help! (2.16) Lennon–McCartney
The Night Before (2.33) Lennon–McCartney
You've Got to Hide Your Love Away (2.08) Lennon–McCartney
I Need You (2.28) Harrison
Another Girl (2.02) Lennon–McCartney
You're Going to Lose That Girl (2.18) Lennon–McCartney

Disc 4, Side A
Yesterday (2.04) Lennon–McCartney
Act Naturally (2.27) Morrison–Russell
Tell Me What You See (2.35) Lennon–McCartney
It's Only Love (1.53) Lennon–McCartney
You Like Me Too Much (2.34) Harrison
I've Just Seen a Face (2.04) Lennon–McCartney
Day Tripper (2.37) Lennon–McCartney
We Can Work It Out (2.10) Lennon–McCartney

Disc 4, Side B
Michelle (2.42) Lennon–McCartney
Drive My Car (2.25) Lennon–McCartney
Norwegian Wood (This Bird Has Flown) (2.00) Lennon–
McCartney
You Won't See Me (3.19) Lennon–McCartney
Nowhere Man (2.40) Lennon–McCartney
Girl (2.16) Lennon–McCartney
I'm Looking Through You (2.20) Lennon–McCartney
In My Life (2.23) Lennon–McCartney

Disc 5, Side A
Paperback Writer (2.25) Lennon–McCartney
Rain (2.59) Lennon–McCartney
Here, There and Everywhere (2.29) Lennon–McCartney
Taxman (2.36) Harrison
I'm Only Sleeping (2.58) Lennon–McCartney
Good Day Sunshine (2.08) Lennon–McCartney
Yellow Submarine (2.40) Lennon–McCartney

Disc 5, Side B
Eleanor Rigby (2.11) Lennon–McCartney
And Your Bird Can Sing (2.02) Lennon–McCartney
For No One (2.03) Lennon–McCartney
Dr. Robert (2.14) Lennon–McCartney
Got to Get You into My Life (2.31) Lennon–McCartney
Penny Lane (3.00) Lennon–McCartney
Strawberry Fields Forever (4.05) Lennon–McCartney

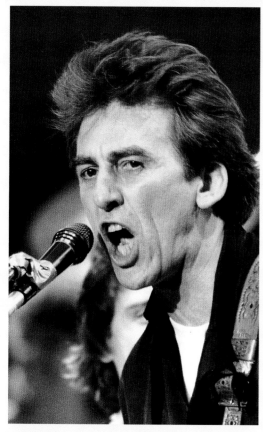

Disc 6, Side A

Sgt. Pepper's Lonely Hearts Club Band (1.59) Lennon–McCartney
With a Little Help from My Friends (2.46) Lennon–McCartney
Lucy in the Sky with Diamonds (3.25) Lennon–McCartney
Fixing a Hole (2.33) Lennon–McCartney
She's Leaving Home (3.24) Lennon–McCartney
Being for the Benefit of Mr. Kite! (2.36) Lennon–McCartney
A Day in the Life (5.03) Lennon–McCartney

Disc 6, Side B

When I'm Sixty-Four (2.38) Lennon–McCartney
Lovely Rita (2.43) Lennon–McCartney
All You Need Is Love (3.57) Lennon–McCartney
Baby You're a Rich Man (3.07) Lennon–McCartney
Magical Mystery Tour (2.48) Lennon–McCartney
Your Mother Should Know (2.33) Lennon–McCartney
The Fool on the Hill (3.00) Lennon–McCartney
I Am the Walrus (4.35) Lennon–McCartney

Disc 7, Side A

Hello Goodbye (3.24) Lennon–McCartney
Lady Madonna (2.17) Lennon–McCartney
Hey Jude (7.11) Lennon–McCartney
Revolution (3.22) Lennon–McCartney
Back in the USSR (2.45) Lennon–McCartney
Ob-La-Di, Ob-La-Da (3.10) Lennon–McCartney
While My Guitar Gently Weeps (4.46) Harrison

Disc 7, Side B

The Continuing Story of Bungalow Bill (3.05) Lennon–McCartney
Happiness Is a Warm Gun (2.47) Lennon–McCartney
Martha My Dear (2.28) Lennon–McCartney
I'm So Tired (2.01) Lennon–McCartney
Piggies (2.04) Harrison
Don't Pass Me By (3.52) Starkey
Julia (2.57) Lennon–McCartney
All Together Now (2.08) Lennon–McCartney

Disc 8, Side A

Get Back (3.09) Lennon–McCartney
Don't Let Me Down (3.34) Lennon–McCartney
The Ballad of John and Yoko (2.58) Lennon–McCartney
Across the Universe (3.51) Lennon–McCartney
For You Blue (2.33) Harrison
Two of Us (3.33) Lennon–McCartney
The Long and Winding Road (3.40) Lennon–McCartney
Let It Be (4.01) Lennon–McCartney

Disc 8, Side B

Come Together (4.16) Lennon–McCartney
Something (2.59) Harrison
Maxwell's Silver Hammer (3.24) Lennon–McCartney
Octopus's Garden (2.49) Starkey
Here Comes the Sun (3.04) Harrison
Because (2.45) Lennon–McCartney
Golden Slumbers (1.31) Lennon–McCartney
Carry That Weight (1.37) Lennon–McCartney
The End (2.04) Lennon–McCartney
Her Majesty (0.23) Lennon–McCartney

Producers George Martin and Phil Spector

22 MARCH 1982 Capitol (US)
23 MARCH 1982 Parlophone (UK)

Reel Music

Side One

A Hard Day's Night (2.32) Lennon–McCartney
I Should Have Known Better (2.42) Lennon–McCartney
Can't Buy Me Love (2.15) Lennon–McCartney
And I Love Her (2.27) Lennon–McCartney
Help! (2.16) Lennon–McCartney
You've Got to Hide Your Love Away (2.08) Lennon–McCartney
Ticket to Ride (3.03) Lennon–McCartney
Magical Mystery Tour (2.48) Lennon–McCartney

Side Two

I Am the Walrus (4.35) Lennon–McCartney
Yellow Submarine (2.40) Lennon–McCartney
All You Need Is Love (3.47) Lennon–McCartney
Let It Be (4.01) Lennon–McCartney
Get Back (3.09) Lennon–McCartney
The Long and Winding Road (3.40) Lennon–McCartney

Producers George Martin and Phil Spector

18 OCTOBER 1982 Capitol (US)

20 Greatest Hits

Side One

She Loves You (2.18) Lennon–McCartney
Love Me Do (2.19) Lennon–McCartney
I Want to Hold Your Hand (2.24) Lennon–McCartney
Can't Buy Me Love (2.15) Lennon–McCartney
A Hard Day's Night (2.32) Lennon–McCartney
I Feel Fine (2.19) Lennon–McCartney
Eight Days a Week (2.43) Lennon–McCartney
Ticket to Ride (3.03) Lennon–McCartney
Help! (2.16) Lennon–McCartney
Yesterday (2.04) Lennon–McCartney
We Can Work It Out (2.10) Lennon–McCartney
Paperback Writer (2.25) Lennon–McCartney

Side Two

Penny Lane (3.00) Lennon–McCartney
All You Need Is Love (3.47) Lennon–McCartney
Hello Goodbye (3.42) Lennon–McCartney
Hey Jude (5:05) Lennon–McCartney
Get Back (3.11) Lennon–McCartney
Come Together (4.16) Lennon–McCartney
Let It Be (3.50) Lennon–McCartney
The Long and Winding Road (3.40) Lennon–McCartney

Producers George Martin and Phil Spector

18 OCTOBER 1982 Parlophone (UK)

20 Greatest Hits

Side One

Love Me Do (2.19) Lennon–McCartney
From Me to You (1.55) Lennon–McCartney
She Loves You (2.18) Lennon–McCartney
I Want to Hold Your Hand (2.24) Lennon–McCartney
Can't Buy Me Love (2.15) Lennon–McCartney
A Hard Day's Night (2.32) Lennon–McCartney
I Feel Fine (2.19) Lennon–McCartney
Ticket to Ride (3.03) Lennon–McCartney
Help! (2.16) Lennon–McCartney
Day Tripper (2.27) Lennon–McCartney

Side Two

We Can Work It Out (2.10) Lennon–McCartney
Paperback Writer (2.25) Lennon–McCartney
Yellow Submarine (2.40) Lennon–McCartney
Eleanor Rigby (2.11) Lennon–McCartney
All You Need Is Love (3.47) Lennon–McCartney
Hello Goodbye (3.24) Lennon–McCartney
Lady Madonna (2.17) Lennon–McCartney
Hey Jude (7.11) Lennon–McCartney
Get Back (3.11) Lennon–McCartney
The Ballad of John and Yoko (2.58) Lennon–McCartney

Producer George Martin

7 March 1988 Parlophone (UK)
Capitol (US)

Past Masters, Volume One

Side One

Love Me Do (2.22) Lennon–McCartney
From Me to You (1.55) Lennon–McCartney
Thank You Girl (2.01) Lennon–McCartney
She Loves You (2.18) Lennon–McCartney
I'll Get You (2.04) Lennon–McCartney
I Want to Hold Your Hand (2.24) Lennon–McCartney
This Boy (2.11) Lennon–McCartney
Komm, Gib Mir Deine Hand (2.24) Lennon–McCartney
Sie Liebt Dich (2.18) Lennon–McCartney

Side Two

Long Tall Sally (1.58) Johnson–Penniman–Blackwell
I Call Your Name (2.02) Lennon–McCartney
Slow Down (2.54) Williams
Matchbox (1.37) Perkins
I Feel Fine (2.19) Lennon–McCartney
She's a Woman (2.57) Lennon–McCartney
Bad Boy (2.17) Williams
Yes It Is (2.40) Lennon–McCartney
I'm Down (2.30) Lennon–McCartney

Producer George Martin

7 March 1988 Parlophone (UK)
Capitol (US)

Past Masters, Volume Two

Side One

Day Tripper (2.37) Lennon–McCartney
We Can Work It Out (2.10) Lennon–McCartney
Paperback Writer (2.25) Lennon–McCartney
Rain (2.59) Lennon–McCartney
Lady Madonna (2.17) Lennon–McCartney
The Inner Light (2.36) Harrison
Hey Jude (7.11) Lennon–McCartney
Revolution (3.22) Lennon–McCartney

Side Two

Get Back (3.11) Lennon–McCartney
Don't Let Me Down (3.34) Lennon–McCartney
The Ballad of John and Yoko (2.58) Lennon–McCartney
Old Brown Shoe (3.16) Harrison
Across the Universe (3.41) Lennon–McCartney
Let It Be (3.50) Lennon–McCartney
You Know My Name (Look Up the Number) (4.20)
Lennon–McCartney

Producer George Martin

15 November 1988 Parlophone/Capitol (UK & US)

The Beatles Box Set

Fifteen album boxed set containing the entire Beatles catalogue.

Producers George Martin and Phil Spector

30 November 1994 Apple (UK)
6 December 1994 Apple (US)

Live at the BBC

Disc One

Beatle Greetings (0.13)
From Us to You (0.27) Lennon–McCartney
Riding on a Bus (0.53)
I Got a Woman (2.48) Charles
Too Much Monkey Business (2.05) Berry
Keep Your Hands Off My Baby (2.30) Goffin–King
I'll Be on My Way (1.57) Lennon–McCartney
Young Blood (1.56) Leiber–Stoller–Pomus
A Shot of Rhythm and Blues (2.14) Thompson
Sure to Fall (In Love With You) (2.07) Perkins–Claunch–Cantrell
Some Other Guy (2.00) Leiber–Stoller–Barrett
Thank You Girl (2.01) Lennon–McCartney
Sha la la la la! (0.27)
Baby It's You (2.43) David–Bacharach–Williams
That's All Right (Mama) (2.53) Crudup
Carol (2.34) Berry
Soldier of Love (1.59) Cason–Moon
A Little Rhyme (0.25)
Clarabella (2.39) Pingatore
I'm Gonna Sit Right Down and Cry (Over You) (2.01)
Thomas–Biggs
Crying, Waiting, Hoping (2.09) Holly
Dear Wack! (0.42)
You Really Got a Hold on Me (2.37) Robinson
To Know Her Is to Love Her (2.49) Spector
A Taste of Honey (1.57) Scott–Marlow
Long Tall Sally (1.52) Johnson–Penniman–Blackwell
I Saw Her Standing There (2.31) Lennon–McCartney
The Honeymoon Song (1.39) Theodorakis–Sansom
Johnny B. Goode (2.51) Berry
Memphis, Tennessee (2.12) Berry
Lucille (1.49) Collins–Penniman
Can't Buy Me Love (2.06) Lennon–McCartney
From Fluff to You (0.28)
Till There Was You (2.13) Willson

Disc Two

Crinsk Dee Night (1.04)
A Hard Day's Night (2.24) Lennon–McCartney
Have a Banana! (0.21)
I Wanna Be Your Man (2.09) Lennon–McCartney
Just A Rumour (0.20)
Roll Over Beethoven (2.15) Berry
All My Loving (2.04) Lennon–McCartney
Things We Said Today (2.18) Lennon–McCartney
She's a Woman (3.14) Lennon–McCartney
Sweet Little Sixteen (2.20) Berry
1822! (0.10)
Lonesome Tears in My Eyes (2.36) Burnette–Burlison–Mortimer
Nothin' Shakin' (2.59) Fontaine–Calacrai–Lampert–Gluck
Hippy Hippy Shake (1.49) Romero
Glad All Over (1.51) Bennett–Tepper–Schroeder
I Just Don't Understand (2.46) Wilkin–Westberry
So How Come (No One Loves Me) (1.53) Bryant
I Feel Fine (2.12) Lennon–McCartney
I'm a Loser (2.32) Lennon–McCartney
Everybody's Trying to Be My Baby (2.20) Perkins
Rock and Roll Music (2.00) Berry
Ticket to Ride (2.56) Lennon–McCartney
Dizzy Miss Lizzy (2.42) Williams
Kansas City/Hey Hey Hey Hey (2.30) Lieber–Stoller/Penniman
Set Fire to That Lot! (0.27)
Matchbox (1.57) Perkins
I Forgot to Remember to Forget (2.08) Kesler–Feathers
Love Those Goon Shows! (0.26)
I Got to Find My Baby (1.55) Berry
Ooh! My Soul (1.36) Penniman
Ooh! My Arms (0.35)
Don't Ever Change (2.02) Goffin–King
Slow Down (2.36) Williams
Honey Don't (2.11) Perkins
Love Me Do (2.29) Lennon–McCartney

Producer Various

21 November 1995 Apple (UK)
Apple (US)

Anthology 1

Disc One

Free as a Bird (4.23) Lennon-McCartney-Harrison-Starkey
John Lennon Monologue (0.13)
That'll Be the Day (2.07) Allison-Holly-Petty
In Spite of All the Danger (2.44) McCartney-Harrison
Paul McCartney Monologue (0.17)
Hallelujah, I Love Her So (1.13) Charles
You'll Be Mine (1.38) Lennon-McCartney
Cayenne (1.13) McCartney
Paul McCartney Monologue (0.07)
My Bonnie (2.42) Traditional; Arr. Sheridan
Ain't She Sweet (2.13) Ager-Yellen
Cry for a Shadow (2.22) Harrison-Lennon
John Lennon Monologue (0.10)
Brian Epstein Monologue (0.18)
Searchin' (2.59) Lieber-Stoller
Three Cool Cats (2.25) Lieber-Stoller
The Sheik of Araby (1.43) Smith-Wheller-Snyder
Like Dreamers Do (2.35) Lennon-McCartney
Hello Little Girl (1.40) Lennon-McCartney
Brian Epstein Monologue (0.32)
Besame Mucho (2.37) Velasquez-Skylar
Love Me Do (2.31) Lennon-McCartney
How Do You Do It (1.57) Murray
Please Please Me (1.59) Lennon-McCartney
One After 909 (False Starts) (2.23) Lennon-McCartney
One After 909 (2.55) Lennon-McCartney
Lend Me Your Comb (1.49) Twomy-Wise-Weisman
I'll Get You (2.08) Lennon-McCartney
John Lennon Monologue (0.12)
I Saw Her Standing There (2.48) Lennon-McCartney
From Me to You (2.05) Lennon-McCartney
Money (2.52) Bradford-Gordy
You Really Got a Hold on Me (2.58) Robinson
Roll Over Beethoven (2.21) Berry

Disc Two

She Loves You (2.50) Lennon-McCartney
Till There Was You (2.54) Willson
Twist and Shout (3.05) Russell-Medley
This Boy (2.22) Lennon-McCartney
I Want to Hold Your Hand (2.36) Lennon-McCartney
Eric Morecambe and Ernie Wise Dialogue (2.05)
Moonlight Bay (0.49) Madden-Wenrich
Can't Buy Me Love (2.10) Lennon-McCartney
All My Loving (2.19) Lennon-McCartney
You Can't Do That (2.42) Lennon-McCartney
And I Love Her (1.52) Lennon-McCartney
A Hard Day's Night (2.43) Lennon-McCartney
I Wanna Be Your Man (1.47) Lennon-McCartney
Long Tall Sally (1.45) Johnson-Penniman-Blackwell
Boys (1.49) Dixon-Farrell
Shout (1.31) Isley-Isley-Isley
I'll Be Back (Demo) (1.12) Lennon-McCartney
I'll Be Back (Complete) (1.57) Lennon-McCartney
You Know What to Do (1.58) Harrison
No Reply (Demo) (1.46) Lennon-McCartney
Mr. Moonlight (2.47) Johnson
Leave My Kitten Alone (2.56) John-Turner-McDougal
No Reply (2.29) Lennon-McCartney
Eight Days a Week (False Starts) (1.25) Lennon-McCartney
Eight Days a Week (2.47) Lennon-McCartney
Kansas City/Hey Hey Hey Hey (2.30) Lieber-Stoller/Penniman

Producers George Martin and Jeff Lynne

12 December 1995 Capitol/Apple C2 7243 8 58497 2 5 (US)
12 December 1995 Apple 7243 8 82587 2 (UK)

Free as a Bird

Free as a Bird (2.42) Lennon-McCartney-Harrison-Starkey
I Saw Her Standing There (2.56) Lennon-McCartney
This Boy (2.16) Lennon-McCartney
Christmas Time Is Here Again (6.08) Lennon-McCartney-Harrison-Starkey

Producers Jeff Lynne, John Lennon (posthumous credit),
Paul McCartney, George Harrison and Ringo Starr

18 March 1996 Apple (UK)
19 March 1996 Apple (US)

Anthology 2

Disc One

Real Love (3.54) Lennon
Yes It Is (1.50) Lennon-McCartney
I'm Down (2.54) Lennon-McCartney
You've Got to Hide Your Love Away (2.45) Lennon-McCartney
If You've Got Trouble (scrapped) Lennon-McCartney
That Means a Lot (2.26) Lennon-McCartney
Yesterday (2.34) Lennon-McCartney
It's Only Love (1.59) Lennon-McCartney
I Feel Fine (2.15) Lennon-McCartney
Ticket to Ride (2.45) Lennon-McCartney
Yesterday (2.43) Lennon-McCartney
Help! (2.54) Lennon-McCartney
Everybody's Trying to Be My Baby (2.46) Lennon-McCartney
Norwegian Wood (This Bird Has Flown) (1.59) Lennon-McCartney
I'm Looking Through You (2.53) Lennon-McCartney
12-Bar Original (2.54) Lennon-McCartney-Harrison-Starkey
Tomorrow Never Knows (3.14) Lennon-McCartney
Got to Get You into My Life (2.54) Lennon-McCartney
And Your Bird Can Sing (2.14) Lennon-McCartney
Taxman (2.32) Lennon-McCartney
Eleanor Rigby (Strings Only) (2.06) Lennon-McCartney
I'm Only Sleeping (Rehearsal) (0.41) Lennon-McCartney
I'm Only Sleeping (Take 1) (2.59) Lennon-McCartney
Rock and Roll Music (1.39) Berry
She's a Woman (2.55) Lennon-McCartney

Disc Two

Strawberry Fields Forever (Demo Sequence) (1.42) Lennon-McCartney
Strawberry Fields Forever (Take 1) (2.34) Lennon-McCartney
Strawberry Fields Forever (Take 7 & Edit Piece) (4.14) Lennon-McCartney
Penny Lane (3.13) Lennon-McCartney
A Day in the Life (5.04) Lennon-McCartney
Good Morning Good Morning (2.40) Lennon-McCartney
Only a Northern Song (2.44) Harrison
Being for the Benefit of Mr. Kite! (Takes 1 & 2) (1.06) Lennon-McCartney
Being for the Benefit of Mr. Kite! (Take 7) (2.33) Lennon-McCartney
Lucy in the Sky with Diamonds (3.06) Lennon-McCartney
Within You Without You (Instrumental) (5.27) Harrison
Sgt. Pepper's Lonely Hearts Club Band (Reprise) (1.27) Lennon-McCartney
You Know My Name (Look Up the Number) (5.44) Lennon-McCartney
I Am the Walrus (4.02) Lennon-McCartney
The Fool on the Hill (Demo) (2.48) Lennon-McCartney
Your Mother Should Know (3.02) Lennon-McCartney
The Fool on the Hill (Take 4) (3.45) Lennon-McCartney
Hello Goodbye (3.18) Lennon-McCartney
Lady Madonna (2.22) Lennon-McCartney
Across the Universe (3.28) Lennon-McCartney

Producer George Martin

28 OCTOBER 1996 Apple (UK)
29 OCTOBER 1996 Apple (US)

Anthology 3

Disc One

A Beginning (0.50) Martin
Happiness Is a Warm Gun (2.14) Lennon–McCartney
Helter Skelter (4.37) Lennon–McCartney
Mean Mr. Mustard (1.57) Lennon–McCartney
Polythene Pam (1.26) Lennon–McCartney
Glass Onion (1.51) Lennon–McCartney
Junk (2.24) McCartney
Piggies (2.01) Harrison
Honey Pie (1.19) Lennon–McCartney
Don't Pass Me By (2.42) Starkey
Ob-La-Di, Ob-La-Da (2.56) Lennon–McCartney
Good Night (2.37) Lennon–McCartney
Cry Baby Cry (2.46) Lennon–McCartney
Blackbird (2.18) Lennon–McCartney
Sexy Sadie (4.06) Lennon–McCartney
While My Guitar Gently Weeps (3.27) Harrison
Hey Jude (4.21) Lennon–McCartney
Not Guilty (3.22) Harrison
Mother Nature's Son (3.17) Lennon–McCartney
Glass Onion (2.08) Lennon–McCartney
Rocky Racoon (4.12) Lennon–McCartney
What's the New Mary Jane (6.12) Lennon–McCartney
Step Inside Love/Los Paranoias (2.30) Lennon–McCartney–Harrison–Starkey
I'm So Tired (2.14) Lennon–McCartney
I Will (1.55) Lennon–McCartney
Why Don't We Do It in the Road (2.15) Lennon–McCartney
Julia (1.57) Lennon–McCartney

Disc Two

I've Got a Feeling (2.49) Lennon–McCartney
She Came in Through the Bathroom Window (3.36) Lennon–McCartney
Dig a Pony (4.18) Lennon–McCartney
Two of Us (3.27) Lennon–McCartney
For You Blue (2.22) Harrison
Teddy Boy (3.18) McCartney
Medley: Rip It Up/Shake, Rattle, and Roll/Blue Suede Shoes (3.10) Blackwell–Marascalco–Calhoun–Perkins
The Long and Winding Road (3.40) Lennon–McCartney
Oh! Darling (4.08) Lennon–McCartney
All Things Must Pass (3.05) Harrison
Mailman, Bring Me No More Blues (1.55) Roberts–Katz–Clayton
Get Back (3.08) Lennon–McCartney
Old Brown Shoe (3.02) Harrison
Octopus's Garden (2.49) Starkey
Maxwell's Silver Hammer (3.49) Lennon–McCartney
Something (3.18) Harrison
Come Together (3.40) Lennon–McCartney
Come and Get It (2.29) McCartney
Ain't She Sweet (2.08) Ager–Yellen
Because (2.23) Lennon–McCartney

Let It Be (4.05) Lennon–McCartney
I Me Mine (1.47) Harrison
The End (2.50) Lennon–McCartney

Producer George Martin

14 SEPTEMBER 1999 Apple (UK)
Capitol (US)

Yellow Submarine Songtrack

Side One (vinyl)

Yellow Submarine (2.38) Lennon–McCartney
Hey Bulldog (3.11) Lennon–McCartney
Eleanor Rigby (2.04) Lennon–McCartney
Love You To (2.57) Harrison
All Together Now (2.09) Lennon–McCartney
Lucy in the Sky with Diamonds (3.27) Lennon–McCartney
Think for Yourself (2.17) Harrison
Sgt. Pepper's Lonely Hearts Club Band (2.00) Lennon–McCartney
With a Little Help from My Friends (2.44) Lennon–McCartney

Side Two (vinyl)

Baby You're a Rich Man (2.59) Lennon–McCartney
Only a Northern Song (3.23) Harrison
All You Need Is Love (3.46) Lennon–McCartney
When I'm Sixty-Four (2.38) Lennon–McCartney
Nowhere Man (2.41) Lennon–McCartney
It's All Too Much (6.24) Harrison

Producers George Martin and Peter Cobbin

13 NOVEMBER 2000 Apple (UK)
14 NOVEMBER 2000 Apple (US)

1

Side One (vinyl)

Love Me Do (2.19) Lennon–McCartney
From Me to You (1.55) Lennon–McCartney
She Loves You (2.21) Lennon–McCartney

I Want to Hold Your Hand (2.25) Lennon–McCartney
Can't Buy Me Love (2.11) Lennon–McCartney
A Hard Day's Night (2.33) Lennon–McCartney
I Feel Fine (2.18) Lennon–McCartney
Eight Days a Week (2.43) Lennon–McCartney

Side Two (vinyl)

Ticket to Ride (3.10) Lennon–McCartney
Help! (2.19) Lennon–McCartney
Yesterday (2.05) Lennon–McCartney
Day Tripper (2.47) Lennon–McCartney
We Can Work It Out (2.15) Lennon–McCartney
Paperback Writer (2.18) Lennon–McCartney
Yellow Submarine (2.37) Lennon–McCartney
Eleanor Rigby (2.06) Lennon–McCartney

Side Three (vinyl)

Penny Lane (2.59) Lennon–McCartney
All You Need Is Love (3.47) Lennon–McCartney
Hello Goodbye (3.27) Lennon–McCartney
Lady Madonna (2.17) Lennon–McCartney
Hey Jude (7.03) Lennon–McCartney

Side Four (vinyl)

Get Back (3.11) Lennon–McCartney
The Ballad of John and Yoko (2.59) Lennon–McCartney
Something (3.00) Harrison
Come Together (4.17) Lennon–McCartney
Let It Be (4.01) Lennon–McCartney
The Long and Winding Road (3.37) Lennon–McCartney

Producers George Martin and Phil Spector

17 NOVEMBER 2000 Apple (UK)
Capitol (US)

Let It Be...Naked

Side One (vinyl)

Get Back (2.34) Lennon–McCartney
Dig a Pony (3.38) Lennon–McCartney
For You Blue (2.27) Harrison
The Long and Winding Road (3.34) Lennon–McCartney
Two of Us (3.21) Lennon–McCartney
I've Got a Feeling (3.30) Lennon–McCartney

Side Two (vinyl)

One After 909 (2.44) Lennon–McCartney
Don't Let Me Down (3.18) Lennon–McCartney
I Me Mine (2.21) Harrison
Across the Universe (3.38) Lennon–McCartney
Let It Be (3.53) Lennon–McCartney

Producers George Martin, Paul Hicks, Guy Massey, and Alan Rouse

15 NOVEMBER 2004 Parlophone (UK)
16 NOVEMBER 2004 Capitol (US)

The Capitol Albums, Vol. 1

Disc One: *Meet the Beatles*

I Want to Hold Your Hand (2.24) Lennon–McCartney
I Saw Her Standing There (2.50) Lennon–McCartney

This Boy (2.11) Lennon–McCartney
It Won't Be Long (2.11) Lennon–McCartney
All I've Got to Do (2.05) Lennon–McCartney
All My Loving (2.04) Lennon–McCartney
Don't Bother Me (2.28) Harrison
Little Child (1.46) Lennon–McCartney
Till There Was You (2.12) Willson
Hold Me Tight (2.30) Lennon–McCartney
I Wanna Be Your Man (1.59) Lennon–McCartney
Not a Second Time (2.03) Lennon–McCartney

Disc Two: *The Beatles' Second Album*
Roll Over Beethoven (2.44) Berry
Thank You Girl (2.01) Lennon–McCartney
You Really Got a Hold on Me (2.58) Robinson
Devil in Her Heart (2.23) Drapkin
Money (2.47) Bradford–Gordy
You Can't Do That (2.23) Lennon–McCartney
Long Tall Sally (1.58) Johnson–Penniman–Blackwell
I Call Your Name (2.02) Lennon–McCartney
Please Mr. Postman (2.34) Holland
I'll Get You (2.04) Lennon–McCartney
She Loves You (2.19) Lennon–McCartney

Disc Three: *Something New*
I'll Cry Instead (2.04) Lennon–McCartney
Things We Said Today (2.35) Lennon–McCartney
Any Time at All (2.10) Lennon–McCartney
When I Get Home (2.14) Lennon–McCartney
Slow Down (2.54) Williams
Matchbox (1.37) Perkins
Tell Me Why (2.06) Lennon–McCartney
And I Love Her (2.28) Lennon–McCartney
I'm Happy Just to Dance With You (1.56) Lennon–McCartney
If I Fell (2.19) Lennon–McCartney
Komm, Gib Mir Deine Hand (2.24) Lennon–McCartney

Disc Four: *Beatles '65*
No Reply (2.15) Lennon–McCartney
I'm a Loser (2.31) Lennon–McCartney
Baby's in Black (2.02) Lennon–McCartney
Rock and Roll Music (2.02) Berry
I'll Follow the Sun (1.46) Lennon–McCartney
Mr. Moonlight (2.35) Johnson
Honey Don't (2.56) Perkins
I'll Be Back (2.22) Lennon–McCartney
She's a Woman (2.57) Lennon–McCartney
I Feel Fine (2.20) Lennon–McCartney
Everybody's Trying to Be My Baby (2.20) Perkins

Producer George Martin

11 APRIL 2006 CD Capitol/Apple (US)
The Capitol Albums, Vol. 2

Disc One: *The Early Beatles*
Love Me Do (2.19) Lennon–McCartney
Twist and Shout (2.32) Medley–Russell
Anna (Go To Him) (2.56) Alexander

Chains (2.21) Goffin
Boys (2.24) Dixon–Farrell
Ask Me Why (2.24) Lennon–McCartney
Please Please Me (2.00) Lennon–McCartney
P.S. I Love You (2.02) Lennon–McCartney
Baby It's You (2.36) David–Williams–Bacharach
A Taste of Honey (2.02) Scott–Marlow
Do You Want to Know a Secret (1.55) Lennon–McCartney

Disc Two: *Beatles VI*
Kansas City/Hey Hey Hey Hey (2.30) Lieber-Stoller/Penniman
Eight Days a Week (2.43) Lennon–McCartney
You Like Me Too Much (2.34) Harrison
Bad Boy (2.17) Wiliams
I Don't Want to Spoil the Party (2.23) Lennon–McCartney
Words of Love (2.10) Holly
What You're Doing (2.30) Lennon–McCartney
Yes It Is (2.40) Lennon–McCartney
Dizzy Miss Lizzy (2.51) Williams
Tell Me What You See (2.35) Lennon–McCartney
Every Little Thing (2.01) Lennon–McCartney

Disc Three: *Help! Original Motion Picture Soundtrack*
Help! (2.16) Lennon–McCartney
The Night Before (2.33) Lennon–McCartney
From Me to You Fantasy (Instrumental)* (2.03) Thorne
You've Got to Hide Your Love Away (2.08) Lennon–McCartney
I Need You (2.28) Harrison
In the Tyrol (Instrumental)* (2.21) Thorne
Another Girl (2.02) Lennon–McCartney
Another Hard Day's Night (Instrumental)* (2.28) Lennon–McCartney
Ticket to Ride (3.03) Lennon–McCartney
The Bitter End/You Can't Do That (Instrumental)* (2.20) Lennon–McCartney
You're Going to Lose That Girl (2.18) Lennon–McCartney
The Chase (Instrumental)* (2.24) Thorne

Disc Four: *Rubber Soul*
I've Just Seen a Face (2.04) Lennon–McCartney
Norwegian Wood (This Bird Has Flown) (2.00) Lennon–McCartney
You Won't See Me (3.19) Lennon–McCartney
Think for Yourself (2.16) Harrison
The Word (2.42) Lennon–McCartney
Michelle (2.42) Lennon–McCartney
It's Only Love (1.53) Lennon–McCartney
Girl (2.26) Lennon–McCartney
I'm Looking Through You (2.27) Lennon–McCartney
In My Life (2.23) Lennon–McCartney
Wait (2.13) Lennon–McCartney
Run for Your Life (2.21) Lennon–McCartney

*Performed by George Martin and His Orchestra

Producer George Martin

20 NOVEMBER 2006 Apple (UK)
Capitol (US)

Love

Because (2.44) Lennon–McCartney
Get Back (2.05) Lennon–McCartney
Glass Onion (1.20) Lennon–McCartney
Eleanor Rigby/Julia (transition) (3.05) Lennon–McCartney
I Am the Walrus (4.25) Lennon–McCartney
I Want to Hold Your Hand (1.26) Lennon–McCartney
Drive My Car/The Word/What You're Doing (1.54) Lennon–McCartney
Gnik Nus (0.55) Lennon–McCartney
Something/Blue Jay Way (transition) (3.29) Harrison
Being for the Benefit of Mr. Kite!/I Want You (She's So Heavy)/Helter Skelter (3.22) Lennon–McCartney
Help! (2.18) Lennon–McCartney
Blackbird/Yesterday (2.31) Lennon–McCartney
Strawberry Fields Forever (4.31) Lennon–McCartney
Within You, Without You/Tomorrow Never Knows (3.07) Harrison–Lennon–McCartney
Lucy in the Sky with Diamonds (4.10) Lennon–McCartney
Octopus's Garden (3.18) Starkey
Lady Madonna (2.56) Lennon–McCartney
Here Comes the Sun/The Inner Light (transition) (4.18) Harrison
Come Together/Dear Prudence/Cry Baby Cry (transition) (4.45) Lennon–McCartney
Revolution (2.14) Lennon–McCartney
Back in the USSR (1.54) Lennon–McCartney
While My Guitar Gently Weeps (3.46) Harrison
A Day in the Life (5.08) Lennon–McCartney
Hey Jude (3.58) Lennon–McCartney
Sgt. Pepper's Lonely Hearts Club Band (Reprise) (1.22) Lennon–McCartney
All You Need Is Love (3.38) Lennon–McCartney

Producers George and Giles Martin

A

ABOVE: **The Beatles begin filming of *A Hard Day's Night* at a theatre converted into a television studio for the purpose of the film, 1964.**

ACKNOWLEDGMENTS AND PHOTO CREDITS

The photographs in this book are from the archives of Associated Newspapers. Particular thanks for the photographers' collective work over the last 45 years. Thanks also to Steve Torrington, Alan Pinnock, Katie Lee, Dave Sheppard, Brian Jackson, Richard Jones, and all the present staff.

Additional photographs/images:
Getty Images:
Pages: 1, 8-9, 10, 11, 12, 13(t), 14, 15, 16, 17, 18, 22, 24, 26, 28, 30, 49, 53, 56 (main), 63(b), 83(t), 82(t), 90(l), 93(t), 124, 126, 153, 161, 162, 163, 164, 167(b), 171, 172, 201, 202, 212(b), 214(t&b), 215, 216(t&b), 217, 222, 223, 224, 225, 227, 234, 235, 239(t,m,b), 240, 242(t&b), 244(t&b), 247, 249(t), 270, 274(t&b), 278, 279(l&r), 327, 335(t), 339, 371.

Corbis:
Pages: 32(t), 45, 72, 81(t), 82, 83(m), 85, 88(t&b), 103, 165, 168(t&b), 169, 170(main), 195 (l &top r), 212 (main), 213, 252(t), 311, 329

Unless otherwise stated, memorabilia shown in this book are taken from private collections. Special thanks to Pete Nash for providing material from his private collection (photographed by www.britishbeatlesfanclub.co.uk) and to Barnes & Noble, Inc. (photographed by Christopher Bain).

Every effort has been made to trace copyright holders but if there are any omissions the publisher will be happy to rectify such omissions or errors in future reprints and/or new editions.

Thanks to the following contributing authors: Alison Gauntlett, Gareth Thomas, and Jane Benn.

Thanks also to Cliff Salter, Duncan Hill, Kate Truman, Harry Chambers, Jill Dorman, and Sarah Rickayzen. Thanks to Bruce Lubin, Nathaniel Marunas, and Devorah Klein at Barnes & Noble, Inc.

Design and layout: Phil Yarnall, Mark Brown, John Dunne, Gordon Mills, Kevin Ullrich, and Rich Hazelton.